ib.

had me a real good time

faces

before during and after

had me a real good time

faces

before during and after

Andy Neill

OMNIBUS PRESS

London / New York / Paris / Sydney / Copenhagen / Berlin / Madrid / Tokyo

This Edition © 2016 Omnibus Press
(A Division of Music Sales Limited)

Cover designed by Fresh Lemon
Picture research by Jacqui Black & Andy Neill

ISBN: 9.781.78305.995.9
Order No: OP56507

Exclusive Distributors
Music Sales Limited,
14/15 Berners Street,
London, W1T 3LJ.

Music Sales Corporation
180 Madison Avenue, 24th Floor,
New York,
NY 10016,
USA.

Alliance Distribution Services
9 Pioneer Avenue,
Tuggerah,
NSW 2259,
Australia

Printed in the EU

A catalogue record for this book is available from the British Library.

Visit Omnibus Press on the web at www.omnibuspress.com

For Laneole, Krissie & The Chuch

Contents

Introduction   ix

Part One: Overture And Beginners
Chapter 1 – East End Boys   3
Chapter 2 – Of Mods And Mac   20
Chapter 3 – Rod The Mod   36
Chapter 4 – Strictly For The Birds   57
Chapter 5 – Beck's Blues   73
Chapter 6 – Immediate Collapse   93
Chapter 7 – Slim Chance   111
Chapter 8 – New Faces   129

Part Two: Flying
Chapter 9 – First Step   147
Chapter 10 – America   164
Chapter 11 – Gasoline Alley   182
Chapter 12 – Tell Everyone   201
Chapter 13 – Every Picture   219
Chapter 14 – A Nod Is As Good As A Wink   239
Chapter 15 – Never A Dull Moment   260
Chapter 16 – Ooh La La   283

Part Three: Last Orders Please
Chapter 17 – Tetsu And Teacher's   307
Chapter 18 – I've Got My Own Album To Do   324
Chapter 19 – Passing Show   346
Chapter 20 – Atlantic Crossing   361
Chapter 21 – Glad And Sorry   375
Chapter 22 – Simply Rod   394
Epilogue   409

Appendices
Selective Discography   421
The Faces at the BBC   439
Concert Listing   446

Acknowledgments   460
Bibliography   463
Source Notes   465
Index   479

Introduction

THROUGHOUT their relatively short six-year tenure, the Faces embodied the perfect balance of sloppiness and discipline, informality and seriousness, sensitivity and arrogance – a good time, rock'n'roll band with no pretensions to grandeur. "There was a lot of that East End thing that the Small Faces had that went into the Faces," Ronnie Lane proudly told journalist Penny Valentine in 1974. "That attitude the Faces had was the attitude that I liked."

The starring cast was made up of five disparate characters – a flamboyant yet shy, sandpaper-voiced front man in Rod Stewart whose distinctive voice earned him the nickname Golden Catarrh from one music paper, a similarly spiky-haired, affable guitarist Ron Wood, a spiritual rascal and affecting songwriter Ronnie Lane, a sharp-witted raconteur and pithy player of the 88s Ian 'Mac' McLagan and a quiet but solid dark horse in drummer Kenney Jones.

While not the best musicians treading the concert stages of the early to mid-Seventies, their unpretentiousness and sheer force of personality more than made up for this. In an age of bland collectivism the Faces had a comedic quality that Ron Wood once described as "the Marx Brothers on the road".

Formed in 1969 out of the remains of the Small Faces and the Jeff Beck Group, the individual Faces had paid their dues over the past five years in such groups as the Outcasts, Jimmy Powell & The Five Dimensions, the Hoochie Coochie Men, the Muleskinners, Steam Packet, the Birds, and the Creation. Thanks to the entrepreneurial might behind them, the Small Faces rose to pop fame in Britain in 1965, yet by the time the group disbanded with the departure of charismatic frontman Steve Marriott, they had little to show for their success. At the same time Stewart and Wood despaired at being treated as dispensable sidemen to bolster Jeff Beck's star. Marrying the light-heartedness of the Small Faces with the contemporary blues approach of the Jeff Beck Group, it was apparent that the Faces were to be a different proposition.

"Of course you compared them to the Small Faces because there were three of them in it," observed DJ and friend, Jeff Dexter, "but it didn't have that kind of rawness of the Small Faces in terms of grooving and dancing. This was more like a pub brawl than a soul band even though they were very soulful."

Initially ignored by the hip cognoscenti in Britain who regarded them as passé the Faces were quick to make their mark in America thanks to the reputation Stewart and Wood had cultivated with Jeff Beck. Through a potent combination of hard work, creativity and a readily identifiable image of approachable lads next door at the best party you ever had, they overcame this initial indifference to become one of the biggest and best loved bands of the Seventies.

Many observers felt the Faces never realised their full potential on record but compensated for this by projecting their music via their personalities. Other bands of the era, notably Mott The Hoople and Slade, shared the same traits, but achieved nowhere near the same intense audience interaction.

"On a good night – and with the Faces you had a 50-50 chance of catching them on a good night – they were absolutely spectacular," says Faces roadie Russ Schlagbaum. "I remember being on stage with them and just being freaked out because they were so good."

This notoriously unpredictable inconsistency as to which Faces you would encounter was mainly down to their legendary fondness for a friendly tipple before, during and after a show. "It all stemmed from the early days when we used to think nobody wanted to hear us," Stewart explained to *Zigzag* in 1971, "so we used to go and get pissed and then go on and have a laugh."

"We were all drinkers," Ron Wood added, "drinking at rehearsals and recording sessions – it was just a natural progression to take it onto the stage – although we didn't know it was going to get out of hand."

The Faces' inclusive brand of boozy blues and soused soul extended beyond the spotlight; along with bands like the Who and Led Zeppelin they perfected the on-the-road practice of annihilating hotel rooms down to a fine art (if it could be defined that way), while indulging in all the typical trappings of the Seventies rock star. But then a seismic change in their happy dynamic occurred when Stewart achieved unimaginable success with his third solo album *Every Picture Tells A Story* and its single, 'Maggie May'.

From the outset concert promoters, particularly in the States, invariably billed the group as 'featuring Rod Stewart'. Although Rod continued to insist his albums were merely a sideline to the Faces they ended up selling more in direct proportion to the group's, leading many outsiders to speculate that he would now ditch the Faces to further his own self interest.

Some saw it as fortuitous for Stewart who had the best of both worlds in having a superb backing band, one that he didn't have to pay a salary to but who nevertheless played his songs on tour and effectively promoted both him and them.

This state of affairs became intractable for the Faces' bassist and founder. Ronnie Lane was "one hell of a character" as his former school chum and band mate Ron Chimes remembered him. As Stewart now readily admits, "When Ronnie left the band the spirit of the Faces left." Lane's subsequent vision of taking his music back to the roots, and his ultimate ambition, playing under a circus big top was an admirable aim. However his single-mindedness cost him dearly both financially and in health.

The Faces continued, recruiting an inscrutable Nipponese, Teacher's toting Tetsu Yamauchi, to replace Lane but the band virtually ceased to function in the studio. Once Wood accepted an offer to join his heroes the Rolling Stones, ostensibly on a temporary basis, it was obvious that the writing was on the wall. While Yamauchi returned to Japan, McLagan and Jones to a reformed Small Faces and then different ventures with various artists, Stewart and Wood went on to greater achievements but it was their time making music and mayhem with Lane, McLagan and Jones that continues to thrill and fascinate – particularly for succeeding generation of musicians – such off the cuff examples being the Replacements, Guns N' Roses, Red Hot Chili Peppers, the Black Crowes and the Quireboys.

Looking back three decades on from turning professional, Stewart summed up his outlook, "At the time I thought it was a quick way of getting my hands on a few bob and I thought if it lasted a year I'd be happy." He certainly achieved that and more.

The motivation to write such an extensive account of the Faces can be traced back to my childhood love of Rod Stewart's early albums followed in quick succession by the Faces. The youngest of four with music always being played around the home, I was unable to afford to buy LPs, the next best thing being to borrow them from the local library. It was in 1972, while scanning the racks, that I alighted on *Every Picture Tells A Story*. On opening the gatefold sleeve and reading through the track listing, I found that it contained 'Maggie May', the song I'd heard being constantly played on the radio for most of the past year.

As soon as my young impressionable ears hooked on to the cascading acoustic chords of 'Every Picture Tells A Story' and that 'tuff 'n' ruff as grit' voice came crashing in, I was hooked. I went back to the library and found *A Nod Is As Good As A Wink . . .* My sister saw the Faces in concert but being just a little too young, I had to make do with playing her copies of *Never A Dull Moment* and *Sing It Again, Rod.* Among the first albums I bought with my own money was *Ooh La La.* Although not long after Rod and I parted company as far as my musical tastes went, I continued to cherish those early albums.

After making the connection between the Small Faces and the Faces – I had 'Lazy Sunday' on 45 – my interest in the period in which they recorded their imperishable music increased. Over the years, I sought out and absorbed as much information relating to both groups and their individuals as possible. In 1976 the first Faces related book, *Rod Stewart And The Changing Faces*, a modest paperback by *Let It Rock* writer and best-selling *Slade In Flame* author John Pidgeon, was published which drew on his interviews with various band members and his first-hand knowledge of their history. It opened the floodgate for a steady stream of Rod Stewart titles that dealt with the Faces mainly in the context of Stewart's involvement. In 2003, *Last Orders Please: The Faces . . . And The Britain We Forgot*, a 300-page biography by Jim Melly, painted the Faces story against the societal backdrop of Britain in the Seventies – despite the fact that much of the Faces story was played out on the highways and byways of America. In reality their success insulated them from the type of dull existence recounted by the ordinary folk to whom Melly talked.

The basis for this book originally grew out of the need for a definitive Ronnie Lane biography – a vacuum that hopefully will be consummately filled by the right author. When that was unforthcoming, I set to work on the broader canvas of the Faces – before, during and after. While I hesitate at describing the resultant work as being 100 per cent accurate I'd boldly venture that it's near enough to being the most definitive account as reports and memories relating to events that happened over four decades ago will allow.

Some housekeeping: throughout the Small Faces and Faces years Kenney Jones' first name was predominantly written as 'Kenny'. In accordance with his preference, the spelling throughout this book adopts an extra 'e'. Similarly, when starting out the band was known simply as 'Faces' but as they are generally referred to as 'the Faces' the more populist choice is used for convenience.

Finally, above all the stories, trivia and minutiae attached to a band and individuals of the Faces' stature, the only thing that it should ultimately boil down to is the music. Those of younger years holding to the (widely held, it must be said) view of Rod Stewart as a superannuated, blonde-chasing irrelevance are directed to *Gasoline Alley* and *Every Picture Tells A Story* forthwith. The underrated homespun delights of Ronnie Lane are best appreciated via the utterly charming *Anymore For Anymore* and *Rough Mix*, his collaboration with Pete Townshend.

As an approximation of the Faces prepares to tour, their songs will be heard in the environment where they were best accommodated – on the stage in front of audiences intent on having themselves a real good time.

As former Faces road manager Charlie Fernandez remarked when looking back to those distant days of craziness, "They had fun. That's one thing I can say through all the history of the Faces, when they went out and whatever they did, it was all in the name of fun."

No band could hope to leave a better legacy.

Andy Neill
London
January 2011

faces

Part One

Overture And Beginners

CHAPTER 1

East End Boys

"London is the largest of the bloated modern cities; London is the smokiest; London is the dirtiest; London is, if you will, the most sombre; London is, if you will, the most miserable. But London is certainly the most amusing and the most amused. You may prove that we have the most tragedy; the fact remains that we have the most comedy, that we have the most farce. We have at the very worst a splendid hypocrisy of humour. We conceal our sorrow behind a screaming derision. You speak of people who laugh through their tears; it is our boast that we only weep through our laughter. There remains always this great boast, perhaps the greatest boast that is possible to human nature. I mean the great boast that the most unhappy part of our population is also the most hilarious part."

– G.K. Chesterton, 'Cockneys And Their Humour',
All Things Considered, 1908

"Honestly we believe so much in being a team, it's not true. And we don't have to work at it either. We're sort of a natural unit. We know what each other is thinking."

– Steve Marriott, *New Musical Express,* 1966

THROUGHOUT the centuries, Cockney humour has defined London's citizenry with its qualities of charm, warmth, light-heartedness and self-deprecation. On the other side of the coin it can be sarcastic, cutting and exclusive to those outsiders finding themselves at the sharp end of the joke. But then such qualities were needed, particularly for those Londoners from the lower classes to stoically soldier through an upheaval like the Second World War.

Of all the areas of the capital to be affected during the Blitz, from September 1940 to April 1941, the East End was undoubtedly the worst hit. In one night alone – March 19, 1941 – a 500-strong Luftwaffe squadron dropped 176 high explosive bombs, mines and incendiary devices on the county borough of West Ham. Exactly a month later, during the heaviest raid of all, a bomb scored a direct hit on the Princess Alice public house at the junction of Romford Road and Woodgrange Road. Just down the road, at 385 Romford Road, opposite Forest Gate police station lived the Lane family.

"The bomb fell on the pub and blew all the windows in on us but we were lucky," Stan Lane (Jnr.) recalls. "We was in the main road and the houses on our side never got hit at all. They're still there now."

Stanley Frederick Lane and his bride Elsie May Milborn started married life in Bonner Road, Bethnal Green, when their eldest child Stanley was born in 1938. With war being declared the following year Stanley didn't volunteer for the army as his services as a lorry driver were needed to deliver vital supplies. When the German Blitzkrieg campaign commenced, the Lanes moved to Forest Gate in a vain bid to escape the relentless bombardment.

Stan Lane: "Where we lived behind was all debris, and the side of Forest Gate going towards Woodgrange Road was all a bomb site. We used to go to the Odeon by the Princess Alice, a tanner for the Saturday morning pictures. We'd come out and play cowboys and Indians and re-enact the film all over the debris. It was like an adventure playground."

By all accounts, the Lanes were a typical example of the 'Blitz spirit' – an extended, tight knit working-class East End family, looking out for each other in the face of wartime adversity.

"They were all characters, all proper characters," Stan says with a chuckle. "Auntie Rene was my dad's sister, Ethel, Rosie, his brothers Lenny and Charlie . . . I saw Uncle Lenny right up until he died a few years ago. When Rosie died we all met in the Approach pub in Bethnal Green, and then went over to the French polishing shop on Robinson Road where they lived when they was kids and we had photos done outside. It's amazing because it hasn't changed because that's all Crown land and it didn't get bombed. All opposite to Uncle Lenny got bombed because when we had the VE Day night party they was getting the old wood out of them homes and we had a big bonfire in the middle of the road."

While the end of the war in May 1945 was greeted with jubilation, the considerable hardships for those less privileged continued throughout the lean years that followed. The winter of 1945–46 brought an acute shortage of coal to the East End and the indignation at the consequent plight suffered by its citizens was summed up in a West Ham council meeting in January as the *Boro' of West Ham, East Ham, Barking and Stratford Express* reported: "After the privations and suffering of six years of war, during which the people cheerfully accepted whatever came to them, it is a poor reward to be left fireless in houses that do not keep out the weather."

Town planning was high on the agenda, with an intense clamour for permanent or temporary accommodation after so many homes had been destroyed. In March, Essex, then England's fourth largest county, was placed in the hands of a Socialist council for the first time in history. "Labour must have power in Essex," read its propaganda. "The future of the County is in your hands. Vast new possibilities confront our county and vast opportunities, too. Great works of reconstruction, rehabilitation and re-planning have to be faced."

It was into this climate of austerity that Ronald Frederick Lane arrived on April 1, 1946 at Plaistow Maternity Hospital. Being an April Fool it seemed somehow natural he should be blessed with elfin features and an impish grin. From an early age, the youngster had pluck within him, as Stan remembers: "Outside our house the buses used to change drivers and conductors and Ronnie would go down and play to them, strumming a little toy ukulele. He was only about five or six. He'd wear a cowboy hat like Roy Rogers and they used to give him pennies and halfpennies and he'd come back in with a big pocket of money. It was a nice little earner. We used to say, 'Are you going out there again tomorrow, Ron?'"

This early musical inclination came from his father's side as Stan confirms: "Dad used to sing and play drums. He'd go in the Approach pub and sing in there. He could also play piano. Dad would say to Ronnie, 'If you can play a piano you'll always have a friend' because all the pubs around the East End had one and if you was skint and you went in and played piano, someone would always buy you a beer and give you a fag, put something in the hat."

On Sunday mornings Stan would take his boys down to the popular bric-a-brac market at Club Row in Brick Lane to rummage through the odds and ends. The brothers were close to their father who unconditionally showered them with his affection.

Stan Lane: "In Romford Road we lived upstairs and there was like a big bay window and me and Ronnie would stand at the top of the stairs waiting for our dad to come home from work. As soon as we saw him we used to run down and he would swing us round – well, he did to Ronnie more what with me being older."

By sad contrast Elsie Lane was far less demonstrative towards her children. "My mum was a funny woman, she wasn't a good mixer. We never got a cuddle off our mother, never sat on her lap. Dad used to give us all our love, but mum wasn't really affectionate towards anybody."

Stan Snr had his own vocabulary of jolly sayings and malapropisms that he was fond of expressing such as "A nod is as good as a wink to a blind horse" and a particular favourite, "There's a difference in scratching your arse and tearing it to bits," which really meant, there's no need to go over-the-top.

Stan Lane: "When it was time for bed and a story, he always used to say to me and Ronnie, 'Come on, let's go up the wooden hills to Bedfordshire.' My dad went to Bedfordshire a lot to deliver bricks up there. I used to go along with him [in the lorry] when I was a kid. Dad drove for his uncle, Charlie Goldsmith, who had a transport business. He always said, 'I'll look after you, boy, don't worry' but he sold up to British Road Service and dad got sold with it. Dad never got fuck all but he was very loyal to his new guv'nor."

As well as being a driver, Stan Snr was a shop steward at the firm's depot on Violet Road, Bow. During one particularly fraught stand off, he had a knife pulled on him by a militant union member. "I think he'd told this guy to quieten down or shut up," says Stan, "and he went for my dad with a knife, slashed his throat but luckily it was only a scrape."

These indelible memories from Ronnie's childhood were later to be immortalised in one of his most evocative songs.

As the Sixties dawned and with compulsory National Service abolished, Britain's male youth could now look at the prospect of becoming a pop star with some semblance of reality. The arrival in 1956 of the skiffle craze – an improvised form of folk and blues launched by the success of Lonnie Donegan's take on Leadbelly's 'Rock Island Line' – had inspired thousands of teenage boys to create their own groups using homemade instruments like washboards and tea chest basses. Yet with rare exceptions, the UK had yet to produce its own convincing brand of indigenous rock'n'roll and was still looking to America for inspiration. Thanks to the overwhelming popularity of instrumental combo the Shadows and their breakthrough hit, 'Apache', in 1960, sales of guitars and drum kits were on the increase. Because of import restrictions the fabled American Fender guitars that Hank Marvin, Bruce Welch and Jet Harris played were out of the price range of the average aspirant British musician. However other more affordable models could be within reach thanks to the hire purchase system of buying on the never-never as it was popularly known at the time.

"I [learned] to play a little on an acoustic guitar and [my dad] was so tickled with it that he went out and bought me a cheap little Broadway guitar," Ronnie told Allan Vorda in 1987. "He brought it home and was bursting to give it to me. My mum said, 'Why did you buy him that? He's never going to do anything with it.' She was so negative."

Ronnie attended Lister Technical College, on Queen's Road West, Plaistow, where he met a lad in the same year, Ron Chimes, known to all as 'Ben' Chimes after Westminster's famed clock tower. "Ronnie was probably one of the best liked kids in the school by both the teachers and the other pupils," Chimes recalls. "The reason we ended up at Lister was because they concentrated on commercial art. Ronnie was not very academic or sporty but he was very good at drawing but then most of that particular class were.

"We used to call him 'Bronco' Lane [after the rugged '50s TV cowboy star played by Ty Hardin] because he had 'Bronco' written on his bike. I think Ronnie had started to play guitar in the last few months we were at school together. I was introduced to a guitarist quite near where Ronnie lived called Steve Taylor. I played piano but at the time I did think about learning guitar so we started to play a bit."

The East London group scene of the early Sixties was highly incestuous with members joining, leaving and forming bands seemingly at the drop of a hat – therefore the exact chronology of Lane's pre-Small Faces groups is hard to nail precisely. As far is known, around this time, he continued to practise and play with some lads from Three Mills School, including Kenny Bennett on rhythm guitar and Alan Hutton on bass, calling themselves the Muleskinners.

Bob Edkins, a mutual friend and guitarist from the period, recalls: "Kenny sat down for hours teaching Ronnie chords. They were doing Chuck Berry stuff really well. Between all the guys – me, Kenny, Alan and Ronnie and most any guitarist in the Stratford area – if you fancied having a rehearsal with someone you'd say, 'Come round and we'll have a plonk.' Even later in the Small Faces, I can just imagine Ronnie saying 'let's have a plonk' because that was the word we used."

Ron Chimes says he never knew Ronnie as 'Plonk' and Edkins' theory as to how this early nickname came about is met with vociferous resistance from Stan: "It was because Ronnie had a big knob!" he attests, guffawing, "It's a family trait!"

Chimes kept in touch with his old schoolmate and introduced him to Steve Taylor. "Ronnie and Steve got on like a house on fire. They did a couple of gigs just as a duo where they played background music at like a restaurant or coffee bar. I said to them, 'What about if I joined the band?' I remember our first gig was at my neighbour's local in Barking and we got paid £1 10s – 10 shillings each!"

Finding the pianos in the pubs where they rehearsed to be substandard Chimes bought a Vox organ. "I learnt to play left-hand bass on the organ because we didn't have a bass player." Ronnie and Steve played matching Hofner Verithin* guitars purchased from either Freemans in Leyton or the J.60 Music Bar at 445–7 High St North, Manor Park, a popular shop with the area's musicians and one that would play a significant role in Ronnie's early career.

Leaving school at 16 Ronnie had already been earning money, working at Battersea Park Funfair, south London during the holidays. He started on the Roll A Penny side stall, working up to the daunting task, considering his size, of brakeman on the Big Dipper. His first full-time job was as a sales assistant at Dunn's men's outfitters in Stratford. He also had a steady girlfriend, Jill Walsh.

Ron Chimes: "Jill was a hairdresser, very good looking, slim and always immaculate. None of us could believe that Ronnie could pull someone like her!"

On one occasion their amorous teenage fumbling on the sofa was rudely interrupted by the unexpected return of Ronnie's parents from Auntie Rene's – another formative experience that would provide the inspiration for a Lane song.

Ron Chimes: "Steve Taylor was in love with Jill, and Ronnie knew that. Being the joker he was, he got Jill to ring Steve up one evening and make out she had the 'hots' for him and that they should meet in secret. Steve was taken aback at first but then decided and agreed to meet up whereupon Ronnie, in the background, shouted out 'Taylor, you bastard!' It was very funny but broke poor old Steve's heart!"

Around the spring of 1963, Stan Lane facilitated an important meeting for his brother. "I'd bought a '63 [Volkswagon] Beetle for £680, brand new on the road," says Stan. "I had it on the book. I thought 'fuckin' 'ell, how am I going to pay for the car?' So I was doing a few shifts at this pub, at weekends mostly."

The British Prince, situated on the corner of Bromley Street and Walter Terrace, in Stepney, held a regular Friday night music session with a jazz band providing live entertainment. Word had reached the ears of 14-year old drummer, Kenney Jones.

---

* The Verithin, Hofner's answer to the then extremely popular Gibson ES335 guitar, was introduced on to the UK market in 1960.

Stan Lane: "Kenney used to stand outside the pub because he wasn't old enough to have a drink. When the drummer in this band used to go and have a few drinks I used to call Kenney in and he used to play and then the publican would sling him out again."

Kenneth Thomas Jones was born on September 16, 1948 at the London Hospital, Whitechapel. An only child, he lived with his parents, Samuel Thomas and Violet Elizabeth in a terraced council house at 34 Havering Street, Stepney, where Violet's mother and father, Mr and Mrs Ward, had resided.*

Stan Lane: "I knew Kenney's dad because he worked for Union Cartage just off Ben Jonson Road, Poplar. We used to go down the docks and pick up all the containers. Sammy was a lorry driver but also he was a warehouseman. He used to shunt the motors backwards and forwards in the yard."

Being an undiagnosed dyslexic, Kenney's education was affected when attending St George's-in-the-East and Stepney Green Secondary School. "It was quite rough, the school I went to," Jones recalls. "There was a music teacher there. She tried teaching us but she was given a hard time because nobody wanted to know about anything poncey like music. I was only interested in woodwork and metalwork really." As a youngster Jones was something of a tearaway, hanging out with local hooligans around the rough and tumble East End.

Kenney Jones: "Me and a mate were washing cars after school and at weekends to earn a bit of pocket money, getting about five shillings a car. One day he said to me, 'Why don't we form a skiffle group?' I said, 'Yeah, great.' After about five minutes, I said, 'What's a skiffle group?!' He said, 'There's going to be one on TV tonight. You'll see.' So I watched Lonnie Donegan on TV playing a banjo. I thought, 'Yeah, that's what I want.'"

When the banjo he had his heart set upon getting from a pawn shop on Bethnal Green Road was sold, Kenney's attention turned to percussion when the shop assistant mentioned he knew someone who owned a couple of drums.

Kenney Jones: "I must have been about 12 at the time. It was the summer school holidays and no one else was in so I started bashing away at these drums, with the windows open. My mum was coming down the

---

* The house, complete with outside toilet, can be seen in the 1968 promotional film for the Small Faces' 'Lazy Sunday', co-starring the Jones' neighbour.

road and she could hear this noise coming from our house. But I just took to it [drums] like a duck to water."

Kenney saw a second-hand set at the J.60 Music Bar. "I caught the bus back home, 'borrowed' ten pounds out of my mum's purse to put down the deposit. I still remember how much it cost – £64 9s 2d."

His parents were initially horrified when the shop's salesman brought the Olympic kit around to the Jones' front room to set up and demonstrate but they eventually gave in and signed the HP form, if only in the hope of the drums keeping their wayward lad out of mischief.

Kenney Jones: "I played all the time – in the morning before school, during the lunch hour, after school. The neighbours all used to complain but my parents stuck by me. I taught myself by playing along to records, the Shadows and a couple of 78s we had round the house, 'Twelfth Street Rag' and stuff like that."

Eventually the enthusiastic young skin basher started checking out other musicians around his manor. "I went to this local pub, the British Prince, trying to look four years older because I was underage," Jones recalls. "I watched the jazz band they had playing there for a few weeks and their drummer – this guy called Roy – came up to me and said, 'Why do you keep on looking at me? Are you taking the piss?' I said, 'No, no, I'm watching you because I'm teaching myself to play the drums.'

"About a couple of weeks later I got a total shock when he announced, 'Now we've got a special guest coming up tonight to play with us, it's a young drummer, here he is, Kenney Jones.' I ended up getting behind the kit to play with these jazz guys. And I was nervous as hell. But after they counted in the number, I was off, it just felt totally natural [to me].

"Afterwards, the barman came over and asked me, 'Are you in a band?' I said 'No' and he said, 'Well, my brother plays guitar and he's looking to start a group. Shall I bring him down next week?'"

Ron Chimes has a different version of events. "Stan had said to us, 'Look I've had a chat with the landlord. Do you fancy coming down and playing a couple of nights a week at the pub,' and we said, 'Yeah but we need to get a drummer.' And Stan said, 'Well as it happens there's a young kid who plays there with a piano player and he's only 14.' Now bearing in mind we were 16, 17 at the time three years was a huge age gap so we weren't that keen."

Kenney Jones: "I'll never forget my first meeting with Ronnie Lane. He walked into the British Prince and he had a really smart suit on with a starch collar and a tie, looking very much like one of the Beatles, but before the Beatles, if you know what I mean. Every time he talked his collar and tie would stay still while his neck moved!"

Jones was shy and reserved next to Lane's boyish enthusiasm but this didn't faze Ronnie who invited the drummer to an audition being held in a hall above a pub in Plaistow.

Kenney had been playing with a local group called the Pioneers whose line-up featured vocalist Terry Dent, Ron Stanley (lead guitar), Mike Gower (rhythm), Micky Willis (bass) and drummer Clifford Smeeth. "This kid kept pestering us to come and hear him play," Gower recalls. "Eventually, because he only lived around the back to where I lived in Albert Gardens in Stepney, me and Ron went round there. Kenney had his kit set up and he basically played along to a couple of Shadows albums, played the drum solos perfectly." The Pioneers rehearsed Saturday afternoons at a church hall on Stepney Way. Kenney would quietly watch until being invited to sit in. The group had a regular Friday night gig at the Kate Odders pub on Duckett Street. While Smeeth attended an evening bricklaying course at East Ham Technical College, Kenney would cover for him during the first set until Smeeth took over.

Ron Stanley: "Kenney was only with us for about a few months. I remember him telling us about this audition. Ronnie Lane had said there was a set of drums he could use but Kenney was insistent he wanted to use his own kit. I drove him over there in my van."

Ron Chimes: "We saw a couple of drummers. Kenney was one, the other was a guy called Phil Kenton, who I worked with at an advertising agency in the West End. Phil impressed us with his technique but as Ronnie put it, Kenney was the one who had the beat. He wasn't the best technically but he was the one that felt right."

As they got to know each other Lane and Jones – both standing at five foot five – discovered they'd been in the Army Cadets at the same time. "I was in the Royal Green Jackets Rifle Brigade," Jones told Rupert Williams. "I don't know who he was with but Ronnie and I had been at this camp for about two weeks in Salisbury, full of hundreds of army cadet kids from all over England. While he was there Ronnie trod on one of these fake landmines they were using and blew himself up over a gate!"

The new group – still without a name – consisted of Ronnie Lane and Steve Taylor (guitars), Ron Chimes (organ), and Kenney Jones (drums). On top of their day jobs, the British Prince offered regular – and long – hours with the group playing there Thursdays, Fridays, Saturdays, Sunday lunchtimes and Sunday nights, earning £10 a week each.

Ron Chimes: "One night we went down to Kenney's house to pick up his drum set to take it down to the gig. Ken's dad wouldn't do any of the lifting because he reckoned he had a bad back. We were using my dad's

11

car which had a roof-rack but by the time we got all the gear on there and in the back there was no room for Ronnie and Kenney. They said, 'What are we then, the outcasts?!' And we said, 'Bloody hell, that's a good name for a band.'"

The Outcasts were just one of hundreds of local groups playing at dances, pubs and clubs performing a mixture of Beatles songs, Shadows instrumentals and current pop hits. Stan Lane: "The Outcasts used to rehearse at the Boy Scouts Hall over the road from the Princess Alice. I was the roadie at the beginning. I used to lug their gear about in the Bedford Dormobile. We used to have Watney's beer crates in the back for seats."

Such was the transience of the Sixties British beat scene that seemingly overnight the Merseybeat-inspired combos of 1963–64 were being supplanted by a new breed of hirsute R&B bands hoping to emulate the success of groups like the Rolling Stones. Moving with the times, the Outcasts played Chuck Berry, Bo Diddley and the more commercial side of R&B in their sets. To relieve Chimes of foot pedal duties, Ronnie persuaded Alan Hutton, who he knew from the Muleskinners, to join the Outcasts on bass. A further twist occurred around early '64 when Lane, Jones and Hutton left to form their own group, which they insisted on calling . . . the Outcasts.

Ron Chimes: "I can't remember why they split, there was a bit of disagreement over something, it wasn't a big falling out, we still spoke to each other. Ronnie, Kenney and Alan got together with a guy called Terry Newman, who was in the year below Ronnie and I at Lister Tech. He was a very good guitarist. So we had this anomaly of two bands both called the same name."

To confuse matters even more the breakaway group then changed their name to another familiar moniker – the Muleskinners. Perhaps feeling intimidated by a guitarist of Newman's ability Ronnie decided to upgrade his instrument and brought his father along to the J.60 to guarantee the HP on a spanking new Gretsch Tennessean.

While gigging at night, Ronnie continued to hold down a succession of diverse day jobs – precariously riding around on a scooter delivering sets of false teeth for a dental firm. A three-week stint as a plumbers mate, ripping up floorboards to fit pipes for a central heating firm, followed. "It wasn't uncommon in those days living in the East End to flit from job to job for an extra few shilling a week," says Chimes.

Thanks to his brother, now married and following in his father's footsteps as a lorry driver, Ronnie landed a job much closer to his heart. Stan

Lane: "I used to deliver guitars to the Selmer's factory up Holborn way. They wanted guitar testers and I put Ronnie's name forward. He went up there and got the job."

Whereas most males of his background faced dull, soul-destroying vocations, to work in the factory headquarters of Selmer Electronics Ltd. at 40 Theobalds Road, surrounded by guitars and amplifiers for eight hours a day, must have seemed like nirvana to the teenage wannabe musician. Ronnie worked in a soundproof room where his job was to test the newly made amplifiers and speaker cabinets.

Meanwhile Chimes and Taylor of the *original* Outcasts continued with a rhythm section of Clifford Goode and drummer Brian Hudson who later joined local East End favourites Tony Rivers & The Castaways.

Ron Chimes: "We were doing a gig at East Ham Town Hall [in July '64] and Steve Taylor took ill with pneumonia. So I quickly rang Ronnie and said, 'Is there any chance that you could fill in?' He said yes so he learnt the set and he did this gig with us which somebody happened to record."[*]

Ronnie enjoyed the experience enough to leave the Muleskinners to rejoin the Outcasts. Ron Chimes: "We only ever did two original songs that Ronnie mainly wrote. One was a Beatle-type song called 'Don't Talk To Me Of Love' that he wrote with Terry Newman."

Shortly after Lane rejoined, the Outcasts played a gig in Rainham, Essex, with Steve Marriott's Moments. Contrary to most received accounts Chimes is positive that this is where Marriott and Lane first met. "He and Steve just clicked because they were both tiny little blokes with a similar sense of humour."

When the Outcasts were offered steady work at Butlin's Holiday Camp in Clacton it meant turning professional. Ronnie, wary of giving up his job, rejoined Jones, Hutton and Newman in the Muleskinners, who were now augmented by singer George Cambridge, formerly of George Cambridge & The Telstars. Having played guitar for roughly two years without making any significant advance – "I could get my hands around a song" – it was while in the Muleskinners, Lane noticed that bass guitarists were at a premium on the local circuit.

"We could never get a bass player," he told Allan Vorda. "Down in the East End it seemed nobody wanted to play the bass unless he was a real loser who couldn't play a lead instrument."

---

[*] A snippet of the surviving tape – with the Outcasts covering a Bo Diddley song – can be heard in the excellent 2006 documentary on Lane's life, *The Passing Show*.

Having convinced his father that the bass would help pay off the payments on his Gretsch, once again Stan Lane Snr accompanied his son to the J.60 to sign on the dotted HP line. Accompanying them was Kenney Jones. "We walked in and this chirpy kid came up and said, 'Can I help you?' It turned out to be Steve Marriott."

If Ronnie had a cheeky exuberance, it paled next to the five foot four bundle of cocky Cockney confidence that was Stephen Peter Marriott, born on January 30, 1947 at East Ham Memorial Hospital to a working-class family living at 308 Strone Road, Manor Park.

"A born leader," as his mother Kay described Steve to Len Brown, "he was small, not the sort of person you'd think of as a leader but he just had that magnetism."

Marriott showed a propensity towards singing and performing from an early age. As with Ronnie, he was bought a plastic ukulele by his father Bill, which along with harmonica, Steve taught himself to play. Such was the young Marriott's plucky determination that, inspired by his hero Buddy Holly, he was playing guitar in his first group by the age of 12.

Thanks to his parents putting him forward to audition for the role, in 1960, Steve spent a year in Lionel Bart's *Oliver!* musical at the New Theatre in London's West End.* Having undoubted charisma, acting appeared to be the natural way forward and he was accepted into the prestigious Italia Conti Academy of Theatre Arts. In lieu of his tuition fees Marriott took jobs in radio (*Mrs Dale's Diary*) and TV (*Citizen James, Mr Pastry's Progress, Dixon Of Dock Green*) as well as having a cameo role in the Boulting Brothers' *Heavens Above!* (1963), and as a chirpy Cockney drummer in two low budget British pop films, *Live It Up!* (1963) and *Be My Guest* (1965).

While at acting school, Marriott continued to pursue his musical career and it eventually won the upper hand. "I was doing well and [my parents] were badly brought down when I started to get interested in groups, going out on the road and not living at home," Marriott told *Rave* magazine in 1966. "But the drama school did me good. It gave me confidence. It gave me front."

Singing, playing harmonica and a little piano, Marriott fronted several groups under such names as the Moondogs, the Moonlites, the Frantics (sometimes billed as Steve Marriott & The Frantic Ones) and Steve

---

* The original cast recording, released through World Records, featuring Marriott as the Artful Dodger, became his recorded vocal debut.

Marriott's Moments. He also released two unsuccessful singles – the Buddy Holly aping, Kenny Lynch composed 'Give Her My Regards' (issued by Decca in March 1963) and, with the Moments, a tepid cover of the Kinks' 'You Really Got Me,' for the American market, on World Artists.

Both recordings masked Marriott's true love of the American soul (James Brown, Wilson Pickett, Garnet Mimms, Bobby Bland) and R&B/jazz (Muddy Waters, Jimmy Reed, Ray Charles, Booker T.) he had been hearing via Radio Luxembourg and clubs like the Flamingo and the Scene whose DJ, Guy Stevens, possessed a formidable collection of blues, soul and rock'n'roll. As Steve absorbed these influences so his abilities exponentially grew as a vocalist of startling power for one so young.

However, Marriott's brash ambition had thus far failed to carry his career as far forward as he would have liked so he'd been forced to hold down a temporary Saturday job at the J.60 as a sales assistant when Lane and Jones came calling.* "I said, 'I'd like to have a look at that bass over there,'" Lane told Vorda. "And [Marriott] said, 'Oh, that's the best bass in the shop. That's a great bass!' He was very enthusiastic and keen about Tamla–Motown. I liked him."

Kenney Jones: "I left them to it and wandered over to this drum kit set up in there, got behind it, and started to play. Ronnie plugged in and started plonking along with me and Steve picked up a guitar and suddenly the three of us were all playing, annoying the other people in the shop. We just sort of clicked right away."

Legend – possibly apocryphal – has it that Marriott and Lane sufficiently bonded for Ronnie to acquire the Harmony Meteor bass for a significantly knocked down price, resulting in Marriott getting his marching orders from the J.60.

That afternoon Lane visited Marriott's parents' council flat at 9 Daines Close, Manor Park, to sample Steve's extensive collection of black American soul, Tamla and R&B records. Suitably impressed, Ronnie invited Steve to the gig the Muleskinners were playing that night. Kenney Jones: "We had a residency at a pub over in Bermondsey. Ronnie and Steve ended up getting paralytic. Steve got up with us, sang a song and then he brought the house down with his Jerry Lee Lewis routine on the upright piano they had. He was jumping up and down on top of it and breaking all the keys on the keyboard.

---

* Advertisements from this period indicate that Marriott was still fronting the Moments at the time, and continued to do so into the early months of 1965.

"We got thrown out of the pub, lost the gig there, the other guys had gone off, they weren't speaking to Ronnie and I because we'd brought Steve along. We were sitting on my drum kit outside on the curb. The three of us just looked at each other and burst out laughing and that's when we decided to form a band together."

Ron Chimes: "When Ronnie and Kenney got together with Steve Marriott, they asked Terry Newman to carry on with them but Terry refused. I don't think he liked the direction they wanted to go in. He eventually joined us and so did George Cambridge – talk about incestuous. So we became the Outcasts with all the members from the other Outcasts!"

With Marriott offering to fulfil guitar as well as vocal duties and to take over the HP payments on Ronnie's Gretsch, the fledgling group still needed a fourth member to realise their vision of becoming the East End's answer to Booker T. & The MG's. Enter James Langwith (a.k.a. Jimmy Winston) whom Marriott claimed to have known through the J.60 and whose parents, William and Esta, ran the Ruskin Arms, on High Street North, Manor Park.

"It was the very week that I left drama school [at the Theatre Workshop, Stratford] that I first met Steve Marriott and Ronnie Lane," Winston told John Hellier in 1996. "I was doing a spot of compering at my dad's pub and they came in . . . Steve wanted to get onstage with the resident group and play a bit of harmonica. He got up, played and was good. We then got chatting over a few beers and it was that night really that the Small Faces were launched . . . Strange really because up until that meeting I had been geared up for an acting career but after just the one meet with them I was prepared to throw it all up in favour of joining a new group."

Born in Stratford on April 21, 1943, Winston was not only the eldest but at five foot six, the tallest in the group. He owned a Rickenbacker but as it was decided there was only going to be one guitarist, Jimmy bought a Vox Continental organ and he, Steve and Ronnie set upon learning the rudiments of their respective instruments. Thanks to the convenience of having a pub as a regular place to rehearse, and a van bought and driven for them by Winston's brother Frank, the still unnamed group were on their way.

After a few warm ups at the Ruskin to get the feel for an audience, their first booking was at the Kensington Youth Centre in Wordsworth Road, East Ham. "They didn't know what to expect," Winston recalled, "we kind of bluffed our way through the set. We only knew five songs but with different variations we got away with it."

It was after one of their earliest gigs that Annabelle, a posh acquaintance of Marriott and Winston's from Kensington, apparently remarked "Haven't you got small faces?!" Thanks to their diminutive stature (bar Winston) and sharply dressed, mod about town appearance (i.e. 'a face') the name – Small Faces – seemed ideally suited although it initially drew derisory comments from friends and acquaintances when asking what the group was called.

With remarkable audacity, having only played a handful of times, the untried group decided to head north to check out the club scene there. From Marriott's recall their first gig was at Manchester's Twisted Wheel, a hardcore R&B and soul venue. According to an account in *CENtral 1179*, Keith Rylatt and Phil Scott's book about 'the Wheel', when auditioning before the club's promoters, Ivor and Philip Abadi, the group were cut short after a couple of numbers. "Unceremoniously they were given the thumbs down and compensated with a pound note for petrol for the return drive back to Sheffield."*

The fast-talking Marriott persuaded a working men's club in the Steel City to put them on but, as he recalled to *New Musical Express*: "Halfway through, the manager stopped us, said he was sorry but we were just not right for a working man's club. Anyway he paid us before we left but strangely there was a woman of about 60 who loved us. She knew all the James Brown numbers we played and kept asking for more."

More receptive were Sheffield's jazz/R&B clubs, the Esquire, and its rival, the Mojo, the latter run by brothers Peter and Geoff Stringfellow. The band went over well, despite the fact they barely knew half a dozen numbers. These included Jesse Hill's 'Oo Poo Pah Doo', James Brown's 'Think', Rufus Thomas' 'Jump Back' and an improvised, free-for-all called 'E To D'. Peter Stringfellow not only paid the group and put them up in lodgings above the club but was eager to rebook them. The Mojo, in particular, would become one of the Small Faces' major Mod strongholds north of Watford.

Marriott was keeping his options open and during this time (the spring of '65) he auditioned at Soho's La Discotheque to join an R&B group from

---

* *CENtral 1179* states the audition occurred on October 2, 1964 and the *Manchester Evening News* advertisement for the Twisted Wheel on this date lists 'The Faces'. Marriott was still being advertised with the Moments at this time, who were booked to play down on the South Coast the following day – a distance of over 200 miles.

Kent called the Manish Boys who were looking for an additional vocalist alongside their singer Davy Jones (who would soon change his name to David Bowie). Marriott and Bowie became friendly as fellow hustlers on the pop scene, and in 1999, on VH1's *Storytellers*, Bowie recalled: "Steve was very short in height but long on big ideas. 'I've got this idea,' he'd say over eggs and bacon. 'Why don't we form this R&B duo and call ourselves David & Goliath. You be David . . .' One night he came up to me in the dressing room and said, 'I've got my mates Ronnie and Kenney together and we're going to form a band. What we're going to do is get these really big amplifiers and this enormous drum kit, kind of like the Who you know, but we're going to be really, really little. We're going to call ourselves the Small Faces.' "

Kenney left his job at Speciality Foods Ltd, a pickle manufacturers situated on Hardinge Street, close to his home, for an opening at Selmer's, found for him by Ronnie, to work on the cabinet and speaker assembly line. Former workmate John Crocker recalls Lane regularly strolling around outside the soundproof testing room playing the walking bass line of 'Green Onions' on a Fender, trailing a long lead connected to an amp.

As well as being the subjects of various caricatures drawn on the walls, the staff were the fall guys in Ronnie's pranks as another ex-Selmer's employee John Weir recalls: "[Ronnie] used to keep us in hysterics most of the time . . . When [he] was working in the soundproof room, he would often lock the door and settle down to read the newspaper, with a cup of coffee and a cigarette. Tom Sayers, the foreman, knew this and would try the door. Finding it locked, he would bang on it with his fist, shouting, 'I know you're in there, Lane. Open this door and come out now!' On hearing this, Ronnie would move a Goliath speaker cabinet aside to reveal a small hole which he had cut in the hardboard wall at the back of the room. He would wriggle out through this, walk around and come up behind, saying, 'Hello Tom, are you looking for me?' to which Tom would reply, 'I swear I will swing for you, Lane!' "

Even Kenney wasn't immune from Ronnie's wind-ups as his carefully assembled amps were often deliberately 'failed' and sent back, much to Ronnie's merriment. After Lane left Selmer's his next attempts at gainful employment included a brief stint working for the Civil Service and washing dishes at a Joe Lyon's Corner House restaurant along with the now out-of-work Marriott, who hung around the Giaconda coffee bar on Denmark Street hustling for work at the nearby publishing houses.

The Small Faces decided to turn pro when, while playing at the Ruskin Arms, they were spotted, either by DJ and A&R man Ian 'Sammy'

Samwell who had written Cliff Richard & The Drifters' early UK hits, including 'Move It', as well as songs for Johnny Tillotson, the Isley Brothers and Dusty Springfield, or Samwell's close associate, Terry Slater (an agent known as Terry 'the Pill'). The group got offered a Saturday night one-off at a hall in central London, The Cavern On The Town, which operated out of the Notre Dame Hall in Leicester Square.

Kenney Jones: "We ended up playing this residency there for another five Saturdays. Word spread, Don Arden got to hear about it and sent down his right hand man Pat Meehan Jnr to see us."

As fate would have it, the night before while walking home, Marriott and Lane got badly beaten up in a random attack. "We were covered in blood, kicked to bits, eyes out to here, lips, ears, everything," Marriott recalled to John Hellier. "We found out later that it was some boys from Loughton who had gone down to Tottenham and smashed up a few cafes so this was a return visit. We didn't know, we had no idea . . ."

Luckily Meehan was not the type put off by the effects of violence. "He said, 'I've heard great things about the group. We'd like to sign you up. Come up to the office tomorrow,'" Jones recalled. "We said, 'We're not interested, we don't want to be managed' but we were up at Don Arden's office the next morning . . ."

CHAPTER 2

Of Mods And Mac

"Mods were small strange creatures, very neat and delicate, and they rode scooters, chewed gum, swallowed pills by the hundredweight. Most of all, they were hooked on clothes. Any money they got, it always went on making themselves look beautiful."

Nik Cohn, *A Wop Bop A Loo Bop A Lop Bam Boom – Pop From The Beginning*, 1969

"It was work, work, work – and I loved it, that's exactly what I'd wanted . . . I just wanted to work and when I joined the Small Faces I joined a band who really wanted to play all the time."

Ian McLagan, interview with author, 2010

B Y 1964, after years of stifling conformity, British youth were finally in a position to shake off the burdensome spectre of the Second World War and enjoy themselves at last. In October Harold Wilson's Labour government overturned 13 years of Conservative dominance by a slim majority. With seemingly equal opportunities open to all classes, it appeared that Macmillan's statement of never having it so good might actually be coming true. Thanks to a relatively buoyant economy, with almost full employment, teenagers now had the income at their disposal to spend on accoutrements like records, clothes and guitars.

Through such outlets as influential pop television show *Ready, Steady, Go!* the subculture of Mod had spread to the furthest reaches of Britain. The roots of Mod – from Modernist – stretch back to the late Fifties. There is dispute as to its origins – some say it came from working-class 'dandies' obsessed with Italian style and cool modern jazz centred in London's West End, others that it emerged out of the clothes-conscious East End rag trade or as an extension of beatnik existentialists. Originally something of a secret society and in thrall to American consumerism over Britain's post-war drabness, the movement seemed to arrive fully formed with its own look (Fred Perry polo shirts, Madras cotton jackets, turned up Levi's, bowling shoes, French Crop hairstyles), transport (Italian mirrored motor scooters), drugs (mainly amphetamine pills – purple hearts, blues and leapers) and music (American soul, R&B and Tamla and Jamaican ska) centred around Soho's clubs (the Scene in Ham Yard, the Flamingo on Wardour Street).

The topical Mod v Rocker confrontations in Britain's seaside towns over the spring and summer of '64 gained nationwide headlines but in the process, once the media co-opted the original purist movement a bastard-ised version of Mod arose with an emphasis on garish fashion with Carnaby Street as its nexus.

In tandem with this reinvention came a new type of group that was more individual in its outlook and approach, taking their lead from Mod fashions and either copying or providing their own take on the obscure American music that Mods dug – the Who being the most obvious example. Hailing from west London with an in-built songwriter and spokesman in Pete Townshend, the Who were moulded to Mod by their original publicist and quasi-manager Peter Meaden whose ideas were taken over by Meaden's usurpers, Kit Lambert and Chris Stamp.

Kenney Jones: "We were aware of the Who through seeing them [during a weekly residency] at the Marquee [Club]. We couldn't believe that there was another group that was just like us in a sense. I mean we were playing different music but it was definitely part of the same thing."

With an average age of 18 the Small Faces were just part of the British post-war generation caught up in the music, fashion and lifestyle of Mod. And here was Don Arden, offering them £20 a week, almost double the average wage for 1965. As Ronnie Lane described it to Penny Valentine: "One minute we was living off brown sauce rolls – the next we had the run of Carnaby Street."

Known variously under such (often self-styled) guises as 'Mr Big' and the 'Al Capone of Pop', Arden's notorious exploits as a much revered and reviled manager, entrepreneur and record label owner are now the fabric of legend. Born Harry Levy in Cheetham Hill, Manchester, in 1926, Arden entered show business as a singer and stand-up comedian. After serving in the British army during World War II, he continued to tread the boards on the British variety circuit until realising, at the age of 28, that there was more profitability in becoming a promoter.

During the early Sixties, Don Arden Enterprises Ltd held the monopoly on bringing American rock'n'roll artists to Britain, among them the Everly Brothers, Bo Diddley, Little Richard (all part of a package supported by the little-known Rolling Stones on their first national tour in 1963), Jerry Lee Lewis, Chuck Berry and Carl Perkins. Arden's first managerial client – or victim, depending on one's viewpoint – was Gene Vincent who by the time he moved to England, was heading into a downward spiral of booze, pills and general erratic behaviour. Eventually Arden and Vincent's management arrangement was acrimoniously terminated.

Realising there were fewer problems and more capital in handling beat groups than untamed rockers, Arden became the Animals' agent in 1964 and managed the Nashville Teens who not only backed the American artists he brought over but were signed to Arden's Contemporary Recordings Ltd. whose output was released on Decca. Arden's management company, Pavion Ltd., with Pat Meehan as director was based on the third floor of an office at 52–55 Carnaby Street. According to Marriott, the Who's co-manager Kit Lambert had shown interest in the Small Faces as had Maurice King who with his partner, Barry Clayman, ran a company Capable Management that handled the Walker Brothers among others. King also owned a club, the Starlight Rooms that Marriott frequented. It was the coincidental connections – Marriott attended drama school with Don Arden's son, David and had appeared in films alongside Arden-connected artists Gene Vincent, Jerry Lee Lewis and the Nashville Teens – that helped seal the deal.

Kenney Jones: "Don Arden offered us a straight wage or a percentage. We had a moment to ourselves and we said, 'No this is silly, we want both.' He said, 'OK we'll give you 20 pounds a week and we take 25 per cent of your earnings.' So we signed a three-year contract with his company."

With an important manager behind them and a recording contract in place, the Small Faces looked poised for success. Arden put them into the studio with Ian Samwell who, with songwriter Brian Potter, dashed off the defiant 'Whatcha Gonna Do About It'. It was catchy, memorable if not entirely original – the title cribbed from a Doris Troy soul classic, the tune from Solomon Burke's 'Everybody Needs Somebody To Love' while Marriott's feedback solo owed a lot to the Who's recent pop art experiments on their second single 'Anyway Anyhow Anywhere'.

When released on August 6, Arden used every scam to hype the record into the charts, including the all-important pirate station exposure on Radio Caroline and Radio London.* To make them look the real deal he

---

* For a more detailed examination of Arden's practices in this area, the author recommends Johnny Rogan's *Starmakers & Svengalis: The History Of British Pop Management* (Macdonald 1988).

handed DJ and Mod about town, Jeff Dexter, a wad of notes to kit his charges out in the latest Carnaby clobber from John Stephen's neighbouring clothing shops. "They were like kids in a sweet shop but their style was all wrong," says Dexter. "I said, 'You can't have stripes and checks together' but Sammy Samwell said, 'Think about it, they look like little clowns and people will recognise them.' I went back to Don's office and told him I thought they looked horrendous but that it was unusual. So I asked him, 'How do you want to package them, looking good or unusual?' Don thought about it and said, 'Fuck it, stick with unusual.'"

Dressed in these gaudy outfits, the Small Faces appeared on *Thank Your Lucky Stars* and *Ready, Steady, Go!* and made their BBC Light Programme radio debut on *Saturday Club*. Three weeks after its release, 'Whatcha Gonna Do About It' entered the *Melody Maker* Pop 50 chart at 45 and peaked at 15 in the *NME* Top 30, not bad going for a group that had only been together officially for ten weeks.

Determined to have their own head the young upstarts insisted their second single should be an original composition, and to this end the dramatic 'I've Got Mine' – which was performed by the Small Faces in a B-movie entitled *Dateline Diamonds* – became the first release under the Marriott-Lane imprimatur. However an irreconcilable schism was developing within the group.

Kenney Jones: "Jimmy Winston couldn't play organ that well. I mean we were all still learning but he started competing with Steve to get attention. Steve was a perfect frontman and Jimmy would be there in the background, going over the top, waving his hands about or whatever. He stuck out like a sore thumb and it became embarrassing."

Inevitably Winston takes a different view, telling John Hellier: "We were earning virtually nothing at the time and agreed to give my brother Frank 10 per cent [*sic. The arrangement was actually five per cent*]. He was going to purchase the van, insure it, tax it, and do all the driving. Everybody agreed that was fine . . . Seeing as I was older than the others it was always me that went and collected the money after a gig. I'd automatically deduct my brother's percentage and pay him. The rest of the band got a bit grumpy about this . . . It was one of those incidents where I got stuck in the middle and I did get into conflict with Steve and Ronnie over this. I'd always been close to my brother and they weren't being fair to him. I think they used this as a bit of a lever . . .

"Don Arden saw it as [five] per cent of his earnings and I think right from the start he was trying to do something about it . . . Arden called me into his office and told me that this wasn't going to work and suggested I put another band together and he would record us.* He kind of gave me an alternative . . . I wasn't particularly happy about the situation, the Small Faces were doing well and the future for the band looked rosy but at the same time we were not getting on, there were a lot of rows and it was becoming a drag."

Little did Winston know that his band mates had already nominated his possible successor who, as fate would have it, had just quit a popular club group, Boz & The Boz People. "There was a review of one of the Boz People's gigs," Ian McLagan recalls, some 45 years on. "The article raved about my playing, which was very kind but they used a photograph of Boz and put my name under it.† So the guys in the Small Faces must have thought, 'He plays a great Hammond and he's really good looking, too' and then they saw me. I'm sure they must have thought, 'Oh well, at least he plays a good Hammond.'"

Ian Patrick McLagan was born on May 12, 1945 at West Middlesex Hospital, Isleworth, with Irish-Scottish ancestry – his mother, Susan Young, was from Mountrath, County Laois, Ireland while Alec William McLagan was born in Shepherd's Bush to a Scottish father.

Ian McLagan: "My dad's family all called him John but he preferred Alec. Everybody else called him 'Mac'. My family all called me Ian but everybody else called me Mac. My brother Mike was always called Mac, too."

Alec McLagan was a keen amateur skater and became speed skating champion of Great Britain in 1928 when aged about 20. Ian McLagan: "He belonged to the Aldwych speed club, which was a roller rink – it might have been an ice rink – which is now the site of the Kensington Hilton. One of his close pals at the time was a guy called Joe Weatherburn and Joe's girlfriend, Paddy, and dad's girlfriend, later wife, Susan, were best mates. They worked at the John Lewis department store on Oxford Street. My mum came over to England from Ireland when she was 16 and lived in at John Lewis."

After marrying, the Weatherburns bought a home in Hounslow where

---

* Arden was as good as his word, managing Jimmy Winston & The Reflections, who recorded the Kenny Lynch-written 'Sorry She's Mine', released by Decca in June 1966, after the Small Faces recorded their own version for their first LP.

† McLagan remembers the article and photo appearing in *Beat Instrumental*, a monthly magazine aimed at musicians. However only a mention-in-passing of Boz appeared in the November 1965 issue, with nothing about McLagan and without an accompanying photo.

their close friends, the McLagans, lived in a rented house two doors down at 32 Taunton Avenue. Ian McLagan: "Mike was born in '43. Joe and Paddy found out they couldn't have kids so they adopted a girl, Gillian, who was pretty much like my sister – still is. Her birthday was within a week of my brother's and they grew up together. When Bill Haley's 'Rock Around The Clock' hit [in January '56], they had their first teenage party. I was the youngest one allowed in, I was only 10-and-a-half at the time. That's where I discovered rock'n'roll and sex because that was my first kiss. So there were two teenage parties, one at her house, and one at ours, same people at both parties, same music, same kisses."

Mac had a happy childhood raised as a Roman Catholic with regular summer holidays to Ireland, although his education suffered from frequent absenteeism. "I went to infant school, junior school, slid into grammar school by the skin of my teeth and got bored with school almost immediately."

Having heard rock'n'roll and with the massive popularity of skiffle, Mac got his first guitar. "I begged for a guitar and eventually I got one for Christmas. It was a Spanish model but I lost interest in it very quickly because it hurt my fingers. I just thought you picked up a guitar and you could play it."

His mother also made him take piano lessons under considerable duress. "I had no desire to play piano, which is crazy really when you think about it. It was only because of my mum who'd never had piano lessons and always wanted them. My grandmother was a fantastic concertina player – she could play anything. But my mum couldn't afford piano lessons so I had to have them.

"I liked the music but piano lessons didn't involve rock'n'roll in any way. It was boring, scales and things. It was a long ride on the bus right out to Cranford near Heathrow Airport. It got so noisy with the planes, the cups would rattle on top of the piano. This piano teacher, Mrs Morgan drank coffee non-stop and she used to put her coffee cup on the keys at the high end. She had a ruler and she would rap your knuckles if you didn't get it right."

Eventually Mac skipped the lessons to hang out at the Temperance billiard hall on Hounslow High Street* with his mates from Spring Grove Grammar School, Alan Worrell and Terry Munro. "We'd meet up there

---

* This venue later became the Attic, a popular club in the area where coincidentally Steve Marriott's Moments held a residency in the summer of 1964. It then changed its name to the Zambezi.

and have cups of tea and cheese rolls and play snooker all afternoon. It was right by Hounslow bus garage so I'd time it right to go home. I saved the bus fare money by walking back home as if I'd been to piano practise."

Like so many other British boys of their generation, Alan, Terry and Mac formed their own skiffle group. "Terry could play a bit of guitar. Alan was on washboard and I played tea chest bass. The three of us had these chequered flat caps because we wanted to be like Gene Vincent's Blue Caps so we were the Blue Men."

Mac renewed his interest in guitar after hearing more of the life-changing sounds coming over from America. "I don't think there was any music on my dad's side that I knew of. My mum wasn't really musical. The only instrument my brother could play was the Dansette – which I inherited – and the radio. He turned me on to Buddy Holly, that was my indoctrination. Gill had more of a record collection so I would play her records."

After his dismal scholastic record at Spring Grove Grammar School, Isleworth, Mac was lucky to pass the entrance exam into Twickenham College of Technology and School of Art on Egerton Road. "It's only now I realise what a great advantage kids of my age had to be able to get into art schools. I was absolutely useless at school, I'd lost interest and I'd been put down a year. I really was the worst pupil and a friend of mine, Cas, who I'd been to junior school with, showed me his portfolio. I couldn't believe he got to paint and draw all day. He was in the junior part of the art school but he was the same age as me but when I did get accepted I was in the year below him. It was just amazing to be able to do lino cuts, litho, still life classes, oil painting and sketching. And also there was the music, girls and drink. It was all happening."

Jazz and blues also reached Mac's ears via the BBC Light Programme's *Jazz Club*, hosted by Humphrey Lyttelton. "I heard Thelonius Monk's *Blue Monk* and one of the tracks off Muddy Waters' *At Newport 1960* album. It was either 'Got My Mojo Working' or 'Hoochie Coochie Man'. They were almost impossible to buy then. I think I went to Broadmead's on Hounslow High Street and the guy didn't know what I was talking about until he looked through his catalogue and ordered them for me."

Developing a passion for rhythm and blues, Mac saw the Rolling Stones for the first time in May 1963 during their trailblazing Sunday residency at the Crawdaddy Club, held in neighbouring Richmond's Station Hotel. "The amazing thing was the sound, they had started playing before I got in [to the club]. I assumed that as they were a blues band, they would be black and American so it was quite a surprise to find that they were white London boys. But the sound, the throbbing bass and the harmonica on top it just convinced me they were black until I walked in. Then it was a case of, 'Well blimey, I love this music, I'm trying to play it, maybe I can.'"

Mac had been playing guitar in a group, the Cherokees, with some art college pals. "It was basically an instrumental group with a singer. I was the guy who wanted to be in the band, I was the no-talent. Dave Pether was a brilliant guitarist. It was basically his band. His mate, Mick Carpenter, who, like Dave, lived in Southall, played drums. Dave and I were the same age and Pete Brown, the bass player, was a year above us. Mick already had a job and he had some money, we were just poor artists.

"Because Dave was a great instrumentalist and soloist I had to learn things like 'Havah Nagilah'. There were all kinds of instrumentals we did where I just strummed. Bit by bit, we listened to blues, Jimmy Reed and all kinds of R&B and it was just like we had to change. I thought, 'Well, everyone's playing guitar' so eventually I got my first keyboard – a Hohner Cembalet electric piano – because I figured I could play the Chuck Berry rhythm on my left hand and didn't have to play too much on the right to tip the chords. I mean I just fumbled my way into it. By now, Pete's mate Nick Tweddell was playing harp, I brought in my friend Johnny Eaton to sing and we changed the name of the band to the Muleskinners from 'Muleskinner Blues'."

Deciding to quit studying graphic art to become a full-time musician, and through the connection of having arranged for the Rolling Stones to play at two of the art school dances on Eel Pie Island (with the Muleskinners supporting), Mac made contact with their booking agent Eric Easton.

Ian McLagan: "I was very cocky, I had more front than Harrods. When I went up [to Easton's office], Bob Knight, who was one of Eric's bookers, saw me. They had a kind of strange combination of acts. Bob was handling Julie Grant and he was actually looking for a band to back her but she wasn't suited to the music we were playing but it was a way of getting gigs. Eventually Bob took us down to the Vox factory in Dartford and we got free amps so we were like, 'now we're a real band with real equipment'."

Thanks to Mac's tenacity the group started to get gigs further afield including a Friday night residency at the Imperial Ballroom (above Burton's tailoring shop) in Eastleigh, Hampshire, in March '64. "I was the group's manager in a way. I mean we were making no money really. £15 was a good night but then I had to take the van rental out, then petrol and drinks or whatever and there's not much left."

Easton got the Muleskinners on the bill of several Rolling Stones' South Coast package dates in the summer just after singer Eaton quit. Ian McLagan: "I had to do the singing and I was playing maracas too. We'd recorded a demo – a cover of Buddy Holly's 'Love's Made A Fool Of You' [at Southern Music in Denmark Street] which was somewhat similar to the Stones version of 'Not Fade Away'. Mick [Jagger] never said anything but it's pretty embarrassing to think about it now."

Mac's face was saved by the recruitment of vocalist and hardcore blues fanatic, Terry Brennan, formerly of the Roosters, a Richmond area group who'd previously boasted Eric Clapton and Manfred Mann's Tom McGuinness in their line-up.

Like many British R&B groups of the period, the Muleskinners were given the unexpected but nerve-racking opportunity to back several of their heroes. In September '64 a visiting blues package was brought over featuring Sonny Boy Williamson and Little Walter. As well as these two greats, the Muleskinners also backed Howlin' Wolf. "We played with the Wolf [in December '64] at the Ricky Tick, Reading, Corn Exchange, Chelmsford and an all-nighter at the Club Noreik in Tottenham. He was such a sweet man. [Howlin' Wolf's guitarist] Hubert Sumlin told me in recent years, 'The Wolf loved you. He wanted to take you guys back to Chicago.'"

The Muleskinners recorded some further demos including Howlin Wolf's 'Back Door Man'. "I think we recorded at the same studio, Southern Music," says Mac. "An Irish guy called Terry got us in there and he kind of produced the session." A tough, Pretty Things-style re-recording of 'Back Door Man' (featuring Mac's Hohner Cembalet) was released on Fontana in January '65. However, with a plethora of similar-sounding R&B groups around the country, the record quickly vanished. This setback was further compounded by the absence of Dave Pether who became hospitalised following a road accident. "We had to keep finding guitarists to cover for him," McLagan explains.

Ever since hearing Booker T. & The MGs seminal 'Green Onions', Mac had been seduced by the warm, sexy and soulful sound Booker T. Jones got out of the Hammond L100. "With piano you had to learn a lot of clever stuff but with a Hammond you only have to put your hand on it and it stays, you don't have to keep hitting it."

Thanks to a Boosey & Hawkes trade advertisement in *Melody Maker* that caught Mac's eye, a trial Hammond L101 was delivered to the McLagan home on Taunton Avenue. After winning his parents round to the idea, Alec was again pressed into signing HP forms for a Hammond L102 and

Leslie cabinet. In a *Beat Instrumental* profile (dated April 1966), McLagan said, "I changed on to the Hammond last April. What a jump! At first I was completely lost. I felt like a little man with a big machine. The controls were a problem after the simple working electric piano. I learned something different every time I played it."

Through Jack Barrie, of Marquee Artists, McLagan left the Muleskinners around June '65 to join an outfit Barrie was managing from King's Lynn, Norfolk, Boz & The Boz People, formerly known as Boz & The Teatime Four.

Ian McLagan: "Boz wanted to sing jazz so I had to learn jazz chords and I wasn't happy with it. We were playing all these kind of jazzy R&B things.* One night we played a US army base and we had to do three of these hour-long sets. After the first, the bass player came over to me in the dressing room and said, 'Do you fancy a smoke?' I'd smelt dope before but never actually smoked it . . . the next set was just another world and I was so deep into it, I was turned right on, the sound was bigger, deeper and wider and the songs went on forever."

McLagan was alarmed to discover that the Boz People displayed even less professionalism than the Muleskinners. "Boz was always a bit of a rascal and he wasn't taking it as seriously as I wanted. We had these dates in Scotland booked and we broke down on the Friday somewhere north of London and Boz just laughed, 'Ha ha, we broke down, oh well, what the fuck, we can't get there.' So the van got fixed and on Saturday we set off again. We got as far as the North Circular as I recall and it broke down again. It was like the Russian flyers in *A Night At The Opera*, you know, 'Well we got halfway there, we ran out of gas so we went back home.' Sure enough Boz started giggling, so I said, 'That's it, I quit.' I got my case and I thumbed a lift back home."

Now out of a gig and feeling despondent, McLagan was ready to quit the business. "My earnings were getting smaller and smaller each week and I was sick of all the travelling and having to lug my gear about." It was then that fate intervened.

"I went to see my girlfriend Irene as I didn't have anything to do Saturday night and I came back on the tube, she was in Manor House, I was in Hounslow. Completely wrong end of the bloody line. On the way back, I met a pal of mine, Phil Weatherburn, who was actually Gill's cousin. He said, 'Hello Mac, how's the band?' I said, 'I just quit' and he said, 'You

---

* The Boz People recorded four singles for EMI's Columbia label in 1965–66 but McLagan cannot recall if he played on any of them during his brief tenure in the band.

should join the Small Faces' and I went, 'Yeah, very funny, Phil.' I'd actually already seen the Small Faces on *Ready, Steady, Go!* doing 'Whatcha Gonna Do About It'. My dad had called me downstairs to watch them and I thought they were great especially Steve's voice and the way they looked.

"On the Monday morning, November 1, about nine o'clock, the phone rang and it was Don Arden saying, 'Can you come up to the office this afternoon? I've got a job for you.' I didn't know what it was for. I thought it might have been for a recording session. While I was waiting in the outer office I looked at the photographs on the wall of all the bands Arden handled – the Nashville Teens, the Animals, the Clayton Squares, the Small Faces and I thought it couldn't be the Small Faces, the Nashville Teens or the Animals, so it had to be the Clayton Squares who I'd never heard of.

"When he finally got me in, Arden said, 'How much are you earning?' and I lied and told him the figure that my dad was earning as a foreman in an engineering works which was £20 a week. I'd actually been on £5 a week with Boz & The Boz People and I was living at home. Arden said, 'You start at £30, you'll be on probation for a month and after a month if the guys like you and they want to keep you on, you'll get an even split.' And I said, 'What guys?' He said 'The Small Faces' and I smiled to myself. I thought, 'Fucking great!'

"Don said, 'Come back at six o'clock.' I think it was probably around five or 5:30 and I walked to the Ship, the pub next to the Marquee. I wasn't allowed to tell anybody, it was all top secret, mainly because I think Jimmy Winston didn't know he'd been fired at that point, and also his girlfriend was the secretary in the outer office but I didn't know that. So after a couple of pints I called my dad who'd just got home from work. I said, 'Look, dad, I can't tell you what's going on but I've got a job with a band and I'm going away, it's really exciting.' And bless his heart he guessed who it was. It was him who turned me on to the Small Faces in the first place.

"So I went back to Don's office and I was two pints down on an empty stomach, I hadn't eaten since breakfast. He invited me into his office again. Then the door opened and the three of them came in. Steve looked at me and just grabbed me. They picked me up off the ground and we all started laughing 'cause we were all the same size."

As a postscript, after a period of time had passed, Mac enquired as to whether he'd passed the audition. "Ronnie said 'Whaddya mean?' so I told him about me being on probation. Ronnie said, 'Did you hear that,

Steve? Let's get this sorted now.' So we went up to the office and Ronnie points at me and says, 'Listen Don, we like this guy. Mac's one of us now, fuck this probation shit.' That's when my money dropped down to £20 a week!"

As with Ringo Starr joining the Beatles or the Who finding Keith Moon, the recruitment of Ian McLagan was the last vital piece of the jigsaw. 'Mac', as the others swiftly fell into line by calling him, got further acquainted with his new band mates that night at the President Hotel, Russell Square, where the group were staying between engagements. The first task was conforming Mac's look to the Small Faces' image.

Ian McLagan: "I was never really a Mod. I thought I was more of a beatnik with the brown corduroy jacket, blue jeans, etc. I loved the music Mods liked and I loved the clothes but I didn't have any money [to spend on them]. The night I joined [the Small Faces] Ronnie worked on my hair and I was sitting in front of the mirror while he was blow-drying it. I looked at him and looked at myself and we both realised . . . because my dad had said, 'This guy looks like you'. We didn't look a lot like each other but we did back then. The following day we went to Carnaby Street and I got kitted out and then on to Sound City where I got my Telecaster and we did *Ready, Steady, Radio* at the Lyceum. That's where Jimmy Winston showed up and there was a bit of a scene. We mimed to 'I've Got Mine' . . . that's why I had to have a guitar. It was bizarre, the crowd were watching and screaming at us while we were miming for a radio show."

McLagan's recruitment certainly raised the Faces up a few considerable notches musically. While bringing a perfect symmetry to the group's look in height it was doubly fortunate that he also shared the others' impeccable taste for American soul and R&B. "The very first thing we ran through together was the Booker T. version of [Mel Torme's] 'Comin' Home Baby'" Marriott said in a December '65 *Beat Instrumental* interview. "I didn't like to expect too much but I was really knocked back, he was so good. At the first booking the Hammond really slew me, it did something to me inside. It's a wonderful sound. I was so moved I could have cried."

On Christmas night, Steve, Ronnie and Mac moved their belongings into a four-storey Victorian terraced townhouse at 22 Westmoreland Terrace, Pimlico, found for them by Arden's company, who covered the £40 a week rent, complete with their own housekeeper and cook. Being an early riser and the youngest, Kenney remained at his parents in Stepney.

The group were ferried to gigs in a green Mark X Jaguar by 16-stone road manager Bill Corbett, an employee of Arden's who had previously driven the Beatles. "We had a portable record player in the car," Mac recalled. "We'd get stoned and play this box of singles over and over . . . 'Billy's Bag' by Billy Preston, all the great Atlantic people and the blues stuff on Pye International."

If they weren't staying somewhere overnight after returning from a show, the three would wind down into the dawn, either playing with their giant Scalextric racing track with cars specially modified for them by Ronnie's brother Stan, or immersing themselves in sounds.

Ian McLagan: "Westmoreland Terrace was Small Faces Central. There was a piano in the basement, the organ was usually left in the hallway and I'd be playing it out there. We'd smoke, have a drink, and turn everything up. I'm amazed we didn't get any noise complaints because we usually had the windows open. Great times."

After the commercial failure of 'I've Got Mine', Arden insisted on bringing in a professional associate for the all-important follow-up. Stepney-born entertainer and comedian Kenny Lynch was known to Marriott since his acting days, and McLagan had backed him when in the Boz People. Lynch knocked off 'Sha La La La Lee' in partnership with American Brill Building songwriter Mort Shuman.* Recorded at Decca's West Hampstead studios and released on January 14, Arden was vindicated when the record got to number one on the *MM* and *Disc* charts (#2 in *NME*) in March. It was a decent enough pop record, despite Lynch's obtrusive high falsetto vocal, but totally unrepresentative of what the Small Faces were about.

"The whole point in recording a commercial record is to try and get our name really established," Marriott pleaded to *Melody Maker*. "If we can score two or three big hits then we'll start making the kind of records we want to . . . we want to get the full force of our stage numbers on record."

This they achieved with *Small Faces*, a product of fast and frenetic industry, completed, like all good mid Sixties' debut LPs, in just three days with IBC in-house engineer Glyn Johns who successfully captured the sheer ebullience of the Small Faces' live sound blasting through 100 watt Marshall's.

---

* With former writing partner Doc Pomus, Shuman penned hits for Elvis Presley, Andy Williams, Dion & The Belmonts and The Drifters to name but several. As well as 'Sha La La La Lee' Shuman and Lynch wrote 'Love's Just A Broken Heart', a Top 5 hit for Cilla Black in February 1966.

Ian McLagan: "We would get in to IBC, have like a couple of hours at the most to record and then jump in the car and go off to a gig. Steve would do 'Come On Children' which was basically a jam and an excuse to sing James Brown or Muddy Waters lines on things like Willie Dixon's 'You Need Love'. There was a lot of freeform stuff going on but basically we were just playing behind Steve's voice."

For one so young, Marriott's throaty vocals possessed all the authority of a dispossessed Chicago bluesman and the swaggering sexuality of the most lubricious soul performer. On top of this his command could make the commercial, Lynch-written pop confections like 'You Better Believe It' and 'Sorry She's Mine' more palatable.

The album appeared in May, at the same time as a new single, the Marriott-Lane composed 'Hey Girl'. While a cut above 'Sha La La La Lee', the record, which cracked the Top 10 the following month, was obviously tailored to commercial expectations and, again, wasn't truly indicative of the Faces' musical direction.

Ian McLagan: "Arden would rush us into the studio, 'A-side, A-side' they were the words. And then once you'd delivered whatever it was – 'All Or Nothing' or something – then it was like 'What about the B-side?' 'We haven't got one!' 'Well make something up' so that was 'Grow Your Own', 'Own Up Time' and 'Almost Grown' – those Booker T. type instrumentals."

Throughout that pivotal year of 1966 the Small Faces maintained a gruelling schedule of concerts, recording, interviews, photo sessions and TV and radio performances. However the strain from the pace Arden was putting them under told when Jones went down with nervous exhaustion and Marriott collapsed from low blood pressure at the end of a *Ready, Steady, Go!* slot.

When 'All Or Nothing' reached pole position in the *Melody Maker* chart on September 8 (and all others the following week), the Small Faces attained the peak of their fame. With the Beatles' unannounced retirement from live performing, and the Rolling Stones having reduced their work-load, for sheer teen scream appeal, only the Walker Brothers could seriously rival the Small Faces for riotous scenes in British theatres and ballrooms.

Ian McLagan: "Sometimes we were meant to play two 20-minute spots or one 40-minute set but more and more often we'd be halfway into the 20-minute spot and the girls would rush the stage. It was incredible the strength young people had, they would bend barriers – it was just beyond belief. I mean you'd want to play. You couldn't hear yourself. The geezers in the audience couldn't hear it either because of the girls screaming. It was strange."

The pubescent popularity of the Small Faces is no better encapsulated than in this letter published in popular teen pin-up magazine *Fabulous 208* by one Dulcie Row from Kingston-upon-Thames, detailing a local record shop appearance by her heart-throbs:

> "Whenever I hear anything to do with the Small Faces my heart misses a beat and my stomach feels empty . . . When I told my friends that the Small Faces were going to be in Kingston, they just flipped, too . . . Eventually *they* arrived! A great scream went up. I was so overjoyed that I was speechless . . . When I eventually got to them I could hardly say anything, and my legs turned to jelly . . . [Kenney] had just finished a cigarette and so I asked him for the filter tip. 'Sure' he said, and gave it to me. Wow! Was this my day! As we went downstairs one of the assistants in the shop was taking away some dirty glasses. I asked her which one was Plonk's, she told me and I grabbed hold of it, but unfortunately a man came along and took it from me . . ."

With such teen coverage and a photogenic image of four midget moppets as Carnaby clotheshorses, the Small Faces got branded with a misleading pop tag, one they would find hard to shake off – with far-reaching consequences.

By the end of 1966, the Small Faces had played nearly 200 gigs, earning up to £1,000 a night, made over 50 television and radio appearances and chalked up four Top 10 (including two chart-topping) singles and a Top 5 album. Yet apart from their £20 wage and expense accounts in quintessential Carnaby Street boutiques like Lord John and Topper shoes, there was little to show for this success – a situation that was becoming of rapid concern to the band members' families.

Ian McLagan: "Our parents got together while we were away on the road and they arranged a meeting with Don Arden at his office. They said, 'Where's all our boys' money?' Arden liked to think he was like James Cagney and he did this sort of Cagney thing where he sat there and told them, 'People in showbiz spend money and they've spent theirs. Oh, and by the way, they're all on drugs.' Of course, after that our parents forgot what they came for. I mean we took speed, Steve, Ronnie and I smoked hash every day, we'd had acid but we never touched heroin which is what

Arden led them to think. So they were horrified, they forgot about the money, and they went away really upset, like, 'My God, what are you kids doing to yourselves?!'

"We knew Arden couldn't be trusted from that moment on, so we hired an accountant and a lawyer. The accountant would turn up at gigs and say, 'Sign this and sign that.' Fucking idiots we were but we didn't know. We were musicians, not accountants or lawyers."

The Small Faces' fiscal situation, coupled with the fact that Arden was not a producer in the creative sense of the word, had reached stalemate. In November, when driving between dates, they heard on the car radio the rough demo they'd delivered of 'My Mind's Eye', a proposed album track, which was now being pushed as their latest single. By year's end the agreement with Arden had been terminated and the group signed a management and agency contract with British impresario Harold Davison worth £12,000.

However, behind the scenes, things were still unsettled on the management and recording front. For many industry insiders it must have come as a surprise to read the *NME* announcement (dated February 11, 1967): "The Small Faces have signed a lucrative long-term deal with Andrew Oldham and Tony Calder's Immediate company, under which the group will, in future, produce all its own records. The tapes will then be leased by Immediate to the Faces current label Decca."

Under the existing arrangement with Davison, the group were committed to yet another British theatre tour, a 32-date affair co-starring Roy Orbison and at the bottom of the bill, the newly formed Jeff Beck Group, featuring singer Rod Stewart. The first date was set for March 3 at the Finsbury Park Astoria, north London.

"I called into their dressing room to say hello to Steve," Stewart told *Melody Maker*'s Mark Plummer in 1970. "I didn't have a clue who the rest of them were."

CHAPTER 3

Rod The Mod

"Rod Stewart is a real find. He is one of the few teenagers who has got on to the real R&B scene."

Long John Baldry, *Melody Maker*, 1964

"I've always been very flash, even when I was at school I had to be the best dressed. I had to prove I was better than somebody else."

Rod Stewart, *Record Mirror*, 1974

DURING the evening of November 2, 1965, British commercial television station ITV screened a half-hour documentary, *Rod The Mod*, following the activities of one of the most flamboyant characters on the club circuit. Rod Stewart was already turning heads due to his self-created image – checked trousers, leather hip-length coat with belt at the back, high-heeled boots, tartan scarf and, most strikingly, a backcombed, heavily lacquered coiffure below which jutted a prominent beak. Singing in a soul septet called the Steam Packet his voice was guttural – harsh but unmistakably distinctive, if still to find its definitive setting. While he was not yet a star, the 20-year-old north Londoner certainly carried himself in a fashion that suggested it was only a matter of time.

Roderick David Stewart was born at home at 507 Archway Road, Highgate on January 10, 1945. His father, Joseph Robert Stewart was born in Leith, the port of Edinburgh, Scotland, while his mother Elsie Gilbart had grown up in London around the Islington area. "My dad left Scotland when he was about 14," Rod's eldest brother Don relates, "and he joined the Merchant Navy and ended up here [in London]. He took up building – he was a master builder by the finish – and he met my mum one night when he went out dancing."

The couple met at the ballroom above the Boston Arms pub in Tufnell Park, married in 1928, and settled in Upper Holloway Road, where their two eldest children, Mary and Donald were born in 1928 and 1930, respectively. By the time Peggy (b. 1933) and Robert ('Bobby', b. 1934) followed, the family had moved to Duncombe Road and then, during wartime, to Archway Road.

For its size, Hornsey was the most heavily bombed area in Middlesex, with nearly three-quarters of the buildings in the borough damaged by enemy action. Robert belonged to the local ARP (Air Raid Precaution) and during Elsie's pregnancy, on August 13, 1944, a German V1 doodlebug hit and demolished the nearby magistrates' court and police station at the corner of Archway Road and Bishops Road.*

While the ever present threat of a raid made a hospital trip risky, the home birth was more a matter of convenience as Don explains, "Dad was working and mum wouldn't leave us on our own. Our grandfather had a butcher's shop out in Kingston-on-Thames and dad said, 'If you move to Kingston, you'll be out of the way of the bombing' but mum and us all, we were only there a few days before we moved back home again. I think because mum didn't want to to be away from dad.

"My earliest memory of Rod is the day he was born. Right up the top of the house was mum and dad's bedroom. It was late afternoon or early evening, dad said come up and have a look at your new brother. I remember my mum and the midwife looking so worn out."

While working class, the Stewarts were not poor; the rented terrace house at 507 had a basement with three storeys. Rod later described his childhood there as being "fantastically happy".

Don Stewart: "Roddy was spoilt rotten by all of the family because of the big age difference, no doubt about it. I was the last to leave home and get married. Rod was about 11 or 12 at the time because I remember the morning I got married I said, 'I'll take you down the West End to have a look around'. And he cried his eyes out, he wanted to know why I was leaving and why couldn't I stop at home?"

Among the first music Rod heard were 78 rpm recordings by Al Jolson, a particular favourite of Elsie's. The extrovert, self-assertive performing style of the Jewish American singer, comedian and actor, who more often than not 'blacked up' for his performances, had a mesmerising effect. "When I was old enough, I was taken to see his films," Rod told Peter Burton, "the ones about Jolson with Larry Parkes – *The Jolson Story* and

---

* The incident log and bomb map for the Highgate/Hornsey area confirms that, contrary to what is frequently reported in biographies, Rod's birth did not coincide with a bombing raid.

Jolson Sings Again. And that's when it really hit home – that was well before I had any idea I was going to come into this business myself. I got so bowled over by him."

Rod took particular note of Jolson's mannerisms – his fluttering hand movements, emphasised by the white gloves he wore, the way he went down on one knee to express the emotion of a song – and the inclusive, supremely confident attitude Jolson displayed onstage which was reflected in his famous catchphrase "You ain't seen nothing yet." All of this would later be integrated into Stewart's own stage performances.

Education held little interest and Rod failed the 11-plus exam in his final year at Highgate Primary School. "School in Highgate weren't the finest days of my life," Stewart told *Disc*'s Caroline Boucher in 1971, "although my mum used to say make the most of them."

In February 1957, Don took his youngest brother to see Bill Haley & His Comets at the Gaumont State Theatre, Kilburn. A deeper impression was made when Bobby brought home a copy of Little Richard's 'The Girl Can't Help It'. However it was not until his 15th birthday that Rod was given his first guitar by his father. Like thousands of other kids of his generation who mastered a few chords thanks to Bert Weedon's guitar bible *Play In A Day* Rod joined a skiffle group with some schoolfriends, calling themselves the Kool Kats, busking their way through songs popularised by Lonnie Donegan and Chas McDevitt.

In July 1960 Rod and a bunch of mates made an undignified entrance at the annual Beaulieu Jazz Festival in the grounds of Lord Montagu's stately home in Hampshire. "We had long scruffy hair and duffle coats, so we couldn't get in," Stewart told Rob Partridge. "But we met this old farmer outside the gate who says to us, 'Ere, you can get in through them sewers over there.' And over this cliff there's the entrance to the sewers, so we crawled through and came up near the beer tent, of all places."

In a tent at Beaulieu Rod lost his virginity. "It was under an old grey blanket . . ." he told *Penthouse* in January 1975. "This great big bird dragged me off . . . She was about 30. Well she was a lot older than me 'cos I was still at school. She was a big woman – a *very* big girl . . . It was all over in about two seconds. She walked away in disgust!"

The scenario of predatory older woman seducing a young, inexperienced schoolboy later provided the lyrical inspiration for one of Stewart's greatest songs.

From a young age, Rod's main hobby was – and continues to be – the decidedly unglamorous pastime of railway modelling, an interest inspired by the view from the Stewart house which overlooked the Highgate marshalling yards. "I remember seeing the TV documentary on the Flying Scotsman," he says "and feeling really sad at the end when they played a bagpipe lament." Rod felt a devoted kinship with the country of his father's birth and remains passionately patriotic about Scotland.

Next to sex, trains and rock'n'roll, football was to be the other lifelong obsession, as he told Frank Clough in 1974, "My dad would talk about the Wembley wizards and show me pictures of men like Bobby Evans, Billy Liddell, Willie Waddell and George Young." Rod found he had a natural ability on the pitch and for a time, he played in the same team as Ray Davies, a fellow pupil at William Grimshaw Secondary Modern School in Muswell Hill. William Grimshaw was progressively minded with courses designed to move pupils into the affiliated Hornsey College of Arts & Crafts on Crouch End Hill where Rod enrolled when leaving school at 15. "Rod was very keen on art," Mary Stewart told John Gray, "but they said he was colour blind so he had to give that up."

Out of art school Rod worked for about two months at Elliott Displays, a silk-screen printing company at 501 Archway Road, run by a friend of the family, where his brother Bobby was employed. Having been an amateur footballer, playing in the Twenties and Thirties in a team called the Vagabonds, Robert constantly urged his youngest to turn professional. Standing five foot 11 inches, Rod was playing for the Finchley youth team when he was spotted by an agent for Brentford FC, the west London side then hovering between the third and fourth division of the English football league, and went for trials as a semi-pro on a low pay of around £6 a week.* "My heart wasn't in it," Stewart told Caroline Boucher. "You had to get up at seven in the morning to clean the first team's boots. So that lasted about five months."

Rod's short-lived career at Brentford is still shrouded in uncertainty. In 1995 the club's Deputy President Eric White told writer/musician Will Birch, "He trained with us for a week or two, and he may even have kicked a ball around with the juniors, but there is no record of Rod Stewart ever having *signed* to Brentford. Unfortunately, nobody at the club remembers his time here."

Faced with menial tasks and the long commute west to the team's training ground in Griffin Park, Hounslow, Rod made the fateful decision to concentrate on music as his primary pursuit, much to his father's disappointment, although he still continued to play the sport whenever the

---

* Ironically that same year of 1961 the abolition of the maximum weekly football wage of £20 enabled footballers the potential to earn more money.

opportunity arose for Highgate Redwing, the amateur side founded just after the war by Robert and for which all three Stewart brothers played at various times.

Around the end of 1961, Rod tried out as singer with a local group from Muswell Hill. Ray Davies and his younger guitarist brother Dave had been scuffling around the area, picking up the occasional gig where they could in their group the Ray Davies Quartet with a line-up completed by fellow William Grimshaw pupils, Pete Quaife (bass) and John Start (drums). Ray initially felt uncomfortable as a vocalist so Rod sang during the group's practises at Start's home on Ringwood Avenue. "I did a very good Eddie Cochran when I was at school," Rod told Rob Partridge. Cochran's 'C'mon Everybody' was the first record he'd bought, something that held him in good stead with Dave who was a fellow admirer of the charismatic American rocker who met his fate in a car accident at the end of a UK tour with Gene Vincent in April 1960.

In his autobiography *X-Ray*, Ray described Rod as "the Elvis Presley of Muswell Hill" but this and a shared love of football weren't enough to keep Stewart and the Davies brothers from parting company over musical and personal differences.* A determined Rod then joined another local outfit, the Moontrekkers who gained a Saturday night residency at the Muswell Hill Youth Club at Carisbrooke House on Colney Hatch Lane with the Davies brothers' group in competition there on Fridays. Under the surname alteration of Rod Stuart, Rod sang with the Moontrekkers up in Scotland and auditioned for Joe Meek but the legendarily eccentric British record producer was far from impressed. According to John Repsch in his biography *The Legendary Joe Meek*, the moment Rod started singing Meek ran into the studio, "waving his arms from side to side and blowing a raspberry".

Don Stewart: "There was an occasion when my dad came round to me, saying 'I wish you'd have a word with your brother because he's just wasting his time and he's not doing anything. Make him get a decent job, he's never going to earn any money.'"

To keep Robert happy Rod flitted through a series of jobs, working for wallpaper manufacturers Shand Kydd Ltd, based at 73 Highgate Road, at a picture framers in North Finchley and "for about three or four weeks", measuring out plots in Highgate Cemetery. "That was all right, we only had to work two days a week, and you didn't spend the whole day digging

---

* In a further coincidence Ray Davies enrolled at Hornsey College of Art in September 1962.

holes; we did a lot of other things there." Stewart later said that the task helped him conquer an early obsession with mortality. "I was scared of dying so I thought the only way round this is to go and work in a cemetery," he told *Penthouse* in 1975. "It kicked it out of me."

By 1962, with the Cold War, nuclear proliferation and the world brought to the brink of Armageddon with the Cuban missile crisis, the romanticism and political conscience attached to American folk music captured Rod's imagination. Eddie Cochran was now replaced as his role model by Bob Dylan, whose nasal, untutored voice and message-laden songs, so at odds with the prevailing formulaic Tin Pan Alley pap, proved a revelation. Dylan's key inspiration Woody Guthrie was another important influence, as were the wandering West Coast folkies, Derroll Adams and Ramblin' Jack Elliott. "Jack Elliott always seemed like he was one of the boys, although he was probably further away than any of them . . ." Stewart told *Melody Maker*. "I could do what he was doing, I could sing in that sort of style."

In what would become the first of several image transformations, Rod wholeheartedly embraced the beatnik lifestyle. He frequented CND rallies and demonstrations at Trafalgar Square and Whitehall – getting arrested in the process, much to his parents' horror – and started hanging out and busking around Leicester Square and Soho, on the Zenith acoustic guitar bought with a £30 loan from his brother Bobby. "When I was playing on my own in folk clubs I was happy," Stewart told *Melody Maker*'s Mark Plummer, "always broke and never paid, but getting all the beer I could drink." He taught himself harmonica and five-string banjo in homage to folk icon and activist Pete Seeger. It wasn't until he saw Peggy Seeger that he realised he'd been playing in the wrong tuning.

Rod embarked on the annual 50-mile 'Ban the Bomb' Easter marches from Aldermaston, Berkshire to London.* However not for the last time there were ulterior motives in Stewart's actions. "I used to wear a chequered armband so I'd get a lift down to the front of the march to be near the cameras," he told *Melody Maker*'s Roy Hollingworth in 1971. "You had to swear blind you were going along because you believed in the cause," he remarked to Caroline Boucher, "and not because you were

---

* The Ban the Bomb marches had started in 1958 but originally commenced from London to the atomic research station in Aldermaston, Berkshire. Starting in 1960 the destinations were reversed.

going to lay someone." One can just imagine his chat-up lines, boasting to an intended conquest of how he toiled at Highgate Cemetery in the shadow of the final resting place of that great 19th century socialist philosopher Karl Marx.

Over the summer of '62 Stewart hung out with some beatniks dossing at an old house in Highgate – becoming known to the local constabulary in the process – and drifted around Brighton among a group of non-conformists, several of whom were squatting on a derelict Thames houseboat 'Louise' at Shoreham-by-Sea, Sussex. On October 16, the occupants – five men and three girls – were evicted by a group of bailiffs and County Council officials bearing a High Court order for repossession.*

Incredibly, a few precious seconds of B&W mute BBC television newsreel survives from a news story on South Coast beatniks; there, seemingly oblivious to the camera, is a 17- or possibly 18-year-old Rod staring into a shop window, looking every inch the itinerant, duffle-coated drop-out carrying a rolled up sleeping bag with CND peace symbol and guitar.

Within the unconventional orbit in which he now moved Rod met troubadour Raymond 'Wizz' Jones, an older folk musician, who busked around Soho, on the Cornish coast and in France. In true Kerouac-style, armed with harmonica, an acoustic and only 3/6d in his pocket, Rod headed out via the cross-channel ferry with some cohorts on a busking trip around Europe. As he recalled to *Rolling Stone*: "We started out in Belgium, lived in Paris in the Saint Germain area of the South Bank . . . [he claimed to have backed Memphis Slim in a Parisian club] then got to Barcelona."

Unable to afford a hotel Rod slept under the arches of Barcelona's Camp Nou football stadium. In St Tropez he and his companions busked for francs, sleeping on the beaches at night. Eventually, they were arrested for vagrancy and repatriated by the British Consul.

Rod returned, tail between his legs. "That was a sad day in the Stewart family," he told Boucher, "when their son was deported back to them." Robert Stewart took one look – and sniff – and ordered his son to the bathroom, taking the clothes he'd been wearing day in, day out for months on end and put them on a bonfire. "He burned the bloody lot. Rod stunk, he did," says Don. "My dad was a hard nut in many ways but

---

* Stewart later claimed that the eviction was effected with the use of water hoses, that the barge was towed away and sunk to ensure the squatters did not return and that the story made the front page of the *Daily Mirror* and the *Daily Sketch*. A good yarn but research confirms this was not the case. Curiously if Rod *was* on board at the time he was one of the few inhabitants not to be named in the local *Shoreham Herald* report.

in others he was a big softie. He would help Roddy out by giving him a coupla quid and then Rod'd be off again!"

As he headed toward retirement from the building trade Robert saw a business opportunity. "Dad used to do a lot of odd jobs like plumbing and things for the whole area," says Don, "and he found out the old lady, Mrs. Lewis, who ran the newsagents near us had passed away so he jumped in and bought it." Robert, Elsie and their errant youngest moved into the two-bedroom flat above the premises at 503 Archway Road. Don made sure Rod earned his keep by pressing him into helping with the newspaper rounds.

Despite the chastening outcome the European sojourn was to provide a rich seam for Rod to mine when writing some of his best songs. As would his first serious relationship with 17-year-old London art student Suzannah Boffey who became pregnant. Rod could not face up to the responsibility of marriage and fatherhood at an early age let alone the couple being practically penniless. A girl, Sarah, was born on November 6, 1963, at Whittington Hospital, but the relationship came to an end and the child was later given up for adoption.[*]

If anything positive resulted from the regretful episode it came from Boffey's friendship with Chrissie Shrimpton, sister of quintessential Sixties model Jean Shrimpton. It was Chrissie who inadvertently provided the next pointer on Stewart's career path by recommending he check out her singer boyfriend Mick Jagger's group, the Rolling Stones, playing at Eel Pie Island.

One of the key music venues of Sixties London, Eel Pie Island was situated in the middle of the Thames, reached by a narrow concrete footbridge from the north bank that carried a sixpenny toll. The large hotel, built in the 19th century, featured a dance hall with a sprung dance floor. Apart from the odd social event the venue had largely been left to decay by 1956 when Arthur Chisnall started to put trad jazz dances on there to cater for the local bohemian community. A regular patron in the early Sixties was art student Ian McLagan.

"Eel Pie Island was quite a scummy place," he says. "It started out as some kind of social experiment. Arthur was such a kind guy. There was no reason for him to do this but one time I got there and he gave me a membership card. He said you don't have to pay any more. I'd show him my

---

[*] In 1982 a tabloid journalist sought to re-establish contact between Sarah Thubron and her natural father. Understandably reluctant, Stewart established only sporadic relations with his eldest daughter through the years. In 2010 a reconciliation of sorts had been effected.

membership card and he wouldn't even look at it, he'd just look at me and go, 'Oh yeah, come in.'"

Among their London club residencies the Rolling Stones played Wednesday nights at the venue over the spring and summer of 1963. "I couldn't play the harp at all – I used to blow it, and wondered why I kept running out of breath," Rod told Pete Frame in *Zigzag*. "Then I saw the Stones and watched Mick playing it and I realised where I was going wrong."

Following London's burgeoning R&B scene, as a semi pro, Rod joined the Dimensions, a London-Birmingham five piece, managed by the Malcolm Nixon Agency. Nixon paired the group up with another of his artists, Brummie vocalist Jimmy Powell, who had cut several singles for Decca. Jimmy Powell & The Five Dimensions started playing regularly at Ken Colyer's Jazz Club, a.k.a. Studio 51, at 10/11 Great Newport Street. "I was just playing harmonica, I wasn't really allowed to sing as such," Stewart told Royston Eldridge, attributing this to jealousy on Powell's part although Rod was still unsure of his own vocal ability.*

The Dimensions, who featured future Renaissance and Steamhammer bassist Louis Cennamo in their line-up, were fairly schizoid in their musical approach. According to Rod, "one half wanted to do Beatle things and the other half wanted to play the blues. We played down Ken Colyer's jazz club and got booed off."

On Friday, October 25, Jimmy Powell & The Five Dimensions played an all-night session at Studio 51 with the Downliners Sect and Cyril Davies' R&B All-Stars featuring singer Long John Baldry. Stewart claimed it was here that Baldry first saw him perform. "He probably came down to see Jimmy Powell and he saw me there . . . I did sing one number that night actually, a slow blues and [Baldry] said, 'Do you want to join the band?'"

However, the oft-repeated version of events has Baldry informally approaching the inebriated singer at Twickenham railway station on a cold, foggy Sunday evening, January 5, 1964, after Baldry had performed at nearby Eel Pie Island with the All-Stars. "I was waiting for my connection and I didn't know Rod from Adam," Baldry told John Gray in 1993, "although he'd been to see my shows many times when I was in

---

* An inaccurate legend built up over the years that during his time in the Dimensions, Rod Stewart played harmonica on Millie's 'My Boy Lollipop', a bluebeat hit in March 1964. Jimmy Powell has since confirmed it was he who played on the recording, arranged by Jamaican guitarist Ernest Ranglin. However, in Will Birch's Stewart *MOJO* article, Louis Cennamo states fellow Dimension member Peter Hogman was responsible. A further source says it was John 'Junior' Wood, future bassist with Tomorrow.

Cyril Davies' band . . . I heard the sound of 'Smokestack Lightning' and I walked along the platform to investigate . . . What I thought was a pile of coats with a nose coming out the end turned out to be Rod! I told him I thought his harmonica playing sounded very authentic and he told me he sang a little, too."

Born January 12, 1941 at East Haddon, Northamptonshire, John William Baldry's imposing six foot seven inch frame earned him the adolescent nickname of Long John. "What started me off was buying 78s by Big Bill Broonzy and Muddy Waters when I was about 12," Baldry said in a 1964 *Melody Maker* interview. After leaving school with the intention of becoming a commercial artist, his fanatical interest in black American music led him to join the Ken Simms Vintage Jazz Band.

Baldry's association with British blues pioneers Alexis Korner and Cyril Davies stretched back to 1957 when he attended early blues and folk shows the pair put on at the 'London Blues and Barrelhouse Club', held above the Round House pub on Wardour Street, Soho. In 1962 Baldry was singing as guest vocalist with Blues Incorporated, the now fabled R&B group formed by Korner, a genial bohemian guitarist of Austrian-Greek stock and Davies, a gruff, balding panel beater who was the first – and finest – blues harmonica player in Britain. Both Korner and Davies had played as an interval act for Chris Barber's Jazz Band.* In March 1962 they started an R&B club at the Ealing Jazz Club, opposite Ealing Broadway station in west London.

As well as Baldry, the regular Saturday night gatherings attracted an impressive roll call of the future leading lights from the British R&B boom. Sitting in with Blues Incorporated on any given night could be Mick Jagger, Keith Richards, Brian Jones, Eric Clapton, Paul Jones and, having hitched down from Newcastle, Eric Burdon – backed by a band that included Jack Bruce and Charlie Watts among its ranks. On May 3, Blues Incorporated took this new electrified blues into the West End, starting a Thursday night residency at the Marquee International Jazz Club on Oxford Street billed as "Britain's only Rhythm & Blues Group". In October Korner and Davies parted company over musical differences. Alexis kept the Blues Incorporated name, while Cyril took over the Thursday night Marquee spot with a new band formed of respected

---

* Another unsung hero of British R&B, with the National Jazz Federation, bandleader Barber was the first to bring black American jazz and blues musicians to Britain in the late Fifties including Big Bill Broonzy, Lonnie Johnson, Sonny Terry and Brownie McGhee, Sister Rosetta Tharpe and Muddy Waters.

musicians who had previously played in Screaming Lord Sutch's backing group, the Savages – Bernie Watson (guitar), Ricky Fenson (real surname: Brown) (bass), Carlo Little (drums) and pianist Nicky Hopkins.

The Cyril Davies R&B All-Stars soon established themselves as the hottest band on the circuit. 'Country Line Special', recorded on February 27, 1963 and released in May on Pye International was (and remains) the key recording of the early R&B scene in England, sounding nothing less than prime, authentic Chicago blues featuring Davies' chugging, wailing harp, Watson's stinging notes, Little's hard-hitting tom-tom rhythm and Hopkins' distinctive fills played on an electric Hohner Pianet. Above all it demonstrated that young British enthusiasts had the ability to perform this exotic music without having to be American. Equally impressive was the single's B-side, 'Chicago Calling', featuring Hopkins' jaunty, piano trills.

Unfortunately, just as the record was released, Hopkins became seriously ill with intestinal problems and was hospitalised for 19 months. His replacement was Keith Scott (another musician to have passed through Blues Incorporated) but there were further upheavals when Davies' forceful single-mindedness resulted in both Watson and Fenson quitting to be replaced respectively by Geoff Bradford (who had briefly served time in an embryonic Rollin' Stones in 1962) and Cliff Barton. Davies brought in Baldry as 'guest vocalist' and a black female vocal trio, the Velvettes to expand the line-up.

Ian McLagan: "I used to go and see Cyril Davies Sunday nights at Eel Pie Island. I loved that band. I remember Keith Scott had a Hohner Pianet and he made it sound great. Cliff Barton was a very sweet guy, he was very encouraging to us [the Muleskinners] considering we weren't half the musicians they were."

Over the summer, the All-Stars gained exposure on radio and television, landing a regular spot on a weekly folk and blues TV showcase *Hullaballoo* that also brought Baldry into wider focus as an entertainer. With a recording contract, an enviable reputation and a full-date sheet, things looked promising despite Davies' uncompromising stance. However, it was not to be. For several years Davies had been stricken with an unexplained illness and on January 7, 1964, he died of pleurisy just short of turning 32.[*]

And so it was with ironic timing that Baldry and Stewart's chance encounter occurred on a rail platform, as Baldry told John Gray. "It turned

---

[*] Other sources cite the cause as leukaemia or lung cancer. Whether his illness suddenly crept up on Davies or he was a fighter to the end it's hard to tell as an All-Stars gig for Thursday, January 9 was advertised in the Marquee's listings in *Melody Maker*.

out he [Rod] was going in the same direction as me: Twickenham to Richmond, changing over to the Broad Street line and going to north London. I lived in [South Hill Park] Hampstead at that time and he lived in Highgate."

Baldry invited Rod to sit in with the All-Stars. "On the morning of the gig, Elsie, his mum, rang me up and said, 'Ere, have you asked my boy to play harmonica and sing with your band? Well, just make sure he gets home on time!' "

The day after his 19th birthday Rod Stewart turned professional. The All-Stars club date on Saturday, January 11, was an all-nighter at Manchester's Twisted Wheel. "The first song I ever sung professionally on the stage was 'Night Time Is The Right Time'. And I took a leaper to do it," Rod revealed to *NME*'s Nick Logan. "I remember Cliff Barton gave me a leaper because I was so scared."

Assuming leadership duties of the All-Stars, Baldry renamed the band Long John Baldry & The Hoochie Coochie Men, with Rod as his subordinate. "I didn't know that much about the blues as such . . ." Stewart confessed to Royston Eldridge. "I never really considered myself as being a blues singer. It was John who introduced me to the blues via Big Bill Broonzy and Joe Williams. My personal favourite at the time was Jimmy Reed."

The Hoochie Coochie Men was a crucial apprenticeship for Stewart. Baldry always looked for the best players and his reluctant deputy must have felt out of his depth surrounded by improvisational musicians of such a high calibre. "That band taught me a lot," Rod admitted to Rob Partridge. Amongst the floating personnel, Barton and Bradford had both been in the All-Stars, while pianist Johnny Parker and his replacement Ian Armit had played with Humphrey Lyttelton's jazz band.

A taste of how the band sounded in the early stages of Stewart's recruitment can be heard on a live recording made on February 28 at Birmingham Town Hall as part of a Blues Festival starring Sonny Boy Williamson and the Yardbirds. Baldry's men competently take on Jimmy Reed's 'Bright Lights, Big City' as a jazzy shuffle while Rod's voice has yet to acquire its distinctive hoarseness.

Ian McLagan: "When John took over Cyril's band, it became more jazzy. I used to marvel at how Geoff Bradford played – he'd be all the way up and down the neck and you just never knew what key he was in."

Mac first set eyes on Rod at Eel Pie Island. "I noticed this guy walking in, he had a big bird's nest hairdo even then. It was all backcombed and he was tall as well with a big nose, very sure of himself, a Jack the Lad. Rod would sing in the break while John went and had a drink. Rod sang sharp [in those days] and it was a bit aggravating but I could see he had talent."

While living at home, Rod continued perfecting his gravel-voiced tones, much to Elsie's consternation. "I sincerely used to wish I'd been born a Negro" Stewart admitted to *Record Mirror* in 1971. "I used to spend hours trying to imitate their sound. It used to drive my mum mad and it hurt like hell at first."

As well as de blooze, Stewart's admiration for the peerless Sam Cooke, whose 'Chain Gang' he first heard in 1960, became obsessional. "I listened to everybody and probably picked up a lot from them all," Rod told *Rolling Stone* in 1970. "Sam Cooke was the only one that really influenced me. Over a period of about two years, that's all I listened to . . . I didn't sound at all like Ray Charles or anybody, but I knew I sounded like Sam Cooke . . . It was the tone of his voice that did it, not the phrasing or whatever, just the tone."

In April, Baldry received an invitation to appear among the guests in a Rediffusion TV special, *Around The Beatles,* produced by Jack Good, the father of British rock'n'roll television with *6.5 Special* and *Oh Boy!* The show was broadcast on May 6 and as a result Baldry's profile increased. "You couldn't talk to him [Baldry] after that," Rod told Boucher. "He always looked after the boys though, you have to say that for him. He'd never let us go short, he'd rather go without himself."

Indeed, Baldry's philanthropic gestures towards his musicians would be his financial undoing throughout his career. Thanks to a proliferation of bookings, sometimes up to three in the course of an evening, Stewart was paid £35 a week – more than double the average wage by 1964 standards. Knocking about with older musicians was bound to lead Rod astray and his liking for a tipple grew. "I was quite content with half a cider before that." It was during the Hoochie Coochie Men period that those around Rod first became aware of his 'short hands, long pockets' tendencies. "He [Rod] was always tight and he was always mean, but never with me . . ." Baldry told Gray. "He never smoked and never drank, unless it was a free one!"

On May 13, Stewart signed a management contract with the unorthodox business partnership of publicist Jonathan Rowlands and agent Geoff Wright. Welsh-born Rowlands had studied stage management at RADA, worked as a comedian and appeared as a film extra and starred in television commercials. If all that failed to cover the rent on his Knightsbridge flat, he had his own light delivery company and would take to the roads across Britain in a small van.

Wright, from the Manchester area, was less multi-faceted, having helped launch Tommy Steele before losing him to Larry Parnes. He had been associated with managing Des O'Connor and Val Doonican and was the chairman of Associated London Scripts, the company looking after the comedy talents of Spike Milligan, Frankie Howerd, and Eric Sykes among others. Rowlands and Wright were operating out of premises owned by Wright at 234 Old Brompton Road, near Earl's Court, when Rowlands proposed they go into artist management.

Jonathan Rowlands: "My memory says that I first met Rod Stewart after a gig he and Long John Baldry did at the City University in Islington. Francis Megahy, who was making a film about Rod [*Rod The Mod*], said I should come and see this singer. I told Geoff about him and we both went and saw Rod at the Marquee. Rod was great, he looked and sounded different and had a presence, all things that we could work with . . . We took him to a restaurant below the De Vere Hotel on the corner of De Vere Gardens and Kensington Road, which was a late night hangout of ours, to discuss management . . . The contract we were offering was standard for that time but we had to get his parents' signatures because Rod was 19 and you couldn't sign unless you were 21 at that point.

"Rod was already shrewd when it came to money. He insisted that the deal not include us taking any percentage of his earnings with Long John Baldry, which were quite substantial, because that was something he'd arranged before we appeared on the scene. He also didn't want to cause any upset with Baldry so we had to make sure John was OK with everything before he would sign."

The next hurdle was securing Rod a recording contract. On June 18, Stewart, backed by the Hoochie Coochie Men, recorded several demos at Radiomusic Recordings, a small basement studio run by Pepi Rush at 42 Berwick Street. (Rowlands appointments diary reads: "Call Mr Stewart to remind Rod to get up in time!") At a total cost of £39, with engineer Vic Keary, Rod and the band laid down 'Keep Your Hands Off Her', 'Just Like I Treat You', 'Ain't That Lovin You Baby', 'Bright Lights, Big City', 'Moppers Blues', and 'Don't You Tell Nobody'.*

---

* Despite legal action taken by Stewart against Wright's company, Independent Music, to prevent their appearance, the demos were later released on an album, *A Shot Of Rhythm And Blues* released by EMI in the UK and Private Stock Records in the US in December 1976.

Baldry, meanwhile, had landed a deal with United Artists and in June, a single 'You'll Be Mine' appeared. The B-side, 'Up Above My Head (I Hear Music In The Air)', a spiritual call and response gospel testifying. Originally recorded by Sister Rosetta Tharpe (with Marie Knight), it marked the unofficial debut of the Stewart larynx (in duet with Baldry).

The gregarious and covertly (considering homosexuality was still illegal in Britain) gay singer took the self-conscious neophyte under his wing. Just as he had appropriated the beatnik look and attitude so Rod became a Mod, ditching the liberal consciousness, long, unkempt hair and scruffy jerseys and donkey jackets for the individualism, immaculately maintained coiffure, and sharp, mohair suits of Modernism. Baldry encouraged Rod to experiment with his image, using his sister Mary's hair lacquer, eye-liner and an exaggerated mincing gait seven years before Glam Rock was thought of. Little wonder people talked about the pair. Through Baldry's connections, Stewart was introduced to all stratum of society – Rod was fond of chasing posh skirt – and under John's influence, occasionally landed himself in the odd spot of bother.

On Sunday, June 28, after the regular Hoochie Coochie Men gig at Eel Pie Island, Baldry, Stewart and Baldry fan Ian Crossley went to the L'Auberge coffee bar, a popular hang-out in Richmond. As they ambled down Hill Street, some innocent larking ended with all three being arrested and charged with using obscene language to the annoyance of pedestrians and insulting behaviour likely to cause a breach of the peace. When heard at Richmond Magistrates Court the following morning, an adjournment was requested so that the three could be legally represented. They were remanded on bail of £5 each until July 13. Pleading not guilty the court heard how the three were wearing "modern dress" and that two elderly couples were walking along the road when Baldry made a comment about "a stout woman", to which Stewart remarked, "Fuck me!" Due to conflicting evidence the three were cleared – no doubt to Robert and Elsie Stewart's relief in seeing their wayward son escape from his latest brush with authority.

Through Hugh Mendl at Decca, Rowlands and Wright met the company's R&B expert Mike Vernon who heard the demos cut in June and gave the thumbs up after seeing Rod perform at the Marquee. Vernon supervised a formal audition (again backed by Baldry's band) at Decca's studios in Broadhurst Gardens, West Hampstead on July 16, resulting in a recording contract. The session for Rod's first single was fixed for 10 am on Thursday, September 10, at Decca's No. 2 studio with producer Ray Horricks and a session musician line-up of drummer Bobby Graham, guitarist Brian Daly, pianist Reg Guest and John Paul Jones on bass.

Jonathan Rowlands: "Everybody showed up on time but there was no sign of Rod. Eventually Geoff rang his parents and Rod's mum said that Rod was still asleep. He'd got in late and forgotten all about the session. We eventually had to pay for a taxi to get him down there."

Unimpressed with the commercial material presented to him, Stewart pushed matters further by cockily insisting on interpreting two obscure blues instead; a take on Sonny Boy Williamson's 'Good Morning Little Schoolgirl', revamped to a breezy, jazzy stroll akin to Georgie Fame & The Blue Flames, and Big Bill Broonzy's 'I'm Gonna Move To The Outskirts Of Town', previously recorded by Louis Jordan and His Tympani Five, Jimmy Reed and Ray Charles among others.

The single was released on October 16 with attendant publicity arranged by Rowlands ("He spends £1 a week on his hair," ran one headline) and Rod's gift for the gab – "All these Negro singers singing about 'Walking down the railroad track' they've never walked down a railroad track in their lives. Nor have I. You've got more to sing the blues about in the Archway Road than on any railroad track I know" (from Decca publicity handout). Despite a plug on *Ready, Steady, Go!* with Rod ineffectually miming on a Vox Phantom guitar (other publicity shots showed him holding a Fender Telecaster) the record failed to move. The fact that the Yardbirds released a more commercial version of 'Good Morning Little Schoolgirl' at the same time didn't help sales.

For a 19-year-old with a shot at success, Rod was both remarkably sanguine and candidly honest in an interview given for the Highgate paper at his local, the Wellington at the junction of Archway Road and North Hill. "I'm not particularly bothered about my new record. Of course I hope it's going to sell and make me a lot of money but I'm not pinning too much on it . . . The pop industry is a rat race and as phoney as everyone thinks it is. I happen to sing rhythm and blues and R&B is the fashion at the moment. I'll stay on the bandwagon as long as it's there," before delivering the pay-off, "Sure I'm in it for the money."

A week after the record's release Stewart was fired from the Hoochie Coochie Men after Baldry arrived late to a gig at the Rendezvous R&B Club, Portsmouth, on October 24. "I had to hold the stage," Stewart told Michael Wale, "and I really couldn't, so when he turned up I swore at him and he sacked me. I cried because I didn't think people got sacked in show business."

However mutual respect over-rode any lingering resentment and a supportive Baldry gave Rod the opening slot on his Thursday residency at the Marquee. Like McLagan with the Muleskinners, Stewart was offered the unique opportunity of working up close with some of the great American bluesmen, sharing stages with visiting artists such as Memphis Slim, Little Walter, Howlin' Wolf, and Sonny Boy Williamson.

Jonathan Rowlands: "Bryan Morrison, who managed the Pretty Things, had an agency on Charing Cross Road and Bryan and myself wanted to put Rod out with a group backing him. We went down to a cafe and I always remember Rod said to us, 'I'm not a solo singer and I'm never going to write a song.' He always had this fixed idea of not wanting to go commercial or selling out."

A *Melody Maker* advertisement for a Marquee appearance on December 3 lists Long John Baldry & The Hoochie Coochie Men supported by Rod Stewart & The Ad-Lib. However, according to Rowlands' diary, Rod was backed by the Soul Agents. For the next six months Stewart fronted this solid but – judging by the records they made for Pye[*] – undistinguished R&B group from Southampton, who were popular around the clubs, earning on average £40 a night. Rod's cocksure image was already attracting notice – an advertisement for a gig at Sheffield's Mojo Club on May 8, 1965 hails him as "King Of The Stylists".

However with a lack of commercial success and his payments being funnelled through two agents, Avenue Artistes Ltd. (representing the Soul Agents) and the Malcolm Nixon Agency, Rod was on the lookout for a better break.

The idea behind the Steam Packet originated when Baldry approached Hammond jazz organist Brian Auger at a Brian Auger Trinity gig at the Twisted Wheel on June 17. "John said would I be interested in coming and having a meeting with his manager Martin Davis and agent George Webb," Auger recalls, "so I came up and met with them and the idea was that the Hoochie Coochie Men had kind of run rough shod over Baldry and he was unable to keep them under control, I think. So John's management were proposing we join forces."

Auger brought his own manager Giorgio Gomelsky to the meeting. A part-Russian émigré, film-maker, and promoter, Gomelsky was quite a

---

[*] None of these featured Rod's vocals because at the time he was still contractually with Decca. The contract was for five years with annual options; the company guaranteeing to issue four sides a year. The agreement was nullified after Decca failed to issue a second Rod Stewart single.

character, having set up the Piccadilly Jazz Club (renamed the Scene) and the Crawdaddy Club at the Station Hotel, Richmond. Famously, he gave the Rolling Stones their regular Sunday residency at the Crawdaddy. After losing the Stones to Andrew Oldham, Gomelsky was not about to make the same mistake twice, mentoring their Crawdaddy replacements the Yardbirds and signing them to a management and production deal.

After agreeing to amalgamate with Baldry, guitarist Vic Briggs was added to the trio of Auger, Ricky Brown and drummer Mickey Waller, a character who was to figure prominently in the Rod Stewart story. Born in Hammersmith in 1941, Waller formed his first band, the Flee-Rekkers, while still at school, followed by stints in Joe Brown's Bruvvers and the ever volatile Cyril Davies R&B All-Stars line-up in 1963. He then joined the Wildcats, Marty Wilde's backing group, and in March '64 depped for Charlie Watts at a Rolling Stones gig in Chatham, Kent. Waller then played in Little Richard's touring band and Georgie Fame & The Blue Flames before joining Auger. No wonder band members nicknamed him 'the Fox' due to his cunning in bagging the best gigs going.

Auger, who suggested bringing in 18-year-old singer Julie Driscoll, who was then employed by Gomelsky to answer Yardbirds fan mail, as a female foil, remembers, "John insisting that this protégé he had, Rod Stewart should join." Baldry magnanimously relinquished much of the spotlight by pushing the nervous performer out front to share vocals with himself and Driscoll. "Steam Packet was just like a white soul revue," Stewart told Nick Logan, "like a white Ike & Tina Turner Show but nowhere near as good."

Their debut occurred in July '65 and the group were added to the bill supporting the Rolling Stones on some South Coast dates and the Stones' first major West End concert at the London Palladium on August 1. In the audience was the Stewart family. "That was when I thought to myself, 'He's going to make it now,'" Don Stewart recalls. "You couldn't get much bigger than the Palladium in them days."

As well as appearances on *Ready, Steady, Go!* and a BBC radio booking on *Saturday Club*, the Steam Packet were seen on American television when they were among the acts filmed in colour at the annual National Jazz & Blues Festival in Richmond for ABC TV's *Shindig!* "[Steam Packet] really worked hard," Stewart told Royston Eldridge in 1970. "We earned good money, too . . . It was a band that was built purely on reputation and live shows."

Brian Auger: "I ran the whole damn thing – we only had one roadie so I was hauling gear, driving the van and picking the others up for gigs. I was also entrusted to collect the money every night so it was exhausting work."

Although the Steam Packet never officially recorded,[*] some demos were taped at the Marquee by Gomelsky, which to Stewart's chagrin would continue to be released by various fly-by-night labels after his fame arrived. Rod was still self-consciously struggling to find his true voice, pushing himself in imitating Sam Cooke and Otis Redding to the point where his voice would occasionally give out.

In November, as part of a deal Rowlands and Wright had arranged with EMI, a Stewart solo single, 'The Day Will Come' was released on Columbia, produced by Tony Palmer. With its Spectoresque production the lyrics, written by Barry Mason, a commercial songwriter who wrote hits for the Fortunes, Engelbert Humperdinck and Tom Jones, harked back to Rod's beatnik era with the threat of nuclear extinction, an *au courrant* subject coming as it did on the trail of the folk-rock protest hit, Barry McGuire's 'Eve Of Destruction'. However, unlike fall-out, the single could be (and was) avoided. A rather pedestrian cover of Sam Cooke's (via Otis Redding) 'Shake', backed by Auger and band, followed in April '66 but was equally unsuccessful.

In March 1966, Rod left the Steam Packet under a cloud. "It was all down to Brian giving me the elbow," Stewart claimed to Logan, "and I will never forgive John for agreeing with him. They thought I was getting too much money . . . I was out of work. That came as a terrible blow. It was really unexpected, because I had really got into singing and it was hard not being able to get up onstage and do it any more."

Auger disputes Stewart's account as 'absolute nonsense'. "Rod didn't endear himself to the band, not least from being a skinflint. Even Julie would help load some of the equipment when we got to a gig but Rod would beat a hasty retreat to the nearest mirror to check his hair. At Klooks Kleek [club] one night he made some incredibly hurtful remarks about Julie in front of everyone in the band room. She saw red and hurled a pint of bitter at him. The glass smashed at his feet but Rod was more angry that his shoes got doused in beer!

"We'd been offered a month at the Le Papagayo club in St Tropez, where all the film stars used to go, it was very chic but the money was

---

[*] The reason proffered was due to the individuals being with different record companies. However during their time together all were within the EMI organisation; Baldry with United Artists (whose product was pressed and distributed through EMI), and Auger, Driscoll and Stewart on Columbia, so it seems strange this situation could not be resolved.

terrible so we had a meeting about it. Julie wasn't present and for some reason, neither was Rod. That was up to his manager to arrange. When we discussed it John still wanted to do it because friends of his like Lionel Bart and Leslie Bricusse were going to be there and I needed a holiday. Eventually, George Webb pointed out that the whole band didn't need to go so it was put to the vote who to take – Julie or Rod. Everybody – *including* John – agreed that we should take Julie. He could have said, 'Well, I'm staying behind if Rod's not going' but he didn't. So how the fuck is it that I fired Rod Stewart from the Steam Packet? The truth is I could not do that, it was Baldry's band and *he* had the last say."

The dust had barely settled before Rod was back in a virtual clone of the Steam Packet. Shotgun Express evolved out of the Peter B's (formerly Peter B's Looners), an instrumental quartet featuring ex-Cheynes and Them organist Peter Bardens, drummer Mick Fleetwood (who had played with Bardens in the Cheynes), bassist Dave Ambrose, and guitarist Peter Green. Stewart and Liverpudlian singer Beryl Marsden were brought in to bolster the vocal department.

The unsteady enterprise was masterminded by Rik Gunnell who, with his brother John, operated regular gigs at the Flamingo and ran a management stable, headed by the cream of London's club acts, namely Georgie Fame & The Blue Flames, Chris Farlowe & The Thunderbirds, Zoot Money's Big Roll Band and John Mayall's Bluesbreakers.

"In those days," Bardens told George Tremlett, "our act included numbers like 'Hold On I'm Coming', 'Knock On Wood', 'Midnight Hour', 'Feel So Good', and '634-5789' . . . and then we'd maybe do a couple of instrumentals, and Beryl would come on to do 'Soulful Dress' or 'High Heel Sneakers', and then she'd go off and Rod would come on and do another song."

"It was too soon after Steam Packet and it was just a poor imitation," Stewart opined to Nick Logan. "I was still getting this terrible feeling of doing other people's music."

All the while Rod continued looking at ways of moving his career up a gear. Thanks to Rod's friendship with Chrissie Shrimpton, Mick Jagger, who was producing tracks for Andrew Oldham's Immediate label, became involved. Around August 1966, Jagger attempted to oversee an opportunist cover version of Lee Dorsey's US hit 'Working In The Coal Mine' but apparently an ensuing studio dispute put paid to the recording. Considering Dorsey's original became a UK Top 10 hit, it would appear to have been a redundant exercise all round.

Towards the end of the year (or possibly early '67), Jagger tried again, pairing Rod with Pat 'P.P.' Arnold of the Ike & Tina Turner Revue who had toured Britain on a package with the Stones. Offered the chance of a solo deal by Oldham, Pat remained in Britain and signed to Immediate. The resultant duet, 'Come Home Baby', a Mann-Weil song recorded by Wilson Pickett, purportedly featured Georgie Fame's brass section and Keith Richards playing guitar and bass.[*] A stand off over studio costs occurred between Jagger and Immediate, resulting in Jagger's eventual dissociation from the label.

Despite the loss of Peter Green (in July '66) to John Mayall's Bluesbreakers, Shotgun Express continued into 1967, recording two singles for Columbia but only the first, the heavily orchestrated pop of 'I Could Feel The Whole World Turn Round', released in October '66, featured Stewart who described it as "a terrible fucking record."

Shotgun Express' demise came at a turning point when faux white soul acts were giving way to a new wave of experimental music. A significant line-up at the Leicester Arts Ball on January 19, 1967 featured the current hip blues trio Cream supported by the fading vestiges of London's R&B scene: Zoot Money's Big Roll Band (who would soon metamorphose into the fully blown psychedelic outfit, Dantalion's Chariot), Shotgun Express and bringing up the bill, the Birds, a west London group now languishing in the doldrums, featuring 19-year-old guitarist, Ron Wood.

[*] Purportedly as no solid details have emerged regarding the recording. Stewart's own unreliable recollection has Keith Emerson, Nicky Hopkins and Ron Wood playing on the session. 'Come Home Baby' would not emerge until 1975 on an American 'Rod Stewart and The Faces' collection of dubious legality.

CHAPTER 4

Strictly For The Birds

"This album is affectionately dedicated to those bands who made it, the ones who didn't and those poor unfortunate souls who wasted the most precious years of their youth sleeping rough on clapped out equipment in the back of broken down Bedford vans, ruined their digestion with motorway grease and were always six months behind with their H.P. payments."

Roy Carr & Charles Shaar Murray, *Hard Up Heroes* compilation
sleeve blurb, 1974

"Onstage we all had that same energy. We were vibrant, spunky, unstoppable, we had attitude, and that was the whole thing. It was a great band."

Ali MacKenzie, interview with author, 2010

FROM its inception in the late 18th century, the Grand Junction Canal was designed as a major transport infrastructure of goods from the North and the Midlands to London. It was originally intended to link Braunston, Northamptonshire to the Thames at Brentford. In 1801, a 13-mile branch or 'arm' connecting Bulls Bridge, Norwood to the Paddington area of west London was opened. Paddington Basin soon became one of the capital's busiest transport hubs, providing an even smoother route to and from the docks. Many transient families of water gypsy origin lived and worked on the canal system. Mercy Leah Elizabeth (Lizzie) Dyer entered the world on a canal barge, the *Orient*, moored in Brentford Dock. Her beau, Arthur (Archie) Wood was the Paddington-born son of a tugboat skipper.

When the couple married in 1934, Lizzie was the first of her generation to decamp to dry land. The Woods settled on a housing estate at 8 Whitethorn Avenue, Yiewsley, part of the suburban west London borough of Hillingdon, near Heathrow Airport – an area mainly renowned for its bricking and agricultural industries. Archie followed in his father's foot-steps by becoming a tugboat captain while Lizzie worked as a cleaner at the huge EMI factory in nearby Hayes. The couple's two eldest boys, Arthur and Edward arrived in 1937 and 1939 respectively. Like Stanley Lane, Archie Wood was not called up during the war as his services delivering vital supplies via the canal system was considered more important.

As a ration-installed, post-war Britain started to rebuild itself, Ronald David Wood was born on June 1, 1947 at Hillingdon Hospital. "I was brought up on evaporated milk and the canals," he told David Wigg of *The Daily Express* in 1972. "But I had a happy home life. We loved having parties. We used to cram 50 people into our tiny little semi-detached house with parties at weekends as well as Christmas [with] the music shrieking out."

Archie played the harmonica and frequently led the sing-alongs behind the old Joanna at his local, the Nag's Head. "My dad had his own band of harmonica players," said Ronnie, "and they used to play at racetracks." As well as a penchant for music Ronnie shared an early flair for drawing and painting with his older brothers who were training to be commercial artists. Despite the age gap Art and Ted were close to their younger sibling who adored them. Ronnie envied his brothers' carefree lifestyle as they brought a never-ending procession of musician and art school friends home to the back room at Whitethorn Avenue. "Art and Ted weaned me on the old traditional jazz like Art Tatum and Bix Beiderbecke," Wood told *Melody Maker*'s Geoff Brown. "They even started me on Jerry Lee Lewis and Fats Domino with the old 78s."

Ronnie's first stage experience came at ten, playing washboard in Ted's skiffle group during an intermission in the Saturday morning preview of *The Tommy Steele Story* at the Regal Cinema, Uxbridge in June 1957. "[Art and Ted] always had lots of instruments knocking round the house," Ronnie told *Disc*'s Caroline Boucher, "and in the jazz days they always had trumpets and trombones so I used to potter about on them at first. I always went for the drums in those days, and they used to sit me at them at parties . . . it's funny, my parents weren't musical or artistic but they saw that we were interested and encouraged us."

The brothers pooled their money to buy Ronnie his first acoustic guitar that he eventually replaced with a guitar bought on HP from Franklin Radio on Yiewsley High Street. Unlikely as it might seem from his later solo work, Ronnie sang baritone in the Ruislip Manor Secondary School choir with fellow pupil and Whitethorn Avenue neighbour, Tony Munroe. As budding artists and musicians, Ronnie and Tony started off playing guitar in the Rhythm and Blues Bohemians with some local lads, harmonica player/vocalist Robin Scrimshaw, drummer Bob Langham, occasional pianist Terry Back and bass player Kim Gardner, who had played in a school group the Renegades, led by Ali MacKenzie.

"We were playing at the USAF camp at West Drayton being no more than about 14 or 15 at the most," MacKenzie recalls. "In walked Ronnie and Tony, they'd come down to see this band they wanted to check out and we just got chatting and within no time at all they asked me and Kim to join them."

In true Sixties beat group fashion, the recruitment of Gardner and MacKenzie was considered paramount because of their respective owner-ship of a separate bass amp and PA. Tony Munroe: "Ron and I didn't have any equipment apart from our two guitars. So my father went out and bought a Vox AC30 amplifier for both Ronnie and I to use. We wanted Ali to sing but he wouldn't join at first." "It's not that I *didn't* want to join them," MacKenzie explains. "It was just that I was happy where I was."

With MacKenzie eventually replacing Scrimshaw, the Rhythm and Blues Bohemians became the Thunderbirds, named after the Chuck Berry song, 'Jaguar And The Thunderbird'.

Tony Munroe: "When we first started out we would rehearse Wednes-day nights at the Yiewsley Community Centre on Tavistock Road. Because none of us could drive we literally pushed all our stuff around in wheelbarrows. It didn't matter what weather it was. We would take all the amplifiers and drums and whatever down to the rehearsal room and then we'd push it back to whoever's house so it was all based round the Whitethorn Avenue area."

Ali MacKenzie: "The Thunderbirds went in for a local competition and we won. The prize was a Saturday spot at the West Drayton Community Centre, so we used to play there every Saturday night. We called it the Nest, the Birds' Nest."

The search for repertoire material was made easier by rehearsals at a local music shop, Rainbow Records, with branches at 15 High Street and 111 Falling Lane, Yiewsley. "They used to let us rehearse in both shops," Ali recalls. "We would literally set up in their shop window after hours." In between perfecting a 12-bar shuffle and Chuck Berry rocker the Rainbow racks would get scoured for the latest American import.

As well as soaking in Art and Ted's respective passions for early Chicago blues and traditional Dixieland jazz, 16-year-old Ronnie followed in their footsteps by enrolling at Ealing Technical College & School of Art on St Mary's Road. Other musical alumni who attended at the same time included Pete Townshend and future Bonzo Dog Doo-Dah Band member Roger Ruskin Spear.

"Ron and I were both studying fine art," says Munroe. "When we were at Ealing Tech, it was very avant-garde, it was a very dramatic and new style of art. We had the most revolutionary type of teachers. My grandmother had passed away and we turned her old room at my house into a studio where Ronnie and I painted and practised guitar. We did this almost every night back then so that was our lives."

It was Ronnie's brothers' lives, also. Ted played drums in a trad band, Colin Kingwell's Jazz Bandits. Having turned professional in 1958 fronting a nine-piece swing and blues band, the Art Wood Combo, Art had started singing with Alexis Korner's Blues Incorporated in 1962 at the Ealing Club. As already examined, both Korner and the venue he started with Cyril Davies had a siren-like hold on the R&B acolytes who flocked to hear this antidote to the watered-down pop and dance bands that filled the ballrooms.

When Blues Incorporated splintered, Art formed a new version of the Art Wood Combo using the already existing Don Wilson Quartet, featuring Wilson (bass), Reg Dunnage (drums), Derek Griffiths (guitar) and organist Jon Lord. With Wilson replaced by Malcolm Pool and Dunnage by Keith 'Keef' Hartley the group shortened their name to the Artwoods and secured residencies at legendary jazz and blues venues, the 100 Club on Oxford Street and Klooks Kleek, West Hampstead as well as landing a recording deal with Decca.

While the Beatles and their commercial ilk swept all before them in 1963, the Thunderbirds took their cue from the sounds happening in Richmond, as had Ian McLagan with the Muleskinners.

Tony Munroe: "We used to go over to the Crawdaddy at the [Richmond] Athletic Ground on a Sunday night to watch the Yardbirds. We basically went just to listen to Eric Clapton. He was the first guitarist I heard that could make a guitar talk. And he was a real Mod. We used to go to this shop in Richmond to buy our Ben Sherman shirts, highly polished black American shoes and white socks, things like that. Our set at the time was all R&B but in our own style. It was more similar to the Yardbirds than the Rolling Stones."

While digging 'the most blueswailing Yardbirds', it was the Stones' undoubted charisma that left the biggest impression on Ronnie. He first saw the band playing at the 3rd National Jazz Festival, held in the grounds of Richmond Athletic Association on Sunday, August 11, 1963.

"It was rocking," he recalled in an interview conducted by Stones bassist Bill Wyman almost two decades later. "I was the last one out of the tent, looking at everybody packing up the gear and I fell over a tent peg and smashed my leg."

Ronnie doubled on harmonica – an instrument he apparently mastered with little effort. When Yardbirds vocalist and harmonica player Keith Relf missed a Crawdaddy gig in March '64 through illness, Ronnie was coaxed by Kim to get up out of the audience and sit in playing harp. He also chatted up the lead guitar player's 16-year-old girlfriend. Malta-born, blue-eyed and blonde-haired Christine Findlay had been dating Clapton for about a year. The daughter of a Scottish Royal Navy officer and half-Italian, half-Swedish mother, Krissie had led a traditionally peripatetic army service family life with her parents and three brothers now settled in Edge Hill Road, Ealing.

"The [Crawdaddy] club had ultra violet lighting," Wood reminisced to John Blake ten years later, "and I made fun of [Krissie] because I could see her bra. So she said she had never seen such ridiculous looking teeth." Within a few months the two of them would be inseparable.

On the same club circuit were Chris Farlowe & The Thunderbirds, a popular draw who had a recording contract with Columbia. It was decided, therefore, to shorten the band name. With its associated connotations to British slang for females and Alfred Hitchcock's popular film of the same title, the name the Birds stuck.

Ali MacKenzie: "It was quite a strange coincidence bearing in mind we had long hair then. It was a related thing from people thinking you were longhaired, dirty, what have you. We were called birds, tarts, etc. There was all that sort of thing."

On the evening of Saturday, May 30, while the Birds were playing the Reading Mod Ball at the Olympia Ballroom with the Falcons and the Storms, fate dealt Ronnie a cruel blow. On the eve of his 17th birthday his first girlfriend, 16-year-old Stephanie De Cort of 12a Hill Lane, Ruislip, was killed after the Morris Mini in which she was a passenger collided head on with a red Fiat at the Oxford end of the Fair Mile at Henley-on-Thames. The occupants of both cars – five persons in all – lost their lives in the worst road accident to occur in the Henley district to that time.

The unexpected death of one so young has the obvious capacity to affect and Ronnie found it hard to unlock his emotions. When Munroe and Robin Scrimshaw took him to a local pub he found that alcohol could provide the solace he needed. In his 2007 autobiography, Wood wrote, "I was unable to accept what had happened to Stephanie, but in the bottle I had discovered a way not to think about it."

As the Birds' popularity grew locally, they started attracting outside interest as MacKenzie recalls: "There were a couple of local faces who used to come down to rehearsals, one of them being Colin Farrell. Colin was a big guy, nice but a bit of a nutter, you wouldn't mess with him. He suggested that his cousin Leo could do us some good and he'd like to see us play so we met."

Leo de Clerck was a local entrepreneur who operated 'Leo's Cavern' clubs out of the Olympia Ballroom, Reading and the Ex-Servicemen's Club, Windsor, as well as at the Zambezi Club in Hounslow.*

Ali MacKenzie: "Leo was larger-than-life, he was tall, six-foot-plus, bold, brassy, confident, very well groomed. When we signed up to Leo's management [in June '64], Bob Langham's mum and dad didn't want him to go into this world of rock'n'roll and all that sort of thing so we had to look for a new drummer. We found Pete Hocking during a Battle of the Bands competition being held at the Uxbridge Blues Festival [at Uxbridge Showgrounds on June 20]. We sort of poached him from [future Blossom Toes/Family/Cockney Rebel/Rod Stewart Band guitarist] Jim Cregan's band, the Dissatisfied. Pete was about 20 when we met, then it went Tony, me, Ronnie and then Kim. We were all about 17. Kim was a little bit younger at 16 but not by much."

Hocking – or 'Hockey Sticks' as he was instantly nicknamed – was persuaded to adopt the stage surname Pete McDaniels in honour of Ellas McDaniel (better known as Bo Diddley). Just prior to turning professional, Ronnie dropped out of art school and was training as an apprentice sign-writer with Art's brother-in-law's company, Signcraft, on St Stephen's Road, Yiewsley. He soon jacked it in when the workload became too much.

Ali MacKenzie: "Leo got us gigs almost immediately, it was great. Obviously we used to play his clubs a hell of a lot because he was getting his own band in but we used to go down very well at those venues anyway. Basically we were playing in and around London and because Leo was with the agent Harold Davison all of a sudden you'd get a gig in Sheffield, Leeds or the North."

---

* Leo de Clerck ran these venues in rivalry with his army buddy John Mansfield, who with his partner Philip Hayward, ran the Ricky Tick Clubs in Windsor, Newbury, Guildford and Staines.

The Birds spent the best part of the next three years, criss-crossing the country, playing up to six nights a week and gaining a popular following in discerning mod venues such as Watford's Trade Union Hall, Sheffield's King Mojo Club, and Bristol's Chinese R&B Club at the city's Corn Exchange. Unlike the Small Faces, whose hectic schedule was eased via a chauffeur-driven Mark X Jaguar, the Birds' negotiated Britain's archaic road system in a Sixties regulation Austin Morris J2. As Kim Gardner told Mike Stax in 1994: "You'd travel for six hours to get somewhere – or seven hours, maybe longer – and get like £20 and then drive all the way back, break down and spend the night in the van 'cos it's freezing cold and there's no engine."

Tony Munroe: "At the time there were only two motorways, the M1 which finished at Watford Gap. It used to take us ages to get anywhere but we did it. If you wanted to take a leak, you had to piss out of the window. We had one van where we made a hole in the floor and pissed through that! We used to live on eggs, sausages and chips at the Blue Boar, which was the only sort of place at the top of the M1."*

Ali MacKenzie: "It was nothing to arrive at the Blue Boar after having come back from up north, go in and see the Pretty Things in there, John Mayall, the Who, all these different bands coming back from a gig and colliding in that sort of area. We drove long distances but when you're 17 or 18 years old you don't give a shit, you're having fun."

In June '64, at the Tony Pike Sound Studio, a two-track recording and demo facility at 31 Dryburgh Road, Putney, south-west London, the Birds recorded Ronnie Wood's first songwriting effort. 'You're On My Mind' was very much in the current R&B idiom, revealing the twin influences of Bo Diddley and the Yardbirds. The group also laid down a cover of Bo's 'You Don't Love Me (You Don't Care)'.

As a direct result the Birds were short-listed for Rediffusion TV's *Ready, Steady, Go!* contest spin-off, *Ready Steady, Win!* The rules were simple enough – various unsigned combos from around England competed through ten heats and a semi-final for the first prize of a recording contract with Decca, a publishing deal with KPM (Keith Prowse Music), an agency deal with the Harold Davison Organisation and £1,000 in prize money for musical gear. The runners up received the consolation prize of a new transit van while the third contenders got £250. With the British beat

---

* Watford Gap was named after a gap in the hills of Northampton, not the Hertfordshire town further south. The Blue Boar motorway cafe opened on November 2, 1959, the same day as the M1 motorway.

boom at its height that summer it could be reasonably assumed that a successful career beckoned.

To enter, groups had to submit a demonstration disc of an original composition then pass a formal audition. The Birds were given the nod and appeared live at Rediffusion's Wembley studio on June 23 (the show was broadcast six nights later). They got the third heat "off to a lively start" (in the words of host Keith Fordyce) performing 'You're On My Mind'. Among the ten million viewers were a large contingent of Birdwatchers from Middlesex but the decision was left to the judges who included Adam Faith and *Evening Standard* show business journalist Maureen Cleave who took a dim view of the proliferation of these long-haired R&B types. When giving her prerequisite regarding the most important attribute a group should have as "clean fingernails", the Birds must have sensed their chances were slim. They didn't survive to the next round, finishing fifth out of a possible six, and the Thyrds from South London went through to the semi-final (The Bo Street Runners from Harrow eventually won the prize).

Dick Rowe – head of Decca A&R and the man who had to live with the ignominy of having turned down the Beatles in 1962 – was interested enough when de Clerck played him the Birds' acetate. With the added weight of a Monday night residency at the 100 Club in their favour, the Birds were signed to Decca and placed with Belinda (Recordings) Ltd, a company set up by Aberbach Music and run by music publisher and producer, Franklyn Boyd, to make independent recordings.[*]

Released in November, 'You're On My Mind' was an unrestrained re-recording of the demo; a surly burst of Brit R&B featuring MacKenzie singing in a more confident drawl with Wood's wailing blues harp on the verses before the song changed tempo, Bo-style, for the chorus, underpinned by Gardner's walking bass line. The snarly treatment given to 'You Don't Love Me (You Don't Care)' on the B-side adapted the Diddley "shave-and-a-haircut, two-bits" rhythm to the Birds' own devillish design.

The group rarely played 'You're On My Mind' onstage which Ali felt was more his comfort zone. "To be honest, I never really liked recording. The atmosphere wasn't there for me like it was at the gigs we were doing.

---

[*] Belinda was the UK arm of the Bienstock publishing empire, Aberbach and Hill & Range, which published Elvis Presley's music. Franklyn Boyd was involved in the early management of Cliff Richard.

It was a totally different thing. With playing live you got instant feedback and energy. It was total adrenalin from the word go."

On Friday night, October 30, 1964, Ronnie was having a drink at the Intrepid Fox, a familiar watering hole for musicians at the Shaftesbury Avenue end of Wardour Street, when in walked a familiar figure he'd noticed around the scene. This guy stood out, if not for his cocksure manner and gravel-throated vocals than his spiky barnet similar to Ronnie's own long, thick Romany thatch that earned him the nickname Cleopatra. The fact that this Mod about town was sporting a check Coco the Clown jacket and a shiner only made him stick out more. Ronnie was being sussed out, too. Before long, the stranger walked up and greeted him with the words, "Hello, face, how are you?"

Rod Stewart had just come from the Rediffusion TV studio on nearby Kingsway where he'd awkwardly plugged his first single 'Good Morning Little Schoolgirl' on *Ready, Steady, Go!* While Ronnie hadn't heard the record he discovered that he and Rod were on the same label. The two found they instantly hit it off, sharing similar tastes in music and humour, especially when the vainglorious singer admitted tripping over as he'd started to mime. Ronnie was rather envious that at 19, Rod had already seen a bit of the world, albeit penniless and starving. Stewart mentioned he sang every Thursday night at the Marquee just up the road and Wood said he'd look in if he didn't have his own gig to do. The pair staggered off into the night with a bond cemented.

On February 12, 1965 the Birds and their west London rivals the Who both auditioned for the BBC Light Programme. While the boys from the Bush just narrowly passed, the Talent Selection Group assigned to listen to the Birds' audition tape were less favourably inclined. "A scruffy-looking lot, to say the least" and "A rather dreary R&B group" typified the response. Ironically, one of the three songs they performed was a staple in the stage act of both bands at the time.[*]

'Leaving Here', a little-known Eddie Holland song written by Holland-Dozier-Holland, had been released as a Motown single in 1963 but only crept out in England on an EP, *R&B Chartbusters Volume 3*.

Ali MacKenzie: "At the time if you heard a song you went down to

---

[*] The other two were covers of Billy Boy Arnold's 'I Ain't Got You' and Bo Diddley's 'Bring It To Jerome' – both British R&B staples.

Rainbow Records and they would import it for you or Leo used to say, 'I've got this from so and so.' Because Leo ran a chain of clubs he would hear stuff or we would say 'get us this' and he would use his contacts and get it in from the States for us."

Some discrepancy remains as to which group was first to pick up on 'Leaving Here'. The Who recorded it during the sessions for their aborted pass at a debut album in April 1965 but their attempt remained in the can. The Birds unleashed their version in March backed by 'Next In Line', a Wood original featuring Ronnie's rather weak lead vocal. Ali's reservations about recording notwithstanding, both sides are a testament to the group's gutsy brashness and what the Birds must have been like to see tearing it up onstage at the time.

Thanks to Decca's promotional department, the group travelled to the Alpha Television Studios in Birmingham on May 2 to pre-record their slot on *Thank Your Lucky Stars*. Unlike the trendy, freewheeling *Ready, Steady, Go!, TYLS*, which started broadcasting in 1961, was a more mainstream affair comprising a bland mix of chart hits, newcomers and plain MOR acts. To illustrate, the other guests on that week's show included Shirley Bassey, the Searchers, Marianne Faithfull and twist king Chubby Checker.

The Birds' farcical appearance was worthy of *This Is Spinal Tap* as Gardner recounted to Mike Stax: "We'd got these new shirts: dark blue shirts with light blue collars and cuffs. We got them from some West End shirt maker that Leo took us to . . . [At the TV studio] they were saying, 'Oh we've got to put holes in your shirts.' And all of a sudden they ripped all our new shirts we'd just got for the show."

The idea was for the group to be lowered on to the set via invisible wires as 'Leaving Here' began and removed in similar fashion at song's end. "They stuck wires and harnesses on us," said Gardner. "I went sideways off the stage and totally missed where I was supposed to land and landed in some lady's lap. And the drummer came directly down and landed backwards on his kit . . . So at one point I'm actually not touching the ground – still playing but I can't quite touch the ground."

The Birds' other brush with national notoriety occurred on Monday, August 2 when American group the Byrds touched down at Heathrow that morning to begin a problem plagued, 18-day British tour. Standing self-consciously among the screaming hordes were the group's British namesakes who had travelled the short distance with their scheming manager and an inquiry agent who delivered the California-based folk-rockers with writs, seeking an injunction to stop them from using the name and damages for loss of earnings. Documents were also served on the tour's promoters, Mervyn Conn and Joe Collins.

"This is obviously a publicity stunt," Conn raged to the Uxbridge *Weekly Post*. "Why have the Birds waited so long in lodging their complaint? . . . And why at the airport of all places? . . . they even tried to get photographs taken of their agent handing over the writs, but we evaded them in the Customs Hall."

The stunt made the papers but was an embarrassment to all but de Clerck. With the Byrds' 'Mr Tambourine Man' having just slipped down from two weeks at number one to second position on the UK singles charts they were hardly about to back down to a bunch of Limey unknowns who hadn't got within sniffing distance of their record sales. "The matter is now in the hands of my solicitors" Conn informed the *Weekly Post*, "and the Byrds' British tour will continue as planned."*

Tony Munroe: "When we played at places kids kept coming up to us saying, 'We went along to buy your record, 'Leaving Here' but they didn't have it so we bought your other one, 'Mr Tambourine Man'. Why didn't you play it?!' That was happening at gigs all over the country. And that really messed things up for us."†

By October, *Disc* reported without any evident surprise that the Birds v Byrds case had been dropped. That same month Decca issued the third Birds single, a cover of Marvin Gaye's 'No Good Without You Baby', featuring Wood's serrated-edge guitar cutting like a switchblade and another impressive vocal from MacKenzie. The B-side, 'How Can It Be', a Wood original featuring more aggressive, raw-edged guitar and a crisp drum sound, was impressive enough for another west London group, the Eyes, to strongly influence their own unyielding, proto-punk sounding 'You're Too Much', released by Mercury in May 1966.

For the third time, the Birds' hard-earned live reputation failed to translate into significant record sales. As befell so many other unsung combos, including Ronnie's brother's group the Artwoods, Decca and the other big companies' safety in numbers attitude of pumping out product from a number of often identikit groups in a misguided effort not to be left behind on the latest transitory trend meant that without the right break the

---

* The Byrds' first British tour was notorious for ill-organisation, unrealistic expectations and the band's stiff, indifferent stage performances winning them few plaudits from audiences and reviewers. The support acts on the theatre dates included Them and Kenny Lynch whose backup band, Boz & The Boz People featured Ian McLagan.
† 'Leaving Here' charted at 45 in *Record Mirror* dated May 29, 1965 – the Birds' only modest success.

records sank without trace to all but that band's fervent following. Yesterday Merseybeat, today R&B, what was the difference?

Then there was the Birds' own bloody-minded outlook to contend with as Munroe confirms: "We didn't care what people wanted to hear, we stayed true to ourselves by playing what *we* wanted to play. If they didn't like it then too bad."

Without a hit to bring in the readies it was business as usual with the Birds constantly gigging, including a New Year's Eve all-nighter at Sheffield's Mojo Club with the Graham Bond Organisation, the Steam Packet and the Mike Cotton Sound. "I remember that night because the police raided us," says Munroe. "We were all sharing the same dressing room and there was a coloured bloke, I don't know which group he was with, and the police found his stash in his coat. The police were asking us, 'Whose coat is this?' and we were all looking at each other, saying 'It's not bloody mine!'"

Ali MacKenzie: "I didn't drink or smoke but Kim and Ron both liked their puff and pills, and Tony, a bit later. I think Pete was on pills before he even joined the band but it just didn't float my boat."

On January 14, the Birds arrived straight from a gig to an early morning shoot at Twickenham Film Studios, being paid £50 each to make the obligatory 'Sixties group in B-movie' cameo in *The Deadly Bees*. A forgettable horror-thriller directed by Freddie Francis, the film starred Suzanna Leigh as a stressed pop singer recuperating at an island cottage who winds up in an Agatha Christie style murder intrigue with the added danger provided by a swarm of killer bees.

Obviously somebody saw the gimmick in putting the Birds with the bees but mercifully the group's appearance in glorious Technicolor occurred during the opening minutes, where they are seen, heavily made-up, resplendent in striking Mod apparel lip-synching on a *Thank Your Lucky Stars*-type TV studio set. Ronnie wears a white polo neck jersey, his Fender Telecaster bearing a black and white check and striped design. The song, 'That's All That I Need You For', was in the usual strident Birds style and was one of three Wood/Munroe compositions written for the soundtrack.[*]

"Thank you, The Birds", the fictional TV compère announces as the song ends, "I'm sure we all wish them the very best on their forthcoming tour of America." Like certain managers from the time who fed stories to the press of their hitless band's imminent American conquest, such a

---

[*] *The Deadly Bees* was not released to cinemas until April 1967, following the Birds split, whereupon it promptly vanished into obscurity, occasionally being resurrected for late night TV screenings.

prospect for the Birds was wishful thinking, particularly in light of events following a gig at the Starlite Ballroom, Greenford in early 1966.

Ali MacKenzie: "Peter Lindsay, who was the promoter there, gave me a thick brown envelope at the end of the evening and said, 'Make sure you give this to Leo.' Now I don't know why Colin Farrell wasn't there because Colin always came with us to the gigs. So I said to Peter, 'Yeah, sure, what is it?' and he said, 'Just make sure Leo gets it.' Tony being Tony sort of snatched it out of my hand and proceeded to open it and there was a wad of money in there.* He said, 'What's this all about?' I said, 'I got this off Peter and he's asked me to give it to Leo.' We're all sort of looking at this money in the dressing room, and of course it was, like, 'Leo's ripping us off, look how much he's earning', the usual reaction. The next day, Colin came round and picked up the envelope and remarked, 'How come it's been opened?' I can't remember how I explained it away. I then got a call, either from Ronnie, Kim or Tony, saying 'Let's have a meeting and get this sorted out.' I think we had a meeting round at Kim's actually and the majority vote was to get rid of Leo.

"My own opinion was that it was the worst thing we ever did, bearing in mind we were picked up in a van or a car, taken to gigs, and given three square meals a day. We had a little bit of a clothing allowance, not as much as the Small Faces but enough. Pete used to get his drumsticks paid for, the boys used to get their strings paid for, repairs were paid for, our tax and insurance was paid and we also got a wage. When we started with Leo we were on £15 a week each but we ended up at about £25. We were working up to seven nights a week and we had our own fan club. I was getting tambourines by the boxful because I used to smash a couple up every night as part of the act so I didn't have to pay for them, I didn't have to pay for anything so as far as I was concerned it was a good arrangement. But the band decided that we had to get rid of him and the majority won.

"We spoke to Kim's dad and he said, 'What you'll have to do is set up a meeting and thrash it out with Leo'. Kim or Ron hid a tape recorder behind the sofa and recorded the whole conversation at Kim's house on Edgar Road. Leo was there, Colin was there and basically everything that we said in our infinite wisdom was a bit unfounded, you know, 'He's ripping us off, he's ripping us off', but that's about as far as it got."

The Birds were eventually extricated from their contract on a technicality. "In those days," Munroe explains, "you could take people on if they

---

* MacKenzie claims the amount was nearly £1,000 but Munroe remembers it more likely being £400.

were under a certain age but it was like an apprenticeship and if you didn't give them gainful education, which might have been only one or two days a week, then it was an illegal contract. So that's the way the solicitor we hired got us out of it. The facts speak for themselves – Leo didn't do anything with any other group apart from the Birds. I think the reason the Birds didn't succeed was because of Leo."

Shortly after breaking away from de Clerck, the Birds formed their own company Popgressive Ltd and signed up to Australian impresario Robert Stigwood's agency.

Ali MacKenzie: "In the cold light of day, we now had to pay for our own petrol, our own stamp, our own insurance, our own digs, etc. My biggest regret after getting rid of Leo was that Stigwood never managed us. Stiggy was only our agent but we'd just come out of one management situation so we didn't want to be tied down to another. Big mistake."

Stigwood was also the Who's booking agent and had set up his own record label, Reaction, distributed through Polydor, primarily to aid the group after their recent acrimonious split with Decca and producer Shel Talmy. Because of their stake in Pete Townshend's publishing agreement with Essex Music, Who managers Kit Lambert and Chris Stamp, then currently operating out of Stigwood's office at de Walden Court, solicited various acts to cover Townshend compositions. The Birds recorded two versions of 'Run Run Run' based on Townshend's original demo. (The Who ended up recording the song on their second album *A Quick One*.) 'What Hit Me', a Wood/Munroe composition was taped at Pye Studios on March 18 but again, was not released. "That was down to Stigwood," Munroe sighs. "He kept saying, 'It's not the right time yet.'"

Surprisingly, for such an abrasive group on record, the Birds were vocally adept in handling a varied stage repertoire mainly comprised of American soul, similar in style to contemporaries the Action. "Ronnie used to sing lead on a Beach Boys song ['Here Today', from *Pet Sounds*]," says MacKenzie. "Tony sang a Smokey Robinson number, 'The Way You Do The Things You Do'. I did 'Tracks Of My Tears'. We used to do the Impressions 'It's Alright', 'Talking About My Baby', 'You Must Believe Me'. Most of our numbers featured Ronnie, Tony and myself doing three-part vocal harmony."

Like Rod Stewart, Ali had a fondness for Sam Cooke. "Sam Cooke was *the* vocalist for me. I first heard him when I was about 12. My sister Josie had one of his LPs which I've still got. Sam Cooke, Jackie Wilson, Marvin Gaye, Dionne Warwick – they were all played around our house on St Martin's Road."

In June the Birds recorded a scorching cover of a Doc Pomus/Mort Shuman song, 'Say Those Magic Words, originally recorded by American group the McCoys – laden with fuzzed, wah-wah guitar, swooping bass, clattering drums and an infectiously commercial chorus. In Ali's opinion, "That was our best record in terms of its production and execution. I was trying not to sound American to a certain degree." The Wood/Munroe written flip, 'Daddy Daddy' was something of an undeveloped throwaway but for the sinister foreboding mood of the arrangement, which descends into a bizarre coda of fuzzed-out guitar and driving drums. Finally released in September, the single proved to be the band's last flight.

Tony Munroe: "It was Stigwood's idea to change the name to Birds Birds. He wanted to lose the association with the Birds and the American Byrds. We all thought the idea was rather stupid."

The accompanying publicity photos show the group, now with short crops – apart from Ronnie whose trimmed mop sticks up – in suits and flowered lapels with Tony holding a toy sub-machine gun, looking like a mod version of the St Valentine's Day Massacre.*

Ali MacKenzie: "Ronnie, Kim and I bought these jackets in a second-hand shop up north somewhere. Tony already had his, a velvet, double-breasted jacket. I don't really know whose idea it was to be gangsters or where the car prop came from. Again it might have been Stigwood."

With another unsuccessful record and after three years living in each other's pockets, things reached breaking point.

Tony Munroe: "We were playing somewhere in east or south-east London. When the gig had finished this gang of hoodlums started to come up onstage and be a nuisance. A friend of the band's, Roger Jeggo, and myself tried to stop it and none of the other guys did anything, they just ran for the dressing room. Roger got the worst of it and had most of his teeth kicked out and we had to take him straight to hospital. I did my nut, I called the others a load of cowards and then the following day, they went and called a meeting with Stigwood, came back and said, 'We don't want you in the group any more.' I'm pretty certain Ron and Kim were behind it. So I said, 'Fine. The way you guys behaved last night I want out anyway.' By that stage Ron and I were always in conflict. He was a better guitarist but he always wanted to do things his way. And also Krissie and I

---

* Ironically, a year later, to cash in on the publicity surrounding the *Bonnie And Clyde* movie, Art Wood's group the Artwoods reluctantly used that very name for a one-off, 'Brother Can You Spare A Dime'. The single's picture sleeve showed the group in an almost identical gangster pose as Birds Birds.

didn't get on. She was manipulative and she turned him against me."

Ali takes the opposite view. "Krissie was a lovely lady. She and Ronnie were living together before the [Birds] broke up – sometimes at his mum's in Whitethorn Ave and then they got a flat in Shepherd's Bush. Krissie taught Ronnie to drive. They had a Morris Minor, which the two of them hand-painted. To my mind, Krissie definitely guided Ronnie and put him on the road to meeting your Jeff Becks, Rod Stewarts and Mick Jaggers. Ronnie knew what he wanted and she helped him get it."

For Munroe, it was a case of out of the frying pan into the fire, when joining another group featuring a future Rolling Stone. "I got a phone call from Peter Lindsay to say I've got Nick Simper, the bass player from the Pirates and an organist, Ken Hensley. I had Mick Taylor's number so I phoned him up and that was the beginning of the Gods. But I only stayed with them for a few months because to be quite honest, I'd had enough of the music business."

Meanwhile, the Birds carried on for several more months as a four-piece.

Ali MacKenzie: "Ronnie had to work a lot harder because we lost a good vocalist so we were down to a two-part vocal but it had an edge to it with the one guitar and that raspy sound that Ronnie used to get. Kim used to add a little bit. He wasn't really a singer but he could hold a note if there were some backing vocals needed."

The band continued to gig and record[*] but by the end of 1966 Ronnie was weighing up his options. "The Birds had reached saturation point," Wood told *Sounds'* Penny Valentine in 1971. "We'd play 17 gigs on the trot in England and then have two days off and go round again and we just ran out of ideas . . ."

Ali MacKenzie: "The business had a bit of a lull. Gigs were going down a little bit . . . I can remember saying to the others, 'We haven't got any jobs for a while, let's have a little break and we'll get together in a couple of months' time,' but we never did."

Present at the Birds' last-ever London gig were Jeff Beck and Rod Stewart. "When Beck left the Yardbirds he was like an old pal we used to meet on the road," said Wood, "and I just rang him up and said, 'What you doing?' and he said to come over and get some ideas going."

---

[*] The uncharacteristically poppy, horn-laden 'Daddy Rides Again', written by Wood, was the last track to be recorded by the Birds in December '66. It remained in the Polydor tape vaults before being retrieved and released as part of the definitive Birds' package, *The Collectors' Guide To Rare British Birds*, in 1999.

CHAPTER 5

Beck's Blues

"The American debut of the Jeff Beck Group promises much heated enthusiasm for the quartet in its six week tour . . . [Beck] and his band deal in the blues mainly, but with an urgency and sweep that is quite hard to resist. The group's principal format is the interaction of Mr Beck's wild and visionary guitar against the hoarse and insistent shouting of Rod Stewart, with gutsy backing on drums and bass. Their dialogues were lean and laconic, the verbal ping pong of a musical Pinter play."

Robert Shelton, *The New York Times*, 1968

"With Beck even the roadies were telling us what to do."

Rod Stewart, *Sounds*, 1970

IN 1967 Jeff Beck must have felt as though he was starting from scratch. Over the past two years he had built up a formidable reputation as the guitarists' guitarist, having stepped into the unenviable vacancy left by Eric Clapton in the Yardbirds with nerve and aplomb, creating whole new avenues of guitar virtuosity that managed to be both commercial and groundbreaking at the same time.

"Jeff was the guy for developing sounds," Yardbirds' singer Keith Relf stated in a 1974 interview with artist William Stout. "He used to get into motorbike sounds on a guitar and detuning, playing with the strings over the top of the nut, and detuning the thing while he was playing . . . He'd go out onstage with the guitar out of tune – but whatever he'd play would be in tune."

Like the others in the triumvirate of distinguished Yardbirds axemen, Beck hailed from Surrey; born Geoffrey Arnold Beck on June 24, 1944 in Wallington. In the mid Fifties he would tune into Radio Luxembourg, trying to catch the latest sounds from America over the faint, crackling signal and was particularly affected by guitar and recording innovator Les Paul. Beck's elder sister brought home Elvis Presley and Gene Vincent &

The Blue Caps records – Scotty Moore and the latter's guitarist, Cliff Gallup, making a lasting impression – and on March 12, 1958, Beck saw Buddy Holly perform on his only UK tour at the Davis Theatre, Croydon.

Like so many other guitarists Beck learnt his craft by playing along to records – not just rock'n'roll but also country, folk and jazz. During his teens he befriended another aspiring guitar player the same age from nearby Epsom, James Patrick Page, who shared a similar passion for early Sun era Elvis, Eddie Cochran, Gene Vincent and James Burton solos on Ricky Nelson's records.

With his Burns guitar (eventually upgraded to a coveted Stratocaster), Beck began playing in 1960 with local Croydon group, the Deltones. Having briefly attended Wimbledon School of Art, Beck drifted through odd jobs including work as a panel beater and car painter at South Croydon Motors – a job that helped satisfy his other obsession, cars, preferably those capable of going very fast.

Beck continued in various outfits, including Epsom group the Nightshift, who were managed by Jonathan Rowlands (then also looking after Rod Stewart) and a brief stint in Screaming Lord Sutch's backing group, the Savages. In late '64 he joined the Tridents, a popular group around west London with a regular gig at the Richmond Community Centre as well as residencies at the 100 Club on Oxford Street, where they supported the Birds. The Tridents were also a popular draw at Eel Pie Island – regularly packing out the old hotel – and on November 8, 1964, they supported Long John Baldry there. Similarly, Beck was in the audience at the Marquee on February 25, 1965 to see one of his favourite blues guitarists, Buddy Guy backed by the Soul Agents (featuring Rod Stewart on vocals).

That same month, the Tridents had just finished played a storming gig at the 100 Club when Beck was approached by Giorgio Gomelsky's associate Hamish Grimes and invited to audition to replace Eric Clapton in the Yardbirds, the rest of the line-up at the time being Keith Relf (vocals), Paul Samwell-Smith (bass), Chris Dreja (rhythm guitar) and Jim McCarty (drums). The group's increasingly commercial approach was anathema to Clapton who quit in order to pursue his blues purist instincts. Ironically Jimmy Page was first offered the job but turned it down because he was secure in plentiful and lucrative session work, so recommended his good friend Jeff instead. "I was just doing nothing, no money," Beck remarked to *Sounds'* Steve Rosen in 1973. "I couldn't even afford guitar strings."

On March 5, a nervous Beck made his Yardbirds debut on a 'Sounds of '65' package at the Fairfield Hall, Croydon, followed a few days later by a pressurised club debut at the Marquee. However within a matter of gigs, he won over the majority of Clapton supporters who had previously seen him as being unfit to fill Slowhand's considerable shoes. During Beck's tenure of almost two years in the Yardbirds,* the group made their most original and innovative recordings.

"It was a perfect excuse for me to experiment on everything that I'd heard – all the influences I'd picked up," Beck told Scott Muni in 1989. "Luckily the group policy was to experiment and not stay with the traditional verse-chorus-verse pop songs. We had to do that in order to get a single played but within that single I used to bend all the rules . . . you can hear that in those early records."

Beck's prowess more than matched the group's expectations, pulling out of the hat an eclectic range that included some of the most imaginative guitar work ever recorded, whether it was the delicate slide on 'Steeled Blues', the Eastern-style riff on 'Heart Full Of Soul', the exquisite volume tone pedal on 'Still I'm Sad' and the double-tracked solo on 'Shapes Of Things' (with added feedback overtone) that inspired a generation of American guitarists. His otherworldly noises during the solo in 'Happenings Ten Years Time Ago' paved the way to imminent psychedelia. On stage it was a similar story with Beck playing guitar behind his head, T-Bone Walker style, and coaxing feedback by laying the guitar atop his amp.

For all their innovation and potential the relentless pace for a jobbing group in the mid Sixties, the endless distances between personal appearances, the lack of sleep and bad food, and invariably inept management, took their toll on the Yardbirds, often resulting in cancelled shows at short notice due to illness, giving them a bad reputation with promoters. Beck was particularly affected and the band were often forced to play without their guitar wiz. His frail condition was exacerbated in October 1966 during the Yardbirds' fourth American tour – a gruelling, financially bereft six-week trek on a Greyhound bus as part of the Dick Clark Caravan Of Stars. By now Jimmy Page had replaced Samwell-Smith, initially on bass but soon moving to play twin guitar with Beck. Unfortunately, this novel and potentially mind-blowing arrangement was destined not to last.† The strain on Beck, which manifested itself by onstage tantrums and abuse of amplifiers that often malfunctioned, culminated in a meltdown in Texas

* As a salaried employee, it should be noted!
† This explosive line-up of the Yardbirds was captured for posterity in a contrived, Who-like auto-destructive scene filmed in October '66 at Pinewood Studios for Michelangelo Antonioni's art-house classic, *Blow-Up*.

near the start of the tour when Beck smashed an amp to bits, stormed off-stage and locked himself in the dressing room.

A decade later Page gave his version of what happened next to *Trouser Press*: "In the dressing room, I walked in and Beck had his guitar up over his head, about to bring it down on Keith Relf's head. But he smashed it on the floor instead. Relf looked at him in total astonishment, and Beck said, 'Why did you make me do that?!'"

While the others continued the tour (with Page now sole guitar player for the remainder of the Yardbirds' formation), Beck flew to Los Angeles for a cooling out period. "Mental exhaustion" was the reason proffered by journalist June Harris in her *NME* column; Beck was more explicit when recalling to *Rolling Stone,* "I had inflamed tonsils, an inflamed brain and an inflamed cock." On November 30 it was announced that he was leaving the Yardbirds due to persistent ill health which was news to the guitarist when he arrived back in London.

With unreliability cited as a further reason behind his departure Beck entered the New Year of 1967 broke, bitter and angry. His dismissal from the Yardbirds coincided with a shift from R&B and soul to the progressive pop of groups like the Move and the nascent psychedelia of the Pink Floyd. Clubs like the Scene and the Flamingo gave way to Tiles, on Oxford Street (for diehard Mods still dancing to soul) and the UFO club, on nearby Tottenham Court Road, which swiftly became the meeting point for the burgeoning British 'underground' influenced by reports of what was happening on America's West Coast. With the new music came new drugs – speed was replaced by pot and a mysterious and powerful hallucinogen, LSD, which encouraged free-form ideas and experimentation. On top of this a black American guitarist, who arrived in London in September '66, was taking London's clubs by storm, giving the holy trinity of Clapton, Beck and Townshend reason to peer nervously over their shoulders. On December 21, both Beck and Townshend witnessed a typically incendiary Jimi Hendrix Experience performance at Blaise's club in Kensington.

"He was unbelievable," Beck told the BBC. "It was like a bomb blowing up in the right place." Also witnessing the shell-shock effect Hendrix had on the hip Swinging London crowd was Ronnie Wood and his girlfriend, Krissie. With his future plans still indefinite Beck, who knew Wood from his Tridents days, mentioned he was thinking of forming his own group. Wood confirmed his interest and phoned Beck the next day.

"We got together the day after I rang and started talking about America and its potential," Wood told Caroline Boucher.

In the December 31 issue of *New Musical Express* it was announced that Beck had signed a recording contract with independent record producer Mickie Most and that he would be jointly managed by Simon Napier-Bell and Most's management partner in RAK Productions, Peter Grant.*

Like Don Arden, Peter Grant's fearsome reputation preceded him. A former wrestler from south London, Grant was six foot five and his weight hovered around the 300 pound mark, appropriate credentials as bouncer on the door of the 2I's Coffee Bar in Soho's Old Compton Street, where so many of the first wave of British rock'n'roll and pop stars were discovered. It was here that Grant first met Michael Hayes (a.k.a. Mickie Most) and the two started a friendship. Grant was employed as a stand-in actor as well as getting the occasional bit part in films and television. Most notably his enormous bulk made him body double for portly actor Robert Morley.

In 1963 Grant was employed as tour manager for Don Arden's visiting American rock package shows. Opting to go into management himself the following year, Grant set up office at 155 Oxford Street with Most – by now, a successful record producer with the Animals, the Nashville Teens and Herman's Hermits – where RAK Productions was based. Grant was managing all-female trio the She Trinity and the New Vaudeville Band, who had a freak novelty hit in both the UK and US during 1966 with 'Winchester Cathedral', when he became manager of both Beck and the Yardbirds. Most's hit streak was set to continue with transatlantic successes for the Animals, Herman's Hermits, Donovan and Lulu. With such a cast iron team behind Beck, what could go wrong?

"I'm prepared to work hard [and] I'm entitled to make a joke of it," Beck told *Hit Parader*'s Valerie Wilmer. "If I can't make a joke of it, I don't want to do it."

To describe Beck as mercurial would be an understatement. Even without hindsight it was obvious at the time that he was not cut out to be a bandleader – or at least in the way a band operated in the Sixties. Writing in *NME* in 1967, Keith Altham presciently observed that Beck had already cultivated a reputation in the business. "At his best, he is a talented, guitar

---

* In early January Napier-Bell, who had replaced Gomelsky as Yardbirds manager in April '66, sold off his interest in that band to Most and Grant. In February a recording deal for Jeff Beck was finalised with Columbia for the UK and most worldwide territories, and EMI subsidiary Epic in the US – the same arrangement in place with the Yardbirds.

perfectionist with a pleasant, conversational manner. At his worst, he's an obstinate, uncompromising character who avoids doing things he dislikes by the simple expedient of walking out on them."

A considerable line of disappointed musicians, promoters, managers and audiences were to experience the worst side first-hand.

Not only forfeiting a band but a marriage as well, Beck relocated to a bachelor pad in Sutton, Surrey where tentative plans began for his new venture. With the Birds in their final flap, Ron Wood and Kim Gardner came along to jam and added to the mix was a familiar face.

"I was in the Cromwellian club," Beck told Douglas J. Noble in 1993. "That was our hangout – our watering hole. And this particular evening, [Rod] was somewhat worse for wear through drink and I just thought there's the guy – the one guy – I would like to play with, have him sing in my band. And I was pretty down as well – totally out of the Yardbirds, nothing going, no money. I hadn't got anything to lose so I asked him if he would be interested and he said, 'Yup!'"

In the early stages Beck's band was set to continue within a Yardbirds framework with a singer (Stewart), two guitarists (Beck, Wood) and a rhythm section. In an ominous move, Gardner was the earliest victim of Beck's 'hire then fire' whims, leaving it to Ronnie to give his mate the bad news. Unruffled, Gardner joined a revamped version of Hertfordshire Mod heroes the Creation, another group like the Birds unable to equate a live following with chart success. With Cream having defined the term 'supergroup', Terence 'Jet' Harris, the Shadows' former bassist whom Most knew going back to his 2I's days, was invited to rehearse as was eccentric ex-Pretty Things drummer and all-round looner, Viv Prince. Due to their fondness for the sauce, however, Harris and Prince were erratic at the best of times and kept missing rehearsals booked at a studio in Goodge Street.

With Grant jumping the gun by booking the band onto the bill of a package tour starring Roy Orbison and the Small Faces, rehearsals moved to Studio 19 on Gerrard Street, Beck tearing up to London in his Corvette Stingray. Having little time for thought, the guitarist brought in drummer Ray Cook, formerly of the Tridents, and Wood was asked to switch to bass. Ronnie liberated a Fender Jazz from Sound City on Shaftesbury Avenue for the purpose. For years Wood said that he grabbed the bass off the wall because it was nearest the shop doorway, while in his autobiography he claimed he managed to persuade the shop manager he needed it for an urgent job that afternoon and never got round to taking it back. Either way, the bass wasn't paid for until Wood's Faces days.

Considering how audiences had been primed by Cream and the Jimi

Hendrix Experience, expectations were impossibly great for the high-profile debut of the week-old Jeff Beck Group on March 3 at the Finsbury Park Astoria. In what can now be seen as the first instance of Beck retrieving defeat from the jaws of victory, it was, in short, a shambles. In a front-page story headlined 'Beck Leaves Tour – Disastrous Debut', *Melody Maker* reported: "The group were obviously under-rehearsed and in the first house on opening night Jeff walked offstage when the power failed.* Rod Stewart attempted to salvage what remained of the act. In the second house they played badly and created a very poor impression. It was a sad occasion and an object lesson on relying too heavily on past reputations." The *Melody Maker*'s man on the scene, Chris Welch, had this to say, "Jeff Beck's new group presented a quite extraordinary performance. It was obvious they had not rehearsed sufficiently and Jeff seemed to have difficulty even playing a good solo."

Looking back, the evening sticks in Welch's mind for a less musical reason: "I was in the front row and I noticed that Rod's zip kept falling down, whether it was deliberate or not, I don't know."

After this public humiliation Beck immediately pulled out of the tour (P.P. Arnold became his replacement), fired the hapless Cook who had specially bought a new £400 kit on HP, replacing him with Mickey Waller and retreated back to the rehearsal room. As if to cause further aggravation, two things followed to taunt the guitarist – the first were Beck's candid (and ghosted) comments about his on the road sexploits appearing in a delightfully tacky tabloid expose printed in the British *Sunday Mirror* newspaper. ("Derby and Nottingham are good scenes. In those areas girls will follow groups within a 50-mile radius and the message is always the same – have sex, will travel.")

The second was the first piece of product from the uneasy Beck/Most coalition, 'Hi Ho Silver Lining', released March 24. Recorded before the band's formation in January with session musicians including drummer Clem Cattini and John Paul Jones (who arranged the zippy strings), its trendy Swinging London-style lyrics were actually written by American songwriters Scott English and Larry Weiss, and selected by Most from a music publisher's catalogue (along with Neil Diamond's 'The Boat That I Row', a hit for Lulu at the same time).

The fact that he had a bona fide vocalist in Rod Stewart at his disposal over a tone deaf guitarist was of no interest to Most, so intent was he that

---

* Ever since dark mutterings about sabotage have attached themselves to the Small Faces and their road crew. When pressed Ian McLagan pleads memory loss.

Beck should be the primary focus from the outset. "He [Most] didn't give a damn about me," Stewart remarked to Harvey Kubernik in a 1974 *Sounds* interview. "It was Jeff this and Jeff that." Stewart was relegated to backing vocals (with Most) on the session.* Bearing the production tricks pioneered by the Beatles (a backwards piano loop brings the song in) and Beck's vocal shortcomings covered by double tracking 'Hi Ho Silver Lining' was jaunty yet serious,† competent if vacuous, and extremely commercial.

Just like the Small Faces with 'Sha La La La Lee' (and even Cream with their surprisingly uncharacteristic chart debut 'Wrapping Paper'), it was wholly unrepresentative, throwing Beck's hardcore following off guard. Having pioneered whole new vistas of guitar craftsmanship with the credible Yardbirds why was Beck recording something more suited to Dave Dee, Dozy, Beaky, Mick & Tich or Most's main money-spinners, Herman's Hermits? In an attempt at damage limitation, Beck told *Record Mirror*'s Peter Jones: "'Hi Ho' was aimed at the people who don't know me. It's different from the stuff I'd done before . . . People who knew me before were surprised at it . . . but it did the trick."

Hopefully they turned the disc over to find 'Bolero' – an elaborate setting for Beck's showmanship. Based on Ravel's *Bolero* (and subsequently re-titled 'Beck's Bolero') this track was the result of a covert session at IBC Studios dating back to May 1966 when Napier-Bell was encouraging the Yardbirds' members in outside pursuits. With a roll call of Beck and Jimmy Page (guitars), John Paul Jones (bass), Nicky Hopkins (piano) and Keith Moon (drums) it was the ultimate dream line-up and, if Beck had had his way, the first supergroup, just pipping Cream to the post. Moon had briefly quit the Who during a combustible period in the group's history and the plan was for he and John Entwistle to join forces with Beck and Page – and if they could be persuaded either Steve Winwood or Steve Marriott as vocalist – in forming a group calling themselves Lead [sic] Zeppelin – a name suggested by either Moon or Entwistle, depending upon the source. The idea foundered when Moon swallowed his pride and rejoined the Who but did not evaporate entirely.

'Hi Ho Silver Lining' climbed to number 14 in May; a competing version on Decca by a London group called the Attack may well have

---

* Rod's backing vocals can be heard clearly on the stereo mix included on the 2005 CD reissue of Jeff Beck's *Truth*.
† The lyric's cautionary tone echoed the same writers' anti-consumerist stance in 'Popcorn Double Feature' recorded contemporaneously by the Searchers.

prevented its progress higher. The song – now a ubiquitous staple of wedding receptions and football terraces – became a source of embarrassment to Beck who was less than pleased when it became an unexpected Top 20 hit again in 1972 when re-released by Most.* As Beck described it, 'Hi Ho Silver Lining' was "like having a pink toilet seat hanging round my neck for the rest of my fucking life."

A packed gig at the Marquee on April 11 went some way to restoring Beck's besmirched reputation. The band had reverted back to a twin guitar line-up of Stewart (vocals), Wood and Beck (guitars), Dave Ambrose (ex-Shotgun Express) on bass and Rod Coombes, formerly of Lulu's backing band, the Luvvers, on drums. Mickey Waller had left for a better paid gig, filling the drum seat in the Walker Brothers' backing band, the Quotations, on a classically mismatched Walkers-Engelbert Humperdinck-Cat Stevens-Jimi Hendrix UK package tour.

However it didn't last long – Ambrose joined a new version of Brian Auger's Trinity and went on to become a successful A&R man for EMI; Coombes moved through Trifle, Juicy Lucy, Stealers Wheel and the Strawbs. Having just been let go from John Mayall's Bluesbreakers, Aynsley Dunbar joined on drums and Wood moved back to bass. "Before I took up bass I was getting in a rut on guitar but bass gave me new ground to build on," Wood told *Beat Instrumental* in 1970. "I got into the thing about what you don't play being as important as what you do play."

With Napier-Bell selling out his management stake in Beck to Grant and the agency arm of NEMS Enterprises setting up gigs, the Jeff Beck Group went out on the road playing clubs and ballrooms. The taciturn guitarist appeared content, telling *Melody Maker*, "We've got a knock-out group now, and we are going down tremendously well. . . . We've got enough numbers off for an hour and we do two half hours."

Although Beck was definite kingpin he magnanimously allowed the billing to reflect Rod as featured attraction with various ads from the period variously reading 'Jeff Beck plus the Rod Stewart Show' and 'Jeff Beck and his Group featuring Rod Stuart' (spelling Rod's surname was evidently a problem with some promoters). In some ads the group was billed as the 'Jeff Beck Sound'. However the prestige of separate status

---

* Beck issued a curt press statement to the effect that he had not authorised its reissue and would not be performing it onstage. Ironically, the first time he willingly resurrected it was for the Ronnie Lane ARMS benefit concerts in 1983.

was not reflected in financial parity due to Stewart, Wood and Dunbar not being under RAK's management aegis.

From their earliest stages the Jeff Beck Group ignored the prevailing spirit of psychedelia that Beck's Yardbirds work had presaged in favour of being an Anglicised Chicago blues band. But as Rod pointed out to *Melody Maker*, "I think we took the Chicago blues a stage further with the Beck group. It was no longer just copying things."

Represented in their repertoire were Buddy Guy ('Stone Crazy', 'Let Me Love You, Baby' – initially played at a fast tempo as a Beck guitar vehicle before moving to the funkier blues as heard on *Truth*), Elmore James ('Talk To Me Baby'), Albert King ('Oh Pretty Woman'), B.B. King ('Sweet Little Angel') and Howlin' Wolf ('You Shook Me', 'I Ain't Superstitious'). A shared love of Tamla-Motown was reflected by beefed up cover versions of the Temptations' '(I Know) I'm Losing You' (a song Stewart and Wood would resurrect in the Faces) and the Four Tops' 'Loving You Is Sweeter Than Ever'. The band also cheekily reworked B.B. King's 'Rock Me Baby' into 'Rock My Plimsoul', helping themselves to a writing credit of 'Jeffrey Rod' in the process. The track became a stage staple and also the B-side of Beck's second single, the Graham Gouldman-written 'Tallyman', released in July.

While a step up from 'Hi Ho Silver Lining', featuring a gorgeous Beck slide solo and session singers' John Carter and Ken Lewis' bright harmony lines behind Beck's endearingly flat vocal, it still bore the stamp of Most's autocratic approach in the studio although at least he allowed the band to play on both cuts. This incompatibility would be a problem for the rest of their existence. "He [Rod] doesn't want to sing the songs we pick as A-sides," Beck simplified for US magazine *Hit Parader*. "And we couldn't release the things he wants to do. So Rod sings on the B-sides."

On July 2, the Jeff Beck Group played their first major London show since the Finsbury Park Astoria debacle – at the Saville Theatre, sandwiched between John Mayall's Bluesbreakers (now featuring 18-year-old guitarist Mick Taylor) and Cream. "It was just about the time of flower power," Rod recalled to *NME*'s Nick Logan, "and we all came on in flowers and kaftans . . . did we look a state – and Aynsley was really insulted. This wasn't the blues to him." Dunbar left to form his own group, the Aynsley Dunbar Retaliation.[*] Their debut came on August 12 at the

---

[*] Stewart sang on the Retaliation's recording of Buddy Guy's 'Stone Crazy' which remained unreleased until appearing on a blues sampler in 1973.

The Faces' first publicity shot, Twickenham, late 1969 (L-R): Ron Wood, Rod Stewart, Ian McLagan, Ronnie Lane, Kenney Jones. "I was ready to get into it," said Lane. "I hadn't got disillusioned, though I did have some fears because Rod had his own solo things to honour – just from the point of view of having all the energies contained. But I thought as long as it was good and made good music, I didn't really give a shit." (WARNER BROS)

Boyish Faces (clockwise from left): Stewart, Lane, Wood, McLagan (with elder brother Mike) and Jones.
(COURTESY MIKE MCINNERNEY/FACES FAMILY ARCHIVES)

The Outcasts, 1964 (L-R): Ron Chimes, Kenney Jones, Ronnie Lane, Steve Taylor, Alan Hutton. (RON CHIMES)

The Muleskinners, 1964 (L-R): Alan Hutton, Kenney Jones, Terry Newman, Ronnie Lane. (ALAN HUTTON)

Jimmy Powell & The Five Dimensions, Rod Stewart's first semi-professional group, late 1963. "I was just playing harmonica," he says. "I wasn't really allowed to sing as such." Rod's roots lay in folk music, learning to play banjo (bottom left) before graduating to his first familiar guise as 'Rod The Mod' (bottom right). (DAVE MCCARTHY, REDFERNS)

The Small Faces, 1965 (L-R): Jimmy Winston, Kenney Jones, Ronnie Lane, Steve Marriott, and (below) in 1966 with Winston's replacement, Ian McLagan (first left). Ronnie Lane: "I don't know if the image of the Small Faces got in the way of the musicianship. There were some people that really liked what we played and others that really only came to see us for the shop front that they saw." (DECCA/UNIVERSAL; LFI)

The Birds, Ron Wood's first group, 1965 (clockwise L-R): Kim Gardner, Ali MacKenzie, Pete McDaniels, Ron Wood, Tony Munroe (front). (DECCA/UNIVERSAL)

Shotgun Express, 1966 (L-R): Rod Stewart, Beryl Marsden, Pete Bardens. (EMI)

Steam Packet, 1965 (L-R): Rod, Long John Baldry, Julie Driscoll, Brian Auger. (REX)

The Jeff Beck Group, 1968 (L-R): Stewart, Wood, Mickey Waller, Jeff Beck and (below) onstage in 1969 with Waller's replacement, Tony Newman, on drums. "Jeff and I were uneasy with one another," said Stewart. "I think Jeff thought I had something up my sleeve, and I always felt Jeff had something up his sleeve." (GETTY IMAGES; RAY STEVENSON/REX)

The Small Faces in front of their communal home at Marlow, Buckinghamshire, 1968. Ian McLagan: "Things were becoming difficult because the sounds we were making on record, we found hard to replicate with just the four of us on stage. I learned afterwards that when 'The Universal' failed Steve Marriott thought he'd let us down." (LFI)

Windsor Jazz Festival where the drummer also played his last Jeff Beck Group commitment the following evening.

An existing recording of the show captures the Beck band at this juncture. "You've heard it all before," Stewart announces with remarkable nonchalance. "We're not gonna play nothing new." The opening number, a cover of the Soul Brothers Six's 'Some Kind Of Wonderful' rumbles powerfully along on Wood's driving bass ("Ron, the bass guitarist, appeared onstage stripped to the waist, and dressed as a Red Indian, complete with feathers," reported *Record Mirror*) and while not retained in Beck's set for long, it would be resurrected in a different guise by Wood and Stewart for the Faces. The set, suffering slightly for the lack of sufficient volume because of a noise curfew, proceeds along a course of heavy blues – not dissimilar to other contemporaries playing at the festival such as Ten Years After, Chicken Shack and, making their live debut, Peter Green's Fleetwood Mac – ending with the proverbial sore thumb of 'Hi Ho Silver Lining'.

Mickey Waller rejoined and a Marquee gig on September 26 pinpointed the difference "the Waller wallop" brought to the band; tight, unobtrusive and holding back just enough to allow the band space to improvise. Beck squeezes every possible permutation of the blues from his Gibson, taking the traditional 12-bar format and straining the very life out of it with a dirty overdriven tone – licks, squeals and big blocks of noise. Stewart's chummy between song patter that would become so familiar to Faces audiences is now in place.[*] But the real revelation is Wood's bass playing. Having only taken up the instrument within the last six months his origins as a guitarist come through in lead lines and driving runs on the Fender Jazz with its heavy wirewound strings giving a distinctive fuzzy tone. His almost jazzy style effectively fills the gaps not already marked out by Beck's marauding axe. Now all that was needed was to get this band to America. In the wake of the inroads made by Cream and the Jimi Hendrix Experience the potential was there to clean up.

However the whole enterprise might well have been derailed by Beck's third single, 'Love Is Blue' originally recorded by Vicky Leandros as Luxembourg's entry ('L'Amour Est Bleu') in the 1967 Eurovision Song Contest. Released in February 1968 to coincide with Valentine's Day and the current penchant for MOR ballads, evidently, Most was covering all

---

[*] A revealing moment occurs where Stewart asks the audience which of the 'hits' the audience wants to hear – 'Hi Ho Silver Lining' or 'Tallyman'. Beck can be heard muttering "Neither!"

bases by turning his client into 'the Engelbert Humperdinck of the fretboard' but the mix of schmaltzy strings, choir ensemble and soaring guitar was better suited to Hank Marvin than Jeff Beck. Musical carping aside, there were simply too many competing versions of the song for it to succeed. (Paul Mauriat's reached the top spot in America; Beck's only scraped into the UK Top 30.)

Of far more worth was 'I've Been Drinking', a slow piano blues based on Dinah Washington's 'Drinking Again', sensitively sung by Rod (with backing vocals from Madeline Bell) featuring delicate touches from Nicky Hopkins and a stinging fuzz solo from Beck who also doubled on bass. This was the first Stewart studio vocal performance par excellence and illustrated what could have been achieved if a sympathetic producer and a ready-made supply of quality material were available to draw upon. Stewart was already starting to write but his low-key, folk influences were no doubt considered inappropriate for an all-out, ballsy blues band like the Jeff Beck Group. While the musicianship was sewn up, a lack of original songs would continue to be a problem.

During this period Beck supplemented his earnings with session work, playing on recordings by Paul Jones and John Walker – who had sold Jeff his battered Fender Esquire back in '65 – and, so the story goes, was approached about replacing the increasingly fragile Syd Barrett in the Pink Floyd, a most unlikely pairing if ever there was.

Having kept him on hold for some time, in March, Immediate Records finally released a Rod Stewart solo single, 'Little Miss Understood', arranged and produced by the song's composer Mike d'Abo at Olympic Studios. While achieving commercial success, replacing Paul Jones as lead singer with Manfred Mann in 1966, d'Abo felt creatively stifled and so was welcomed into Immediate's stable. Richly arranged with violin and female backing, with Waller on drums, Rod vocalised well on a song struggling under the weight of its own pathos. "Mike's a great guy, but he would try and tell me how to sing . . ." Stewart complained to Nick Logan. The B-side, 'So Much To Say', carrying a d'Abo/Stewart writing credit, featured d'Abo playing laid-back piano over which Rod moaned the blues. The record attracted positive reviews but again failed to chart.

While it seemed that Stewart's talent was being overlooked, Lou Reizner, an expatriate American and head of Mercury Records' London operation, was taking note. Founded in Chicago in 1945 by Irving Green,

Berle Adams and Arthur Talmadge, the independent Mercury Record Corporation soon became a direct challenge to the major labels, boasting a quick distribution with pressing plants in both Chicago and St Louis, Missouri. The company proved successful with their pop, jazz and classical divisions and launched subsidiary labels including Wing, Smash, and Blue Rock Records. In 1962 Green sold Mercury to Philips but retained his post as president, and two years later he appointed jazz trumpeter, arranger, composer and producer Quincy Jones as vice president of the company – the first African-American to hold such a post.

Reizner had carved quite a career himself. Born in 1933 and raised in Chicago, where he attended junior college, he gained a first degree in sociology from the University of Colorado. "I wanted to be a social worker or something," he told *Sounds'* Martin Hayman, "but music was always my first love." Reizner had first-hand knowledge of the Windy City's blues scene, being friends with the likes of Willie Dixon and observing the Chess family operation. In the late Fifties, Reizner moved through Europe, picking up several languages along the way and with acting aspirations and standing at six foot four, ended up in Italy on the set of *Ben Hur* with a bit part.

Deciding the film business wasn't for him he returned to Chicago and started in record production, cutting sides at Audio Recorders in Arizona, the studio home of Duane Eddy and Lee Hazlewood. Having travelled and worked all over America and Europe, Reizner was appointed by Irving Green to set up the international arm of Mercury Records in London. In 1968 Philips launched Mercury as a separate division, giving the label greater independence in the British market. Reizner's signings included Welsh group the Eyes Of Blue (whom he also produced), the Buddy Miles Express, and Van Der Graaf Generator.

In April '68, Reizner first met with Jonathan Rowlands to enquire about Rod Stewart's recording contract.

"I knew Lou as his office was nearby on Chesterfield Street," says Rowlands. "He ended up living right next door to me in Albert Court, Knightsbridge. Lou mentioned how he'd like to be involved with Rod but lamented he couldn't because Rod was tied to the Jeff Beck Group. I said, 'No, he's not, he's signed to me.' So that got Lou interested."

Meanwhile, frustrated at his sideman role in the Beck Group with little financial reward, Wood was tempted by Kim Gardner to join him in the Creation during March. The group, whose original 1966 line-up had featured Kenny Pickett (vocals), Eddie Phillips (guitar), Bob Garner (bass) and Jack Jones (drums), were particularly popular in Germany; their second single, 'Painter Man' with its banal, nursery rhyme chorus, was translatable enough for it to become a number two hit there. Since Gardner's recruitment on bass in February '67 (Garner moved to lead vocal to replace Pickett), the group had been semi-resident in Germany, releasing further recordings through Polydor. However around September, Phillips bowed out and the Creation were effectively in limbo.

When Gardner returned to England at the end of that year, he and Ronnie messed about between Wood's Beck commitments, recording some tracks with former Artwoods keyboard player Jon Lord and John 'Twink' Alder, drummer with British psychedelic group Tomorrow.*

"Jack [Jones] asked me if I wanted to carry on [The Creation]," Gardner told Mike Stax in 1997, "'cos there was only him and me at that point. But him and Kenny [Pickett] were always really good friends, so we put some rehearsals together . . . I asked [Ronnie] if he wanted to make some money, 'cos the money was really good. So Kenny came back and off we went again."

Ronnie toured around the Continent in relative comfort, copying Phillips' distinctive stage pyrotechnics of controlled feedback and playing electric guitar with a violin bow.† Wood also helped Pickett aerosol spray designs onto canvases that would then be set alight. True pop art!

The group continued to record material produced by Shel Talmy – 'Midway Down', 'The Girls Are Naked', 'For All That I Am', 'Uncle Bert' were all supreme examples of period English psychedelia but wielding a hard edge, similar to the work of the Small Faces from the same time.

When the Creation finally broke up in June '68, Wood was readmitted to the Jeff Beck Group (John 'Junior' Wood, formerly of Tomorrow, had been holding down the bass job) while Gardner hooked up with pianist Tony Ashton and drummer Roy Dyke of Liverpudlian group, the Remo Four, thus forming Ashton, Gardner & Dyke.

Despite returning to the same ill scenario he'd left, Ronnie was clear-eyed about his reasons. "I only went back with Beck because I wanted to go to America."

---

* The four songs, basically jams in a heavy Booker T. style, engineered by future producer of renown Gus Dudgeon, were credited to the West Coast-sounding Santa Barbara Machine Head when released on an Immediate Records anthology, *Blues Anytime Volume 3* in 1968.

† Some might be surprised to learn that Phillips was employing this trick well *before* Jimmy Page adopted it in the Yardbirds and Led Zeppelin.

America made the Jeff Beck Group. "Until we did that first album *Truth*, and then we went for our first American tour," said Rod, "we had no real expectations of what we were going to do and that's when we busted the States open."

1968 was the year when LPs outsold singles for the first time in America, and when album oriented FM underground radio stations replaced AM transmitters as the medium of choice for the new 'serious' rock audience. With *Truth* the Jeff Beck Group were in a promising position to maximise their introduction to the States with a varied album that played to their strengths.

Largely a distillation of the band's stage act for the past year, with the exception of studio concoctions 'Ol' Man River', 'Greensleeves' and the previously released 'Bolero' to break the mood, the four days of sessions at Abbey Road in May with engineer Ken Scott cut to the quick without the need for overindulgence or fussy embellishments – only Nicky Hopkins and John Paul Jones were brought in to add keyboard parts.* From the opening funky yet heavy reworking of the Yardbirds' 'Shapes Of Things', featuring a breathtaking duel between Waller and Beck in the solo and Beck showing off a dazzling array of tricks, the hip swaggering 'Let Me Love You, Baby' with a great Stewart performance, his vocal asides displaying a new-found confidence, a delicate yet powerful arrangement of Tim Rose's melancholic 'Morning Dew' to the final wah-wah splurge and Waller drum rolls on 'I Ain't Superstitious', *Truth* epitomises the model of power rock trio with dynamo singer; heavy metal in its perfect form – if that isn't a contradiction in terms.

Without fanfare, the Jeff Beck Group made their American debut in New York City on June 14, playing two nights supporting the Grateful Dead at the Fillmore East. From audiences of 200–400 in English clubs and ballrooms the band now faced crowds numbering in the thousands. "I suffered from the most frightening experience [on opening night] . . . the voice just went," Rod told *Zigzag*. "I just went to open my mouth on 'Ain't Superstitious' and nothing came out. So I remember in those days Woody and I used to have a little bag we carried around with us all the time and it used to have a little bottle of brandy in it. So I ran back, got the bag, had a quick shot of brandy . . . I sort of crouched behind the amp and had a quick swig. Beck was covering for me, he was playing a solo, but

---

* There had been talk in the British music papers the previous year about Beck's supposed plans for a 35-minute guitar concerto to fill an album side. Whether this was an attention-seeking ruse is unclear but luckily wiser heads prevailed.

there was definitely a sort of embarrassment all round . . . everyone was looking for the singer. And sure enough, as the brandy hit the bloodstream, back came the vocals."

Considering that opening act, the Seventh Sons, were booed off by a typically demanding Fillmore audience, Stewart's stage nerves were only quelled when the band received a standing ovation. In his *New York Times* column, influential music critic Robert Shelton's review helped spread the word. "All told an auspicious beginning for an exciting group."

"His [Rod's voice] was amazing in those days . . ." Beck marvelled to Steve Rosen. "He had so much overtone . . . it was wild and it was raucous and was everything rolled into one. When he sang a blues, it just moved me, it was beautiful." As well as singing the blues Rod would strap on a guitar to provide the strumming rhythm on 'Beck's Bolero'.

During the band's five-night New York stint at Steve Paul's Scene Jimi Hendrix stopped by to jam.* On the opening night, having just finished another lengthy Cream tour, Eric Clapton showed up for a blow, giving the club's patrons cause to test their sobriety in seeing three of the world's greatest guitarists all squeezed on to the small stage.

The Beck band shared bills with familiar names from the psychedelic ballroom scene – Sly & The Family Stone, Moby Grape, Blue Cheer, the Steve Miller Band – playing at all the key late Sixties' American venues including Detroit's Grande Ballroom, San Francisco's Fillmore West and the Shrine Exposition Hall in Los Angeles. Boston Tea Party promoter Don Law remembers Beck giving a pep talk to raise flagging enthusiasms: "Jeff Beck . . . he had Rod Stewart and Ronnie Wood. And he was chewing them out! 'You wankers! We gotta play this thing better than we're playing it – these people came to hear the record' . . ."

Truth cemented Beck's reputation in the States when rush-released in July, selling around 150,000 copies and eventually peaking at number 15 on *Billboard*. Although it failed to chart in Britain when released in October the album increased Beck's diehard following and introduced Rod Stewart to his widest audience yet. "I learned so much with that band. That was where there was a change in my voice," Rod told Nick Logan. "I learned phrasing, how to blend with three or four other instruments." Having spent the past four years feebly aiming for success, he was now part of a dynamic and important rock force – albeit one continually beset by internal disputes, as Stewart made plain to *Rolling Stone* in 1970:

---

* Beck, Wood and Waller comprised an impromptu backing band for Hendrix at a festival show at Randall's Island on 16 June.

"That was a lot of the trouble with Beck; neither Ronnie nor I got enough attention. It wasn't all Beck's fault, either, it was the management, the record company, too. Nobody at Epic [Records] even knew Jeff Beck; they didn't even know they had us under contract when we made our first American tour. They'd come around to see a concert once, and somebody from Epic actually came up to me and said, 'Hey Jeff, you sang great, fucking good guitar player you got in the group too.'"

Accompanying Peter Grant on the first few tour dates was Jimmy Page. Since Beck's departure, the Yardbirds had soldiered on, concentrating mainly on the American market. Unfortunately, they too had been saddled with Mickie Most who, in his directive to find hits, had the group record such inappropriate fare as 'Ha! Ha! Said The Clown' and Harry Nilsson's 'Ten Little Indians'. Their 1967 album, *Little Games*, was an uncomfortable mix of pop novelties, straight blues and more experimental material. The Yardbirds played their final show in the unremarkable surroundings of Luton Technical College on July 7, 1968. Watching the Jeff Beck Group from the wings, Page and Grant observed with interest how well audiences responded to interplay between the singer and guitarist with a driving rhythm section, and on their return to the UK, set about finding musicians with a similar dynamic.

According to separate accounts from Wood and Waller, after returning from the States in early August, Grant offered each a place in the New Yardbirds. If true it would indicate Beck's insecurities were already set to mess up a good thing.

Rod and Ronnie's first trip to America had been a real eye opener. As working-class London kids, they had finally reached the home of the music they loved, a place that symbolised all that they could only dream of. However, there was a price to pay. Both tell stories of sharing rooms on the road with little money, stealing eggs from hotel kitchens to keep from starving. As Stewart explained, "By the time we got to LA we'd been there three or four months and I was desperately homesick." As well as family and friends, and despite a plentiful supply of willing female company, the lads were pining for their girlfriends back home. Rod had started a relationship with Krissie's friend, Sarah Troupe. Like Krissie, Sarah was from a well-to-do family; her father was high up in the Admiralty and her mother had been a debutante. Sarah and her mother lived in a flat in Wilton Crescent and then a house in Notting Hill Gate where Rod became a constant presence.

Having caught the Beck Group's shows at the Shrine and become acquainted with Rod while both were staying at the Continental Hyatt

House – the now legendary rock star's home away from home – dubbed the 'Riot House', Lou Reizner had done his homework and was ready to make an offer.

"I met Lou when he was on the way to his barbers in Mayfair," says Jonathan Rowlands. "We discussed it as we walked and actually agreed terms while he was getting his hair cut. By now, Geoff Wright had more or less stepped out of the picture and I was looking after Rod myself. It was very hands-off management. Rod was in and out of these bands, he made his own money and he had me if there were any problems to resolve. When he toured with Jeff Beck, Peter Grant did all that but he wasn't signed to Peter or Mickie. So as only a de facto member of Beck's band, Rod was free to sign with Mercury.

"The original management contract was, I think, for a year with an option and we kept taking up the options. The Gunnell brothers had tried to poach Rod [in 1966] but he re-signed with me so it was probably now of a 'grin and bear it' nature on his part. Tony Calder at Immediate [Records] was less than pleased. He became very unpleasant when he realised he'd forgotten to renew his recording option and Rod was a free agent."

The three-year contract between Stewart and Mercury Records was signed on October 8, with an option for a further year's extension.

Jonathan Rowlands: "As far as I'm aware, I had put in a clause that the terms should be governed by the laws of England because I didn't know the laws of Delaware which was in the original contract and Lou agreed to that. Possibly he was thinking further ahead, I don't know." Two weeks later Rowlands boarded the Queen Elizabeth and relocated to America where he continued his show biz adventures.

"I never made any money off Rod despite what he may think which doesn't worry me because there wasn't really any money to be made from him at that time . . . It wasn't worth taking commission off 90 quid, for example. The only commission I ever got was when I signed him to Lou for the Mercury deal. Rod told me he wanted a Marcos sports car, which cost £1,000 and Lou gave me £250 commission on top so it never cost Rod a thing."

To capitalise on the momentum from *Truth* and their earlier visit, the Jeff Beck Group started a second American tour in Chicago on October 11. Making his debut a week later at the Fillmore East was official fifth member, Nicky Hopkins.

Born Nicholas Christian Hopkins in Perivale in 1944, the Royal Academy of Music trained pianist joined his first group, Screaming Lord Sutch & The Savages, in 1960. In May 1963, while with Cyril Davies' R&B All-Stars, Hopkins was hospitalised for a lengthy spell with serious intestinal trouble. In light of his poor health, Hopkins took on session work after being discharged in December '64 and became *the* session pianist of choice, playing on recordings by the Who, the Kinks, the Rolling Stones and the Beatles' 'Revolution' among hundreds of others. He had, of course, played on 'Bolero', 'I've Been Drinking' and *Truth* as well as several studio jams with Beck and Jimmy Page* and had sat in with the Beck Group at their Sunbury Festival appearance in August.

"Really it just got too much by '68," Hopkins told Chuck Pulin in 1973, "because it got very wearing and very boring and the sessions I was really interested in – well I'd be really tired by the time I got to them. Like I'd start at 10 am and go through until midnight and then go on to Stones sessions and work through the night . . . I just got fed up recording 24 hours a day and I wanted to go on the road so I said, 'The next person who asks me to join I'm going to do it' – and it was Beck."

The band returned to the scene of previous triumphs such as the Fillmore's East and West, Grande and Shrine, sharing bills with the likes of Ten Years After (who belonged to the same booking agency run by Terry Ellis and Chris Wright). While in Los Angeles, Beck, Hopkins and Stewart appeared on an album *Permanent Damage* masterminded by Frank Zappa and featuring his all-female protégés the GTOs (Girls Together Outrageously) consisting of a gaggle of LA rock star courtesans. This mainly comprised a few stray notes and vocals behind the girls' tuneless brayings. Considering Beck had earned himself a reputation as "scourge of the groupies" it only seemed fair to give something back.

In New York he caught up with Peter Grant and Jimmy Page who were bearing the completed master tapes for the first Led Zeppelin album in an ultimately successful bid to secure a deal with Atlantic. Beck was more than taken aback at what he heard, as he recalled to John Tobler and Stuart Grundy: "He [Page] said, 'Listen to this. Listen to Bonzo, this guy called John Bonham that I've got.' And so I said I would, and my heart just sank when I heard 'You Shook Me'. I looked at him and said 'Jim, what?' and the tears were coming out with anger. I thought, 'This is a piss-take, it's got to be.' I mean, there's *Truth* still spinning on everybody's turntable,

---

* These recordings, credited to Jeff Beck & The All Stars, were given an unauthorised release on the Immediate compilation series *Blues Anytime* in 1968.

and this turkey's come out with another version. Oh boy . . . then I real-ised it was serious, and he did have this heavyweight drummer, and I thought 'Here we go again' – pipped at the post kind of thing."

Returning to England Beck pleaded exhaustion, resulting in a string of further cancelled dates and a third American trip around Christmas for shows with Vanilla Fudge going begging. Grant didn't have to look far. Eagerly stepping into the breach was Page's new band.

In their year-end round-up *Rolling Stone* praised, "The Jeff Beck Group was the best thing from England this year with the exception of Traffic. Deluged by British blues bands, they said it with a rock and roll difference, a good record, characterised by new sounds and a respectable tour . . ."

On February 11, Ronnie was at home celebrating Krissie's 21st birthday when the phone rang. It was Grant informing him that his services would not be needed on the forthcoming American tour. The same call was made to Mickey Waller. Wood wrote in his autobiography, "I said, 'OK, if you think you can beat us, go right ahead,' put the phone down and thought, 'Bloody hell, what am I going to do now?' and then, 'Peter Grant is a shit.'"

CHAPTER 6

Immediate Collapse

"I started Immediate to prove to the big companies an independent company could be successful – to give them a kick up the arse – and that's what it did."

Andrew Oldham, *Sounds*, 1972

"It suited Andrew's purposes to keep us in the studio. And so the road thing really suffered. By the time we came out of the hole, after being in the studio for a year, the road sounded terrible to me. That's when I thought, 'It's got to be over.'"

Steve Marriott, interview with John Hellier, 1984

HAPPY To Be A Part Of The Industry Of Human Happiness. Immediate Records' credo was a succinct if naïve aphorism in defining the modus operandi of one of the first British independent record labels, launched in August 1965 by Rolling Stones manager and all-round maverick, Andrew Loog Oldham.

"We believe that success lies in dispensing with accepted tradition and going against the current trend," Oldham declared to *Record Mirror*, "which is to deal with pop merchandise in a stiff and unimaginative manner. We want to give an aura of youth. There's no room in the business for an old-club atmosphere. One must adopt streamlined American methods of selling and promotion."

Oldham had plenty of experience of the "old-club atmosphere". In 1962, when he first entered the music business as a PR, the four main record companies – EMI, Decca, Philips and Pye – had the industry completely sewn up. The recording and music side of these major public companies was only a small part of their operations, with each having interests in all manner of electric products, mostly for home use, but both EMI and Decca also invested much of their profit in defence technology.

The organisations were run with strict formality by a directorship that knew little or next to nothing about pop music except the immense profits it could bring, and generally viewed colourful interlopers like Andrew Oldham with utter disdain.

Born in London in 1944, instinct, style and a knack for being in the right place at the right time had taken Oldham on a Zelig-type route from Tin Pan Alley, the 2I's, window dressing for Mary Quant, scamming on the Côte d'Azur, handling PR for the likes of Mark Wynter, Bob Dylan (on his first British visit) and the early Beatles to co-managing (with Eric Easton) the Rolling Stones in April 1963. Their rapid success set him up at the age of 20 as a self-confident, fast moving hustler with a capacity for shock and outrage, ruffling many feathers in the process.

"Andrew was very much the man on the ball in those days," says former *NME* journalist and PR, Keith Altham. "He was so tuned in to what was going on. If there was anything happening Andrew knew about it."

As the epitome of the new breed of flamboyant showbiz entrepreneur and in obvious emulation of his idol Phil Spector and Lester Sill's Philles label and Berry Gordy with Tamla-Motown, Oldham was looking to launch a comparable outlet in the UK. At the time of Immediate's conception, Oldham was independently producing the Stones' recordings on a tape lease deal with Decca as well as discovering and recording artists for the label, usually with derivative examples of Mick Jagger and Keith Richards' incubating songwriting. Like the image he sought to project, the label was to be cool, hip and progressive, reflected in the jagged logo lettering concocted by renowned stage designer Sean Kenny.

Oldham's track record in the business was enough to secure Philips' co-operation in the manufacture and distribution of the label's output. An examination of the first dozen or so releases by artists as diverse as Nico, the Golden Apples Of The Sun and John Mayall's Bluesbreakers, as well as the British licence of American hits by the McCoys ('Hang On Sloopy') and the Strangeloves ('Cara Lin') reflected the label's eclecticism and unorthodoxy.

Assisting Oldham in the venture was Tony Calder, who worked in the press office at Decca and as a DJ in the evenings at various Mecca venues like the Locarno, Basildon and the Palais, Ilford (where he first encountered and managed a certain Stephen Marriott) as well as a Monday night residency at Southampton's Royal Pier. Oldham's path first crossed with Calder's when the latter's firm CFP (Calder, Forester & Perkins) was helping to handle the promotion on the first Beatles single, 'Love Me Do', and the pair set up a partnership. Once Immediate was up and running, their operation moved out of Ivor Court in Gloucester Place to a suite of offices at 63/69 New Oxford Street.

"I don't think you could have got two more madder people than Andrew and Tony at the time," says Rolling Stones and Immediate promotional film-maker Peter Whitehead. "They had this office which was opulent and very kitsch. I think Andrew saw himself as an Arab prince. You went into this office that was thick with smoke and other things. There were always crazy people around there."

With the Rolling Stones now firmly established and vindication being achieved when Chris Farlowe's 'Out Of Time' gave Immediate its first chart-topper in July 1966, Oldham was looking to expand his creative empire. Hearing industry gossip of the Small Faces' dissatisfaction with their management, Oldham followed developments with interest. His connections with the group stretched back to 1964 when a Tin Pan Alley-haunting Steve Marriott was occasionally roped in to play on sessions by the Andrew Loog Oldham Orchestra – a floating, pick-up band of session men and various Rolling Stones assisting in fulfilling Oldham's fanciful notion of becoming "an English Phil Spector". Oldham was also reported to have produced an unreleased Marriott version of Jagger-Richards 'Tell Me' (off the Stones' first album) for Decca.

By the end of 1966 the Small Faces' stature was confirmed in the music paper polls – in *Melody Maker* the group came third in the British section (behind the Beatles and the Stones), in *Disc & Music Echo*, they ranked fourth in the 'Top Group, Britain/World' category while in *Record Mirror*, they finished second behind the Beatles in 'Britain Male Vocal Group' and fourth in the 'World Male Vocal Group' categories. In December Don Arden sold his management rights in the Small Faces to Harold Davison (a director of the Grade Organisation) and Tito Burns became the group's agent. Among the acts the Harold Davison Organisation represented were the Rolling Stones, Dusty Springfield, the Searchers, the Dave Clark Five and the Hollies. Marriott and Lane went label shopping, first approaching Chris Blackwell, of Island Records, another of the earliest British independents. However, Blackwell declined, pleading commitment to the Spencer Davis Group and Island's other acts.

Having spent the best part of a year living together ("It did get a bit much," says McLagan. "We were in each other's pockets") and with Arden controlling the lease, Ronnie, Mac and Steve moved out of Westmoreland Terrace into separate flats; Mac to Princes Mews off Bayswater Road, Steve to William Mews, Knightsbridge (the first of several addresses he was evicted from after complaints about rowdiness), and Ronnie to Spear

Mews, Earl's Court. It was at Ronnie's that the band met with Oldham. "I liked Andrew's flair," Marriott told John Hellier. "We all did, thought it was great. He had a lot of style."

Kenney Jones: "Andrew said, 'The Small Faces have *got* to be on Immediate' so through his connections with this young American lawyer Eric Kronfeld, who later became an executive at Polygram [Records] in the States, he bought us out of the arrangement we were in with Harold Davison and all these other people."

As part of the label's philanthropic ideals, Oldham encouraged the Small Faces to interact with the Immediate family. "They wanted us involved with all their artists," Marriott told Hellier, "wanted us to produce for artists, write for artists, the whole thing, you know." As an example of this, both Steve and Ronnie sang and played on Chris Farlowe's recording of their composition, 'My Way Of Giving', which was produced by Mick Jagger and released in January 1967.

After the intense schedule endured under Arden, the freedom they now enjoyed was a double-edged sword. The Small Faces could not have foreseen that, contrary to his self-assured demeanour, parading around London in shades and a black-windowed Phantom V Rolls-Royce, Oldham had reached the top of his mountain and it was to be a slow, painful descent. A prodigious drug intake, not to mention electric shock treatments to cure his depression and panic attacks, had blurred reality for the once astute player. In February '67, Mick Jagger and Keith Richards fell victim to an infamous drug bust at Richards' Sussex home Redlands and with the Stones' camp under surveillance, instead of standing by to fight their corner, Oldham's paranoia directed him to California, assisting Lou Adler and John Phillips in setting up the Monterey International Pop Festival. Consequently, Oldham's days as the Stones' manager were numbered and his role in the administration of Immediate was not as hands on as it had been at the outset – with predictably disastrous results.

The Small Faces' first single for Immediate was the soulful 'I Can't Make It'. Because of an outstanding contractual issue, it was leased to Decca and released on March 3. Unfortunately, thin exposure because of the supposed suggestiveness of the lyrics meant it rose no higher than 21 on the *NME* chart. Throughout April and May the group ensconced themselves in Olympic Sound Studios at 117 Church Road, Barnes, south west London which swiftly became their second home.

Kenney Jones: "We stopped playing as many gigs, came off the road and got into the studio . . . We never had a producer; Glyn Johns was our engineer, but he would suggest and come up with things like a producer would. After our time at Decca where we had to make an album in, like, a day, there was no pressure. We had a lot more time to try things out."

In April, Immediate released '(Tell Me) Have You Ever Seen Me' by the preposterously named Apostolic Intervention, a group from Hertfordshire featuring 15-year-old drummer Jerry Shirley, who recalls, "Steve wanted to call us the Nice but Andrew Oldham said, 'You're not calling them that', and then the next thing, he gives the name to P.P. Arnold's backing band." Originally called the Little People, having supported the Small Faces on occasion, the group were brought to the label thanks to Marriott's patronage. "I became very friendly with Kenney," says Shirley, "I would study his playing and we'd talk drums all the time . . . Ronnie was a bit funny towards us – I don't think he was too pleased that we were recording a Small Faces song because he left halfway through the session at Olympic . . . I didn't really know Mac, I only saw him at gigs. With Steve and me, it became very much a social thing."*

Marriott and Shirley's association was ultimately to lead to something more than mere socialising.

A further managerial twist occurred when Robert Wace and Grenville Collins, personal managers of the Kinks, in themselves a bundle to contain, built an extra rod for their backs by taking over the Small Faces' representation from Oldham and Calder to avoid a potential conflict of interest from the group being signed to their label. The arrangement didn't last and Immediate Enterprises eventually assumed full management and publishing duties in July.† On May 27 *NME* formally confirmed that the Small Faces had switched labels and that 'Here Come The Nice'/ 'Green Circles' was to be their next single.

Ian McLagan: 'Here Come The Nice' came from a [American alternative satirical poet] Lord Buckley thing. Steve had a very catholic taste in music, more than my own, and he turned me on to Lord Buckley who did this kinda rap, 'Here Come The Nazz', meaning Jesus, the Nazz was

---

* Marriott also produced a version of 'Get Yourself Together', recorded by the Small Faces on their first Immediate album, for his former flame and drama school friend, Adrienne Posta, for a projected Decca single. However it never appeared. "I'm finished with the pop business and all it stands for," Posta dramatised to the *Daily Mirror* in June '67. "From now on I'm purely an actress."

† Wace's connection with Oldham resulted in him recording an Immediate single, a quaint period piece, 'The Changing Of The Guard' under the pseudonym the Marquis Of Kensington.

Jesus.* So Steve took that and adapted it to 'Here Comes The Nice' . . . That was Steve's catchphrase, 'it's nice to be nice', meaning it's good to be stoned so the nice was a dealer. I mean I'm amazed how well it did when you hear that line, 'He's always there if I need some speed.' It was obvious what the song was about."

The lysergic influenced 'Green Circles', featuring some thundering Jones fills, was replaced by the raunchy, straightforward 'Talk To You' for the B-side. As the crafty but infectious 'Here Come The Nice' slipped past the BBC, reaching number 10, the group's first Immediate album appeared in June, titled simply and pointedly, *Small Faces*. Decca retaliated with *From The Beginning*, an unauthorised collection of hits and studio left-overs, as well as a single, 'Patterns' which, because of the group's refusal to promote it, failed to chart.

The Immediate album's varied nature – from straightforward power pop ('My Way Of Giving', '(Tell Me) Have You Ever Seen Me', and 'Get Yourself Together'), Fats Waller-style trad ('All Our Yesterdays' – one of five Lane vocals, featuring Marriott memorably introducing "Ronald Leafy Lane" as the "darling of Wapping Wharf launderette"), stoned imagery (McLagan's 'Up The Wooden Hills To Bedfordshire', his writing and vocal debut) to the Calypso-flavoured 'Eddie's Dreaming', named in honour of Georgie Fame's trumpet player Eddie 'Tam Tam' Thornton (who appears on the track) – was reflected in a wider instrument palatte – piano, harpsichord, mellotron, horns, bells, percussion were all thrown into the mix. Marriott and Lane's development as songwriters, the band's improvement as musicians and the technological advance from four to eight-track recording added up to markedly improved results when compared against the Decca material.

Ian McLagan: "Glyn Johns was a great engineer. He really knew how to get the right feel, the right sounds, where to place the mikes. He had a no-nonsense attitude in the studio. Come midnight he would grab his coat and say, 'That's it, I'm off, you guys can carry on for as long as you like but I'm going home.' He'd leave us to it, he was being sensible but we were like kids in a toy shop."

In August, a song inspired (from some accounts) by the stinging nettles in Little Ilford Park and with a melody Ronnie lifted from a hymn 'God

---

* The Buckley phrase was also adopted by another top line British Sixties group – in 1966, the Yardbirds rewrote an Elmore James blues for their first studio album and called it 'The Nazz Are Blue' as a vehicle for Jeff Beck. The song influenced both Alice Cooper and Todd Rundgren who used the name Nazz for their first bands.

Be In My Head', restored the Small Faces to the Top 5 and became one of their most identifiable songs, much to McLagan's everlasting regret: "Ronnie wrote 'Itchycoo Park' with a serious intent but Steve made it more poppy on the chorus [sings] *'it's all too beauty full.'* It was meant to be Ronnie's comment on how acid had opened his head, that it was all too beautiful and that there was another way – 'don't go to learn the word of fools' – but Steve took it in a much lighter direction."

The song bore all the hallmarks of that hot, idyllic summer of '67 as typified by 'All You Need Is Love' and 'San Francisco' sitting atop the UK charts at the time – languid feel, hip sentiment (with drug references subtle enough to slip by uncensored) and a hazy, otherworldly sound achieved by phasing, a new studio technique developed by Olympic tape engineer George Chkiantz, which the group first used on 'Green Circles'.*

'Itchycoo Park' got to number three in September and was in step enough with the zeitgeist to reach 24 in the *Billboard* US Top 100. It might have got higher if paranoid radio censors hadn't insisted the song advocated drug use and encouraged kids to drop out of school.

"The Small Faces were hugely respected," says Glyn Johns. "They were a great live band and if they had of gone to America they would have cleaned up in my opinion. I think they would have been just as big as anybody else from that era."

Much has been made of the Small Faces' failure to get to America. To this day, McLagan believes that Don Arden, knowing his clients would be out of his direct control and at the risk of being influenced by another manager, deliberately offered them Dick Clark-style tours playing well down on a mismatched bill of artists sharing a Greyhound bus for two months, knowing full well they would find the prospect unappealing and decline. While there is some substance to this, the situation was far more prosaic.

After the initial British Invasion onslaught in 1964, an outcry arose from American entertainers who claimed unfair competition from British acts impacting on their record sales and bookings. While it was relatively straightforward for an American artist coming to Britain, the reverse situation was far more complex, involving the combined red tape of immigration and labour laws plus the added might of the unions. The necessary H–1 work visa was only given to "artists of unique distinction and merit" which allowed acts like the Beatles, the Rolling Stones, Gerry & The

---

* Explained simply, phasing – or tape flanging as it is also known, is achieved when the signal running from one tape machine is slightly out of sync with another.

Pacemakers, Dave Clark Five et al to tour backed up by the weight of their record sales.

At the end of 1964, the US Department of Immigration changed its laws, resulting in British artists being allowed in only on the far more restrictive H-2 visa whereby the onus was on their representatives to prove their client was performing a job which no American citizen was capable of doing. While the H-1 applicant needed only a single work permit, H2 required individual approvals from each city or state the act intended visiting. Much delicate negotiating had to be undertaken – most of which involved bowing and scraping to ignorant officials who couldn't determine one long-haired group from the next – before they were allowed in and even then some, initially at least, were banned from performing live.

In the Small Faces' case, without the necessary promotion (none of their Decca era singles had been successful in America) a lack of a proven track record and a potentially daunting battle with the American Federation of Musicians conspired to make a Small Faces tour logistically unlikely. A slight relaxation of the laws and a modest chart hit ('Itchycoo Park') eased matters. By the end of '67, Cream, the Who, the Jimi Hendrix Experience, Procol Harum and Pink Floyd were making inroads into the developing American underground ballroom circuit.

"See, since Andrew had a record company, he didn't have to work hard as a manager, did he?" Marriott told Hellier. "We were on his label and under his management. So it suited his purpose to have us turning out records he just has to market rather than manage us on the road and worry about all that kind of shit."

This was unfair to Oldham, who had spent much of the year on the West Coast observing how the business was changing and who successfully got the Nice to America in early '68. By rights, it should have been the Small Faces. However, that became academic when, on November 13, 1967, McLagan was busted at Heathrow Airport after customs officers found a small quantity of cannabis resin on him as he was flying to Greece on holiday.

Mac was taken to West Drayton police station and charged with being in unlawful possession and, because he had presented his passport, with the attempted illegal exportation of a dangerous drug. He was released on bail to appear at Uxbridge Magistrates Court and then remanded for a week while the substances were analysed. The smuggling charge was dropped and on November 22, McLagan pleaded guilty and was fined £50 – a lucky escape considering the sentences (albeit successfully quashed) handed out to Mick Jagger, Keith Richards and Brian Jones for drug offences that year. At the time, US immigration laws disallowed persons with a drug conviction from applying for a visa for one year. By which time, it would be too late for the Small Faces.

Ian McLagan: "So we never got to America which is a great shame. The Who went over opening for Herman's Hermits, Jimi Hendrix was playing before the Monkees, I mean these were awful bills but it got them a foot in the door."

If 'Itchycoo Park' was the result of a genuine Marriott-Lane collaboration, 'Tin Soldier' was a Marriott tour de force, featuring one of his most impassioned vocals and a fantastic ensemble performance, with Pat Arnold's high, soul shakin' voice on the backing chorus. In December, it entered the *NME* chart at 25, marching to ninth position.

Ian McLagan: "So now we were playing around with sounds and ideas and that's how something like 'Tin Soldier' came about. We had more tracks to play with, there's a Wurlitzer on there, a Steinway piano and B3, double-tracked guitars from Steve and that's just the intro! The only thing I don't like is that echo delay that Glyn put on the verses. But otherwise, everything came together on the recording, great song, great performance from us as a band, amazing vocal from Steve. 'Tin Soldier' is *the* Small Faces song. For me, it's our finest moment."

1967 had proved a halcyon year in music and popular culture spearheaded by the Beatles' astonishing artistic advance with *Sgt Pepper's Lonely Hearts Club Band*. Taking a reported 700 hours to record, its seismic effects dictated the way the industry was to develop with groups spending more and more time cocooned in the controlled environment of the studio. The Small Faces were not immune to the album's influence. As documented in Derek Taylor's book *It Was Twenty Years Ago Today,* Donovan recalls first hearing *Sgt Pepper* with Steve, Ronnie and Marianne Faithfull. "Ronnie shouted, 'I've got it', and I said, 'Let's play it' and it was astounding."

After three years of British artists dominating its charts, America's pre-eminence was reasserting itself, particularly on the West Coast with the likes of Buffalo Springfield, Jefferson Airplane and the Doors achieving Top 40 success while crucially maintaining credibility with the emerging 'rock' audience. Meanwhile in Britain the brave new world exemplified by Jimi Hendrix, Cream, Pink Floyd, Procol Harum and Traffic fought for singles chart supremacy against the schmaltz of Engelbert Humperdinck, Tom Jones, Frankie Vaughan and Val Doonican. The Small Faces, like other 'English-sounding' contemporaries the Who and the Kinks, weren't entirely comfortable with this new, serious and often superficial direction as the comedic parody inherent in 'Itchycoo Park' made evident. "I feel inclined to blow my mind, get hung up, feed the ducks with a bun" indeed!

Faced with the risk of being left stranded by a constantly evolving and competitive scene, their own desire to break out of the straitjacket that pigeonholed them as a teenybop group, coupled with the influence of various mind expanders, the Small Faces started creating what would become their ultimate artistic achievement, *Ogdens' Nut Gone Flake*.

If the group seemed content within the febrile artistic environment at Immediate, things were also stable on the domestic front with Steve, Ronnie and Mac all marrying within months of each other. On January 4, 1968, Mac suddenly got hitched to 20-year-old dancer Sandra Sarjeant.

Born Althea Sarjeant to a French West Indian father and English mother, Sandy attended tap and ballet classes near her home in Kensal Green, north London. In 1965, she won a dance competition to appear on *Ready, Steady, Go!* and became a weekly fixture on the iconic show until its demise in December '66. Sandy also regularly danced on a German TV show, *Beat Club* and such was her Teutonic popularity, she recorded a 1966 single for Polydor, 'Can't Stop The Want'.

"I met the Small Faces at *Ready, Steady, Go!*" says Sandy, "and I used to see them down Carnaby Street when they were buying clothes or visiting Don Arden's office. I went to the house in Pimlico a few times and Mac and I sort of fell in together. We gelled quite well and that's how we started going out but not for very long. When I became friends with Pat Arnold and we shared a flat off Baker Street, I saw Mac again and that's when the real romance began. The Small Faces came over to Bremen to appear on *Beat Club* and we were flying back to London when Mac suddenly proposed.

"We didn't tell anybody because those were the days when pop stars had to be single. Mac got the licence and two days before, we went over to see my mum and he asked her for my hand which was very sweet. The next night Mac's parents came over to our flat in Hanover Terrace Mews. When he told them, his mum said, 'What am I going to wear?' We got married the next morning at Marylebone Registry Office, then Mac had to go off to do *Top Of The Pops*. I went out shopping and in the euphoria, forgot my keys and locked myself out so I had to wait for him to come home. This all happened within a week of Mac proposing."

Ronnie wed 21-year-old model and actress Susanna Hunt on April 24 at Kensington Register Office. The middle child of a farming family from Brenchley, near Tunbridge Wells, Kent, Sue was living with her parents in

Sedlescombe, a small Sussex village, when she moved up to London at 16 and took a three-week course at the Cherry Marshall Model Agency*and started to model professionally. Gaining a manager in Harvey Freed, Sue went into singing as a means of becoming an actress. After being spotted by a TV producer, she was given a regular role in British comedy sitcom *Hugh And I*. Under her stage name of Geneveve, Sue received some publicity for her two-day engagement to David (Screaming Lord) Sutch, which was supposedly broken on Freed's orders, released two singles 'Once' and 'Nothing In The World' on CBS, and appeared as a panellist on *Juke Box Jury*.

Playing bottom of the bill on a Small Faces tour, during her brief flush of pop stardom in the summer of '66, Sue met Ronnie "backstage in some big theatre up north," she recalls. "He was standing on his own, deep in thought. There was a connection straight away. At least from my side but I don't really remember how long it was between us meeting and the time that we kind of really got together."

Sue had a flat in Sloane Square not far from where the Small Faces were living in Westmoreland Terrace. "It was a very happy atmosphere. The band was very creative. They hardly went out except to play a gig. Otherwise they were at home constantly making music – there was always someone sitting down with a guitar and wanting to jam, writing or just playing on their own."

However, Sue was aware of occasional friction. "I knew it was there but I didn't really take much notice of it. Steve and Ronnie were very different personalities. Steve was very outgoing and flamboyant; Ronnie was more sensitive and inward. Very deep and very caring."

The witnesses at Ronnie and Sue's wedding were Marriott and his girl-friend, 23-year-old Jenny Rylance, a tall, willowy blonde from Cumberland who previously had a four-year, on-off relationship with Rod Stewart. Steve and Jenny's courtship had been tempestuous (she claims he wrote 'All Or Nothing' with her in mind while he admitted 'Tin Soldier' was designed to woo her) but the couple eventually tied the knot at Kensington Register Office on May 29, a month after Ronnie and Sue's nuptials.

Kenney was engaged to 17-year-old Jan Osborne, London-born daughter of composer and arranger Tony Osborne, who had worked with Gracie Fields, Shirley Bassey, Eartha Kitt and Judy Garland. Jan had attended Arts Educational School (at the same time as a young John

---

* Pattie Boyd, Pat Booth, Brenda Walker and Anthea Redfern belonged to the same agency.

'Mitch' Mitchell) and Italia Conti with Steve Marriott, as well as singing in a duo with her elder brother Gary, releasing two singles on Pye in 1965 as Gary and Jan Lorraine.

"We were brought up in and around the entertainment business because of daddy's connection with people like Adam Faith and [his manager] Evie Taylor," says Jan, "and he was resident bandleader on BBC-2's *Open House*. Daddy knew Pete Townshend and John Entwistle's fathers because of the bandleading connection."

It was a coincidental Who link that brought Jan and Kenney together on December 21, 1966 at the opening of the Upper Cut, a club in Forest Gate, east London, owned by boxer Billy Walker.

Jan Jones: "The Who were playing there that night. I went with Adrienne Posta, my friend from acting school, who knew Kenney. We saw him chatting to Roger [Daltrey]. Adrienne forgot to introduce me and I was so annoyed I tapped Kenney on the leg to introduce myself. Unfortunately I kicked him too hard and sent him sprawling. After the gig we all went to the Golden Egg on Oxford Street and Kenney drove me in his Mini. That was the first time he asked me out. All I remember is we ended up back at my parents' place in Hampstead. Kenney was very pissed and I made him tomato soup, which he promptly threw up on the bathroom floor but forgot to tell me. My father announced it the next day – the bathroom was near his study and he said, 'Next time you bring a boyfriend home and he's sick can you get him to clean his own mess up?' From then on Kenney and I were an item."

With wives, girlfriends and dogs, the band hired cabin cruisers at Henley for blissful excursions down the Thames armed with guitars and a cassette machine to get the creative juices flowing.

Ian McLagan: "That's when I got involved with the songwriting. With Steve and Ronnie it was hard to get a look-in but I was there so they couldn't deny me, ideas would come and some were mine and we would work on stuff. Many of the songs that made up the story on the second side of *Ogdens'* – 'Happiness Stan', 'The Hungry Intruder', 'The Journey' and 'Happydaystoytown' – originated from that boat trip.

"We had some songs already written and others we worked on at Olympic. Most of the album was done there except for the instrumental, which we re-cut at Pye because the track got lost. Then when they found it again, it had got stretched so Glyn did an edit so I don't think we used anything from Pye. We also recorded at Trident when Olympic was booked up but *Ogdens'* was all pretty much done at Olympic."

Released on May 24, *Ogdens' Nut Gone Flake* unerringly capped the spirit of experimentation in British pop that *Sgt. Pepper's* instigated the previous summer. It was inventive, innovative and most importantly it never took itself too seriously in an era where that became the default setting. The album bore all the period trappings as encapsulated in the gimmicky circular, four-fold sleeve (which caused retailers to complain that the record would roll off their display shelves), the in-joke title ('Nut Gone' replacing 'Nut Brown' to hint at the type of tobacco required during listening), the 'Sus' brand of rolling papers, the psychedelic painting created by Mac's art school pals Nick Tweddell and Pete Brown, and the 1lb box and faded portraits, reflecting British psychedelia's Edwardian fascination.

While the whimsical segued concept of Happiness Stan's (no doubt named with Ronnie's father and brother in mind) Tolkien-esque journey to find the missing half of the waxing and waning moon awkwardly remains of its time, the vital ingredient of humour lifted it above the po-faced pretentiousness that affected similar works from bands such as the Moody Blues. The Small Faces originally approached Spike Milligan to provide the spoken narration but his agent turned them down. After seeing him in a popular Gale's Honey television advertisement, the master of gobbledegook, comedy actor and writer 'Professor' Stanley Unwin was asked to do the honours using 'Unwinese', his characteristic mangling of the English language.

Although the band could do 'heavy' as well as the latest johnny-come-lately, there were many more strings to their bow – the contrasting hard but delicate shades of the gorgeous 'Afterglow (Of Your Love)' featuring another devastating Marriott vocal, the instrumental title track (a revisiting of 'I've Got Mine', the group's flop second single which they still held in high regard) featuring Mac's electric piano played through a wah-wah, 'Rollin' Over', a storming rocker incorporating Georgie Fame's brass section, and 'Song Of A Baker', which developed from Ronnie's growing interest in Sufism as well as his and Sue's visits to the Balearic island of Ibiza.

Sue Tacker (formerly Sue Lane): "Ronnie and I rented a farmhouse there. It was set in this olive grove and it was just very calm and peaceful. We got to know some of the locals, one of whom was a guy called Chris Smith. The Spanish houses had these great earthenware ovens and Chris used to cook these great loaves of bread for us in the traditional Spanish way. So I think that's partly where 'Song Of A Baker' came from."

Steve and Ronnie's cockney Music Hall roots were tapped for the delightful 'Rene' (named after Rene Tungate, a local lady of ill-repute well-known to Marriott) and, of course, the infectious 'Lazy Sunday', an idea of Steve's, inspired by the frequent confrontations with his long-suffering neighbours in Eyot Green, Chiswick. The words came to Marriott in a taxi on the way to Sunday lunch at his Aunt Sheila's home in West Ham and completed on the khazi – while he "sussed out the moon," no doubt. "Chas & Dave on acid" was Marriott's later succinct description.

Ian McLagan: 'I seem to recall when Steve brought ['Lazy Sunday'] in it was a lot slower and then by the time it got recorded, we'd turned it into a bit of a piss-take. Steve decided to sing it in that exaggerated cockney accent."

From the outset, the band considered the track a novelty to lighten the album but the joke was on them when Immediate made the decision to release it as a single without their knowledge.

"We were away in Europe," says Kenney, "and we got one of the music papers and we saw that Andrew Oldham and Tony Calder had put it out. Here we were trying to be taken seriously and then we had a hit with 'Lazy Sunday' [a UK number two in May]. I mean, really in a way it was our fault in the first place because we wrote these songs but it was like we were back at square one."

Ogdens' was a commercial as well as critical triumph, staying on the UK album charts for 19 weeks; six of those in the top slot. The album found favour with other musicians, not least Rod Stewart and Ronnie Wood of the Jeff Beck Group. "*Ogdens'* was a masterpiece, but a bit before its time," Stewart told Royston Eldridge in 1970, "*Tommy* got in where *Ogdens'* should have scored."

There's a certain irony in how the thematically linked 'Happiness Stan' encouraged Pete Townshend to develop his ideas for what became *Tommy*. "*Ogdens' Nut Gone Flake* was a world shaking record," Townshend remarked in 1969. "When they first played it to me the only material I had heard to which it could be compared to were concept pieces like *Pet Sounds* or *Sgt Pepper's*. I was jealous of the Small Faces; they were becoming a real extraordinary sonic force to be reckoned with."

Townshend's long-standing friendship with Ronnie Lane flowered when they discovered a mutual interest in spiritualism during the Who and the Small Faces' problematic tour of Australia in January '68.* "I was

---

* A detailed account of this challenging tour, entitled *A Fortnight Of Furore*, was self-published by this author in booklet form in 1998.

reading a couple of Sufi books," Lane told Jody Denberg, "and [Pete] was reading this book about this guy called Meher Baba that had this thing called Sufism Reoriented. So I started to learn about Baba and he seemed like an all right guy, and Pete and I had fun."

Meher Baba, meaning 'compassionate father', a name given to him by his early followers, was born Merwan Sheriar Irani in Poona, India in 1894. Being spiritually transformed, from July 10, 1925 (until his death in 1969) Baba took a vow of complete silence, communicating by alphabet board and hand movements. His simple and moral philosophy of life, most familiar from his oft quoted "don't worry, be happy" message, resonated with a messianic following that spread eventually into the West.

Sue Tacker: "Pete started sending Ronnie and I these notices in the mail about Meher Baba meetings where this guy Don Stevens was going to be reading Baba's discourses and inviting us to go. This went on for a while and we didn't go. But from when we lived in Spear Mews, we started reading Inayat Khan's books so you could say we were seekers in a way. We were looking for something that would answer our questions about life. A lot of people in the Sixties were interested in finding something that made sense to them spiritually. Because no way could we go along with the traditional kind of church stuff. We knew there was something bigger than that. We were looking for answers basically. So we said, 'let's go to this thing, why not?'

"Pete had given his Wardour Street studio to the Baba group to use for the meeting. So we went up there and Don was reading Baba's discourses and he would stop and explain each little sentence and stop and answer questions about what it meant and so forth. And it was just absolutely riveting to us and we both kind of recognised that this was what we'd been looking for and it made sense."

"I don't know why but Ronnie and I don't seem to have the time to get together," Marriott ominously admitted to *Disc & Music Echo* in April. "I've written a few things and so has Ronnie but it's not the same as writing together as two minds and it doesn't really come off."

Over the summer of '68, following the vogue of getting it together in the country and noticing with increasing alarm that, despite a successful album, there was little money in the kitty, Steve, Ronnie and Mac, together with wives and pets, rented a secluded, two-storey house near the river in Marlow, Buckinghamshire, previously owned by *Three Men In A Boat* author Jerome K. Jerome.

Ian McLagan: "We actually only lived in half the house, it was that big. It was very relaxed, very peaceful. We'd set up the equipment outside and work on ideas. Our neighbours were these two old ladies but they were far enough away not to complain. Steve recorded 'The Universal' on his 12-string in the back garden at Marlow. That's his dog, Seamus, and my dog, Rufus, in the background. I'm not even on 'The Universal'. It was mainly recorded on cassette and the other instruments were overdubbed at Olympic."

Although chiming with the 'one man band' sound of Don Partridge (who achieved top five hits with 'Rosie' and 'Blue Eyes' that year), it seems unfathomable how Marriott could have seriously considered 'The Universal' hit material.* Slight, self-indulgent and, unlike 'Lazy Sunday', lacking a memorable chorus, with brazen drug references to "hippy trippy name droppers" and knowing where to "score", it unsurprisingly failed to climb higher than 18.

Ian McLagan: "I learned afterwards that when that single failed, Steve thought he'd let us down. I don't know whether that's true or whether it was something he said. I mean after 'Lazy Sunday', another 'Tin Soldier' was what we needed. The thing is we were finding it hard to replicate our singles onstage. We couldn't play 'Itchycoo Park' well and things were getting more difficult because the sounds we were making on record, with overdubs and backing vocals, with just the four of us [onstage], it was getting harder to pull off."

Added to this the situation with Immediate had festered into something ugly. The June 5 issue of *Record Retailer* reported: 'Small Faces handling own management following closure of Immediate Artists'. According to Marriott, "[They] wanted us to re-sign, and we wouldn't at the time. We were saying, 'No, we want this much dough to re-sign', and they, for some reason, decided not to pay us what they owed us, let alone what we were asking to re-sign. And for about two months we didn't have anything."

Ian McLagan: "Whatever money Arden considered we owed him, when we moved to Immediate, that debt was paid by Andrew Oldham and Tony Calder. They paid Arden and then we owed them so we never got clear, we never got money or royalties.† Steve got a lump sum up front

---

* Even at the time of his unfortunate death, Marriott still considered 'The Universal' as his favourite Small Faces recording. The song's full and proper title is 'Hello The Universal' but Immediate left off the opening word on the original label copy.

† Interestingly, considering the past contretemps with Don Arden, during this time, Lane produced and Marriott arranged 'Man In Black', the third RCA single for Arden's clients, Skip Bifferty, released in July 1968. The group featured singer Graham Bell and organist Mick Gallagher who went on to play with, among others, Ian Dury & The Blockheads and the Clash.

from his publishing to buy a house but when I tried to get £800 as a deposit on an £8,000 Georgian double fronted house on a couple of acres in Fifield, Essex, I couldn't get it, there was no money there for me."

Marriott's move from Marlow to his dream home, Beehive Cottage, a 16th century oak-beamed thatched abode in Moreton, Essex was only made possible thanks to the rest of the deposit being borrowed from the Small Faces' latest booking agent, Arthur Howes. Ronnie also used an advance against his publishing to buy into the property.

"We started converting the barn into our own home," says Sue, "but that's when the falling out between Steve and Ronnie started. I guess Steve didn't give Ronnie enough credit in the writing and Ronnie not having a pushy personality so much you could sense that there was an issue about whose name got the credit for what. They would have horrible arguments over that kind of stuff . . . It got a little silly really and when you introduce that kind of negative energy then it puts a block on the creativity that was happening in the early days between them . . . but at the same time I think they were both going off in their own directions."

A glimpse of Marriott's discontent was evident as far back as 1966 in an uncharacteristically portentous interview given to teen bible *Rave*: "I am different as a person, it is true. I am not pleased with my musical achieve-ments. In fact I get less and less personal satisfaction from live per-formances. I am more interested in writing. I feel that if I can write songs I will be giving something back to life. I am scared that otherwise I'll look back in 20 years and see nothing but selfishness. Live shows are full of screams and adoration we don't deserve."

"We never really heard what we were playing for a couple of years, and when the screaming stopped we were so loud . . ." Lane admitted to Nick Logan. "There was no subtlety in it at all."

By the autumn Steve had become friendly with 'the Face of '68' Peter Frampton, guitarist and singer with the Herd. The two had a lot in common – in professional terms, at least; both inspired teen worship, were underrated as guitarists and felt undervalued in their respective groups and were seeking peer respect.

At Marriott's invitation, Frampton started sitting in at Small Faces gigs, fuelling rumours of a merger. "The reaction to that idea was terrible . . ." Marriott told Hellier. "It just didn't go down too well. Ronnie didn't want it, no one wanted it. So that's when I first thought, 'Well, Christ, I want to play live, but not the way I feel about it now.' I'd just lost a lot of confidence."

By December, Frampton had left the Herd and was invited to Paris to play with the Small Faces on recording sessions backing French superstar Johnny Hallyday, which led to heated arguments.

Ian McLagan: "That was Glyn Johns' idea as it turns out and really it was a rotten idea and a rotten album frankly."

The same day they returned to London, on New Year's Eve, the Small Faces were among the acts playing a multi-artist Gala Pop & Blues Party at the cavernous Alexandra Palace.

Ian McLagan: "Steve got Alexis Korner up onstage with us at the end of the show, which was strange because we weren't a blues band . . .* Steve got Alexis to sit in on a vamp of 'Lazy Sunday' of all things – on the fade which just repeats in A – and after about a minute of that, he walked off the stage and left us there with Alexis, it was a fucking disgrace. So there was this almighty row later in the dressing room and Steve basically said, 'I'm leaving the group.'"

---

* Korner had jammed with the Small Faces when both acts appeared at the Bilzen Jazz Festival, Belgium in August 1968. Marriott also made a low-key appearance as part of Korner's band on some Scottish dates.

CHAPTER 7

Slim Chance

"I thought it's the hardest thing in the world to assemble a group of guys who get on well together, musically and socially. So even though we'd decided to part company, I thought why break up a friendship that had grown really strong after working together for five years. So in the end we decided to stick with each other."

— Ronnie Lane, *Rolling Stone*, 1971

"The old ego ran away with Beck. He was never really a bastard to me. He was always, like, friendly but it was down to the pay. We never earned a great deal."

— Rod Stewart, *New Musical Express*, 1971

"AFTER *Ogdens'* it was a case of, well, follow that," Kenney Jones reflects. "It was an album we were all proud of but I think Steve felt it couldn't be followed. And all of us were sick of the image we had in the Small Faces, especially Steve as the frontman. So when [Peter] Frampton came along, I think he saw it as an opportunity to get more serious."

The idea had been forming in Marriott's mind for some time. During the previous summer, when Frampton had expressed dissatisfaction with his role in the Herd, Steve had played musical matchmaker, bringing him together with Marriott's young protégé, drummer Jerry Shirley, formerly of Apostolic Intervention, who was now playing in a group called the Wages Of Sin. In the early hours of New Year's Day, Shirley received a phone call. "Steve told me that he'd just walked out of the Small Faces and asked if he could join Peter and myself in the band we were putting together. It was a shock for me at first because I was such a fan of the Small Faces, I didn't want them to split up."

Jan Jones: "Kenney was particularly pissed off because Jerry, who's a lovely guy, was always asking for advice more and more of the time . . . I remember afterwards Kenney saying something along the lines of, 'Ah, it all makes sense now.'"

111

When Greg Ridley, bass player with Spooky Tooth, was approached by Marriott to join, Humble Pie fell into place.

"I told Andrew [Oldham] what I was going to do," Marriott recalled to John Hellier, "and asked him what he thought of me and Peter playing together 'cos I was broke. We were all broke – desperately broke – and I couldn't get out of that [Immediate] contract. Not unless he [Oldham] wanted to give it away and I'm certain he wasn't about to do that."

In a *Melody Maker* interview given the week of his flounce out at Alexandra Palace, Marriott let slip to Chris Welch that, ". . . all we [the Small Faces] want to do is get better musically and stay together. We'd have broken up long ago if we didn't want to work as mates and improve . . . There's been a bit of a minor disaster going and nothing has really been happening for us. But we've got a new album together in our heads. It's down on tape but we haven't been able to record in the studios. It's very frustrating, but we've got to get our business scene sorted out."

"It was a surprise to me when Steve said he was leaving," Lane told Penny Valentine in 1972. "I never recognised the problems at the time, or that the band might eventually split or perhaps I didn't want to recognise it. We were certainly in a lot of financial trouble . . . but I thought we were all going to concentrate on getting out of that situation."

It was estimated the Small Faces were approximately £10,000 in debt at the time. From most accounts, the root cause of the band's money problems centred on when Arden sold his management and agency interests (and associated debts) in the Small Faces to Harold Davison, which were, in turn, inherited by Andrew Oldham. "See Arden didn't pay us any money because he said he was paying off money, and apparently he didn't pay them," Marriott told Hellier. "So at the end of the day we were left with bills that we thought were paid years ago. . . . And we were paying and paying . . . that's where our money was going, to pay them back."

In a *Melody Maker* interview just after the split, McLagan admitted, "We messed ourselves up. We got into the habit of living well and didn't want to change. I lived in an eight guineas a week flat and we always used Daimler car hire." When the author suggests that much of the group's lost earnings might have been legitimately swallowed up in expenditure on clothes, transport, studio costs and high living, Mac indignantly retorts: "How could we spend that much on clothes when we were earning serious amounts of money? In the time we were together we never received any record royalties. We must have lost in the region of at least a million quid so you do the math, buying a few shirts ain't gonna cover it!"

"Kenney had a different car every week – a Lotus, an MG, Mini Coopers, a Zephyr which he let his dad drive – and as many shirts as he could carry," Gary Osborne, Kenney's former brother-in-law, recalls, "but then you found out later that the cars were leased and he didn't have a pot to piss in. I remember asking, 'Where's all the money?' and Ken said, 'Don's looking after it.'"

For all the muck that sticks against Arden, Jones now adopts a resigned stance, considering him "a necessary evil in a sense. I have to say he was a great manager at the time. If it hadn't been for Don having a plan for us I don't know how far we would have got." Indeed, without the connections available to the 'Al Capone of Pop' the Small Faces might never have gotten further than the East End, let alone released a record. They enjoyed a year of pop star trappings – a house in Pimlico, chauffeured car, expense accounts but it was a Faustian pact.* With Immediate Records, Andrew Oldham offered the perfect environment for the Small Faces to grow artistically and for Marriott and Lane to find their feet creatively as songwriters, resulting in the group's best work. However round-the-clock studio time was costly and recoupable against royalties, as is standard practice in the industry 'of human happiness'. But attention to detail when it came to accounting was never Oldham's concern. Suffice to say, without either manager, the Small Faces career might have been a lot shorter than it already was.

The rumours could only be held off for so long and talk of unrest in the Small Faces camp came with the February 8 edition of *Disc & Music Echo* posing the question: 'Is Steve Marriott quitting the Small Faces?': "I don't know whether the Faces are splitting yet, or not," an impassive Tony Calder told the paper. "One minute they are getting on fine. The next they are talking about going their separate ways. I do know, though that the other three have been getting a bit uptight about the Peter Frampton thing."

Tracked down to Essex, Marriott was evasive. "You're the 80th person to ask me that! I'm looking forward to a great future. Leaving the Faces? I could never be out of a group, and I wouldn't want to be part of a double act either."

---

* In 1967 the Small Faces entered into litigation against Arden over unpaid royalties and a judgment in their favour was granted for £4,023.7s. However, due to Arden's request to have the amount repaid in instalments and then defaulting on that arrangement, the group didn't receive their money until 1977, a full decade after the case was first brought to court.

When reports of the Small Faces' disarray reached him, Pete Townshend pledged support by offering Ronnie, Kenney and Mac the use of his home studio. The February 22 issue of *Disc* reported that they had been recording there that week. "Ronnie asked me to play lead guitar for them as a favour," Pete said. "They don't quite know what's happening. They were making the disc to see how things would work out without Steve. Although Ronnie's voice lacks Steve's projection, they still sound very much like the Small Faces . . . I think that if Ronnie, Kenney and Mac don't find another guitarist they really like, they will break up completely."*

It was a typically benevolent gesture on Townshend's part. Apart from his close friendship with Lane, it solidified the strong links existing between the Who and the Small Faces. Both had enjoyed a raucous camaraderie when touring Australia and Britain together and were inextricably tied to the Mod movement that now seemed light years away as the curtain fell on the Sixties.

Ian McLagan: "When we were doing stuff with Townshend, we were thinking of a new group name and I came up with Slim Chance and told Ronnie about it way early on. He never gave me credit for it but that was my title. In fact I remember saying it in Pete's house in Twickenham."

It was an ironic reference to the bleak forecast for the remnants of a once successful group now without its charismatic leader, lacking a manager, deep in debt and legally bound to a rudderless label hovering on bankruptcy. Track and Apple were two of the hipper record labels that Ronnie, Kenney and Mac approached for a deal. "We went to see Ringo, actually," says Mac. "We thought we'd be perfect, I mean you want to sign an act that's already proven, you know? But they [Apple] weren't really interested. Ringo was playing us stuff they were putting out and it was a waste of time really."

"We had a terrible time trying to flog ourselves," Lane confirmed to Penny Valentine. "As far as they were concerned we were just a bunch of silly boys and Steve was the real face in the band. I thought that was a pretty short-sighted view."

To all intents and purposes the Small Faces had split but several previously arranged bookings had to be honoured and with being stony broke, there was little option but to fulfil them despite Marriott being out of sorts with the others. According to Mac, a German tour and several British gigs actually felt like a weight being lifted. "I was doing the group

* The recordings – made for private use, after all – have never surfaced, that's presuming they were kept.

accounts on the last dates, because we were ripped off so much I decided to take the reins and so we all got paid." On Saturday, March 8, as the last notes of 'Tin Soldier' faded over the nondescript surrounds of the Springfield Ballroom, Jersey, in the Channel Islands, the Small Faces walked off-stage for the last time.*

"We're quite excited about it [Marriott's departure]," McLagan told the *Jersey Evening Post*: "We can't wait for it to happen so that we can get started on our own. We want to learn a lot of new numbers and then decide on a new name. The Small Faces will be dead and buried forever we hope . . . Steve's replacement won't be a singer as such. He will be a good guitarist who can sing."

With expert timing, Immediate administered the last rites with a double A-side, an edit of 'Afterglow (Of Your Love)' from *Ogdens'* backed with a new track, 'Wham Bam Thank You Mam'. Among a batch of songs recorded as relations with the label started to deteriorate, 'Wham Bam' was a raucous riff rocker, betraying a Free influence, and an accurate indicator as to Marriott's future musical horizons. Lane hated the song and as a further manifestation of the ill feeling floating about, Marriott and McLagan came to loggerheads during the recording.

"I told Steve where to go and walked out of Olympic," Mac recalls. "The next day I went back and all was forgiven. But then Steve played me what they'd done after I left and he'd got Nicky Hopkins in. I love Nicky but the message from Steve was clear, 'Go on and leave if you like but I can always get Nicky Hopkins to replace you.'"†

Hot on the single's heels Immediate issued an album, *In Memoriam*, a hastily concocted half live, half studio affair featuring tracks earmarked for a follow-up to *Ogdens'* which, according to accounts, carried the working title of *1862*, the date on the church hall next to Marriott's cottage. *In Memoriam* was swiftly withdrawn after the band's objections to the title. "It made us sound like we were dead," says McLagan. It was eventually to be replaced by *The Autumn Stone*, an uneven double compilation (retailing for the price of a single LP) which mixed most of the *In Memoriam* tracks with hit singles from both the Decca and Immediate years.

Ironically, several of the new tracks – ostensibly unfinished and carrying

* The advertisement in the *Jersey Evening Post* read: 'Don't miss this opportunity of seeing the last performance of the Small Faces before they disband.'
† There are two versions of the song – one at mid-pace featuring McLagan's piano and organ while the Hopkins version is much faster and more dynamic and generally referred to as 'Me, You And Us, Too'. It can be found on the *Best Of The Immediate Years* German CD (2007).

working titles – were excellent. Two brassy instrumentals, 'Collibosher' and the jaunty 'Wide Eyed Girl On The Wall' were both possibly backing tracks waiting for a vocal,* the cautionary 'Call It Something Nice' was influenced by Lane's spiritualism ("please don't grow to depend on me, don't lean on me 'cos I might let you down" carried, in light of Marriott's position, an ironic weight), while an evocative, folk shuffle through Tim Hardin's 'Red Balloon' and an ethereal, acoustic Hardin-ish number, 'The Autumn Stone', featuring a beautifully languid Marriott vocal, indicated the lighter nature of early Humble Pie. It also showed that the creativity surrounding *Ogdens'* remained undiminished for a group whose members were still only in their early twenties. Little wonder that Lane never forgave Marriott for leaving the band when he did, for on this evidence, there was more that could have been achieved with the Small Faces.

After weeks of secrecy, the formation of Humble Pie was exclusively revealed in the April 26 edition of *Melody Maker*. "I've never been so excited about anything as I am about the group . . ." Marriott enthused to Chris Welch. "We're going to be a heavy music band." Of his former bandmates, he soberly assessed, "My quitting is the best thing for them and for me. It will give both of us freedom."

"I'll always remember reading, on the front page of the papers, 'Steve Marriott quits the Small Faces to play with better musicians' which still annoys me to this day because we were great musicians," Kenney declared.†

The Small Faces and the Herd weren't the only top British chart group to lose a key member during this period; Trevor Burton quit the Move as 'Blackberry Way', a song he despised, climbed down off number one, Pete Quaife left the Kinks during a creatively rich but commercially barren phase for the group and most significantly, Graham Nash of the Hollies departed for California's West Coast and a harmony-led trio completed by

---

* Another instrumental – or possibly, backing track – recorded at this time, named 'The War Of The Worlds' – perfectly captures the group as they had always wanted to sound – a grooving Anglo version of Booker T. & The MGs.

† Marriott's supposed tactless remark over playing with 'real musicians' stuck in Jones' craw and he continues to refer to it in interviews. However, no such quote appeared in the British music press at the time. If anything, Marriott's comments from this period only reveal how respectful he was of his former comrades. In a January 1971 *Sounds* interview, he stated, "I read an article from a British paper that said Ron Wood had heard I'd said 'now I'm going to play with some real musicians' when I left . . . For him to think I'd turn round and say something like that – well it really upsets me. I never would."

ex-Byrd David Crosby and Stephen Stills, formerly of the Buffalo Spring-field. In each case the individuals departing wanted to be taken more seriously and provided with a greater challenge as musicians.

The reception afforded to the 1968 *Super Session* album involving Al Kooper, Mike Bloomfield and Stills ominously predicted how popular the supergroup genre would become. The origin of the species, Cream, now disbanded, left the field open for other competitors to exploit the blueprint. At the same time Humble Pie assembled, Eric Clapton and Ginger Baker teamed up with Steve Winwood and Ric Grech to form Blind Faith, a short-lived enterprise that collapsed under a combined weight of egos, drugs and expectation, a clear case of too much, too soon. Even the band name carried an in-built irony (or conceit, depending how one looked at it) by anticipating the audiences' Pavlovian response to whatever was offered – the very situation that had driven Clapton from Cream in the first place.

With a clean slate and a band name suggesting equanimity Marriott thought he could subjugate his ego for the good of the whole. Of course, it wouldn't last.

For Lane, Jones and McLagan, 1969 proved to be their winter of dis-content. "No one had any money," Mac confirms. "Everyone was on their uppers, really." He and Sandy were living at her mother's council house in Mortimer Road, Kensal Green when Sandy discovered she was pregnant. "Mac had about £100 put aside in premium bonds but we didn't have any money to buy a pram or a cot or to buy me maternity clothes." The couple packed their belongings into Mac's red Mini Cooper and moved to an £8 a week, two-room cold water flat, found for them by Kenney, on the first floor of a Victorian terrace at Finborough Road, Earl's Court.

Sandy Sarjeant: "The main room was quite big and part of it had been turned into a galley kitchen. There was a downstairs toilet and even further down was the bathroom, which we shared with the people in the downstairs flat. Boz [Burrell] eventually got the flat above us."

Because of the toilet's location, and Sandy's condition, a Victorian chamber pot was kept under the bed in case of middle-of-the-night emer-gencies. It also came in handy for other uses.

"One morning, really early, there was a knock on the door. Mac went out on to the balcony to see who it was and these men were standing outside trying to serve him with legal papers," says Sandy. "I just remember he grabbed the bed pot, which had been used during the night, and threw it all over them. We never saw them again after that."

When not fending off bailiffs and creditors, the McLagans' attention turned to brightening up their surroundings.

Sandy Sarjeant: "While we were living in Marlow, when Mac and I talked about buying our own house, which seemed like this big dream, Mac bought some quarry tiles, and we used to sit there, day after day, painting them. He was very arty and I'd always been quite good at drawing so we brought out the artistic side in each other. Those were the happiest times in our marriage when Mac and I did that flat up. We made things together, we used to buy sort of junk furniture and clean it up and varnish it. Mac sanded the floor and I made a rug. Mac's mum bought us two little antique chairs and I reupholstered them."

Pitching in to help with the redecorating were Ronnie, Sue, Kenney, Jan and a sheepish Peter Frampton, who frequently visited with his girl-friend Mary.

Ian McLagan: "I had this song I was working on called 'Growing Closer' and Pete liked it. He had a Revox two-track, same as I did, so we made a track out of it and we recorded it at my place, going backwards and forwards from machine to machine. When Humble Pie got together, Pete asked me to join. I went out there because I thought it was an interesting idea but I don't think Greg [Ridley] liked me because he had gone out with Sandy years before. He didn't take kindly to me and I didn't take kindly to the band really. I'd just done that, I'd just done Steve, thanks very much! So the end result was Humble Pie cut 'Growing Closer' on their first album [*As Safe As Yesterday Is*] but I'm not on it."

Also helping the McLagans through the lean times was their close friend, Billy Nicholls. "Billy was a lifesaver," says Sandy. "Mac and I had done up the front room. We were sleeping and living in this one room and we needed to get the bedroom ready because the baby was coming so it took all our efforts. Billy turned up and because we only had one ladder, I climbed on top of this cheap horrible wardrobe. I think I was about seven months' pregnant. While I was painting away, the whole thing started to go with me on top of it. Luckily Billy saw it and caught me otherwise I don't know what would have happened."

Born in Shepherd's Bush in 1949, Nicholls came from a musical background and started writing songs from an early age. Through George Harrison he met Ray Tolliday, the promotions man at Immediate Records who in turn arranged a meeting with Tony Calder and Andrew Oldham. Billy was installed in a small room at the company's New Oxford

Street offices to compose and demo songs in a quasi Brill Building, which is where he met and befriended the Small Faces. As well as singing back-up vocals on many of the *Ogdens'* tracks, in the spirit of Immediate's family vibe, the Small Faces reciprocated by playing on Nicholls obscure and highly-prized 1968 album, *Would You Believe.* It was during these sessions that he noticed all was not well within the group.

"One of the last tracks I recorded for the album was 'Girl From New York' at IBC. I asked Steve if he would help me. I thought it would be the Small Faces coming down, because they were on the single, 'Would You Believe', which Steve and Ronnie produced, but Steve brought in Jerry Shirley and a bass player. Peter Frampton wasn't there because Steve wanted to play guitar himself so I knew something was up. The track turned out great but it felt a bit strange."

Among Mac and Sandy's pop biz friends helping make light of their situation was Keith Moon and his pretty blonde wife Kim. The couples socialised upstairs at Ronnie Scott's Jazz Club, where, on May 1, Mac witnessed the Who's deafening live baptism of *Tommy* to an invited audience in the downstairs club (coincidentally, where Humble Pie were unveiled in August).

Kenney, meanwhile, shifted between Stepney and the Osborne family residence in Gainsborough Gardens, Hampstead.

Gary Osborne: "Kenney was virtually living with us and obviously, if you've got a girlfriend and mother under the same roof, there were huge rows. Kenney and Jan were deeply in love but they were both immature. Ken would pack all his stuff up in the car and drive off home and the next day he'd be back. Sometimes he'd only go round the block and come back and they'd start again.

"Of course he was not earning any money now. There was at least a year and a half after the Small Faces where Ken was absolutely skint and he suddenly thought, 'What the fuck am I gonna do?' By this time I was working as a staff A&R man at RCA and my father was still quite a popular conductor, arranger, musical director – doing jingles and film themes so both myself and dad would book Kenney on sessions wherever possible. And that wasn't some charitable act – Kenney was a damn good drummer, one of the better ones that played on his own records, which you couldn't say about a lot of the pop bands in the late Sixties.

"Some of the sessions were not at all rock'n'roll – mine were sort of pop but my dad's were commercials. Advertisements in those days had to have one and a half seconds' silence – no clicks, no synths, no drum machine, there's a discipline in there so this was really helpful to Kenney's development as a drummer because he was doing things that he normally wouldn't have done, that he wouldn't *had* to have done. He was playing very light, playing with brushes. So I think that advanced him as a musician. And whereas the fee at that time I think was about £12 for a standard three-hour session, a commercial was £12 for an hour . . . Ken didn't pay any rent because he was living with us and his mum so that got him through that tough year."

Jan Jones: "Things were really bloody tight. I worked in the Bally shoe shop in Hampstead and as assistant press officer at Fenwick's [a women's fashion department store] in New Bond Street to keep things going. It didn't affect us quite as much as it did Mac and Sandy because Kenney was doing sessions and bringing in about ten quid a week although some weeks he didn't earn a penny. I'd look after the money. Out of what he or I earned, I'd allocate Kenney two quid a week which was just enough for a packet of fags and some petrol for the car. I think Ronnie had a little bit more from his publishing."

It was the payments from the Performing Rights Society and Sue's acting and modelling work that kept Ronnie afloat. "It saved my bacon, it really did," he confirmed to Nick Logan.

Sue Tacker: "At the beginning the [Small Faces] split was a shock for Ronnie but then, it was like a sense of relief, at least that was my perception . . . But my memory of how it affected him was that it was risky but what wasn't? Ronnie didn't care about risk, it's like here today, gone tomorrow, it didn't matter, it didn't mean anything. He didn't cling to money, he didn't care really."

Stan Lane illustrates just how casual his brother's attitude was – a trait that was to follow him for the rest of his life. "When he and Marriott bought the place in Moreton, [the previous owner] had started to turn the barn into a replica of the main cottage. But all it had was the upstairs and the underneath was a big area like a warehouse. My dad French polished the windows and all that inside. But then Steve and Ronnie had this big row and Ronnie just walked away and left it."

Ronnie and Sue moved from the Essex countryside to a small flat in Elsham Road, Shepherd's Bush, coincidentally just around the corner from where Mac's father grew up.

Sue Tacker: "We would often make visits out to the East End to visit Ronnie's mum and dad or go down to the market at Brick Lane where Stan had a stall. Ronnie's mum had this sort of, at that time, mystery disease – this thing where, in a way, the family didn't understand what was going on with her so they just pooh-poohed it as people do when they don't understand things. They couldn't understand her mood swings, thinking it was psychological, that it was manipulative. Actually the poor woman was really suffering and she was not a happy person really. You could tell that she was sweet underneath but she was in a bad way physically and she had not been diagnosed with multiple sclerosis yet so it was kind of awful."

Stan Lane: "I think mum was about 32 when the disease showed. It started off just in the foot and then it gradually got worse but she never got to the stage where she was incontinent or nothing like that, it was just that she couldn't walk. About the time Ronnie started to be successful with the Small Faces, the council moved our parents out of Forest Gate into a high-rise block of flats in Plaistow. They put them on the 14th floor or something and the only way mum could get down was the lift and it always used to break down. We had to carry her up and down the stairs. So that's when Ronnie bought mum and dad a bungalow in Collier Row."

Meanwhile, Ronnie, Kenney and Mac carried on playing together but were in danger of splitting for good. According to McLagan, "It didn't sound that great. I mean we missed someone as a real singer and a real guitarist. The three of us said let's stick together if we can but obviously if someone gets an offer and something happens, then take it . . . We left it open."

"Just after Steve left, I was in a right state," Lane admitted to *NME*'s Gordon Coxhill. "One thing we didn't want to do was keep the name and gradually fade away to nothing. I wasn't even sure that I wanted to stay with Kenney and Ian . . . we rehearsed, just the three of us mainly because we had nothing else to do. I changed my mind from day to day."

At one point, Ronnie approached Billy Nicholls: "I was absolutely shocked when he said, 'We need another guitarist now that Steve's left. Will you join? Can you play electric guitar?' I said, 'I haven't got an electric guitar. I can't play electric guitar.' So he gave me Steve's first guitar, an old Framus with a sliding pick-up, which I've still got. But suddenly Ronnie Wood appeared on the scene and he fitted in absolutely perfectly. He was just meant to be."

Having been sacked from the Jeff Beck Group in February 1969, supposedly on the grounds of allowing their playing to deteriorate, although closer sources suggest their removal was engineered by Beck and Nicky Hopkins respectively, Ronnie Wood and Mickey Waller were at a loose end.

"I decided I wouldn't waste my time any more," Waller told Bob Dawbarn, "either I would get a group together or forget it."

The pair started jamming with Leigh Stephens, former guitarist from West Coast proto-heavy metal merchants Blue Cheer who had a US Top 20 hit in 1968 with an ear-splitting desecration of Eddie Cochran's 'Summertime Blues'. On leaving the band, Stephens decided to try his luck in London and looked up Waller whom he'd met when the Jeff Beck Group played California.

Meanwhile, Beck recruited ex-Sounds Incorporated drummer and session man Tony Newman while Doug Blake, who hailed from New Zealand and rather eccentrically played in fingerless gloves and bare feet, replaced Wood as bassist for a third US tour set to start on February 14 but postponed to March 1 in order to break in the new line-up. Beck's hubris was repaid with a disastrous opening night in Alexandria, Virginia, whereupon the next concert was cancelled and Blake promptly sacked. With a tour booked and profits at stake, Peter Grant swallowed his immense pride and placed a call through to Wood in London who, sensing the urgency afoot and unperturbed by Grant's ferocity, exploited the situation by demanding his own fee.* He flew out and reclaimed his place in time for two gigs in the New York area on the 7th.

"By that time Ronnie was well pissed off," Stewart told *Zigzag*, "and from then on he just used the Beck group as filler while he looked for another band."

Itching to play guitar again, while on the road, Wood heard Aretha Franklin's superb treatment of the Band's 'The Weight', which featured distinctive slide bottleneck from Duane Allman, a young session musician at Muscle Shoals, Alabama, whose prowess provided a major inspiration. "I heard Duane Allman and felt a natural pull towards it . . ." Ronnie told *NME*. "It was like a new style of bottleneck, because he started playing slide guitar using regular tuning. I'm glad I started learning that [difficult] way because when I went to open tuning it was easier."

Three weeks into the tour Beck's unpredictability flared up again when he cancelled the remainder of the dates and returned to England, primarily to record a second album. There was some basis to this decision, as Stewart told Penny Valentine in 1971. "The trouble with the Beck band – its downfall really – was that we kept the old material all the time." The band

---

* Wood has since claimed he received a whopping £2,000 per gig but considering this was more than the potential band gross for a single show, the rate was undoubtedly far less.

was coming apart fast, a process documented on *Beck-Ola*.* Beck delegated Stewart and Wood to write original material, an ironic situation considering he'd only just given the latter his marching orders. Recorded over four days in April '69 at De Lane Lea studios, Stewart's assertion to James Johnson in 1974 that "Woody and I would slave for months putting the album *Beck-Ola* together, doing the arrangements for Jeff" was plainly exaggerated.

The cover reproduction of Magritte's *La Chambre d'Ecoute* suggested Beck had embraced surrealism but the sleeve's caveat: "Today, with all the hard competition in the music business, it's almost impossible to come up with anything totally original. So we haven't . . ." promised anything but. Released in June in the States (September in the UK) where it reached number 15, *Beck-Ola* was rushed and uninspired, blighted by brevity and bad mastering.†

Having personally witnessed the band wowing audiences in the States, Mickie Most replaced the flash but subtle approach of *Truth* in favour of bludgeoning hard rock that would play well in American concert halls and on FM radio. The invention used to rework 'Shapes Of Things', for example, was overlooked in favour of bombastic rearrangements of two Elvis Presley songs, 'All Shook Up' and 'Jailhouse Rock'. The album's only delicate moment came in the form of Nicky Hopkins' stately 'Girl From Mill Valley', a beautiful, affecting piano instrumental, inhabiting a similar feel and space to Floyd Cramer's 'Last Date'; it would not have sounded out of place on a Band album. Of Stewart and Wood's efforts, 'Spanish Boots' and 'Plynth (Water Down The Drain)' were the first to feature Rod's 'been down so long it looks like up to me' lyrical bent, while 'The Hangman's Knee', like Led Zeppelin's 'Gallows Pole', nicked from a centuries-old folk song. It wasn't the most auspicious introduction for a songwriting partnership that would soon blossom into impressive productivity.

On April 25, the Jeff Beck Group played what was to be their last British gig – an all-night show at London's Lyceum. Significantly, among the audience stood Ronnie Lane, Ian McLagan and Kenney Jones, invited along by their new friend, Ronnie Wood. While jamming with Waller

* The album's unofficial full title was *Cosa Nostra Beck-Ola*, a play on the popular Rock-Ola jukeboxes that were linked to the Mob during the Twenties.
† Although the 2004 CD reissue has gone some way to alleviating this.

and Stephens, Wood kept his options open and just as he had done with Beck, took the plunge and made an important phone call.

"We were hunting around and Ronnie Wood turned up who we didn't know . . ." said Ronnie Lane. "He just phoned up. I'd seen him round Steve Marriott's now and then. He always had a smile on his face. I always remember him as a smiling head."

Sue Tacker: "Ronnie and Ronnie Wood became fast friends. Ronnie Wood was a breath of fresh air – he was just so funny and bubbly and light-hearted and I think it was really nice for Ronnie to have him around."

Ian McLagan: "I first met Woody at Steve's place in Chiswick in 1968. Steve was always hanging out with other guitarists. I wasn't aware of what Ronnie had done before. Apparently his girlfriend Krissie used to work for Don Arden when we were with him. Anyway, eventually the two Ronnie's got together and I would go over to Ronnie [Lane's] flat in Elsham Road. He had a Wurlitzer there and I'd sit in and we'd play and work on these songs."

"We jammed together and we weren't very good but Ronnie was all right," Lane told *Rolling Stone*. "Not brilliant but we thought, why not? He'd just come off the bass and to be honest at first we wondered if he was the man for the job. But we thought, 'Well, none of us is brilliant, so we'll work at it together.'"

"[The Small Faces] hadn't been publicly recognised as good musicians," Wood told Penny Valentine in 1971, "but then again I'd seen what was in it from a musical point of view and I think if people had looked hard enough they would have seen there was something there . . . They had a very simple approach and were into things I was digging at the time – things like Booker T."

Around May, Ian Stewart, the Rolling Stones' chief road manager and piano player, offered his aid. Stewart, known to all as 'Stu', had originally founded the Stones with Brian Jones before Andrew Oldham decided that his face didn't fit and six members was one too many. Small, stocky, with a protruding jaw, Stu looked more like a garage mechanic than a rock musician but his boogie-woogie licks captivated those who heard them and his forthright opinions often contained good advice for those within rock's premier hierarchy to whom he became a dear and valued friend. Stu had shared a house in Surrey with Glyn Johns and first met the Small Faces at Olympic while the Stones were recording in the next studio.

In 1968 the Stones invested in a warehouse at 47 Bermondsey Street, south-east London to use as a rehearsal and storage facility. Because they spent so much time at Olympic the basement space wasn't being utilised, so Stu offered it to Ronnie Lane to rehearse in.

Ian McLagan: "Ronnie and Glyn Johns were good pals and Glyn and Stu had always been tight so Ronnie would go and visit Glyn and hang out. Stu had faith in us, he said, 'I know you've got no money now but you can use the studio as much as you like and pay us when you get a record deal.' That was how things happened in those days."

Ron Wood gave a slightly different version of events to Penny Valentine: "I was down the Stones studio, just getting it together on the guitar. Mickey Waller just happened to be there and I phoned Ronnie and said, 'Why don't you come down and play on decent amps?' I didn't think he'd turn up but he turned up with Mac, then Kenney came later. So we had another go and that one worked out a bit better."

Ian McLagan: "We started to have these jams and Ronnie [Wood] was bringing people down like Mickey Waller and Leigh Stephens. I mean Woody was playing guitar so I don't know why he brought Leigh down and we had Kenney so I don't know why he brought Mickey down. It was all in flux until we decided 'well let's not tell those other people what we're doing' so we started rehearsing as a four piece. Quite soon really we didn't need those people around, it wasn't helping that all they wanted to do was jam, we wanted to work on songs."

Leigh Stephens hasn't a particularly fond memory of the rehearsals, as he recalls: "Ronnie, Mick and myself were trying to see if we could put something together or so it seemed at the time. In retrospect I think Woody was just using it as an opportunity to audition for the Faces. I was renting the Stones' rehearsal basement and we were fooling around with a few things when, to my surprise, in walks Rod, Ronnie Lane and Mac. They proceeded to commandeer Woody and jammed on a thing, leaving Mick and myself to sit and watch . . . Anyway after a while they all packed up and I got stuck with the bill."

There's a story that Ronnie Wood often likes telling of Mick Jagger phoning the warehouse to offer him the job of replacing Brian Jones in the Stones and how Ronnie Lane intercepted the call, bluntly telling Jagger, "Ronnie is quite happy where he is, thank you very much." It's a good yarn but is it entirely plausible? Wood was then primarily known in the business as a bass player, his stints as a guitarist had been with two obscure groups the Birds and the Creation that had long since broken up. By now Ian Stewart was well enough acquainted with Wood to have put his name forward but, by his own admission, Wood was only just starting to regain his chops on the guitar, whereas Mick Taylor, on

Stewart's recommendation, was a recognised guitarist with John Mayall's Bluesbreakers. Jagger has never confirmed or denied the anecdote and without Ronnie Lane around to corroborate it, Wood is given the benefit of the doubt.*

Ronnie and Krissie were renting a country cottage, the Old Forge in Henley-on-Thames where the rudimentary band spent weekends rehearsing and writing. "We used to sit out in the field and that's where we got lots of things together which were done on the first [Faces] album," Wood told Penny Valentine.

Occasionally Rod Stewart would drop in on his mate to see how things were shaping up. "Rod started turning up on Sundays," Lane told *Rolling Stone*. "We'd get well pissed, shout and make a lot of noise. We became good drinking partners with Rod."

"Ronnie Wood asked me to go down and see them rehearse, which is what I did," Stewart told *Rolling Stone* in 1970. "I wasn't too impressed at the time. I thought they were putting together some nice things, but that there was no direction to what they were doing."

In late May, Mickie Most teamed up two of his artists – using the Jeff Beck Group to provide the powerhouse backing for Donovan on several tracks recorded at Advision Studios, including the funky 'Goo Goo Barabajagal', released as a single the following month. Ironically, that spring, when looking for a touring band, the hippie troubadour saw the possibilities and approached his friend Ronnie Lane. "Donovan came over to Finborough Road one night and offered us the job of his backing group," says McLagan, "but we thought the idea was ridiculous."

On June 4, Nicky Hopkins suddenly quit. "We were doing a Donovan session for *Barabajagal* and I left," Hopkins told Chuck Pulin. "I said, 'Sorry, man, I've had it.' [Beck] said he was expecting it anyway and he was sorry the money got fucked up – because we never got paid . . ."

Relocating to the West Coast, Hopkins appeared on Jefferson Airplane's *Volunteers* and Quicksilver Messenger Service's *Shady Grove* albums and played live with both bands, eventually joining Quicksilver full time. He

---

* Wood also tells a similar story of bumping into Jagger and Charlie Watts just prior to the Rolling Stones' Hyde Park free concert in honour of Brian Jones, who died two days earlier, and wishing them a good gig, not realising how close he could have been to joining them. Another nice anecdote but there's just one problem – on July 5, the date of the concert, Wood was in America with the Jeff Beck Group.

also contributed to the Steve Miller Band albums *Brave New World* and *Your Saving Grace*, produced by Glyn Johns.

Now back to a four-piece and barely on speaking terms, the Jeff Beck Group embarked on one last lucrative swing around America, starting in the New York area on July 2. Steve Weiss, Peter Grant's American business partner, poured fuel on the flames when decreeing that many of the dates – such as the Newport Jazz Festival – were promotional by nature and therefore Rod, Ronnie and Tony Newman's wages would be fixed, sparking a revolt by the feisty Newman. To further aggravate matters, Led Zeppelin played on a couple of shows – an abject reminder of what the Beck Group could have achieved.

Also touring were Vanilla Fudge, an indulgent outfit whose clinical musicianship captivated Beck. He had already made eager overtures to the rhythm section of Tim Bogert and drummer Carmine Appice about forming a band once contractual matters were sorted. It was naturally assumed Stewart would be the vocalist.

The original Jeff Beck Group played their last concert on July 26 at the Grande Ballroom, Detroit and returned to England. A second night at the Grande and six other US dates were cancelled – including a scheduled appearance on August 17 at Woodstock. "We'd been doing two festivals a week," Stewart told Nick Logan, "and we just thought 'Oh another festival' . . . we blew it because we [could] have made the film – we were bigger than [Joe] Cocker at the time. That must be one of the biggest regrets of my life – and Beck's."*

The Jeff Beck Group were also provisionally added to the line-up of the 2nd Isle of Wight Festival of Music, featuring the headline appearance of a reclusive Bob Dylan, which would have come as an added blow for Stewart. In disarray, Wood permanently joined up with the ex-Small Faces and Newman went back to session work and joined progressive outfit, May Blitz.

"It was weird, [the Beck Group] never actually broke up," Rod told Royston Eldridge in 1970. "When we came back off the last American tour we knew that Woody was going to leave and Beck didn't know what I was going to do. I never knew what he was going to do because we'd never ask each other. He'd never turn round and say, 'Are you going to leave or are you going with Woody?' And I'd never asked him what he was going to do. It just fell apart, we drifted apart, we never phoned each other up."

---

* Ironically, Nicky Hopkins played at Woodstock with Jefferson Airplane.

To say relations were strained between Stewart and Beck at the band's demise was not to overstate the case and admiration for each other's considerable talents was tempered with bitter barbs sailing back and forth over the years. In 2010, Beck told the BBC: "[Rod and I] got on great at first until it said 'Jeff Beck Group'. Everywhere we went, there was no mention of the [vocalist], but I was the one selling the tickets and people were paying to see me. I just thought, 'Well, wait a minute, I've taken you from obscurity, you're now on a big stage with me, just behave yourself and we'll see what happens'. So you can understand, someone with a massive ego being left out . . . I blew out Woodstock – the most famous gig blown ever, I think, and he hated me even more after that."

CHAPTER 8

New Faces

*"We wanted Rod to join and he was only waiting to be asked. In the
same way Kenney, Ronnie and Mac didn't want to split up, Rod and I
wanted to stay together as well. It was like a natural continuation for us to
get together. They didn't join us, we didn't join them, we just came
together."*

— Ron Wood, *Music Now*, 1970

"Find myself a rock'n'roll band, that needs a helping hand"

Rod Stewart, 'Maggie May', 1971

AN unwitting catalyst in bringing Rod Stewart a step closer to joining
Ron Wood in the ex-Small Faces was Ronnie's brother Art. When
the Artwoods commercially unsuccessful tenure with Decca ended in
1966, the group signed to Parlophone and then, in September '67, to
Philips. After a non-starter as the St Valentine's Day Massacre, the group
called it a day; Jon Lord to form Deep Purple with Ritchie Blackmore,
Keef Hartley to John Mayall's Bluesbreakers and his own band. Retained
by Philips, Art was offered some recording time along with well-paid
engagements at the annual Oxford and Cambridge May Balls. Only
problem was he didn't have a band. While the Jeff Beck Group was
between tours, Art asked his little brother to help. Ronnie, in turn, roped
in his Birds and Creation mate Kim Gardner, now playing with Ashton,
Gardner & Dyke, as well as inviting Kenney and, as Art knew him, "little
Mac."

"I called the group Quiet Melon because I wanted a name that wouldn't
immediately be associated with the Artwoods," was Art's unenlightening
explanation as to the origins of the ad hoc unit's name.

From all reports, the university gigs were a hoot and provided a bit of
light relief during an uncertain period not to mention some much needed
readies. "We were on two hundred quid [for each appearance], which was

good money," Art recalled to *Record Collector*. "We played for three-quarters of an hour, doing mainly standards plus a few of our own songs, a lot of blues numbers, and then came offstage, ready to have a beer and go home. So everyone started having a few drinks, and throwing strawberry pies at each other, when the promoter came up to us and said that P.P. Arnold wasn't going to play, and would we go back on for another £250. Well, we were back up there as soon as he said it."*

Among those along for the crack were Rod Stewart, John Baldry and friends such as Gary Osborne. "I'd seen Rod down at the Cromwellian when he was part of the Steam Packet and Shotgun Express so I kind of knew him peripherally. I just got in the van and went along as part of the entourage. The college people had no idea who was coming – they didn't know that they had half the Small Faces who, although they were now finished, were still a name and the guys from Jeff Beck's band. I very much enjoyed those gigs.

"I'd never met Woody before those Quiet Melon gigs but I got on really well with him because he and I snuck off and had a little spliff. Woody was not the subtlest, 'Oi, has anybody got any puff.' That was a bond between Woody and I – that we both liked a smoke."

Jan Jones: "I can only remember the one gig in Cambridge, everyone pissed as farts, they were just playing these old songs. Art was leading the show and Rod was there but I don't know why. He wasn't out on the stage, you couldn't see him . . . he was unbelievably shy. Maybe he was supposed to sing but couldn't hack being up front or he was just there as a mate of Woody's, there for the laugh and decided to sing a few songs."

And where was Ronnie Lane? "Ronnie Lane couldn't come because he went to India to find a mystic," Mac flippantly remarked to Chris Welch a week after the gig. "He's blown all his bread on the trip."

McLagan was half serious. On January 31, 1969, Avatar Meher Baba died – or 'dropped his body' as Baba followers refer to his passing.

Sue Tacker: "The Meher Baba Trust in India arranged for people to go to his samadhi [tomb-shrine] at Meherabad . . . They allocated weeks for parties to visit from different countries, I think the first was America, the second from Europe. I just wanted to go right away. I was still doing modelling and acting but for some reason my schedule was, like, 'I really have to go now' so I did. I borrowed money from my agent and went

---

* Because of the spontaneous nature of these gigs, there was no mention of Art Wood or Quiet Melon in the Rag Ads for Cambridge paper *Varsity* or Oxford paper *Cherwell*. The band reportedly also played at the University of Surrey, Guildford.

with about five or six other people. It was only for a week, I believe. Ronnie ended up going on the third trip. Ronnie and I had met Michael McInnerney by then. I guess he had work commitments and couldn't go so by happenstance, Ronnie went to India with Michael's wife, Kate."

Born in Liverpool in 1944, Michael McInnerney moved to London with his family in 1952, settling in East Ham to be near the docks where his father worked, and attended Lister Technical School. "I was there at the same time as Ronnie Lane," McInnerney recalls, "although we didn't know each other. We both left at 16 to make our way in the world. I was really surprised when I later found that out. It was a strange connection, a bit of serendipity."

Showing an early interest in art, McInnerney started as a tea boy at the advertising agency Gerrards in Holborn and Saward Baker in Great Portland Street. He then took a graphic design course at the London College of Printing where he became the art editor for CND founder member George Clark's magazine, *People & Politics*. Clark also helped to run the London Free School in Notting Hill Gate and introduced McInnerney to photographer and liberal activist, John 'Hoppy' Hopkins. With turbulent changes occurring in art and society, Mike dropped out of the LCP during his final year (1966) and at Hopkin's invitation, became art editor for *International Times*, the underground newspaper co-founded by Hopkins and Barry Miles. Mike also designed the posters for gigs and events connected to the movement including UFO and the British underground's Coming Out Ball, the 14 Hour Technicolor Dream, held at Alexandra Palace on April 29, 1967.

The following month, Mike married his girlfriend, 18-year-old Katharine 'Katie' Lambert, a solicitor's daughter from Lewes, Sussex, in a full-scale hippie ceremony in Hyde Park. The couple met in 1966 when, to earn some extra money in the evenings, Mike was managing Bunjies folk club on Litchfield Street, off Charing Cross Road, a basement coffee bar where Bob Dylan, Paul Simon and Al Stewart had performed. Rebelling against her bourgeois upbringing, Kate was something of a free spirit who had already experimented with hard drugs and spent time in a rehabilitation centre.

The couple's wedding clothes were made by Karen Astley, a regular at UFO and the eldest daughter of television composer and arranger, Edwin 'Ted' Astley. Karen had studied dress design at Ealing College of Art where she met her boyfriend and future husband, Pete Townshend.

Mike McInnerney: "Kate and I moved to this great little flat at the top of a mansion block on Shaftesbury Ave behind the Shaftesbury Theatre.

Mick Farren [of The Deviants and later writer with *NME*] took it over after we left. It was just a good little hub in the centre of London for various events. One of the things that we did was a party for Simon & Marijke, [two of the psychedelic Dutch artistic collective known as The Fool]. Pete came along – we'd met before on occasions at places like UFO – and that's when we sat down and started talking about Meher Baba. At that time we were looking for ideas to explore. It was that period. I first heard about Baba through [fellow designer] Dudley Edwards when we went along to a Baba meeting at the Poetry Society building in Earl's Court during the summer of '67 and came across a small group of people who met regularly, including Delia de Leon and Tom Hopkinson.

"The Baba thing was intriguing and it appealed to me because it involved older people . . . I don't know why but Delia having met Baba seemed to be really appropriate, it seemed to come from a real bit of history; a history of love for a perfect master and there was something about that generation as well which I found really touching . . . who still had these beliefs and faiths. I really liked that."

The McInnerneys moved out of central London into a flat on Richmond Hill. "We started to hold Baba meetings there which people came to including Pete and Karen. This would be late '67 – early '68."

Mike and Kate then moved to a flat in Willoughby House, a large Victorian villa situated just over the Twickenham side of Richmond Bridge, where actress Lillie Langtry reputedly enjoyed secret trysts with the future king, Edward VII. After their marriage in May '68, Pete and Karen Townshend moved into a three storey Georgian townhouse over-looking the Thames just down the road on the Embankment opposite Eel Pie Island. Now closely connected, Pete commissioned Mike to design and paint the elaborate album sleeve and libretto illustrations for the Who's *Tommy*. Having given up the lease on the Elsham Road flat after their trips to India, Ronnie and Sue found a place on Russell Road, next to the Olympia Exhibition Hall in West Kensington. "I remember visiting them there and they were both reading *Lord Of The Rings*," says Billy Nicholls, "and it was there that I first saw a photograph of Meher Baba. They told me he was the Avatar. At that time, I was a bit sceptical and couldn't quite believe in anything other than the here and now."

The couple temporarily lodged with the Townshends before moving into a ground floor flat at 3 Heatherdene Mansions, on Cambridge Road, just around the corner from Willoughby House, at the side of Richmond Bridge.

Michael McInnerney: "Pete and Karen brought Ronnie and Sue along to our Baba meetings. They were good neighbours to Kate and I. The weekends we would go off with the dogs; Ronnie had Molly, a half Alsatian, half Welsh collie and Pete had a spaniel Towser and we would walk along the river. It was a really lovely time."

After all the recent upheavals – the Small Faces split, the end of his and Marriott's partnership, no band, no money, his mother's illness – in a serene atmosphere within a stone's throw of the river where he could indulge his love of fishing, surrounded by lively, intelligent friends from the welcoming Baba community, it seemed that Ronnie had found the perfect surroundings.

If the Jeff Beck Group had failed to secure the same amount of recognition in Britain as they had in America or if the Small Faces found it hard to shake off the albatross of a pop tag, it was not without the selfless efforts of disc jockey, John Peel. Born John Ravenscroft in Heswall, Cheshire in 1939, Peel started his radio career in America while based in Dallas, Texas in the early Sixties and built a name for himself at various American stations by cannily capitalising on the colonial craze for anybody talking with a British accent. In 1967 he returned to Britain and, with American radio credentials, was hired by pirate station Radio London where he adopted the name John Peel. Moving to the BBC's new flagship station Radio 1, Peel was given his own two-hour Sunday afternoon programme *Top Gear* where his reputation as a discerning purveyor of the new music over the Corporation's staid airwaves was consolidated. A respected man of eclectic and eccentric tastes, Peel had spun *Truth* and *Ogdens' Nut Gone Flake*, extolling the virtues of both to his devoted listeners.

Always open to finding and promoting new talent that caught his ear, in partnership with business manager Clive Selwood, in 1969, Peel set up Dandelion Records, named after one of Peel's pet hamsters, ostensibly to release an album by Bridget St. John. It set the trend for the independent label, which continued releasing records until folding in 1972, an altruistic if indulgent and certainly financially deprived outlet for Peel's catholic tastes.

After being tipped off by *OZ* editor Richard Neville, Peel saw an unknown band named Python Lee Jackson play at underground venue, the Arts Lab on Drury Lane. Python Lee Jackson, made up of expatriate Australians, formed in Sydney in 1965 but after various personnel changes, had split in 1968. However a revived line-up comprising guitarist Mick Liber, drummer David Montgomery, bass player John Helman and keyboard player/singer David Bentley, relocated to London in an attempt – like compatriots such as the Easybeats and the Bee Gees – to break into the competitive British scene.*

Liber, originally from Ealing, had played in a group Frankie Read & The Casuals that worked the same circuit as the Birds before he emigrated. "It was Ronnie Wood who phoned me up and got me my first session [after returning to the UK]," Liber recalled to rock writer/researcher Nick Warburton. "It was a strange session. I had to go to this studio 'cause Ronnie couldn't make it and they played me a basic track and said, 'Can you play some fills?' And I said, 'Well, there's no vocals so I don't know where the fills go.' And they said, 'Just imagine where the vocals go and play some fills like that!'"

In April 1969, having landed a distribution deal for Dandelion with CBS, Python Lee Jackson recorded some demos for Selwood at R.G. Jones studio in Morden, south London, which impressed Selwood sufficiently for him to book a proper session at the CBS studios in Bond Street. According to Selwood's recollection, the session deteriorated because of a stereotypical Australian thirst for the amber nectar. After another session at R.G. Jones the band were given one last shot at CBS. But when the band rehearsed, Bentley felt unsure as to his abilities in handling the key on a song he had written, 'In A Broken Dream'.

"We had a 'manager', a slick car salesman with pretensions to become Andrew Loog Oldham or Brian Epstein," Montgomery told Warburton. "He told us he knew this singer Rod Stewart very well, having sold him a Lotus or Ferrari or something, and he was sure he could get him to join the group or at least sing on the recording date."

Bentley taught Stewart the lyrics at Montgomery's Chelsea flat before going back into the studio. "The band hadn't done much playing in London. Everyone was feeling uptight and the first run-throughs of 'In A Broken Dream' were less than promising," says Bentley. "In upshot, John Peel, who was producing the track for his Dandelion label, sent out for beer – and we drank quite a lot of this stuff in the interests of heightened relaxation. Rod, as always, sang well but, because the lights had been doused, he missed the last verse, repeating the first one instead, filling in at one point with a hummed 'mmm mmm mmm' which subsequent cover versions have faithfully copied."

"It was John Peel's fault," was how Stewart remembered it to *NME*'s

---

* A full and detailed examination of Python Lee Jackson's history can be found at www.nickwarburton.com

Nick Logan in 1972. "He said come down and show this guy how to sing this tune. So me, being very naïve and in no particular group at that time, I went and showed him how to sing."

For such a random exercise, the song was an unexpected gem; a moody, bluesy piece with a Procol Harum feel thanks to Bentley's Hammond organ and scanning, melancholic lyrics. With Liber's screaming guitar licks and Stewart's expressive vocal ("I was really trying to sound black"), it could pass for a great lost Beck Group out-take – of the type that would have greatly benefited *Beck-Ola*. A couple of other tracks were cut at the session – a Beck-like cover of B.B. King's 'How Blue Can You Get' and a loose jam – later given the title 'Doing Fine' – over which Stewart, being a huge Motown fan and a particular admirer of David Ruffin, improvised the lyrics from the Temptations 'Cloud Nine', a US Top 10 hit in 1968 but still to enter the UK charts at the time of the recording.

In lieu of a session fee, Rod requested a set of carpets for his silver Marcos from the used car salesman of a manager. Of more significance it was the start of a long-standing association and friendship between the disc jockey and singer. "I didn't particularly want to release anything with a session singer," Peel told Danny Holloway, "because it wouldn't have been representative of what the group were truly like."

With its unusual commercial potential one could speculate how 'In A Broken Dream' might have set Stewart up as a solo singer in a way that 'Space Oddity' did for David Bowie if it had been released under his name at the time. Or it may well have left him a one-hit wonder – a fate that befell Bowie until his chart fortunes revived in 1972. Either way, the song remained in the can until the following year when Dandelion sold the tapes to songwriter and producer Miki Dallon of Young Blood Records who re-released it to no response. And that was that. For now.

Lou Reizner was fast losing patience. Nine months had passed since he had gained Rod Stewart's signature on a Mercury Records contract. Rod had received an advance of £1,000 – an enviable amount in the days when record company advances generally weren't forthcoming in Britain – but still there was nothing to show for it.

"We'd done the deal and then Rod started complaining that we hadn't paid him enough money," Reizner told George Tremlett, "and then he did not want to leave the Jeff Beck Group to go solo after all [which was what I'd been expecting he would do] – and then Peter Grant started saying that he could have got him a much better deal with Atlantic than

Rod had done with us . . . and then it all started to become very difficult around June and July 1969 because now that he'd got his car what Rod really wanted more than anything else was his house. He wanted more money so that he could get this house in Highgate, which was the first he'd ever owned."

According to Jonathan Rowlands, Stewart's obduracy was only assuaged when Mercury eventually agreed to pay him an extra amount after some persuasive talking from Reizner to company president Irving Green that this young upstart was worth persevering with.

Of course Rod offered a different explanation when talking to Nick Logan in 1971. "I was at a loose end. I'd left the Beck group, and this was the only thing I'd been able to do. Make an album and hope for the best . . . I was offered the chance to make it while I was with Jeff but turned it down because I didn't want to offend him."

In actual fact the album was recorded before the last Beck tour at Lansdowne Studios in west London and Olympic Studios in just a week and a half – Stewart exhibiting typical financial shrewdness in realising that excessive studio time ate into profits. Rod brought in Wood, McLagan ("Poor old Mac was a bundle of nerves because he didn't want to play on it," Stewart told Logan. "He didn't feel he was good enough") and, of course, "Old Mother Waller". Since the idea of forming a band with Wood and Stephens had fallen through, in May, Waller had continued his peripatetic musical adventures by joining blues-rock band Steamhammer. "That didn't really work out," Waller told Bob Dawbarn. "They were so keen. I mean they'd travel to Manchester just for the joy of playing even if the money wasn't good. I tried to get along with it but I couldn't."

Steamhammer's line-up also featured guitarists Martin Pugh and Martin Quittenton. "Rod came along to see us play, and really liked Martin's guitar work and that's how we got involved [in Rod's solo album]," Waller told John Gray.

Having worked for five years towards this goal, *The Rod Stewart Album* captured a singer hungry for the prize. "That was a weird album. I was so naïve when I went into the studio, yet I knew exactly what I wanted," Stewart told *Rolling Stone*. "I had ideas of riffs. I said, 'Go in, mates, play a riff, make a progression and do this', and then I took the track from it and wrote the words. Which is a great way to do it, because the backing track always conjured up something for you, and you can write the words around it . . . I had no idea what the words were going to be, but I had an idea what the song would be about."

The album opened with the tentative acoustic chords of 'Street Fighting Man', which run behind Waller's thumping drums, Mac's piano and Wood's loose bottleneck runs. From the first verse it was a startling rearrangement, punctuated by Wood's rumbling, trebly bass so familiar from the Beck Group. As a further reminder of that band, after the first couple of verses the song adapts the same solo section as 'Shapes Of Things' with Wood's overdubbed soloing over the top. The song halts momentarily to resume with the familiar Stones arrangement featuring Wood's impressive chunky bass solo and in a tip of the hat, in unison, Mac and Woody revive Nicky Hopkins' piano riff from 'We Love You'. Overall, it was an inspired reworking and ranks among the best cover versions of a Rolling Stones song. Stewart claimed that he chose it because he "wanted somebody to hear the words. Such fine lyrics." It was a perceptive observation and one that still holds. Both Jagger and Stewart's abilities as lyricists during their run of creativity remain all too easily overlooked because of their image as flamboyant, posturing vocalists.

'Man Of Constant Sorrow', an American folk song popularised by Bob Dylan on his first album, features a masterful light and shade vocal while, again, a simple but effective arrangement enhances the mood with Rod strumming acoustic guitar. It marked the first of several superlative interpretations of Dylan songs attempted by Stewart (who claimed a trad arr. writing credit) and pronounced his love for Americana. This was further evidenced by 'Blind Prayer', which concerned the sad story of one of life's unfortunates, the only son of a lawyer orphaned by the death of his parents at the age of "four or perhaps five", then blinded by an illness "by the time I was ten".

"'Blind Prayer'" was entirely imagination, and I think that's where songs came from, they come either from imagination or from experience. Can't think of any other source," Stewart told *Rolling Stone*.

Mike d'Abo's 'Handbags And Gladrags' had already been recorded by several other artists including Stewart's fellow hoarse Brit soul shouter and Immediate label-mate Chris Farlowe who had a minor hit with the song in 1967, as well as pop groups from the obscure (Double Trouble) to the familiar (Love Affair). D'Abo wrote it as an appeal to a teenage girl that the way to fulfilment was not through being trendy and superficial, there are deeper values involved. As on 'Little Miss Understood', Mike d'Abo played piano and tastefully arranged the track. And as with 'Little Miss Understood', 'Handbags And Gladrags' is a little melodramatic in bringing the message home, a trait which hasn't affected its surprising durability – it was the track most reviewers remarked upon at the time and has become one of Stewart's best loved songs – belatedly released as a US single in 1972.*

'Old Raincoat . . .' is a rollicking, good-time rocker and a pure blueprint for the Faces, being a dry run both lyrically and musically for 'Three Button Hand Me Down', propelled by Wood's lead bass and Mac's honky tonk piano. "On that number, 'Old Raincoat' we tried to record two basses but Ronnie [Wood] got so drunk he fell over," Rod revealed, probably truthfully.

'I Wouldn't Ever Change A Thing' is the first of Stewart's wistful reflections on his footloose days as a nomadic beatnik, concluding, despite the unsure interjections of a friend (sung by Lou Reizner), that it was all worth it. While having a spellbinding melody, the arrangement is unnecessarily busy with heavy prog-style keyboard work from Keith Emerson.

'Cindy's Lament', set to a swaggering riff typical of the time, appears to be the diary of an obsessed stalker being given the brush-off. The protagonist runs the gamut of derision from the object of his desire's family and friends but the pay off comes with "if only they knew that you've already spent one night with me, honey".

As the album began with an inspired cover version so it ends with 'Dirty Old Town', a folk tune written by Ewan MacColl as a paean to Salford in greater Manchester where he was born and raised and a song well known to Rod from his days scuffling around Soho and Europe. The warm arrangement, reminiscent of Tim Hardin, features picked acoustic guitar from Quittenton, jazzy runs from Wood, Mac's gentle Hammond and a harmonica presumably played by Rod. It was sometimes easy to forget Rod's true roots after his recent guise as a blues rock shouter with the direct, aggressive Jeff Beck Group and his comment to Royston Eldridge in a 1970 interview, "I was listening to guys like Jack Elliott, and Guthrie and Dylan when he first came out. That's what I used to listen to because I never really considered myself a blues singer."

In 'Street Fighting Man', 'Man Of Constant Sorrow' and 'Dirty Old Town', he'd discovered a gift for taking well or little known material and interpreting it to his best means – managing to combine songs by artists as disparate as the Rolling Stones and Ewan MacColl and successfully sequencing them onto an album that was unusually refreshing in its variety. "I was out to try to prove myself as a singer more than anything,"

---

* In obvious homage to Stewart's vocal, Welsh group Stereophonics revived the song as a B-side in 2001, around the same time as the arrangement by Big George became indelibly associated as the theme to the award-winning British comedy *The Office*.

was Stewart's assessment of his debut. It was a formula that would stand him in good stead over a run of albums that, by and large, forged his reputation as an interpretative singer of the first rank and a songwriter of occasionally rare sensitivity.

Despite Reizner's producer's credit, Stewart insisted the on-the-money arrangements and crisp sound were all his own work. "I produced it as well," he told Caroline Boucher. "The only success I've ever had was doing things off my own bat and not listening to producers and record companies."

"It was writing, producing and singing my own album that really brought me together," Stewart told Nick Logan. "Up until then I don't think I had improved over a period of four years . . . And this came through jumping in at the deep end and putting an album together, trying to make it sound different, writing my own songs – there were [five] originals on that – because if you do none of your own songs it has just gotta sound like nobody else."

However within a year of its release the artist in Rod was restless. "I don't think my songs are good enough on the first album," he told *Rolling Stone*. "I tried out my own songwriting . . . and I didn't think my songs were up to much. I know my limitations now."

Released in the US in December, *The Rod Stewart Album* – which Stewart wanted to call *Thin* after an unusual adjective in common usage within his vocabulary at the time (it can still be seen in small letters at the sleeve's bottom left hand corner) – picked up airplay thanks to the Beck connection and eventually broke into the *Billboard* Top 200 reaching number 139. "When it sold 30,000 copies, I realised somebody must like what I'm doing," he told *Rolling Stone* in 1973.

Released by Philips' progressive subsidiary Vertigo Records in February 1970, the album was re-titled to the more imaginative *An Old Raincoat Won't Ever Let You Down*. While Vertigo had a reputation in the true fashion of the times of elaborate or conceptual sleeve designs, some creative spark in the art department interpreted the title a literal step too far by creating a gatefold sleeve showing an old tramp cavorting with three young children – an image that would not have gotten to the ideas stage in this modern age.* *NME* said: "Of course Stewart has worked with the Jeff Beck Group for over a year but *Raincoat* would seem to emphasise that he is much more than just another rock singer." *International Times* went so far as to call it, "A rock heirloom even" while esteemed critic Greil Marcus wrote in

---

* Significantly, when Stewart's solo canon was remastered and reissued by Spectrum in the UK in 2004, *An Old Raincoat . . .* reverted back to *The Rod Stewart Album*.

Rolling Stone, "Unlike so many of the records of 1969, issued with a flood of hype and forgotten after a dozen playings, this one is for keeps. Many LPs are a lot flashier than this one, but damn few are any better."

"When I did the first solo album, Ronnie Wood and I could have got a band together with Mickey Waller but it couldn't happen," Stewart told Nick Logan. "I am very lazy; I wouldn't like the responsibility of my own group. I am pressurised by the record company to get a band together but I never will."

With the Jeff Beck Group defunct and 'the new Small Faces' still gestating, Kenney and Mac found the odd bit of work playing on sessions including Marsha Hunt's 'Desdemona'. In August, Art Wood used the studio time Philips were offering at Pye Studios and recruited his drinking buddies to cut several tracks. ("Plonk Lane cycled from Clapham to Marble Arch complete with guitar for recording sessions after his car refused to start" reported *Melody Maker*'s 'The Raver' column on August 16). "We delivered the tapes and Philips said they weren't good enough and called a halt to my free studio time," Art told *Record Collector*. "I told them I'd done my bit, and it was up to them if they didn't want the stuff.

"We had this agent, a promoter called Rufus Manning [of Cambridge-based agency Rufus Manning Associates] who took over and went round trying to get us a deal but no one wanted to know at all," Art recalled. "They all thought the music was all right but that it wasn't hit material."

It was a damning indictment that in the age of the super group, Quiet Melon's personnel wasn't enough to guarantee a deal, which speaks volumes of how the British industry viewed the Small Faces and the Jeff Beck Group in 1969. Perhaps because of Rod's involvement Mercury showed an interest and a news item, appearing in *NME* dated September 13, stated: "Art Wood is forming a new group called Quiet Melon, which will make its disc debut on Mercury shortly."

However it was not to be and Art valiantly packed the music business in and moved back to being a graphic designer. It took until 1995 for history to judge Quiet Melon when two tracks, 'Diamond Joe' and 'Engine 4444' were released on a limited edition CD and 12-inch single.* While

---

* Both releases also contained an early attempt at nailing the backing track to 'Diamond Joe', preserved on acetate. Two other tracks Art Wood mentioned in the *Record Collector* interview, 'Right Around The Thumb' and 'Two Steps To Mother' were presumably deemed not good enough to release.

admittedly a demo, it's not difficult to see why record companies weren't buying. Both songs, carrying an intriguing railroad theme, were fairly undistinguished and Wood and Stewart's call-and-response vocals rub uneasily against each other. The true value of this curio was in illuminating how the Faces' easy, laid-back groove fell into place once Lane and Jones locked in with Wood and McLagan and how Stewart's distinctive vocals floated above it all with ease.

By now Rod was a regular fixture at the Bermondsey rehearsals to watch his mates who were gaining in confidence. But there was still an obvious ingredient missing – the vocals. "Woody had been asking me for a long time 'do you want to join, do you want to join'" Stewart told Royston Eldridge, "and I was . . . listening and thinking 'they're getting better and better' which they were."

"When we went back to the Stones' studios to start rehearsing for the road, after we decided to get the band together, Rod used to creep in upstairs and listen with Stu and he'd be very shy about coming down," Wood told Penny Valentine. "I used to say come down because he didn't know what he was going to do. We were just entirely working with the musical side and singing ourselves, which was really a racket. We'd always say, 'Oh, we'll take care of vocals later.'"

"We weren't really worried who was going to sing," Lane told Valentine, "we just wanted to get the band together and worry about that afterwards, and get back on the road – something we really missed in that time . . ."

Ian McLagan: "Rod would hang out in what was basically the control room if [the basement] was ever used as a studio and he was too shy to come down, he didn't want to intrude. I mean we knew he was there and I was happy that he stayed in that room, quite frankly, and so was Ronnie [Lane]. We'd all taken turns at singing and it was going OK. We only had two originals at that point, 'Shake, Shudder, Shiver' and 'Flying' which Ronnie [Lane] was singing and we rehearsed my song, 'Growing Closer' . . . I mean we just did what we could but we needed a singer. Kenney eventually said to Rod, 'Well come and sit in,' and he did. And once he did . . . I mean we were doing what we could on our own. It was just early days but as soon as Rod started singing it was very apparent. Obviously he was good."

Kenney Jones: "Ronnie Lane sang great, he had a nice, touching voice but from where I was sitting, after Steve Marriott, there's a large hole there. Rod used to sit on the amps waiting for us to finish and when we finished we'd go to the pub and cause havoc and whatever. Rod was like a member of the band without actually being one."

Ian McLagan: "Rod knew all of Muddy Waters' *At Newport* and so did Ronnie [Wood] and so did I. Steve Marriott, too, it was a bond that we all had. So when Rod wanted to sit in we'd play 'Feel So Good', 'Got My Mojo Working', 'Hoochie Coochie Man' 'Got My Brand On You', we had six songs we didn't have before. And Rod was great, of course he was great and it meant we could play. Actually the version of 'Feels So Good' [on the Faces *Five Guys Walk Into A Bar . . .* box set], which I recorded on cassette from those days, has Rod playing guitar as well. And Woody plays harp on it."

The Bermondsey rehearsal tapes – obviously rough in quality – capture the band's transition into something more significant than a bunch of mates playing for a lark – although humour was never far from the surface as captured in the banter between takes, another crucial factor in Stewart's acceptance. The cover of Willie Dixon's 'Evil' (written for Howlin' Wolf) has the feel of the Quiet Melon tracks but the telepathy is apparent, while 'Shake, Shudder, Shiver' is pretty much developed, with a familiar, repeated phrase that anticipates the riff in J.J. Cale's 'Cocaine'. Future show closer, 'Feel So Good', as Mac has stated, a common denominator from Muddy's *Live At Newport* album, was down pat with Rod's bawdy vocal, Woody's slide licks and the call and response section.

This band now needed to get out on the road. As if to taunt them, the good time, no frills rock'n'roll of 'Natural Born Bugie', the debut single by Humble Pie sat in the Top 5 in September and an American tour had been arranged for Marriott and co. by Oldham. But what were Lane and co. to do about a singer? The answer was staring them in the face but Stewart had a solo recording deal. Surely he wouldn't be interested in joining a band. Or would he?

"I remember I was at the Spaniard's Inn pub up at Highgate with Kenney just before he was going to rehearsals," Stewart told Nick Logan, "and he said 'Why don't you join the band?' And I said 'All right.' We all drove down to Ronnie Wood's and they put it to the 'board'. Everybody wanted me to join I think, but they didn't want it to happen again like it did with Steve."

Whether Rod was putting a positive spin on events is unclear as his introduction to the group was by no means what "everybody wanted" for the very reason he mentioned.

Kenney Jones: "I didn't tell anyone first that I was going to ask Rod to join the band so when I told the others, Mac and Ronnie Lane hit the roof, they gave me a right bollocking, 'We don't want another Steve Marriott, we don't want another fucking prima donna in the band.'"

With Woody obviously on his best mate's side, it was left to the placid drummer to convince the truculent team of Lane and McLagan.

Kenney Jones: "Ronnie was renting a flat in Gloucester Place Mews from Alvin Lee of Ten Years After at the time so we all went back there and had a meeting up in his bedroom about it."

Sue Tacker: "Rod really wanted to be in the band and was hoping they would invite him. There was one night when they were going to have a meeting to decide but in order to do that they had to get Rod out of the way. So I had to take him out in the car and drive him around and then come back later and try to act like it was all perfectly normal. He probably wasn't fooled for a minute. I'm sure he knew what was going on. Rod was quite nervous. It struck me at that moment he was quite sensitive and insecure in a way, not this extrovert character. So then we came back and they said to his great relief, 'We'd like you to be in the band.'"

It must have been a long drive for Sue as Jones has a memory of sitting up all night, thrashing it out until he'd finally convinced the others.

Ian McLagan: "Ronnie [Lane] and I definitely didn't think it was a good idea because we just had a singer leave us and the last thing we needed was another. Ronnie and I only needed to discuss it once – we didn't need to mention it again. 'Rod? Fuck no, we don't need some bastard coming in, taking over the band and then leaving'. But the thing is when he started singing with us it was so great, we thought 'Sod it.'"

"I've often said this but, to my mind, I felt it was the difference between success and failure," says Jones. "Rod was just what the group needed."

The October 18 edition of *New Musical Express* made it official in a small piece – 'New Lead Singer Joins The Faces' – buried in their news pages. "In an attempt to present a new image, the group is to change its name, but a new title has not yet been set."

"I took the plunge," Rod told *Rolling Stone* a year later. "It was definitely a blind plunge, because I didn't know what I was getting myself into. I was more impressed with them as people – I said, 'What a nice bunch of guys – I'll join that band!' Literally that's what I said, and that's exactly what I did."

Part Two

Flying

CHAPTER 9

First Step

"We had this fabulous brief from Mo Ostin at Warners in America saying 'Just go out there and sign what's happening now in England' and I remember thinking, 'What a fabulous position to be in.' It wasn't a matter of trying to find the biggest names around at that time. It was very personal. We were only really looking for the people we admired as musicians. It would be unthinkable today."

— Martin Wyatt, co-founder of Warners Bros. Records UK division, 2010

"All we can do is let our music speak for itself, and that way find our own audiences. To me, all this supergroup crap is just the same sort of hype as we had with the Mod thing, only people who should know better are taking it too seriously."

— Ronnie Lane, *New Musical Express*, 1970

THE recruitment of Rod Stewart promised much for the Faces. They were all roughly the same age, shared the same musical tastes – their mutual passion for American blues and soul had remained undiminished since 1964 – and crucially, they each betrayed a dry, frequently sarcastic and occasionally cruel brand of humour. But there was still much to iron out in intensive rehearsals. "I had a few doubts about the Faces to begin with," Stewart confessed to *Disc*'s Caroline Boucher in 1971. "Me and Woody used to leave and think, 'Christ, we'd better ring Jeff [Beck], this isn't going to work.' Me and Ron had come from the so-called underground then; the Faces were more pop and it was hard to match the two at first."

While this dichotomy was being reconciled, any attempted rapprochement with Beck would be ill-timed after a tyre blew on the guitarist's 1923 A-Ford hot rod in the early hours of November 2, 1969. He was rushed to the intensive care ward of Royal West Kent Hospital, Maidstone with serious injuries. At one point there were fears Beck might be para-lysed for life. Starting a lengthy convalescence, and with hopes of forming his dream supergroup with Vanilla Fudge's Tim Bogert and Carmine Appice seemingly dashed, Beck expressed surprise when learning that the singer he expected to join them had already moved on. "He [Rod] never came to see me in the hospital even. When I came out of my coma, I picked up *Melody Maker* to find out he'd joined the Faces, thank you very much!"

This comes across as a revisionist snipe because the news of Rod's move had been announced prior to Beck's accident. Still it underlines the incredulity that many in the business felt at Stewart throwing in his lot with a defunct pop group. "When this band started we had a ridiculous barrier to get over," Wood told *Music Now* in 1970. "We couldn't lash out and get things we needed. We had big debts from the old Small Faces and various other things. We started the new band with enthusiasm but all the problems hanging over our heads could have made us give up. We just put our heads down and ploughed through it all."

The task of breaking through these seemingly insurmountable obstacles was taken up by the man destined to become the Faces' manager, a diminutive, sparse haired, cherubic faced gay Irishman named Billy Gaff. Gaff faced his sternest test in getting the former Small Faces out of their existing contracts and bagging a record deal.

Born in County Kildare on June 6, 1942, William Gaff's first brush with the entertainment business came when attending boarding school at Newbridge College, where he was elected president of the dramatic society, and later at Woolwich Polytechnic, studying economics for three years. "I produced three major plays including *Under Milkwood* which I narrated and directed with a full cast which I think was the first time any amateur group had done it with a set and in costume," he recalls. "[Actress and drama tutor] Rose Bruford turned up to see it and said that she wanted me to go for an audition. I spent three days at the Rose Bruford Training College of Speech and Drama in Sidcup, which at the time, next to RADA, was the next best [in Britain] but I was a wreck and had a fit of nerves on the day of the audition."

After his brief dalliance with the footlights, the 20-year-old Gaff was at a loss as to what to do next. "My parents had paid for me to get through school and college but I hadn't made any progress and they were con-cerned. Then I went down to the P&O office and got a job as a steward on board the *Oriana* and I saw the world on a nine-month cruise."

Returning to London in 1964, Gaff looked up the contacts he had made when booking acts as Social Secretary at Woolwich Poly and started working, off and on, for the Robert Stigwood Organisation. While at a friend's house playing poker one night, he met Colin Huntley, who promoted gigs at a pub, Cook's Ferry Inn, in Edmonton, north London. Ironically the very first band Gaff saw playing there were Long John Baldry and his Hoochie Coochie Men featuring Rod Stewart.

"I didn't think much of Rod in those days," Gaff freely admits. "He wasn't really doing much. He just played harmonica and sang a few songs with John who I was more impressed by."

Some time during 1965 Gaff was at Cook's Ferry Inn when he saw the Herd, a group from Beckenham, Kent, whose line-up then comprised Terry Clark (vocals), Gary Taylor (guitar), original Rolling Stones drummer Tony Chapman and Andy Bown (playing bass before switching to keyboards).

Billy Gaff: "They didn't have a manager so I offered to do it even though I knew little about the business. Luckily neither did they. Peter Frampton wasn't in the band then. Peter was a friend of Andy Bown's and I think he was only 16 when he joined. I remember having to go to his father and I said, 'If you don't let your son do it, he'll never know what he might have missed' because Peter said there was no way I'd ever talk his father round but I did . . . The Herd had no record deal at that point [their contract with Parlophone had lapsed] but they were incredibly successful, we used to pack 'em in on the road. I was manager in all areas, literally – I set up the gear, I drove the van, I did everything.

"One night, these guys Alan Howard and Ken Blaikley, who'd had a bit of success with Dave Dee [and previously the Honeycombs], saw the Herd and approached me, saying they'd really like to produce them and all the rest of it. I said, 'OK fine.' And of course, bit by bit, they talked the boys into dumping me. I didn't have a clue, I was heartbroken but I don't think I had any contract with them or if I did it wasn't valid. Of course they went on to have hit records and Peter became a teenybop idol, 'The Face of '68' or whatever."

The Herd regularly performed at the Marquee Club which is where Gaff met a talented young musician named Jimmy Horowitz. Born 1945 in Liverpool, Horowitz was playing organ (under the name Jimmy Horrocks) in a band called the Five Proud Walkers that included Richard Hudson and John Ford on drums and bass respectively (the band evolved into psychedelic act Elmer Gantry's Velvet Opera). Billy Gaff: "Jimmy wanted me to manage them but after what happened with the Herd, I didn't want to get involved just for the sake of managing a group."

Gaff and Horowitz formed a close, mutually beneficial friendship and shared a flat at 79a Warwick Square, near Victoria Station, that Ralph Horton, the co-manager of struggling singer-songwriter David Bowie, had just vacated. Stigwood sent Gaff out over the summer of 1967 road managing for Cream. Gaff also assisted with Stigwood's other acts including the Bee Gees, duo Marbles (featuring Graham Bonnet) and the comedy stable overseen by agent Beryl Vertue (who had joined forces with Stigwood's agency) that included Frankie Howerd and Bill Oddie.

Horowitz continued to look for opportunities as a musical director and joined Long John Baldry's backing band. Since Rod Stewart's departure under cloudy circumstances in March 1966, the now five-piece Steam Packet played their summer season at St Tropez. However Brian Auger had reached the end of his tether with Baldry's unprofessionalism and decided to form a new version of the Trinity with Driscoll, ex-Shotgun Express/Jeff Beck Group bassist Dave Ambrose and drummer Clive Thacker (going on to have a UK number one in 1968 with 'This Wheel's On Fire'). Baldry then signed a deal with Pye and recruited an R&B group from Middlesex called Bluesology, who, through the Roy Tempest Agency, had backed various visiting American soul and R&B artists. The band's pianist was 19-year-old Reginald Dwight, who would later choose the stage name Elton John by combining the first names of Baldry with that of Bluesology's saxophonist, Elton Dean.

Billy Gaff: "I knew John Baldry well by then. He was always hanging around the Marquee with [Marquee club managers] John Gee and Jack Barrie and everyone else as indeed was I . . . I talked John [Baldry] into taking Jimmy Horowitz because Elton had just left Bluesology because he didn't like the middle of the road direction John was going in."

Having spent the best part of four years slogging away without any commercial success Baldry changed tack and moved into cabaret, cashing in on the British record buying public's inclination for ballads by recording Tony Macauley and John Macleod's lachrymose 'Let The Heartaches Begin', which topped the UK charts in November '67. The faithful who were drawn to Baldry's authenticity in interpreting black American music, as well as fellow musicians and friends like Rod Stewart, were suitably aghast, but for Baldry it was a case of paying the rent.

While with Bluesology, Horowitz steadily made a name for himself. "I was producing this record for Decca called 'I Lied To Auntie May' [co-written by Andy Bown and Peter Frampton] by a group called the Neat Change," Gaff explains. "It needed a string arrangement so I asked Jimmy to do it. The record got great reviews so I started managing him, building up his reputation in the business as a songwriter and arranger.

"Jimmy was arranging and composing for Virginia Vee, an American singer living in France, and won two International Song Contests in Poland and Rio de Janeiro with her. He worked with Dusty Springfield, Peggy Lee, Cilla Black, Lulu . . . Burt Bacharach was doing a show in London for Dusty and he used Jimmy as conductor and arranger."

Horowitz's credentials as a pianist and arranger also got him regular session work which is how he encountered RCA A&R man Gary Osborne, who recalls, "I met Jimmy through Stewart A. Brown, the former lead singer of Bluesology. Jimmy did a fantastic arrangement on Stu's version of [Elton John & Bernie Taupin's] 'I Can't Go On Living Without You' that I produced but it was never released, unfortunately. Jimmy said he had this manager who worked for Robert Stigwood and that's how I came to meet Billy Gaff. One night I was down at the Speakeasy with Kenney [Jones] and Billy was there and I said, 'Billy, come and meet my sister's boyfriend.' I introduced him to Kenney, they got talking and then he introduced Billy to the other Faces and it went from there."

Of all the trendy nightclubs that sprang up in central London during the Sixties the Speakeasy was arguably the most popular. From its opening in December 1966 the basement club at 48 Margaret Street, near Oxford Circus, became a late night refuge where groups, managers, producers, agents, roadies, music journalists and assorted hangers-on could dance, drink, eat, pull and chinwag about the latest industry gossip while hip imported records issued forth from the DJ booth or a visiting American band blasted away on the small bandstand. Other clubs, most notably the Revolution in Mayfair, vied for their custom but 'the Speak' held firm as the after hours rendezvous of choice for London's pop elite.

"Kenney told me about the problems the Small Faces had so I offered to look into it for them and be their manager," Gaff recalls. "A couple of nights later at the Speakeasy I met Kenney again and he had with him Mac and Ronnie Wood who I knew from the Birds because of the Stigwood association. We decided there was nothing to lose on either side so once I'd talked to Ronnie Lane I met with the Small Faces lawyer to sort it all out."

"It took Billy Gaff to get us out of the Immediate deal," Ronnie Lane told *Rolling Stone* in 1971. "Nobody else really wanted to know. He just turned up and said to Kenney, 'I'll get you out of it.' Well, 150 others had said the same thing and not done anything about it.[*] So we thought, 'Give

---

[*] According to Ian McLagan in his autobiography *All The Rage* one of these interested parties was the Beatles' and Rolling Stones' then business manager Allen Klein.

him a crack of the whip, why not?' Three days later he had us out and we asked Rod to join."

Gaff confirms that at the time of his introduction, "Rod wasn't in the band yet and everybody reckoned that without Marriott it was a lost cause and they were probably right. Andrew Oldham was kind of on the sidelines because Immediate was going under and I think as a result of that the contract was null and void so they were free. But then it was all Don Arden, he became interested when he found out the Small Faces were getting back together again with Rod Stewart. Arden always thought he had a claim on everybody he'd ever been involved with, even if the paperwork had lapsed but nobody wanted to go there because he wasn't the easiest person to deal with. Arden wasn't too happy, he tried getting them back and he was shouting and ranting but I managed to get the band away from him with great trauma. They were not getting any money from Arden, they certainly weren't getting any money from Immediate, they were stony broke."

Gaff started looking for a record label and thanks to a familiar figure he was guided to the right choice. "Ian Samwell was a good friend of mine through Jimmy Horowitz and Long John Baldry so we all knew each other quite well. He had produced the Small Faces' first hit and I think he was hoping to produce them again. When he found out that I was involved, he said, 'Billy, that's fantastic' and he recommended Warners."

Warner Bros. Records was established in California in 1958 by Jack Warner as an in-house operation of the American movie studio Warner Bros. Pictures. The company had been acquiring song publishing catalogues since the late Twenties to provide a ready-made source of musical content for their films but this profitable enterprise was hit by the double whammy of the Depression and radio broadcasting and was forced into licensing its valuable catalogue – which included George and Ira Gershwin and Jerome Kern copyrights – to outside companies to release on film soundtracks.

By the late Fifties confidence in the record business had returned and Warner Bros. Records was launched in order to re-enter the market, initially aiming at the more discerning album business with a selection of film and television soundtracks, MOR, spoken word and comedy as well as experimenting with embryonic stereo recording. The company ran at a loss until it broke into the pop market with the Everly Brothers, Peter, Paul & Mary and comedians Bob Newhart, Allan Sherman and Bill Cosby.

In 1963 Warners bought Reprise Records, Frank Sinatra's financially adrift label, and along with the artist roster, inherited its president Mo Ostin who was to prove an important and influential figure within the operation. By the late Sixties, having merged with Seven Arts Productions, Warners-Reprise was established as one of the world's largest recording organisations, covering the musical spectrum from Sinatra and Dean Martin to the Grateful Dead and Tiny Tim.

In Britain, Warner-Seven Arts-Reprise had a pressing and distribution deal through Pye but was looking to go independent. In 1969 Ostin entrusted the setting up of the company's British operation to Ian Ralfini and Martin Wyatt, an illustrious music industry double act who, by that time, had worked their way up to running the A&R and publishing side of MGM.

Wyatt entered the music industry in 1958 working for song publisher David Platz and his company Essex Music from their offices at 4 Denmark Street. He first encountered Ralfini while at Pye Records around 1960. "We did about three or four years at Pye," says Wyatt, "and then David [Platz] enticed me to go back to him which was exciting because I took over the Curtom catalogue – Curtis Mayfield, the Impressions and all that stuff." Meanwhile Ralfini was working with Tony Newley who had a hit musical with *Stop The World – I Want To Get Off* and was writing a second show, *The Roar Of The Greasepaint – The Smell Of The Crowd*.

"That didn't last for too long and then Ian and I got together again at a company called Alan Freeman & Associates run by Pye producer Alan A. Freeman," Wyatt continues, "and we took over things like the English end of French Vogue – Petula Clark, Sacha Distel, people like that."

In 1966 the pair moved to Robbins Music. "Robbins was affiliated with MGM so they moved Ian and I into MGM Records in late '68 . . . we had Jethro Tull and bits and pieces. There was the Verve label as well; Ian and I signed Caravan [to Verve] so we had a few things like that which were quite successful."

Ralfini and Wyatt had worked the Reprise catalogue while at Pye. "So we had an association with Mo Ostin going back to the early Sixties," says Wyatt, "and that's why when he was looking to open the Warners office in England Mo came to us which Ian and I were very flattered by. He wanted us to sign acts that hadn't yet made it in America. We inherited Family, they were the first British band signed directly to Reprise. I knew Fleetwood Mac and I knew a couple of the Small Faces, and by coincidence, both bands were on Immediate Records. We were aware that Immediate was on the verge of folding so our initial focus was on those bands."

153

As a matter of convenience the pair also took over Immediate's premises at 67/69 New Oxford Street.

Martin Wyatt: "Andrew Oldham and Tony Calder had started to have the offices refurbished because I remember we had to get builders in to finish the work off. Ian inherited Andrew's office and I got Tony's. Andrew's office was octagonal – typical Oldham, he always had these ridiculously palatial offices – and you had to walk up these marble steps to double doors, open the doors and then walk down, he liked the idea that you had to walk down into his office. It had wood panelling and concealed blinds inside all the windows. And there was like a secret door connecting to next door so Ian and I had adjoining offices to each other."

With the publishing offices of DJM (Dick James Music) at 71–75 New Oxford Street and Mickie Most and Peter Grant's RAK Music Management empire at 155 Oxford Street, a significant chunk of the British music industry was located on a small stretch of road on either side of Tottenham Court Road tube station, a stone's throw from London's Tin Pan Alley in Denmark Street.

In August Ralfini and Wyatt signed Fleetwood Mac to a three-year contract with Reprise, despite reported interest from Apple Records. The band, then at the height of their early success and led by guitarist and songwriter Peter Green, had come out of a brief but disenchanting spell with Immediate (although they achieved a UK number two with Green's haunting 'Man Of The World' while with the label). "Fleetwood Mac's manager Clifford Davis was a good friend," says Wyatt, "and had been working at the Gunnell agency for a long time. I knew the Gunnell set-up very well so it was kind of an obvious move." As an indication of the creative freedom offered by Warners, the terms of the contract allowed the group to bring new artists to the label and handle the production themselves.

"When finding and signing new acts, what Ian and I were supposed to do was share them out [between Warners and Reprise]," Wyatt explains, "so we now needed a band for Warners."

A discrepancy remains in the participants' memories regarding the involvement of Warners A&R executive Joe Smith in negotiations over the Faces; Gaff recalls Ralfini not being interested in signing the band and that it was Smith who was behind the deal, while Wyatt claims that it was down to himself and Ralfini and that Smith did not get involved until the actual terms were being agreed. However, both parties confirm that Ian Samwell was a catalyst in the deal.

Martin Wyatt: "We initially brought Ian Samwell in to Warners to act like a talent scout more than anything. He had his nose to the ground, telling us what was going on out there. Sammy wasn't actually working with us then but he definitely helped to encourage the Faces about Warner Brothers and us."

According to Rod Stewart in a 1971 *Disc & Music Echo* interview, "Warners Records didn't want to sign us up – it was only Ian Samwell saying, 'That band's going to be big one day' that did it. I'm pretty sure nobody else wanted us."

Wyatt agrees on the last point. "I don't recall that we were competing with any other major label for the Faces, I think it was kind of almost fore-gone that we were going to have them. The point is both Ian and I knew Billy Gaff quite well and we had sort of good relations and the fact that we knew a couple of the band as well it just seemed to be very comfortable, it was just a question of getting the deal right."

The one snag, of course, was Stewart's existing contract with Mercury Records. Martin Wyatt: "As far as getting the OK for Rod to sign [with Warners] I think Billy did most of the sorting out. We were aware Rod was with Mercury but the prospect of having the Faces with Rod singing, I mean it was such an exciting project . . . We loved the demos that we heard* and at the time I think we just sort of blanked the idea of Rod being on another label. We knew it was going to be a hassle but I think we were confident that we could sort of blast through that.

"Joe Smith got concerned when he realised Rod had already recorded a solo album and made it quite strong in the contract that Rod would support and play with the Faces and promote the product. I remember that part being quite tough."

Eventually a compromise was reached in the form of a verbal gentle-man's agreement with Mercury granting Rod special dispensation to record with the Faces on Warners in return for honouring the terms of his original deal. The only comparable example of a similar dual artistic situa-tion was Neil Young being allowed to record with Crosby, Stills & Nash for Atlantic Records while being signed to Warners-Reprise in America – although the situation was different – and less problematical – because Young was already within the same overall corporate structure, Warners having bought Atlantic in 1968.

---

* An eight-track Ampex tape recorder had recently been installed in the Stones' Bermondsey rehearsal studio but Mac says, "I certainly don't recall recording there, but we did cut 'Shake Shudder Shiver' and 'Flying' at Olympic with Glyn Johns engineering." Unfortu-nately, no further information has surfaced as to the contents of the demo tape.

Martin Wyatt: "I don't recall the negotiations being that tough. I've got a feeling the Faces' accountant Milton Marks may have been there even though Billy negotiated the deal. He [Marks] always seemed to be around at that time because he was involved with the Fleetwood Mac signing as well. At first he came over to us as being just an ordinary type of accountant but you wouldn't mess with him. He had a history, I think he was involved with boxers and things. He was a tough talking guy."

"I remember Milton Marks saying to me, 'Oh, so you've started a band then, how are you gonna pay for it?'" Kenney Jones told John Gray. "I told him we were gonna get an advance, go out on the road and make records. He said, 'Oh yeah, and what kind of money?' He was real sarcastic. So I came out with a figure of £30,000 and he went 'Ha, telephone numbers!' So when Billy asked me how much advance I thought we should steam in for, I said £30,000. He didn't think he could get that much and I said I didn't want a penny more or a penny less . . . He went off, got 30 grand out of Warner Brothers and I took great delight in showing [Marks]. But he still ended up being the accountant for a while."

According to McLagan, the Faces inked the three-year worldwide deal with Warners on Saturday, November 1, 1969,* which, as he remembers, was "four years to the day after I joined the Small Faces. Funnily enough we signed in the back room of the same office where we signed with Andrew and Tony."

Martin Wyatt: "The actual contract signing, when they all came in, was much more of a fun meeting because by that time they were sold on coming with us."

"When Kenney and I walked into the office," Jan Jones recalls, "the first thing Ian Ralfini said was, 'Hello Jan.' Ian had managed Gary and I when we were with Pye Records as Gary & Jan Lorraine and Martin Wyatt I knew from the Cromwellian days. I think that surprised the rest of the Faces – you know, 'We've signed a big contract with these guys, how do you know them?' I suppose they didn't realise that Gary and I had been around in the business."

Gaff was now officially installed as the Faces' manager, taking only five per cent in an agreement that, remarkably, was bound with just a handshake. "When I offered to manage them I said I'd do it without contracts and that's what I did."

"When the Faces got their record deal, Billy was so pleased," Herd organist Andy Bown recalls. "They had been really skint so they all went

* The October 25 edition of *Melody Maker* reported that the Faces had just signed the deal.

out and bought sports cars. Ronnie Lane bought a Mercedes 190 convertible, Ron Wood had a red Jaguar XK150, Kenney had an MGA and Mac got a green Triumph TR4. We had a sort of celebration dinner and I remember we drove up to the Golden Egg on Oxford Street and parked up as you could do then."

"I was ready to get into it," Lane told Penny Valentine. "I hadn't got disillusioned, though I did have some fears because Rod had his own solo things to honour – just from the point of view of having all the energies contained. But I thought as long as it was good and [we] made good music I didn't really give a shit."

As well as a manager and record deal, the Faces gained their first roadie in Peter Buckland. Born in Hanwell, Middlesex in 1944, Buckland trained as a precision engineer but spent the majority of his leisure time checking out bands on the bustling London club scene, becoming acquainted with Aynsley Dunbar.

"I met him when he was with John Mayall's Bluesbreakers," Pete recalls, "and then Aynsley left them and was with the Jeff Beck Group for a while which is how I first met Rod Stewart and Ron Wood. I had a good job so I could get time off work and when Aynsley formed his own band, the Retaliation, because he couldn't really afford anyone, I'd help out on the road."

Buckland also managed part-time a blues trio from south London called Boilerhouse, featuring 17-year-old guitarist and songwriter Danny Kirwan, who ended up joining Fleetwood Mac.

Pete Buckland: "As I recall, I took Peter Green and Mick Fleetwood down to the Boilerhouse which was a boiler room in the basement of a local church where the band used to rehearse, and introduced them to Danny because I thought Boilerhouse was never really going to go anywhere and I thought Danny needed a bigger canvas if you like. Greeny and Mick were just absolutely blown away by him."

Having dipped his toe in the pool, Buckland became acquainted with some of the other road managers in the business, particularly Bob Pridden, chief roadie for the Who. Thanks to the two bands touring together, Pridden was a good friend of the Small Faces, particularly Ronnie Lane.[*]

Pete Buckland: "It must have been April or so of '69, somewhere

---

[*] Lane was inspired by Pridden's characteristic habit of humming nonsense verse for the "root di doo de doo . . ." chorus of 'Lazy Sunday'.

around then, I got a call from Bob asking me if I'd be interested in working full-time for this new group being put together from the remains of the Small Faces. I said, 'Yeah for sure, let me know when it comes up.' Later on that year, sometime around late October – early November, Bobby said, 'It's together. I've told the boys about you and they want to meet you', so I went round to see them at Billy Gaff's flat in Warwick Square. I was given all sorts of horror stories about how vile the Small Faces were and how difficult they would be to work with but I instantly got on with everyone. I had no problem at all so that was it."

The Faces were about to go into the studio when Buckland was hired. "The initial rehearsals at Bermondsey were more for the album," said Pete, "but because there was a gig in the offing I wanted to do something where we could actually play with a PA so we did some rehearsals at Hanwell Community Centre in west London."

For a band that was to play in some of the world's most celebrated venues in front of capacity audiences, the Faces' first ever gig was less than what might be termed glamorous. Rufus Manning, the promoter who had booked the Quiet Melon university gigs, had an existing booking at a United States Air Force base in Cambridgeshire. "If you've ever seen *Spinal Tap*, the scene where they play the Air Force base, that was the Faces' first gig, exactly the same thing," Buckland recalls, shuddering at the memory 40 years on. "I had the chief guy, the American version of the wing commander or whatever, come up to me and say, 'They're playing a bit loud, aren't they?'"

"There was about 35 people in this enormous gym, sitting around tables and eating sandwiches with their children and their wives in tow," as Lane described it to Penny Valentine. "They didn't know what hit them 10 minutes later. It really was a classic gig. During the set we got steadily more and more pissed, and it ended with Rod waltzing across the stage, tripping over the mike lead and going straight through a double bass."*

In December the Faces started recording their first album at De Lane Lea at 129 Kingsway, opposite Holborn tube station. Although the band insisted on producing themselves, the sessions were overseen by Martin

---

* As with the retelling of so many 'Faces on the road' stories, Billy Gaff's memory tallies with Lane's recollection of the double bass being broken on stage but both McLagan and Buckland distinctly remember Stewart and Wood destroying it in the dressing room when trying to get it to the stage. A picture of the instrument, post Faces' handiwork, can be found on the poster packaged with *A Nod's As Good As A Wink*.

Birch who was engineer-in-chief at the studio; he had been behind the board with Mickie Most for the brief and fractious *Beck-Ola* sessions and had worked with Fleetwood Mac on their *Then Play On* album and 'Oh Well Parts 1 & 2' single over the spring and summer which, possibly on Wyatt's recommendation, is how the Faces came to record at that particular studio.

Initially Ronnie Lane had approached his close friend, Glyn Johns. "After the Small Faces broke up, I was put in an awkward position because I was asked by both Steve and Ronnie to produce their first albums," says Johns. "I felt loyal to both sides and I did not blame one or the other. But because I'd known Peter Frampton for a long time and although I wasn't overly fond of Steve Marriott he was such a great artist, I agreed to produce Humble Pie. I can't really tell you why I chose Steve over Ronnie – it might have been that I thought the Faces really weren't quite together at that point."

First Step* only took around two weeks to complete thanks to the past nine months of solid rehearsal, although Stewart noted to Nick Logan that McLagan and Lane "wanted to do things over and over again".

The album opened with a louche cover of Bob Dylan's 'Wicked Messenger'†, brimming with implied menace. Mac's intro evokes Garth Hudson's heavy organ sound on Band tracks like 'Chest Fever', Woody's slide lines cut to the bone, Stewart contributes a strong, gritty vocal alongside Lane's occasional harmony line while the drums are pushed up front. The track's live feel is emphasised by Rod's offhand "one more" before the final repeated bars and a Jones signature drum roll.

In view of the Dylan songs that Rod interpreted, when enquiring of McLagan whether it was Stewart who suggested the band should cover 'Wicked Messenger', he says, "Possibly but we were all Dylan fans. I remember rehearsing that and playing it a lot at Bermondsey." The song soon became a live favourite although curiously Stewart claimed in a 1970 *Rolling Stone* interview that it wasn't one he liked to sing.

A reduction in voltage, 'Devotion' was a positive reflection in seeking solace through troubled times and Lane perhaps wrote it for Sue who had helped him through his recent personal turbulence. The song's almost gospel-like flavour made it a highlight of the band's early live sets particularly Wood's beautifully understated solo and Stewart and Lane's shared

---

* The original UK pressing of the album listed the title as *The First Step* on the label.
† Recorded by Dylan on his 1967 album *John Wesley Harding,* the song's full title was 'The Wicked Messenger'.

vocals. Ian McLagan: "'Devotion' was all Ronnie Lane's pretty much. We rehearsed that at Bermondsey as well if I remember."

'Shake, Shudder, Shiver', supposedly written by Lane about his freezing cold flat in Elsham Road, was already well-developed from the Bermondsey rehearsals but is fairly unremarkable save for some tasty Wood slide lines that weave in and out of the mix.

The proverbial black sheep of the album, Lane's 'Stone' was certainly the most uncharacteristic track the Faces would ever lay down. Based on Meher Baba's theory of creation – a chart he drew known as the Circle of Evolution – which Ronnie set to words and music, the philosophical message is offset by the hillbilly arrangement, featuring Rod on banjo and Woody on harmonica and Stewart's vocal exhortations, but then knowing Lane that was precisely the whole point. More successful was Lane's simpler re-recording of the track (with fellow devotee Pete Townshend on acoustic) for the limited edition album *Happy Birthday*, released in February 1970 marking what would have been Baba's 75th birthday, which was also released on Townshend's 1972 solo album *Who Came First*.

"I was never a fan of 'Stone'" Mac admits. "It just went on and on and on. But you know Ronnie was never daunted by what anybody thought of his songs."

'Plynth (Water Down The Drain)' was resurrected from *Beck-Ola* as 'Around The Plynth' – this time a Wood bottleneck tour de force although at nearly six minutes there was a feeling of filler. Wood's playing inhabits a similar mood to Jimmy Page's work on 'Hats Off To Roy Harper' (released on *Led Zeppelin III* around the same time). The frantic slide runs in the solo bounce from channel to channel before coming to an exhausted halt at Stewart's "Slow down" command with a phrase from the Rolling Stones' 'No Expectations'.

Whereas the *Beck-Ola* arrangement of 'Plynth' was controlled to an extent by Tony Newman's tight, funky backbeat, 'Around The Plynth' belonged firmly in the Mississippi Delta with Stewart's ghostly wails and vocal improvisations, McLagan's sparse piano fills and Jones' cymbal crashes.

As well as the great blues bottleneck players like Robert Johnson and Elmore James, and rock names like Duane Allman and, yes, Jeff Beck, Wood's slide playing was influenced by Ry Cooder who had taught Keith Richards the rudiments of open tuning. Cooder had also played on Captain Beefheart's magnificent *Safe As Milk* and one could speculate whether Wood had heard the Magic Band's more unearthly slide noises but then again, Beefheart was probably too outré for Wood's tastes.

The hypnotic, rippling picked guitar phrase of 'Flying' opens the second side. It was another of Stewart's "imagination" songs, continuing a familiar lyrical theme of yearning to be home following the character's five-year spell in the county jail "hungry, tired and poor".

Fitting in with the slower swagger of 'Wicked Messenger' and 'Shake Shudder Shiver', 'Flying' features some effective soaring harmonies from Lane, Wood and Stewart and despite a marked lack of a distinctive melody, it went on to figure prominently in the Faces' early live sets.

'Pineapple And The Monkey' was the first of two instrumentals on the album and the first in a line that the band would usually reserve for B-sides. "'Pineapple And The Monkey' was Ronnie Wood's and we worked on it out at his place in Henley over a period of days," said McLagan. "It's very organ heavy, very Booker T." Indeed the track swings in a most Booker T.-like fashion with Woody's crisp Steve Cropper style licks, wonderfully soaring Hammond swirls from McLagan and laid-back Al Jackson/Duck Dunn rhythm from Jones and Lane. Out of all their attempts 'Pineapple And The Monkey' came closest to realising the Faces 'British Booker T. & The MGs' fixation.

The tranquil 'Nobody Knows', another song emanating from Lane's Baba immersion, contains some simple yet affecting philosophical sentiments similar to the "*nothing is everything*" line Pete Townshend later used for the Who's 'Let's See Action'. Its contradictions give pause for thought yet remain oblique but such is the nature of spiritual texts from Indian mystics.

With a writing credit of Jones/McLagan, 'Looking Out The Window' – another instrumental in the style of Booker T. – comes off less memorably than 'Pineapple . . .' and smacks of a publishing reaping exercise.

The first bona fide 'Faces classic', 'Three Button Hand Me Down', rounds off proceedings. A close relation to 'An Old Raincoat Won't Ever Let You Down' from Rod's solo album, it was clearly based on the Soul Brothers Six's 'Some Kind Of Wonderful', a *Billboard* Top 100 entry in 1967 written by John Ellison which had been covered by the Jeff Beck Group (and later Grand Funk Railroad). The deep resonating bass sound is its notable feature. According to Mac, "On 'Three Button . . .' there's two basses, both Ron and Ronnie are playing bass on that."

Of all the songs on *First Step* 'Three Button . . .' best summed up the Faces light-hearted, devil-may-care approach with Stewart's witty verses about certain women – "a filly from Boston, a barmaid from Houston, not forgetting the one in Detroit" – coming between him and his hand-me-down suit, wrapped around an archetypal, arms-round-shoulders, bawl along chorus.

Overall *First Step* was, as its title suggests, a tentative exercise. "We had nothing to do for months but rehearse and rehearse which is one of the reasons why the first album had a sterile feel to it," Lane told *Rolling Stone*. If anything it illustrated how the rhythm section's style of playing had altered since the Small Faces, and that they were still exploring their capabilities. Production wise, the rather eccentric panning on the vocals and instruments occasionally jars but then, the album was a product of the early Seventies when rock connoisseurs considered headphones a must for the listening experience.

"I wasn't over pleased with *First Step*," Stewart told Penny Valentine. "I don't think any of us were. It didn't come together the way we wanted it to; it ended up sounding like tracks that had been cut over a four-year period and put together on an album."

In a more revealing interview with Royston Eldridge in 1970, Stewart intimated at the hierarchal set-up within the Faces. "It wasn't a good album. There were a couple of good tracks on it. . . . me and Woody didn't like to sort of say what we thought much because we were the new lads and they didn't want to try and tell us . . ."

The cover picture was taken at Willoughby House, Mike and Kate McInnerney's residence. "I don't remember bringing the Mickey Mouse props along with us," says Mac. "I get a feeling the doll must have been at Mike and Kate's house although Ronnie Lane is wearing a Mickey Mouse T-shirt so maybe they were his. Ronnie [Wood] brought the *First Step* guitar songbook with him."

Mike McInnerney: "I suppose Willoughby House was a place to gather – all the lads had been over at one time or another. Martin Cook, a photographer who was another local Baba follower, took the picture. The inside black and white photograph was taken in the garden."

"We're all supposed to be playing our instruments," Mac explains, "except Ronnie Lane had his hands in his pockets, he's actually pulling his hands out of his pockets, he didn't get what we were meant to be doing.

"We ended up getting extremely drunk while the pictures were being taken. Kate made this bowl of punch but what she didn't tell us was that she'd put some wood alcohol into it. I remember we all ended up jumping up and down on this low table and smashing it into splinters."

The memorable afternoon provided Mike with an opportunity to observe how the band interacted. "It was a great marriage between the individuals. Rod was a lovely bloke but at the same time I noticed he was always lurking off to one side. He had ways of building walls around himself and Woody with his jokes – a kind of defence mechanism, I suppose."

Not that anyone was looking for any hidden significance at the time – in an era when album covers were habitually scanned for clues – but hindsight reveals that, squeezed on to the McInnerneys' cramped sofa, Rod sits uncomfortably removed from the others.

CHAPTER 10

America

"We realised the potential because Rod and I had done so much work in the States and we were thinking, 'This'll go down well in the States and this won't' . . . Because at the time we had nothing to live up to in England, there was nothing going for us here."

– Ron Wood, *Sounds*, 1971

"It seemed to me that the Faces started out with a certain amount of energy and it never really left. It wasn't a band that sort of built up, it was there from the beginning and just more people eventually found out about it."

– Charlie Daniels, interview with author, 2010

As the Seventies dawned the music industry no longer resembled the naïve, developing animal of a decade previous. The Beatles had broken up, Bob Dylan was in hiding, and the Rolling Stones were revitalised by touring America for the first time in three years. However it was a different America they returned to, a country divided by race riots and violent protest over the ongoing Vietnam War. The feeling of hope and optimism that had characterised the mid-Sixties was symbolically snuffed out by events like the Manson murders and the Altamont Festival. Although the latter fiasco was designed as a non-profit event, mainly to counteract accusations of the Stones' shameless profiteering, its organisation epitomised the thinking of the next generation – greed over consideration for the audience. Many lost souls from the so-called 'Woodstock Generation' would find themselves estranged during the 'me' decade as the Seventies came to be known, summed up by Steve Winwood in Blind Faith's memorable line, "I'm wasted and I can't find my way home."

After the high profile Monterey and Woodstock festivals the business was dramatically transformed from inside, with previously archaic modes of operation replaced by forward thinking and an understanding of rock music's market potential. No longer would artists be at the mercy of the usual foibles that had characterised record companies. A&R men, previously the image of respectability in suit and tie, were increasingly mistaken for the musicians on their rosters, with long hair, loud shirts, dropping the word "man" into every sentence. Largesse was extended from the drinks cabinet in the company boardroom to flying a plane load of journalists from London to New York to behold the debut of their latest signing – as happened at New York's Fillmore East in April 1970 to the unfortunate Brinsley Schwartz, who were branded a cheap hype as a result.

Art and profit made uneasy bedfellows. Despite the anti-corporate image they promoted, many of the left-field singer-songwriters who valued artistic validity over commercial reward had a ruthless negotiator behind them, not least Neil Young and Joni Mitchell who were managed by Elliot Roberts and budding business supremo David Geffen. With the advent of the rock festival, elaborate sound systems and FM radio, the potential to sell tickets and 'shift units' increasingly became the motivating force of the rock industry throughout the Seventies.

Putting cart before horse, the Faces game plan was to crack the States first before concentrating on Britain. "Of course we wanted to go to America, didn't everybody?" says Billy Gaff.

Early in the New Year, Gaff, Rod and his girlfriend Sarah Troupe flew to New York on a modest publicity junket for Stewart's first solo album and to pave the way for the release of *First Step*. "I think I only had $100 in my pocket when we went over on that promotional visit," says Gaff. "While we were in New York I got to meet Jeff Franklin at American Talent International who became the Faces' American agents and they set up the band's first American tour which was due to begin in late March."*

While Rod was familiar with the Big Apple, it was Sarah's first trip across the Atlantic and she was naturally excited. However she hadn't counted on Rod's macho ways as Sandy Sarjeant recalls, "Sarah told me she sat in a hotel room on her own for most of the time she was there, poor girl, because Rod couldn't let people see that he had a girlfriend. It was that whole rock star thing."

After Rod packed his devoted but deflated partner back to London, he and Billy went on to Philadelphia and Chicago. "It was snowing there and absolutely freezing," says Gaff. "We were going to radio stations. It was a real eye opener. In Boston Rod and I went to the Boston Tea Party to

* In England, the group were logically placed through Gaff with the Robert Stigwood Organisation.

165

appear on WBCN and it was one guy in a back room full of electronic equipment, broadcasting with two turntables and a microphone in the middle and we had to sit on a beer crate I think, to give the interview. I couldn't believe it. We were used to the BBC. Of course you listened back to it and it sounded so fucking professional.

"When we got to California Joe Smith at Warners did everything he could possibly do for us. To be honest with you Mercury Records were so cheap and shabby on that trip but when we got to Los Angeles it was a totally different ballgame. I remember Rod saying, 'What am I doing on Mercury, why aren't I with Warners?'"

In San Francisco Rod was interviewed for a *Rolling Stone* article during which he mentioned some of the songs he intended to cover on his next album and stoked up expectations for the Faces. "It's going to be an interesting combination, me working with the Small Faces. Everybody knows what they've done, like 'Itchycoo Park' but that's all they remember them for. So they were always considered a teenybopper group; they've had Top 10 records, but always kept their respect. The Stones have always had Top 10 records, too.

"Ronnie Lane writes beautiful songs for the Small Faces; most of the commercial junk was the Steve Marriott influence . . . They're marvellous guys and it's a relaxed group to be in. It's going to be great, you'll see."

The unnecessary dig at Marriott was the first of several Stewart directed at his predecessor via the pages of the music press as the Faces were getting off the ground. Although Marriott was far from the shrinking violet type, surprisingly he appears not to have risen to Stewart's jibes in print. However when interviewed by John Hellier in 1999, Marriott's first wife Jenny revealed he had his own way of bringing Stewart down to size. "Steve always said [to Rod], 'You had my band but I had your woman.'"

Thanks to memories of the Beck Group and the album's quality, sales of *The Rod Stewart Album* shifted up a gear. "It ended up doing nearly 100,000 sales just in America," Gaff says, "which for a first outing was quite a good figure. That was a lot of albums. You either sell nothing or you shift 100,000. If you do 100,000 you've definitely got some interest."

Back in England, on January 9, Lee McLagan was born at St George's Hospital on Hyde Park Corner. After witnessing the birth of his son and heir, Mac slipped away and spent the rest of the night at Ron and Krissie's latest flat on Lower Sloane Street, wetting the baby's head many times over with champagne, cannabis and cocaine, the new rock biz drug of choice and one that was to attain an insidious hold on the Faces' circle.

During these early months, the band cautiously tested the waters via several low-key university dates and a Swiss and Scandinavian tour. "The first couple of gigs were a bit rough," Stewart told Chris Welch, "but you can't expect anything else really. Led Zeppelin on their first gigs were bad. We just need a bit of time."

"When we first joined up the idea really was to be into nice taste things – Gladys Knight & The Pips – we were all into the same records – but it certainly got more rock'n'roll much more than we initially expected it to," Lane told Penny Valentine.

From the outset the Faces were a band that valued excitement, spontaneity, communality and glamour – attributes sorely lacking among the heads down, technically disciplined, turgid approach of the British progressive rock scene that sprang up after the first creative flush of psychedelia. Whereas the Small Faces had once played to ballrooms of hysterical girls they were now confronted with passive audiences sitting on the floor, attuned to precise musicianship, self-indulgent solos and superfluous light shows.

"We are out to enjoy ourselves, but a lot of groups and audiences take themselves far too seriously," Lane complained to Welch. "Everybody is trying to be so cool. Even the students are duds sometimes – 'Oh yeah. Entertain us.'" The situation was exacerbated from sometimes being billed as the Small Faces. "The band is nothing like the old Faces," Jones told Welch. "Only the name is the same. The music is completely different. Some of us wanted to change the name completely so we all agreed to keep it as the Faces without the Small bit."

With Marriott long gone and the addition of the considerably taller Stewart and Wood, the name was obviously outdated but as Gaff explains, "When I signed the Faces to the Warners deal, Joe Smith insisted on keeping them as Small Faces in America because although the band weren't hugely well known, the name was recognised. We reluctantly agreed because we needed some money up front when we signed the deal and they wouldn't give us as much if we changed the name but gradually the 'Small' prefix was dropped."

The confusion over the name wasn't the only thing to cause headaches as Martin Wyatt recalls, "When the band came in with the picture for the sleeve, I remember we all sat down and discussed it. I didn't give the Mickey Mouse thing a second thought, I just thought it was a good, fun picture, you know? Then after the album came out in America Disney came down on us like a ton of bricks saying, 'Who gave you permission to put Mickey Mouse on the cover?'"

In Britain, *First Step* was released in March, preceded by a single 'Flying' b/w 'Three Button Hand Me Down'. Chris Welch was effusive in his *Melody Maker* appraisal. "Kenney Jones' drumming is a relentless driving force behind Rod Stewart's shouting vocals. And the guitar, organ and bass convey a mood of menace mingled with despair. Smiling faces will be back in the chart soon." Welch's optimistic forecast was to be wide of the mark. Despite appearances on *Top Of The Pops* and *Disco 2*, the 'serious' late Saturday night rock prototype for the more familiar *Old Grey Whistle Test*, the single failed to chart – either side was admittedly overlong for the conventional BBC Radio 1 playlist – and the album was largely ignored. But then – paradoxically – commercial acceptance was the very thing the band were keen to avoid. As Jones told *Music Now*, "I had four years of doing commercial records, *Top Of The Pops* and all that other crap. Now I am enjoying some freedom. We are all much happier now than we have ever been before."

The Faces' official London debut came on March 1 at the Lyceum Ballroom with the support bill including two names from Rod's past, Brian Auger with his new band and Silver Metre, formed in San Francisco by Mickey Waller and Leigh Stephens that might have included Ron Wood if events had taken a different turn. Among the sparse Sunday night attendees was a recuperating and no doubt curious Jeff Beck. "[The Lyceum gig] didn't bring us down because we knew we were in the early stages and the band weren't that together although it went down very well," Wood told Penny Valentine. "And if there were any really bad goofs the band was always capable of turning round and going, 'Arggh what a *horrible* mistake' while we were actually playing and laughing it off rather than getting screwed up." Talk about starting as you mean to continue.

Bob Dawbarn was impressed enough to offer encouraging words in *Melody Maker*: "The new revitalised Faces are even better than the older and smaller variety. That is the glad tidings I bring from their performance at London's Lyceum. The group sounds heavier and tighter than of old and much of the credit must go to guitarist Ronnie Wood. Rod Stewart not only sounds just right as the new singer but is one of the best pop showmen. In fact the whole group has lost none of its stage presence and looming talent while adding a wider musical dimension."

Of the four British music weeklies operating at the time, *Melody Maker* – and in particular Chris Welch – was the most supportive of the band during its formative stages. "I don't know whether I was the first journalist to write about the Faces," says Welch today, "but when they got together, expectations were high. It had to be good. Certainly I was expecting it to be great. They'd all been through the mill with the Small Faces and Rod had been battling away to rise up out of the Steam Packet era . . . the Faces was kind of a lifeline for him. I went to one of their first rehearsals and they looked to me as though they were really looking forward to starting afresh. I think the others were more nervously excited whereas Rod and Ronnie Wood never seemed to take things too seriously."

If Stewart and Wood weren't taking things seriously their women certainly were. "When the Faces got together, it soon became very clear that it wasn't just the boys, the girls were going to have their say as well," says Sandy, who would be left to look after two month old Lee by herself. "I remember being up in Hampstead and Ronnie having to tell Krissie that the band were going off on their first American tour and she had a real tantrum, throwing abuse at Ronnie because he swore he wouldn't go anywhere without her because before he'd gone off on these long tours with Jeff Beck and left her behind. So she was shouting and screaming at him, saying he couldn't go and us girls had never seen anything like it. The only way he got round Krissie was by buying her a fox fur coat."

"We are looking forward to playing, touring and especially going to America," Ronnie Lane told *NME*'s Gordon Coxhill. "That's where it's got to be for us, unless we make it big in the States, I don't think we'll call ourselves a success . . . We are looking on this group as a long-term prospect and I can't see any splits for quite a while. I don't go along with all this fluidity in groups, it just doesn't rub with me. That happens when you get stars in groups believing their own publicity, something we were guilty of in the old days.

"It won't happen with us because nobody emerges any stronger than the rest. We all have something to offer, and although it might be easier to sell the group on one name and one face, we aren't doing it that way."

On the same page as Lane's comments was an interview with Free, a band whose simple earthy bluesy sound appealed to the Faces, particularly Rod. "We just want to be a good group," drummer Simon Kirke told Jan Nesbit. "People are getting tired of supergroups who just come together for a few weeks. They're just myth groups you read about them but never get to see [them] . . . The Americans like their music more blatant, they want a good rave about." Both bands could have been speaking on behalf of the other.

The Faces were determined to go over in America without hype, refusing to hire a publicist, preferring to, using a well-worn phrase, "come in through the back door" as so many other British acts had done. They were also wary, if not quietly enjoying some degree of schadenfraude at what had happened to Humble Pie on their first American tour in late 1969. Having slogged hard for no reward the unprepared band returned to England just as their manager Andrew Oldham and Immediate Records went into voluntary liquidation.*

For the three ex–Small Faces, the prospect of finally getting to play in America was mind blowing. When returning from Australia in February 1968, their flight had been forced to divert to San Francisco, requiring an overnight stay in transit. "I was worried that because of my drug conviction they would put me in a holding cell for the night but they didn't even check our passports," says Mac. "As soon as I got to my hotel room, I turned the radio on and flicked through all the different stations. In Britain there were only three TV channels that shut down before midnight but here there were so many and they ran all night. I was just knocked out by it all. Ronnie, Kenney and I couldn't wait to get back there."

The Faces put in a rigorous series of rehearsals at the Stones' warehouse in Bermondsey in preparation for the tour, interspersed with frequent excursions to the local a few staggered steps away.

"We called it Going To The Pub," says Mac, "The landlord at the King's Arms loved it when we walked in because we drank spirits like brandy and ginger or vodka and tonic which were more expensive than pints. Woody once heard him tell the locals in the public bar next door, 'They're nice boys, all shorts!' We noticed how Rod would always get there first and open the door for us so he was the last one to the bar. It was always time to start rehearsing again when it got to his round!"

On top of this Rod maintained a hectic schedule by completing his second solo album, *Gasoline Alley*. "The whole album was written, conceived and recorded in two weeks, just before we left for the first Faces tour of the States," Stewart told Nick Logan. "I finished mixing it at two o'clock on a Tuesday morning and was off to America at eight the next day."

On March 24, 1970, the Faces, accompanied only by Billy Gaff, Pete Buckland and Buckland's hired help, Terry Smith, flew to New York and on to Toronto to start their first American and Canadian trek at the Varsity Arena supporting Detroit rebel politico rockers MC5 and boogie merchants Canned Heat. Over the course of the tour the group opened for blues 'n'

---

* A detailed account of the Immediate Records creditors' meeting held in London, published in *Rolling Stone* (issue dated April 16, 1970) makes for frequently amusing if poignant reading considering how the company had formed with worthwhile intentions.

boogie acts like Savoy Brown and Johnny Winter and often found they were blowing the competition off stage. "We just went on and played rock'n'roll and relaxed," Lane told Penny Valentine, "because as an opening act you've got nobody chewing your heels and nobody to follow."

When the Warner Bros. advance came through the band invested in new equipment, including a Hammond B3 organ and two Leslie cabinets (costing just under £2,000 in total) and a Hohner Pianet for Mac, but a meagre tour budget required compromising.

Pete Buckland: "On that first American trip we brought over Kenney's drums, a 100 watt Hi-Watt amp and two 4x12 cabinets for Woody, a 200 watt Hi-Watt and two WEM bass cabinets for Ronnie Lane. For Mac, I think at first we had one 100 watt Hi-Watt stack for the keyboard. We also took a small PA and a couple of odd cabinets we used for monitors. This was to cover us for the small venues that didn't have PAs."

The tour concentrated on the East, the mid-West, the Pacific Northwest, the West Coast, and then further dates back East, all interspersed with smaller shows in states like Virginia and Maryland.*

Billy Gaff: "It was a gruelling schedule but we were young and had an awful lot of energy. America was such a different ballgame to everywhere else, everything was so fucking organised, everybody wanted to get on with stuff. The record companies were brilliant, the promotions side were absolutely incredible, the agency. There was so much to do that trying to keep up with it all was the problem. There were radio stations, interviews, they never left a stone unturned and it was so exciting, completely different to England."

"We had strict ideas about the States," Wood outlined to *Music Now*. "We had a direct approach – we knew how to go in. We organised the first tour so that the places of most importance – the gigs that had to be really good – came at just the right time . . . If we had gone straight into the Fillmore East and given a dud show it would have had a bad effect on the band, it could have smashed the confidence."

The tour risked getting off to a bad start regardless thanks to the unpredictability of air transport. As Gaff recalled, "We were at Toronto and we were due in Boston that night. But we couldn't get there because of an air strike. The only flight we could get was going to New York so I said, 'Let's get to New York because there's no way we'll be able to make the gig at Boston.' So we got on this Eastern Airlines flight and can you

---

* The full schedule for this tour – and indeed all Faces tours – can be found in the book's Concert Appendix.

171

believe it, the fucking flight was diverted to Boston because of fog. I thought, 'It's our lucky night.' We needed the money if nothing else because the budget was so tight."

Ian McLagan: "We hadn't realised Boston in March was going to be so cold. I had a thin leather jacket on and Ronnie and Kenney only had these little coats but Rod and Ronnie Wood had overcoats so they knew. When we got to the Boston Tea Party the doors were locked and there are photographs of us out in the cold shivering. We eventually got in and during the soundcheck I discovered that my B3 had a double transformer so it was transformed into English voltage but they couldn't adjust it, it needed a cycle changer and a transformer. It wasn't quite in tune so if Ronnie was playing in E, I was playing almost in F. It sounded horrible so every song I was like learning for the first time. All these strange keys – if it was in G, I'd be playing in A flat.

"I went out and bought this other keyboard which was horrible but eventually the organ got fixed for the second night. I still use the same B3 on the road today and I've asked several people if I can just get rid of the other transformer and they say no, it's built that way, you can't change it."*

The Boston Tea Party was the city's prime underground rock club, originally a synagogue and art film theatre before opening as a live music venue at its original East Berkeley Street site in 1967. By the time the Faces came through it had shifted to an old warehouse on Lansdowne Street. Promoting the shows there was Don Law, now a major player behind Live Nation, America's biggest concert promoter. Over three nights the Faces opened for Lee Michaels and Frosty, an organ and drum duo from Los Angeles. With the Tea Party holding only about 1,500 people the venue provided an intimate setting for band and audience.

Ian McLagan: "The announcer there was Charlie Daniels, the 'Master Blaster' from Alabama, this tall, slim black dude who wore a bandanna around his head. Rod and Woody knew Charlie from when they'd played the Tea Party with Beck. He looked very cool and he became a really good friend to us. The audiences in Boston were great, especially the women."

As so many other British bands found, having long hair, playing in a

---

* Pete Buckland's memory differs from McLagan's. "We didn't bring Mac's B3 and Leslies over as at that time multi voltage/cycle B3s and Leslies weren't available in Britain. Initially we had a B3 and two Leslies provided at each gig. I eventually rented the equipment from a company in Boston and we took it around with us. We bought two Hohner Pianets in the States as they constantly needed tuning and were quite fragile. Also after trying out both Rhodes and Wurlitzers we went with a Wurlitzer."

rock'n'roll band and talking with an English accent were the ultimate aphrodisiacs for the young American women, newly dubbed 'groupies', who followed bands around or lay in wait when they came to town. Despite recently becoming a father, McLagan didn't hesitate in diving into the carnal pool along with the others. "American girls were lovely and willing, they were much more upfront about sex than English girls," he says. "It's only years later you realise there were so many women around because a lot of the guys were off in Vietnam. AIDS hadn't been invented and the menfolk were away and we were there looking pretty snazzy."

While AIDS was not yet a serious curse, less deadly social diseases were widespread and certain band members caught STDs, removing any doubts as to their infidelity. "They brought things back with them," Sandy Sarjeant confirms with a weary sigh. "Mac came back all excited about Thousand Island dressing, which you couldn't get in England at the time, as if catching a dose of the clap was no big deal."

Whereas Stewart and Wood were recognised from the Beck band, Kenney, Mac and Ronnie Lane were virtual unknowns. It was advantageous for the three ex-Small Faces because unlike in Britain they didn't have an image to overcome, the audiences took them for what they were.

"The first few gigs were naturally a bit shaky but after that, well, they couldn't have been better," Stewart told Penny Valentine. "I'm sure everyone says that when they do America but the band became tighter as we went along and American audiences really do have this power to make you or break you."

This was certainly true of the punters in Detroit who, as at New York's Fillmore East, were among the most critical and discerning about what they liked or more pertinently didn't like. "When we got to the Eastown Theater, that was pretty amazing," recalls Mac. "We didn't realise it was going to be so good. We opened for Savoy Brown for two nights but once we had the crowd, we won them over."

The tour's only serious hitch came when the band crossed the border back to Canada from Detroit to play a club in Toronto on April 5. Ian McLagan: "That's the only Faces gig I didn't play. We were at customs and when they found out I had a drug conviction they took me into a room, strip search, bend over, finger up the bum and everything. 'Thank you Mr McLagan, you can put your clothes on now,' and they escorted me on to New York where the next gig was."

The Toronto gig proved something of a damp squib as most potential fans elected to attend the opening of *Woodstock* the same night. While he waited for the others to arrive to play two nights at Ungano's, a hip club on West 70th Street, Mac had a chance to take in the city. "New York was happening. The first time I got there I took tons and tons of photos of the streets and the bums and the hookers and the people. I was so fascinated."

While staying in New York the band bumped into other English groups on the road like Pink Floyd and Led Zeppelin with whom the Faces spent a riotous evening and, as Mac told Chris Welch in a transatlantic phone call, they found an English pub that sold Watney's Red Barrel but at an exorbitant ten shillings a pint.

Another city, another party, but a fortnight in and the band were feeling bored and homesick. "Mac had called me and he was crying, he was really homesick," says Sandy. "He really missed me and the baby and asked would I phone him that evening British time to wake him because he would love to wake up to the sound of my voice. Of course I was chuffed to bits 'cause here I was stuck in a cold-water flat with the baby and he was there in America. So I phoned but they put me through to the wrong room and there was a hell of a party going on. Some girl answered and I said, 'Can I talk to Mac, please?' and she said, 'Who's calling?' and I said, 'His wife' and she put the phone down on me. Well, I was devastated. Of course the wives and girlfriends knew about what went on when the guys were on the road, we weren't that naive but we didn't want our noses rubbed in it.

"Mac told me about this one girl that he'd been with who wouldn't leave him alone. These girls were expected to leave pretty quickly after but this one didn't. He didn't know what to do to get rid of her so he said he was going out to do some shopping, thinking that she would get the hint but she didn't. I think she expected that 'OK, while you're on tour, I'm your girl.' He told her 'I'm married' and showed her photographs of Lee but she wouldn't go. While they were in a big department store, this girl stole a bottle of perfume and got caught while Mac was with her. He had no idea what she'd done and he was shitting himself because he thought he was going to get arrested and deported in the middle of the tour."

After playing Philadelphia's legendary Electric Factory the band reached Chicago where Kenney visited the Ludwig drum factory to invest in a new kit. "When we had that year off the road after Steve split, I did a lot of sessions and that affected me badly, believe it or not," Jones told *Record Mirror*. "When we got back on the road I had forgotten how to be a rock drummer and I had to re-learn it all. I was being so careful in my playing at first that I couldn't get into giving the skins a good thump."

That evening Mac went on a vain mission to visit Silvio's blues club on

Chicago's edgy West Side. "One driver said he would take me there," Mac relayed to Welch, "although he didn't think it would be safe – then he promptly vanished!"

Mac enthused about the following the Small Faces had in America. "In England we don't expect it and yet in the States a lot of people remember our old records, although the Small Faces never toured here. It's really heart-warming." Surprisingly there were no audience shouts for 'Itchycoo Park' on the tour or if there were the band ignored them. Mac signed off with, "We have enjoyed playing here. It took me a little while to get into it but in the last few days we have been working regularly and that gets us all going. And the audiences have been standing up, screaming and making silly noises."

While in America Warners issued *First Step* which hovered around but failed to break into the *Billboard* Top 100 albums. An edited 'Around The Plynth', an odd choice by the record company for a single did exactly what the song described; it wasted away. *First Step* received a tepid review from Joel Selvin in *Rolling Stone*: "The basic weakness with the album is that although the music is original, it is also highly derivative. The final effect leaves one considerably less excited than the [band] line-up promises . . ." Ironically in view of the sloppy reputation the band were to cultivate, Selvin considered, "The Small Faces play with more control than soul. They know exactly what they are doing and do it well, as good musicians should but . . . they lack the drive and power to make their music without subtleties."

The band played two nights at the Action House on Long Island before a mid-tour break that was spent in Wilton, Connecticut where close friend Billy Nicholls was house sitting for Andrew Oldham. After the collapse of Immediate and having received a British tax demand for around half a million pounds Oldham and family decamped to America to the large house that he'd bought from friend and business associate Bob Crewe. However the stir crazy Oldham felt like a caged animal among the tranquillity of Wilton and left his "monastery" under the care of Nicholls, who felt disillusioned after the collapse of the artistic utopia Immediate had promised.

"Andrew asked if I'd look after the place because I had nothing else happening at that time," Billy recalls. "He said that there was a Hammond organ and a piano in the house to write on so I went over and stayed for about six months on my own – maybe Andrew visited a few times. One night I got a call from Mac or Ronnie [Lane] and they said that they were going to be touring America quite soon and could they come and stay as they had a week off. So I said, 'Yeah, provided you don't bring any women with you,' because, as I told them, 'If you bring women down to this house, I'll catch it when I get back to England because I know all your wives and girlfriends.' Funnily enough, Steve Marriott's wife Jenny visited during the week the Faces stayed. I don't know why but she was happily married then so that was OK.

"I'll never forget their visit coincided with Paul McCartney's [first solo] album *McCartney* coming out. The band got some gear out, set it up in the garage, rehearsed the song and that's when they started doing 'Maybe I'm Amazed' on tour."

McLagan recalls hearing the song for the first time on the drive out to the house. "It was a very, very hot Sunday and Ronnie Lane and I were driving from New York out to Connecticut. Ronnie heard 'Maybe I'm Amazed' on the car radio and I said to him, 'That's the sort of stuff Paul McCartney should record,' and at the end the DJ announced, 'That was Paul McCartney,' so we were primed. We said to Billy we've got to get that record."

The band kicked back at the old, oak-beamed house, surrounded by woods and lakes, ordering copious supplies of food and booze from the local convenience store on Oldham's account. "I remember calling Sandy and spending an hour on the phone because it was Andrew's phone," says Mac. "'Fuck him' was our attitude."

Nicholls errs on the side of caution as to whether Immediate artist royalties paid for the house but he openly states it was haunted. "One night, while I was asleep, this small, black, bald headed creature was standing by my bed. It placed something in my ear like a small bellows, which made a whooshing sound and paralysed me. It kept on doing it until I said the name 'Meher Baba' and then it stopped. A real wake up call, you might say. I think after the first night the band stayed, I came down to the kitchen for breakfast and Ronnie Lane was sitting at the table, white as a sheet. He said, 'I've just had the worst experience. I dreamed we were at a gig and there was this blue, bald headed man going through the audience just taking people over. And everyone was being taken over except me and then he tried to take me over'. It was then that I told Ronnie about my earlier experience."

"Of course, when Ronnie told the others, there was a lot of piss-taking going on, people with white sheets over their heads. It was very funny but scary at the same time. I had rebelled against following Baba up to that point but the incident with the apparition in Connecticut made me realise there must be something more."

"I can't believe Ronnie believed all that," McLagan says, laughing. "We were just drunk, we just wanted to do something and he had gone to bed so he had to be woken up."

While hanging with Billy, the band made a trip in to New York to see New Orleans soul funk band, the Meters whose tight, syncopated, Allen Toussaint-produced grooves and rhythms on seminal tracks such as 'Cissy Strut' and 'Look Ka Py-Py' would prove as equally important to the Faces' sound as Booker T & The MGs.

Billy Nicholls: "We decided to go to the Apollo in Harlem which then was a no go area. In fact we were all going to go but I think some of the guys decided not to because we couldn't find a cab willing to take us uptown. But we were intent on going so eventually we persuaded a cab driver. This black driver told us to duck down and keep our heads real low. When we arrived he told us to run in, saying, 'Once you're inside you'll be fine.' So that's what we did. That was a fantastic gig, Little Eva was playing, the Flirtations I think were on the bill. It really knocked us out – the Meters just walked on in jeans and T-shirts and I think that really influenced the band a lot – especially the way Kenney played drums."

The band returned to the midwest for their next set of gigs, laying the ghost of Andrew Oldham and Immediate Records behind them. Oldham's behaviour became ever more erratic during the label's final gasp; bringing a $7.2 million lawsuit charging breach of contract against the might of Clive Davis and CBS who distributed the labels product in America in one last desperate throw of the dice.[*] "In the end I just lost interest because it became like a business," Oldham resignedly commented to Penny Valentine in 1972.

The next 25 years would be one long dark night of the soul for the former hustler and svengali with various attempts to re-establish himself in the music business. The trials and travails of Immediate Records were largely absent from two subsequent volumes of autobiography, named with typical Oldham irreverence *Stoned* and *2Stoned*, apart from the following passage, which left no doubt as to who figured on Oldham's shit list. "My life was not complicated by having to manage . . . gutter scum-line inbred, ungrateful midgets, although the Small Faces would come under my vomit-watch . . . I say vomit-watch as Ian McLagan and

---

[*] Relations between Davis and Oldham had been less than cordial after an incident where Oldham accompanied by a henchman burst into a board meeting in progress and yelled at the suits that Amen Corner's '(If Paradise Is Half) As Nice' was number one in England and "you motherfuckers have three weeks to do the same here!"

Ronnie Lane made my Small Faces experience much ado about all-or-nothing, while the calm and manners of Kenney Jones and the loving madness of Steve Marriott made the journey worthwhile."

"Whatever people say about Andrew he had enormous flair," former music journalist and press agent Keith Altham praises. "It was his intuitive feel at that time and his capacity to take risks when other people weren't, simply because he was in tune with what was going on and he knew that it would happen and that it would be a success. He was part of a whole new attitude."

In Detroit a further two-night stand at the Eastown Theater was a triumph with an extra date added. The Motor City's notoriously demanding audiences took the Faces' honest, uncomplicated rock'n'roll to heart and rewarded them accordingly.

Billy Gaff: "Bob Bagaris, the Detroit promoter, was fantastic . . . he and Bill Graham were the only two people where if the Faces did a great show, they would double the fee. When I was picking up the money for the gig, which was a couple of thousand dollars probably, I remember Bill giving me double. He said, 'We thought it was fucking Xmas.'"

Another central figure among Detroit's incendiary rock'n'roll scene was photographer Tom Wright. Born in Alabama in 1944, Wright had lived in England in the early Sixties when his stepfather was posted to the US army base in Ruislip, Middlesex. Tom enrolled in a photography course at Ealing College of Art and was entranced by the school's bohemian attitude. "It was an eye opener because what I saw was four storeys of beautiful women. I also learned that you could smoke in class. In America, everyone was figuring out how to get out of going to class; at Ealing there was a line waiting for the custodian to open the door in the morning."

Tom met and befriended graphic design student Pete Townshend. Wright and his roommate, Campbell 'Cam' McLester introduced Townshend to the potent influences of American R&B and jazz and pot – both rare commodities in the Britain of 1962 and ingredients that were to transform Townshend's qualities as a musician and songwriter.

After being busted for possession in late 1963, Wright drifted through Europe before returning to America, working as an underwater photographer in Florida when the Who rolled through town on their first American tour in 1967. Wright left his job and travelled on the road with the group, taking a series of striking onstage and offstage shots. Wright became

The Faces pictured backstage at the Weeley Festival of Progressive Music, 1971. Their devil-may-care spirit clashed with the 'heavier' bands of the time. Ronnie Lane: "We are out to enjoy ourselves, but a lot of groups and audiences take themselves far too seriously. Everybody is trying to be so cool." (LFI)

The Faces sign with Warner Brothers, London, November 1, 1969. Pictured countersigning is Ian Ralfini, head of Warners' UK division. "[Ian and I] had this fabulous brief from Warners in America saying 'Just go out there and sign what's happening now in England," said fellow WB employee Martin Wyatt. (DICK BARNATT)

Rod in the middle of a discussion featuring the Faces' colourful manager, Billy Gaff (right) whom Stewart dryly referred to as "the management." Standing behind is arranger Jimmy Horowitz (left) and Russ Shaw, from Warner Brothers. "When I offered to manage them I said I'd do it without contracts," Gaff stated, "and that's what I did." (KATE GADD)

"When the Faces got together, it soon became very clear that it wasn't just the boys," says Sandy Sarjeant. "The girls were going to have their say as well." (Clockwise L-R): Mac and Sandy (with Rufus the dog); Ronnie and Sue; Ron and Krissie; Kenney and Jan. (PICTORIAL PRESS; HARRY GOODWIN)

"It's in E..." Faces photo session at the Nichols Arboretum in Ann Arbor, Michigan on their first US tour, May 1970. Ronnie Lane: "[America is] where it's got to be for us, unless we make it big in the States, I don't think we'll call ourselves a success..." (TOM WRIGHT)

The Faces onstage at Dudley Zoo, June 1970, with road manager Pete Buckland standing stage right. Also on the bill was the Edgar Broughton Band. Broughton branded the Faces a bunch of "drunken East End tarts". (PETE SANDERS/REDFERNS)

God Rest Ye Merry Gentlemen (not forgetting the women), Christmas carols for BBC *Top Gear* radio programme, December 1970. [L-R back row]: Marc Bolan, Faces champion John Peel, Robert Wyatt and Mike Ratledge (from Soft Machine), Rod, Kenney, Pete Buckland [L-R front row]: Romie Young (friend of Sonja Kristina), Sonja Kristina (Curved Air), Mac, Ronnie, Ron and Ivor Cutler. (BARRY PLUMMER)

Ron, Rod and John Baldry in a publicity shot to promote Baldry's 1971 album *It Ain't Easy*, co-produced by Stewart and Elton John. (WARNER BROS)

Rod and Ron present the cake at Kenney and Jan's wedding, Los Angeles, March 9, 1971. (JAN JONES)

Portraits taken on the road in America, 1971. (CRAIG PETTY; MICHAEL OCHS ARCHIVE/GETTY IMAGES)

After playing to large audiences in America, the Faces often performed to modest crowds back home, such as (above) at the Greyhound, Croydon. "The audiences [in England] were alright but we were doing tiny amounts of people," says Pete Buckland. "I mean after that first American tour some of the gigs were dire." (ROBERT ELLIS/REPFOTO)

Rod and ever-present bottle of wine on stage with Ronnie Lane; (right) Ronnie performs 'Richmond' on *Top Of The Pops*, April 1971. Lane's more folky style was in direct contrast to the Faces' boozy, bluesy sound.

(BARRY PLUMMER; CHRIS WALTER/WIREIMAGE)

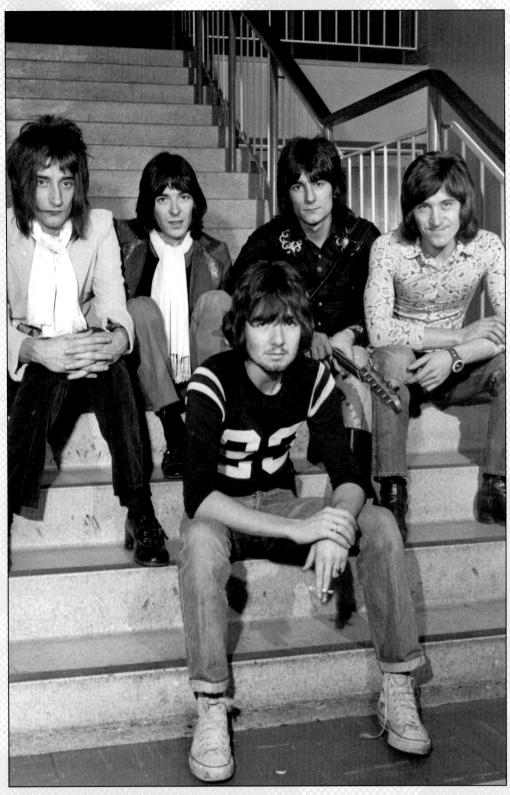

The quiet before the storm: the Faces at BBC TV Centre to record *Top Of The Pops*, December 2, 1970. "We turned over a few tables and got banned," said a straight-faced Stewart, "a complete accident." (HARRY GOODWIN)

the Who's American tour manager in 1968 during which the band played the Grande Ballroom, an old Twenties ballroom situated on Detroit's west side.

"When we reached the Grande I was just blown away by what was happening there," says Wright. "It was unlike anything else happening in America. The tour finished, I moved out of my apartment in New York and moved into the Grande and Russ Gibb employed me to be the stage manager."

Touring British rock bands playing the Grande were expected to put on a show or "kick out the jams" in the parlance of the Motor City's legendary MC5, or risk being either booed off or upstaged by local talent. Some of the British bands experiencing this trial by sword included Cream, the Jimi Hendrix Experience, Traffic, Led Zeppelin and the Jeff Beck Group.

Tom Wright: "Rod Stewart took everybody by surprise because everybody had come to see Jeff Beck. When he sang, you could tell he was putting everything he had into it. Then a few months later Beck came back to the Grande and that's when I first started getting to know [Rod]."

The Grande held its last dance in February 1970 but "when Stewart came back with the Faces he and Woody knew what to expect from a Detroit audience," Wright continues. "They were sort of comfortable with everything and got a warm welcome at the Eastown. The band just kicked ass. They were dressed for the part – Rod with the feather boa and the velvet jacket, Ron Wood looked like a star even when he was starving, you know?

"After the show while they were packing up and doing stuff I started talking to Rod. He said something about, 'Didn't you take some pictures of the Who?' I said, 'Yeah, but the ones I really like are the ones that I took in Europe.' And he said, 'Well, let's have a look,' so I started showing him pictures from when I lived in places like Paris and Spain. Rod saw one I took of this wet brick street in Paris that was real foggy. He said, 'Oh my God, I've just finished an album and it's going to be called *Gasoline Alley*. This is the perfect picture for the cover.' So he said, 'Let me call some people.'

"He phoned the Mercury people in California and then wound up calling the guy in Chicago who was in charge of printing the covers but he said, 'We've already printed up about 100,000 of the watercolour.' So Rod was very apologetic but he said to me, 'We're leaving tomorrow afternoon but why don't you shoot some pictures of us in the morning?'" By now, it was about two in the morning so I didn't sleep at all – I took a couple of hits of speed and started polishing the cameras."

When the Grande shut down Wright had moved out to a farm belonging to Detroit group the Third Power. Also living there was Roydon Walter Magee III, a 21-year-old business college graduate with a wild frizzy Afro from Oxford, Michigan – a small town north of Pontiac. Known to all as 'Chuch' – a childhood nickname his father had given him that stuck fast – Magee had been thrown out of bible school in Bethel, Tennessee for dealing pot to his fellow students. In return for free room and board at the farm, Chuch worked as the Third Power's roadie. Chuch was always up for anything and so for Wright's Faces assignment, he was pressed into 'borrowing' the Third Power's Cadillac limo and acting as chauffeur.

Tom Wright: "In Mac's book he's got it that I just made this photo session up out of thin air by telling each of the band separately that the other members had agreed to it but I can only assume that Rod didn't bring it up with Mac because the other guys seemed to know all about it. It was early for them, for sure. And I was speeding like a freight train so they said go and tell Mac because nobody was sure if he knew what was going on. And that's when Chuch and I went and banged on his door and he got real pissed off that we woke him up. So we loaded the band up in the old limousine, which was really used for funerals, and went to this park, the Arboreum, in Ann Arbor, a cross between woods and a park, which was 40 minutes away. It was beautiful weather and by then everyone was drinking champagne and smoking joints. It was great and we followed them right to the airport where I took more photos. They were heading for California."

The images from Wright's first Faces photo session remain among the most memorable and effective ever taken of the band. They look like a proper gang, lying in the grass, standing in profile, Rod in feather boa and for the first time on camera, pulling gurning, Jacques Tati-like faces. "The people at Warners saw those shots and they were disenchanted because you couldn't see Rod right off which I thought was the strength of the photos," says Wright.

For their sheer chutzpah Wright and Magee made an indelible impression on the band and along with Charlie Daniels would be among the lasting American friends the Faces made on the road. For Chuch it was the beginning of an unimagined adventure.

While on the West Coast, the band played four nights at Bill Graham's Fillmore West, in San Francisco, again with Lee Michaels, billed as 'Small Faces with Rod Stewart'. Between gigs the band explored 'the City by the Bay' in a rented Ford Torino leading to one of the first instances of on the road carnage in Faces folklore. Pete Buckland, who was to figure in many such incidents, recalls: "I think Kenney, Woody and Rod were with me, I don't think Mac and Laneole were there. We were driving around San Francisco, and because we'd seen *Bullitt* with the car chase scene, the guys said, 'Shall we have a go at it?' So I said, 'Yeah, all right.' 'Well, we'll get out and *you* do it.' So they stood on this cross street. I got to the top of this hill, nailed it down, hit the cross street and the front end all bottomed out, sparks and all that stuff flew off it. The car then took off and went through the air, landed so heavily it somehow ripped the sump out of the thing and there was this massive cloud of smoke and oil behind me. Everything stopped, the power steering went, the engine stopped and I had to sort of manhandle this thing over to the side of the road.

"This was late at night, like 11 o'clock or midnight, and we'd been out drinking or something and luckily there was nobody else around. The boys came down the hill giggling their heads off so we got a cab back to the hotel and left the car for dead on the side of the road for the car hire company to come and collect. They didn't think it was very amusing but since I would always take out the maximum insurance, we weren't presented with a bill."

Having come up with ideas for songs during the endless hours of touring doldrums, the Faces entered Western Recorders in Los Angeles. Whether these tracks were first passes at songs that ended up on what became *Long Player* is hard to ascertain. The only concrete result was the instrumental 'Rear Wheel Skid', issued as the B-side of the Faces' next single.

Pete Buckland: "All I remember is that nothing great was done as it turned into a bit of a party – very strange for a Faces session! And Mike Love of the Beach Boys coming along and being very annoying."

After another week of shows, the shattered but ebullient band finally arrived home. The ten weeks away had proved the Faces could stand each other's company in such a hothouse atmosphere – they had to share rooms a lot of the time – and of course the constant playing had sharpened them up as musicians. It also benefited Rod by improving his vocals as well as polishing his style as a front man before large audiences. Whereas before if a gig failed to work it fell on Beck; now Stewart felt responsible.

"The tour didn't half go on a long while," Lane told Welch, "but it was a great experience . . . it's all been said before about the States. It is quite an uptight place and the audiences are bloody good. And that's all been said before."

CHAPTER 11

Gasoline Alley

"All groups need an identity and that identity usually stems from the
  lead singer. I'm not a great singer, but I think I have an identity of my
own vocally. And a group needs a sound that is instantly recognisable."
                                    – Rod Stewart, *Disc & Music Echo*, 1970

"I think we've always had the same attitude to our work . . . Some
people are incredibly serious about the whole business and some people
just throw it away. I think we've always been in the middle which is the
best way to be. You don't feel too much pain then."
                                    – Ronnie Lane, *Sounds*, 1972

IN June 1970 Mercury released Rod Stewart's second solo album
Gasoline Alley in the States – the advance US date confirming all
energies were being directed toward the American market where Rod's
ready-made audience lay. While Stewart still nonchalantly regarded his
solo efforts as "a sideline to the Faces" *Gasoline Alley* was nothing short
of outstanding, confirming his maturity as a vocalist, songwriter and
interpreter.

Rod recruited virtually the same musicians as had played on his debut
album – Wood, McLagan, Waller and Quittenton, with the addition of
Pete Sears on piano. With Waller and Sears only in town for a limited time
after the Faces-Silver Metre Lyceum show before heading back to the
West Coast, the whole album was wrapped up in a productive fortnight at
Morgan Sound Studios. Opening in late 1968 at 169–171 High Road,
Willesden Green, north west London, Morgan was one of several independent recording facilities. Trident and Advision were the other notable
examples that sprang up in the capital, offering up-to-date recording
techniques at competitive rates – a factor that appealed to the thrift conscious Stewart. Behind the desk was Mike Bobak, an engineer who would

prove crucial in translating Rod's ideas over his next four albums. Best of all, a bar was about to be built in the downstairs area, the first London studio to have one.

Lou Reizner claimed a co-production credit on *Gasoline Alley* although he was hardly in the studio, being away in America at his brother's wedding, a situation that led to a temporary falling out with Stewart. "Irwin Steinberg said he would give me $12,000 to produce the album," Reizner told George Tremlett, "and then whatever part of that I didn't spend Rod could have the difference . . . and it was then that his Scottish ancestry came out and he became very mean and frugal in producing the LP . . . and there were all sorts of scenes in the studio. The cost of producing the LP turned out to be £3,500 – and Rod kept the difference."

Gasoline Alley defined a particular brand of English folk that was built on more of a rock foundation than traditionally inclined groups like Fairport Convention, with frequent nods toward the rusticity of the Band. To enhance the folk feel and in a further throwback to his busking days, on three of the tracks, 'Only A Hobo', 'Lady Day' and Jo's Lament', Rod picked acoustic. Curiously the album featured only three of his own compositions whereas the first featured five; Stewart preferring to interpret outside material – or it may have been for the simple reason that these were all he had completed at the time. "I'm not a born writer," he was at pains to reiterate. "I have to be under stress to write anything; on a deadline." Stewart's doubts about his abilities were misguided because the songs were among the best to carry his name. Unlike other contemporaries preoccupied with mystic revelations or fantasy scenarios, Stewart's writing was based in the real and the personal, inspired by the candidness he admired in artists like Bob Dylan and Joni Mitchell.

As with 'An Old Raincoat Won't Ever Let You Down' and 'I Wouldn't Ever Change A Thing', the opening track, 'Gasoline Alley', an inspired Stewart-Wood collaboration looked back wistfully to Rod's drifting days in Europe. " 'Gasoline Alley' is nowhere in particular to me," he told *Rolling Stone*. "It was about a feeling I had when I was in Spain and I couldn't get back to England. I wanted to get back to England but I didn't have the money to get back." The title came from a remark a girl made at San Francisco's Fillmore West. "We were talking and she said something like, 'I must get home, because my mother will say, "Where have you been, down Gasoline Alley?"' Stewart actually thought such a place existed but no matter, the name provided the perfect evocative metaphor for the background he emerged from, its lyrics conjuring up a scenario of the boy who left home full of fanciful ideas who takes stock and realises he was better off back where he started, "down the Gasoline Alley where I came from".

To achieve the memorable arrangement, with chiming guitars closely tracking the melody line, Wood overdubbed 12-string acoustic and six-string electric, adding a distinctive slide part to provide the icing on the cake. "Woody and I have a really good combination," Stewart explained to *Rolling Stone*, "because he writes beautiful melodies, but can't write words. I can't write melodies at all, but I can words."

As the tempo slows to a halt, the last stray slide notes moan like a lone wolf's howl in the dead of night as an old freight train carries this penitent vagabond homeward.

While most were familiar with the Rolling Stones' version of 'It's All Over Now', their first British number one in 1964, Stewart was keen to acknowledge the original by the Valentinos, an R&B group from Cleveland, Ohio featuring the song's writer Bobby Womack, another of Rod's key vocal influences, along with the Temptations' David Ruffin. The emasculated suitor now getting his own back suited Stewart's style to a tee and the song was soon appropriated as the Faces own, becoming a spirited live favourite guaranteed to get an audience up on their feet. The track swings fast and loose, riding along on Waller's trademark wallop, McLagan's honky tonk piano and Wood's swooping bass and slide, the reprise of the 'Gasoline Alley' hook being a nice touch, and even a whistle blown by manager Billy Gaff, his only illustrious contribution to a Faces or Stewart record.

'Only A Hobo' was adapted by Bob Dylan from 'Poor Miner's Farewell', a tune by Aunt Molly Jackson and recorded by him in 1963, first (under the pseudonym Blind Boy Grunt) on a collection of folk ditties entitled *Broadside Ballads Vol. 1.* and for his third album, *The Times They Are A-Changin'*.[*] In a 1971 *Zigzag* interview Stewart said he picked the song up from *Paths Of Victory*, the 1964 album by American folkie Hamilton Camp. However he may well have known it from a recording of Dylan's Witmark publishing demos given to him by Paul Nelson, his friend and Dylanologist at Mercury in the States. Stewart's version masterfully marries the subject's sad, melancholic nature to an inventive arrangement by Quittenton using Dick Powell, a violinist discovered playing in Borscht 'n' Tears, a Russian restaurant on Beauchamp Place. Stewart would revisit the same Hamilton Camp album for another inspired arrangement of a Dylan song on his next album.

---

[*] This Columbia version remained in the can until the Bob Dylan archive release, *The Bootleg Series Volumes 1–3* in 1991.

Rod had admired his gravel voiced contemporary Chris Farlowe's original version of 'Handbags And Gladrags' and by way of acknowledging both singers' Immediate past, chose to cover Marriott-Lane's 'My Way Of Giving', recorded by Farlowe in 1967. Stewart was not so keen on the Small Faces version, which he described as "monstrous" in the *Zigzag* interview, possibly as a dig at Marriott or a way of distancing the old Faces from the new. To "keep it in the family" the Faces played as a group on the track, and it's a great performance, rivalling if not eclipsing the Small Faces original, although during the final chorus the normally reliable Jones beat goes off time.

'Country Comforts' was one of three Elton John-Bernie Taupin compositions that Silver Metre recorded on their only album and Stewart's version preceded Elton's own. "I didn't even know he wrote it," Stewart told Pete Frame. "I got it off Jack Reynolds who was the singer in Silver Metre." Reynolds, who suggested the song when Rod felt the album needed another slow number, provides the underlying vocal beneath Stewart's on the second chorus. Like Stewart, John and Taupin had a fondness for Americana that, in this case, was heavily influenced by the homespun simplicity of the Band. Although Rod and Elton had yet to become acquainted, Stewart's artistic license with the lyrics apparently caused some friction for a time.

Stewart nostalgically returned to another of his past musical heroes, Eddie Cochran, with 'Cut Across Shorty', translating it from a fast-paced Fifties rocker to a traditional folk tune. Powell's fiddle takes centre stage while Wood plays some complementary slide lines in the race to the fade. In the final verse sharp-eared listeners might notice a line was missing. "That was Woody's fault," Stewart told Frame. "He suddenly forgot one change when we were laying the track down, but I think it's great . . . it doesn't sound wrong."

'Lady Day' was the first of two autobiographical songs; a bittersweet reflection from a lover spurned in a one-sided affair that many mistook as some kind of elliptical tribute to Lady Day herself, Billie Holiday. While it's hard to imagine lady-killer Stewart as a jilted party in real life, the lyrics capture his down-at-the-heel desolation – "no perfect picture to place against your whitewashed wall" – in terms of almost perfect melancholy.

Wood coaxes tasteful slide, Powell bows violin and added to the mix is Quittenton's effective contribution on gut-stringed guitar. "He [Quittenton] has the most incredible collection of chords," Stewart told Nick Logan, "he'd just knock everybody out in the studio with what he'd come up with."

'Jo's Lament', based on an old folk tune, seems at first inspection like a sequel to 'Cindy's Lament' off Stewart's first album. In fact it was a *mea culpa* to Rod's long lost love Susannah Boffey who he had put in the family way as an irresponsible 18-year-old.* Contrite yet aware that forgiveness is unlikely, the lyrics nevertheless suggest he looks back fondly on the affair: "... in a funny old way I was sure I had it made".

The album closes with 'You're My Girl' (I Don't Want To Discuss It)', which had been performed live by Delaney & Bonnie And Friends but Stewart's version was closer to that recorded by Los Angeles band Rhinoceros (who supported the Jeff Beck Group) on their 1968 debut album. The track was recorded as a live take with Wood, Lane and Jones – Mac was "not available due to bus strike" according to the tongue-in-cheek sleeve note – and along with '(I Know) I'm Losing You' (off *Every Picture Tells A Story*), is the closest the studio came to capturing the early Faces' freewheeling swagger. It's tough, commanding and downright funky with the band fully locked into a Stax-styled groove. At one point Stewart can't suppress his delight at such a taut, raunchy performance; "perfect" he exclaims with obvious delight.

Gasoline Alley was an unqualified success on all fronts. Musically it contained the right balance, blending vulnerability with a hardness that followed on from the light and shade of *The Rod Stewart Album*. The choice of songs reflected Stewart's attention to detail, a careful selection of obscure or neglected material covering different styles, his uncanny awareness of what melodies could be reworked to suit his voice, and his skill at sequencing the tracks with remarkable precision and clarity. "With the Faces it is five guys who have equal say but on my own it is just my responsibility," Stewart told Nick Logan. "On a group album I couldn't tell Mac what to play but I can when it's my own album."

What else came over as an obvious progression was the increased sensitivity and improvement in Stewart's vocals, right down to the sheer verve in his "now listen" style asides. "I've started doing things off my own bat, instead of relying on other people to tell me what to sing," Stewart told *Melody Maker*'s Richard Williams. "It's worked out OK and I've got a lot more confidence." After a chequered apprenticeship, Rod had found his niche and in *Gasoline Alley* he achieved his first significant career landmark.

---

* Rod's youthful transgression obviously loomed large in his memory – he wrote about Boffey and his misspent youth again in 'I Was Only Joking' on his 1977 solo album *Foot Loose & Fancy Free*.

If the Faces found America open and receptive to their brand of good time rock'n'roll, the English audiences they played to over the summer of 1970 continued to be a tough hurdle to surmount, as was the stigma of being regarded as the leftovers from formerly successful groups. In the eyes of the so-called arbiters of taste at the time, the Faces were not cool. The band's inherent sense of fun, their lightheartedness and unpretentious attitude – a natural continuation from the Small Faces – was interpreted as arrogant and unprofessional by denimed dullards and grim faced 'serious musicians' whose solemn approach to rock as a contemporary art form could bore an audience to death with a single drum solo. Or was it that they weren't 'right on' enough and prepared to fight for the cause, whatever that was? "All those people still believe in that," Lane remarked to Chris Welch. "We came out of it years ago and know what a load of crap it is."

Other acts breaking America at the time who valued straightforward rock'n'roll over navel contemplation – Elton John, Humble Pie and even the Stones after their '69 American 'comeback' tour – found the diffident attitude British audiences displayed annoying. "It wouldn't slay me if we did a gig here [in Britain] and people didn't get up off their feet," Steve Marriott told Penny Valentine. "What would slay me is if they *did*."

The distinction over stimulants was another factor that distanced the Faces from the 'heads' who preferred pot, acid and Mandrax to beer, brandy and Blue Nun. While not averse to a puff and a toot, when 'Going To The Pub' was considered the ultimate in uncool, the Faces revelled in schlepping the short distance from the bar to the stage, glasses in hand. If the audience wouldn't get them off they would groove on each other to provide the requisite sparks.

"It was an awful slog in England at first," Pete Buckland confirms, "because the Faces were perceived as a bunch of drunken East End yobs and they were really being slagged off. The audiences were OK but we were only playing to tiny amounts of people. I mean after the first American tour when we came back and we did some gigs, it was dire. Places like Cook's Ferry Inn."

A World Wildlife Fund benefit show on June 5 among the unusual surrounds of Dudley Zoo in the Midlands highlighted this divide. The line-up also featured Tyrannosaurus Rex, just about to transform into T. Rex and, leading the hairy brigade, the Edgar Broughton Band, Quintessence and Sam Apple Pie. Providing the sounds and acting as MC was Jeff Dexter who recalls, "Edgar Broughton did his thing and brought the house down, got everybody waving their arms in the air, singing along to his anthem 'Out Demons Out'. And then when the Faces, who were being hailed as this new happening band, came on as headliners, they started playing and after about three numbers the audience began booing and lobbing things up on stage, calling for Edgar Broughton to come back on. There had been a lot of hospitality backstage and the band, having been there all afternoon, were actually quite drunk by that time.

"The Faces were really getting jeered and they were feeling really defused about it. Robert Plant who happened to be at the gig was wandering around and he decided to help out by getting up on stage when the Faces were really getting a lot of grief. And of course all the Midlanders, seeing their boy made good with Led Zeppelin, started cheering. Planty started telling the audience the Faces weren't just a bunch of London oiks, they were friends of his and so he and Rod and the band did a song together and that won the crowd over – the Faces were saved by Robert Plant. I talked to the band afterwards and they were pissed off about the whole thing but then again they were very drunk."

Lane referred to the incident a short time later in an interview with Welch. "We were getting a bit boisterous in a dressing room with an underground group recently, clowning about a bit I suppose. As we were going somebody heard them say, 'What a lot of East End tarts – they don't know where it's at'. But I dig being really gross now and then . . . Really the band isn't going in England, is it?"

However their small army of supporters was growing, as illustrated by this letter sent to the *NME* mailbag from Annette and Jean of Birmingham: "Last week we witnessed one of the most brilliant performances of any group on the scene today. We refer to the Faces . . . If people would take the trouble to listen to their music they would hear just how much they have advanced from their Small Faces days. We hope they will achieve the success they deserve."

One of the few British underground figures to give the Faces their due was John Peel – Rod, of course, having done the DJ a favour by singing on the Python Lee Jackson session. The Faces first appeared in session on his *Top Gear* programme back in March, recording four songs off *First Step* which sounded far looser than their studio counterparts. From January 1970, Peel started hosting a weekly series, *The Sunday Show*, recorded in front of an invited audience at the BBC's Paris Studios on Lower Regent Street. The Faces appearance (taped June 25) captures their early dynamic, opening with a fairly sluggish 'You're My Girl', 'Wicked Messenger', 'Devotion' and an invigorating 'It's All Over Now'. With the stiff Beeb audience only just warming up, the band's brief set finished with traditional set closer 'Feel So Good'. Rod commanded the songs with authority; his now trademark vocal ad libs and audience participation routine all part and parcel of the Faces' live experience. At one point between numbers, Peel, in his inimitable fashion, mildly rebukes his listeners with a "stern lecture", calling anyone who wrote the Faces off as "a teenybopper group, whatever that means" because of the Small Faces connection, "a damn fool frankly because they're a great group and it's really nice to see a group that enjoys playing."

"John Peel never liked people who drank," says Mac, "until he met us, bless his heart."

Offstage the band's personal circumstances had improved from the previous year's dire straits. Thanks to his album sales in America Rod was able to invest the money he'd been putting into an offshore bank account in Jersey to buy his first home – a detached house on Ellington Road, Muswell Hill, next door to his brother Bobby.

"Mac and I used to go over there and spend evenings with Rod," says Sandy Sarjeant. "We would decorate for him, paint his doors. Rod reminded me of a naughty schoolboy. He would do something and I might show my disapproval and he would go, 'Oh, Sand', you know and put his head on my shoulder and try and wheedle his way back in until he made me laugh. They were the happy times; the bonding and the jokes."

Mike McInnerney: "There was one really lovely evening in 1970. Ronnie had brought Van Morrison's *Moondance* back from America. I'd not heard it and Ronnie came over to the flat and said, 'Look you've got to come and hear this. Just listen to the bass.' So my first introduction to the album was not Van Morrison's voice – it was the bass. What made the listening experience so special was how Ronnie talked about what this bass player [John Klingberg] was doing. Traditionally, the bass on a record would always be in the background but Ronnie brought it into the fore-ground by the way he was talking about it. Whenever I hear *Moondance* now, all I hear is the bass."

This period of contentment was captured in *London Rock*, an hour-long independent film that also featured Marc Bolan, Linda Lewis, Matthews Southern Comfort, and Fairport Convention.* While there was no actual footage of the Faces performing, the film showed Ron and Ronnie Lane playing a slide blues exercise the narrator calls 'The Moaner' at Lane's flat –

---

* The film, a co-production of Metromedia Television and Trans Atlantic Films, was due to be networked throughout America in September. Although according to a mention in *Disc*, the Faces' representatives stepped in to prevent it being shown as the band were dissatisfied with the results.

a picture of Meher Baba on the wall, Ronnie, Sue, Woody and Krissie walking along the Twickenham towpath, Rod driving his silver Marcus over to visit Mac, Sandy and Lee at Finborough Road, Kenney and Jan driving around the East End and Rod, with Mac playing acoustic guitar (and his collie Rufus barking along) singing 'Nobody Knows' at an outdoor location, possibly Rod's back garden.

The members also talked about how crucial audiences were to their performances and the star process. Ronnie Lane: "The business needs stars but musicians don't need stars, it's a drag when you start believing your own publicity."

By August *Gasoline Alley* was lodged in the *Billboard* Top 30, going on to sell over 250,000 copies and reactivating interest in Rod's first album. In *Rolling Stone* Langdon Winner praised it in an influential review. "As I listened to *Gasoline Alley* for the first time, I found myself saying again and again, 'He *can't* understand *that.*' But he does." Winner concluded by calling Stewart "a supremely fine artist". The British release occurred a month later, meeting similar plaudits. "Rod Stewart has given us a state-ment to rank with his first solo album as an expression of personal truths and experiences . . ." Richard Williams wrote in *Melody Maker*. "Rod's voice is an extraordinary tool, seemingly shot to pieces and at times barely seeming to exist, yet retaining a power and depth of communication with which few can compare." But despite the album's obvious quality and universally positive reviews, Stewart's reduced profile in Britain could only bring it in at a disappointing 62, spending just one week on the UK album chart.

The sleeve had totally changed from the American version. While Vertigo chose a suitably evocative back street scene over the ugly painting, they lost kudos for deleting the track credits that listed each musician's significant contributions. A single in the form of an alternate version of 'It's All Over Now' (backed with 'Jo's Lament') flopped completely.

Having spent three months away, the Faces were itching to consolidate their American success. A few dates were arranged for August followed by a longer, seven-week trek in the autumn – both reportedly set to net in the region of $530,000. In time for their departure, Ronnie Wood and Ronnie Lane took delivery of their new, customised Zemaitis guitars. Born in London in 1935 of Lithuanian descent, Antanus 'Tony' Zemaitis became a guitar manufacturer more by accident than design. Originally a professional cabinet maker working on antiques, and unable to afford a guitar, he made his first model back in the early Fifties by borrowing and copying an acoustic, adding improvements along the way. Word of his abilities spread and Zemaitis designed guitars for folk and blues performers like Davy Graham and Jo-Ann Kelly.

Working out of his home in Balham, south west London, Zemaitis spurned the chance of becoming wealthy through mass production in favour of painstakingly hand crafting each individual instrument to a specific design, spending up to two to three months overseeing each stage of its creation. "My early guitars were all acoustic 12-strings," Zemaitis told *Sounds* in 1970, "but more recently I've made about eight instruments for the Faces – electric six-strings, 12-strings and basses."

"It's interesting in that if I hadn't introduced Woody and Laneole to Tony who I knew through a friend on the folk scene, he probably wouldn't have got into making electric guitars," says Pete Buckland. "In the years that I knew Tony before I started working with the Faces he was anti electric guitars, despite me saying he should try making one. It took quite a bit of encouragement from Woody and myself for Tony to make his first solid body electric."

Zemaitis built up a prestigious client list, among them Peter Green, Eric Clapton and George Harrison, but it was the Faces' patronage that would do more to introduce Zemaitis' unique and beautifully made instruments on to a wider stage.*

The American dates included a return to the Boston Tea Party and an appearance at the Goose Lake International Music Festival, held on a dairy farm near Jackson, central Michigan, between August 7 and 9. Heading the stage crew was Tom Wright and his deputies Chuch Magee and Russell Schlagbaum.

Born 1949 in Ottoville, a farming community in north western Ohio, Schlagbaum first met Magee in autumn 1968 when Russell was in a local band and Chuch was attending business college in Van Wert, Ohio, as a means of obtaining a 2-S deferment from being drafted. In 1970, after joining up with the Third Power as their roadie, Chuch invited Russ to help out on their summer dates.

"There was no money but the Third Power's lawyer would help me with my draft case," Russ recalls, "so I moved out of the flat and joined Chuch on the road. At the same time Tom Wright and his friend Patrick Culley were commissioned by Dick Songer to design, build and operate a stage at Goose Lake. Songer was a self-made millionaire in construction by

---

* For more general and technical information on Tony Zemaitis' instruments, the author directs the reader to http://www.zemaitisclub.com/

the age of 30, and he wanted to build an amusement park and operate it in his retirement. He'd read about Woodstock and he thought the best way to launch this park would be to have a big rock festival. Tom was given a free hand to design and build the stage set up – one of the earliest permanent festival sites specifically designed for rock'n'roll."

The line-up for the impressively organised three-day event included Jethro Tull, Ten Years After, Mountain, Bob Seger, and the Stooges. MC5 and the Faces were late additions to the bill. "The biggest audience the Faces ever played to was at Goose Lake, 250,000 people," Kenney Jones recalled to Rupert Williams. "That was the first time I saw everyone lighting their lighters. It was a starry night and once the stars faded, looking out from the stage, it was like you were playing in space."

"The Faces were probably the highlight of the weekend," says Wright. "They were supposed to play the Fillmore East in New York the night after they played Goose Lake but Rod had his manager call Bill Graham to say, 'We're sorry but Rod's got laryngitis and he's got no voice so we won't be coming.' Graham went ballistic because they had already sold the show out. Everybody was talking about what a great place the Fillmores were but Rod knew from his earliest experiences with Beck that the key to America at least in the rock'n'roll world was Detroit. Stewart loved it so much. He spent Saturday night sitting on the side of the stage with me, drinking Blue Nun, watching the other acts."

Russ Schlagbaum: "Tom, Chuch, and I thought that events like Goose Lake would be ongoing – you know, rock'n'roll in Michigan over the summers and spend the winters in the Bahamas. But the Monday night after the festival ended, the Governor of Michigan went on prime time news and pledged to the citizenry to close the venue down to protect the morals of the youth. He succeeded and as a result, Dick Songer was ruined and lost all of his contracts to build highways for the US government."

With only a few gigs scheduled after returning to England, work commenced on the Faces' second album at Morgan Studios, again with no producer at the helm. "We always produce our own material, usually with Rod in the box, as he doesn't put his voice on till after, and we find that decisions taken amongst us work the best," Lane explained to *Record Mirror*'s Valerie Mabbs, revealing that he wanted to get a studio together for the band near his Richmond home – a dream that would take another two years to be realised. "Producing is a musical thing," Mac added, "and most producers wouldn't know one note from the other, or be able to play it. We don't really know the notes, but we can play them."

While the band were at Morgan, Kenney repaid a debt of gratitude to his future brother-in-law Gary Osborne for keeping him afloat with session work during the recent hard times by playing (with Wood and McLagan) on Osborne's single, 'Three Day Nation' b/w 'Heavies' released on August 21.

"I wrote 'Three Day Nation' about the very first Isle of Wight Pop Festival [in 1968] that I attended," Osborne recalls. "I was very much into this idea that for three days, these festivals that were happening could feel like a nation within a nation. I asked Kenney, Woody and Mac if they'd play on it and very graciously they said yes. I just paid them session rates – it probably cost more to get their roadies to deliver the gear there and back. CBS decided they would put the single out to coincide with the [third] Isle of Wight and we got to do *Top Of The Pops* under the name Gary Osborne & The Heavies. Kenney and Mac were on there with me but not Woody, as I recall.*

"Normally, being on *Top Of The Pops* would have guaranteed some kind of chart action but we got no airplay, perhaps because of the song's drug references. The record company also felt that the timing was a big mistake because it was the week of the Isle of Wight and they reckoned that anybody that might have been interested was over there. I think that was probably just an excuse for the fact it was a shit record!"

Osborne is doing himself a disservice. While the lyrics pay hackneyed lip service to "heads", "freaky ladies", and "the fuzz" the arrangement has a nice power pop feel with some strident, Townshend-like 12-string acoustic chords from Gary, Woody's choogling lead and bass, Mac on piano and Kenney's solid beat. While the dated sentiment was intended as sincere, 'Three Day Nation' could alternately function as a parody of the whole hippie trip.

In early September, the Faces played several Scandinavian dates including an appearance at a chaotic open-air festival on the Isle of Fehmarn. With *Woodstock* in the cinemas and the recent Isle of Wight attracting over half a million people, the performers lined up for the three-day marathon included Ten Years After, Taste, Sly & The Family Stone, Procol Harum, Ginger Baker's Air Force, the newly formed Emerson, Lake & Palmer and headliner Jimi Hendrix. However as was now customary at such circuses, poor organisation, financial irregularities, crowd violence and a marauding

---

* The show was taped August 26 and broadcast the following evening. While working at RCA, Osborne recalls Wood and McLagan playing on other sessions but cannot remember specific details. "Billy Lawrie, Lulu's brother, did a solo album that I produced and I think they may have played on some of the tracks."

biker gang ensured the name, the Love and Peace Festival was some kind of ironic joke. "It was dreadful," Rod told *NME*. "It peed down with rain and the front four rows were just tents with people's heads sticking out of 'em."

"It was pissing with rain, it was horrendous weather," Billy Gaff confirms. "Horrible, horrible gig. In fact we nearly didn't go on but we did."

"The story I heard is that somebody shot the promoter, got the money and set fire to his trailer," Mac recalls.

The inclement weather temporarily cleared when Hendrix appeared the following afternoon. Having cancelled his headlining appearance the evening before due to the elements, he was booed as he walked on and faced an uphill battle against the miserable conditions – a final, tragic endnote to his performing career.

Billy Gaff: "We didn't see Hendrix, he played the day after we got back to London. And then a couple of weeks later I picked up the paper and read that he'd died."

Ironically that same evening – September 18 – the Faces had their first real British breakthrough, headlining the Lyceum after the Kinks pulled out due to Dave Davies' illness. From all accounts the band's boozy bonhomie struck the right chord among like-minded Kinks fans and perhaps enlivened an audience left numb by the news announced that morning.

"We've just done three London gigs and they've all brought us up," Stewart told Nick Logan. "I think we're playing now to a different generation from when the Faces were doing 'Lazy Sunday'." Rod was fulsome in his praise for his chums. "And apart from all that, Ronnie, Mac and Kenney are such great guys. They really are."

At the end of the month the band went back to America, opening a six-week tour on October 1 in Vermont – invariably being billed as 'Small Faces with Rod Stewart'. The budget had stretched enough to allow the hire of John 'Pee Wee' Peverett and Denny Brown as extra road crew to assist Pete Buckland.[*]

Thanks to the success of *Gasoline Alley* and the band's growing reputation, the gigs were mostly sell-outs, breaking house records along the way at venues like the Fillmores and Eastown Theater. Indeed, within the past nine months, the band had played the Detroit area an astounding 11 times. "To get as far as we have in one year is incredible," Stewart boasted to

---

[*] All are thanked on the sleeve of *Long Player* although Peverett's name is misspelt as Peyrett. John Peverett's brother, 'Lonesome Dave' Peverett was in Savoy Brown and a founder member of Foghat.

Sounds' Royston Eldridge, "to be a headline band in the States now which we are, there aren't many groups that have done that, like Zeppelin, Cocker and the Beck group, that's the only three I can think of in the last few years that have gone over there with one or two tours and headlined. Ten Years After it took them ages, it took Jethro Tull ages, you know, five or six tours before they could play top of the bill at the Fillmore [East] which we did."

The Faces' juicer image was now firmly cemented with Bill Graham famously introducing the band with "Ladies and gentlemen, the Mateus Wine Company presents . . . the Faces!" At the venues where they felt most at home, bottles of cheap plonk were passed out from the stage to get audiences loosened up. Mac would be positioned stage left, the top of his keyboards covered in empty glasses and an ashtray; to his right Kenney pounded away, his face an intense study of concentration; standing in front of the drums was Ronnie Lane, his Zemaitis bass almost twice his size, pacing back and forth, encouraging the audience with handclaps and getting his chance to shine on 'Maybe I'm Amazed', sharing the mike with a towering Rod for the second verse, his arms outstretched to mimic the singer's gestures, their contrasting heights adding a splash of hilarity to an already joyous sight.

Stage right the cowboy-shirted, bog-brushed haired Woody would be laying down solos – slide glass on second finger – face grinning and grimacing at each bent note. And standing centre stage was the tall, thin, pineapple-headed singer with the sandpaper voice, mincing, and strutting with the poise of a modern day Al Jolson, grappling the mike stand like a drum majorette, head thrown back to hit the high notes, singing his hale Highgate heart out, and leading the audience in a singalong. "Are you with me?" he'd bawl like an army commander to an affirmative roar, at the end of a number, rhetorically enquiring, "Ow was that? Awlright?"

"There have been times when it's been a bit of a strain to go onstage," McLagan admitted to Caroline Boucher, "but the good thing is that Rod very rarely has a duff night. If I feel I'm having one the rest of the lads pick it up pretty quick, and with five, one person can have a bad night and the other four can take it."

An audience tape of the Faces' Fillmore West show on October 28 captures a band overcoming their nerves and triumphing, playing as *Rolling Stone* described it, "loud, but with care." The set-list at this time was built mainly around *First Step* and *Gasoline Alley* and the songs sound much freer, particularly the *First Step* material. For 'Gasoline Alley' itself, Wood played in open tuning, explaining to Penny Valentine, "I manage to get the same kind of sound [as the record] by using guitar on open strings and fiddling around." This 'fiddling around' was partially covered by Lane and McLagan, arms around each other's shoulders sharing a mike to bawl along on the chorus, falling about like a couple of closing time soaks. An extended 'Three Button Hand Me Down' featured Wood and Lane on duelling basses, while the reward of an encore brought 'Feel So Good' and, having exhausted their repertoire, Stewart and Wood led the band back to Beck territory with 'Blues Deluxe'.

As well as the odd appreciative female scream at Mr Stewart's stagecraft, what is also apparent is the lack of any extraneous waffle. "If there's more than a minute between numbers Rod goes potty and the rest of us get very edgy," Wood explained to Valentine. "I've sat in an audience and watched a band like Grateful Dead, for instance, constantly tuning up. I have to admit audiences don't seem to mind but it makes my nerves bad. When we go out on stage there's no time for messing around tuning up – if the thing's not in tune when you go out there then beware!"

While the audiences were responsive, Lane still found the country "too uptight". "We had a lot of preconceived ideas about America even if they didn't have any about us," Lane told Penny Valentine. "Although it did me a lot of good personally to work there I get homesick for England every time. There's a lack of roots in the States, it's got a big glossy exterior but nothing underneath. I get very patriotic about England when I'm over there."

Despite Lane's ambivalence America knocked the band into shape and reports of their success filtered back across the Atlantic to give previous doubters cause to rethink. Returning home on a high, after having played venues the size of the Santa Monica Civic Auditorium and Detroit's Olympia Stadium, the first gig the Faces played was at the Marquee, attended by family, wives and girlfriends.

"My mum babysat for Mac and I, so we dropped Lee off at her place in Willesden," Sandy Sarjeant recalls. "At the gig there were these American groupies who had followed the band back from the States. They were sitting on the side of the stage, bold as brass, with their legs open, obviously wearing no knickers. I mean the wives were there but they didn't care, they looked at us like, 'What are you gonna do about it?' So now we could see with our own eyes what was happening when the guys were away.

"After the gig Mac and I got in the car to go and pick up Lee. Looking back now, I can see it was really difficult for Mac because he was the only one in the band then who had a child and he'd want to relax and party afterwards but there was me saying, 'No, we've got to go.' So we were driving away and I said, 'Where are you going?' and he said, 'Home' and I said, 'What do you mean home? We've got to pick up the baby!' He'd completely forgotten. So we ended up having this big argument and Mac got really pissed off and slammed the steering wheel and the horn got stuck all the way there."

In November, grudgingly bowing to Warner Bros.' wishes in the UK, a preview from the album sessions was issued even though the band placed little store in the singles marketplace. 'Had Me A Real Good Time' was an effective summation of the Faces *raison d'être* with an easily identifiable, singalong chorus, encapsulating the band's soused brand of camaraderie. "Ronnie Lane and I got the idea [for 'Had Me A Real Good Time'] from an old Fats Waller thing that I brought back from the States," Wood told *Sounds'* Royston Eldridge. "We worked out something but let it lay for a while until we gave it to Rod to come up with some words and what he came up with seems to fit it fine. I don't expect it to be big but if it just shows that's all we need."

The track bopped along nicely, breaking temporarily to the sound of clinking glasses, a few lines of 'Auld Lang Syne', and Wood's "Well, I'll be off then" comment – before vamping into another key, Rod ad-libbing how "the skinny girl made it clear that she only came here for the beer – and that's a fact". The flip, 'Rear Wheel Skid' was a competent but dull 'jam in the studio' instrumental – showing the influence the Meters' Joseph 'Zigaboo' Modeliste had on Jones as a drummer – and the first of several to end up on a Faces B-side. 'Had Me A Real Good Time' failed to chart despite a *Top Of The Pops* plug, for which the band gladly got into the mood of the song. "We were pissed out of our minds when we did it," Stewart told *Music Now*. "You're supposed to turn up at about eight in the morning at the studios, we stayed in the pub until it shut at three o'clock and then went in to record the programme. All the places where we were supposed to stand were marked with chalk crosses, none of us were allowed to move an inch. As soon as I started throwing the mike stand around they rushed on and stopped me."

From all accounts the band's rambunctious behaviour extended into the upstairs BBC staff club. "We turned over a few tables and got banned – a complete accident," a straight-faced Stewart told *Melody Maker*.

On November 19, the Faces recorded five songs before an audience for *John Peel's Sunday Concert*. In appreciation for all that the DJ had done for them in Britain, on December 8, the Faces (with Pete Buckland) sang in the ensemble Peel recruited for the recording of the Boxing Day edition of *Top Gear*. The choir included members of Soft Machine, Marc Bolan (and his wife June Child), Curved Air singer Sonja Kristina, Scottish humorist/ singer Ivor Cutler rounded off by Peel, his girlfriend Sheila Gilhooly (affectionately nicknamed "the Pig") and show producer John Walters. Peel later recalled the session in his weekly *Sounds* column: "Sonja sang 'Silent Night', our Rod took the first verse of 'Away In A Manger' and we did 'Good King Wencelas' with Ronnie Lane as the King and Wyatty as the Page."

The three former Small Faces had a welcome Xmas present with the news that the revenue from the American tours had gone some way in wiping out the bulk of their existing debts. On top of this the tide was turning in their favour in Britain. The Faces' allies in the music press such as Penny Valentine of *Sounds*, *NME*'s Nick Logan and Caroline Boucher of *Disc & Music Echo* predicted that 1971 would be the Faces' break-through year with Rod being singled out as one of Britain's best vocalists.

However, the whole building up process of Rod and the Faces could have been completely scuppered by an interview that Stewart gave to the underground newspaper *International Times* that was published in December 1970. Founded in 1966, the weekly broadsheet rapidly became a thorn in the side of the British establishment who tried to shut it down on numerous occasions. While not attaining the notoriety of its contemporary *Oz,* thanks to that paper's highly publicised trial for obscenity in 1971, *IT* was widely read and disseminated among the British left and reached a wide readership among the counterculture. From near enough its inception the paper had solicited interviews with rock figures and advertising from the music business, a symbol of the capitalism it professed to despise, to boost circulation and keep it from going under. From today's vantage point it seems strange that the views of a then marginal rock singer like Rod Stewart would have appeared in a radical organ more attuned to John Lennon's increasing politicisation, the MC5's righteous baiting of the Nixon administration and A.J. Weberman's endless scrutiny of Bob Dylan's dustbins.

However, *IT* had given both *An Old Raincoat . . .* and *Gasoline Alley* good reviews and Stewart's albums were released on Vertigo, regarded as a hip and progressive British record label. The interview, conducted at the Warner-Reprise offices by one J Mandelkau, followed a leftist bent with Rod's views on the state of America, greedy promoters and Edgar Broughton. When asked about his thoughts on the political situation in

Britain, Stewart replied with, "I think Enoch is the man. I'm all for him. This country is overcrowded. The immigrants should be sent home. That's it."

Stewart's response was in reference to the notorious "Rivers of Blood" speech given by shadow defence secretary Enoch Powell, the MP for Wolverhampton South West, at a meeting of the Birmingham Conservative Association that took place on April 20, 1968. Powell's constituency was in an area of the British Midlands that contained a large population of Asian immigrants, and his inflammatory address attacked the incumbent Labour government's immigration policy, throwing oil on the flames of the race issue in Britain. With dependents from the former Commonwealth countries like India and war-torn Pakistan a hotly contested topic, Powell's address was politically insensitive to say the least.

While Stewart's interview was not banner headlined – being buried away on page 17 in an edition that dealt with race in the form of the Black Panthers, White Panthers and Mick Farren's interview with black British jazz band Noir – the Powell remark was printed in bold within the conversation. While coming from the same kind of working-class Labour voting background as the London dock workers who went out on strike in support of Powell after he was sacked for speaking out, the fact that so many of Rod's heroes were from minority backgrounds, or the early Sixties leftist folk protest movement, made his deplorable remarks ironic as well as moronic. But what is more surprising is that Mandelkau did not probe Stewart further on his typically forthright opinion – whether his stance was prompted by a hardened but realistic attitude to the plight of those fighting to create a life for themselves amid the squalor in the poorest areas of overcrowded Britain or whether he was simply being racist. Curiously, his remarks appear to have provoked no comment (within the pages of *IT* or the music papers, anyway); *IT* continued to review Stewart's output positively, and that Stewart (or a representative) didn't rush to protest he had been 'misquoted'.

Perhaps he wasn't considered important – or regarded as imbecilic enough to be taken seriously. In an age of the sitcom *Till Death Us Do Part* with its bigoted central character Alf Garnett, *The Black And White Minstrel Show*, a popular weekly British variety show where white performers performed in blackface like Rod's hero Al Jolson, and the generally right-wing 'skinhead' movement, an extreme youth subculture that had evolved from Mod, such casual racism was not unusual. However if Stewart had made the same statements exactly a year later to a more mainstream publication when his profile had significantly transformed, then the resulting brouhaha would undoubtedly have been more widespread and potentially catastrophic to his career.

Rod's left-leaning friends weren't about to let him off lightly and he admitted he lost a few. In a 1973 *Disc* interview with Peter Erskine, by which time he was vocally supporting the Liberal party, Stewart explained how careful he had to be over patriotism, agreeing with Powell on certain points, but that, "beneath it all, I think he's a racist." As it happened, it was not until 1976, spurred by David Bowie's verbal fascination with fascism and Eric Clapton's drunken onstage rant in favour of Powell's abhorrent views, that Rock Against Racism would finally come into being and musicians would be called to account on their position. One would have thought that the Powell incident taught Rod a lesson but it was not to be the last occasion where he opened his mouth without thinking.

In America, an equally noteworthy but less controversial Stewart conversation appeared in *Rolling Stone* with a five-page cover story on the singer. "The interview lasted for six hours," he said, "and I was grilled by one and sometimes two and three people at a time. They got into things that I had never thought through for myself."

For the first question Rod was asked if he had considered going out solo after the success of his albums. "I'm just not responsible enough to put a band together and keep it together . . . And even if I chose a band, I'd choose the same guys I got in the band now anyway."

If there was any disgruntlement that Rod had forgotten *they* had chosen *him* to become their singer, it had yet to manifest itself and despite the habitual problems with American promoters over billing, all seemed rosy on the surface.

"I don't think it's inevitable to have a front man," McLagan reasoned to Caroline Boucher, "but I think it's good because Rod can handle it. I can't be up the front doing all that because it doesn't suit me. I much prefer to be behind Rod because that's the way it is. It would bug me if it got to the point where the rest of the band was forgotten – that would be a drag. But one thing we've got that the old band never had is that this band is more of a group."

CHAPTER 12

Tell Everyone

"We've still got a few more things to do yet – a few more pegs to climb up. I don't think we're there yet. I feel we've got a really nice strong foothold, but we haven't got that much history . . . it's only a couple of years old, and one year of that was like struggling, rehearsing, going to the States. But now the reason I think we've got a good stronghold is because we're getting recognised in Britain."

– Ron Wood, *Sounds*, 1971

"Faces . . . will be remembered as not merely a genuinely great band but as the band that in the early Seventies saved rock'n'roll from becoming a highly secular brand of pop music dominated by poeticising simps."

– John Mendelsohn, *Los Angeles Times*, 1971

"THE Faces' second album, as far as I'm concerned, has got to be better than *Gasoline Alley*," Rod had told Penny Valentine in October 1970 as something of a declaration of intent. However, despite reports stating it would be in the shops in time for Christmas, the New Year rolled around and there was still no sign of it in the racks. "With my albums it's just me in charge of the production and the musicians," Stewart almost apologised to *Record Mirror*. "I make all the decisions. With the band, there are five of us and everybody's views have to be taken into account. So it's bound to take longer and be more involved."

While this process might have helped preserve the balance of group harmony, the results proved too democratic for their own good when juxtaposed against the spontaneity of Stewart's albums. However, there was an air of general dissatisfaction with the results – particularly from Ronnie Lane who tended to have the final say, causing the odd moment of friction. "I once suggested we should record 'Go Now' for an album track," Stewart disclosed to Valentine. "I thought it was right for a new treatment and I knew they'd pick it in America and that would make them listen to the album as a whole. Ronnie Wood agreed but Ronnie Lane didn't like the idea. I think he felt the Moody Blues were too established in Britain and that everyone would still have to remember their version. So I was outvoted again."

If *First Step* had sounded clinical, the songs having been written and rehearsed over several months, for *Long Player* the band followed the Rolling Stones' example of going into the studio with only the basic kernel of an idea and building it up – even though some of the songs dated back to the jams at Ronnie Wood's Henley cottage.

"The set-up was pretty nice at Morgan but we just had so many troubles with the board there," Wood lamented. "The headsets kept going wrong and it just got on top of us. Apart from that the bar there was open 24 hours a day so anytime anything went wrong it was, 'Let's go down and have a drink while they're mending it,' and that went on for months."

With the problematic hole in the album waiting to be filled, in the lead up to Christmas, dates in Germany and Switzerland were cancelled as was the Faces' appearance at a charity benefit at London's Roundhouse on December 20 with the Who (rising star Elton John replaced them). Lane hung out with Pete Townshend at various sessions that month – playing with Townshend and Keith Moon as an ad hoc group dubbed 'Tommy & The Bijoux' backing Mike Heron of the Incredible String Band on the inevitably Who-like 'Warm Heart Pastry', included on Heron's solo album, *Smiling Men With Bad Reputations*.[*]

Townshend, Lane, and Billy Nicholls were also invited by Mick Jagger to add backing vocals to several tracks, including 'Sway' off the Rolling Stones' forthcoming *Sticky Fingers*. While at Olympic, Glyn Johns played Ronnie the tracks he'd engineered for the Stones including those recorded in the downstairs reception room of Jagger's Victorian country estate, Stargroves, near Newbury, Berkshire, using the Rolling Stones' eight-track recording unit installed in a custom built truck.

With mobile recording still something of a revolutionary idea, and thanks to Johns' expertise, Lane was knocked out by what he heard. In January, the Faces spent a weekend at Stargroves – the Stones' mobile manned by Martin Birch – where 'Bad 'N' Ruin' and 'Tell Everyone' were recorded. Based around a nagging riff that McLagan came up with, 'Bad 'N' Ruin' boasted a killer backing track, featuring overdubs of Woody's slide and Mac's B3 – requiring Stewart to come up with a set of

[*] Produced by Joe Boyd at Sound Techniques Studio, Chelsea, the album was released by Island Records in May 1971.

lyrics, a somewhat thankless task when he discovered the others hadn't allowed for where the vocal breaks were going to fit.

As Wood explained to Penny Valentine, "You can lose such a lot doing the whole thing over again in another key – a lot of feel . . . I mean 'Bad 'N' Ruin' was a track and Rod fitted words to it and that worked out OK but it could have been better and he put the vocals on [separately] to the one that follows – 'Tell Everyone' and you could tell that too."

For 'Bad 'N' Ruin' Stewart drew upon his first person "wayward son returning home, tired, broke but a lot wiser" experience that had become something of a touchstone in his writing. The line about being at Cannon Street, passport in hand, could well have been where Rod ended up after being repatriated at the end of his Continental capers, although the "burglar in the first degree" lyrical sleight was most likely borne of imagination.

'Tell Everyone' was pure Ronnie Lane, a simple but uplifting song of spiritual devotion, no doubt inspired by Meher Baba's philosophies. "I have little snippets of memories of Ronnie creating different songs," says Sue Tacker. "Mostly the songs were in his head, he had a book full of song ideas. I don't recall him using a tape recorder. He would riff on something and get it going and then he might run it past someone else who happened to come by. I sometimes helped a bit here and there, that line 'May the smile on your face, come straight from your heart' was something I had jotted down somewhere. I was very attracted to the whole creative process, and to see these ideas come into being was just a wonderful experience."

"Ronnie writes very personal songs, which is why I'm trying to get him to sing them," Stewart told *Rolling Stone*. He should have applied more persuasion as, all things considered, 'Tell Everyone' worked best coming from its writer. "I don't recall the other guys mocking Ronnie's spiritual interests," says Sue. "I don't think he would have either hidden it or made it obvious. Ronnie was so natural, so real and honest. He was what he was – he didn't make pretences. In other words he wouldn't necessarily have hidden any of those things from them but neither would he have said, 'Hey, guess what happened to me?'" As it was, Lane would revisit 'Tell Everyone' in a solo capacity.

Still regarded by many as primarily a bass player, within two years Ron Wood demonstrated his diversity by moving from guitar onto slide and pedal steel guitar. "During that period with Beck, when I did the bass only, I never picked up a guitar," Wood claimed to *Melody Maker*'s Geoff Brown, "and as soon as I did it gave me a whole different viewpoint."

'Sweet Lady Mary', which could have sat comfortably amidst Stewart's solo work, invoked the memory of a Spanish dalliance – perhaps again from direct experience, and featured Rod picking acoustic alongside Wood's pedal steel, an instrument he had only recently learned to master. His playing was influenced by certain country rock pickers particularly 'Sneaky' Pete Kleinow of the Flying Burrito Brothers.

'Richmond', written by a homesick Lane during the Faces' first American tour, was a lilting folk tune featuring Wood on dobro. Wistfully evocative of the tranquil borough by the Thames, the song might have been better suited as a Lane contribution to a Baba album – as per his re-recording of 'Stone' as 'Evolution'. The metaphor about the pretty women all looking like the flowers in someone else's garden, "I'll not act on love for anyone but you", while heartfelt and touching, seems disingenuous when considering what went on during a Faces tour.

'Had Me A Real Good Time' was the same basic take (with a few vocal and mix variations) as the single but whereas the 45 faded after nearly four minutes, the album version lumbered on for an extraneous two minutes featuring the tenor sax of Bobby Keys (who was recording next door at Olympic with the Rolling Stones) and Caribbean jazz trumpeter Harry Beckett. Born in 1943 and raised in Slaton, Texas, the larger than life Keys first came to England in late 1969 as part of the transient group of musicians backing Delaney & Bonnie and toured as part of Joe Cocker's *Mad Dogs & Englishmen* troupe. Having played on sessions for the Rolling Stones and George Harrison, he was now established within the British rock hierarchy, becoming an auxiliary member of the Stones, as well as forming a close friendship with Lane, Wood and McLagan in the process.

'On The Beach', a country blues recorded on a Revox tape machine in the spare room of Lane's Richmond flat, was an impressionistic account of a Charles Atlas-type encounter near the ocean, sharing a title with the post-apocalyptic novel by Nevil Shute. "If Ronnie Lane came round for a drink or something we'd often end up strumming and I'd say, 'This is my latest thing' and he'd say, 'Yeah great how about this for a middle' and that's how I'd work," Wood told Brown. "With Rod it's much more – not pre-planned – but determined. He'd say, 'OK, we'll meet Thursday night. You get the song together. We'll make it a fast rocker, and give it to me and I'll write some lyrics.'"

Ian McLagan: "At the very end of 'On The Beach', you can hear a whistling sound – that was the Revox. You wouldn't hear it while you were recording but when you played it back, that noise would occur if you stopped the tape straight after recording. I don't know what caused it but it was a fault of that particular machine."

Apart from McLagan's one-note piano overdub, the track was released as is. "Ron and Ronnie couldn't recreate the feel when they tried to record the track again in the studio," Stewart explained to Pete Frame.

'Maybe I'm Amazed' and 'I Feel So Good', recorded at New York's Fillmore East the previous November using the Electric Lady Mobile Unit, were selected as a means of representing highlights from the Faces' act.*

Ian McLagan: "We played two concerts that night and recorded both. I never liked 'Feel So Good' from the live stuff [on *Long Player*]. 'Maybe I'm Amazed' is OK." After the excessive nine minutes of boogie woogie that 'I Feel So Good' occupies, the album ended on something of a low key with a solo Wood picking Sir Henry Wood's rendition of the immortal William Blake hymn 'Jerusalem' on his Zemaitis, impertinently claiming a writing credit in the process.

Having spent a costly six months trying out studios and engineers, *Long Player* finally appeared in March '71. "It was my idea for the title," says Mac, "and the cover was partly my idea as well. It just developed from those old jazz 78s that were housed in rough cardboard. We went to Dobell's [on Charing Cross Road] or somewhere like that and bought a few 78s and went to the Warners office in London and told the art director what we wanted. He got it, he understood what we wanted to do, even the stitching, and they put together a beautiful cover – very deco."

"With *Long Player* I remember dealing with the printers Garrod & Lofthouse, trying to get the cardboard and the stitching round the sleeve, like the old 78 sleeves, just right," says Martin Wyatt. "That was the period when after signing a band, we followed it all the way through. Ian [Ralfini] and I would sit there and check the artwork. I'd go to the cutting of the disc, I even approved the test pressings."

Ian McLagan: "Later that year, when I was vacationing in Mexico on the Gulf Coast, I was sitting on the beach and this guy walked out of the water, just out of the blue, and said, 'Ian McLagan, right?' I said, 'Yeah.' He said, 'I worked on your album cover.' It was just this tiny little island – five miles by a mile – and this guy knew who I was. I said to him, 'I wish

---

* In his *Rolling Stone* interview, Stewart revealed the Faces intended to record tracks live at the Marquee. While the Fillmore recording ended up being used for *Long Player*, a German crew did film the band at an invite-only performance at the club on December 7, 1970 broadcast the following month on WDR-TV as *Swing In – The Faces*.

the guy at Warners in LA had done a better job. They messed it up.' The American cover was absolute rubbish."

The retro, art deco-style sleeve design wasn't the only quality issue connected with *Long Player*. Despite some terrific tunes, the album as a whole didn't gel; the inclusion of the live tracks throwing the unevenness of the studio cuts into stark relief – it should have been either one or the other. The album's other fault – ironic, in view of later criticisms – is that despite an apt title, the running time of 45 minutes was a little *too* long. Also the mastering produced a samey feel; not benefited by the tracks being recorded in at least three different locations – one on a domestic Revox with submerged vocals.

"The main problem was that we could never get that sound and feeling in the studio that we got on stage . . ." Lane later admitted to Penny Valentine. "We had a very haphazard idea about recording. *Long Player* took so long I almost completely lost interest in it."

Thanks to the Faces' loyal supporters in the music press willing them on, their reviews were prepared to largely overlook these deficiencies. In *NME* Nick Logan called *Long Player* "the best British group LP so far of the year; a joyous celebration of the finest, most exciting aspects of British rock . . . sizzling with energy, laced with home grown humour and good nature, and endowed with plain musicianship." Bill McAllister of *Record Mirror* raved, "*Long Player* happens to be a superb album simply because it keeps within its limitations, because it is never excessive and because the Faces are the best rock'n'roll band in the world today."

In his *Rolling Stone* appraisal, John Mendelsohn, a frustrated musician and iconoclastic rock writer (two non-mutually exclusive qualities), was less forgiving of its flaws. As a committed Anglophile and card carrying Small Faces fan he insisted on comparing the new band to the old, acerbically, if unnecessarily, noting, that "consistently good casual fun and occasionally splendid though [*Long Player*] may be, it's by no stretch of the imagination going to save anybody's soul . . . Magnificent musically as he is most of the time, Stewart is not quite a match for the memory of Steve Marriott in the context of this particular band . . ."

Overall, *Long Player* brought Ron Wood's abilities into sharper focus, thanks to the distinctive sustain and tone of the Zemaitis guitars he used. "I used to tell [Woody] he would never make as good a guitarist as he was a bassist," Stewart told Nick Logan, "but he's proved me wrong." Some were quick to detect a basic R&B feel in Wood's playing, similar to Keith Richards' style. In his 1987 book *The Works,* Wood revealed the Faces would have pre-gig dressing room warm-ups to *Get Yer Ya Ya's Out* during this period and it wasn't entirely coincidental that Robert Johnson's 'Love In Vain' was introduced into the Faces' set shortly after that album's release in September 1970.

The Stones comparisons continued to dog the band, particularly in the common musical reference points each shared, Stewart's renditions of 'Street Fighting Man' and 'It's All Over Now' on his album (and in a live context, 'Honky Tonk Women' which, along with Ry Cooder's slide riff from 'Memo From Turner', were dropped into Wood's lengthy 'Plynth' work-out) and Rod's stage movements supposedly aping Jagger's. "Oh, it's bound to happen," Stewart insouciantly told Penny Valentine. "It happened to Mick, everybody said he was copying James Brown. You always get comparisons. The lads will bear me out . . . I've been doing what I'm doing now for the past four years. I suppose when you're thrust in front of the public eye they automatically think you're copying, they never think anyone else could have been doing this kind of thing before."

In January '71, Billy Gaff tested the waters by promoting (with John Martin) larger Faces concert dates at selected venues around England as well as the usual club and college gigs, although three shows were cancelled, supposedly due to Rod having laryngitis, as was a gig at Birmingham Town Hall on January 27 because of the band's gear being in transit from Paris.

With most of the forthcoming American tour being advance sell-outs, the band members could afford to move up the property ladder. Just before Lee's first birthday, Mac and Sandy left Finborough Road behind for an Edwardian house on the Kingston side of Richmond Park, Woody and Krissie moved to a lodge at 2 Ravenswood Court, Kingston Hill and Kenney and Jan to 25 Hillcrest Avenue, Temple Fortune, in north London. Thanks to Meher Baba's teachings Ronnie and Sue viewed the material world with healthy contempt, and so preferred to stay put in their £6 a week flat in Cambridge Road.

Sue Tacker: "It was right on the river and we were near our friends so we saw no reason to move. Those poor neighbours of ours, we were always playing music loud and I don't think there was any soundproofing so it was like an echo chamber. We were on the ground floor and usually it's the people above that bother you. I think we did annoy some people upstairs . . . Mike McInnerney made this beautiful cloudscape with an airbrush all over the living room walls and ceiling."

With his royalties starting to pour in, Rod bought a £32,000, four-bedroom, mock Tudor house on Broad Walk, Winchmore Hill, where he and Sarah resided in well-ordered splendour. Sandy Sarjeant: "I remember Mac, Lee and I went over there one evening just after Sarah had passed her driving test. We ran out of wine so she said, 'Can I drive the Marcos to the shop, Roddy?' and Rod said, 'No way.' But she kept on at him, 'Oh please, Roddy, please' and eventually he said 'OK'. So off she went and crashed the car – because it was cheap and made out of fibreglass, the whole thing practically disintegrated. You should have seen Rod's face when he found out."

The motor mad singer eventually shelled out £6,500 for a chrome yellow Lamborghini Miura – and presumably hid the keys from his other half. Stewart's loyalty wasn't affected by his newly won possessions, and he never forgot the debt he owed to John Baldry, as was demonstrated when he allowed the impecunious singer, with his boyfriend and pet goat, to live rent free at his house in Muswell Hill. Rod also pledged to reactivate Baldry's career, which had languished in cabaret hell for the past four years, and he and Billy Gaff were instrumental in getting the singer an album deal through Joe Smith at Warner Bros. Although both had paid their dues as Baldry's sidemen, it wasn't until a party at Billy Gaff's flat the previous Christmas that Rod and Elton John were first introduced and, at Gaff's instigation, the two agreed to produce each side of an album for their mentor.

Gaff had moved further into management after leaving the Robert Stigwood Organisation. "There was a bit of a problem between Beryl Vertue and myself," he says. "I think the reason was because I got on very well with her artists, Bill Oddie in particular, who was so much fun. After I was let go, I wrote a solicitor's letter and I got a few bob from David Shaw, who was Robert's right-hand man, as a settlement. It wasn't that much but it kind of set me up."

Bringing business partner Robert Masters with him from RSO, Gaff set up Gaff-Masters Ltd in June 1970, operating from his premises at 79a Warwick Square, with the Faces, John Baldry, Jimmy Horowitz and Horowitz's wife, singer Lesley Duncan as his clients. He also hired a PR man, Mike Gill who had previously worked for publicist Keith Goodwin's company KG Publicity, specifically with the occasionally difficult Dusty Springfield. Gill, always dapper and with the air of a slightly self-satisfied estate agent, brought a touch of class to the Faces' image as deep and dirty rockers. It certainly suited the aspirations of the group's singer, though Gill's smooth patter might sometimes have been at odds with the rest of the band.

On February 5, the Faces' third American tour opened in Virginia, closing in the New York area almost exactly two months later. Supporting was Savoy Brown who, after breaking through in America with their unremarkable brand of British blues boogie three years earlier, were now on their last legs, and the Grease Band. Having split with Joe Cocker exactly a year earlier, the Grease Band played their debut show at London's Royal Albert Hall, supporting Leon Russell, just two days before flying to the States. Henry McCullough, the band's guitarist remembers, "We were terrified."

Any first night nerves were dispelled once the boisterous Faces came crashing into the dressing room, dispensing booze, good cheer and other pick me ups. "I always felt slightly embarrassed about liking Rod Stewart and the Faces," the Grease Band's drummer Bruce Rowland told Rupert Williams, "but you couldn't help yourself, it was such a good time show . . . And they were such characters offstage . . . Any time one of them said the word 'man', they had to put money into a swear box."

Unlike previous tours, the six-week schedule took in the South and North East for three weeks, then on to the West Coast after a week's break in between. With *Long Player* reaching 29 in *Billboard*, the venues were bigger although in an untried area like New Orleans, the Warehouse was only half full. In the usual strongholds like Detroit it was business as usual with the originally planned two nights at the Eastown Theater being rolled into one show at Cobo Hall. *Melody Maker* sent Richard Williams out to cover the gigs in Boston and Jersey City. At the latter, the second show started late and because the Grease Band over-ran the Faces set was abruptly curtailed.

"When the appointed time of closure arrived," Williams reported, "the audience was anxious for an encore and the band was equally anxious to deliver it. Backstage aggro involving nightstick-waving Rentacops, union-minded stagehands, peeved roadies, and gawping groupies took place during which the stagehands, at the cops' behest, switched off the power."

Most pissed off at this, instead of snapping the soft metal mike stand in half over his knee as he usually did at the end of a concert, Rod threw it full force into the stage backcloth and stormed off, closely followed by the others, while an angry crowd spent the next 15 minutes chanting in protest, throwing coins at the stage. Jersey cops were not the sort to be trifled with and one was heard to snarl, "If there's any trouble, that guy who slung the mike's going to jail for incitement to riot." Fortunately, the Faces' limo was speeding back through the Holland Tunnel before anything truly ugly developed.

After a show at Gaithersburg, Maryland on February 28, the tour break enabled Rod to return to London to oversee completion on John Baldry's album, *It Ain't Easy*. Started in December and recorded mostly throughout January at Morgan Studios, Stewart and Elton, together with Baldry, brought in a large amount of friends to help out. For the side that Stewart produced, which embraced everything from folk to the Fugs via the blues alongside the usual suspects of Wood and Waller, old acquaintances from the Hoochie Coochie Men, Ian Armitt and Rick Brown, played piano and bass and Sam Mitchell, guitar and pedal steel. On mandolin was Ray Jackson, from Lindisfarne, whom Baldry had seen perform at the Marquee, while Maggie Bell from Stone The Crows, a dynamic Glaswegian singer in the Janis Joplin mould, provided duet vocals on a Delta version of Leadbelly's 'Black Girl' and Ron Davies' 'It Ain't Easy', off Davies' 1970 album, *Silent Song Through The Land*, also covered contemporaneously by Three Dog Night, Dave Edmunds and David Bowie.

In the liner notes to the album's CD reissue, Baldry recalled the carousing surrounding the sessions, particularly on the night of his 30th birthday, when Rod "showed up with cases of Remy Martin cognac and several measures of good quality champagne!" Little wonder that Baldry recorded his vocal to opening track (and single), 'Don't Try To Lay No Boogie Woogie On The King Of Rock And Roll' "whilst laying on the floor." Elton's side was inevitably less ramshackle, featuring a delightfully lubricious take on Randy Newman's 'Let's Burn Down The Cornfield' and a West Coast country rock style arrangement of the Faces' 'Flying'.

Released in July *It Ain't Easy* was an enjoyable, if schizoid project – either side bearing the unmistakeable trademarks of its particular producer – which helped Baldry reconnect with his roots, and steered him back on the right road with a tour of America – his first ever visit to the land of the music he loved – in the offing. Most importantly, it provided the right cast of musicians for Stewart's next significant set of recordings.

Regrouping on the West Coast to resume the tour, Ronnie Wood told *Record Mirror* via a long distance call, "There's no complaints here about the reaction. All the gigs have been great except Knoxville where the police were a bit strange. They wouldn't let the kids dance, and that's what they like to do at our gigs. They had the truncheons out before we'd even started playing.

"I don't think the fact that Rod and I were with Beck means as much here now. It helped right at the start because [audiences] knew what to expect, although what we've given them has been a good deal different. We're a much subtler band than Beck's group. But the band's come well into its own now. It's got a definite personality and that's what's getting the interest."

Having been engaged for the past four years, Kenney and Jan used the time off in LA to make it official on March 9. "We were going to get married before then," says Jan, "but Kenney's family and mine swamped me, I just couldn't do it. So there we were in America and it seemed like a good opportunity. Ian Ralfini helped with the arrangements; he was in LA for that part of the tour when we decided to get married. In fact it was 'Uncle Ian' who gave me away. Russ Shaw, a very gay American guy working for Warners, helped organise the details. Russ got us the Little Brown Church, in Coldwater Canyon, for the actual ceremony. We had trouble getting a licence because if you were aliens, as we were, you had to have a doctor's certificate to prove that you didn't have any contagious diseases.

"That night was Warner Bros. big official party for the Faces on the *Grand Hotel* lot [at MGM] before the set was going to be dismantled, so that became our wedding reception. Everyone was there including Ahmet Ertegun. The guy from Warners who sorted everything gave a speech and Ron and Woody came down the stairs with this American style wedding cake. Of course, it went everywhere. It was a really messy affair."

The next night the Faces headlined the near capacity, 18,000-seat Inglewood Forum – their biggest show yet – finding favour with the *LA Free Press'* Richard Cromelin. "Loose as a pack of young London pub crawlers and slightly sloshed by pre-show [it appeared] and onstage swigs of wine, the Faces delivered their unique and distinctive brand of rock, transforming and extending the rich, warm spirit of good old bar-room drinking music into the monumental proportions of R&B based killer rock'n'roll, sacrificing not a bit of the former's spontaneity, camaraderie and downright soggy joy."

With Warners pressing them for a single, the band assembled at Sunset Sound with Bill Lazarus engineering. The favoured choice was a reworking of 'Maybe I'm Amazed', which had, by now, become a genuine stage favourite. Paul McCartney's original recording, standing out amid the undeveloped song sketches on his first solo LP, had never been released as a single in the UK or US and neither would the ex-Beatle perform it live for another year, which enabled the Faces to make it their own, albeit temporarily. This new studio version opened with Mac playing the melody of the chorus on piano before Wood came in on 12-string and Lane, as usual, sang the opening verse, his voice double-tracked, as was Stewart's in parts. Intriguingly, McLagan also recalls another track being recorded "out in the alley by the side of the studio, using the traffic from Sunset Boulevard in the background, don't ask me why!" Whether the band were aiming for the same effect the Stones achieved with 'Country Honk' on *Let It Bleed* at the very same studio two years earlier is anybody's guess.

While 'Maybe I'm Amazed' was issued on 45 in America, the band, particularly Lane and McLagan, were less then pleased with the results and the single was "indefinitely postponed" in Britain. The B-side featured the group breezing through a Meters-style style workout, with Wood's Cropper-style licks, that kept its working title of 'Oh Lord, I'm Browned Off.'

While in California the band gained a new tour manager in 23-year-old Richard Fernandez from East LA, who had worked for various bands around town since high school, most notably Crabby Appleton. "I was one of the first guys to work for SIR* and we were always delivering instruments and equipment to bands coming through town – to gigs or the studio," says Richard.

Pete Buckland: "In the early days I did everything but it came to the stage where I couldn't and I had to start delegating . . . I either needed to spend all my time with the band or with the crew to organise the shows. I mean I loved the guys but I didn't particularly want to deal with them all the time. So I decided to get a tour manager in and I asked a very good friend, Larry Vallon, who handled marketing and production with [top Southern California promoters] Concert Associates [and is now senior vice president with AEG Live], in Los Angeles if he knew of anyone."

"I went to school with Larry Vallon," says Richard. "My brother Charlie and I got into the business through helping him. He would need a stagehand or something and we'd be there. I'd rung Larry and said, 'I don't know what's happening but I just want to go in and see the show.' The morning they played the Forum, Larry rang and said, 'They've just sacked one of their crew and they need somebody to finish the tour.' This was like something you pray for and all of a sudden, it happens.

---

* Studio Instrument Rentals (SIR) was founded in Los Angeles in 1967 as a musical equipment rental and production facility. It now has branches all over America and is recognised as the leading facilitator of its kind in the entertainment business.

"So I went over there and met Pete Buckland. I said, 'Can I help you guys set up?' and he replied, 'No, it's OK, just watch what we're doing, I'll introduce you to the band.' After the show, I said to Pete, 'Well, can I help you guys with the equipment?' and instead, he handed me six airline tickets and said, 'The band are staying at the Beverley Wilshire. They've got a noon flight to San Francisco.' So suddenly I realised, 'Oh, he wants me to tour manage these guys. I can do this.' I took the tickets and said, 'I'll see you at the airport,' and Pete went, 'No, I'll be gone already with the equipment.' I got the band to the airport, on the plane and from my work at SIR and just watching and listening to Teddy Slatus, Johnny Winter's road manager, I sort of knew what to do.

"Three weeks later the tour finished up in New York and we were staying at Loew's Midtown. I was getting ready to come back to LA to start a Johnny Winter tour. Billy Gaff called me and said, 'Richard, can you come up?' I went to Billy's room and he asked me, 'How do you fancy coming to London to work with the boys?' Well, you could have knocked me over with a feather. I never ever thought I'd be working in England let alone for a well-known band. So I spent a week in LA getting my act together and then I flew to London."

Fernandez was the first American to join the Faces' organisation. "One of the reasons we would hire Americans was they worked a lot harder and they tended not to get pissed and break up hotel rooms which Buckland was one of the worst for doing," says Gaff. "I liked the fact that they were always much more professional and also of course, because we spent so much time in the States, we didn't have to worry about visas and unions and things like that."

With just a fortnight's break after returning home, the Faces flew to Germany to make up for the gigs cancelled the previous December. A documentary crew followed them around Hamburg, capturing Rod's rather self-conscious a cappella rendering of 'Lady Day' and 'Gasoline Alley' amid a rundown area of the city.

After boarding for a time at Rod's homes in north London, at Woody's invitation, Richard Fernandez moved out to Richmond staying at Ravenswood Court before shifting in with Ronnie Lane at his Twickenham flat. Mike McInnerney describes the fact that three of the Faces lived near each other in Richmond-on-Thames where much of Mac, Woody and Rod's early musical adventures had been played out as two worlds colliding. "It was great that the guys were able to be in this kind of rowdy rock'n'roll milieu and in a sense Richmond was a real haven for them," says McInnerney. "I know it was for Pete [Townshend] – the occasions he came back from American tours you could just feel the journey unwinding out of him; just trying to get back to some kind of normality.

"What was enjoyable was they were all interested in art so they were fascinated in what I was doing as an illustrator, a designer. My friends tended to be musicians, they weren't fellow artists, so most of the chat was about music. Kate and I used to hang out a lot more with Mac and Ronnie [Lane]. We would end up going out sometimes with Ronnie and Krissie, having dinner at their place or meeting up at someone's flat. The Faces were hilarious company. They loved wordplay. I remember after they got back from a German tour, they found it amusing that they had been drinking a beer called Schitt and the titles of the places – especially if it had the word kunst in it, you know, juvenile stuff . . . They were a fairly physical band – into people like Jacques Tati, gurning and the [silly] walking especially Rod and Ronnie Wood who were a real double act."

Billy Nicholls: "We socialised a lot, hanging out in each other's kitchens. We even got a team together in Marble Hill Park for Sunday football. We were called the Marble Hill Academicals. Rod, of course, was good. Ronnie Wood wasn't bad actually. Ronnie Lane was useless. We'd go ice skating and then wander back to Ronnie Lane's flat."

To promote the British release of *Long Player* the Faces appeared miming three songs (with Rod's live vocals) – 'Tell Everyone', 'Sweet Lady Mary' and 'Bad 'N' Ruin' – on *Disco 2* and on April 28, they pre-taped the following evening's *Top Of The Pops,* appearing in the album segment introduced by DJ Tony Blackburn who, on his Radio 1 show, had made no secret of his dislike of Rod's singing. "Something has to be done about the sad state of pop on television," Stewart told *Music Now,* "and it's up to bands like us to let them know." This time the Beeb jobsworths were taking no chances. "We wrecked the bar last time," Stewart told Pete Frame, "so they've insisted that we have a security guard with us from now on."

For 'Richmond', a wispily bearded Lane played a Gretsch Shobro, Woody perched his National Steel astride his lap, while Rod mimed the one note bass on an upright, pausing at one point to cover a grinning Lane in toilet paper. Mac and Kenney took their places for 'Bad 'N' Ruin', Woody playing an improbable 'Toilet Seat' shaped guitar, Lane in constant motion with his Ampeg bass, while Mac grooves away behind the Hammond. Rod has his earthy but glam look down just perfect; pink jacket, blue shirt, studded belt, rooster barnet – the lads' counterpart to the haughty charisma of Marc Bolan and T. Rex, who hogged the number one spot with 'Hot Love' throughout that month. Both tube appearances perfectly capture the Faces' early enthusiasm just before events were to overtake them dramatically. Even Kenney's ill-advised moustache can't spoil the effect.

With only the Kinks for company in embodying an accessible, street level beer and football image – Rod's team Arsenal won the league championship and FA Cup double that season of 1970–71 – the Faces' boozy brand of boys next door Britishness was crystallised; a solidarity with the great unwashed, sharing their love of a pint, a flutter and a roar from the terraces on Saturday afternoons. In many respects the Faces' showboating style echoed the entertainment presented in the old music halls that flourished in London during the century before the advent of television; the suggestions of bawdiness, the impression that the performers were reacting spontaneously to the mood of the audience and – more than anything else – the heroic struggle to guarantee that everyone, in the words of the song, had 'a real good time'. "Listen," Rod would advise the audience with mock seriousness, "one thing you're going to have to get straight with us is that if you ask for an encore, you can't have one (*pause*). You have to take *three* so don't anybody try to leave."

A performance at the Roundhouse on April 29 during the Camden Festival helped spread the word. "If anyone still doubts that the Faces haven't yet 'made it'," wrote Chris Charlesworth in *Melody Maker*, "talk to one of the 2,000 or so who visited Thursday night's show at London's Roundhouse . . . where Rod and the lads gave probably their best British concert yet. They must be one of the funkiest, tightest bands around, laughing and joking through numbers while all the time maintaining a beat that shook the old engine shed at the foundations." Charlesworth, who in the past year had established himself as *MM*'s most vocal Who supporter, was clearly impressed, concluding with, "For a live show, it has long been my opinion that the Who couldn't be topped – but watch out Who, the Faces are breathing down your necks."

"[The Faces'] music, happily extrovert even when making a particularly sensitive point, totally involved the audience," Bill McAllister wrote in *Record Mirror*, "so that they played not so much for us as with us." Not all were converted – Steve Peacock of *Sounds* being one, although he admitted his opinion was in the minority. "Perhaps I'd built [the Faces] up too high in my imagination but I felt very let down . . . Rod Stewart sang well, of course, Ron Wood got off on some nice guitar breaks and Ian McLagan on keyboards did more than anyone to hold the thing together. But the overall effect sounded a bit ragged and disjointed and it all added up to less than what you'd expect from a band with such strong individual personalities . . . As soon as they got something going, Ronnie Lane would stop playing or something else would go wrong and anything they'd managed to build up would just deflate."

"That [Roundhouse] gig was very nice," says McInnerney, "because it didn't feel like anything other than the guys looning around as they usually did, having a good time and transferring it to the stage. They weren't doing a carefully choreographed show. The idea of being slightly shambolic or just on the edge of falling apart in concert was actually quite exciting, it gave a real tension to their performance."

Throughout a packed schedule in May, the Faces concentrated solely on British audiences. To illustrate the relationship with their fans, at Watford Town Hall, they let kids without a ticket through the dressing room window. Patrick Stoddart, writing in the Watford *Evening Echo,* was blown away. "Stewart struts unpretentiously around the stage using that huge soul packed voice of his on anything from the Beatles to Tamla to Mississippi Delta Music and he doesn't give a hoot for trends and the trendies who expect the Faces to adopt fashionable poses." At Leicester the Polytechnic gig was advertised as "second only to the Stones in direct onstage appeal by a UK band", although it was difficult to imagine Jagger & co. having quite the same common touch.

On May 9, Rod flew to New York briefly for the mastering of *Every Picture Tells A Story* (his first two albums were mastered in Chicago), while Ronnie Lane, Kenney and Jan, and Ronnie and Krissie were among the guests on a chartered flight to the south of France for the media circus that was Mick Jagger's nuptials to Bianca Pérez-Morena de Macias in St Tropez on May 12.

The following day, the band taped another typically loose but atmospheric John Peel concert – the highlight being their arrangement of the Temptations '(I Know) I'm Losing You' – which had now entered the set after the band developed the song at Olympic for Rod's next solo album – although it would have been the ideal choice to have further enlivened *Long Player* or as a standalone Faces single. A cancelled gig at the Nag's Head pub in Wollaston, near Northampton, where John Peel was resident DJ on Friday nights, was rescheduled to May 14. However, only Ronnie Wood showed up, sitting on his own in the downstairs lounge bar. When the others finally arrived, claiming they'd got lost, they were harangued by an irate Peel for letting down the organisers whom he considered friends. Such was Peel's influence, and the debt the Faces owed him, that a make-up gig was hastily arranged, with the band's management actually paying the organisers to play. Warners provided 400 albums to be given away to the first arrivals. The landlord 'Big' Bob Knight recalls that in the middle of the band's set in the packed upstairs hall, Rod called for "a tea break". The lights were brought up, pints were ordered from the bar and passed through the gasping punters while the band casually chatted to those at the front. Tea break over, the lights went down and the band continued delivering a powerhouse set.

On May 15, the Faces played before 15,000 at the first of several one day Garden Party festivals held throughout the Seventies at the Crystal Palace Bowl in south east London. Sandwiched between Mountain and Pink Floyd, in the first of his flamboyantly attired makeovers, Rod took to the stage in a pink satin suit, rendering the rest of the band soberly attired by comparison. The freaks and college types waiting for the Floyd weren't accustomed to shaking a leg, and reports vary as to how well they went down. "Once again, I'm afraid I didn't really enjoy the Faces," Steve Peacock stated in *Sounds*, "but this time I found a lot of people – even devout fans – who agreed that they didn't 'really get it on'." The band's insistence on using their own PA resulted in Eddie Waring's commentary of the 1971 Rugby League cup drifting through the amps. After an encore of 'Had Me A Real Good Time' the band hightailed it to the nearest hostelry, leaving Pink Floyd to play through torrential rain.

Such was the Faces' accessible nature that Bournemouth music fanatic Tim Derbyshire recalls encountering the band having a kick around on the beach before their gig at the Winter Gardens and being invited to join in. A few days later, at the Croydon Greyhound, author Johnny Rogan noted the first eyewitness account of the perennial stage ritual of Rod kicking footballs into the crowd.

Instead of a slot at the first of the annual National Jazz and Blues Festivals to be held at Reading, the band took off on holidays; Ronnie and Sue to Ibiza. Sue Tacker: "At first we would go there for holidays but then we got the house and my recollection was that it was some kind of a long lease that allowed us to refurbish the place. It belonged to a local farmer. At one point I had to go out there alone to get the building and repair work done probably because Ronnie was away on tour."

Returning from a wet week in Cornwall, crashing his Lamborghini on the drive back, Rod met up with the others in their Bermondsey local before rehearsing a new act for their next American jaunt. He talked to Penny Valentine about his forthcoming album, originally envisaging *Every Picture Tells A Story* as "a completely light album, late night-type music . . . I'd really like to do vocals with a classical guitar player – bit of a folky scene – to make the division between the stuff I'm cutting solo and the material with the Faces much wider."

Included on the album was a song that was to change things irrevocably – and one that was almost left off the record. "'Maggie May' had no melody," Stewart recalled, "it had plenty of character and some nice chords but there was no melody to it."

CHAPTER 13

Every Picture

"I'm well satisfied with the album. It obviously isn't the best I could do, but if it was there wouldn't be much point in going on any further."
— Rod Stewart, *New Musical Express*, 1971

"We never foresaw the Rod thing being quite so big. Everything was going along great then bang! It's a wonder we survived, but I suppose we're an extraordinarily close group and regardless of the offers that Rod got after the launching of his solo career, he swore blind that the band was still his cup of tea."
— Ron Wood, *Sounds*, 1972

THE summer of 1971 held much for both the Faces as a group and Rod Stewart as a solo artist. After battling indifference in Britain for the first year and a half of their career the Faces were on the verge of a major breakthrough, a direct result of the hard graft they'd put in touring America almost continuously since their formation. On both sides of the Atlantic Rod's profile was now higher than ever before — either through radio listeners discovering him via his solo albums or concert audiences seeing the Jack the Lad singer onstage when the Faces came to town. Little would band or singer have known that events were to accelerate beyond anyone's comprehension after Stewart's third solo album, the magnificent *Every Picture Tells A Story*, was released in July.

By not fixing what wasn't broken Rod's creative purple patch continued apace. Wisely, he adhered to his now customary blueprint — inspired choices of material to revive, inventive arrangements and, in keeping with his work ethic, a fast turnaround, a total of two weeks' recording spread over a five-month period between January and May '71 with Mike Bobak engineering. The usual gang of musicians — Waller, Wood, McLagan, Quittenton — were again joined by Pete Sears and Dick Powell with additional recruits, Sam Mitchell and Ray Jackson, both of whom played on John Baldry's concurrent *It Ain't Easy* sessions.*

"I think Rod had hit his stride as a producer by the time we started *Every Picture Tells A Story*," Sears told Mike Walton. "There was also a strong camaraderie building amongst the small core group of musicians by that time . . . [Rod] was pretty much firmly in control . . . He would listen to our ideas, however, especially from Martin Quittenton and Ron Wood . . . The day of a recording session, we'd all go over to his house in the afternoon and sit around his piano with acoustic guitars and listen to what he wanted to record. Then we'd go over to Morgan Studios, have a few beers in the downstairs studio which had been converted to a full bar, go upstairs and start recording. The takes were very spontaneous; it was all about the feel rather than perfection."

For *Every Picture* . . . Rod contributed just three originals as he had to *Gasoline Alley* but again quality not quantity was the maxim as 'Every Picture Tells A Story', 'Maggie May' and 'Mandolin Wind' rank among his finest work. The deftness of his songwriting evidently came as a surprise to Stewart who, in an interview context at least, continued to downplay his compositional skills. "I've never had a lot of confidence in my own things," he humbly remarked to Penny Valentine. "Those tracks were really put in to fill the album up. I've always thought of myself the way other people have – as a singer more than a songwriter. I mean I'm not really like your Neil Youngs or your James Taylors, am I?"

The jingle-jangle of ringing, acoustic 12-string chords herald the title track – a sort of prequel to the character in 'Gasoline Alley' – wherein the protagonist struggles with his image in front of a mirror, a reference to Rod's own self-consciousness during his schooldays and beyond. His dad accepts his son's need to flee the nest but cautions him against losing his head "to a women that'll spend your bread".

The escapades described were so obviously Rod's Continental experiences neatly rolled into a song – busking on the Left Bank, being moved on by Gendarmes, sleeping under bridges near the Eiffel Tower, not bathing, slumming it on the beaches, "getting desperate, indeed I was." Rod's poetic license took over for the Peking ferry verse and the politically incorrect

---

* *Every Picture Tells A Story* was the first of Rod's albums to be released on Mercury in the UK albeit in a single sleeve. Stewart's hastily compiled credits on the US gatefold carelessly omitted Sam Mitchell while Ray Jackson was merely named as "the mandolin player in Lindisfarne. The name slips my mind." At least he remembered Mickey Waller whose name was accidentally left off *Gasoline Alley*. Martin Quittenton was misspelt as Quittenson.

description of his saviour, a horny, slit-eyed lady Shanghai Lil who "never used the Pill, she claimed that it just ain't natural."

Rolling along on an exhilarating backing track (the occasional vocal exclamation can be heard buried in the mix), propelled by Waller's driving rhythm, with Wood's 12-string and nifty lead embellishments between verses and Sears hammering the '88s halfway through, the final philosophic pay-off was the repetitive closing chorus of "every picture tells a story, don't it?" featuring "vocal abrasives" from Maggie Bell and John Baldry. "It's very uncanny because [Maggie's] phrasing's almost identical to my own," Stewart told Nick Logan. "She's like a cross between me and Paul Rodgers. She has such incredible control; a lot more I would say than Janis [Joplin] ever had."*

Rod found 'Seems Like A Long Time', written by Ted Anderson, on American Midwest folk duo Brewer & Shipley's 1970 album *Tarkio*. For the gospel feel, similar to what the Stones were producing at the same time on *Exile On Main Street*, Rod corralled Madeline Bell and Doris Troy into the studio to lay down some soulful testifying.

As Eddie Cochran's 'Cut Across Shorty' had been revitalised on *Gasoline Alley*, so Arthur 'Big Boy' Crudup's 'That's All Right', covered by Elvis Presley on his debut Sun single, was delivered in a wickedly loose, honky tonk arrangement similar to 'It's All Over Now'. The acoustic bottleneck, played by Sam Mitchell, paid direct homage to Crudup's original, while Wood recycled his lick at the end of the solo for the Faces version of 'Memphis'.

Rod discovered Doc Watson's version of the traditional hymn 'Amazing Grace' and had been saving it to record for some time, so he wasn't best pleased to learn that folk singer Judy Collins had covered it on her *Whales And Nightingales* album in 1970. Elektra also released it as a single. "I was going to record 'Amazing Grace' and call the album that," Stewart told Pete Frame in *Zigzag*, "and then she [Collins] went and recorded it . . ." As a compromise, Rod used it as a brief two-minute link track featuring Sam Mitchell on bottleneck and left the song unlisted on the sleeve.

By coincidence, Collins had also covered 'Tomorrow Is A Long Time' on her 1965 *Fifth Album* – one of two Bob Dylan songs out of three on that record which Rod ended up recording. Stewart picked the song from the same Hamilton Camp album where he'd found 'Only A Hobo' and

* Joplin, who had shared stages and dressing rooms with Stewart and Wood during the Jeff Beck Group days, died of a drug overdose on October 4, 1970.

like that track's imaginative arrangement, he concocted another sublime folk-country setting, with Dick Powell's violin, Wood's pedal steel and his own strumming and double-tracked vocal on the chorus contributing to the melancholic feeling of longing.*

In the first of three brief instrumental interludes spread over Stewart's successive albums, the classical guitar prowess of Martin Quittenton was given a platform. "[Martin's] just amazing, he can play so much . . ." Stewart marvelled to Richard Williams. "The last I heard he was selling ice creams, then he went back to work in a record shop. He's completely devoted to his guitar. I told him he could make a fortune doing sessions in the States, but he says to me, 'Oh no, Rod, I couldn't miss my lessons.'"

Stewart described their working relationship in *Zigzag*. "The way we do it is, I get Martin up from the South Coast where he lives the day before we're going into the studio and say, 'This is the song and I'd like to do it in this tempo'. And he'll say, 'What do you think about this riff, and this little bit?' and so on – and we do a little work on it before we go in. The guy is really gifted, and I pay him well because he's worth every penny of it."

Quittenton was such an integral part of the melody to 'Maggie May' that Stewart felt obliged to share a co-writing credit, something he had only done (on his own albums) with Wood before. Stewart's "since you've been away, it's been so long" guide vocal† – later released on *The Rod Stewart Sessions 1971–1998* compilation – reveals he was still to come up with the song's somewhat risqué lyrics which tapped into another pivotal experience – his sexual deflowering at the hands of an older woman at the Beaulieu Jazz Festival, an episode Stewart was more obtuse in discussing at the time. "It's the story of a schoolboy hooked on a hooker,"‡ he slyly told Nick Logan on the eve of the album's release. "We tried for a *Blonde On Blonde* sound, piano and Garth Hudson type organ and very loose drums."

Richard Williams also picked up on the Dylan vibe when treated to an

---

* Rod had also considered covering 'Bob Dylan's Dream' from *The Freewheelin' Bob Dylan* before deciding "that may be too personal to him." Other contenders were the Who's 'The Seeker' and Chris Farlowe's 'Out Of Time', but, as Rod admitted to *Zigzag*, "I don't think I could improve on the way he [Farlowe] did it."
† Rod's guide lyrics also included the line "I don't mean to tell ya, that you look like a fella" which got recycled for 'Stay With Me' as it was being developed.
‡ 'Maggie May' was the title of a traditional folk song, emanating from the Liverpool docks, about a prostitute robbing a sailor. It inspired a West End musical of the same name composed by *Oliver* creator Lionel Bart, which opened in 1964.

album playback as the sessions were being wrapped up. "The overall sound is, once again, reminiscent of Dylan," he conveyed in his *Melody Maker* report, "and there's a celeste splashing notes at the end of the lines which is strongly reminiscent of 'Can You Please Crawl Out Your Window?'"

Rod had prevaricated over including the track on the album, deeming 'Maggie May' as merely filler with scant thought to its prospects as a standalone single. If anything more regard was directed to the remarkable 'Mandolin Wind', a poignant mood piece that reflected on strength through adversity. The folk-style backing features Stewart's 12-string strums, Quittenton playing the descending classical acoustic figure presaging each verse, Wood on pedal steel, slide and bass, and Jackson once again excelling.

Everything about the song is an unqualified triumph and it seemed also to summarise perfectly a trait of Rod's own personality – the difficulty he had in conveying personal emotion so diffusing the situation with a light-hearted joke. While acknowledging that "romantic words" don't come easy to him, he offers what little he has – "except, of course, my steel guitar" – and in so doing ramps up the tenderness quotient all the more effectively.

An area of controversy that continues to dog 'Mandolin Wind' is its authorship. In later moments of uncloaked bitterness during his long struggle with illness, Ronnie Lane would claim that he wrote the tune but that Stewart took it with no acknowledgement of his contribution. While the melody and arrangement certainly share the same kind of folk influence that Lane would explore on his own recordings, it seems unlikely that he would have stood by and allowed one of his songs to be brazenly appropriated in such a fashion – especially after his experiences with Steve Marriott where Lane's contributions to that partnership were often unacknowledged, leading to much antagonism after they split. For Stewart to use an idea of Lane's to his own means, without so much as a credit, knowing full well the hostility that would result, seems unlikely.*

The album's obligatory Faces ensemble performance was a sublime version of the Temptations' '(I Know) I'm Losing You', a Top 10 US hit (and R&B number one) in 1966. Starting with Wood's solo Steve Cropper-

---

* As an insight it's worth noting that Lane also claimed 'Had Me A Real Good Time' was taken over by Stewart and Wood. That might be the case but Lane was co-credited for his contribution when, as happened with other well-known groups, he could so easily not have been.

style guitar figure and Lane's funky, repetitive bass note, McLagan's piano, recorded in stereo, comes in replicating the guitar riff originally played by the Temptations' manager/arranger Cornelius Grant. Rod's rasp matches the anguished drama of David Ruffin's and in another masterstroke the arrangement suddenly stops for Wood and Lane's breathy a cappella "imm imm imm imm" harmonies. With a powerhouse delivery from Jones, the track swung with vigorous abandon, managing to replicate successfully the chops of the Funk Brothers' playing on the original.

During his late 1970 *Rolling Stone* interview Stewart had used the former Temptations singer as an example of a great artist who picked the wrong material and in *Zigzag* the following spring, he revealed that the two had talked after a Faces show in Detroit (which Ruffin was unable to gain admittance to, such was the band's popularity in the Motor City) and tentatively planned on working together, the might of Motown being the main obstacle. Whether it was Berry Gordy or Ruffin's well-documented personal problems, the project never came off although the two would sing together publicly before the year was out. In interviews prior to the recording of *Every Picture* . . . Stewart also revealed he planned to write with Free guitarist Paul Kossoff – or at least get him to play on the album. Owing to Kossoff's unavailability or the early signs of his erratic nature – fuelled by a chronic drug intake that would eventually claim him in 1976 – it was another collaboration that didn't occur.

As 'Dirty Old Town' had ended *An Old Raincoat* . . . on a minor key, so Tim Hardin's resigned 'Reason To Believe' wrapped the album up in a beautifully crafted, Dylan-esque arrangement with Sears stately piano, jazzy bass courtesy of Danny Thompson (from Pentangle), Powell's fiddle solo and Mac's purring Hammond beautifully underscoring the melody.

It soon became apparent that *Every Picture* . . . was something special and the reviews were unanimous in their praise. "Practically impossible to fault . . . it's certainly the best album he's cut" (*Sounds*); "You won't hear a better rock and roll album in 1971" (*Melody Maker*); "His are just about the finest lyrics currently being written . . . eloquent, literate and moving – a superb writer" (*Rolling Stone*). Michael Wale, writing for no less an authority than the *Financial Times* considered it "musically the best album since George Harrison's *All Things Must Pass*."

Within four weeks *Every Picture* . . . had sold half a million and was sitting at number 20 in the *Billboard* listings. Along with the healthy sales of Elton John's *Tumbleweed Connection*, the album helped generate interest in

John Baldry, who undertook a three-month American tour with the *It Ain't Easy/Every Picture* crew of Waller, Mitchell, Sears and Armitt. "It was good to see John getting to America," says Billy Gaff, "The only real problem was his drinking. Some nights he got pissed off with the audience and told them what he thought of them. The drinking made him very difficult."

Before leaving for the States the Faces rehearsed a new repertoire, dropping certain numbers and introducing new ones including, at Rod's suggestion, a rocked up version of the Everly Brothers' 'When Will I Be Loved'. Parts of the act required streamlining – Jones had no less than three drum spots – while Wood's 'Plynth' slide solo extravaganza was riveting but often excessive. Set opener 'You're My Girl' was sometimes up to 10 minutes in length so 'Three Button Hand Me Down' was brought forward to commence proceedings on a more direct note. The band played two warm-ups – at Aylesbury Friars Club and Kingston Polytechnic – before their fourth major American jaunt opened in Philadelphia on July 9.

Touring with them were Deep Purple, whose records were also released by Warner Bros. in the US. The two bands were like chalk and cheese in terms of sound, image and musicianship, although organist Jon Lord was like family thanks to his close association with the Woods, while Ritchie Blackmore had plied his rapid fire guitar virtuosity since the early Sixties, playing sessions for Joe Meek, for whom an embarrassed Rod had once unsuccessfully auditioned.

"It ought to be a lot of fun and a really good tour because the Faces are a good band and no one will be trying to blow anyone off," drummer Ian Paice told *Sounds'* Jerry Gilbert. These were to be famous last words. The Faces and Deep Purple were popular enough in various areas for the billing to reflect their respective popularities. The Faces headlined in Philly and Chicago, while in areas like Ohio, Florida and Texas, Blackmore, Lord & co. closed the show. A form of competitiveness developed with Deep Purple, as underdogs, out to prove themselves, particularly as their two previous US tours were blighted by illness. "That tour cracked it for us," Paice recalled to Purple biographer Chris Charlesworth. "The Faces were lovely guys but they were always so arseholed that they didn't play well at all. They were already sitting back on their laurels. But we were straight in there. We did a 45-minute set and slated 'em."

"When the tour started, the Faces arrived off the plane and went straight to the [Philadelphia Spectrum]. They were still drunk from the plane flight from England," said bassist Roger Glover. "We went down very well throughout the tour and, more often than not, we went down better then them."

The Faces weren't about to let these showboating upstarts get off lightly. At the end of one show, Rod did his usual shtick of inviting the audience back for a party, only this time he chose to direct them to Deep Purple's hotel. "It was absolute chaos," Glover told Charlesworth. "There must have been 3,000 kids in the lobby, up the elevators and on the stairs. When I finally got to my floor there were 400 people waiting outside my room."

One thing both bands had in common was a penchant for mischief particularly, as has become legendary within rock circles, Blackmore. Arriving in Minneapolis, Warner Bros. threw a party at the hotel, as Deep Purple's co-manager John Coletta recalled. "It was in the presidential suite and they had tables and tables of expensive food [laid out]. I was standing talking to Billy Gaff when I happened to notice that Rod and Ritchie were standing together . . . Suddenly they both picked up cheesecakes and threw them at whoever was nearest to them. The whole place erupted . . . there were soda siphons, bottles of champagne and food going every-where. It was just crazy.

"Russ Shaw from Warner Bros. was trying to stop it but they just got hold of him and carried him to a bathroom and threw him in a tub. Then Ritchie came in with a big laundry bag on wheels and they dumped Shaw into it. They ran him down the lift and took him down to the swimming pool."

The sudden arrival of the cops brought the impromptu floorshow to a close. "We were staying at a lot of Holiday Inns, particularly on the early tours," says Mac. "Those places needed to be burned down. Every town you went to, it was just the same room in the same configuration. You didn't know where you were but it didn't matter really. It helped that the hotels were usually by a motorway so you didn't get too many complaints from the people around you but it was nowhere near anywhere you could get to. There were no local bars or anything. It was only the hotel bar and it created total boredom but for some reason it actually helped because the hotels *were* anonymous and you could deal with it. You knew where the toilet was, where your bed was, where the lamp switch was, you knew there was always a bar of soap, a towel . . . But apart from that they were fucking identical and they were horrible – horrible colours and they were all the same and you wanted to hurt them just a little. They needed it, you know?"

A common on-the-road stunt was for a room's contents to be emptied and re-arranged outside in the corridor. After receiving a guest complaint the hapless hotel manager would emerge from the lift to be confronted with the band casually sitting around in their 'room' – chairs, cabinets, and bed with bedside light on – an ungainly obstruction but impeccably presented.* The green and yellow Holiday Inn flags had their uses as converted stage backdrops for Faces shows. In Chicago, at the Holiday Inn on Lakeshore Drive, Faces fan and photographer Craig Petty remembers, "It was an insane party the whole time they were staying there. It ended in a larger hotel room with a showing of a film the guys were trying to make of themselves on the road. It became a total wreck, the police showed up. Luckily we had a room right across the hall as legit guests so we got out of any trouble."

By this time a spare suite had been designated as the "party room", a fixture of every Faces tour from then on. Before, the after show carousing tended to start in someone's room which made things awkward if its occupant suddenly had his own private party developing and wanted the place cleared. With an empty room or suite, the festivities could continue unchecked for as long as desired while allowing any band member to discreetly slip away, either alone or with that night's catch, without disturbing the good vibes.

Occasionally the band would venture away from the madness around them. When the tour reached San Antonio they caught up with their friend Tom Wright and his sidekicks, Chuch Magee and Russ Schlagbaum. Since working on the Goose Lake festival the previous year, Chuch and Russ had started their own modest company Rent A Roadie, hiring themselves out to bands including Michigan hard rock group Frijid Pink, who had a freak US million-selling hit with a desecration of 'House Of The Rising Sun', and were living in a large old farmhouse in Ypsilanti. To help meet the rent when off the road, Russ would go back to Ohio to work with his brother on the family farm.

Russ Schlagbaum: "Tom's mother and stepfather had bought this beautiful big old mansion built in the Twenties by S. S. Kresge, the guy that started the K-Mart chain. It was a huge home, one of the grandest in San Antonio, way up on the highlands overlooking the valley. So the three of us lived there redecorating for five or six months. During the course of it, the Faces played San Antonio and Tom invited them back to the house which the band were most impressed by as it was absolutely gorgeous, all decorated and furnished.

---

* A picture of such a lay out can be seen among the images on the poster packaged with *A Nod's As Good As A Wink . . .*

227

"There was a little sun deck on the top floor and the guys were up there, strumming acoustic guitars, working on some tunes. Tom is an archivist, always recording stuff and of course he was taping it. They worked through some song – I can't remember what it was – and when they were done playing, Ronnie Lane opened Tom's cassette recorder and put the cassette in his pocket.* Tom freaked out, he kept going on at me, 'You've got to find Ronnie Lane and get that cassette back.' I said, 'Well it's not mine.' He said, 'But there's some really good stuff on there.' So that was one of my chores, I'd had orders from Tom Wright! Chuch and I were the gofers basically.

"My bedroom was the master suite and I discovered Ronnie Lane lying on my bed rolling a joint or a cigarette. He'd wandered off on his own in search of a quiet place and found my room. I think the partying that was going on he wasn't that into, he'd done all that shit, it was really old hat to him by then. I remember he was propped up against the wall with his legs crossed and he apologised, 'Oh, I'm really sorry is this your room?' that kind of thing. I said, 'Don't worry,' even though I was a bit miffed as I thought he was going to set my bed on fire. I sat down and said, 'Tom would really like to have a copy of that cassette.' Ronnie said, 'Oh no, there's a new song on there and I've been fucked over too many times by people stealing stuff. I'm going to have to hang onto it.' And that was my first acquaintance with Ronnie Lane. Chuch latched on to Woody and Mac, he got really friendly with those two."

The next night Tom and Chuch followed the band to Houston where the aerial shot used for the front sleeve of *A Nod Is As Good As A Wink . . .* was taken at Sam Houston Coliseum. A friendly dispute as to who took the actual photo developed over the years. According to Wright, "Chuch continually claimed he took the picture but he was my helper. At that point, I had three Nikons and mostly what I shot was B&W and I would carry one camera that had colour but in this case I had an extra one. On the encore the audience came towards the stage and we were both up in the balcony behind, shooting pictures as fast as we could so I never contested that with Chuch because he needed something to feel good about at that point."

The photo instantly became part of Faces folklore, capturing the band's

---

* The song could well have been 'I Came Looking For You' – an early version of 'Last Orders Please', which Lane and McLagan demoed a night or two earlier in New Orleans. It can be heard on the *Five Guys Walk Into A Bar . . .* box set, irreverently described in Mac's track annotation as "From a quick shag at the Marie Antoinette Hotel."

warm informality – Ronnie Lane is murmuring something to Rod – and the communality with their audience. "I still get people coming up at gigs telling me they can see themselves in the picture," says Mac, "including the guy saying something to Woody."

Rod always had an eye for a pretty face with legs to match – one that stood out from the usual ladies he encountered in the same city on each tour – so when Warner Bros. threw a party for the band at the Bumbles club in Los Angeles on July 29, his behaviour was no different. His relationship with Sarah was now in terminal decline, due largely to his non-committal stance. Rod was about to encounter his next long-term partner.

The Harrow-born daughter of an RAF Squadron Leader, 21-year-old Deidre ('Dee') Ann Harrington had arrived in Los Angeles earlier in the year with her friend Patsy Jones on the first step in a grand adventure to see the world. As Dee recalls: "Patsy went out with Jack Oliver who was the head of Apple Records. We'd gone to his goodbye party at the Speakeasy and he said, 'Well, why don't you both come over?' We didn't have any money, but we worked and put the money down on a flight and three months later we were in LA."

Dee had a little experience of the entertainment business, having worked for movie producer Nat Cohen, at Anglo-Amalgamated Films on Wardour Street. "I'd also been at Lucy Clayton's modelling school at the same time so I was slightly out of the music biz, if you like, I was more into the film and fashion worlds." Just prior to leaving for California, Dee was working as a PA above a record shop in Westbourne Grove, part of a chain of Disci shops set up by Barry & Sylvia Class, who had a management and agency company as well as a label, Trend Records.

"Jack Oliver went to work for Peter Asher who looked after Linda Ronstadt and James Taylor so Patsy and I went to a few gigs. One day, Jack said to me, 'I've a friend coming into town. He's a bit homesick, he's from England, would you cook him a nice English roast dinner?' Because I did all the cooking and Patsy did all the cleaning, I said, 'Yeah, sure.' I didn't even ask 'Who is it?' So that evening, Kenney Jones arrived and I cooked him a roast chicken dinner. I had a girlfriend, Suzy Worth, back in London and she was very into the Faces but I'd not paid any attention to them. I always remember before I left for the States, Suzy said to me, 'Have you seen that life size cut-out of Rod Stewart in the Disci window?' and I said, 'Who?'

"I'm not sure how Kenney knew Jack but he invited us to a party being held at this club. It was a real eye-opener [for me], a real kind of 'Wow' moment, you know? Kenney sat with Jack, Patsy and me in my home-made dress. Rod and Ronnie Wood came in, making faces and just enter-taining people. It was quite interesting to see how all the focus was on them, not particularly the other guys, none of whom really paid very much attention to these – groupies, I presume they were. These herds of done-up women were throwing themselves at Rod all night and he just kind of peeled them off him.

"Towards the end of the evening Rod came up to our table and asked me to dance [to Aretha Franklin's version of 'Spanish Harlem'] and so we danced and he never took me back to the table, it was like he stopped me from going back there. I found him shy and that he liked to make you laugh – he was very funny – so there was this mix of shyness and fun that I liked. We left the club and walked to the Whisky A Go-Go on Sunset Strip. The police stopped us and said, 'You can't walk up here.' Because I was on a tourist visa I had to take my passport everywhere we went because I just looked like a child at 21. So we ended up back at Rod's hotel and we talked and talked until the early hours. And that was the beginning of our relationship.

"It just happened that way, I certainly didn't go to America to meet an English rock star. I could have bumped into Rod on the street or down the Speakeasy. The next day the Faces were playing Long Beach Arena and I went there with Rod and Kenney in a limo. Then I went up to San Francisco with them. Rod and I spent these mad few days together. Then he carried on the rest of the tour and I stayed behind in LA. That was what I wanted because I thought you can't just meet somebody and go off with them like that even though we really enjoyed each other's company."

Although he was unlikely to have admitted it – heaven forbid – Rod was smitten with his new lovely. Like Sarah before her, the working-class rock'n'roller made good saw something in Dee. "Long legs and tits," she says with a laugh. "Rod was four years older than me and his upbringing had been very different to mine, plus he'd been out there striving to be successful in the music industry and so he'd had all that experience. I was interested in black American music – Otis Redding, Stevie Wonder – and those were the kinds of artists he listened to."

The tour played four more dates – the Mississippi River Festival at Southern Illinois University, Atlanta Civic Auditorium, Boston Common and Washington D.C. Armory, supported by Grin, featuring a precociously talented young guitarist and singer-songwriter Nils Lofgren. In Boston, the band reconnected with their old friend, Charlie Daniels, the 'Master Blaster' MC from the Tea Party, which had closed earlier that year.

"The people who were doing the outdoor shows on the Common had hired me to be the MC for this particular concert which featured the Faces," says Charlie. "The band didn't know that I was going to be the announcer until they got there and that's when they said, 'We wanted to have you travel with us but no one knew how to get a hold of you.' Rod said that whenever they'd played in Boston, I always gave them the best introduction so that's why they wanted me to come and bring that energy and have it onstage with them every night. They were pretty much at the end of the tour – they had one more gig to do in Washington but they were going to come back to the States in the fall so when they told me that someone would contact me to sort everything out, I didn't really pay that much attention until it actually happened."

After the show, Charlie and Rod went to watch the Who – in town performing the third of four nights at the 4,500-seater Music Hall. Although some reports say that he came on and sang during the encore, Rod stayed where he was in the wings, particularly as the band were having a bad night with arguments over the sound system. At one point, Daltrey sent Townshend's speaker stacks toppling off the stage, knocking a roadie unconscious. Both the Who and the Faces would be unintentionally pitted against each other on a London stage within a matter of weeks.

With sales figures continuing to climb, Mercury decided to release a single from *Every Picture . . .* opting for 'Reason To Believe'. As a further reminder of how its merits were underestimated, 'Maggie May' was relegated to flipside status. But not for long – the slow pace and pregnant pauses of Rod's superlative Tim Hardin cover posed a problem for DJs, causing one in Cleveland to flip the record over and give the B-side a spin. He continued to playlist the song, and soon other DJs across the country followed suit.

Its progress in the UK was slower. Booked for his first ever solo *Top Of The Pops* appearance on August 18, Stewart insisted that his fellow Faces should be on camera with him despite Lane and Jones not being on the record. Lane wasn't even in the studio to begin with so the band's friend, visiting Los Angeles scenester Rodney Bingenheimer, who had been hired by Mercury in the US to do publicity for both Stewart and David Bowie, was roped in for the camera rehearsals. The record hovered outside the *NME* Top 30 and with no previous chart form of Stewart's to indicate otherwise, that was where it seemed destined to remain.

August was a fairly quiet month, with no gigs on the horizon until a festival in Belgium on the 22nd, so with time on his hands Rod's thoughts drifted back to the willowy English beauty he'd met in LA. "I decided to move back to England," says Dee, "mainly because I'd run out of money but also because Rod had rung to ask when was I coming home. We arranged to meet at a pub in Lancaster Gate and then he took me out to lunch in Kensington Church Street and back to his house. I was so shocked that he had bought a beautiful home and had decorated it with such great taste. Rod really had an eye for all that; oak panelling, a four-poster bed and, of course, the cars in the drive. The night we met in LA, he had a dinky toy of the yellow Mura two-seater Lamborghini in his pocket."

A month to the day of their first meeting, Rod drove Dee in his latest acquisition, a white Rolls-Royce, to rendezvous with the other Faces at Weeley, near Clacton-on-Sea, Essex, for their appearance at the three-day Weeley Festival of Progressive Music, which had attracted a Bank Holiday weekend audience of over 100,000. With such a ponderous name, and with the bands to match, it was little wonder that the Faces stood out among the likes of Principal Edwards Magic Theatre, Colosseum, King Crimson (featuring 'Boz' Burrell, Mac's old bandleader, on bass and vocals) and their old sparring partner, Edgar Broughton. Playing on Sunday's bill, sandwiched between Head, Hands & Feet (featuring ace picker Albert Lee) and T. Rex, each Face was strikingly attired, particularly Rod, resplendent in bright pink satin suit, matching scarf and no shirt, clutching a bottle of Mateus ("good for the voice," he would insist) and Ron Wood in a navy and yellow jacket, a lapel badge of a guitar-playing rocker and yellow strides, against his silver metal Zemaitis guitar. Ronnie Lane wore a white polka dot jacket and cream trousers, Mac, a green jacket and tartan shirt and Kenney an American Nudie-style shirt.

In the backstage caravan that acted as the band's dressing room, the atmosphere was riddled with tension, not least over Rod's new live-in lover now entering the Faces' inner circle. "When I first met the others, it was pretty awful," Dee remembers. "I had this tiny little pink Angora knitted dress on that was a bit like a jumper and this big Afghan coat. You could have cut the air as I walked in. The girls ignored me – it was like the playground really – and the boys wouldn't have wanted to step out of line and so consequently, they didn't talk to me either.

"They'd all been close to Sarah and now, here I was in the wives' camp. But I didn't know any of that. When I was coming into their world, Rod had warned me. He said, 'I don't want you to listen to anything they've got to say because they're troublemakers.' I was a bit surprised by that but I said, 'All right.' Rod just protected me from it and he was right really. The less you know, the happier you'll be."

"There was definitely a frostiness towards Dee at first," Jan Jones admits, "because we were still friends with Sarah. It was a girlie solidarity thing going on. Rod had met Dee on the road so in our eyes she was like a groupie who'd done good. She wasn't one of the wives that supported her man when they had nothing like we had. So there was an attitude towards Dee but it wasn't very long before she was one of the girls."

If the atmosphere backstage was charged, the audience's ferment boiled over when the Faces turned in an exuberant, show-stealing set as confirmed by *NME*'s bold front page headline 'A One Group Festival And They Were The Faces . . . "No group generated the excitement of the Faces – 15 minutes before they went on the crowd were clapping empty beer cans together or anything they could lay their hands on in anticipation of a good set. The cans did the trick – the Faces were in a good mood and an audience who half an hour previously had looked like they were about to fall asleep stood up as the group leapt on stage . . . Those who may have previously thought the crowd were slightly apathetic can have been left in little doubt that all they wanted was a good band, excitement and a bit of a show.

"The Faces provided all this and lots more. After they'd finished my sympathies were with the follow-up band. T. Rex. After all who could possibly follow or match the sheer brilliance of the Faces who were undoubtedly at their best." The Weeley crowd voted with their throats, heartily jeering Bolan who faced an uphill battle to get them on side.

It's interesting to compare how Stewart and Bolan were poised in Britain at this juncture. While Rod was considered the bright new hope, a credible rock singer in the Joe Cocker mould, Marc was seen as having ditched his underground credibility in a blatant attempt to capture the teenybop market and rule the pop roost – 'Get It On' was still firmly lodged in the Top Five after four weeks at number one – with T. Rextasy a bona fide phenomenon by the end of the year. However *Every Picture . . .* held T. Rex's *Electric Warrior* down in second place and that same week, Rod received his first US gold disc for sales exceeding over one million dollars' worth of albums. To remind himself not to take it too seriously, he hung the award in his downstairs loo.

With the acclaim from Weeley washing over them, on September 5, the Faces played Queen Elizabeth Hall as part of a week of shows staged by young Midlands promoter Peter Bowyer who was to promote the Faces

British concerts with Gaff Management over the next few years. "Tonight we're gonna lift off the roof of this conservative establishment," Rod promised.

"I'd dropped acid and gone to the gig just to have a good time," Jeff Dexter recalls. "When I got backstage Peter Bowyer said, 'There's no one here to introduce it, you're on!' I said, 'Are you sure?!' The opening act was a duo called Ricotti & Alburquerque. The words were kind of spinning around in my head and on my tongue but I couldn't say them properly. I kept cracking up and started to take the piss out of myself and ended up taking the piss out of the band, which I didn't intend. Of course the guys in the Faces thought this was highly amusing. I remember they were particularly great that night. Rod had a fabulous pair of satin strides on – he liked his attire, that boy. And he had a fabulous blonde on his arm, I remember being quite impressed with that too."

Two weeks later Dexter observed the Faces up close again when compering (with Rikki Farr) the 'Goodbye Summer' charity concert held at London's Oval Cricket Ground in Kennington, just south of Vauxhall Bridge, on September 18 in aid of the Bangladesh Relief Fund. The open-air concert featured (in order of appearance) Cochise, the Grease Band, Lindisfarne, Quintessence, Mott The Hoople, America, Eugene Wallace, Atomic Rooster, the Faces and the Who. Blessed with perfect weather and organisation, the event was adjudged a success on all fronts with over 31,000 basking in late summer sunshine for the first ever rock show held in an arena where cricket had been played since 1845. After almost being anaesthetised by Atomic Rooster, the crowd were well up for the band of the moment who arrived onstage to a standing ovation in a blaze of colour – Mac in a fire engine red suit, Woody in a tiger striped yellow and black satin jacket and a bare chested, black scarfed Rod wearing a Granny Takes A Trip-designed leopard skin suit.

"There were problems early in the set, particularly with monitors," Pete Buckland recalls. "I believe it was a WEM system every act other than the Who was using that was cobbled together for the event, although after the first couple of numbers it was OK out front." The Faces got into their stride as dusk fell with 'It's All Over Now', had the crowd up for 'Maggie May' (which was hovering just outside the Top 10 that week) and were the only act to be brought back for an encore with an elongated 'Had Me A Real Good Time' which segued into the refrain of 'Every Picture Tells A Story'. The band left the stage to uproarious cheers and while the delay between the previous acts had lasted no more than roughly 15 minutes, tellingly, there was an unplanned hour's interval before the Who appeared.

"The Faces played such a good set," says Billy Nicholls, "and I thought to myself, 'This is going to be interesting.' Then the Who came on with their new sound system and it was like someone had notched it up. I remember Rod looking very stone faced because he could tell the difference. The sound, lights, everything was so much clearer and better. The Faces were fantastic, they played a great show and it was great to see the two bands together but it was very typical of the Who to do that."

Jeff Dexter: "The Faces were great fun, it was refreshing having them come on after bands like Atomic Rooster. I'd already got rather high and then for some reason, I hit the booze with the Faces and I wasn't very good at holding the bottle at that time. At the end of the Who's set, when Keith Moon lobbed this brand new cricket bat I'd borrowed from Surrey Cricket Club into the audience, I tried to put the last record on and I really couldn't do it, I kept falling over.

"We attempted an auction at the end of the night, which I was supposed to host. There were lots of things donated including Rod's leopard skin suit, which, completely out of my head, I wore to see if anyone would bid for it but nobody really bid enough so I was carried off in the back of a car still wearing it. It's now with an ex-girlfriend of mine."

The Oval event raised a total profit of £18,336 with the Who donating 25 per cent of the gross box office receipts. Over and above the charitable outcome, the post mortem in the *Melody Maker* devoted more space to, literally, who topped Who. In his lengthy review, Chris Charlesworth wrote: "The choice of the Who and the Faces to finish off the night was a stroke of genius, not only because both rely on visual excitement to build up their act, but because there was undoubtedly a certain amount of rivalry between the two camps. The Who have long claimed the crown for the most exciting live act on the road – both in this country and across the Atlantic – while the Faces have challenged them for the greater part of this year. Few, I feel, will disagree with me when I say that the Who retained their title.

"Not that the Faces played badly – they warmed up into one of their spontaneous chunks of excitement comfortably – but the Who played and sounded better . . . While the Faces establish their friendly rapport with the audience, the Who are surrounded by a charisma which elevates them much higher than the 20 foot high stage."

Faces fanatic Roy Hollingworth inevitably posited the opposing view, going so far as to compose an Open Letter to Pete Townshend published in *Melody Maker* the following week, daring to criticise the Who for being "too predictable" and "too perfect . . . and that's why I'll say the Faces were ten times better."

"Roy was big mates with Rod at the time," Charlesworth recalls. "He even had the same hairstyle. I think he was being controversial for the sake of it. I watched the show from the side of the stage, while he was right back on the members' balcony opposite, a good 300 yards from the stage, so I had the better view."

While this battle of the bands and critics was being debated, the *MM*'s readers voted Rod as Top British Male singer in the paper's annual poll. Ignoring his own view of how "the wives got in the way", on September 27, Ron made an honest woman of Krissie in a ceremony at Northampton Register Office. Perhaps to avoid the stigma of having lived in sin, Krissie gave her parents' address of 66 Barley Lane, Northampton. The couple swapped turquoise rings while best man Rod and Art Wood Snr proceeded to get uproariously drunk until Rod had to be delivered home.

Meanwhile, 'Maggie May' leaped from number 11 to three. By the following week, it was at pole position where it stayed for a consecutive five weeks and held the top spot in the *Melody Maker* and *NME* charts for six weeks. Meanwhile *Every Picture . . .* reached the top of the UK and US album listings, replacing Carole King's *Tapestry*, which had sat at number one in *Billboard* for the past four months. But the most unprecedented achievement occurred when the charts for the weeks ending October 9, 16 and 23 revealed that Rod was top of both the UK and US album and singles charts *simultaneously* – a feat neither Elvis nor the Beatles ever accomplished and one not matched since – leaving Rod Stewart the only artist in the history of popular music to attain this unique triumph.

In the midst of these astounding stats, the Faces rarely ventured far from a BBC studio. They recorded a three-song live session for *Top Gear* on September 28, previewing 'Stay With Me' (which was, by now, a familiar part of their act) and 'Miss Judy's Farm' from the current album sessions, and the hit single that continued to blare incessantly from the nation's tellys and transistors. A day later the band brought John Peel with them to Television Centre, persuading the reticent DJ to mime Ray Jackson's mandolin part on camera for their second 'Maggie May' *Top Of The Pops* appearance. Dressed for the occasion in a wine red velvet suit and black scarf, Rod disappeared from the camera's gaze at one point so that the others might share the limelight. During 'Peel's solo', Ronnie in his navy and yellow suit retrieved a soccer ball, passing it to Rod who demonstrated his skills before Ronnie Lane clumsily booted it off set.

For the third *TOTP* appearance on October 20, the same day a shell-shocked Rod learned that 'Maggie May' had sold over a million copies in America, the band swapped instruments – with Woody on keyboards, Kenney on bass, Ronnie on drums and Mac on guitar. "It'll never happen again, it's a fluke thing," Stewart told Penny Valentine. "I'm pretty confident I could make another top album again because there's enough material. But not a top single . . . I think I know what the market wants and I certainly can't say the same about singles – I couldn't turn out another hit single to save my life." Maybe not one a shade over five minutes whose subject matter, mystifyingly evading broadcasters and even the eternally vigilant British morals campaigner Mary Whitehouse, candidly described a runaway schoolboy's seduction by a voracious Mrs Robinson-style vamp.

On October 26, the band pre-recorded a 45-minute special, under the working title *Festival*, which eventually aired the following April as the first in a new series called *Sounds For Saturday*. With friends among the audience at the BBC TV Theatre cheerleading them on, the small screen communicated a taste of the Faces' informal charm, casually commanding a television studio as if it were a pub snug and yet, thanks to their extrovert singer's extraordinary success, these carefree musicians were all now on the verge of superstardom.

By November, the album and single had sold vast quantities in Canada, Australia and New Zealand. To celebrate their golden boy's achievements, Philips executives threw a Rod Stewart Day on November 5, to which 100 reporters, flown in from 12 different countries, were invited to the Amsterdam Hilton where a bewildered Rod was feted by record company reps eager to associate themselves with this new phenomenon. He was bestowed with a Gold Disc for UK sales of 100,000, five Gold Discs (for sales in European territories), two Silver Discs, the 1970 Edison award as top male singer on the Continent and, most prestigious of all, a platinum disc presented by Mercury president Irwin Steinberg for over one and a half million album and tape sales. Rod also won Radio Luxembourg's award for the top male record performance. A tie-in Faces' Guy Fawke's Party in the form of gigs in Groningen and Rotterdam was cancelled – officially because Kenney was ill with flu. However, behind the scenes, lines may already have been drawn over the undue attention their singer was receiving.

Rolling Stone summarised things when awarding Rod their Rock Star Of The Year Award for 1971: "In an era where most rock musicians wear faded jeans and too many of them look like they are in danger of falling asleep at the microphone, one man has kept the tradition of the rock star alive . . . He is a great rock singer, a great stylist, funny, intelligent and sensitive and he makes great albums. On top of that, he looks like he always wanted to be a rock'n'roll star and now that he is, he ain't ashamed to show it."

CHAPTER 14

A Nod Is As Good As A Wink

"I definitely think we felt that everything relied on this album – for the group's future. Especially with Rod becoming a ridiculous success. We had to come out with something good."

– Ron Wood, *Sounds*, 1971

"Every band needs a singer and every singer needs a band. We are just one band playing together. No one's trying to outdo the others. It's natural for people to single out the singer, but Rod gets embarrassed when it gets out of hand."

– Kenney Jones, *New Musical Express*, 1972

IT would be a gross understatement to say that Rod's phenomenal success, which continued unabated during the final months of 1971, caught the Faces' camp unawares. The first week of November saw John Lennon's *Imagine* leapfrog one place above *Every Picture . . .* in both the UK and US album charts but the following week, Rod was back on top. Simultaneously 'Maggie May' remained at the crest of the singles listings before being dislodged by Slade's first chart-topper 'Coz I Luv You'. At the end of the month, both album and single were still embedded in the US Top Five and in the year-end round-up of 1971's best selling records, 'Maggie May' came runner up to George Harrison's 'My Sweet Lord' and *Every Picture . . .* finished behind Simon & Garfunkel's *Bridge Over Troubled Water*.

It was discomforting, albeit inevitable, that journalists habitually asked Rod if he could withstand the now tremendous temptation to strike out on his own. Looking back to this period McLagan insists, "There was no problem [with the rest of the Faces], we were part of a fucking hit, you kidding me? We were happy to play it and all those other songs off Rod's albums. We were multi-faceted. Rod had his solo deal and we had our album deal. Actually it couldn't have been better because without us he wouldn't have had the hits because we were performing them every night but at the same time, because of the hits we were getting more people coming to see the band, you know? So it was very amicable actually."

"There's no bad feeling because we've got a very rare thing going," an optimistic Jones told *NME*'s Julie Webb. "When groups split up it's usually because the singer goes solo but that wouldn't happen with Rod. He doesn't like to see his name in the papers more than us and when people started billing us as Rod Stewart and the Faces we soon put a stop to it." Although it seems unlikely that he would not have revelled in seeing his name continually in print, Rod proved that actions speak louder than words by invoking a nine-month ban on interviews, although inevitably it served only to increase the clamour surrounding him.

With this in mind, Rod seemed even more determined that the third Faces album had to overcome their dual identity. It's fascinating how the interviews Stewart gave before his media silence carry a sense of déjà vu, echoing the same hopeful statements he'd made prior to the release of *Long Player*. "This has to be the one to do it, it really has," he declared to *Record Mirror*'s Bill McAllister. "I'm not too sure what's gone wrong before but we've never really gone into a studio as a group and got the kind of atmosphere and sound that we know we can get." As *Long Player* had shown, band autonomy had led to mixed results. What was needed was somebody who could corral the group's collective ideas in a way that would match the busy productivity and creative riches of Rod's albums.

"We're using Glyn Johns . . ." Stewart continued. "He's about the only guy we would use . . . He won't be in complete control, though, he'll co-operate with us and we'll all put in ideas." Never a truer word being spoken in jest, Stewart told Penny Valentine that the band's favoured arrangement with Johns as co-producer was "£10 and all the beer he could drink."

Ian McLagan: "When Ronnie Lane originally suggested Glyn, I was keen until it turned out that he wanted a bigger percentage. I fought it – it wasn't that I didn't want Glyn, it was just that I didn't want to pay him more than I was getting myself. I don't remember the numbers, but if he got three percent we were getting two or something like that. Glyn was worth whatever he got but it was just that I didn't consider anyone was worth more than any one member of the band and if Glyn got the same as us I would have been quite happy. I lost that battle but the great thing is Glyn did the best possible job for the Faces."

Born February 15, 1942, in Epsom, Surrey, Johns' illustrious career in recording began in the early Sixties as a staff engineer at IBC Studios on

Portland Place as well as working with a group, Ricky Tyrrell & The Presidents for whom he occasionally sang. During his time hanging around the nascent London R&B circuit Johns became closely associated with the Rolling Stones – for whom he produced their first demo tape at IBC in 1963 – and went on to be chief engineer on all of the band's seminal recordings between 1966 and 1971 (from *Between The Buttons* to *Exile On Main Street*) and the Who – engineering their Shel Talmy-produced first album *My Generation* and early singles in 1965. Johns started working with the Small Faces at IBC in 1966 and after turning freelance and moving his work base to Olympic Studios, he continued to oversee their recordings for Immediate – his intuitive grasp of how a recording should sound resulting in their best work like 'Tin Soldier' and *Ogdens' Nut Gone Flake*.

By the late Sixties, Johns was among the most respected engineers/producers in the business – manning the desk for the Beatles' ill-fated *Get Back* project (which eventually became the Phil-Spector-doctored *Let It Be*), Led Zeppelin's debut, the Steve Miller Band's first four albums and, just prior to working with the Faces in 1971, the Who's most consistent album, *Who's Next*.

Having worked alongside these top names (with egos to match), Johns' business-like, no-nonsense approach in the studio made him the kind of outspoken mediator that the Faces – who had made plain their disenchantment with producers – needed. *A Nod Is As Good As A Wink . . . To A Blind Horse*[*] was completed in a comparatively quick but efficient time – from late August to October – as compared to the nine months it had taken to deliver the lacklustre *Long Player*. "At first we weren't too sure about Glyn," Kenney told Bill McAllister. "You know, neither side really knew what the other wanted or expected."

"I've always felt that when working with a band my role is to try and represent each member equally," says Johns. "I was terribly impressed with Ronnie Wood who I hadn't known prior to those sessions and I was thrilled to be reunited with the rhythm section again."

From the first track Johns worked on in Studio One at Olympic with newly appointed tape op Phil Chapman, the results spoke for themselves. "We got 'Stay With Me' down in about two takes . . ." Jones enthused. "But it's all down to Glyn for the technical things, that's where he comes into his own. The fact that he has such good taste and a fine ear is a bonus."

Mac described Johns' working methods: "Glyn would walk up to the

---

[*] In the UK, the album was released with the incorrect title *A Nod's As Good As A Wink . . . To A Blind Horse*.

amp and listen, moving backwards and forwards until he heard where the sweet spot was and then he'd put a microphone right there. Now there was no excuse for it not to sound just like he heard it. There'd be limitations with the mikes but he'd always use the right one. He was very sure, you know? There wasn't a lot left to chance with Glyn, he knew what he was doing."

Johns was not only technically adept, he was also astute at picking a band's best material and *Nod's* presented the Faces in a way that the first two albums merely hinted at. From the opening gruff guitar chug of 'Miss Judy's Farm' to the final marimba cascades on 'That's All You Need', the nine tracks conveyed not only a fine range of moods but also a distinct sense of cohesion.

As the band came crashing in on 'Miss Judy's Farm', in the same spirited fashion as 'Bad 'N' Ruin' had introduced *Long Player*, the contrast to the muddy fidelity on that album was like night and day. The song's slow-fast, start-stop arrangement showed an increased awareness of song dynamics, too. Another of Rod's 'imagination' stories, this one concerning a bunch of emasculated workers on a poodle-pampering harridan's Alabama sweatshop, the lyrics, a close relative of Bob Dylan's 'Maggie's Farm', were as witty as they were bawdy, involving a threat to burn the place down being thwarted by the appearance of Miss Judy's allies, the National Guard.

Just as Rod liked to draw on his youthful experiences for subject matter so Ronnie Lane harked back to adolescence for his high calibre contributions to the album. The first, 'You're So Rude', co-written with McLagan, was a delightfully louche recounting of Ronnie and girlfriend Jill Walsh being caught in flagrante when Ronnie's folks unexpectedly returned home early from visiting his Auntie Rene.

"I wrote the music before Ronnie wrote the words," says Mac. "I played him the whole thing and he literally wrote the lyrics within 10 minutes. I still have the sheet that he wrote them on and the words are slightly different, he only made a couple of adjustments. Actually they're written on the back of a Faces schedule and it's funny to see on such and such a date 'Rehearsal' and on another date 'Rehearsal'. I thought the Faces didn't rehearse but there you go . . ." The band groove along nicely on the Booker T. style outro with Ronnie Wood adding harmonica.

The wistful 'Love Lives Here', an evocative lament about an old home being torn down, co-written by Wood, Stewart and Lane, could have come straight out of the Ray Davies songbook. But whereas Davies would have placed a preservation order on it, Lane used the building's demolition as a metaphor for a broken relationship.

That's all you need: the Faces' backstage trailer, 1971. "It's something that happens immediately we all get together – that's probably why we always look so shattered," said Wood, "because travelling to the gig is like a party and doing the gig is a party and on the way back it's a party… and when we've all had a few… it just becomes uncontrollable." (DICK BARNATT)

Ronnie and Rod, brothers in arms, somewhere in America. "Rod was one of the last people I would have thought I'd end up spending my career with," said Wood, " … we lead completely different lives. But there's always this constant factor between us…" (COURTESY MIKE MCINNERNEY)

The Faces' breakthrough British gig at the Weeley Festival, August 29, 1971. 'A One Group Festival', ran *NME*'s headline the following week. "And they were the Faces …" (ROBERT ELLIS/REPFOTO)

Howzat! The Faces at the Bangla-Desh benefit concert at the Oval cricket ground, September 18, 1971. Rod's leopard skin suit from the boutique Granny Takes A Trip was donated to a charity auction. (GIJSBERT HANEKROOT/REDFERNS)

Ron, Ronnie and Rod havin' a laugh onstage, US tour, 1971. Mike McInnerney: "The Faces weren't doing a carefully choreographed show. The idea of being slightly shambolic or just on the edge of falling apart in concert was actually quite exciting, it gave a real tension to their performance." (CRAIG PETTY)

Rod and girlfriend Dee Harrington relax at home in Winchmore Hill, 1971. "After the success of 'Maggie May' everything changed practically overnight," said Dee. "Once the fans discovered our address, it became ridiculous. We couldn't go out the front door in the end." (MANCHESTER DAILY EXPRESS)

Rod and his hero, Temptations singer David Ruffin, duet on 'Losing You' at Cobo Hall, Detroit, December 8, 1971. (MARTY TEMME ARCHIVES)

"Take me back, down to Gasoline Alley where I was born..." Rod, Mac and Laneole share a stool and the vocal spotlight, while the Faces' ladies look on, the Roundhouse, May 6, 1972; (top right and below) At the London Hilton, Chuch Magee, Mac and Kenney inspect the postcards from the Stones' *Exile On Main Street* and (below) the band and Billy Gaff receive gold discs for *A Nod Is As Good As A Wink...* In the centre is Warner Bros President Joe Smith. June 1972. (ROBERT ELLIS/REPFOTO)

The Faces on the road in America – Rod listens to backing tracks – most of his lyrics were written on flights; Mac and his multi-purpose tuxedo before the Hollywood Bowl show August 25, 1972; Ron and Ronnie at a soundcheck, both holding their custom made Zemaitis instruments. (CHARLIE DANIELS)

Rod brought to his knees on the Faces' perspex stage, Empire Pool, Wembley, London, October 29, 1972. Ronnie Lane: "The Faces got to be so good that I would stand on one side playing the bass and I was in awe of the band I was playing with." (REX FEATURES)

Gypsy Ronnie contemplates his future with Alana, daughter of Lane's partner Kate McInnerney. (MIRRORPIX)

Onstage at the Edmonton Sundown, London, June 6, 1973 – Ronnie Lane's last gig with the Faces. (ROBERT ELLIS/REPFOTO)

On the lash at Tramp, *Ooh La La* launch, April 1973. Ian McLagan: "Ronnie said, 'Why don't you come with me and we'll get another band together?' I said, 'I'm in the band I want to be in with you. I don't want you to leave.'"

The song's sentiment was married to a beautifully delicate arrangement, featuring a touch of harpsichord and a refrain that the Stones later unconsciously lifted for 'Fool To Cry'.

Throughout the sessions, the band continued their tradition of recording tracks under daft working titles, with Phil Chapman's studio diary noting, on October 4, that work was done on 'The Hoover's Not Working'. If 'Last Orders Please' was just such a working title it perfectly fit the song's rollicking bar room feel – featuring Lane on his Shobro and Wood on slide acoustic bass – as a soused Lane ruefully ponders the bottom of his glass and the bittersweet aftermath of two old flames' paths crossing. He even slips in a reference to an all-time favourite, the Miracles' 'Tracks Of My Tears', a song Ronnie adored in common with his friend Pete Townshend, who admired Smokey Robinson's use of the word 'substitute' in the song enough for it to inspire one of his own.

If 'Miss Judy's Farm' had been a tongue-in-cheek portrayal of an all empowering, ball-breaking woman, the stiletto was firmly on the other foot in 'Stay With Me', the emancipated male protagonist firmly in control of a drunken brief encounter and, as was so often the case on the road, anxious to sever the coupling at the first opportunity the next morning. Indeed, the denouement suggests the all-too-familiar scenario wherein he has difficulty recalling the name of his conquest.

Stewart's predilections in this area had already appeared in 'Had Me A Real Good Time' where he sang of being "escorted by a friendly slag 'round the bedroom and back". Alongside his views on immigration, no-one could accuse Rod of identifying with the emergent Women's Liberation movement, symbolised in Britain by Germaine Greer's book *The Female Eunuch* and publications like *Spare Rib*, which railed against the borderline misogyny presented in rock songs like 'Stay With Me' and 'Brown Sugar', to name but one from the Stones' catalogue of transgressions in this department. But then again, one could just imagine, if faced with accusations of being sexist, Rod replying in true *Spinal Tap* style, a wide gurn spread across his mug, "What's wrong with being sexy?"

In his defence, with a few adjustments, Stewart's lyrics could be dressed up as both a male *or* female viewpoint before an ill-advised one-nighter or mere reportage – a matter of fact, on-the-road vignette of the type of filly that flung themselves at his – and many other – bands. Within the political and cultural transformation of the early Seventies, however, the reductive male chauvinist pig sentiments expressed by the likes of Stewart, Jagger et al appeared antediluvian at a time when a major rock figure like John Lennon was, under his artistic partner Yoko Ono's influence, embracing feminism with the daring 'Woman Is The Nigger Of The World' (although, admittedly, it would take Lennon some time to practise what he preached).

Elsewhere, sensitive Laurel Canyon troubadours like James Taylor wore their vulnerability on their denimed sleeves. By the time of punk and beyond into the Eighties, when 'new men' began to get in touch with their feminine side, the sentiments of 'Stay With Me' appeared positively primeval unless, of course, you were forming a rock band in LA.

Leaving aside the unfavourable taint of sexism, 'Stay With Me' is great funky fun – "let's go upstairs and read my tarot cards" perfectly encapsulated the type of cosmic groupie like the GTOs that Rod and Ronnie encountered when touring the States in the late Sixties, their readings making little difference to the sensual outcome. Perhaps the closest studio recording to convey the raucousness and sloppiness of the Faces live with its contrasting tempos and cocksure, Stones-like swagger, 'Stay With Me' remains a Faces musical highpoint even though for some it remains a hard beast to love.

" 'Stay With Me' was written in a Georgia hotel room [in March '71] with Kenney pounding away on the telephone books," Wood recalled to Barbara Charone in 1974, "so we had the feel for that one before we went into the studio."

Ian McLagan: "It's very hard to remember how the arrangement on 'Stay With Me' happened – I think it just came from Ronnie [Wood]. I've been asked a bunch of times over the years, 'Oh man, the Wurlitzer sound, how did you get that?' The answer is Glyn came over and adjusted the volume on the Wurlitzer while I was playing, tweaked the amp until it sounded great and then went back into the control room to try and replicate the sound he heard out in the studio."

Like with 'Love Lives Here' Ronnie Lane's affecting 'Debris' acted as a letter to his childhood – in this case paying loving homage to his beloved father Stan.

Just as American singer-songwriters evoked their surroundings with juke joints, roadstar cafe's or the New Jersey turnpike, so Ronnie recreated monochrome images of East London in detailed brush strokes – bomb sites, Club Row, union meetings – even down to grammatically incorrect cockney – "you *was* looking for a bargain."

"One morning, just before *A Nod Is As Good As A Wink* came out," Mike McInnerney recalls, "Ronnie and I decided to go off and photograph the old East End, to do a little driving tour of the haunts from our school-days before they disappeared . . . He was talking about wanting to write this song about his dad. The way he was talking about it there was quite a strong sense of the East End after the war. It's a real little picture of a kind of London experience. That's what I loved about Ronnie's writing; it's global but it's London . . . With Rod you felt his writing was being influenced by more of a show tradition; another culture, another place. But with Ronnie you really got a sense it was from here."

For all the Faces' hot blooded bluster, 'Debris' proved that they could do justice to Lane's subtler writing just as well. Johns beautifully captured a stirring performance from each with Lane's touching vocal, Wood's wonderfully expressive 12-string and lead fills, Mac's melodic touches on Wurlitzer, Jones drums the right side of restraint and best of all, Rod's beautifully complementary back-up vocals.

The loping groove on 'Memphis' reduced the uptempo Chuck Berry original down to half-speed before accelerating up a gear with Wood excelling throughout, his overdubbed licks fed though a Leslie speaker. "It has a frantic ending because we got fed up with playing it – not deliberately," Jones explained to Julie Webb. "The fact it sounds so fast at the end is purely accidental." Developing out of a studio jam, with Rod's vocals added later, 'Memphis' jaunts along engagingly but at nearly five and a half minutes there was a feeling of filler. That's the way it appeared to McLagan who was never fond of the track.

"It was the wrong idea. I love Chuck Berry's original but I don't know why we did that, it's the weakest track on the album. Some people really like it, I certainly don't. It's waffle." Much to McLagan's chagrin, the song soon became a mainstay of the band's live set.

Rod had provided a glimpse of the British class divide in 'Had Me A Real Good Time', a narrative theme he returned to in 'Too Bad', wherein he and his chums – presumably the other boys in the band – gatecrash a posh do but are shown the door when "my regional tongue gave us away again." Whether it was based on an actual event remains unrecorded but there's a sting in the tail with his complaint about how "we always get the blame".

'That's All You Need' was in the same vein: a first person sketch of two brothers, one a violin-playing success, the other on the scrap heap until the other man's grass provides a revelation. Wood's raspy slide solo on his black Zemaitis Disc Front replaced 'Around The Plynth' as his solo spotlight in the live act. The song's fade featured a wry nod and wink back to 'Richmond' (from *Long Player*) and a calypso-style fade. When asked if the steel drums being credited to British comedian Harry Fowler was an in-joke, Mac replied, "I don't know. All I can think of was . . . [*imitates the drum pattern at song's end*] that was me."

A Nod Is As Good As A Wink . . . appeared in America in late November (December in the UK), the title emanating from one of Ronnie Lane's father's idiosyncratic sayings.* Its release was delayed slightly by the printing of the gargantuan poster, designed by Mike McInnerney, and folded to fit snugly into the Ronnie Wood-designed sleeve; the 'Faces' logo based on Holiday Inn lettering. It was the largest insert ever to be made available with a record.

"Ronnie [Lane] commissioned me to do the poster," says Mike. "It measured six foot by four foot six inches and was printed to a size four foot by three foot. The artwork was like a wallpaper idea; re-creating a patchwork of moments to accompany the printed lyrics, expressing something of the rock'n'roll life – from on the road excesses to more intimate moments and private family occasions as well as outside interests. I had to find pictures that I could cut exactly to size. I just remember nights of Kate and I going down to Olympic to listen to the album while the band were making it and taking the artwork to show them. They were blown away by it."

An array of 352 pictures – including shots dating back to early childhood – were loaned to McInnerney by the band and associates to use in the montage as well as his own images, some of which were cut from magazines and art books. Alongside the family snaps and generally innocent clowning moments were those of a seedier nature, namely candid Polaroids of groupies in various states of undress or in compromising situations. "About a third of the pics came from me as I was an avid snapper," says Pete Buckland. "When the SX70 came out, which we all bought, I became known as 'Polaroid Pete'."

In America where 400,000 copies had been printed (250,000 of which had already sold), rack jobbers, clearly with time on their hands, "closely scrutinised" the poster and complained to Warner Bros., refusing to continue distributing the record until the insert was withdrawn from all unsold stock.

Mike McInnerney: "I remember Pete [Townshend] scolding me for

---

* Although the phrase had cockney origins, it gained much wider exposure through *Monty Python's Flying Circus*. In the much loved 'Nudge Nudge' sketch during episode three in the first series of the surreal British comedy, originally broadcast on October 19, 1969, Eric Idle uses the line, "A nod's as good as wink to a blind bat."

including the picture of myself with [prominent Meher Baba associate] Delia de Leon in amongst all the other questionable stuff."

Less objectionable were the 18-inch high Faces marionette figures, specially handmade by Edwin Belchamber for the rear sleeve, which, according to press reports, were to be exhibited in various department stores around England. "I still have mine," says Mac, "although I have a broken hip and the organ is smashed. Until a few years ago, I still had the boots and the shirt. Rod still has his model and I know Ronnie Wood has. I don't know about Kenney but Ronnie Lane smashed his as soon as he saw it. He hated it."

With the burdensome spectre that Stewart's inexorable rise had created, an underlying sense of urgency surrounded the release of *Nod*'s. If it failed to live up to expectation, the Faces as a separate entity might have ended there, with a worse case scenario of the group being regarded as, whisper it, Rod's backing band. It was fortunate that Stewart's song wellspring hadn't been exhausted by *Every Picture* . . . and Lane's creative muse had burst into startling bloom, revealing a fine and disarming songwriter who, with 'Debris' alone, demonstrated his ability to mix the kind of folky sensitivity found on Rod's albums into the Faces robust framework. Allied to this, the clarity of Johns' production highlighted the band's abilities in their best light.

The album received the praise it deserved. *NME* called it "superb . . . What was lacking in their previous album has been rectified – every track has something to offer – and the nice thing is that no one member of the band is hogging the spotlight . . . In fact nothing is spoilt." Over at *Melody Maker*, Faces man Roy Hollingworth was ecstatic. "It's . . . it's hard to type cause the floor's heaving and boots are being smacked against the boards. . . . Whooo-ha!! . . . What a befitting end to the year of the Faces, what a befitting album, what a crazy encore to a set that has been playing all year." Curiously *Rolling Stone* writer, producer and future Bruce Springsteen associate Jon Landau considered the album a major letdown compared to the previous two. "Well now this doesn't make any sense at all . . . It is apparent that when Stewart takes charge of his music he elevates the musicianship of everyone around him; when he submerges himself in the artistic group democracy of this particular band he only succeeds in bringing himself down to the level of the group's lowest common denominator. Thus, at the same time he is riding the success of an intensely personal and beautifully crafted solo album he participates in the making of another almost completely devoid of personality, character, depth or vision."

Landau was in the minority of dissenters for, as Hollingworth gleefully summarised, "At last the lads have got it all down on wax."

"It's not just the sound, Glyn featured everybody," Mac says. "He utilised everyone's talents. *A Nod Is As Good As A Wink* was a fucking good album."

Olympic Studios proved an ideal location for the Faces to record as those members of the group less inclined towards punctuality needed only to travel the short distance from the Richmond area to Barnes. However, they hadn't reckoned on Johns the disciplinarian. "Glyn had lots of problems with us and we had lots with him – just misunderstandings really," Wood told Penny Valentine. "Like we're used to having the run of the studio, kicking the engineer and all that, and Glyn's got so much self-pride he thought we were taking the mickey out of him." Johns wasn't used to having five pairs of extra hands manning the faders while mixing 'Stay With Me'. Nor was he used to a formidable phalanx of bottles, glasses and cans vying for space with the amplifiers and instruments. Helping pour the drinks amid frequent trips to the nearest off-licence[*] was a new recruit, hired by Pete Buckland to replace 'Pee Wee' Peverett, and who was soon to become a permanent fixture within Ronnie Wood's orbit – Chuch Magee.

Having spent the summer in Texas, Chuch, Russ Schlagbaum and Tom Wright faced enduring the freezing cold of Michigan. From memories of his experiences in southern Europe, Wright suggested spending the winter in the south of France, Italy or Spain. "For a farm kid from Ohio it might as well have been the moon," says Schlagbaum. "Chuch and I now had deferments and were free of the draft so we pooled all our money and set it aside. Neither Chuch or I would have made the move without Tom who was extremely paranoid about flying because of a horrible experience he'd had over Cleveland with the Who or the James Gang. He wanted to go by boat and he discovered that you could book passage on a freighter from Houston to Rotterdam."

With Wright's friend Patrick Culley along for the ride, the four left Houston in August, the journey to Europe taking two weeks. "Holland was dreary – nowhere to stay," Russ continues, "so we bought a '57 Mercedes Benz for $150 from a kid at the American Embassy, packed the car solid including Tom's photo archive and darkroom materials, as he intended

[*] The British equivalent of a liquor store.

sending his pictures over to the record companies in England, and drove out through Belgium into France. After seeing Paris we headed down to Le Mans and ended up living at a fortified farm working on a chateau."

By mid-October, Chuch was itching to be with his girlfriend (and first wife) Nicky who, thanks to Wright's tip, was studying at Ealing Art College. "Nicky had done two years of art college in Ohio and was good enough to get a grant and be able to transfer to Ealing," Russ explains. "Chuch said, 'Fuck this, what we set out to do from the very beginning was to somehow work in the rock'n'roll scene not collect eggs on a farm.' He took about $100, probably all the money he had left and hitch-hiked over to London, got into Victoria Station with no idea where Ealing was or how to get there so he changed his money into sterling and took a taxi which, of course, practically ate up all his money.

"He gets to Ealing – the taxi driver short changes him on the fare and then drives off with his suitcase still in the trunk. So there Chuch stands in Ealing, he's got virtually no money left, and only two phone numbers on him: his girlfriend's and Ronnie Wood's. He calls Nicky but she's out so he calls Ronnie Wood who just happened to be home. He tells Woody the story of what happened. Woody says come on over, so Chuch went over to Ronnie's house in Kingston and that was the start of their whole thing. It's funny how Chuch started working for the Faces purely because he was flat broke and had nowhere else to go."

The trappings of success had made Rod an in-demand pillar of his well-heeled community in Winchmore Hill as he told Penny Valentine with some degree of bemusement. "All of a sudden I'm the hero of the street I live in, with all these very well-off over 30-year-olds inviting me to meet their bank managers, use their swimming pools, go riding with them. It gets on my tits a bit but I can't be rude to people however hard I try."

Dee was determined not to be a kept woman, going back to work for Barry and Sylvia Class. "Rod would say, 'How can you get out of bed and leave me?' I'd joke back, 'It's easy.' It wasn't, of course, but I needed to make my own way; I didn't want to be somebody that just coasted along on the coat-tails of somebody famous."

Equally resolved to keep his feet firmly anchored, on weekends Rod would roar off in the Lamborghini, either to watch Arsenal at Highbury on Saturday afternoons with his dad or to play for Highgate Redwing in the Finchley & District League, usually in the half-back line, and Sunday morning as a forward. Rod's VIP status notwithstanding, he would often be brought down to earth with a literal bump from a foul tackle. His assailant, smirking at the spiky-haired star sprawled on the muddy pitch, sarcastically remarked "I'd stick to singing if I was you, mate" before tearing off. All would be forgiven with a convivial pint at the local on Highgate Hill afterwards. Rod was even known to get his round in.

Unfortunately these simple pleasures became less accessible, thanks to the "he's not the same now that he's famous" brigade or intrepid fans discovering where Rod played footie and disrupting proceedings. "After the success of 'Maggie May' and *Every Picture Tells A Story* everything changed practically overnight," Dee confirms. "Once the fans discovered our address, it became ridiculous. We couldn't go out the front door in the end. And then Rod's accountant Milton Marks said, 'You've got to do something with the money you've earned otherwise it will all go in tax. You've got to find somewhere bigger to live.'

"Rod started ringing me at work, saying that Perry Press, estate agent to the stars, had found a house for us to look at. I would trot off to the office in the morning, sit down for five minutes and then the phone would go and I'd be off to look at these very nice houses in a Rolls-Royce. I had to leave the job because it was getting a bit iffy. On the way back from one place, Perry said, 'There's a house in Windsor that's for sale. I haven't made you an appointment but we could probably just nip in and have a look.' We couldn't see it from the road but the big gates were open so we drove down this mile long driveway and saw the house from the car. Rod just went, 'Yeah, Perry, I want to look at it,' so the next day, we went back to have a proper inspection and that was it."

For £89,000, Rod bought Cranbourne Court, a white Georgian mansion on Winkfield Row, set in 17 acres of ground near Windsor Castle. The titled owner was Lord Bethell, Lord-in-Waiting to the Queen, who showed the unconventionally attired but charming young couple around the magnificent house and grounds. "Thirty-two rooms, eight bathrooms, a lodge house, a coach house, a 40 foot high entrance hall . . ." Dee marvels almost four decades on. "It took a lot of decorating. I don't think Rod's brother Bobby had another job the entire time [it took to paint]."

Lending a somewhat reluctant hand was the dependable Chuch Magee, daydreaming of the delights awaiting him on his first American tour as a Faces roadie. "Chuch was living in a bedsit with Nicky, getting £15–£20 a week working for the band," says Russ. "Rod asked him to help paint his mansion but that didn't last long because the fucker wouldn't pay him. He said, 'But you're being paid by the band, aren't you?' and Chuch said, 'Well yeah but that's for Faces work, not this.' So Chuch stayed out in the gate cottage long enough for him to drive the Lamborghini a couple of times and that kinda shit. He got fed up with it real quick – 15 quid a week and expected to paint Rod Stewart's house all day long."

For their third extensive American sojourn of 1971 the Faces returned in late November as bona fide superstars playing to sold-out venues, earning five times per gig as they did on their first tour in 1970. The three-month slogs of yore were replaced by a far more agreeable three-and-a-half-week schedule, although, as Wood complained to Penny Valentine, "Between every gig is a two-hour flight through God knows how many time changes. It really wears us out." Tour supports were Cactus, the band formed by Vanilla Fudge's redoubtable rhythm section of Tim Bogert and Carmine Appice after Jeff Beck's accident, and Bull Angus who were replaced (on the last six dates) by English progressive group Audience.

Four numbers from *Nod*'s – 'Miss Judy's Farm', 'Stay With Me', 'Memphis' and 'Too Bad' – were added to the Faces' 90-minute set. "The whole act's changed now," Wood told *Record Mirror*. "We've just kept the choice numbers from the old act. It was a bit nerve wracking, getting the new numbers together. The old ones were like friends to us somehow, but the time was right for a change."

The wording at venues had been a recurrent problem right from the first US tour with the group variously advertised as 'The Small Faces with Rod Stewart' or 'Rod Stewart & The Small Faces'. Now, because of Stewart's stratospheric popularity, something he could not have foreseen, there was an underlying aggro that made the situation much more difficult for promoters and management.

As Billy Gaff explains, "Then and even now, it makes sense. If a promoter is going to pay a bunch of money to have a rock'n'roll show come to town they're going to use everything they can to sell tickets. When we got to a city I would have to call the promoters in advance and plead, 'For Christ's sake, get Rod's name down, just put 'Faces' up there'. And of course, several times they didn't do it and all fucking hell broke loose. I knew it was happening and I tried to sort it out. Rod knew what was going on and tried to keep the peace, Woody was easy-going about the whole thing, Kenney didn't care too much but the other two were violent. I got bottles thrown at me. They never had the balls to say it to Rod's face so it would always be my fault."

At St Louis, the tour's first stop, the entourage stayed at the Stouffer's Riverfront Towers, where Craig Petty recalls, "More crazy shit happened

. . . the Stouffers was a round hotel and so the halls were circular and the elevator went up the centre. The Faces had a whole floor and the soccer ball came out and it was just a round and round soccer game. The party room got so crowded that they had a whole table of empty bottles and stuff. At one point it was like 'we have to move this stuff out of here' but it wouldn't fit through the door so we turned it over sideways, let everything spill on the floor, kicked all the bottles out into the hall and then got the elevator up there, threw all the trash into the elevator and sent it down to the lobby."

When questioned as to who was generally responsible for instigating the mayhem, Petty says, "I would say Mac and Ronnie Wood. Ronnie Lane could be a little standoffish once in a while, he would be a little more private but once you got him started, he would really go for it. Rod would be up for a lot of the stuff but then once it began he would all of a sudden disappear. Kenney was there a lot of the time but he tended to turn in early."

Also observing the havoc at close quarters was Charlie Daniels who travelled as the tour's MC. "I had my own notoriety in Boston as the Master Blaster but to step outside the kind of gypsy lifestyle I had and be invited to announce each show was such a magical experience as far as I was concerned. I'd never had, like, a nine to five job, most of my time I spent working with horses or trying to be a photographer so to be able to travel in limos and Learjets and stuff like that, hanging with pretty women . . . Whatever it might be, I wanted to do it as well as it could be done so if I was gonna be an announcer I wanted to have fun on stage and keep it real."

After bringing the band on, Charlie would do his bit in getting the audience off. "I played tambourine and jumped around in the background, but without trying to get in the spotlight. After some review mentioned 'the tall, elegant dancer with the Faces', I think it was Billy Gaff or somebody came to me and said, 'You've got to stop moving around like that, you're distracting from Rod!' "

The tour's ultimate triumph was a sold-out concert at Madison Square Garden on November 26, the day after Thanksgiving, attended by 20,000, some of whom paid scalpers $100 for their tickets. And to think this band had struggled out of a south London rehearsal studio deep in debt two short years before. Determined that a good time be had by all, the group footed a $12,000 bill for the installation of video screens located above either side of the stage to project the images being filmed by the Joshua Television company. Gaff-Masters commissioned Mike McInnerney to design a gigantic 20 to 30 feet square 'A Nod Is As Good As A Wink' banner for the stage backdrop (this and the video screen were used for the bigger venues). For the band's carefully choreographed arrival – as Faces entrances would now be – a four-trumpet fanfare brought three costumed characters – two dancing bears, Mickey Mouse and Donald Duck – cheerfully romping about the stage while Charlie built up his announcement.

Suddenly there were the Faces, led out by a beaming Rod in his pink satin suit. "'Ello, New York, how are ya?!" he shouted over the standing ovation. "Don't forget, we're the same group that played Ungano's 18 months ago so don't expect anything different! We're just here to play some rock'n'roll!" To loosen the mood, cases of wine, which the crew had smuggled past security, were distributed out to the audience before stewards intervened. They were unable to stop a couple of dozen plastic footballs being kicked into the arena during Kenney's solo in 'Losing You'. When *Melody Maker*'s Chris Charlesworth asked Jones the following day via a transatlantic call if he considered it the Faces best gig to date, the still clearly overwhelmed drummer replied, "Yes, I think it was. The nice thing about it was we really played more together than ever. We worked well all night more or less as a team. It was a big gig which we hadn't played before, but we treated it like any other small concert, which was a good thing to do."

Dancing and cheering at the side of the stage, drinking in the moment, were the wives and girlfriends. "The guys at Warner Bros. had said that we should go over," says Sandy. "We all went back to the hotel afterwards to celebrate. Rod put his face in and disappeared but then that was no surprise because he became quite separate, particularly when Dee was around."

Now the band's only bachelor and perhaps overcome by the sense of occasion, Rod had been doing some contemplating. "I'd flown out with Krissie the day before [the MSG show]," Dee recalls. "I found a really great wood-panelled suite at the Sherry Netherland, which was like the dining room at home in Broad Walk. I think we shared it with Ron and Kris. Rod and Ron arrived and within an hour, Rod asked me to marry him. I was a bit shocked. I thought, 'This is a bit quick' but at 22, you're kind of swept off your feet, really. So we had a bit of an engagement party that night. I can't even recall who was there but I remember Billy Gaff was. He organised so much for us."

The next morning Rod, Dee, Ron and Krissie caught an early flight to Los Angeles, checking into a shared suite at the Beverly Wilshire. "All the girls were meant to be flying home together," Sandy recalls. "So we get up in the morning to find Kris and Dee had gone on to California without saying anything. You can imagine . . . Sue, Jan and I flew back to London feeling pissed off. And of course it creates a bad feeling which affects the guys."

Facing the prospect of marriage Rod was determined to expunge any unsavoury ghosts from his fiancée's past. Shortly before their first meeting in LA, Dee had done some topless test shots for *Playboy*. "My friend Patsy took her modelling portfolio with her to LA and I accompanied her to agencies and photographers. One day, while I was waiting outside, this guy came out, looked me over and said, 'Hi, I'm Brian Hennessey, I'm commissioned to do the centrefold of *Playboy*. Would you like to be in it?' I said, 'Oh no, I've never taken my clothes off!' I wasn't really like those LA girls. I hadn't got any of that going on.

"He said, 'Well, it's $500 for one picture,' and I said, 'I'll do it!' Patsy and I couldn't get any work because we didn't have Green Cards. We'd been turned down as bunnies so that was all I really got offered the whole time I was there. When Rod arrived back in LA he got Brian to come over and he tried to have the pictures destroyed. Rod had a kind of love-hate thing with them. He kind of liked them and then he didn't."

As the tour wended its way up to the Pacific Northwest, Dee and Krissie flew home and the partying continued. On December 8, at Detroit's Cobo Hall, for the encore of 'Losing You', David Ruffin walked on to duet with Rod. He narrowly missed one of the first instances of a recalcitrant McLagan's form of revenge on skimping promoters.

Ian McLagan: "As the band got bigger, it got written into our contracts that the halls were supposed to supply a nine foot Steinway and for it to be tuned – once when it was loaded in and then checked again before the gig. If this wasn't met then any damage would be the responsibility of the promoter. Before the Cobo show I checked the piano and it was a Steinweg so I was well pissed off. What I didn't realise was the Steinweg is actually an old Steinway."

Just before Ruffin made his entrance Mac chopped the instrument into kindling but hadn't accounted for the unplanned encore that was now short to the tune of one piano. Back at the Detroit Hilton Rod and Ruffin sat and sang for an hour to a captivated audience around the piano in the lobby.

"I always brought my camera with me," says Charlie Daniels, who captured various on-the-road moments on this and future US Faces tours. "Laney also liked to check out the local cities that we were in so sometimes we would go off together to wander about just to see where we were. When you were at a concert it would be all the same – the halls, the people etc. It could be anywhere. It wasn't until you left the hotel the next day that you realised you were in, say, Detroit. I have this shot of Laney sitting in some little diner, looking like Bob Dylan with his beard and sunglasses."

The following night the Faces barely sold out Toronto's 13,000-seat Maple Leaf Gardens, receiving an uproarious reception despite playing sloppily, according to *Melody Maker*'s Canadian correspondent, and the police's heavy-handed attitude. Backstage in Montreal they got invited to a private party by a local actress. "We all went back to her apartment," Daniels recalls. "It was a bit more upmarket than what we were used to with all these theatre people. The guys in the band were getting more and more rambunctious but before anything got broken, they made their excuses and went back to the hotel. Because we had the next night off, I ended up staying and having a thing with this woman who didn't want me to leave and so I missed the flight to Baltimore.

"I arrived just as the band were coming back from the gig and I wasn't sure how this was going to go over. Rod looked at me and said, 'It was a good chance to see if you were worth what we've been paying you. We really missed you tonight on stage.' So everything was cool but the message was 'don't let it happen again'."

While in Virginia, some of the tour party dropped mescaline. "There was a small lake adjoining the Boar's Head Inn and we were sitting down by the dock," says Daniels. "A bunch of reporters came down wanting to interview the band but that was the last thing the guys wanted to do. In order to get away from them we paddled out into the water in this rowboat tripping out of our heads until they finally left."

The tour closed on December 17 with a show before 11,000 at Chicago's International Amphitheatre. The crew flew back to London minus Richard Fernandez, who had made the decision to return home to Los Angeles. He continued to work for the Faces on their frequent American sojourns and thanks to a fateful recommendation from Glyn Johns having produced their debut album, became tour manager for a new group called the Eagles.

With a six-week break ahead, Sandy arrived with Lee for a family Christmas holiday. "I met Mac in Detroit and we flew to New York and stayed a couple of days. We went up to Harlem to see Stevie Wonder at the Apollo. That was pretty risky for the time – there were hardly any white faces in the audience and I was holding a baby as well. Afterwards Mac was talking to Stevie backstage. He asked, 'Who's with you?' and Mac said, 'My wife and baby son.' So he said, 'Do you mind?' He came over and touched my face and Lee's face and then touched the back of Lee's neck. It's a family story now how my eldest son had the back of his neck rubbed by Stevie Wonder.

"We then flew to California and had a week in Malibu before driving down to Mexico. Woody and Krissie spent Christmas in Hawaii but they left early because they always needed to be around people whereas I cherished the time Mac and I had together alone away from band business in a little hotel on the Gulf Coast."

Actually the Woods were one step away from being thrown out of their hotel after other guests were less than polite towards the charcoal-haired English rock star and his ditzy blonde companion. "Kris was a real enigma to me," says Sandy. "To this day I don't know whether she was incredibly stupid or incredibly bright playing dumb. Sometimes I would think, 'Oh my God, how could you be so thick?' and then other times it would be like, 'Where did *that* come from?'"

As 1972 began, Rod and Dee continued restoring their new home with the help of Rod's family. "We had a New Year's Eve party in the house in Broad Walk for the local Highgate people who were Rod's friends and then the removal people arrived and off we went to Windsor. All of our belongings fitted into just a corner of this massive house."

Expecting their first baby, Kenney and Jan fitted in a month's holiday to South Africa, visiting Jan's aunt. As an example of how drumming and politics should not mix, Jones came back with a hopelessly naive vision of apartheid. "Conditions for the black man are definitely looking up out there," he informed *Beat Instrumental*. "There really needn't be any colour bar at all but Parliament is run by the Afrikaaners . . . and they are the ones who practice segregation. If the million or so English people got into power I'm sure everything would change."

While waiting for the Faces to re-emerge, various members bided their time with session work. On February 5, Kenney and Mac, with Ric Grech, formerly of Family and Blind Faith, on bass, backed Chuck Berry, released as the self explanatory *The London Chuck Berry Sessions*.* At AIR Studios, Ronnie Wood overdubbed his guitar contribution to 'The Philosopher' on John Cale's *The Academy In Peril*.

---

* A year later, Kenney was among the musicians backing Jerry Lee Lewis at Advision Studios, produced by Steve Rowland and released as the Mercury double album, *The Session*.

Even in the band's absence from *Top Of The Pops*, 'Stay With Me' climbed to six in the UK Top 10, with *Nod's* reaching second position behind T. Rex's *Electric Warrior*. "'Stay With Me' was the obvious single in a way," Wood told Penny Valentine, "we just threw it out before we could get worried over it being right or wrong – it's solid us." Not that the Faces were about to cater to the singles market. "It would be a rut for us as a band," Wood explained to *Record Mirror*. "It's all right for some people, the kind of artists who just go out to make commercial chart singles, but this band is very much a stage act, we like to have as much freedom as possible, and *having* to have a new single out by a certain time to follow-up your last hit would be a drag."

A pair of shows in Hemel Hempstead and Brighton acted as warm-ups for a three-night stand in early February at the Rainbow* – London's hippest new rock venue and previously the Finsbury Park Astoria, the scene of the Small Faces-Jeff Beck debacle five years earlier. The show represented the Faces first British gigs since October. Reviewing for *Cream* magazine, Pete Roche arrived to find support act Ashton, Gardner & Dyke, who'd achieved a Top 5 hit the previous year with 'Resurrection Shuffle', struggling to win over the vociferous hordes impatient for the main act. The Faces took to the stage in a Mike McInnerney designed, life-size painted cut-out of a vintage yellow Rolls-Royce. "Or it might have been gold coloured," Mike recalls. "The prop, carried by hand, chauffeured the band onto the stage, and was meant to symbolise their rise in fortunes but I think it might have crashed at some point!"

Against a backdrop of Joe's Light Show, imported from the Fillmore East, the flamboyantly attired Faces commanded the stage, playing with a brio, vigour and confidence that had built up over the past two years. The set progressed through 'Maybe I'm Amazed', with Ronnie Lane standing on an empty crate to reach the mike, 'Memphis', for which Rod produced a telephone prop to enact the opening long distance information verse while 'Country Comforts' featured Ric Grech playing fiddle. Returning for the encores, the band booted footballs out amid distinctive chants of "Rod-nee, Rod-nee" that were soon to become ubiquitous at all British Faces shows.

"At times it seemed as though the whole thing might fall apart," Roche wrote, "for whatever their musical shortcomings no one could ever accuse the Faces of slightly disciplined arrangements – but Rod and the two Rons, that skilful inside-forward trio, would move together at stage

---

* One of the Rainbow shows was shot on 16-mm film by Warner Bros.

centre, put their heads together in mid-beat, thump their feet together and the whole thing would start climbing again, bass and drums pumping, Wood's guitar winding and whining, Stewart's voice soaring and the knees-up chorus of the Faces Supporters Club roaring them along in fine style – 'Awright! 'Ere we go then! Stay with me – staaay with me . . .'"

As a surprise for the band during the finale, while they stood at the front of the stage acknowledging the crowd, Janet Webb, the large lady who would appear at the end of *The Morecambe & Wise Show*, suddenly burst on and slung them out of the way like it was her show.

In March, a year on from their first visit, the Faces returned to Germany for three riotous shows. No doubt they wished they'd stayed at home. At the Berlin Deutschlandhalle, the band's gear was held up by snow and when they went on stage to explain, a barrage of bottles greeted them. "They still have Teddy boys, y'know?" an incredulous Rod told Pete Harvey. "I hit a guy around the head with a mike stand. There was blood and all that." The following night in Dusseldorf the reception was no warmer when the Faces arrived two hours late.

Despite the demands fame placed on them, Elton and Rod once again volunteered split production duties on *Everything Stops For Tea*, John Baldry's follow-up to *It Ain't Easy*. However, fame fatigue appeared to have caught up as the lethargic results failed to match the earlier winning combination – neither artistically nor commercially.

Elton's side came off better with enjoyable versions of Australian rock band Daddy Cool's 'Come Back Again' and John Kongos' 'Jubilee Cloud'. Stewart oversaw Baldry's overly camp Nöel Coward-isms on the title track and employed the *It Ain't Easy* crew for a rocking version of Willie Dixon's 'You Can't Judge A Book', during which Baldry ad libbed references to Elton's dress sense, Rod's hooter and Billy Gaff's carousing. On the traditional 'Mother Ain't Dead', he and Stewart duetted (as Baldry pointed out in his spoken preamble) for the first time since 'Up Above My Head' in 1964 while Rod plonked banjo. In a further link to their past, Baldry revived the gospel 'Lord Remember Me' which the pair had sung with Julie Driscoll in Steam Packet. Drawing on his art school back-ground, Ronnie Wood contributed the pen and ink sleeve illustration depicting Baldry as the Mad Hatter from *Alice In Wonderland*.

Baldry embarked on a two-month tour of the States to promote the album, released in May, and when he wasn't drunkenly haranguing them, he found that American audiences generally appreciated his eccentricities. For his *Top Of The Pops* appearance plugging the album's single, a cover of the Dixie Cups' 'Iko Iko', in true camp fashion, Baldry, wore a diaphanous ankle-length kaftan with Rod and Elton as bridesmaids. By coincidence T. Rex appeared on the same show, thus the triumvirate of superstars dominating the British pop scene of the early Seventies were gathered together in one glamorous summit. "I always knew that Rod was going to become something very, very special," Baldry told *Disc*'s Mike Ledgerwood. "I just didn't know under what circumstances . . . Roddy needed the States to succeed on the level that he has done. I honestly don't think it could have happened for him otherwise."

CHAPTER 15

Never A Dull Moment

"Glamour is something that is missing on the rock scene today. I think it's important . . . The Faces are a very good band musically and what we do on top is extra."

— Rod Stewart, *Melody Maker*, 1971

"The audiences got bigger, the money got bigger and the band became more important as a result. The work didn't get any easier, but it didn't get any harder to be honest. You just kept going because there was so much to do but then, there always was. Nothing changed. I know that sounds ridiculous because we were able to take limos but we always had limousines. In America you didn't travel any other way. So no, nothing really changed."

— Billy Gaff, interview with author, 2010

"GOD, I hope people's attitudes don't change towards the band," Rod had remarked in 1971, "it would be really heartbreaking to come as far as we have and for my stuff to go and mess it up . . ." Fortunately, *A Nod Is As Good As A Wink . . .* had gone some way toward stemming the insidious perception of the Faces as 'the band behind Rod Stewart the superstar'. This was due in no small part to their switched-on record label.

In January 1971 Warner Bros., Reprise, Elektra (and eventually, Atlantic) came together to form the Kinney group of record companies in Britain,* operating out of the same offices in New Oxford Street. Alongside the head partnership of Ian Ralfini and Martin Wyatt, the progressive set-up comprised some of the most creative and experienced individuals in

---

* Kinney National Company, an American conglomerate that owned car parks, office cleaning firms and other concerns, bought Warner Bros.-Seven Arts in 1969 for around $64m. To comply with American anti-trust laws, each company – Warner Bros., Reprise, Elektra and Atlantic – operated separately in the US.

the business, including A&R man Ian Samwell, promotions boss Bill Fowler and, as Director of Special Projects, Derek Taylor, the urbane journalist and press officer who had formerly overseen (and indulged in) the chaos surrounding the Beatles' Apple organisation.

Charging into the circular reception area, dominated by a wall decorated with large blow-ups of Indian chiefs and designed by Mica Ertegun, wife of Atlantic founder Ahmet, the Faces in various combinations would threaten to bring the building's organisational efficiency to a grinding halt. "Warners had money to spend so we really made the offices look pretty spectacular," Wyatt recalls with fondness. "Warner-Reprise only had one floor at the beginning but eventually we bought up the other floors because we expanded at such a rate. The big thing for Kinney at that time was the publishing side. There was only about nine of us when the offices first opened but within about a year we were employing around 30 people.

"My memory of that whole period was like continual good times," Wyatt continues. "The Faces' ladies used to call me up, especially Jan as the ringleader, and say, 'Are you going to the boys' gig in Brighton?' or wherever. And she and a couple of the others, Dee, Krissie, would sweetly ask, 'Can we cadge a lift from you then?' So all of these vivacious blondes would jump in my car. We'd drive down to the gig and of course, the guys would be, 'Oh fuck off, Martin, what did you bring the bloody birds for?!'

"The band used to take the piss out of me no end. I remember one time they arrived and I was just going out to lunch and they asked, 'Any chance we could nab some records?' so I instructed my secretary to let them have a few LPs. The office girls were all potty about the Faces. While I was gone, they charmed their way into my office and piled every single thing that was in there on top of my desk. I had a business meeting after lunch and when I came back with whoever it was, I opened the door and all you could see was this column of chairs, lamps and things balancing precariously on top of one another, going up to the ceiling. And the record cupboards were bare and the booze cabinet had been hit."

When quizzed as to whether he noticed any evident signs of disharmony, Wyatt states, "There was a little bit of disgruntlement because of Rod's success. I never saw it get nasty, it was just the general moans that people have always got in bands . . . Of course we used to try to make sure that the release of a Faces album was far enough away from the release of a Rod album so they didn't conflict with each other."

In the spring of '72, Rod started his fourth solo album – the eagerly awaited follow-up to *Every Picture Tells A Story.* "[Mercury] won't allow me to slow down the rate of my solo career," he remarked to Bill McAllister. "You can't blame them really, it's a case of make hay while the sun shines when it comes to business." Nevertheless, four albums in as many years, together with three Faces albums, now seems absurdly industrious, even by Seventies standards. Wyatt recalls Warners' president Joe Smith's keenness in trying to negotiate Stewart out of his existing Mercury deal that was renewed for a further year. "It was a continual battle. There was a great promotions guy over at Philips, Tony Powell, who was close to Rod and worked really hard on promoting his stuff so he was invaluable [to Stewart]."

A frequent visitor to the Kinney offices was gregarious DJ Jeff Dexter, who observed, "I always found Rod to be quite shy, trying to get beyond the normal level of pleasantries. He would be 'Rod Stewart' rather than being just 'Rod the geezer' whereas Ronnie Lane was always up for a laugh. They all loved the pub and that's where they'd always end up. There were a couple of boozers in Soho where they drank and one right round the corner from the Kinney offices. Ron [Wood] was always the first to buy a round. He was very good at holding court, always felt comfortable with one arm on the bar and of course, he made lots of friends because he'd always offer a drink to someone first. Kenney was quiet and Mac was always sweet, a nice fella but Ronnie Lane and Ronnie Wood, I remember as being the most convivial."

As an extension of the informal musical sessions conducted in each other's homes, the two Ronnie's were collaborating on the soundtrack to *Mahoney's Estate*, a.k.a. *Mahoney's Last Stand*, a film funded by the Canadian Film Board. The script, such as it was, about an unconventional misfit running a farm, was co-written by French-born, Montreal-raised actor Alexis Kanner, who had come to prominence on British television during the Sixties in the BBC police drama *Softly, Softly* and cult sci-fi series *The Prisoner* as well as exercising his wit in a regular column for *Fabulous 208*. Kanner became part of the Small Faces circle, directing a promotional film for 'The Universal' and was squiring Annie Lambert, half-sister of Kit Lambert and part of the Meher Baba circle. Thanks to their continuing friendship Kanner invited Lane to write the score. "That was a really good experience for Ronnie," says Glyn Johns, "and he and Woody both enjoyed it as they had a great relationship with Alexis. There was some good stuff there."

Billy Nicholls: "I had been away in America and the night I got back, Ronnie called up asking me to go to Olympic. I was jetlagged out of my skin but I turned up and we worked on 'I'll Fly Away'. I believe that came from when Ronnie and I were listening to [US bluegrass country rock group] the Dillards. Even Glyn sang on that when he was supposed to be engineering. Gallagher & Lyle were there as well so quite a few singers were around the mike that night."

Johns was concurrently producing singer-songwriters Benny Gallagher and Graham Lyle, formerly of McGuinness-Flint, at Olympic. The duo were to play an early role in Lane's subsequent solo career as was Bruce Rowland, the drummer on the sessions. Like most incidental film music the soundtrack covered a spectrum of moods from the sleazy R&B instru-mental 'Tonight's Number' featuring all of the Faces (bar Rod), brass players Bobby Keys and Jim Price and Pete Townshend on guitar, to a high calibre Lane original, 'Just For A Moment', one of his most affecting songs. The *Mahoney* sessions were sporadic by nature and continued off and on into the following year. The soundtrack, slated to appear in 1973 under the punning title *Wood Lane* was not released until September 1976 as *Mahoney's Last Stand*. The film, starring Kanner in the lead role of Leroy Mahoney, premiered at the Canadian Film Festival whereupon it sank into obscurity.[*]

In early April, the Faces with assorted wives and entourage flew from London to San Juan, Puerto Rico for a holiday and the three-day Mar y Sol festival, held over Easter weekend at Vega Baja and featuring an array of rock and jazz acts – many of them fellow Warners artists including Alice Cooper, Emerson, Lake & Palmer, the Allman Brothers, Cactus, the J. Geils Band and John Baldry. The event, memorably described by *Creem* as "an ugly slice of New York City against a postcard backdrop", teetered on disaster. Only half of an expected 60,000 attended, most of them Puerto Rican locals – a blessing in disguise as a capacity crowd camping out on the site might have resulted in a full-scale emergency. The usual in-hospitable conditions at such gatherings – unhealthy and expensive food, inadequate sanitation – was compounded by a scarcity of water in searing 100 degree heat and the Puerto Rican authorities who gained a last-minute court injunction to have the festival shut down. Such was its dis-organisation that the promoter Alex Cooley fled straight back to America

[*] A true maverick, Alexis Kanner went on to make other films including the 1981 cult movie *Kings And Desperate Men*, starring his fellow *Prisoner* actor Patrick McGoohan and featuring Margaret Trudeau. Kanner died of a heart attack in December 2003.

with the proceeds one step ahead of gung-ho authorities intent on throwing him in jail.

Three weeks later the Faces returned to the States to play a whirlwind eight-city tour of the South mostly at places where they had not played before so the visit was more of a promotional nature though both Rod and the Faces' reputations were enough to sell tickets. They were supported by the recently reformed Free, who were last minute replacements for Fleetwood Mac. Along for the ride was *Rolling Stone* reporter Robert Green whose journal was both revealing and lurid – in much the same fashion as his similarly named counterpart Robert Greenfield's chronicle of the Rolling Stones' summer juggernaut around America for the same paper. While it candidly exposed the bacchanalian excesses of a rock'n'roll tour, the more perceptive could have detected between the lines the ever-widening divisions within the group. The three-page article titled, without any reference to the Faces, 'Rod Stewart at Work and Play in the Holiday Inns of America', opened on a fraught chartered flight between dates where Rod and Billy Gaff are sitting at the front of the plane, away from the rest of the group at the back. Rod is listening on earphones to a tape of the previous night's show as well as going over lyrics for songs that would end up on *Never A Dull Moment* – Stewart always claimed his best inspiration occurred on flights.

Throughout, Lane and McLagan were getting progressively drunker and sarcastic, disrupting his concentration, much to Rod's forced jollity. After a near miss of a landing, a bellicose McLagan is on his feet, shouting towards the cockpit, "Where is that cunt of a pilot? What's wrong with him?" No wonder at such times Gaff admitted to "being a complete nervous wreck that I've kind of shut a lot of it out, you know?"

Added to Gaff's woes were the associated headaches in transporting the circus troupe brought in by promoter Jeff Franklin to entertain audiences during the changeover between acts – a similar concept to the 'rock'n'roll band with travelling circus' idea that Mick Jagger had proposed in 1971 as a follow-on from the Stones' 1968 *Rock 'n' Roll Circus* television special.* "The circus thing didn't go down well," says Mac. "I couldn't bear to watch, it was hopeless. The fans didn't care for it, they wanted music, they wanted us. It was worse than having a comedian because at least a comedian can tell a couple of jokes and get off the stage but these people

---

* Coincidentally, Mott The Hoople attempted a similar operation in England at the same time with old music hall comedian, Max Wall. Led Zeppelin had circus acts performing before they took the stage at Wembley Empire Pool in November 1971.

had an act to do. There was a Japanese woman hanging by her hair and trapeze acts and all kinds of stuff. The idea was that we were a bit of a circus on the road and you know, it seemed like a good idea at the time but it sucked actually."

Green expertly nailed the kind of sycophantic record company type that attached itself to the rock'n'roll band of the moment while chasing free booze, drugs and pussy. Rod accidentally stumbles on a bunch of them in the dining room of the Riverbluff Holiday Inn, Memphis and beats a hasty retreat. "Someone told me the bar was in there," he mutters, "I don't know how the hell I got into that."*

The Party Room was also well evoked with Rod and Ron, arms draped around each other's shoulders, bawling along on 'When Irish Eyes Are Smiling' and 'On Top Of Old Smokey' while rubber Holiday Inn welcome mats are frisbeed over the balcony into the empty pool. But by far the most outré incident was a graphic description of a naked groupie, lying on a motel bed in Clemson, South Carolina, inserting various objects including an empty wine bottle, a banana, a room key, a bar of soap, even her own fingers into various orifices while the Faces and onlookers watched – or in the case of Ron Wood, filmed it on his portable video unit.

Show over, the uninhibited young woman told the room, "Look I could dig on a rape trip, but I just don't want to get hurt too bad, you know?" There being no takers, she then offered to have sex with anyone who wasn't carrying diseases to a Rod Stewart tape. At which the incredulous singer let out a heavy sigh, shook his head and got up and left followed, one by one, by the room's other occupants. The girl simply shrugged, got dressed and left, no doubt willing to repeat her performance for the next bunch of rock'n'roll renegades passing through.

Charlie Daniels: "I know the wives got on the guys' case when that article was published. They would read all this crazy stuff of what happened on tour when they weren't around. I don't remember Kenney being involved in much of the after show craziness, maybe he'd hang out for a little bit backstage after the gig or something. And Rod was never really involved with the groupies, he was more into talking about the gig that just happened or singing and drinking and carrying on in a kind of 'mates' way. Rod liked to party as much as the others but he was never the last one up, he would go to bed to save his voice. The band drank before a show, while they were onstage, and it would continue afterwards until it

---

* Green failed to get an interview with his quarry so had to make do with recycling Rod quotes from the 1970 *Rolling Stone* interview.

was, like, five or six in the morning and they would still be looking for someone who might have a drink in their room. Most of them never got up before three or four in the afternoon."

If the novelty of the constant carnal come-on had worn off, Rod still liked to see how far these girls would go. With a little help from his 'assistants', the 'Doctor's Surgery' would open. "I can't remember where it actually started or how long it went on for," Charlie recalls, "but it would be in the Party Room where everyone was hanging out. Either Rod or Woody would be 'the Doctor' and we'd get 'the patients' ready for an examination. It was just like a game of stripping down some beautiful ladies and having a little bit of fun. No one ever really took it seriously, maybe the ladies might have, but certainly no one in the band did because in most cases we'd sort of frolic with these women and then leave to go on somewhere else."

The opening night rustiness in Memphis gradually dissipated and for assistant tour manager Mickey Heyes, one of the best ever Faces gigs occurred in of all places, Auburn, Alabama. "The whole band knew it. I remember Ronnie Lane shuffling to the side and turning round to look at us and he had this grin as if to say, 'Can you fuckin' believe we're this good?' It was just unbelievable."

With plans of bringing the Faces 'Rock 'n' Roll Circus' to Britain dashed due to "organisational difficulties making it impracticable," Rod continued recording *Never A Dull Moment* at Morgan Studios with the usual clan of Waller, Wood, Quittenton, McLagan, Pete Sears, Dick Powell and Ray Jackson.* *NME*'s Nick Logan paid a surreptitious visit to a session where 'I'd Rather Go Blind' and 'Italian Girls' were being worked on and noted that once Woody and Mac had laid down their contributions, they left to join Ronnie and Kenney at Olympic for a *Mahoney's* session. As a trusted personal and professional contact, Logan was hoping to trump the other music inkies with an exclusive but Rod, still insisting on a low media profile, would only agree to a few words in the downstairs bar.

In the eight years since becoming a professional singer, like contemporaries, Marc Bolan and David Bowie, Stewart had jumped on just about every conceivable bandwagon going – rock'n'roll singer, protest folkie, scruffy beatnik, R&B testifier, blues shouter and now, soulful stylist. At

---

* Thanks to Rod's cavalier attitude toward correct album credits, Jackson was not listed on the sleeve. Some musicians' contributions were also attributed to the wrong tracks.

27, an age that, by somewhat morbid coincidence, had seen Brian Jones, Jimi Hendrix, Janis Joplin and Jim Morrison succumb to the pressure of the business, Rod was wearing fame remarkably well. "If you can't handle success [at that age]," he informed David Wigg, "you might as well give up." "Rod has worked hard over the years," Faces publicist Mike Gill gushed. "He's now in the position to do exactly as he pleases. He can be as ostentatious as he likes, he can collect antiques and can still go into a pub and ask for a pint of bitter."

Except it was still rare to hear him ask, 'What're you 'avin?' as former *Melody Maker* writer Chris Charlesworth recalls. "I'd lived in Englefield Green near Egham where my local was the Fox & Hounds and this was near to where Rod lived, on the outskirts of Windsor. Rod and Dee used to go to that pub and I went back there from time to time as I had friends in the village. Rod was notorious for not buying a round and a bit of resentment had built up, especially as when anyone asked him what he'd like he usually opted for a large brandy. One night when he left the pub he found he'd left the lights of his Lamborghini on and the battery was flat. He went back inside to ask for a push but everyone told him to sod off so he had to call a cab to get home."

"I always joke if I had a tenner for every time somebody asked me if Rod was a skinflint, I'd be very rich," says Dee. "I suppose he was careful with money and quite rightly so as far as I'm concerned. When we lived in 'The Big White House' as he referred to it, I'd say, 'Well I'd like to get maybe a part-time job or something that I can do' but Rod would say, 'You can't go to work, people will talk about us. They'll say, 'You know that man who lives in that big house, he's so miserable he sends his wife off to work.' And I suppose, in a way he was right. They'd all be twitching behind their curtains in Ascot. So he was damned if he did, damned if he didn't."

With the emergent 'glam' look in rock'n'roll, the Faces cut a dash style-wise, strutting across stages in eye-catching outfits bought from King's Road boutiques like Granny Takes A Trip.

"The Small Faces wore loads of Granny's stuff, beautiful shirts and jackets," says Mac, "but Granny's changed – there were three different Granny Takes A Trip tailors – the original guy was absolutely brilliant, I mean really well-tailored clothes, made to your adjustments. I was married in one of his jackets. Eventually they were taken over by two Americans, Marty [Breslau] and Gene [Krell]. It was still good clothing but different styles. It wasn't just Granny's – there was Alcazura, there were all kinds of shops. I mean you used to go out and buy whatever you could. Three-piece suits and there were great shoes back then too. I mean clothes today are absolute rubbish. There's fuck all now, it's terrible."

Unlike Marc Bolan, who exuded an aura of untouchable star arrogance, his old London rival, the fast emerging David Bowie with his image of otherworldly alienation or the Liberace-style razzamatazz of Elton John, there was a street level accessibility to the Faces. Kids were going to the barbers and asking for 'a Rod', his distinctive spiky feathercut, the precursor to the dreaded mullet, sprouting up on image-conscious men (and women) on both sides of the Atlantic. If able to afford it, they were starting to copy his dress, too. Whereas in America the Faces were appreciated as a good time rock'n'roll band – no more, no less – who had graduated to the Stones, Who and Led Zeppelin echelon, in Britain there was much more of a societal element involved.

If, culturally and socially, the Sixties began in 1963, kick-started by the Profumo Affair and Beatlemania, they ended almost exactly a decade later in 1972, once the day-glo optimism of the Wilson era was subsumed under the economic devastation and grim darkness – literally thanks to the power cuts caused by the miners' strike – of Edward Heath's Tory administration. The situation in Northern Ireland, exacerbated by the Bloody Sunday shootings in January, brought the IRA bombing campaign to the mainland* while unemployment and militant trade unionism was on the rise. But amidst the crises and disillusionment, here was a working-class lad into music, fashion and football and his rapscallion mates who were now reaping the rewards from doing what they were good at. If they could get away with it, then why couldn't the young kid watching enviously as this wayward gang clowned about on *Top Of The Pops*?

One such example was Glen Matlock, then a 15-year-old shop assistant working Saturdays in the Let It Rock boutique on the King's Road, run by clothing designers Malcolm McLaren and Vivienne Westwood. "The first I knew of the Faces was when I was about 14," he says. "I lived in Kensal Green, at the top of Ladbroke Grove. I went in this record store on Portobello Road and found this record that looked like an old 78. I'd had loads of 78s at home because we had an old radiogram. So I thought this was kind of like that and of course, it was *Long Player*.

"I put it on and I thought, 'This is totally different to what I'm used to' – it was sorta bluesy rock'n'roll soul music which was kinda linked in with the Motown-y stuff the bunch of skinheads round my way listened to, and

---

* The Faces were scheduled to play Dublin's National Stadium but cancelled twice that year due to "heavy commitments".

way different to Uriah Heep and the stuff my mates at school who wore greatcoats liked. I didn't realise it was the same blokes that were in the Small Faces. There was something about [the Small Faces]. I didn't quite understand what it was then but they looked great, they was really young, they looked really English, a total London kinda thing, but I didn't even really understand I was a Londoner at the time but that was what I was picking up on, y'know? They was all a right laugh on *Ready, Steady, Go!* and it was always Ronnie Lane. He had something about him and when he was in the Faces, he was always this individual kind of character. Then I saw the Faces on *Top Of The Pops* and went to see them at the Rainbow. I just thought Rod and Ronnie Wood looked great, whatever they wore. It was a whole attitude with the band – don't take it too seriously but seriously enough."

The Faces cross generational appeal can be seen in Peter Clifton's film of the band's Camden Festival show at the Roundhouse on Saturday, May 6 – appropriately enough the day of the Cup Final between Leeds and Arsenal* – with a sold-out audience of 2,500. A mix of older rock heads and enthusiastic younger kids crammed up against the stage, with 20 reported fainting cases much to Stewart and promoter Peter Bowyer's concern. "If cup final tickets were at a premium on Saturday, the tickets for the Faces at London's Roundhouse cannot have been far behind," wrote Chris Charlesworth in *Melody Maker*.

It was a triumphant gig with the usual lengthy delay for the band to head from dressing room to stage. Ronnie Lane: "Sorry we was late but Rod's hair dryer broke." Charlesworth was among the first writers to note that the band seemed reluctant to alter a winning hand. "There's no denying the Faces on established material, which is probably what the fans want, but new songs wouldn't be amiss in the place of 'All Over Now' and 'Maybe I'm Amazed' which are a bit too evergreen . . . The attitude of the band seems disinclined to change and it's difficult to blame them. And it doesn't detract from the fact that the Faces are the happiest, funniest and possibly the funkiest live band around."

In complete but typical contrast, the Faces turned in a short, lacklustre set at their next appearance – the Saturday night headlining slot at the Great Western Festival at Bardney near Lincoln, a four-day event plagued by rain that was held over the end-of-May Bank Holiday. "When we do Lincoln," Rod told Nick Logan, "we won't have played for three weeks.

* Unlike the previous year, Rod's beloved Gunners failed to triumph and Leeds won with a single goal.

But we'll be good, I tell ya. It doesn't matter how long we might have been off the road, the boys rise to the occasion . . . like [Manchester United striker] Denis Law when he plays for Scotland." Ah yes, Scotland. That afternoon Rod and Dee attended the England-Scotland international at Hampden Park, Glasgow. "Don't talk to me if England win," Rod warned Logan. It was an ill portent when the Caledonians got beaten one nil. "There was just too much expected of [the Faces]," Rod reflected. "Plus the fact that I wasn't in a good mood because I'd had a row with the old lady."

John Peel's tongue-in-cheek introduction ("those five loveable mop-tops") made Rod worry that the Faces were no longer appreciated at Peel Acres now that Stewart was hugely successful. By the same token Peel was no doubt wary of losing another friend to the star process – as had happened with Bolan and Bowie. "If Scotland ever lost a football match Rod would be unhappy about anything and everyone – not just me," says Dee. "And John Peel didn't hold it against Rod as I remember him coming to dinner shortly afterwards at the house."

The sluggishness of the Faces' performance could be attributed to something much closer to home than the result of a football match. Mac's personal life was in disarray after Sandy walked out on their four-year marriage, taking infant Lee with her.

"Thinking about it now," Sandy says, "it was very difficult because Mac and the others were on a completely different mindset from the average person. They'd be away, rushing from one place to another and then to come home and expect to instantly conform to normality. It's horrendous to live like that. Mac had just come back from America and as usual we'd gone to the airport to meet him and welcome them home. He had an appointment with [Faces accountant] Milton Marks and I tried to wake him, 'Mac, you're supposed to meet Milton', but he wouldn't get up. This went on and on and finally I lost my rag and shouted at him, 'For fuck's sake, Mac, get up! Your boiled eggs are getting cold.'

"So Mac finally came down and sat at the table. He cracks open his boiled egg and explodes, 'It's cold and it's hard' and the whole lot went up in the air. Lee, who was sitting in his high chair with his boiled egg, started to cry and Mac said, 'You spoil that baby and so does your mother.' And I said, 'Right, that's it, fuck you, I'm leaving.' I packed a bag and I left. And that was it. I suppose it was all an accumulation of everything that had built up and it all happened over these two bloody boiled eggs.

"I got incredibly pissed off because I'd had a life, I'd had a career, not that I minded playing second fiddle to Mac, I didn't have a problem with that. I fully supported him, I used to make his clothes for God's sake. But as time went on it got worse. Lee didn't have sensible hours. He fitted in around us which didn't matter when he was a baby but it was going to become a problem as he got older. Lee's bedtime was not at seven every night, it was more like one or two in the morning. After a gig they all needed to unwind and Mac would want to party and there was me saying, 'No, I've got to go home because of the baby', and things like that. It was very, very difficult."

"I remember one time when Sandy was around at Willoughby House," Mike McInnerney recalls. "Mac had just gone off on another American tour and she said, 'I wish Mac worked at home' because she saw me working from home and Kate was in the kitchen. She really missed him. All the wives and girlfriends didn't like their guys being away on tour much."

As well as the domestic strain, Sandy was acutely aware of the resentment within the band that was fast encroaching because of Rod's solo success and how this was affecting the attitudes of those around them. "In the Small Faces days they used to get pissed off with each other. They would have an argument but it was a completely different thing . . . there wasn't this kind of competitiveness . . . there was a lot of shit that went on, there were times when one girl didn't talk to another and there were stupid things like that. The whole thing was absolutely ludicrous and I suppose it was jealousies – jealousies at what one girl could get away with by blackmailing her man and so then another partner would try it."

"When I left Mac I went to my mum's and I stayed there. And then Mac's mum phoned my mum to say why had I left because Mac had just bought me a new washing machine! But I did go back, I went back for about a week but I couldn't stand it. In his book Mac says I was already having an affair but that's not the case."

Sandy preferred to walk away than accept a divorce settlement. "Mac and I didn't sit down and discuss it, which is really what we should have done. I think we were both kind of stubborn and I just think Mac thought, well, 'Why would I be leaving him?' I don't know. I mean, I've obviously spoken to him since and really I was pissed off with the whole behaviour of everybody including myself. I didn't like myself very much, I didn't like some of the thoughts and feelings I had and I just didn't want to be there, I really didn't want to be there."

Sandy's plain-speaking and down to earth nature would be missed within the Faces camp and her departure symbolically spelt out there was trouble in paradise.

In June, at the London Hilton, the Faces were presented with gold discs representing a million sales for *A Nod Is As Good As A Wink* . . . As the royalties and concert proceeds poured in, the band spent lavishly on home comforts while much of the country was adversely affected by the Heath government's austerity measures. Kenney bought a two tone Rolls-Royce and a five-bedroom house in Kings Meadows, Coombe Wood Road, Kingston Hill, undertaking extensive renovations before moving in. Dylan Jones had arrived at London's Welbeck Street Clinic on May 31 and several Faces dates were cancelled for Kenney to be with his family. "When Dylan was born Kenney's mum Violet asked if we would keep the middle name Thomas because it had always been in the family on the men's side," says Jan. "We were stuck on a first name and it was Ronnie Lane who came up with Dylan."

Having spent time moving from one location to another, Ronnie Wood wanted a proper home and found it in the Wick, a 20-room, four-storey Georgian mansion perched on Richmond Hill, then owned by the actor John Mills. Designed and built by 18th century architect Robert Mylne in 1775, the house was based on three oval shaped rooms with a master bedroom upstairs, a drawing room off the ground floor, and a dining room in the basement. On either side of the dining room was the kitchen and what were previously maids' quarters. The Wick was originally the home of 18th century portrait artist Sir Joshua Reynolds, who painted the stunning view of the Thames flow path through the woodland.

The only sticking point was the asking price of £140,000 – a problem that was resolved when, in echoes of his doomed arrangement with Steve Marriott on the eve of their partnership splitting, Ronnie Lane agreed to buy the three-bedroom coach house – Wick Cottage as it was known – situated at the bottom of the sloping terraced garden. The setting had its attractions for Ronnie – on a visit to England in 1931, Meher Baba had stayed at the neighbouring Star & Garter Hotel on Nightingale Lane[*], he was just a shout away from his mate Woody and the garden also conveniently offered enough space to park his new toy.

Rather than follow his bandmates' example of accumulating material assets, Ronnie was determined to invest his money in a venture that could give something back. "I know big houses and big cars won't make me particularly happy," he told David Wigg. "I like the work I do a lot. That makes me happy if it's going well."

---

[*] It is now the Petersham Hotel.

Having observed the workings of the Rolling Stones Mobile Studio, Lane bought a 1968 Airstream trailer from Cerritos, California, which he had shipped to England, intending to convert it into a mobile studio at a cost of £40,000. Through an introduction from Pete Townshend, the task of construction was handed to Ron Nevison, a transplanted American from Philadelphia. With experience of both front-of-house and studio mixing desks, Nevison had worked with many acts, including Eric Clapton and Traffic. "The Airstream caravan was just an aluminium shell, there was nothing inside really," he says. "I put in a 16-channel Helios console and I had the Helios people do the wiring inside. I designed the whole space for the speakers, installed hard rubber flooring and seating in the back. It was nice and compact.

"At that time Ronnie was still living with Sue in Twickenham so much of the work was done at the cottage. I had all the workmen come in and that's where we not only built the studio but we put microphones in and did some recording just to check it all out. Ronnie had [the Airstream] painted silver, put a big LMS logo on the side, bought a Land Rover to tow it and we were away."

"Ron Nevison rang me up and asked would I like to come down to the Wick Cottage and record something," Billy Nicholls recalls. "I had nothing written so I put this three-chord reggae type thing together. Ronnie Wood, Mac, a drummer called Ron Berg and I started playing and it ended up as 'Kew' [later released on Nicholls' 1974 album *Love Songs*]. That was the first song recorded on the Lane Mobile Studio."

The Faces' management had also moved up in style. Billy Gaff lived in a lavish home in Fulham – inevitably dubbed 'Billy's Gaff' by the band – and with the departure of business partner Robert Masters, he moved out of Warwick Square to premises above the Marquee at 90 Wardour Street. With the Faces as the jewel in the crown, he set up GM (Gaff Management), which included on its books Atomic Rooster, Byzantium, Greenslade, Andy Bown, Lesley Duncan, Long John Baldry, Chris Jagger, Rory Gallagher and Status Quo.

Billy Gaff: "David Oddie, who'd been with the Robert Stigwood Organisation, came over on the agency side and we brought in Andrew Heath to look after our publishing interests and it went on to grow into quite a decent sized publishing company. Jimmy Horowitz was in-house producer and he used to help Andrew with the publishing. Colin Johnson, Status Quo's manager, worked out of the office, too."

Also working out of the office was Shirley Arnold, who had been poached away from the Rolling Stones for whom she had been working since 1963, first as their fan club secretary and then helping to oversee the band's day-to-day organisation. Shirley was employed as the Faces' Girl Friday and was to become embroiled in their daily escapades – whether she wanted to be or not.

On July 21, Rod's *Never A Dull Moment* was issued and raced straight to number one on both sides of the Atlantic simultaneously, going gold on its day of release in America with one million advance sales. "I was very worried about this album," Stewart admitted to Penny Valentine, "because *Every Picture* . . . was like trying to climb a mountain and this followed closely to that and *Nod's*. You know, if you've sold so many albums everyone's looking forward to the next one and you've got something to live up to. I try not to let that affect me when I'm working and the sessions were very relaxed up until the last week. Then the record company kept phoning and saying . . . where was the album? Then it became a panic and everyone stopped falling over each other and the drinking had to stop."

The album was packaged in an elaborate fold-out sleeve, featuring live shots from the Faces' southern US tour, alongside some of the contributing personnel grouped within a goal mouth, simultaneously entwining Rod's two loves of music and football. The hand coloured cover, created by Mercury art designer John Craig, parodied an advertisement for athlete's foot medication from the Thirties with a head shot of Rod, taken by celebrated rock photographer/designer Ed Caraeff in Puerto Rico earlier that year, superimposed on. Craig then added in the art deco background.

Rod's morose expression echoed the mood of many of the tracks. 'True Blue' was inspired by the aimlessness of the kids he saw in America, the tune recalling the feel of ennui in his hero Otis Redding's '(Sittin' On) The Dock Of The Bay' and lyrics bemoaning his inability to prosper. This might have been viewed as something of a contradiction in view of his current success but Stewart had a way with words that suggested he was sincere even if race-horses, Porsches and private jets were now well within his grasp.

The backing track, cut at Olympic with the other Faces and Glyn Johns, provided the usual balance of looseness and refinement, slipping into top gear for the turbo charged finale, featuring Rod's revved up Lamborghini recorded outside Morgan Studios. When 'True Blue' was diverted from the track stockpile for the Faces' next record to end up on a Stewart album there was substance to the growing suspicion that Rod was holding back his best material. "I think the others were a little pissed off when songs like

'Losing You' and 'True Blue' went on to Rod's albums," says Gary Osborne. "I heard comments about that at the time. But you couldn't deny that the success Rod was having reflected on them and helped them to become more successful."

The punningly titled 'Lost Paraguayos', featuring Quittenton's flamenco flourishes and Woody's rich acoustic and dancing bass, featured another witty Stewart lyric of wanting to abscond from dull, drab England – apt for the times – for the sun of South America. The humorous lines about the potential trouble resulting from attempting to transport a younger lover over the state border were written with Chuck Berry's experiences in mind.*

For the album's obligatory Bob Dylan track, Stewart chose another obscure and unreleased gem, 'Mama You Been On My Mind' found for him by Paul Nelson. Dylan recorded it during the sessions for *Another Side Of Bob Dylan* in 1964 but it was left off, being performed in concert and covered by Joan Baez and Johnny Cash.† In following Rod's inspired Dylan interpretations to date, 'Mama' was enhanced by a down home, Tex Mex-style arrangement, featuring an accordion solo played by 'Brian' over Gordon Huntley's pedal steel and Spike Heatley's jazz bass.

'Italian Girls', a kind of companion to 'Every Picture Tells A Story', recounted Rod's adventures with a girl out of his league at the Turin Motor Show when he was wandering the Continent. Now the owner of two Lamborghinis, it wittily combined his twin passions for motors and miniskirts and who could resist the line "she was tall, thin and tarty and she drove a Maserati faster than sound." Following in the Stewart tradition of incorporating instruments not generally associated with rock, the track morphs into an Italian-operatic style fade featuring a balalaika player, referred to as Mr. Bibbs who, according to Stewart, although English, turned up at the session in full Russian gear, weaving nimbly around Powell's Puccini-like violin. One could almost hear the Chianti being poured as Rod laments his latest botched romance.

With 'Angel' Rod pulled another masterstroke, plucking a relatively unknown Jimi Hendrix song from the posthumous *Cry Of Love* collection and emphasising the melody without sacrificing the beauty of Hendrix's original. Like 'True Blue' it was a virtual Faces performance but for Waller

---

* In 1959, Chuck Berry was arrested and later fined and jailed when convicted of violating the Mann Act by transporting a minor over the state line for immoral purposes.
† Dylan's original version was eventually released in 1991 on *The Bootleg Series Vols. 1–3*.

in place of Jones, complemented by Ronnie Lane's Ghanaian mate Speedy Acquaye on congas.[*]

The remainder of the album reprised the Side 2 format of *Every Picture . . .* a solo acoustic interlude followed by a hit single. 'You Wear It Well', another Stewart-Quittenton composition, cleverly masquerading as a sequel to 'Maggie May' yet simultaneously sounding fresh, rather like, as an example, the Kinks following 'You Really Got Me' with the similar yet different 'All Day And All Of The Night'. The 'Maggie' ingredients were present and correct – same tempo, 12-string acoustic, Woody's lead lines, Mac on Hammond, and an inventive instrumental solo – in this case, Powell's violin over Ray Jackson's mandolin. The cleverly observed lyrics – slipping in a sly "homesick blues and radical views" nod to Dylan – found Rod pouring his heart out in an effort to reconnect with a gracefully aging old flame.

Rod had wanted to revive Etta James' 'I'd Rather Go Blind', familiar in Britain through Chicken Shack's excellent (thanks to Christine Perfect's vocal) version that entered the Top 20 in the summer of 1969, as far back as *Gasoline Alley*. "That was the one number I was worried about," Stewart admitted to Nick Logan, "because it had been done twice before . . . Only reason I did it was 'cos I thought it might be different to hear a guy singing it." The backing captured in one take, Rod excels on vocals and Woody gets in some sharp licks against a tasty backdrop of Mac's Hammond and the laid-back, Stax-like horn section, arranged by Jimmy Horowitz.

Having been a fan of Sam Cooke since his mid-teens, Rod had always insisted he was too reverential to attempt covering anything from the master's catalogue. Revising his view, 'Twistin' The Night Away' was considered fair game and so the album bowed out with the good time, rollicking rocker driven along on Mickey Waller's thumping snare, his solo press roll near the end snapping the listener to attention. 'Twistin' was guaranteed to get people up at a Faces show and it swiftly became the encore in their live set.

Never A Dull Moment continued in the same rich vein of Stewart's previous albums, with several excellent songs and performances. The album's

---

[*] Acquaye was a member of Afro-Rock band, Akido. Lane produced their self-titled 1972 album on Mercury. According to Lane, it "wasn't very good because I couldn't keep the fellas together. The playing was great at rehearsal, but the following Thursday I was sitting in the studio waiting. In walks the leader with a totally different bunch of fellas who started rehearsing a whole lot of new numbers." Bassist Biddy Wright later joined Ronnie Lane's Slim Chance.

only flaw was its slightly formulaic, unadventurous appeasement to those demanding another *Every Picture* . . . The normally unquestioning Stewart and Faces supporter Penny Valentine found the album "rather disappointing . . . *Never A Dull Moment* comes off as a pot pourri that never quite gels into something solid and decisive. It opens with a punch and then fizzles out, so that suddenly you're left without those highlights, those moments of drama, that telling force that Stewart has always possessed."

To no one's surprise, 'You Wear It Well' became the album's lead-off single, reaching number one on September 2.* For the first time in months, Rod, garbed in candy-striped blazer, became a familiar sight on *Top Of The Pops*, while his fellow Faces clowned around him. Looking like a rabbit trapped in headlights, Martin Quittenton was invited to mime his parts, as was Dick Powell, something that justifiably put Mickey Waller's nose out of joint. "My mother got into an argument with her neighbour after she said I was Rod Stewart's drummer," Waller told John Gray. "This neighbour had watched *Top Of The Pops* and seen Kenney miming along to my playing and she called mum a liar which really upset her, particularly as my father had just died. It was never explained to me properly why somebody else was miming to my drumming."

Hot on its heels came an opportunistic reissue of 'In A Broken Dream', the recording Stewart had made in 1969 with Python Lee Jackson, which, in September, reached number three; it had already charted at 56 in the *Billboard* Top 100, selling over 100,000 copies on the Crescendo label. "It's not very good but then I wouldn't want to stop it coming out," Stewart told Mark Plummer. "I'm not getting anything out of it . . . Say to send me a few bob or put the money into a charity or something. I don't see why the record company should make it all."

For producer Miki Dallon of Youngblood Records who owned the rights, it was a case of recouping his investment, having spent time and effort overdubbing and remixing the track which he'd released three times in Britain before hitting the mark.

The success of both singles and *Never A Dull Moment* had the cumulative effect of resurrecting *Every Picture Tells A Story* back into the Top 30. Stewart's ubiquity through 1972 assured that he was voted Best Male Singer in *Melody Maker*'s annual poll for a second year running.

---

* In a glorious week for singles, Slade's 'Mama Weer All Crazee Now', Alice Cooper's 'School's Out', Hawkwind's 'Silver Machine' and Mott The Hoople's 'All The Young Dudes' sat below Rod in the Top 5.

The Faces 'Rock'n'Roll Circus' American tour continued in July with a short sweep through the east and north-east, beginning in Boston. Of all the major British rock groups, only the Who were off the road that summer with the Faces, Led Zeppelin and the Rolling Stones all cleaning up – the Faces dates averaging over $75,000 per show. Despite the larger venues – 14,000 packed the Spectrum in Philadelphia – the carnival-like communion between the Faces and their audience was as boisterous as ever.

Starting his first Faces tour was Charlie Fernandez, Richard's younger brother, who was brought in to drive the equipment truck and help set up the gear with Chuch. "When a position opened up, Richard put my name forward and I got the call from him telling me to meet them in Boston," says Charlie. "I was with Richard's assistant Mickey Heyes. We'd only just walked in to the Sheraton Towers when we ran into Richard, Chuch, Mac and a few of the band. They told us, 'Go throw your bags up, we're going out' . . . All I remember of that first evening is that we ended up at somebody's apartment and just continued drinking. That was what the band was like – they accumulated friends everywhere. They had this reputation of being party animals and they were. So that was my introduction to the Faces and that's how it went on."

This reputation inspired a jingle that was distributed to radio stations: "It's a booze-up/It's a ball/the wildest party of them all/Faces in the USA/Join the party/Right away." Gaff's press assistant Peter Burton wrote a tour report for *Sounds* portraying the now typical scenes following a Faces show: "The lobby of Philadelphia's Marriott Motor Inn seemed to be under some kind of siege. Slowly the gaudily dressed American matrons and their paunchy husbands retreated upstairs to their rooms as more and more young people drifted into the foyer. 'Hey,' they'd ask, 'do you know where Rod Stewart's room is?' Or – 'Say, we hear that The Faces are having a party here tonight.'"

On July 8 the Faces were scheduled to appear at a one-day festival in the Pocono Mountains, Pennsylvania. By the early Seventies the idealistic nature of the original late Sixties festivals had been replaced with an attitude that was openly and cynically avaricious with an audience of 200,000 sitting through heavy rain, knee deep in mud watching a lifeless procession of bands while the promoters grossed over a million dollars. Black Sabbath cancelled, feigning illness, while a hapless Badfinger waited around for eight hours only to be told they couldn't play.

"All the bands stayed at the same hotel and there was definitely a lot of egos clashing all over the place," Charlie Daniels recalls. "That night there was a bank of really heavy fog coming in and so the schedule had got completely offset because the helicopters could only get the performers in and out when the fog lifted a little. I think we were supposed to be on at about 8pm before Emerson, Lake & Palmer and that got changed to 10 and then midnight and it just kept getting later and later.

"Chuch and Charlie were trying to get set up and ELP's manager Dee Anthony wasn't letting anybody up there because he wanted all his bands to go on first. He was physically manning the stage. Pete Buckland spoke with him and got the same result and when Billy Gaff insisted that we keep to the original schedule, Dee Anthony threatened to beat the shit out of him."

According to Daniels, when Rod personally intervened, Anthony appeared to calm down and agree to the original arrangement but then just as the Faces were about to go on, ELP struck up their interminable noodling. "Rod got really pissed off that he'd been tricked so he said, 'Come on, let's go out onto the stage'. We trooped on there and all of a sudden people saw the Faces jumping around and they all started cheering and shouting, 'We want the Faces' and 'Get off the stage' to ELP. So we kind of got our own back. Rod felt it was a breach of contract and wanted to leave and go back to the hotel but the others, especially Laney, really wanted to play, no matter where, so the band decided to stick it out."

After the audience had been lulled into torpor by ELP, the Faces didn't hit the stage until 5am by which time the dawn fog was slowly lifting. Mac's regular piano hacking gave vent to everyone's frustration. Reviewing for *Sounds*, Chuck Pulin felt the Faces deserved an award "simply for managing to get a dawn weary, wet, dirty audience up on their feet."

Nearly a year on from their European sojourn, with Tom Wright having returned back to San Antonio and Chuch now entrenched in the Faces' set-up, only Russ Schlagbaum remained in France. "Having made all this money, the Faces bought a Tycobrahe PA system back from America so they needed another full-time crew member," says Russ. "That's when Chuch rang me and said, 'If you don't come to London now, they're going to hire somebody else.' So I came over from Bordeaux with the Mercedes packed with all of our gear. I arrived in England about £50 in debt but I had a job offer of £15 a week working for the Faces. When I came in to the crew Charlie Fernandez moved on to help John Barnes who became the band's chauffeur cum tour manager. His dad, Cyril owned a limousine company and drove Rod around. So I did Charlie's job which was looking after Kenney's drums and Ronnie Lane's bass.

"Chuch was among those road guys who invented the term 'guitar tech' – before that with most guitarists they didn't have guys tuning their instruments they did it themselves backstage. Same with 'drum tech' we made those roles up as a way to justify our existence, I think."

Russ's first major Faces show came on August 12 at the annual Reading Festival where they topped a bill that included Electric Light Orchestra, Focus, Man and Edgar Broughton – the man who had branded the Faces a bunch of "drunken East End tarts".

"The Faces seemed to be playing it down," wrote *Sounds*' Steve Peacock, never the greatest of Faces admirers, "and though their cheers and stomping was immediate – rather than a spontaneous growth like the Broughtons – they got it on. They are sloppy but for this gig the rhythm section kept it together well, Ronnie Lane playing better than I've seen him for a long time and it was only occasionally that Rod or Ron Wood would take a break for a giggle."

Rod reflected the current vogue for glitter by wearing a gold lamé outfit with matching bare midriff top. 'You Wear It Well' and 'Maggie May' were joined together into a medley and for 'Twistin' The Night Away' Mac led an impromptu twisting contest. His playing was suffering from over-indulgence in booze and cocaine to numb the pain of his domestic upset, a condition exacerbated when his doctor prescribed Valium. "Mac could never get his banking and stuff done because he would never wake up until six o'clock in the evening," Russ recalls. "I remember Chuch and I would go over to his house and Mac would say, 'Damn, I've missed the banks again. Can you guys loan me a fiver?'"

Charlie Daniels: "He was in a really depressed state. I didn't sense the depth of what was happening but I knew something was up because every moment when he wasn't drinking or performing he was awake and on the phone. I refused to let him get into a slump so when I'd see Mac I'd say, 'You're so fantastic' just to keep him pumped up."

It was a far from ideal condition in which to undertake a three-week American tour – the Faces' third US visit of 1972. The country was still torn apart over Vietnam and in an election year, perhaps to distance himself from his previous right-wing utterances, Rod considered staging a benefit concert for George McGovern, the Democrat candidate running against Richard Nixon.*

Alongside the video screens the presentation envelope was pushed further with a Perspex reflective stage (giving the impression of being floodlit from underneath) and a fully equipped bar and bartender in Mickey Heyes.

---

* The concert never occurred and Nixon was re-elected in November 1972.

"We always had drinks onstage," says Mac, "it's just that we never actually had a bar, so it was a case of setting up a bar, and dressing Mickey and later on, John Barnes as a barman. In fact the crew were dressed as barmen too. I got the idea from seeing a Fats Waller film. He had these six male dancers in very close formation, like in a triangle doing this kind of shuffle and they wore smart pants, like tuxedo pants with a stripe down the side and waistcoats. So I had these black satin waistcoats designed on the King's Road with 'Faces' written on the back in gold and the guys had to wear white shirts and had like a black band round their elbows to hold the cuffs up, like a card dealer wears. They hated wearing them and the shirts eventually disappeared but it looked good having all the crew in uniform."

Travelling with the entourage was Tom Wright who joined up with the tour for the first couple of Southern dates. "Tom had this technique of taking photos, then he would go back to his hotel room and develop all the pictures in the bathtub," says Russ. "[It] was the height of technology [in 1972]. Tom, Chuch and I would be up all night drinking wine, smoking dope, and making 8 × 10s to show the band of the previous night's performance. They were blown away."

On August 25, the band sold out the Hollywood Bowl, a prestigious show that opened with a piper in full Scots regalia parading across the stage to herald their entrance. Mac marked the occasion by hiring an old-fashioned tuxedo complete with sneakers and a handy carnation to snort his blow from. As a special thank you the band played a smaller gig at the Hollywood Palladium two nights later where a banquet and drinks were laid on before the Faces took to the stage of the packed club; McLagan speaking for the others when remarking "it reminded me of the Marquee." Based in Los Angeles for a week, the band flew out to do shows around California.

"We went to see Elvis at the Las Vegas Hilton," Charlie Daniels recalls. "I think they'd planted these women in the audience who would scream and run up to the stage and put a scarf around the King's neck. And we were just up – cheering, yelling and stuff. It was Elvis after all! There was a lot of attention being drawn to us but we weren't causing any problem. They had these black ashtrays at the Hilton and someone had put coke in one of them so this ashtray was being slid up and down the table. We were just having a really good time but these goons kept telling us that we were being too loud and if it didn't calm down, we were gonna have to leave. Of course that just made the band be more outrageous, they had no intention of calming anything down and I think we got thrown out.

"Warner Bros. had arranged for an after show party upstairs in one of the suites. A lot of the record company people wanted to go back and have like a big LA kind of gathering and stuff like that but Woody, Laney, Mac and myself stayed on. The promoter had given everyone in the band a bottle of special Cognac and on the flight, we were up above the clouds, it was like a full moon night and we were drinking this Cognac and maybe having a little snort or something – and the whole thing was so magical. Here I was this person from Alabama, had never done whatever – cruising along in this Learjet, it's four in the morning and I'm hanging out with this beautiful woman who I'd hooked up with at the Beverly Wilshire and these bunch of guys who I loved as brothers. The whole thing was just so unreal, you had no idea what it felt like to be in that situation at that particular time."

The tour wound up on the opposite coast on September 11. Billy Gaff, who had been recovering in hospital after a car accident, flew in with his leg in a cast to oversee the grand finale in New York. As the noise of 18,000 people rang through Madison Square Garden the Faces had reached their performance pinnacle. They just didn't know it yet.

CHAPTER 16

Ooh La La

"Can you show me a dream? Can you show me one that's better than mine?"

– Ronnie Lane, 'Glad And Sorry', 1973

"To see out a dream, Ronnie had to smash something up to do that. And Kate was a really good companion for that dream."

– Mike McInnerney, interview with author, 2010

"I WISH I could give the Faces a lot more attention than I do," Rod confessed to *Disc*'s Mike Ledgerwood in August 1972. "They know I'm deadbeat after doing my own [album] – so they've started the new album without me . . ." Almost a year had passed since the recording of *A Nod Is As Good As A Wink*. Due to 1972 being spent mostly on the road in America, and Glyn Johns' production commitments with the Eagles and other projects, the follow-up had largely been neglected.

While on tour, a vague Can Can theme had been decided upon with a working title, *How Ya Gonna Keep 'Em Down On The Farm After They've Seen Paree?* from the popular American tune of the same name. Then Rod suggested *Ooh La La* from the song's line, "Imagine Reuben when he meets his Pa/He'll kiss his cheek and holler 'Ooh La La!'"

On August 5, the band and Johns commenced cutting tracks at Olympic. Although the actual studio time wasn't lengthy, the whole process ended up taking six months. "It seems like ages since we started the first sessions," Mac told Ray Telford in a February 1973 interview as the album was finally drawing to a protracted conclusion, "but then we did have 10 tracks laid down really early on last year but half of them had to be blown out for some reason or other which meant we had to re-record them and that's very time consuming."

McLagan neglected to mention the other aggravating factor, namely the laissez-faire attitude he and the two Ronnie's had to punctuality and sobriety. "Rod would get really pissed off because he and Kenney wanted to work and the other guys liked to mess around," says Dee Harrington. "They wouldn't turn up to the studio until really late and all this money for studio time was being wasted. Glyn might book the sessions from, say, seven to midnight and Rod and Kenney would be on time but the others wouldn't turn up and when they did roll in, they were usually off their heads. Kenney and Rod were quite similar in a funny sort of way, chatting about their cars and houses, they were more straightforward and practical whereas the others were loose cannons."

This also partly accounted for Rod's absence, knowing as he did that progress would be slow. "They're a really great bunch of guys, so understanding," Stewart told Mike Ledgerwood. "I mean, can you name another band that would let the singer stand down and go away and make the album without him? They sent me three tracks the other night that were beautiful. I had nothing to do with them, they laid them down on their own entirely. And they just said, 'This is what we're going to do. The key might not be right but we can change that. You just write the words.' I mean they could have been on the other side of the world."

As far as his bandmates and Johns were concerned, Rod might as well have been on the moon. "Glyn liked to utilise everyone's talents and I think Rod didn't like him because of that," says McLagan. "Rod didn't like that *Nod's* was a proper *band* album . . . So Rod had nothing much to do with *Ooh La La*. We cut tracks for two weeks before he'd even deign to come to the studio."

"I didn't really feel Rod gave the others enough credit," says Johns. "To be fair to him he was having a lot of success as a solo artist in parallel to the records we were doing. But he did treat them rather like they were a backing band and that pissed me off. I never thought he was that great to begin with and I told him, 'As far as I'm concerned you're the bloody singer in this band so shut up and get on with it.'"

Stewart's previous assurances that his solo career was merely a sideline to his primary role as the Faces' singer were becoming noticeably less pronounced. When asked by *Record Mirror* why he kept making solo albums, Rod replied, "What you should ask me is why do I keep making albums with the group. Apart from the fact that I'm under contract to make solo albums, I like making them cause . . . I need an outlet like that. The band don't really want to get into recording old Dylan tracks. I'm a folkie at heart – they're not, they're rock and rollers."

Ironically, of all the Faces' albums, *Ooh La La*, in which he played a significantly reduced role, would have much in common with the mellower, more reflective qualities of Stewart's recordings.

Apart from the odd session, a month's break loomed on the schedule. Exhausted by the jet set rock'n'roll treadmill of constant travel, enormous venues and deafening PAs, Ronnie Lane was looking to newer horizons.

"For us living in London at that time, the countryside was considered attractive – a bit like *Withnail And I*, getting out of the city," says Mike McInnerney. "Wales was seen as this romantic place so Kate and I bought Whitehall Farm in Montgomery, Shropshire, on the border of Wales and England. Our daughter, Alana had just been born – she was only a few months old by the time we left Willoughby House. Just after we moved Kate and I set up this sort of country house weekend with lots of people coming from different places; Pete and Karen Townshend arrived in their huge Winnebago, Billy Nicholls, Ronnie and Sue.

"Things seemed to be going sour between Sue and Ron. Poor old Susie she wasn't having a good time of it. There was definitely something going on there and she was very unhappy, there's no question. I think Ronnie wanted to leave London but I don't think Susie did. So an impasse must have been developing between them. Ronnie helped us with the deposit on the farm, using dollars he'd earned on a recent American tour. He liked the idea of the countryside, the lifestyle and the community. There was a lot of music going down there [in Wales], gentle rolling hills, a sheep rearing area – very nice, very pretty. At this party Ronnie suddenly decided he wanted to go off to Ireland. I had to stay at home because I was doing some commissioned work so Kate and the baby went away with Ronnie and Billy and Molly the dog."

Billy Nicholls: "Kate asked if I'd go with them to Southern Ireland and do some playing. I said, 'Yeah, that sounds like fun.' We took Rosie, Ronnie's Defender 110 Land Rover to Anglesea in Snowdonia but it was too high for the ferry. We camped in the Land Rover that night and in the morning drove to Fishguard where we took the night ferry to Ireland. The next day we drove to Mick Jagger's mansion, Castlemartin and stayed there for about a week. It was just myself and Ronnie playing on acoustics at the White Horse Inn, the local pub in Kilcullen, singing some of Ronnie's stuff, Dylan, Dillards, Everlys . . ."

Sue Tacker: "When Ronnie and Kate were in Ireland, I didn't think anything of it. These were your friends, it was just the way things were. I couldn't go, I was working, I believe but then I had a free weekend and I thought 'I'll go and surprise them.' So I got a flight and a taxi out to the house and when I got there, the atmosphere was very strange. Maybe I was extremely naïve or stupid but I didn't realise what was going on at first. I guess I didn't want to. I came back home and I was so ill, I was in bed with a fever for days. Subliminally the realisation hit me that Ronnie and Kate had got together."

Billy Nicholls: "Even though it was great playing in the pub, we decided to travel and sleep in the Land Rover or in bed and breakfasts. And that's what happened for the next two weeks after Sue left. One night Ronnie was driving down this country lane, more like a path, in Tipperary. We didn't realise it had been raining for weeks. We got to the end and there was a gate that wouldn't let us go across the fields. So he started to reverse but didn't realise that the camber was about a six foot drop either side and we just slid. Even though we were in a four-wheel drive Land Rover with a big fender, it rolled over onto its back and I smashed my head.

"I held the door up, while they were down there, blood was pouring off my head onto everybody. I thought they were all badly injured but it was just me. One by one I got everyone out and we staggered to a local pub. At first the locals refused to take us because there was so much blood everywhere and it was on closing time. But eventually they called us back and they were the nicest people you could ever hope to meet. They got me into St Vincent's Hospital, run by nuns and Ronnie and Kate slept on the police constable's floor. They came to pick me up. I'd had stitches put in and that's when I sussed out that something was going on between them. We caught the ferry back and drove to the farm. The next day Ronnie and Katie dropped me off at the train station. Even though we had been through a lot together in Ireland, it felt strange as they waved me goodbye."

Sue Tacker: "Ronnie came back home on his own and then drove back to see Mike and Kate in Wales. I followed him up there with my friend Annie Lambert. And while we were there, Ronnie and Kate made this rather quick announcement that they were leaving together. And it was like, 'What do you mean you're going?' 'Yeah, we're going now. So bye, see you some time.' It was as casual as that."

As the news spread, a feeling of sadness enveloped the once tight-knit Baba community. As Sue explains, "With hindsight, Ronnie went through a big change in his life and in a way it wasn't really surprising that he and I ended up splitting. I still to this day don't really know why – I guess he just needed something different. It came as a shock in the lives of the big family that had built up because Kate and Michael were part of that and when I say family – it really was very, very close. We had all come to Meher Baba and we were in the sort of honeymoon phase of falling in love with his teachings.

"It was such a wonderful period. The people that were involved in it felt so bonded. As neighbours we saw each other every day, so it was really upsetting to everyone, not just for myself and Mike, when Ronnie and Kate walked off into the sunset which is basically what happened."

Billy Nicholls: "Ronnie and Kate came back and went straight to the Wick and told Ronnie Wood what had happened. I didn't realise until I got back to Richmond from Wales. I went up to the Wick and Sue was there, crying her eyes out. It was terrible."

After Kate left with Alana, Mike sold Whitehall Farm and travelled around, staying at Pete and Karen Townshend's retreat in Goring-on-Thames while sorting himself out. Sue stayed at the Wick for a time while considering her next move. Both in a position of vulnerability after their partners had left them, she and Mac had a brief rebound fling that fizzled out after he followed her to Toronto where she had gone to stay with friends while tending her wounds. Mac had started to pull himself together, moving out of the home still undergoing renovations that he'd shared with Sandy and Lee and buying a five-bedroom Gothic style house in half an acre overlooking Richmond Park on Fife Road, East Sheen.

On October 29 the Faces played a Stars' Organisation For Spastics charity concert sponsored by the *Daily Express* at the Empire Pool, Wembley. Support acts were punk progenitors the Pink Fairies and the New York Dolls, a sassy, flamboyant bunch, recommended to Stewart by Paul Nelson, who, in his capacity as A&R man at Mercury in the US, signed them to the label the following year. The Dolls exuded a similar cavalier, rock 'n' roll street attitude to the Faces (but without the success and recognition to back it up) with guitar player Johnny Thunders sporting an outsized Stewart-Wood style feathercut.

It was a gig that changed the outlook of Glen Matlock who was among the 10,000-strong audience. "As headliners, the Faces were fantastic but what stuck in my mind were the New York Dolls. Their guitarist Sylvain Sylvain was on roller skates, roller-skating up and down the stage. They did three or four numbers and then Johnny Thunders broke a string. Spare guitar? No! Spare string? No! And everybody's yelling 'Fuck off you Yankee queers' and they're going 'Well fuck you, you Limey fuckers.' Somebody must have gone and begged a string off of Ron Wood's roadie because Thunders came back, put it on and started tuning at full-blast, began playing and broke another string and then the same thing happened all over again and they just fronted it all out. It was great."

Because Rod's version of 'Angel' (from *Never A Dull Moment*) was getting considerable airplay on American radio, Mercury issued it as a single on November 10, with the non-album B-side, a cover of Jerry Lee Lewis' maudlin bar-room lament, 'What Made Milwaukee Famous (Has Made A Loser Out of Me)'.* Now an integral part of the Faces' set, with its memorable chorus, 'Angel' eventually nudged its way up to number four in the UK; 40 in the US.

A *Top Of The Pops* recording had been booked for November 15 but there was a problem. Ronnie Lane, no doubt intent on keeping a low profile, was away in Ibiza and refused to return just to plug a song of Stewart's – albeit one that he'd actually played on. In keeping with the Faces' humour, but with an underlying sense of irony, a life-size cardboard cut out of Lane was substituted instead.

"Ronnie flew me down to Ibiza for a couple of weeks and had a roadie drive his Land Rover over with recording equipment and a generator because the house didn't have electricity," Ron Nevison recalls. "It was a neat old farmhouse and I remember hanging microphones in the cistern and using that as an echo chamber. I didn't know Kate that well, she was like a hippie, she was totally different from Sue who was more of a career girl at that time. Ronnie and Kate were like soulmates. I just remember drinking lots of cheap, Spanish wine, smoking a few joints and having a really good time."

While in Ibiza, Ronnie composed several songs for *Ooh La La*, their philosophical nature at odds with the ballsy all-out rockers associated with the Faces. The busking trip to Ireland had convinced him that while he might be limited as a musician, as a songwriter the possibilities were endless. "It didn't occur to me at the time but Ronnie was writing all these songs that with the Faces, he would never have got to sing," Mac points out, "so he was becoming less and less interested in what we were doing."

With the fallout from this deeply traumatic period still thick in the air, the Faces commenced rehearsals at the Fishmongers Arms in Wood Green, north London, for a series of UK shows. Russ Schlagbaum: "Ronnie Lane

---

* The track, a leftover from the album sessions, was originally intended as a bonus for cassette and eight-track buyers – cassettes being more expensive than records in 1972. Because of copyright difficulties it was not released that way in the UK. Another casualty from the *Never A Dull Moment* sessions was an early version of Crazy Horse's 'I Don't Want To Talk About It', which Stewart would revive on *Atlantic Crossing* in 1975, earning him a UK number one when released as a single two years later.

always used to dress so impeccably with his three-piece suits – 'three-piece' that was his nickname. We knew he had run off and left Sue so all of us were, like, 'What the fuck is Ronnie thinking?' In he walks with Kate in tow and baby Alana in a wicker basket. His ears are pierced, he's got all these bangles, he'd turned into a gypsy. And he's walking around, miles away from everybody. He's not joining in the frolics like they would do, falling over each other and all that shit. He was completely aloof and everybody was wondering, 'What the fuck's happened to Ronnie Lane?!' "

Kate McInnerney is still regarded by many who were close to the Faces inner circle as a Yoko Ono-type figure, the solicitor's daughter casting the successful but impressionable East End dreamer under her spell in some gypsy lifestyle pipe dream. "Kate was using Ronnie to live out her fantasies, I believe that absolutely," says Schlagbaum. "You know, Ronnie fell in love with her or fell in love with her ideals or whatever but he was a big boy and he should have known better. Kate knew how to manipulate him."

The tour opened north of the border in Dundee on December 7. Support act on each of the 10 dates was Kenney's brother-in-law Gary Osborne and his singing/songwriting partner Paul Vigrass and their five-piece backing band, Stumble. "We had an album out and an American tour planned," Gary recalls, "but then [MCA record company boss] Russ Regan left to work for 20th Century Fox and they pulled the plug on us. Billy Gaff, remembering how I had been instrumental in introducing him to the Faces, threw us a lifeline by asking us to be the support act on their Christmas tour."

Having been close to the Faces set-up for some years Osborne couldn't fail to pick up on the tension brought about by recent domestic upheavals. "They were travelling in separate groups; Rod, Woody, Mac and Kenney would travel to the gigs in a hired plane and Ronnie Lane was driving around in a Land Rover with Katie and the baby. There was dissent because Ronnie had run off with Mike McInnerney's wife and that didn't seem right because everyone liked Mike. So they weren't coming in together. You only had to have one of them arrive late and the others would start fuming, like 'Why is he bloody late?' Well, sod that, tomorrow we'll be late' and then the others would say, 'Tomorrow, *we'll* be late.' So there was this competition to see who would be the last to arrive, which, of course, meant they were going on later and later every night so we didn't actually see them a tremendous amount."

Faced with rowdy northern audiences impatient for the Faces, Vigrass &

Osborne were forced to improvise a routine where they threw the leftover food from the backstage buffet out to the audience to buy some time. "It was the end of my performing career because I realised the sandwiches were going down better than the songs," Gary quips.

Also along on the tour assisting the road crew was Clapham-based journalist John Pidgeon, a writer for *NME* and monthly music magazine, *Let It Rock* who was documenting his experiences for a tour diary originally intended for publication in *Rolling Stone*. Hired by Pete Buckland, he was given the most onerous task, lugging Mac's Leslie Cabinet. Soon exposed to the tour pranks dished out to 'the new boy' Pidgeon took these with good grace and a lasting friendship developed with the band – particularly McLagan with whom he later formed a songwriting partnership.

Having not played together, apart from the Wembley one off, the Faces were frequently lethargic, out of tune and more concerned with looning than musicianship. The lean and hungry band that broke out at the Weeley Festival was now content to mark time.

"Some nights were absolutely dreadful," Schlagbaum confirms. "You'd look out at the audience going mad and think, 'Are these people listening to the same band I am?' Hearing it onstage every night, you would know when the band weren't cutting it."

On December 9, Rod, with Ronnie Wood, appeared at London's Rainbow Theatre in two charity concerts of Lou Reizner's adaptation of the Who's *Tommy*. Having kissed and made up since their disagreement during the *Gasoline Alley* sessions, Reizner had hired Rod as the Local Lad character singing 'Pinball Wizard' for his grandiose all-star revamp of Pete Townshend's rock opera, recorded at Olympic and financed to the tune of £60,000 by estimable rock mogul Lou Adler. As well as the Who, the cast also featured Sandy Denny, Graham Bell, Steve Winwood, Maggie Bell,* Richie Havens, Merry Clayton, Ringo Starr and Richard Harris. Released on Adler's Ode label at year's end, backed to bombastic effect by the LSO and English Chamber Choir, the ghastly, overblown arrangement of 'Pinball Wizard' removed all traces of the original's wit, subtlety and simplicity and much to Rod's dismay it became singled out for attention from the rest of the album.

The following night in Blackpool the Faces resorted to their usual antics

---

* For *Never A Dull Moment*, Rod had lined-up Maggie Bell to reprise the kind of spirited duet they had sung on 'Every Picture Tells A Story.' There was also talk of Rod producing an album for her but the tragic death of Stone The Crows guitarist Les Harvey by electrocution on May 3, 1972 put the kibosh on these plans.

when authority reared its head. As Russ recalls, "We were in a hotel and the manager put us all in a wing that had been closed down for the winter and he wouldn't turn on any heat. We're in our rooms and it's fucking freezing cold so we went up to the bar. Then they closed the bar so we're back in one of our rooms making quite a ruckus. The manager comes in with this Alsatian, making threats, you know, 'If you guys don't straighten up, I'll set the dog on ya.' So Ronnie Lane pulls out this great big jack knife and says, 'Come on let him loose, let's see who comes out best.' Ronnie had the little man complex, he certainly wasn't going to take any shit from this guy. We weren't being that bad but, of course, the worse they treated us, the worse the band behaved.

"The next morning, Chuch and I were driving this big Avis ten ton Bedford with all the gear in it and Chuch said, 'I'll fix these bastards.' There was this long retaining wall, maybe six or eight feet high with a decorative post at the entranceway, extending all the way along the parking lot. Chuch swerved the truck and caught the corner post and knocked down the entire brick wall. Rips off the side of the truck – it had a kind of bumper rail along the side so you wouldn't go underneath. He bent that all up. Chuch would do stuff like that. I would never behave so badly! So we scooted the hell out of town in a hurry. I think they sent a bill for the wall."

But at another tour stop even authority couldn't suppress a smile. "Usually the party would always end up in Billy Gaff's room even if he was asleep," says Russ. "They would end up somehow getting the door open through a pass key or something, roust Gaff out of bed and then end up wrecking his room and leaving him there in a pile. They loved to do that. They would charge everything to his room. So we were in Billy's room, it wasn't too raucous but it was rather noisy . . . it was late and there were probably complaints from the neighbours. Suddenly there's a knock at the door and everybody scrambles and hides like schoolchildren. Rod and Ronnie Wood climbed in this sliding door closet. So somebody opens the door and Billy says, 'What's the problem, sir? Everything's fine here, everything's under control' and just as he's about to get it all settled, this sliding door opens and Rod and Ronnie stick their noses out and go into 'Chattanooga Choo-Choo', imitating the hand crank and the whole bit. Even the security guy had to laugh."

On December 16, the tour reached the capital with shows at the Sundown theatre chain, newly opened by the Rank Organisation, in the London suburbs of Brixton and Edmonton. The Ronnie and Kate situation prompted an unintended but nonetheless amusing incident at one of the concerts as Jan Jones recalls, "The wives and girlfriends never used to travel with the band that much. Not like nowadays where the partners seem to go everywhere. The boys do lose a lot of the camaraderie if the women fall out and also why pass up an opportunity with all these girls throwing themselves at your feet, so I can understand them not wanting us there. But Ronnie Lane changed that all around with Katie. From then on, it was always going to be difficult. There she would be, dancing by the other side of the stage.

"I don't know which gig it was but Krissie wandered onstage one night, out of her head, looking ethereal with her blonde hair. She had this long chiffon thing on and she was so pissed that the shoulder had fallen off and her tit was hanging out. She tapped Woody on the back while he was playing, he spun round, looking completely surprised and she said to him while pointing at Ronnie Lane, 'If you do to me what he did to her . . .' The next night the crew wore T-shirts reading 'If You Do To Me . . .'"

It just went to prove that the wives could easily be replaced, not that Krissie or Jan were exactly pure as the driven snow. While Ronnie was off hobnobbing with Mick and Bianca Jagger and the Guinness family in Ireland, Krissie began a low key liaison with George Harrison. Meanwhile, Jan was embroiled in a lengthier affair with Ron Nevison, who recorded the London concerts on the Lane Mobile Studio. "The airstream was parked up our drive so Ron constantly had a reason to be at the house, running backwards and forwards," says Jan. "He was a flirt, a big Gemini flirt. He'd had a quick fling with Krissie before me. Our affair wasn't full on so there was a lot of clandestine behaviour. I know it started when Ron was working on the airstream and it was at its peak when the Faces were at Olympic because that's when I started sneaking about."

After one of the Edmonton shows a football was produced and the Faces took on the Sundown crew in the unseated area downstairs, which degenerated into mayhem when each team went on the attack with fully blasting fire hoses.

The tour wound up in Manchester's Free Trade Hall before which Rod first got to meet his idol Denis Law at Old Trafford where Manchester United were playing Leeds United. He described the encounter in his short stint as a guest *Melody Maker* columnist. "I went downstairs to the dressing room to meet him [Law] because he'd been taken off at half time. He'd been kicked to death and his knee was swollen. It was the first time in my life I really didn't know what to say . . . I was so overwhelmed by it all. As it turned out he was a really beautiful guy. Meeting him was probably the best Christmas present I had, that and the set of bagpipes I got."

The New Year opened for Ronnie Wood with ten days of solid rehearsal in the basement of the Wick for Eric Clapton's eagerly anticipated come-back to the concert stage at the Rainbow on January 13. Reclusive and in the grip of heroin addiction for the past two years, Clapton was coaxed out of his stupor by a philanthropic Pete Townshend who put together a stellar group of musicians, dubbed the Palpitations by Clapton, to back him. The line-up featured Clapton, Townshend, Wood, Steve Winwood (keyboards), his fellow Traffic bandmates Jim Capaldi and percussionist Rebop alongside an additional drummer, Jim Karstein from the Crickets. Ric Grech, a common friend to all, volunteered to play bass, allowing Ronnie to move over to play slide guitar.

As show time came and went for the first house with no sign of the badly strung out Clapton, there were fears that he might be a no show. Eventually the reluctant guitar hero made it, mumbling something about his girlfriend Alice Ormsby-Gore having to let his stage suit out. Both shows – staged by Great Western Festivals to mark Britain's entry into the Common Market – were recorded on the LMS by Glyn Johns and selec-tions were released on the heavily doctored *Eric Clapton's Rainbow Concert* album in September. "We did it on eight-track that night and there wasn't enough mikes to go round," Wood told Penny Valentine. "Only one drum kit was picked up and a couple of the vocals – mine and Jim Capaldi's – were lost altogether."

Determined to eliminate the usual problems of unavailability and expense associated with studios, Woody got into the home studio kick and employed Ron Nevison to construct his own, at a cost of £25,000, in his basement.

Ron Nevison: "I had gone with Woody when he went to see the Wick, I'm not sure if it was before he bought it but it was before he moved in because I remember we were mooching around one of the bed-rooms, Woody said he was looking for Hayley Mills' knickers! I had three or four of the maids' quarters in the basement knocked into a single space and made that into a control room. I installed a 16-track Studer and a Helios board probably bigger than the one that I put in the LMS. It ended up being a fun studio." Subsequent events would make that quite an understatement.

After building Wood's studio, Nevison went on to became an in demand engineer, being hired by Pete Townshend that summer to record tracks for the Who's *Quadrophenia* album on the LMS as their own studio in Battersea, Ramport, was still under construction.

In February, Rod received the final batch of *Ooh La La* backing tracks which required lyrics. Working best under pressure he took himself off to Switzerland to meet the deadline, then returned to Olympic to overdub his vocals with Glyn Johns, a frustrating process for all. Russ Schlagbaum, who was on hand to pour the drinks, recalls, "Rod said, 'I'll do the vocals but I'm not going to work with Glyn, all I need is an engineer to run the tapes'. So Phil Chapman was brought in. Phil brought up the backing track to 'Just Another Honky' and a couple of other things that Ronnie Lane had written. Rod was out there making snide comments like, 'Who wrote this tripe?' The session lasted less than an hour before he left, complaining, 'I can't get the vocal sound right.'"

With the Faces limbering up to go back on the road, Stewart was determined that some of the new songs be rehearsed to counteract the criticism they'd received for lax playing and the rigidity of their set-list. As a result several European dates were postponed to accommodate this. Things unexpectedly flared up at a recording of the BBC's *In Concert* at the Paris Theatre on February 8. An internal memo reported: "Halfway through the recording, in front of an audience, the group walked offstage and returned to the dressing rooms. They were unhappy about repeating all their old material and, in fact, some members of the band had not wanted to accept the booking until their new material was ready for a stage performance, but they had been talked round by the other group members and the agency. After about 20 minutes they were persuaded to finish the recording but the final result was a bit of a shambles and no one was really happy with it."

A re-booking, taped on March 29, passed without incident, becoming the Faces' final radio recording for the Corporation. The original aborted session stayed in the BBC archives after producer Jeff Griffin decided it "was not as good as we would all have wished."[*] Among the new songs rehearsed were 'Silicone Grown', 'Cindy Incidentally', 'If I'm On The Late Side', 'My Fault' and 'Borstal Boys' off *Ooh La La* as well as Free's 'Stealer' and John Lennon's 'Jealous Guy', based on Donny Hathaway's live arrangement. A version of the latter, preceded by some amusing

---

[*] By clerical accident the abandoned concert was exhumed and rebroadcast on BBC digital Radio 6 in January 2003. It was soon bootlegged under such titles as *Too Drunk For The BBC*.

Derek & Clive style banter, was recorded by Ron Nevison using the LMS during a boozy weekend at Stargroves, along with Luther Ingram's 1972 R&B hit, 'If Loving You Is Wrong (I Don't Want To Be Right)', an apt choice considering the marital infidelity rife around the Faces camp.*

The day after the aborted BBC recording, a taster for *Ooh La La* appeared. "'Cindy Incidentally' happened while I was playing piano," says Mac, "and really it came from while I was playing 'Memphis' backwards because if you listen to the opening riff [to 'Memphis'] and then you hear the riff to 'Cindy' it's more or less the same. Rod and Ron said, 'What's that? What's that?' and Rod put the words to it. There wasn't much to the song, really."

A mid-paced shuffle, 'Cindy Incidentally' was deceptively simple, featuring an appealing *carpe diem* lyric of hitting the high road at the first opportunity because "this dream can pass just as fast as lightning". The melody in the verses recalls Dylan's 'I Don't Believe You' and a double-tracked Stewart vocal originally featured some Lane "shoop shoop" style harmony,† harking back to the Small Faces' 'I Feel Much Better'.

Those expecting an ardent singalong like 'Stay With Me' were caught wrong footed. "Normally [the Faces] have the impact of a joyful steam-roller on me," Penny Valentine reviewed. "I think half the problem is a lack of an immediate hook-line to get your teeth into . . ." On the flip was a moody instrumental, 'Skewiff (Mend The Fuse)', so musically reminiscent of Wood and Lane's *Mahoney's* soundtrack that it may well have been cut during those same sessions.

'Cindy' climbed to number two – failing to dislodge Slade's 'Cum On Feel The Noize' – and in an ironic move, considering how he had treated Rod as a spare part, Mickie Most capitalised by reissuing Jeff Beck's 'I've Been Drinking', previously the 1968 B-side of 'Love Is Blue' in April. Now exposed on its own considerable merits the single, issued on Most's hit stable RAK Records, scraped into the Top 30.

Ooh La La appeared in the UK on April 20 and thanks to both Rod and the Faces' immense popularity it reached number one (surprisingly, it only reached 21 in the US). The album came housed in a gimmicky, paper-engineered sleeve designed by Jim Ladwig of AGI, the Chicago-based

---

* Both songs were remixed and included on the *Five Guys Walk Into A Bar . . .* box set in 2004. They were dated as being recorded on January 4, 1973 but research indicates the tracks were taped later in April after the *Ooh La La* sessions had wrapped. 'If Loving You Is Wrong . . .' was later recorded by Stewart on his 1977 album *Foot Loose & Fancy Free*.
† These were removed from the final version but while going through tapes, McLagan found this early mix and included it on the *Five Guys Walk Into A Bar . . .* box set.

design company behind Rod's albums, which enabled cover star Ettore Petrolini to open his mouth and roll his eyes, rather like a Terry Gilliam animation from *Monty Python's Flying Circus*.

Ian McLagan: "[Petrolini] was like one of the Marx Brothers in a way, or a Max Wall character. He would sing a song and then he'd stop and tell a story and the place would break up and he'd start singing again. I only found this out a few years ago when an Italian fan got in touch with me. I was in this tiny little restaurant once in old Naples and the walls were covered with photographs from the stage and cinema, including one that showed a guy in a tuxedo on a huge stage with a cast of hundreds, the orchestra, dancers, violins, singers, etc. I said to the waiter, 'Is that Petrolini?' And he went [*feigns OTT Italian accent*] 'Oh, Petrolini!' We didn't know that at the time, it was just a photograph to us."

The inside gatefold featured an old-fashioned, high-kicking Can-Can girl above a Tom Wright photo composite of the individual members with Ronnie Lane pointing up her skirt. "We worked it out she would have been about 90 when the album came out," says Mac.

Ooh La La counterbalanced generic 'Faces-style' raunch and uncharacteristic laid-back moments dominated by Lane's introspection. A honky-tonk roll from Mac introduces 'Silicone Grown', a tongue in cheek rocker whose melody owes a debt to Larry Williams' 'Boney Moronie'. But whereas Williams' heroine was skinny as a stick of macaroni, Rod's character – perhaps a curtain call by Rita from 'Stay With Me' – carries a lot up front thanks to surgical enhancement. Like 'Stay With Me', 'Silicone Grown' is bawdy and irreverent with enough double entendres – 'keeping abreast of time' and 'more front than the Haig Museum' – to impress Max Miller.

Following 'Cindy Incidentally', 'Flags And Banners', credited to Lane/ Stewart is most reminiscent of the folk feel of Rod's albums; the Faces sounding like an Anglicised version of the Nitty Gritty Dirt Band with Rod playing banjo and Lane singing in a high register of a nightmarish dream he'd experienced. "I don't know the exact details," Mac says, "except that it happened when the Small Faces were first formed. They'd been smoking dope and I think Ronnie nodded off. When he woke up, he remembered he'd been having this dream about wearing Southern Grey in the American Civil War."

'My Fault', a fairly mundane plodder with Stewart and Wood singing verses of defiant character stubbornness in unison, featured some nifty interplay between Wood and Jones. As the song drifts off with a resigned shrug, a shrill klaxon heralds there's a riot goin' on in the mess hall. "I think it might have been Rod or Ronnie Wood's idea but they found a klaxon and they set it off in the studio. It was fucking loud!" says Mac.*

Inspired by such classic US rock'n'roll prison songs as Elvis Presley's 'Jailhouse Rock' and the Coasters 'Riot In Cell Block # 9' (both written by Leiber-Stoller), 'Borstal Boys' cleverly transplants the scenario to the British prison system of borstal, a perceptive slice of social comment to show how it sometimes failed to reform young offenders like the song's character. With a powerhouse performance from all, it ranks among the Faces' musical high points as a band.

"Fly In The Ointment', a favourite saying of Ronnie Wood's, is a funky but forgettable instrumental that McLagan claims was recorded in awkward 5/4 time so Rod wouldn't be able to sing over it. Russ Schlagbaum: "Kenney used his son Dylan's miniature drum kit for that track. I remember setting it up, it was a really tiny kit with a 12-inch bass drum. They all marvelled at how great it sounded. I think Kenney used one of his real snares but the bass drum and the toms were these little toys."

The soulful 'If I'm On The Late Side', another Stewart/Lane co-write, may have been inspired by Lane's newfound passion with Kate or, as in 'Debris', a memory from his East End background – Maryland and Silvertown are both districts then within the County Borough of West Ham.

The sound of light chatter and a car driving off behind Mac's solo piano ushers in the pensive 'Glad And Sorry', sung together by Wood and Lane. Lane's lyrics are among his best and, like 'Nobody Knows' off the first Faces album, were inspired by Baba's philosophies.

With a mesmerising piano figure from Mac, rich acoustic sounds (another testament to Johns' production) and a tasteful Wood solo, the song assumed an added poignancy in light of how Lane's life would develop. Opening on a false start from Wood's Leslie'd guitar, 'Just Another Honky', another deeply philosophical Lane tune, of the "if you love someone, set them free" nature, may have been intended as a form of *mea culpa* to Sue or as an excuse to himself in justifying his recent actions.

With the album having reached something of a wistful air, the mood wasn't alleviated with 'Ooh La La', a wry, regretful folksy ditty addressed from an errant grandson to a grandfather whose sage advice regarding the fairer sex he'd ignored, leaving him wishing he "knew then what I know now", an easily identifiable sentiment. Set to a gentle folk strum with

* The sleeve note reads 'Thanks to Phil Chapman for the Klaxon' but he has no memory of the session.

parping harmonium and a great saloon bar piano solo from Mac, the song fades out on some delicious acoustic soloing from Wood who sang lead on the track – his first solo vocal performance since the Birds days.

Ian McLagan: "When Rod heard 'Ooh La La' he said, 'I don't like it and anyway it's in the wrong key.' Ronnie Lane had sung it because it was basically his song. Rod then came back after a week or something and we'd recut it in *D* to suit him but he said, 'Nah, I still don't like it.' He said to Ronnie Wood, 'You should sing it' which is why Woody sang it."

With its varied moods and some of Ronnie Lane's finest writing, *Ooh La La* stands as, for this writer, the best album in the Faces' erratic catalogue. "I feel with this album more than any of the others there are no throwaways. Every track stands up," Wood told Penny Valentine. "In fact we slung a couple off because for once we actually made more tracks than we needed – a bloody miracle."

Its main flaws are a slightly disjointed feel and the paltry running time of 30:22 – ironically, *Long Player* had been criticised for overrunning at 45 minutes. Ideally, if 'Just For A Moment' and other quality Lane songs from the time, such as 'Done This One Before' were added to the mix or if Rod had held onto 'True Blue', it could have ranked in the classic album stakes. As it was, if Wood's comment was referring to the tracks cut at Stargroves, neither would have exactly lifted the album. Of the outtakes, eventually released on the Faces box-set, 'Insurance' was the title given to a somnambulistic backing track over which Rod was unlikely to have wanted to sing, although 'The Cheater' and 'Wyndlesham Bay' (an alternate version of 'Jodie', eventually released as a Stewart B-side) were certainly worthy of consideration.

At the time, critics considered *Ooh La La* a letdown, especially considering 18 months had elapsed since *Nod's*. In a review headlined 'Something Amiss With The Boys' *Sounds'* Billy Walker summed up the general consensus: "The Faces are such a damn good band that giving them the elbow, no matter how mildly, is thought to be the pastime of madmen and fools but *Ooh La La* . . . for all its fine music and incredibly inventive cover is a rather disappointing album . . . You can't fault Rod's vocals throughout the whole set and it's hard to see where the Faces have missed out here too, they play with a great deal of depth but the excitement and wonder moments aren't there."

Ooh La La was launched with a pre-release playback party at the Warner Bros. offices and a more upmarket gathering at Tramp, on Jermyn Street, the London nightclub of choice for the well-heeled, A-list rock stars and footballers on the razz. The band had graduated to the Mayfair set from the less refined Speakeasy and it was now their playground of choice, along with the likes of Mick Jagger, Keith Richards, Ringo Starr and Keith Moon. Surrounded by tarted up Can Can girls flashing their frilly knickers, the band posed for the press with glasses in hand, a dishevelled Ronnie Lane looking particularly worse for wear. Dishevelment was the word Lane gave to a tedious, incoherent blues that was spontaneously recorded and given away as one side of a free flexi single (the other previewed tracks from the album) to readers buying the April 7 edition of *NME*.

"We were all in quite a state at the time – quite a pissed state actually," Wood told the paper. "Everybody was mucking about with this old blues number, so we shouted to Glyn to turn the tape on. The Stones were in the next studio and Mick and Keith came in to listen for a laugh."

Before leaving for America, the band fitted in four British dates around towns and cities left off the previous tour. These included Sunderland on Friday, April 13. It was a week since the FA Cup semi-finals where Sunderland beat Arsenal 2–1 to progress to the final against Leeds.* John Peel, a staunch Liverpool and Faces supporter, cherished the memory of that night as one of his favourite ever gigs when both band and audience bonded in one unholy communion. "I'm supposed to have danced in the wings with a bottle of Blue Nun in my arm," Peel later recalled. "And I'm a person who never dances. Never, never, never."

The day after the show at Worcester Gaumont, Roy Hollingworth interviewed Rod at his home in Windsor and found him in a bored, surly frame of mind. When the journalist gave his favourable verdict on *Ooh La La*, Stewart registered surprise. "It was a bloody mess . . . But I shouldn't say that should I? . . . It was a disgrace but I'm not going to say anything more about it." Hollingworth tried diverting the conversation to a lighter bent but Rod was on a roll – he hit out at the Faces sticking to the same material, their problems in playing the new songs live and the wasteful work pattern in the studio. Stewart later claimed he'd been misquoted but the damage had been done.

When the interview, carrying a banner headline 'Rod: Our new album is a disgrace . . . a bloody mess', was printed prominently on page three in the *Melody Maker* dated April 21, all hell broke loose. "It was very mean

---

* Sunderland went on to win the FA Cup with a single goal, becoming the first Second Division side to lift the Cup since West Bromwich Albion in 1968.

spirited of Rod to slam *Ooh La La* in the press immediately after it came out," says McLagan. "He was making his own albums, fair enough but he didn't have to slag ours off and he had no right to because it wasn't a bad album . . . The irony is he could have contributed more to it but he didn't so he had even less of a reason to criticise."

Amid ill feeling emanating from Rod's outburst the Faces ninth US tour started just days later with Jo Jo Gunne supporting.* From the beginning it was, to borrow a familiar phrase, never a dull moment especially as Lane deliberately disobeyed the band's unwritten 'no wives on the road' edict.

Russ Schlagbaum: "The other guys were really pissed off, they felt that Kate was putting all this shit in Ronnie's head. I got the shock of my life because my girlfriend Barbara Morice, who was Ronnie's secretary, came over with Kate. In Columbus, Ohio, there were a load of girls that I knew from college around, I was working for one of the world's biggest rock'n' roll bands and I'm all set up. I walk into the lobby of the Holiday Inn and there stands my English girlfriend who I thought I'd left behind in Richmond. It was like 'Holy fuck, what do I now?' I thought it was very odd that Ronnie would bring someone over to play au pair but then leave the child with a hotel caretaker or some sort so that Kate and Barbara could go to the gig. They all travelled round in this great big Ford station wagon and I have to give Laney credit because he busted his ass to drive those distances from gig to gig with these women and a kid until the end of the tour in Indianapolis."

On May 10, the intractable situation came to a head at Nassau Coliseum, Long Island. As Schlagbaum recounts: "It started at the hotel earlier in the day. Charlie Fernandez came in, saying, 'Whoa, something really weird is brewing'. The band got to the gig, had an argument in the dressing room before they went on and while they were walking on stage. I'm standing there, holding Ronnie Lane's bass. He walks right by me and goes over to Mac and throws a glass of wine in his face, walks back and while I'm putting the bass on Ronnie, Mac picks up a tambourine and throws it as hard as he can. Ronnie ducks and it just misses him. The audience had no idea, they're thinking it's all part of the act. The band carried on arguing throughout the set and afterwards, they locked themselves in the dressing room for hours. Chuch and I were pissed off because we wanted to get back to the hotel for the party and the women but the keys to the truck were in the dressing room so we couldn't leave. We said, 'Can't we get

---

* Jo Jo Gunne featured former Spirit members Jay Ferguson and Mark Andes. Andes would later go on to play in Ian McLagan's Bump Band.

in?' and [Faces tour manager] John Barnes said, 'Absolutely nobody can come in.' They had this huge row and that's when Ronnie decided he was leaving the band.

"The next gig was in Roanoke, Virginia and nobody was speaking to Ronnie except Woody who was his usual bubbly self, you know, 'Let's put all the bad stuff behind us and have some fun.' Woody was always desperate that everyone should have a good time. Laney always used to wander round in circles onstage so that his guitar cord would end up in a huge knot, which was always a problem for me but that night he just stood still back by his amps and played bass."

Mac, who was celebrating his 28th birthday, remembers Lane coming up to his face during the gig and swearing at him whereupon an enraged McLagan kicked him up the arse and chased him off the stage. Alongside "Fuck the gig!" and the even more endearing "Bollocks, you cunt!" "I'm leaving the group" was a common Faces catchphrase – a mock cry wolf uttered whenever there was any minor hassle or pressure to deal with, usually with drink in hand and tongue firmly in cheek. But now Ronnie Lane was implacable as Mac recalled, "When he said, 'I'm leaving the group', I said, 'Oh, for fuck's sake, Ronnie.' He said, 'Why don't you come with me and we'll get another band together?' I said, 'I'm in the band I want to be in with you. I don't want you to leave.'"

An uncorroborated story has it that after a gig on the tour, the resentment directed at Stewart from Lane descended to a confrontation where Rod, all satin and white gloves, sized up the bass player in his East End barrow boy clobber and remarked, "What are you trying to be – a spiv or a Ted?" to which Lane retorted, "Well I'd rather look like a fucking Teddy boy than an old tart who's going through the change." Lane later acidly remarked he knew it was time to move on when Rod "started buying his clothes from Miss Selfridge."

For Lane it must have seemed a bitter irony – feeling he had no alternative but to leave the band he'd formed, ten years on from finding Kenney Jones in the British Prince; not least because of his ongoing concerns over the wisdom of inviting the vocalist to join in the first place. It is unfair to lay all the blame at Rod's feet for being the catalyst behind Lane's decision, and it should be reiterated that Stewart did not want Lane to leave the Faces either. Onstage they were something of a double act – Ronnie doing his best to make 'the LV' (lead vocalist as Rod was sardonically referred to) crack up while Rod would piggyback Ronnie around the stage or help keep him vertical. Most crucially Lane's levelling humour kept Rod's excesses in check. During the fraught vocal overdubs for *Ooh*

La La, Rod made it known to *Circus* reporter Barra Greyson that, in his opinion, "Ronnie's the real songwriter."

Going further back to the *Never A Dull Moment* sessions, Rod had expressed concern for his comrade, telling Nick Logan, "I saw Ronnie Lane the other day and he was looking a bit bleary eyed. I must ring him up and persuade him to take an early night." Although in the same interview, he did admit having problems interpreting Lane's compositions. "Ron [Wood] and I have this incredible thing between us. We could both be on opposite sides of the world and Ron could phone and play me a tune, and I could put the lyrics to it. Whereas I don't have that same thing with Ronnie Lane because of the chords and the structures he uses. I can't get into them."

"They always took the mickey out of Ronnie's songs," says Jan Jones. "Kenney used to laugh about it. He'd come in from Olympic and I'd say, 'How did it go?' and he'd say, 'We've got the statutory Ronnie Lane song, 'rinky-dinky-dink . . .' Musically Ronnie and Rod were like chalk and cheese but I loved the blend of Ronnie Lane and Rod's voice."

The Faces were predominantly a band built for the stage but, as Mac points out, "apart from singing the opening verse of 'Maybe I'm Amazed', Ronnie didn't really get to do anything with the band so it was no wonder he felt frustrated."

Russ Schlagbaum: "Everyone thought Laney was insane. 'Why the fuck would he leave the Faces right at their peak? He's got to be out of his mind. It must be the woman he's with.' Of course, Kate had a lot to do with it but Ronnie was on the alert from the very beginning. Ronnie saw through the Rod thing and he told Mac and Kenney, 'Rod's gonna leave you in the shit like Steve [Marriott] did', but they wouldn't have it. They didn't want to get off the golden cart at that point."

Ronnie's brother Stan takes a similar view. "I used to say to Ronnie, 'You only jump off the boat if it's sinking.' And for the first time in his life he was making plenty of money. But I think that Kate was a bad influence at that time because she wanted to be a hippie and live on a farm and all that shit. I think she was the force that dragged Ronnie away from the Faces plus he was pissed off with Rod so I think between the two of them it turned him."

'Faces Go To Town' ran the front page of the May 19 edition of *Sounds* announcing that the band were to play three major London concerts at the Edmonton Sundown on June 1, 3 and 4 as a prelude to a full scale European tour with dates to be recorded for a proposed live album. But of far more drama and consequence was the paper's announcement a week later:

'Plonk Quits Faces'. "Following speculation about the future of the Faces, Ronnie Lane announced this week his decision to leave. Prior to leaving for a holiday in France, he said 'It's time for me to move on. I feel the need for a change.'"

The resultant hoopla surrounding the gigs involved fans queuing for over seven hours for tickets with the 3,500 capacity audiences being jammed against the barriers and the inevitable cases of fainting. Such was the fervour that a fourth and final show on June 6 was added. Ironically the Edmonton shows were some of the best the Faces played. "Ronnie was feeling good, his anger had passed," says Russ. "It was accepted – he was leaving, there was no changing his mind and that was it. There wasn't a lot of tension – or there appeared not to be."

"All I mainly recall of Edmonton is the bar onstage," support act Andy Bown says. "I couldn't believe Rod had his wine frozen at the correct room temperature in an ice bucket. I thought what a spoilt bastard but nowadays that's nothing."

Aware of the sense of occasion, Gaff Management hired Mike Mansfield Television to videotape the final night. After a long wait in which an announcement was made that the Faces had been stopped by police on the way to the gig, a line of Can Can girls came on for a vibrant display before the Faces finally took their places on the wide, palm-treed stage with white rubber flooring – Rod in sparkling vest and long tartan scarf with a green feather boa tied around his waist, the two Ronnie's fags clamped in mouths and Mac with candle atop the Steinway to add atmosphere as well as being handy for lighting ciggies. Kenney sat behind his new Ludwig 'liquorice allsorts' kit. If it weren't for the presence of 'Farewell Ronnie' signs scattered among the ubiquitous tartan scarves in the audience, it was difficult to determine this was Lane's last gig – as if the subject was verboten. The encore of 'Memphis' over, Lane joined the others to take his final bow, joining in on the traditional 'We'll Meet Again' singalong as the five Faces left the stage together.

"That last night at Edmonton was absolutely fucking fantastic," says Stan Lane. "I was up in the balcony and it was moving. I was shitting meself because I thought it was all going to collapse. Ronnie left there that night and he came with me in the motor and we went to Tramp. He sees Marc Bolan, goes up to him and says, 'You haven't got a job for an out of work bass player, have ya?'"

faces

Part Three

Last Orders Please

CHAPTER 17

Tetsu And Teacher's

"There's only one Ronnie Lane and it's impossible to look for another one. The guy's a character and we'll never replace 'im."
— Rod Stewart, *New Musical Express*, 1973

"It was always the case you just wanted to get out of the hotel to play and after the gig you just wanted to get wrecked. Then the next day you had to get to an airport and another flight."
— Ian McLagan, interview with author, 2010

RONNIE Lane's departure from the Faces came as a shock — but then the summer of 1973 saw significant personnel upheavals in other major British rock bands. Ian Gillan and Roger Glover both left Deep Purple, a tired and emotional Ray Davies dramatically announced he was leaving the Kinks — a temporary lapse as it turned out — Mick Ralphs departed Mott The Hoople to form Bad Company, Brian Eno walked from Roxy Music and David Bowie 'retired', famously disbanding his Spiders From Mars on the stage of the Hammersmith Odeon.

More of a surprise — given that this was a band characterised by a tight-knit London bond — was the candidate selected as Lane's successor.

Tetsu Yamauchi presents a challenge for any biographer — because of the language barrier and his media reticence, details are scant regarding his background. From what can be established, he was born Tetsuo Yamauchi in Fukuoka, Japan on October 21, 1946 and grew up in Tokyo. He first came to London in 1968 with a Japanese group called Samurai who spent the next two years travelling around, recording an album on Philips, *Green Tea*. Free were popular in the Land of the Rising Sun and after their temporary split in 1971, Paul Kossoff and drummer Simon Kirke recorded an album with Yamauchi and session keyboard player John 'Rabbit' Bundrick at London's Island Studios — released in February '72 as *Kossoff,*

Kirke, Tetsu, Rabbit. Returning to Japan and recording a solo album, Tetsu received a hasty telephone call in July 1972 from Free's manager Johnny Glover and was asked to replace bassist Andy Fraser who finally quit for good during the band's Japanese tour supporting ELP.

Tetsu kept in the shadows while Free disintegrated due to Paul Rodgers' and Bundrick's volatile personalities and Kossoff's alarming drug use, though his almost complete inability to speak English was a contributing factor. Yamauchi played on the band's final album *Heartbreaker*, released January 1973.

With Free in terminal stasis, and Lane serious in his intentions, the first approach was made to Fraser, although memories conflict slightly. "We wanted to get Andy Fraser because we liked his playing, those sliding bass lines," says Mac. "I'd never met the guy and still to this day I've never met him. But Simon Kirke said, 'Fuck no, you don't want Andy Fraser in the band, take Tetsu, he's much better and a much nicer guy.'"

According to Pete Buckland, Fraser was actually offered the gig "but he turned it down so I think it may well have been Kirkey that recommended Tetsu."

"We didn't steal [Tetsu] from Free or anything," Rod explained to Penny Valentine in August '73, ". . . the relationship between us and Free – we adore each other. I think Paul [Rodgers] is still one of the best singers around and it was a real ego thing for me to have Tets in the band. But it was done nicely. I mean we said to Tets, 'Go and talk to them and if they're upset in any way, you must stay . . .'"

Another contender for the vacant position was Phil Chen, a Jamaican born, Chinese bassist whom the band knew from his stint in London's R&B clubs in the mid-Sixties with Jimmy James & The Vagabonds. "Phil's name did come up but I can't remember why we didn't go with him," says Buckland.

"I had a telegram from Shirley Arnold while I was in Jamaica recording with the Butts Band," says Chen, "and they wanted me to join the Faces but I had one more week in the studio so they got Tetsu instead."

Pete Buckland: "With Tetsu the sound changed a lot because Ronnie Lane was a unique player. At his best Tetsu could sound really good but he was inconsistent. Not that the Faces were consistent as a band but they all played very, very well but loose. Tetsu would play badly but loose, if you see what I mean. He was undoubtedly a great player when sober. Unfortunately he wasn't sober that often.

"When you've had a bass player who played some of the most beautiful lyrical bass and was so much a part of the fabric of the Faces as Laneole was, you can't replace them really. It would have been better with just a good, adaptable bass player like Phil Chen. I think Phil would have fitted in a lot better musically than Tetsu."

McLagan disagrees: "Tetsu was a bad choice but it wouldn't have worked with Phil either. We hired Tetsu without listening to or meeting him. The thing is the band was in the States at the time [when Lane said he was leaving]. If we'd have been in London it would have been different, we could have called a few people and had auditions but we were in the middle [*sic*] of a fucking tour. Ronnie [Wood] was calling Simon [Kirke] and just trying to figure out what to do. It was all too rushed."

To recruit an untried musician to replace a key creative member in one of the world's biggest rock bands in such a peremptory manner was asking for trouble. But that was only the start of their problems. Having been subjected to the heavy boozy, druggy combative atmosphere surrounding Free, and taking the Faces' public image at face value, Tetsu, it could be said, was no stranger to the demon alcohol.

"At the first rehearsal he brought a bottle of Teacher's in with him," Mac recalls. "Rod said to us, 'He's trying to impress us, he's going to offer it round,' but he didn't, he drank the whole bottle himself. Rod swears blind that one time on tour, he saw Tetsu's breakfast tray being delivered with a bottle of Teacher's on it!" A story of a more apocryphal nature has it that the only Japanese word the Faces knew was kampai – "Cheers!"

During the final Edmonton date with Lane, Kenney had collapsed from severe flu, and although he was able to finish the show a doctor subsequently diagnosed he and Rod with "extreme exhaustion" and ordered them to rest. A European tour was duly postponed. Away from the prying eyes of the British music press, Tetsu made his Faces debut in Turin, Italy on July 16. Two weeks later, his British baptism of fire occurred before a packed audience at Manchester's Hard Rock Cafe. It was an endurance test for all with obstructed views, poor sound and sweltering heat making the instruments go out of tune. Draped in scarf with platform heels and denim cap atop his tall frame, Tetsu was the image of Zen calm, picking out runs on his Fender Precision, but such was the sauna-like temperature onstage that Kenney collapsed about 25 minutes in after exerting himself during his solo in 'Losing You'.

"Chuch and I carried Kenney back into the dressing room," says Russ Schlagbaum. "We tried to revive him, got an oxygen tent and all that shit. The other band members went into a slow number ['I'd Rather Go Blind'] without a drummer. Chuch came back and said, 'Come on, go out and play the drums, they need a drummer.' I could have gone on but I said no because I was busy trying to revive Kenney who had to be taken off to hospital in an ambulance and treated for heat exhaustion.

"So I missed my big opportunity. They brought some guy on [John 'Willie' Wilson from support act Sutherland Brothers And Quiver] and he was bad. I was listening from backstage and I thought, 'Fuck, I should have gone out there' because I knew the arrangements from listening to them every night."

"Kenney got in the wars a lot," Jan Jones recalls. "At one show, I think he was just doing an ordinary fill and he poked himself in the eye with a drumstick and went over the back [of the drums]. He got a glass in his head at another gig. Someone threw a glass on stage but he carried on playing. He thought it was sweat pouring down."

A more pressing problem presented itself the following month when the Musicians' Union and the Home Office refused Tetsu's application for a work permit. The MU claimed that Yamauchi was depriving a British musician of work, saying, "There are enough British musicians out of work without bringing in foreigners to fill any vacancies."

It seemed odd that Yamauchi had been playing in Britain for two years, technically illegally, without any hassles but then Free weren't in the lime-light or as big an earner as the Faces. Equally inconsistent was that the Faces' organisation employed an American-born road crew. "Chuch and I both came in without permits, on visitor's visas but it was a lot easier in those days," Russ explains. "I think Billy Gaff's office claimed that because the band used American equipment they needed American technicians."

"It's our British fans who'll suffer because we make most of our money abroad," said Rod, who believed, without basis, that the Faces were being made an example of by the authorities. "The ban on Tetsu just means we won't be able to play over here. It's silly of the government, too, because we earn millions of dollars for the country every year."

With both sides in deadlock, the Faces' imminent appearance at the 12th National Jazz, Blues and Rock Festival at Reading on August 25 was touted as potentially their last British gig. "We ain't gonna get rid of Tetsu – no way – even if he was on the other side," quipped Stewart, who had a novel if impracticable solution to the dilemma as he told Penny Valentine. "I had this brainwave about maybe playing concerts in Jersey and flying people out there or getting boats to go out. Or we could play at Dunkirk and have boats going backwards and forwards – oh, that'd be great, wouldn't it?"

A Faces spokesman made it clear that whatever the outcome the band would still honour the Reading date, without Tetsu if necessary. Thanks to some nimble legal negotiating, the perpetually grinning bassist was able to appear with the others before an audience of around 40,000 (although the legal attendance was limited to just over half that number). While the scarf-waving segment of the crowd got behind them the Faces turned in an indifferent 70-minute performance, coming on late and drunk, Rod in yellow satin and tartan.

Reviewing for *The Times*, Michael Wale considered the Faces "a disappointment", presciently observing, "One wonders how long this group that has obviously lost its impetus can continue. Despite this, Rod Stewart still stands out as a personality and surely must now make his own way in rock."

Ron Nevison recorded the show on the LMS for a possible live Faces release – something that had been on the agenda for a while now. Initially no Faces tracks were to be included on the *Reading Festival* album planned by GM Records due to the band's low opinion of "the quality of the tapes" (or, reading between the lines, their performance). Eventually, a pedestrian version of 'Losing You' was selected featuring Jones' interminable drum solo. Whereas the studio cut had displayed his considerable prowess with economy, Jones extended showboating in the song was now an excuse for the others to indulge in whatever took their fancy or let the sadistic side of their humour take over.

"They used to take the mickey out of Ken during his solo," says Jan. "He always used to look around for the signal to wind it down and they'd be standing on the side of the stage, drinks in hand, smiling at him with no intention of coming back on so Kenney would have to string it out. He would look over to where I was standing and I remember this look of panic in his eyes as if to say, 'Go and get them now!' That's when I did get cross and said to them, 'Hurry up, he can't take much more.'"

Apart from a new introduction to the set, the Temptations' 'I Wish It Would Rain', featuring a guest horn section, which would be used as the B-side of the Faces' next single, the Reading tapes were shelved. "Reading wasn't good . . ." Stewart opined to *Disc*'s Rosalind Russell. "Tetsu was playing the wrong kind of bass – he was playing lead bass instead of with the drums. But we got it sorted out."

Stewart had revealed to *NME* that Mick Jagger expressed interest in coming on at Reading for a guest duet on 'Love In Vain' and 'It's All Over Now' but this didn't occur despite the Stones and Faces now becoming thick as thieves.

As well as Ian Stewart's early connection, Jagger in particular held the Faces in high regard, perhaps seeing them as a complement to the Stones' own basic brand of R&B. Glyn Johns, a common denominator to both groups, recalls, "going to a Faces concert at the Rainbow in north London [in February '72]. I gave Mick a lift home and he was so blown away by the Faces that he was more or less saying they were a better band than the Stones. I told him he was talking rubbish. I think on reflection if you've been in a band for a long time, you're bound to go through periods of feeling restricted by what that band is and you get frustrated if you see something else that's really impressive. I think that's what Mick was going through. But to say they were better, well that's nonsense, they were two different bands."

Stewart had once claimed to be in competition with Jagger although one could hardly imagine the imperturbable legend from the Dartford Delta quaking in his boots. Over-riding any hint of rivalry, the two socialised and Mick also became very close to Ronnie Lane whom he called "an incurable romantic" and Ronnie Wood, regularly dropping into the basement studio at the Wick where Wood was putting ideas together for a solo album. For Woody the most significant bond was struck in the summer of '73 when Krissie noticed Keith Richards sitting at a table in Tramp looking like he wanted to be somewhere else and invited him back to the Wick.

Another close social acquaintance in Faces' circles was Keith Moon. The Who and the Small Faces' connections were well documented and Woody had known Moonie, as he was known to all, since his West London days with the Birds. A former model, Keith's vivacious wife Kim had received the amorous attentions of Rod the Mod at the same time as Keith who became jealous of the singer as a result. Both Woody and Mac could often be found at Moon's madcap mansion, Tara House, an ultra-modern glass bungalow consisting of five interlocking pyramids in seven acres of grounds on St Ann's Hill, Chertsey, Surrey – or drinking at the Golden Grove, the pub at the top of its long drive. Likewise, Keith and Kim were frequent visitors to the Wick along with Keith Richards and Anita Pallenburg, George and Pattie Harrison and other windswept rock couples.

On a whim Mac had invited Keith and Kim to accompany him to the Faces' headlining festival appearance at Frankfurt's Radstadion on July 22. Keith handled the stage introduction: "And now with their new bass player, Tetsu, he's Japanese but don't hold it against him unless he asks ya and that's especially for you women at the front. Ladies and gentlemen, the finest rock'n'roll band in Frankfurt today, the Faces!"

During the encore of 'Borstal Boys', Keith reappeared to hit a cymbal alongside Kenney. The next day Mac and the Moons flew back to London and back to Tara to continue the merriment where they left off. A year on from his split with Sandy, Mac had consoled himself with various lovelies all too willing to help a rock star through the blues but now he found himself harbouring feelings for Kim that went beyond mere friendship. That summer, she reached breaking point with Keith's unpredictable behaviour and walked out on him, taking their seven-year-old daughter Mandy with her. Kim had left Keith before on several occasions but after constant imploring and promises of good behaviour from her errant husband she had given in and returned. This time, however, there was no going back.

At the same time Kenney and Jan's marriage was in jeopardy due to her ongoing affair with Ron Nevison. Eventually, Kenney sussed what was happening. "On this occasion it was genuinely innocent," says Jan. "Ron was still living in the flat above Mac's garage in East Sheen and he was in bed quite ill so I dropped him off one of those electric fires. I was on my way to Harrods, that's where I told Kenney I was going but he was questioning me an awful lot. I thought, 'Hmmm, OK, I think you're on to it but as I'm not up to any mischief today, I'm not worried.' Kenney did a bit of detective work and followed me but as I said in my defence, 'Because you keep going on and on, saying there's something going on when there isn't, I didn't want to cause trouble so I parked round the corner.' Mac must have known what was going on but I don't think he would have said anything.

"I took this electric fire in and within seconds there was a loud bang and it was Kenney, he'd smashed the door down and come flying up the stairs, shouting and ranting. If he was expecting to catch us in the act he should have at least waited. So I just said, 'I'm sorry about this, I just brought the fire' and I got up and left.

"I don't know if Kenney had a fight with Nevison after I'd gone. I went to Harrods and came back home. Then Kenney came home and he kept going on and I sidestepped around it. But the worst bit was later on that afternoon, a big bouquet of flowers arrived from Kenney to say he was sorry. The affair just petered out, it was over by the time I decided to confess. I'd just come out of hospital, I'd been very ill and I was recuperating at my mum's in Hampstead and that's when I told Kenney. He may well have gone off, had his punch-up with Nevison and well, you can't blame him. Kenney was boozing an awful lot and he could get into fisticuffs when he overdid it. I knew how to wind him up so I was not blameless in all this."

313

Rod had sung of never being a millionaire in 'True Blue' but that oversight was close to being remedied by the summer of '73 when he seemed more omnipresent than ever. A compilation, *Sing It Again Rod*, appeared in August which he personally compiled at Mercury's invitation, flying to New York to re-mix certain tracks, as well as working with Shakey Pete Corriston on the die-cut sleeve design of a whisky shot glass.* The inner live shots were photographed by Steve Azzara at Nassau Coliseum the night Ronnie Lane announced his departure from the Faces. In the UK *Sing It Again Rod* went straight in at number two behind Peters & Lee's *We Can Make It*, the first time Philips had the first two places in the album charts since 1957; a week later it was in top place.† Jon Landau wrote in *Rolling Stone*: "*Sing It Again Rod* is, like all such greatest hits albums, a compromise, because any Stewart fan has long ago digested the material. However it was put together with great care, is brilliantly edited, intelligently, if imperfectly, selected, plenty long and well-paced, and as much fun to listen to, if a bit less unified, than most of his solo albums and all of his Faces records . . .

"His next move should be a genuine solo album – one on which he takes the big chance and writes the whole damn thing himself."

On August 31, a stand-alone single, 'Oh! No, Not My Baby', Rod's cover of the Maxine Brown soul classic, written by Goffin & King, was released. The song had been a hit for Manfred Mann eight years earlier and an R&B hit in 1972 for Merry Clayton. Recorded over two days with the usual line-up of Waller, Quittenton, Pete Sears (bass) and Ronnie Wood (guitar), and with a saccharine Gamble & Huff Philly style string arrangement from Jimmy Horowitz, 'Oh! No, Not My Baby' pointed towards the future Stewart sound – slickly polished, commercially palatable but lacking the true grit and inspiration of his earlier work. Housed in a sleeve in the colours of the Royal Stewart tartan, with no other lettering, the single reached number six. The preening promotional appearance Rod made to promote it on the *Russell Harty Plus* chat show was particularly narcissistic.

The velvet suits, five o'clock shadow and everyman image of previous years was replaced by chiffon, satin and a lion's mane of hair streaked at the swank Sweeney's salon in Knightsbridge. His flamboyant style – which he described as "gypsy, sloppy, not very smart" – came from slinging bits together: a pair of satin trousers, an embroidered silk shirt, long scarf, or a

---

* The title was to be *Play It Again Rod* until it was discovered that Fats Domino was bringing out a compilation called *Play It Again Fats*.
† *Sing It Again Rod* only reached number 31 in the US.

tartan outfit. Tartan was now ubiquitous. "It's not just a craze," Rod declared. "I really dig wearing it. It's beautiful, original, at least in this business. I reckon I look pretty good in it too – the rest of the boys think the same! But they wouldn't dare copy me!"

Actually, while he and Woody always looked like glamorous brothers, Mac and Kenney were falling into line with Stewart's mid-Seventies chic – Mac wearing tartan suits and chopping his hair into the spiky style while Kenney's locks grew longer at the sides and frosted on top. Tetsu, pencil thin and unlike Ronnie Lane as tall as Rod, was just Tetsu.

In *Disc*'s 1973 Poll, Rod was voted both Top British Male Singer and Top World Male Singer (Faces finished third in the respective group categories). There were offers of film roles and a solo concert with the musicians who played on his solo albums to consider. Asked by *NME*'s James Johnson whether he didn't need the Faces as much as they needed him, Rod cautiously replied, "Well, I don't know whether they need me but I know I need them. If something was to happen I could always make my own albums but I'd be lost without them. I get depressed if I don't see the boys for a while. There'll always be a Faces and I think I'll always be in it. I hope so anyway. Unless they kick me out of course . . ."

Ironically, recognised singers from successful groups were achieving individual success in 1973 – the most prominent being Roger Daltrey with his Top 5 single, 'Giving It All Away' written by star-in-waiting Leo Sayer. Bryan Ferry got in the act of albums of cover versions then in vogue (Bowie's *Pin-Ups*, the Band's *Moondog Matinee*, etc.) with *These Foolish Things* and his version of Bob Dylan's 'A Hard Rain's A-Gonna Fall' entering the Top 10.

Waller, Quittenton, Sears, Wood, and McLagan commenced work at Morgan Studios on Stewart's latest solo album. "Right now I don't feel either my albums or the Faces' albums are as good as they could be," Stewart told Penny Valentine. "So the next album is the last I'm going to make on my own and next year we start making them together. Rod Stewart/Faces albums – that's what we're going to see." Early reports revealed that Paul McCartney, Elton John, Mick Jagger and the Sutherland Brothers had submitted material and Rod was threatening to follow though on his intention of recording 'I've Grown Accustomed To Her Face' from *My Fair Lady*.

"I've always been worried about the band but I've got to the point now where I think it's time to start thinking about myself a bit more. I've got to be careful what I say here . . . The thing is that from now on in we must combine albums. The band are suffering and I'm suffering with the

315

situation at the moment. We've been channelling too much talent in the wrong direction. Everything's gone at bloody tangents. We've got to channel all our energy in one direction to make really good albums."

With hindsight such remarks can be seen as Stewart's last attempt at maintaining an illusion of creative democracy within the Faces, for as McLagan indicates: "Ronnie Lane had been the core of the band. Ronnie worked with Rod, he worked with Ronnie Wood and he worked with me. There was the Lane-Wood songs and the Wood-Stewart songs so Woody was also in the middle. But once Ronnie Lane had gone, what we were left with was the Stewart-Wood songs and . . . nothing. Ronnie Lane had been the balance but now Rod could do whatever he wanted. The fact that he lost interest in recording with the Faces, well that was not good."

With America providing 80 per cent of their income, it was imperative to get the red tape surrounding Tetsu sorted and after much negotiating his permit was finally granted days before a four-week tour of the south and West Coast, supported by Rory Gallagher, opened in Florida on September 16. "We were in Fort Lauderdale, just got off the plane, straight into rehearsal," says Charlie Fernandez. "There was this pile of what appeared to be packing blankets spread out on the floor. I just strode over it and went to say 'Hi' to everybody and they said, 'You just trod on our new bass player.' Tetsu was asleep underneath."

Asked if the attitude of American audiences had changed, Rod told *Disc*, "No, if anything it's got better. We seem to have got into the bracket where the crowd knows what to expect – which doesn't mean we're too predictable, I hope."

The band's behaviour was becoming somewhat predictable offstage with only the Who and Led Zeppelin rivalling the Faces in the hotel demolition stakes. "We get pissed off with taking the blame for a load of other bands knocking down whole walls and that," Wood told *Record Mirror* in a feeble attempt at protesting innocence. "Most hotels won't book us in now. We used to book in as Fleetwood Mac in the States but there's still places where they know our faces so we just can't go to those." The manager of the Executive Inn, Evansville, Indiana obviously couldn't tell his bands apart and called in police after discovering torn out ceiling tiles, broken lighting fixtures and fire hoses and furniture pulled into a hallway, causing $1,500 damage. This was relatively restrained compared to the infamous "train incident" a week later at the Hilton Garden Inn in Tucson, Arizona.

"We'd done the gig," recalls Pete Buckland, "and as the final announcement of the night Charlie Daniels would say, 'Thank you, ladies and gentlemen, thank you for paying your money. If there are any ladies in the audience that would like to come back for some dictation we're staying at . . .' So consequently loads of people came back and it soon got out of hand. It was one of those sorts of big motel places, a very large area with a train that ran around the outside. The train was actually padlocked to the track. I had my trusty Swiss army knife with a metal cutting saw on it and I cut through the chain or whatever and managed to get the carriages going really, really quickly – we all loaded in and of course we got to the first bend and it all came off the track."

Ian McLagan: "It was just total boredom. We had nothing to smoke and I think it was Chuch who suggested we get a can of beer and a shot glass each, a shot glass being one ounce and a can is 12 ounces. Fill the shot glass, drink it down when the second hand hits 12, wait one minute, fill up your shot glass and then drink the next one and keep on doing that for 12 minutes. Because we were bored, we'd been travelling all that day and we wanted to get fucked up. It gets you very drunk very quick."

Meanwhile in the Party Room: "I think it was Woody who decided that he wanted to get into the adjoining room and he just broke the doors down," Buckland continues. "Stuff got thrown out the windows and the hotel ended up calling out who I think were the National Guard. There were helicopters hovering overhead and guys in helmets coming through the place."

"The next morning I was lying on the bed still a bit pissed from the previous night," McLagan recounted to *Sounds*, "and there's this voice outside the door: 'OK kid, get up.' I didn't move at all because I thought it was someone larking around. Then 'Police, open up or we'll break down the door.' 'I don't give a shit, break the door down.' I said, 'It's not my property.' Eventually I got up and opened the door and it was the police so I was very polite . . . They were checking on every room we had booked to see if there was any damage."

Amazingly none of the tour party ended up behind bars in the conservative state, unlike what befell the Who's touring party a month later in Montreal when a hotel suite was subjected to a destructive makeover. John Barnes simply produced a wad of notes, reportedly $1,500 worth, and calmly asked, "Will that cover it?" As Buckland states, "In those days if you were English, you could get away with bloody murder."

Asked if there was one champion wrecker within the band to rival Keith Moon, Mac says, "No but we all had our specialty. Mine was putting towels in the toilet, flushing it and flooding the room and unscrewing the doorknob from the inside so when you shut the door, there was no way you could get out. That was always a favourite as was unscrewing the phone receiver and taking the microphone out. A few twists of a wrench you could disable the bed that as soon as someone sat on it, it would fall apart.

"When I was at my angriest I bought a bullwhip and I used to carry it around coiled up. I'd go into a hotel lobby, crack the whip and say, 'McLagan here, where's my room key?' Horrible boy. Actually Rod bought one as well. I got on planes carrying mine and they'd say nothing but Rod put his in his suitcase and when his luggage got checked, they confiscated it. It was like if you had a gun in your hand it's OK but don't conceal it."

For those outside the entertainment business it looked like nothing less than delinquent behaviour and outright hooliganism. But for a bunch of young musicians living in a twilight zone out of sync with the rest of society, it was the most extreme form of catharsis. At least the routine was cushioned by luxury. A well-drilled procedure involved a private Learjet (FACES painted on its side in vast letters) ferrying the tour party between gigs, a fleet of Cadillacs and Mercedes limos delivering the band to the venue just moments before showtime.

The concerts at Anaheim Convention Center and the Hollywood Palladium were recorded and engineered by Gary Kellgren who had built New York's Record Plant in the late Sixties before opening its West Coast operations. Ian McLagan: "My memory is that after the second Anaheim show, because Ronnie Wood and I had done a load of blow, we thought, 'That was the much better show' but after we listened back to the tapes we went, 'We were so wrong!' And that's been an education to me ever since, I realise, 'just listen to the tape, never mind what you *think* is on the tape.'"

Based at the Beverly Wilshire during the California leg, Rod continued work on his album between partying at the Roxy and Rainbow. Some bad vibes arose when, at a midnight reception held at the swank Green Cafe, in between the sandwiches and hors d'oeuvres Rod was feted in an obvious display that detracted from the other Faces. "When Rod walked in he seemed to glow, like he was luminescent," recalls Chris Charlesworth, then based in Los Angeles as *Melody Maker*'s US editor. "The girl I was with just melted when I introduced her to him. Not a good idea. Her eyes were like saucers. I swear she would have followed him anywhere, done absolutely anything for him, if only he'd asked."

"The two record companies involved caused a schism from the

beginning," says Russ Schlagbaum. "When the band got to an airport or went to a gig, Warners would supply a limo and Mercury would supply a limo so Rod would have his own limo. You'd get to a hotel and Rod would check into a suite – the rest of the band would be in standard rooms. Mac said, 'I'm not fuckin' paying for Rod Stewart's suites, if he wants to be a flash git like that, he can pay for them himself.' After that US tour, Mac went to Billy Gaff's office and got the tour accounts and saw the cost of the hotels had been split evenly. He said, 'I'm not paying for Rod's lifestyle. I want new accounting. You either split this out and make Rod pay for his own bills or I'm going to come up there with a hatchet and destroy your office.'"

While on tour, Mac had persuaded Kim to join him incognito in LA. At this point their blooming relationship was still under wraps, as Kim was seeking some independence after living with a madman for so long. She and Mandy moved into a house in Campbell Close, Twickenham, rented for them by the Who's office.

"I would visit them unbeknownst to Keith," recalls Peter 'Dougal' Butler, Moon's driver and personal assistant. "Mac would call Kim there while he was in America. Keith didn't realise she was seeing Mac to start with. I can't remember how he found out – it might have been when she rang him and he heard Mac in the background. I remember driving Keith in his lilac Rolls-Royce over to where Mac lived in East Sheen and he was so nervous because he knew Kim was there. I mean everyone knew why she'd left Keith because he was so unmanageable. I did feel sorry for him because he was heartbroken – absolutely heartbroken. I said, 'I'll stay in the car,' but in actual fact I did go in but waited in another room. He was there for a couple of hours with Kim and then with Mac. When Keith got in the car he was OK but as we drove off, he just cried his eyes out. He said, 'I've lost her.' He and Mac still met up socially but Kim was never mentioned. In that scenario, they just carried on as though nothing had ever happened but Keith always thought he could get Kim back."

Moon's darker side flared up on Kim's birthday when he hired a well-known music biz heavy, Reg King, to put the frighteners on Mac, threatening to break his fingers. Fortunately word reached Pete Townshend who paid the guy off before any harm could be done. Kim would have to endure a lot more of Keith's persistent harassment before he finally got the message.

With a break of six weeks before the Faces' forthcoming UK tour, Wood high-tailed it to Munich where the Stones were recording at Musicland Studios. He also contributed a song, 'Let 'Em Say What They

Will' to Alvin's Lee & Mylon Le Fevre's *On The Road To Freedom* on which he played guitar, bass and drums. Ronnie also spent time hanging out rehearsing and recording at George Harrison's home studio at his Oxfordshire mansion, Friar Park in Henley-on-Thames. Tabloid rumours emerged of Woody creating sweet music with Pattie Harrison in return for Krissie's dalliance with George.

There were domestic rumblings in the Stewart household too. "Elton was our neighbour and so was Ringo," says Dee. "Elton would come over to the house a bit and I used to ride up to Ringo's in Ascot, which used to be John Lennon's house [Tittenhurst Park] and see if Maureen was around. She was like a vampire, she didn't get up when it was light. I was riding around Windsor Great Park with the dogs and the horses and everybody was carrying on and I still didn't really know about any of that. I was very young, 23, 24, I just did my thing, that's all I knew how to do. Before coke entered the picture Rod never smoked a cigarette, he never had any dope, he made everybody leave their drugs outside the front door if they came round but then our relationship suffered greatly in the end by the fact that he succumbed and joined in with everybody else.

"We were arguing in the bedroom which had these sort of porcelain statues and I remember while we were shouting at each other I picked up one of these statues, I wasn't going to throw it at him or anything and underneath it was a packet of coke and I said, 'See what I mean?!' I can understand why he was hiding it from me but I just thought it was funny that out of all of the rooms and places to hide it . . ."

Dee packed a bag and moved back to her parents while Rod was seen out cavorting with model Kathy Simmonds and Joanna Lumley, a sophisticated actress and model whose credits included *On Her Majesty's Secret Service* and *Coronation Street*. The two met while giving out prizes at the *Sun* newspaper awards and they soon became an item. Rod told the *Evening News*: "We come from the two ends of the social scale. I'm dead common and she's dead classy. We have nothing in common but we find a lot to talk about."

Preceded by a week's rehearsal at Shepperton Studios, the Faces first proper full-scale UK tour, supported by John Baldry and band, commenced with London dates at East Ham Granada on November 29 followed by the Kilburn Gaumont State, then the biggest cinema in Britain. It was also where Rod had caught a glimpse of his future at Bill Haley's concert 16 years earlier. Ronnie designed and drew an advertisement for the tour publicity inspired by a Norman Rockwell painting he'd seen in the States. By now British audiences resembled a tartan army, or the Tartan Hordes as

Rod dubbed them. "I love to see them singing and swaying like the Scots supporters at a Wembley football match. Really great." The sold-out shows and the party atmosphere was still present and correct – with few going home unhappy – although reviewers noticed the lack of spark in some shows, commenting how the Faces were predictable and "sounding a bit tired".

A single and album arrived at year's end, both putting this sense of lethargy on record. 'Pool Hall Richard', a Stewart-Wood concoction, was 'Pinball Wizard' transferred to the snooker table, the inspiration, conjuring up the Hounslow hall where Mac hung around in his youth, no doubt emanating from the lengthy marathons held around the elaborate snooker rooms in the band members' homes. Melodically it was unmemorable: Chuck Berry-by-numbers with some nice Johnnie Johnson trills from Mac but as a rocker, it lacked the velocity of 'Borstal Boys'. The fans and the Warner Bros publicity cue smashed it to number eight in the UK but the single wasn't released in the US, ostensibly due to record company politics. For many critics it felt like the Faces were going through the motions. They were none too enamoured of the long-promised Faces live recording either. *Live! Coast To Coast Overture And Beginners* emerged in December; a month later in the UK after being on sale on import. As a prelude to the complications in the impending legal battle over Stewart's recording contract, the LP was released on Mercury and the cassette and eight-track versions on Warner Brothers.* In an arrangement that fulfilled both contractual obligations simultaneously the sleeve credited Rod Stewart/Faces.

"When Rod came on stage just off the cuff, he said, 'Good evening, we've got four sets of fingers and one throat.'" Wood told *Sounds'* Rob Mackie, "and I thought that would be a good title, but the title had already been printed on the sleeve as *Overture And Beginners*. Don't know what that's got to do with it!"

The album's number three chart placing belied its attempt to capture the excitement of the Faces on stage. Like so many other releases from the period – Mott The Hoople's *Live*, Bowie's *David Live*, etc. – it seemed to exist perfunctorily for the sake of there being a Faces concert document. In balancing the nine tracks, four came off Stewart's albums, four were from Faces releases with 'Jealous Guy' remaining neutral. Unlike McCartney's 'Maybe I'm Amazed', the Faces never really put their stamp on Lennon's

---

* The cassette included the *Reading Festival* version of 'Losing You' – which, in fact, originated from the same autumn '73 LA live recordings – as a bonus track.

song. A better choice would have been Free's 'Stealer' in which the whole band excelled. A curious flatness to the sound was picked up on by Pete Erskine in *Sounds*: "While this album never falls below a very high standard it never actually exceeds it." *Rolling Stone*'s Jon Landau was more scathing: "The Faces long ago moved from enjoyable looseness to undisciplined laxness. This live album is particularly distressing not only for its lack of ambition but for its tedious repetition of stale formulas."

Stewart was again quick to disown a Faces album, revealing he had to redo most of his vocals. "Some people seem to like that album. I don't have much love for it," says Mac. "I recently discovered an invite to a party and found it was the same night as the Hollywood Palladium show. So we'd be a little wrecked after the gig then we went to this party till . . . I think it was close to three by the time we left and then on to the Record Plant to start mixing. Good idea!"

The British tour continued without incident – on December 11 in Manchester, footballers Denis Law, Paddy Crerand and Mike Summerbee presented the band with Gold Discs onstage[*] – until the penultimate show at Oxford's New Theatre. John Baldry and band had been kicked off the tour when their boozing got out of hand and were replaced by Strider, a four-piece signed to Gaff Management, who had played at Reading with the Faces. Lead guitarist, Gary Grainger, recalls: "There was major panic the morning of the gig. Tetsu had gotten pissed the night before and crashed out, lying on his arm. He'd slept on it for about seven hours and all the circulation stopped so he temporarily lost the use of his right arm. They weren't sure if he could play or not and one of the roadies – it might have been Pete Buckland – was asking Lee Strzelczyk, our bass player, if he could fill in and Lee was shitting himself."

Told by a doctor that there was no chance that Yamauchi could perform, promoter Peter Bowyer, unable to bear the prospect of a late cancellation, turned physiotherapist by instructing Tetsu to exercise his fingers by squeezing an orange and practicing playing bass on the drive to the gig. Massage and exercise techniques followed backstage and to impatient cries from the crowd, the now traditional intro music of David Rose's 'The Stripper' blared over the PA as the band finally got on stage. With encouragement from Rod, who explained the predicament, Tetsu struggled through the gig with the use of only two fingers.

---

[*] At that time, Crerand was assistant coach at Manchester United, Summerbee played for rivals Manchester City and 'the Lawman' had committed the unthinkable by returning to City for a season.

The Faces, 1973, with new recruit Tetsu Yamauchi. "At the first rehearsal Tetsu brought a bottle of Teacher's in with him," Mac recalls. "Rod said to us, 'He's trying to impress us, he's going to offer it round' but he didn't, he drank the whole lot himself." (GETTY IMAGES)

Kim Moon and Mac backstage at a rock festival in Frankfurt, July 1973. Later that year, having had her fill of his unpredictable behaviour, she walked out on husband Keith. (ROBERT ELLIS/REPFOTO)

""All togetha nah... we'll meet again..." The Faces acknowledge their audience, UK tour 1973. (ROBERT ELLIS/REPFOTO)

Ronnie Lane and Kate McInnerney, Fishpool Farm, Wales, 1974. "I think Ronnie's love of that freewheeling gypsy lifestyle was influenced by the poet Jean Michel or Jack Kerouac," says Mike McInnerney. "It was also a leftover from his fairground days." (MIRRORPIX)

"The Faces was like the good old days of the Wild West in America…" describes Faces road manager Charlie Fernandez. "It was like a hurricane passing through. Everyone had a drink in their hand around the clock." (GEMS/REDFERNS)

Ronnie Lane and Slim Chance (featuring Benny Gallagher and Graham Lyle – right) under the Chipperfield's Big Top, Clapham Common, November 11, 1973. (BARRY PLUMMER)

Rod, Ron, and Keith Richards at Wood's solo show, Kilburn Gaumont, London, July 14, 1974. "The gas about playing with Keith is how smoothly our styles meshed," said Wood. "I'd always thought we had that street feel in common." (DAVID WARNER ELLIS/REDFERNS)

Rod in communion with 'the Tartan Hordes' as he dubbed them. Very few bands had a close identification with their audience like the Faces. (ROBERT ELLIS/REPFOTO)

'Sweet Little Rock 'n' Roller': Keith Richards guests during the Faces' last UK concert, Kilburn Gaumont, December 23, 1974. (GRAHAM WILTSHIRE/REDFERNS)

The Faces line-up backstage at Madison Square Garden, New York City, February 24, 1975. "Sometimes I forget why I love rock and roll," wrote Jan Hodenfield in the *New York Post*. "Rod Stewart and the Faces made me sit up and remember." (MIRRORPIX)

Charlie Fernandez helps pour the drinks backstage; (bottom right) Kenney onstage behind his Tartan-design Premier drum kit. (BILL VETELL/MIRRORPIX)

The hired string section and conductor Jimmy Horowitz (foreground right) backstage, and additional guitarist Jesse Ed Davis (bottom right) on the Faces last US tour, 1975. (Bottom left) Rod with new flame Britt Ekland, 1975. The pair set up home in Hollywood, leading to the next phase in Stewart's career. (MIRRORPIX; ROBERT KNIGHT ARCHIVE/REDFERNS)

The original Faces reunite for the first time since 1973 at Rod Stewart's Wembley Stadium concert, July 1986, with Bill Wyman filling in for Ronnie Lane who was diagnosed with MS in the late Seventies. (BRENDAN BEIRNE / REX FEATURES)

Ronnie Lane with his third wife, Susan Gallegos. In 1994 the couple moved to Trinidad, Colorado where Lane saw out the last few years in his battle against the debilitating disease. (MIRRORPIX)

Mac proudly holds *Five Guys Walk Into A Bar...* the Faces box-set he produced, Virgin Megastore, New York, August 17, 2004. *All Music Guide* wrote, "There has never been a box that captures an artist so perfectly." (KRISTIN CALLAHAN/LFI)

Take three-fifths Faces (Jones, Wood & McLagan), add a former Sex Pistols bassist (Glen Matlock, far right) and Simply Red singer (Mick Hucknall, second right) and what do you get? The 21st century model 'Faces' meet the press, London 02, August 2010. (PRESS ASSOCIATION)

And then there were three. The surviving Faces onstage at Hurtwood Park Polo Club, Ewhurst, Surrey, September 5, 2015. "It was so loose," said Rod. "I was thinking, 'If this is what it's like when we're all relatively sober what must it have been like when we were completely pissed?!'" (RICHARD YOUNG/REX SHUTTERSTOCK)

Stewart read the riot act, telling Yamauchi to sort himself out – though whether he understood the singer was another matter. "At one gig, Chuch was actually holding Tetsu because he was so pissed," Grainger recalls. "We were in the wings cracking up because Chuch had his hands between the Ampeg speakers holding him up because he kept toppling."

The tour culminated in 'a special Christmas party' at the Edmonton Sundown on Christmas Eve. Woody invited a full house – including Rod and his new lady Joanna Lumley – over for Christmas dinner. "I wasn't really comfortable around all the excess," Jan Jones admits. "Neither Kenney or I were really into drugs and that's why we got left out of a lot of things because those people don't really want outsiders around – it's like a secret society and besides they're all on a different level. So that's why Kenney never wanted to go round to the Wick even though we lived across Richmond Park. It was different if I popped in to see Krissie during the daytime, where we were just the girls but when it was a party at the Wick, Kenney and I felt decidedly uncomfortable.

"Woody was and is a great host. He noticed that Kenney wasn't talking very much with David Bowie. It's assumed that famous people know each other. Woody kind of stopped and said, 'You know David, don't you Kenney?' and Bowie allowed himself to be introduced to Kenney. That really wound Kenney up because Bowie used to help carry Kenney's drums in during the early days of the Small Faces so of course he knew him. Cocaine did awful things to people with their delusions of grandeur."

CHAPTER 18

I've Got My Own Album To Do

"Everybody has to level out and I can't expect to have another album as
successful as Every Picture Tells A Story. *That was a freak album . . .*
Yet Gasoline Alley *was the best for me. If I could capture that again I'd*
be well pleased . . . I look at it like all good footballers should – I want to
retire at the top. It doesn't tend to happen in this business and it's sad
. . . I want to disappear [snaps fingers] like that."

– Rod Stewart, *New Musical Express*, 1973

"I'm pleased with [the album] because I accomplished more than I set out
to do, but I know that still in the back of my mind there's more to come
out."

– Ron Wood, *Melody Maker*, 1974

"AS for Ronnie Lane I don't really know what he's doing," Rod
remarked to *Disc*'s Peter Erskine in August 1973. "I think he's
living in Wales now. We haven't seen him since the Edmonton gigs so I
don't really know. I don't think he'll ever set the world alight with his
songs, but he could be successful. He just wants to sing his own songs his
own way."

This backhanded appraisal from Stewart concisely summed up Lane's
post-Faces modus operandi. "Ronnie and I talked about his situation,"
Glyn Johns recalls. "He was worried because, despite having just left the
Faces, he was skint and didn't know what he was going to do so I said,
'I'm free on Wednesday, I'll book the studio and we'll make a single and
that will start you off.' So we went in to Olympic [on September 19,
1973] and cut 'How Come'."

Lane and Johns gathered an ad hoc backing band of musicians whom
Ronnie dubbed Slim Chance, the name that the Faces could so easily have
ended up with. The original personnel comprised Ronnie playing rhythm
guitar with Kevin Westlake (who co-wrote 'How Come'), Billy Livsey

(piano), Chrissy Stewart (bass),* Bruce Rowland (drums), Jimmy Jewell (sax), Benny Gallagher (accordion, organ) and Graham Lyle (mandolin, harmonica).

Gaff Management handled promotion despite the fact that Lane had made Gaff's job all the more difficult while in the Faces. 'How Come', released by GM Records on November 9 as a maxi-single, featured a superior re-recording of 'Tell Everyone' (from *Long Player*) and 'Done This One Before', a high quality original that reconfirmed Lane's abilities as a lyricist. A catchy, happy-go-lucky jig, like a sprightlier 'Ooh La La', 'How Come' got Lane's solo career off to a promising start when, thanks to a series of British TV plugs and airplay, it eventually reached number 11 in February '74.

But having spent time in the fast lane, Ronnie felt determined he was not going to be manipulated by the standard razzmatazz of the music industry. "I don't think Ronnie wanted to be a hugely successful solo artist," Johns confirms, "that desire certainly wasn't apparent to me."

Having spent all his 27 years as a city dweller, Lane had a hankering for a less pressurised existence, a feeling of freedom that the long distances he'd driven between Faces gigs with just lady and baby only reinforced. "I think Ronnie's love of that freewheeling gypsy lifestyle was influenced by the poet Jean Michel or Jack Kerouac – a hangover from the Sixties," says Mike McInnerney. "It was also a leftover from his fairground days – how a fair or circus would come to town and then pack up and move on to the next place."

Following on from the unwieldy Rock and Roll Circus concept dreamed up by Mick Jagger in 1971 – taking the Stones, Who and Faces on a travelling road show around America – Ronnie's idealism led him to the notion of a show playing under a Big Top. "Think of all the advantages of playing in the same venue each night in terms of sound and showmanship," an enthusiastic Lane told *Sounds*. "I plan to make the show an entertainment with possible dancers and a variety of musical acts. Nobody knows what will work and what won't because nobody's tried it before."

While plans for a proper travelling circus developed, Lane's Slim Chance played a dry run on Clapham Common on November 11, hiring an ex-Chipperfield Circus tent with a capacity of 2,500. When asked by Erskine how he got the idea, Lane commented, "It came from my total

---

* Stewart had played with a later line-up of Spooky Tooth and Stumble, the backing group for Vigrass & Osborne who supported the Faces on their 1972 UK tour.

inability to carry on the way I was carrying on . . . I was confident in the
Faces as a bass player and as a backroom writer, but I wasn't confident in
terms of singing, 'cos it was never the sort of band that I had a powerful
enough voice for . . . and also I always felt that people had come to see
Rod and I was imposing myself on them. That made me nervous."

Ronnie, Kate and Alana were still living at Wick Cottage – Billy Nicholls
took over the flat in East Twickenham – but the birth of Ronnie's first
son, Luke Kito in August '73, made him all the more determined to make
the break. With the money he made from selling the cottage to Ronnie
Wood, Lane put down a deposit on Fishpool Farm, set in 100 acres of
sheep-grazing land near the village of Hyssington, on the Shropshire-
Montgomeryshire border.

Having been an important part of one of the world's biggest rock'n'roll
bands, only to abandon it to establish a new direction, Ronnie was treading a precarious path. Entering this atmosphere of insecurity was Russ
Schlagbaum who left the Faces' employ in November '73 to work full-
time for Lane.

"When Tetsu came in there was definitely a real void," says Russ. "The
band were struggling to make it happen and I think they knew it wasn't
working like it had worked. After the late '73 US tour I made the decision
to go and work for Ronnie Lane. I was getting paid £30 a week and
Kenney said, 'What do you want to go and work for Ronnie Lane for?
He's never going to amount to anything.' At that point he and Mac were
still pissed at Laney for leaving. I didn't really get to know Ronnie until I
went to work for him. It took a while because he was always drifting
around, lost in thought a lot of the time.

"Ronnie was in this transitional stage between December '73–March
'74. He didn't really have a full band together and he was still working on
his latest songs. The farm in Wales wasn't finished because he planned to
convert one of the barns into a studio and take his mobile up there. The
LMS was actually booked for about six to eight weeks at Headley Grange
with Ron Nevison doing Led Zeppelin [*Physical Graffiti*] and then Bad
Company's first album. So there wasn't a lot happening. That's when the
Faces were touring Australia, which I was peeved about because they'd
been talking about it the entire time I'd been with them.

"Pete Buckland hired this American guy named Art Margain to replace
me. I don't know how they found him, I think he was from California and
worked for Pacific Presentations. On the Faces' '73 UK tour in Liverpool
he started a fight with the bouncers and got his jaw broken. One morning,
I got a call from Pete in Auckland, New Zealand saying, 'Look, this guy

turned out to be pretty useless, we had to ship him home. Can you come out and finish this tour?' So I said, 'Yes, of course I'd love to but I've got to ask Ronnie Lane.' Ronnie was going back and forth between Wick Cottage and Wales at that point. The whole place [in Wales] was derelict. He hired these builders, the Tanners of Montgomery, to excavate the cottage out from the side of a hill. They put in plumbing, electricity, etc. and while they were doing all this work there wasn't a telephone, I don't think they even had electricity wired in yet so I had to send Ronnie a telegram.

"He gets in his Land Rover, drives down to his local, the Drum and Monkey and calls me up from a payphone. I laid out the scenario and said, 'I would really love to go do this tour, can I have three weeks off to do it? The mobile's booked, you're not recording until May, I've never been to Australia, probably never get the chance to go again, etc, etc.' And Ronnie said, 'Aw, Russell, if you go now, you're really going to leave me in the lurch.' He said, 'You make up your mind, you decide' and then he hung up. So I was left standing there and immediately the phone rings again and it's Ronnie. He said, 'Russell, this is Ronnie. I'll make it easy. Since you're even considering going off to work for that cunt Rod Stewart, you're fucking fired!' He fired me over the phone, I thought, 'Great, I'm gone. I'm going to Australia, fuck it.' So off I went. The next day I flew for 32 hours to Sydney, Australia and picked up the tour there."

By the mid-Seventies Australia had gained a reputation for being inhospitable towards visiting entertainers. Led Zeppelin were subjected to an early morning police raid at their Perth hotel in early 1972, the same year that Joe Cocker was busted and deported, and the Stones were dogged by voyeuristic pressmen looking for sleaze in 1973. Even 'Ol Blue Eyes found how unforgiving the country could be when, during a concert in July '74, he described the gentlemen and ladies of the press as, respectively, "bums and parasites" and "buck-and-a-half hookers". As a result the hostile unions refused to allow Sinatra's private jet to be refuelled, effectively leaving him stranded. Frank threatened to cancel his remaining three concerts until a truce was called. Safely back home, Sinatra told a New York audience, "A funny thing happened in Australia. I made a mistake and got off the plane."

Mac and Kenney had their own tales to tell from six years earlier when their infamous tour with the Who ended with both groups narrowly avoiding deportation after an incident on a commercial airline that got blown out of all proportion.

The Australian tour had originally been booked for July '73 so expectations were primed for when the Faces arrived in Sydney. In answer to Stewart's pre-tour request, local radio station 2SM pushed a wheelbarrow of ice cold Tooheys into the press conference. "Are you going to be breaking up any hotels this time?" was one of the first questions thrown at them. Exhibiting remarkable fortitude in the face of provocation, Mac finally snapped, "The only thing that'll get broken will be that reporter's head if he doesn't get on his way."

The open-air, afternoon show at Western Springs Stadium, Auckland on January 27 attracted 15,000, culminating in McLagan taking his hatchet to the Yamaha piano foolishly supplied in place of a Steinway by Phil Warren, Aussie promoter Paul Dainty's New Zealand representative. Returning to Australia, the opening show in Brisbane was cancelled due to extensive flooding brought on by Cyclone Wanda, the region's most severe flood in a century.

From all accounts the Australian dates – variously billed as the Faces featuring Rod Stewart – saw an upswing in the band's dynamic. "That was a great tour," Pete Buckland recalls. "We went down there with great trepidation as to how we were going to be received because of what had happened with the Small Faces but we did fantastic business and the shows were really good. We had an absolute ball. A bit of wreckage along the way, too."

"It was like the good old days of the Wild West in America," describes Charlie Fernandez, "when Jesse James and his men would ride into town, take all the money, have all the women, and ride into the next town and do the same thing. It was like a hurricane passing through. Everyone had a drink in their hand around the clock."

"There was a lot of time off on the Australian tour," Schlagbaum recalls. "We were holed up several days in the Sydney Hilton or somewhere like that, getting very bored. Pete usually was the one – the band would start something, they would give like the signal and do something and that would set Pete off, he'd go on a rampage, get totally out of control, as would Chuch, he was out of his mind in those days . . ."

Charlie Fernanadez: "In Sydney, Chuch hung all the hotel furniture out the windows tied to guitar leads. You'd be walking back to the hotel and see stuff hanging outside and you'd think, 'God, people must think we're horrible.' Rental cars were always a target. Chuch and I had a rented station wagon and all of a sudden he wanted to go off-roading in it. At that point there were no off-road vehicles, so here we were going through the small hills of Australia, destroying this station wagon. I was thinking, 'This is fun if you're a kid but aren't we supposed to be adults?'"

Pete Buckland: "I think it was my rent-a-car. They brought it back and the engine was barely running and in the end, it sort of blew up with lots of oil on the floor. I had to call up the car hire guy to come and pick it up the next day. We all watched from our windows as he opened the bonnet and he just freaked out when he saw the wreckage of his engine."

When the rescheduled Brisbane show was cancelled (the band donated $2,000 toward the flood relief fund), Rod and the Faces' popularity Down Under warranted two indoor shows in Melbourne and Sydney being added to the end of the Australasian itinerary. The tour then moved on to Hong Kong for a football stadium show on February 12. "Woody and I tried to score some blow from this guy showing us round and what we got was heroin and we didn't want that," says Mac. "We tossed it. The only other thing I recall about Hong Kong was going to this fabric makers who had all this beautiful brocade and fantastic silks. I had red, gold and all kinds of clothes made out of them."

Flying to Tokyo, a welcoming committee was waiting as Charlie Fernandez recalls. "We walked through the arrivals hall, came in through the gate and there's this long line of fans waiting. Half these kids had their hair bleached to look like Rod and they're all holding signs up saying 'Welcome Tetsu & The Faces'. The promoter made up 'Tetsu & The Faces' sweatshirts for everybody."

Russ Schlagbaum: "We were in Japan for about a week. We stayed in Tokyo and went out by train to do Osaka. At the Hilton these little Japanese girls would camp out in the lobby for days. You'd give them money to have breakfast because you knew they hadn't eaten. You'd come in at three in the morning and they would be waiting there, you'd get up for breakfast at noon and they're still there. They would have these lines of English like 'I want to be your friend', 'I always want to be by your side', 'Please can I come to your room?', that's all they could say. They'd jump in the elevator with you but the hotel security would throw them out.

"On that tour I noticed how cocaine had taken over and it wasn't quite so much fun anymore. I remember witnessing Rod mistreating this waiter in the hotel who, of course, hardly spoke English, and Rod was just really tearing into him. It embarrassed me to the point that I had to get up and leave."

Tetsu handled between song announcements in his native tongue at the concerts, which received a polite but restrained reception, typical of

Japanese audiences but weirdly unnerving to Western performers used to a rowdy reaction.

A second Osaka concert was cancelled ostensibly because Rod was suffering throat pain but others claim this was down to his prima donna behaviour. "Rod looked at things from a very businesslike point of view," says Charlie, "and he did start separating himself from the band. From what I saw when we were in Australia and Japan Rod would just show up for his part, like his attitude was, 'I don't need to be here.'"

"They nearly had me fly out to Japan because there was something funny going on with Rod and they thought it would cheer him up," says Dee Harrington who, after Stewart's brief relationship with Joanna Lumley ran its course, reconciled with the singer shortly before the start of the Far East tour.

"After the last concert in Japan," Wood told *Disc*. "Rod and Mac and everybody were playing football up the corridor in the early hours of the morning. Some American guy with a towel wrapped around him comes out of his room and hits Rod over the head with a shoe-tree. So Tetsu was up like this [*imitates Kung Fu pose*] . . . and a great big bundle started up."

Despite enthusiastic audiences and reviews, Mac opened fire in a *Melody Maker* interview by phone from Melbourne, being generally contemptuous of Australia and its Sheilas in particular: "All the Australian girls have got broken noses and big tits . . . And they're dressed like tennis stars – a bit muscular in the legs. Australian girls have an inbuilt sense of no rhythm. Very sad. It's a bit like Belgium over 'ere in some ways . . . We just wanna get onstage, do the job and get 'ome. There's no history 'ere. No culture . . . We're really bored to tears."

The Britain to which the Faces returned could hardly have been further from the sunshine utopia of Australia. A nation crippled by strikes, bombings, television blackouts, power cuts and three-day weeks inspired the joke: while America had Johnny Cash, Bob Hope and Stevie Wonder, the UK had no cash, no hope and no bloody wonder. In February Edward Heath was ejected from power as the global recession continued to deepen.*

The Middle East oil crisis led to the scarcity of plastic but of more concern than the resultant vinyl shortage was the moribund state of the

---

* By 1975 inflation would top 24 per cent, interest rates hitting 11.25 per cent.

music scene. With few exceptions 1974 saw rock'n'roll's vitality and inventiveness sink to its lowest ebb since 1962. The UK charts were dominated by the superficial detritus of the glitter boom (Gary Glitter, Mud, Alvin Stardust), lightweight entertainers more suited to cabaret (Gilbert O'Sullivan, David Essex, Leo Sayer) and pop pap (the Rubettes, Paper Lace, the Wombles), while a prototype boy band from Glasgow, Bay City Rollers, who took Rod's tartan look to its extreme, snatched the transient teenybop crown. Having turned their backs on 'glam rock' Bowie was busy reinventing himself yet again while Bolan's pre-eminence diminished as T. Rex vainly attempted to crack America along with rivals Slade. Hardy perennials like the Rolling Stones and the ex-Beatles were in creative stasis.

Elsewhere, bulky concept albums (*Quadrophenia, Tales From Topographic Oceans, A Passion Play, The Lamb Lies Down On Broadway*) were often as indulgent as the drawn-out concerts performed by heavyweights like Led Zeppelin, Yes and Pink Floyd. Almost as depressing was the passive idolatry of their audiences.

As if reflecting this torpidity the Faces were inactive for much of 1974, leading to unfounded rumours that Ronnie Wood was joining the Stones as Keith Richards' replacement or that he was leaving the Faces to form a backing band behind Rod Stewart. Adding to rumours of a split, Tetsu toured with Stomu Yamashta's East Wind band, and on May 5, Rod came on as a guest before 45,000 packed sardine-like into Elton John's concert at Watford Football Club. As with the major show starring the Who, staged at Charlton Football Ground two weeks later, the event was excessively overcrowded, and a hard lesson was learned on May 26 when 650 were injured and a young fan, Bernadette Whelan, died after being crushed at a David Cassidy concert at White City Stadium.

The tapes of Stewart's next album were due to be delivered to Mercury when Warner Bros. secured a court injunction saying that because his existing contract had expired on October 8, 1973, he was now a Warners artist. "I got the injunction the day the album was finished and I was busy buying a bottle of Scotch for everyone who'd played on it," Stewart told *NME*'s Nick Kent. The injunction extended into mid-May to allow Rollgreen Ltd, Stewart's company, time to prepare their case.

The legal wrangling delayed the album's release for five months so Rod took it easy over the summer – decorating his mansion with help from brother Bobby and collecting antiques and scale model railways with the enthusiasm of, well, a train spotter. His passion for Scotland continued to burn, so much so that he thought nothing of hiring a private jet to follow

Willie Ormond's squad's adventures in the 1974 FIFA World Cup in West Germany.* He also made himself available to help out his best mate.

Having tired of the nagging record company question as to whether he'd ever considered making his own album, in a remarkable burst of productivity, Wood laid down a total of 25 tracks over six weeks in the basement studio of the Wick. "It's funny," he told *Melody Maker's* Brian Harrigan, "because solo albums have always put me off for years. I never really wanted to enter those sweepstakes. I just blundered into it. I didn't spend much time thinking about it."

The idea developed back in July '73 after Wood attended the Great Western Express Festival to see Sly & The Family Stone's headlining appearance and was "absolutely floored" by Sly's drummer Andy Newmark. Shortly after, at a festival in Frankfurt where the Faces and Sly & The Family Stone were appearing, Wood and Newmark made plans to reconnect in London. At Andy's suggestion Atlantic session bassist Willie Weeks, who had played with Aretha Franklin, Roberta Flack and Donny Hathaway, was approached to complete the funky rhythm section.

The loose sessions for what became *I've Got My Own Album To Do* started with a basic line-up of Wood, McLagan and Newmark, with Mick Taylor playing bass, as well as guitar and keyboards, before Weeks' arrival. "I cut three or four demos at the Wick with Chuch engineering, God bless him, while things were being set up," says McLagan. Wood invited Gary Kellgren from the Record Plant over to co-produce (the pair credited as 'The Penguin Brothers') while Ron Nevison engineered most of the sessions on a basic eight-track set-up. "Doing it at home was good," Ronnie told Lisa Robinson, "because, although it had certain restrictions, I found enough room to overdub a track and the vocals and that was about it."

"The guys arrived from the States all ready for work so I got out my little cassette machine and started doing songs," Wood told *Sounds*. "I had about eight ideas to see through and about another 20 just hanging around." Most of these came from a backlog of material originally intended for Rod or the Faces.

The de rigueur Seventies model of assorted rock star cameos emerged when various heavy friends like Mick Jagger, Eric Clapton, George

---

* The previous September, while in Houston on the Faces' US tour, Rod arranged an expensive phone link to Hampden Park to receive a live commentary from Allan Herron, chief sports writer for the *Sunday Mail*, of Scotland's World Cup qualifier against Czechoslovakia. Scotland won 2–1.

Harrison, Paul McCartney and Keith Richards dropped by to help.

Ian McLagan: "Paul McCartney came to my house for a social visit, it was very odd. I said, 'I have to go to the studio' and Paul said, 'Oh really?' He knew full well what I was doing because he wanted an excuse to get into Woody's studio to persuade Andy Newmark away from us to be the drummer in Wings. He already had Jimmy McCulloch who came over with Paul and Linda. Kim and I had only just started to live together and in my kitchen, in front of everyone, Jimmy tried to pull her. Great guitarist, useless human being! So we went over to the Wick and Paul played piano on a version of Jimmy Reed's 'Ain't That Lovin' You Baby.'"[*]

"Keith [Moon] and I were there the night [July 24 '73] they started recording 'It's Only Rock 'n' Roll'," confirms Dougal Butler. "Mick Jagger was playing guitar with Woody, David Bowie sang backing vocals, and Kenney played drums."

"Kenney might get a call at two in the morning saying can you come and lay a drum track down," says Gary Osborne. "That's how he came to play on 'It's Only Rock 'n' Roll'. It was originally going to go on to a Woody thing and so they were messing around and Kenney said, 'Can you hurry up so I can go back to bed.' They kept saying, 'Can you play a bit more like Charlie Watts?' and Kenney was getting quite cross, you know, 'You wouldn't wake Charlie up at two in the morning!'

"When it was decided to make it a Stones track, Jagger took it away and all the guitars were replaced except Woody's 12-string acoustic. Charlie said, 'Kenney sounds more like me than I do. Why do you want to change it? Why don't you just leave the drum track as it is?' so they did, they just built the whole track up around Kenney's drums."

Released in July '74, 'It's Only Rock 'n' Roll (But I Like It)' became a Top 10 hit (16 in the US). In a typically canny trade off, Jagger let Wood keep 'I Can Feel The Fire', the reggaefied track the pair worked on that prominently features his vocals. Halfway through the sessions, the other Glimmer Twin arrived with the force of a thunderbolt. Richards moved into Wick Cottage, to be near proceedings but also to avoid the harassment he was undergoing at his home on Cheyne Walk from the Chelsea Drug Squad. "The gas about playing with Keith is how smoothly our styles meshed," Wood enthused to Barbara Charone. "I'd always thought we had that street feel in common."

"I realised I couldn't do all my own compositions on my first outing. So

---

[*] One of several tracks to be shelved from the sessions, several others were held over for Wood's second solo effort, *Now Look*, the following year.

then Keith [Richards] suggested the old Freddie Scott number 'Am I Grooving You?' and so we did a couple of days of cover versions, Ann Peebles 'I Can't Stand The Rain' and James Ray's 'If You Gotta Make A Fool Of Somebody.'"*

Richards also donated two songs, 'Act Together' and 'Sure The One You Need' (both credited to Jagger-Richards) while 'Mystifies Me' started life as a Stewart solo track with improvised lyrics.†

The sessions were relaxed and convivial, with a faint irony in that here were names from the British R&B era revisiting their roots in the lap of luxury just a rolling stone's throw away from the west London clubs where they'd started out as hard up blues crusaders.

The round the clock proceedings were also a byword for unbridled decadence with most of the £40,000 recording costs spent on booze and other substances. "I didn't spend all those nights in the studio like Chuch did," says Russ Schlagbaum. "I refused to be called out of a warm bed and have to tromp over to the Wick. It did happen one time. Woody couldn't get a hold of Chuch and he called me up at about one o'clock in the morning, saying, 'Hey, Keith's here. Can you come over and rig up some stuff?' So I went over and I go down the studio and find everything's there, everything's working and there's nothing for me to do. Then Woody sends me up to Fulham to pick up a coupla hundred quid's worth of blow or something – that was the real purpose of getting me there. So I did his drug run, came back and said, 'Woody, I'll do anything for you except this because if I get caught it means deportation and I lose everything. So don't ask me again.'"

Apart from Kenney and Jan, Dee Harrington was one of the few to abstain from the ritualised coke snorting. When asked if she accompanied Rod to the sessions, Dee exclaims, "Did I go to The Wick?! Frightening carry-on. It's quite funny when your chosen friends are the Rolling Stones, Led Zeppelin, the Who and various other people are all down there in that basement. I always used to say if the floor could have swallowed me up. It was just beyond anything I could imagine. It's ridiculous to think that I was a bit like a child bride, a bit of a princess, somebody that had been wrapped in cotton wool and when they were brought out they couldn't cope. It was very far removed from my and Rod's existence.

---

* 'If You Gotta Make A Fool Of Somebody' was popularised by Freddie & The Dreamers, reaching the Top Five in the UK in 1963.
† This can be heard as 'Think I'll Pack My Bags' on *The Rod Stewart: Sessions 1971–1998* box-set.

Those people really lived a rock'n'roll lifestyle which made us look a bit ridiculous."

Ian McLagan: "I'd get back to the house at 10 in the morning or even in the afternoon sometimes after Ronnie and I went for a drink in the pub after a session. It was a warm summer and I had a hammock in the back-yard. If I got home before dawn I'd climb in and swing it with a stick until I was fast asleep and wake up in broad daylight. Wonderful times."

Four days of rehearsals at Shepperton Studios to rearrange the act preceded the Faces' headlining appearance on July 6 at the Buxton Festival on Moor Farm, appearing with the five-piece Memphis Horns, who had recently recorded with Stewart. "It was a buzz rehearsing together but when it came to the stage I was the one leading them," says Mac. "They weren't sure where they were going and I had to give them directions. I remember it being a fucking horrible gig, it was a right mess." The supporting bill featured Humble Pie but McLagan has no recollection of crossing paths with Steve Marriott. The following day Rod flew to Munich to attend the World Cup final, watching West Germany defeat the Netherlands 2–1.

Ronnie Wood used Shepperton to rehearse for two London concerts, billed as 'Ron Wood – If You Gave Him Half A Chance', at Kilburn Gaumont State on July 13 and 14. Having participated in Eric Clapton's Rainbow comeback, Wood felt able to carry his own show, promising "a good night's boogie. We'll recreate the atmosphere of the studio things we did, I hope." Alongside the rhythm section of Newmark and Weeks, Mac played keyboards, Keith Richards was on guitar (Jagger was rumoured to be appearing but was in the States) and an ill-at-ease Rod came on to provide backing vocals for 'If You Gotta Make A Fool Of Somebody' and 'Mystifies Me,' as well as shaking a tambourine on 'Take A Look At The Guy'.

Ian McLagan: "The first night was brilliant. There was more tension on the first show, which had gone by the second and things got a bit sloppy. Willie messed up his solo and it didn't hang together as well."[*]

The reception was varied with some naively expecting the gigs to exceed or at least, equal the atmosphere generated by a Stones or Faces show. Woody's confidence could have done with a lift – not only did the poor reviews sit squarely on his shoulders but things were turbulent on the

---

[*] The second night was recorded and filmed and despite being sold to TV stations in Japan and Australia an edit of the show was only ever broadcast on ABC in the US.

home front as Krissie had moved out and shacked up with Jimmy Page at Plumpton Place, his Elizabethan manor house in Sussex. Page's extracurricular interests beyond the incestuous world of rock'n'roll fascinated Krissie and while her liaisons with Eric Clapton and George Harrison had been little more than brief dalliances this was far more serious, especially when marriage was being mooted. As usual, Woody ignored the problem, hoping it would go away, staying up for days on end in the Wick studio with his inseparable crony, Keith Richards and assorted hangers on. Wood's mum Lizzie would drop by to cook breakfast in the late afternoon, his sister-in-law, Doreen, Art's then wife, looked after day-to-day matters while Liesel Schiffer, who was also Mac's housekeeper, having known him since the Small Faces' Westmoreland Terrace days, cleaned the place.

Mixed at the Record Plant, Sausalito and mastered at Apple Studios in London, *I've Got My Own Album To Do* appeared in September, the title, according to Wood, coming from a comment either Jagger or Harrison made when leaving to go home having spent hours in the basement. Other observers consider it a sardonic comment on Rod's attitude to recording with the Faces. When asked his opinion of Wood's effort, Stewart grudgingly praised, "It was OK for a first attempt . . . there's a couple of vocals on there that are just horrible, y'know, and the lyrics – well, Ronnie's just not a good lyricist yet. But it's coming on."

Wood and Stewart were also working on a book project compiling all the nonsense verbiage – such as that which appeared on Stewart's album sleeves – with Wood's illustrations, which they'd collected since their Beck days. Just such one appeared on *Never A Dull Moment* – "Far be it from us to affiliate any previous constructions on past editions – notwithstanding any resemblance between this and the last phonographic achievement" – a convoluted plea to resist the impulse to compare it to what had come before. With a temporary truce called in the battle over Rod's recording contract, when Mercury released *Smiler* in October, it was hard to do otherwise when it became clear the consecutive run of superlative Stewart albums had finally been broken.

"*Smiler* is an album that I would rather forget," says Billy Gaff. "It was pretty poor with that horrible tartan sleeve and because Mercury knew it was their last album, they didn't bother to promote it as much. They couldn't care less. We were coming off millions and I'm not even sure it went gold in America."

Smiler only reached 13 in the US but entered the British charts at number one, more a reflection of Stewart's unassailable status than its quality. Recorded at various locales over a six-month period, as usual the ever-dependable Mike Bobak engineered at Morgan Studios. "Rod used to hit him over the head affectionately, saying, 'Better get it right this time,'" says Dee who sat in the vocal booth while Rod overdubbed his contributions. "Rod used to work on a week to week basis," Mickey Waller told John Gray, "and we'd record about one track a week. Rod would decide what number he wanted to do and if Martin [Quittenton] or Ronnie [Wood] or I were involved, we'd go over to Rod's house in Windsor and work it out."

"Mickey was so nice, he came down to the house quite a bit," says Dee. "When Rod and I argued and we'd break up, he used to get Mickey to call me and say, 'If Rod rings you, will you talk to him?' I used to take Mickey's car keys because he drank a lot. He would collapse in the billiard room and sleep under the snooker table because I wouldn't let him drive home."

To the barks of Waller's dog Zak, *Smiler* started by playing one of its strongest cards, a carefree romp through Chuck Berry's 'Sweet Little Rock 'n' Roller' with Pete Sears' Johnnie Johnson trills and courtesy of the Richards' influence, Woody's Berry licks to the fore. With a suitably raucous Rod vocal, the track swings like a noose. A brief harpsichord instrumental, 'Lochinvar' from Pete Sears linked to 'Farewell', the album's single, featuring Sears on harpsichord, Ray Jackson on mandolin and Ric Grech on fiddle; a pleasant, catchy tune but reliant on the tried and trusted Stewart-Quittenton 'Maggie May'/'You Wear It Well' formula. The song, which had actually been carried over from the *Never A Dull Moment* sessions, nonetheless provided Stewart with another UK Top 10 hit.

'Sailor', an unmemorable rocker about a philanderer jilting his bride at the altar features excessive wailing from Irene and Doreen Chanter, session choristers of choice on so many British recordings from the mid-Seventies. Whereas covering 'Twistin' The Night Away' felt unforced, attempting a Sam Cooke medley of 'Bring It On Home To Me'/'You Send Me', laden with a syrupy Jimmy Horowitz string arrangement, was an ill-advised move. 'Let Me Be Your Car', an uptempo Elton John-Bernie Taupin vehicle, stars Elton on piano and dominant vocal, reducing Stewart to a supporting role. As wrong-footed as the sterile Cooke medley is the weak gender reverse of Aretha Franklin's ('You Make Me Feel Like A) Natural Man', recorded in Sydney during the Faces' Australian tour, with the overdubbed Memphis Horns. Chris Barber's Jazz Band play New Orleans style on 'Dixie Toot'; 'Hard Road', an undistinguished rocker written by former Easybeats, Harry Vanda and George Young chugs along to negligible effect (their classic 'Friday On My Mind' would have been a far more inspired choice for Stewart to cover but David Bowie got there first on *Pin-Ups*); and 'I've Grown Accustomed To Her Face' (from the musical *My Fair Lady*) that Rod had talked about recording as far back as *Every Picture . . .* turns out to be simply a Quittenton instrumental, exquisitely played but incongruous nonetheless.

The album's finest moment is a tender arrangement of Bob Dylan's 'Girl From The North Country', off *The Freewheelin' Bob Dylan* and re-recorded with Johnny Cash on *Nashville Skyline*. Horowitz's string arrangement is an inspired touch without being overly obtrusive behind Stewart's sensitive vocal. It would have been a classy note on which to end but that accolade went to a twee, calypso-flavoured Paul McCartney confection, 'Mine For Me' that McCartney passed on to Rod via Woody.

Smiler served notice that there would be few musical surprises on future Rod Stewart albums. Of equal concern was the fact that in the two years that had elapsed since *Never A Dull Moment*, only three originals (co-writes with Wood and Quittenton) were considered worthy enough to include but none approached Stewart's previous artistic benchmark.[*] While he had always seen himself as an entertainer in one form or another, the inspired song selections, sympathetic arrangements and quick but effective production were now supplanted by a vacuous slickness that had little more than Rod's unique vocal timbre to recommend it.

His image had changed for the worse, too. The funky but chic days of velvet suits, scarves and Blue Nun were replaced by the satin-clad 'coke fag queen' look epitomised by the *Smiler* sleeve photo. "We all used to joke about Rod's attire," says Jan Jones, smirking at the memory, "you know, the naff yellow satin sprayed-on trousers. He used to wear women's knickers, too, because he didn't want a visible panty line. People have an image of Rod Stewart as this elegant figure but I recall somewhere in the States, him lying down on a pier and me squeezing the blackheads on Rod's back. Kenney told me how when the band were receiving a B12 shot on an American tour, they were lined up with their trousers down and Rod insisted a plaster be put on afterwards. The doctor said, 'Where do I put it?' because Rod had such a spotty arse, he wasn't quite sure where the injection mark was."

---

[*] Unusually, Stewart recorded more tracks than would fit on the album and these leftovers – versions of Gerry Rafferty/Joe Egan's 'You Put Something Better Inside Me', Labi Siffre's 'Crying Laughing Loving Lying' and Cole Porter's 'Every Time We Say Goodbye' and a Stewart original, 'So Tired' (also recorded as 'Missed You' and superior to much of what ended up on *Smiler*) – were first released in the UK in 1995 on the *Handbags & Gladrags* compilation of Stewart's Mercury years.

Portraits proliferated of a vain rock star posing around his capacious Ascot estate – its estimated worth now trebled – next to his Excalibur SS Phantom, Mercedes 600 and 1932 Rolls with all the trimmings. In fact the publicity junket surrounding *Smiler* seemed to involve journalists being ushered into luxurious suites or shown around Rod's vast home to ensure good reviews. Having been in the business for a decade he was not about to be hypocritical, telling Peter Dacre, "I can't stand people who are two-faced about money; who pretend they're not rich when they are . . . I've earned everything myself. I've worked hard for it and I'm going to enjoy it in the next five to ten years."

Smiler and its attendant press campaign marked a decisive turning point when many of his original supporters began to reconsider not only Stewart's music but also his motives. Part of the problem was the personal PR man that Rod had hired. "I can't remember how Rod found Tony Toon," says Billy Gaff. "He just turned up out of the blue. He worked for the Sunday tabloids, he had nothing to do with me at all."

If the intention was to show austerity-hit Britain how this rags-to-riches rock singer still held the common touch, for many it had quite the opposite effect, turning him into a figure of mockery and ridicule, even among his contemporaries in the business. The articles and comments became increasingly snide, especially those in the iconoclastic *NME* which was fast developing an amusing line in pinpricking rock stars' egos. "Rod was becoming defensive," says *Melody Maker*'s Chris Charlesworth who interviewed Stewart at the St. Regis Hotel President's Suite in New York when he was promoting *Smiler*. "In the past he'd been chatty, friendly, but now he was behaving as if he expected the interview to turn into an argument. 'Well, what do you want to know?' he asked when I arrived. He was unnecessarily abrupt, almost aggressive, and I'd been a supporter. Maybe he didn't trust us writers any longer."

In many ways Rod was his own worst enemy. Allied to his Capricorn characteristics: stubbornness, conservatism, difficult to get to know, tremendously loyal to friends and immensely practical, insecurity was another. "I really need an audience – the bigger the better," Stewart told James Johnson. "It's a great boost to the ego – that's something that everybody needs. Also I need to be told how good I am. And everybody needs that."

Even the easygoing Woody found out what could happen when a rock star displayed his status symbols in an economically depressed climate – a bunch of envious local yobs sent his Mercedes saloon crashing down the hill into the hotel opposite the Wick.

In late summer Rod and Ronnie undertook separate promotional sweeps through America – in view of the ongoing legal dispute between Mercury and Warners the record companies were happy to keep them apart. With the flurry of solo activity one might have expected a solo album from Mac, who creditably admitted he had nothing creative to offer. "There are so many bleeding albums around already that I've never listened to, it's not worth it," he told *Disc*. "I've no aspirations in that quarter."

So it came as a surprise when a Kenney Jones solo single – a cover of Jackson Browne's 'Ready Or Not' – appeared on October 4. But then in an era where the whims of major groups were obsequiously indulged – each of the Moody Blues and even Keith Moon releasing ill-advised solo albums – it wasn't that unusual. Recorded at Morgan and released on GM Records, Kenney drummed and sang while his brother-in-law Gary Osborne produced and played acoustic, Jimmy McCulloch was on electric, Mark Griffiths (formerly of Matthews Southern Comfort) on bass, and Peter Wood (Sutherland Brothers & Quiver) on keyboards.

"Kenney asked me to produce it because even during the Faces years he would still do sessions because there was lots of down time while Rod was off doing something else," Osborne states. "I also sang on it with Paul Vigrass because like most drummers, Kenney can't really sing . . . The B-side, 'Woman Trouble', was better. I co-wrote that with Kenney and Billy Lawrie, Lulu's brother. Mike Mansfield even did a video. It was not going to be a hit but it was a nice song."

"I wanted to do the solo thing because it was a challenge," Jones told *Popswop*. "I needed to do something that wasn't connected with the Faces . . . I'd like to continue recording on my own as well as with the Faces. It'll stop me from getting bored when the Faces aren't working. If I stop drumming for a few weeks, I find I stiffen up. I have to keep on playing." An album was planned if the single proved successful but blushes were spared when it quietly sank.

On September 13 the Faces reconvened for a six-week European tour commencing at the Palais de Sport, Paris. "We'd been six months without regular gigs while everyone was doing their solo bits," Mac told *Record Mirror*, "so at the beginning of the tour it was like being in a new group." Support act on all the dates was Strider.

"We all went to this very swanky restaurant after the Paris show," Strider's Gary Grainger remembers. "A bit of a row started and Billy Gaff was trying to calm it all down. The band went, 'Fuck this, we're going home.' The rest of the French dates were cancelled. I can't remember why, someone had got upset or something had gone on. Back in the bar at the hotel, we were like, 'What's going on? Have we done something?' And they said, 'No, no, everything's fine, we're going home, we'll see you in a week's time.' I remember Mac and Kenney being behind the decision and when I later worked with Rod, I brought the subject up and he said, 'Woody and I never felt we could overrule Kenney or Mac because the Faces was their band,' which I was surprised by. I thought it was much more of a co-operative thing."

The tour resumed the following week in West Germany. The band was improving with each show although attendances varied. "Because of the audiences, the band were kind of playing a rockier set then they were in the UK," Grainger confirms. "There wasn't as much of the singalong stuff. Rod was singing great, it was a joy to watch. We used to stay behind and catch nearly all the shows because they were playing so well.

"They were always friendly and funny all in all. They'd come in and say, 'Got anything to drink?' and they'd bring in some brandy and port or whatever. Rod and Woody used to sneak out and watch when we played 'Little Wing', the Jimi Hendrix song. I had loads of neck in them days and I'd go and stand right on the edge of the stage, almost defying anyone to come up and play the solo . . . I don't even remember doing it really. The other common denominator was I played a silver-fronted Zemaitis like Woody's. I knew Tony Zemaitis because my cousin Danny did all the engraving so there was a kind of contact there . . . we just used to swap guitars, jam and hang out and stuff."

"The road crew were fun as well. You'd say, 'Would you like a drink, Chuch?' and he'd say, 'Yes, just a crate of champagne and a small 7-Up for me, please.' At one show we had adjoining dressing rooms. There was a small corridor between and all the stuff from the Faces' rider . . . they were slinging it at these doors. It went on for about five minutes – full, empty, the whole lot got smashed. It was just this shower of drink. Rod used to be a terrible instigator and he loved mischief like that. So that was on the agenda at any given time. When we were going through customs at Gothenburg, a few of us were in the car with Chuch and Pete Buckland. They let the first Volvo estate through, we were in the second when a guy stepped out and went 'in there' pointing to this locker. Chuch had this Mars Bar size block of hash and some blow so he ate the hash and bunged the rest up his nose.

"He was OK during the strip search but on the long drive, Pete would say, 'How're we doing, Chuch?' because obviously we were on the wrong side of the road, it was getting dark and he wanted to overtake and there would be no answer from the passenger seat. So I would say from the

341

back, 'Yeah it's clear, Pete' and then after about five minutes Chuch piped up, 'Yeah it's clear, Pete.' It got funnier and funnier. By the time we got to the hotel in Stockholm, Chuch was completely gone. The next day we all went into the sauna and a couple of the guys had nailed the door closed. They'd gone in fully dressed, drinking, which you weren't supposed to do. Chuch was in there just sweating all this hash out of his system. It was a fun tour."

Having tried it out at Munich's Musicland Studios, and the Wick, the Faces re-cut 'You Can Make Me Dance, Sing Or Anything' at Olympic. "I was doing a session at Morgan Studios with Paul Vigrass," says Gary Osborne, "and we saw Rod in the bar. He asked us, 'Could you help out on a track?' The track was already laid down and Rod said, 'Just sing on the chorus.' That year I sang on the Rubettes 'Sugar Baby Love' and got paid £30 for a record that sold four million copies. I got another £30 for singing on David Essex's 'Gonna Make You A Star' – another number one. I didn't even get a drink out of Rod for 'You Can Make Me Dance . . .' let alone 30 quid."

Although all five members' names ended up on the label, 'You Can Make Me Dance . . .' sprang from a Stewart-Wood collaboration. "It started off as about four different riffs," Wood revealed to *NME*, "and Rod had to come in and sew them all together with words." Released in November, credited to 'Faces/Rod Stewart', the full title, 'You Can Make Me Dance, Sing Or Anything (Even Take The Dog For A Walk, Mend A Fuse, Fold Away The Ironing Board, Or Any Other Domestic Shortcomings)' was the longest to ever grace the UK chart, demonstrating how humour rarely left the Faces.

Unlike the unadventurous 'Pool Hall Richard', 'You Can Make Me Dance . . .' was a progression with a fun and funky rhythm that Jones gets his chops into and another sweet Philly string arrangement from Horowitz. Wood's choppy parts came from pretending "I was Barry White's guitarist." Stewart's self-effacing lyrics pay homage to the Isley Brothers' 'This Old Heart Of Mine' and 'I'd Rather Go Blind', while the strings and "keep on loving me babe" refrain were inspired by 'You're Messing Up A Good Thing' by the Faces' inspiration, Bobby Womack.

The B-side 'As Long As You Tell Him', a Stewart-Wood co-write, was even better – an Al Green-style soul ballad supreme with some fine Stewart vocals, Mac's glowing Hammond and tasteful Wood slide and Stratocaster licks.

NME led the plaudits: "At last, a single from the Faces that bears comparison with the best Rod Stewart solo records . . . On this new one,

Ron Wood plays some great guitar all the way through, like Steve Cropper mixed with Little Beaver of the Miami session band." Wrote *Melody Maker*: "The song sounds like it wants to charge away and bulldoze everything in its path, but the Faces treat it with uncharacteristic restraint . . ."

A 24-date British tour, supported by Strider, opened on Friday, November 15 with a three-night stand at south London's Lewisham Odeon. Despite an enthusiastic partisan atmosphere, the first night failed to activate, resulting in no encore. Rod had strained his throat so the second show was postponed and moved to the following Monday when a surprise in the form of Paul and Linda McCartney popped up on the 'Mine For Me' encore.

The all-night partying was ever present although hotel managers in cities within driving distance from London breathed easier as the band preferred to commute home after gigs. At Lewisham, Mike Mansfield's cameras filmed a live clip of 'You Can Make Me Dance', shown on the December 12 *Top Of The Pops*. Mansfield's crew were also shooting an hour-long *Smiler* TV documentary. If as some suspected Rod was moving further away from any street cred he previously held, this embarrassment of a film, shot in London, Los Angeles, Glasgow and Inverness, written and narrated by Russell Harty and financed by Stewart for a reported £60,000, confirmed their worst fears. It showed Rod at home, at airports, on stage, having a sing-song with Elton at a showbiz party in LA and a rather contrived scene of him wandering around the fruit stalls of Covent Garden, presumably to show Rod as ordinary working class as the barrow boys, albeit one dressed like a King's Road jet setter.[*]

A pall hung over the two Birmingham Odeon shows after the IRA bombings on November 21.[†] "Thank you very much for turning up tonight," Rod announced, "because we didn't expect too many people to be here." The Faces' infectious brand of good cheer helped to relieve the tension. Midway through the tour Stewart tore the ligaments in his shoulder muscle during a charity football match. Despite his injury he was determined that the show should continue, especially with Scotland on the itinerary. On December 14 Rod's in-store appearance at Bruce's

---

[*] Apart from an edited American TV screening in 1975, the film was indefinitely shelved due to Rod's "fast-moving way of life making it out of date" and claimed as a tax loss.
[†] Explosive devices were placed in two central Birmingham pubs, the Mulberry Bush and the Tavern in the Town, resulting in the most serious terrorist blasts in Great Britain to date; 21 fatalities and 162 injuries. A third device failed to detonate.

Record Store in Dundee attracted a crowd of 3,000 resulting in Reform Street being cordoned off and his car nearly overturned. In Glasgow, where the band played four sold out nights at the Apollo, he received two gold discs for *Smiler* (as artist and producer with sales exceeding 150,000) and a Friend of the City award from Sir William Gray, the Lord Provost of Glasgow.

For the European and UK tour, Kenney took the Scottish theme to heart by switching from his Ludwig 'liquorice all-sorts' kit to a Tartan design Premier set with matching circular rostrum. By now Tetsu had seamlessly integrated into the rhythm section and the band sounded tighter than on the '73 shows – perhaps because the perpetually grinning bassist had cut down to just one bottle of Teacher's a day.

In early December events conspired when during a party at Robert Stigwood's mansion in Stanmore, north-west London, Mick Taylor informed Mick Jagger of his intention to quit the Rolling Stones after five and a half years, feeling disenchanted with his role in the band. At Warner Brothers' Christmas party thrown at Searcy's in Knightsbridge, Jagger and Wood were photographed engaged in a hushed tête-à-tête, fuelling speculation that an announcement was on the cards. "I don't think it'll happen, I really don't," Stewart told *NME*'s Nick Kent. "I mean I'm saying that even though we haven't had a heart-to-heart or anything . . . Ronnie's my best mate. There's never been anyone closer to me than Woody. I'm taking bets that it won't happen. I know him too well."

On December 21, at the first of three consecutive nights at the Kilburn Gaumont State, the Faces were preceded by a belly dancer, an inept dancing troupe and a drag act before the curtain lifted to reveal the lads descending down a flight of white steps. The tartan terraces were disappointed when the band didn't return for an encore while at the second show, Stewart insisted on dragging Gary Glitter onstage for a guest appearance. The two had met at Tramp and become acquainted to the extent that he and Glitter were onstage guests at Elton John's Xmas Eve gig. On the last night – for what turned out to be the Faces' final British concert – Keith Richards swaggered on for 'Sweet Little Rock And Roller', 'I'd Rather Go Blind' and the 'Twistin' The Night Away' encore as Christmas tinsel fell.

Gary Grainger: "Keith used our bass player's Ampeg because we had the same amps as the Faces. Afterwards when Strider played a Christmas gig at the Marquee, Lee switched on his amp and discovered everything was turned up full. That's the way Keith plays."

Pete Buckland: "For the finale of that last Kilburn show I got a bunch of young ladies dressed in schoolgirl outfits to enter via the upstage stairs and walkway we had built, much to the band's surprise as I hadn't told them. It's in the video that Mike Mansfield shot."[*]

At tour's end it was claimed by a Gaff Management spokesman that the Faces' UK tour was the biggest grossing of 1974. Box office receipts raked in well over £100,000 – good going in a depressed economy and a perfect way to end a year in which predictions of the band's imminent demise had been widespread. To attempt to put the kibosh on the rumours, on New Year's Eve Ron Wood gave a statement over the phone to *NME*: "People would obviously think that I'm joining the Stones due to my supposed social connections with them. This, however, is just not true – for though I respect them immensely, my position in the Faces is of far greater personal importance."

With optimistic talk of a single and album being recorded in the New Year and an American tour already on the schedules, there was no reason to think 1975 would be anything but a bumper year for the Faces.

[*] The concert, shot on videotape, was edited to a 65-minute TV special intended to be shown worldwide but was only screened in the US and UK the following year. It has since been widely bootlegged under such inaccurate titles as *Rod Stewart And Faces: The Final Concert With Keith Richards*. Billy Gaff: "I haven't got the master tapes, I don't know where the fuck they are. I paid for all that to be made."

CHAPTER 19

Passing Show

"I'd rather make my church the open road."
— Ronnie Lane, '32nd Street', 1975

"If Woody has to go, there'd be no point in me carrying on; we share each other's tears. But ever since then there's been no doubt in my mind that Woody is here for the duration."
— Rod Stewart, *Rolling Stone*, 1975

"I HAD no idea about a circus tent and all this gypsy shit — I thought Ronnie was out of his mind, I really did." Russ Schlagbaum's blunt opinion reflects the precariousness surrounding Ronnie Lane's decision to take the Passing Show — a circus tent with assorted musicians, families, and circus performers — nationwide over the summer of 1974, predating Bob Dylan's similar Rolling Thunder Revue concept by 18 months.

While austerity was widespread in the UK as a whole, the hermetically sealed world of rock was, paradoxically, staging ever more overblown superstar spectaculars. Going against the grain, Lane was determined to communicate the good-time bonhomie of his time in the Faces via lower voltage to smaller audiences.

"If you think about Ronnie's career," says Russ, "the Small Faces went straight in to the screaming girls deal during Beatlemania and then the Faces got successful fairly quickly. So when he went to Ireland and started playing in pubs with Billy [Nicholls] and they're sitting right there with the audience all joining in, it must have been wonderful for him, it was a whole new arena."

Schlagbaum had returned to work for Lane after a rapprochement was effected through Ronnie's secretary, Barbara Morice. "Barbara and I were living together at 2 Cambridge Court just down the street from Ronnie's old flat in Heatherdene Mansions," Russ recalls. "Barbara said, 'You've got to go see Ronnie.' I replied, 'Fuck him, he fired me.' She said, 'Well he's been trying desperately to find a replacement, he's depressed he can't find anybody, he wants you back but he's too proud to ask.' I said, 'Fuck it, if he wants me back he can call or come see me. I'm not going to see him.' So after a relentless three or four days of her badgering I finally went around to see Ronnie at his local next to Wick Cottage.

"I'd made good money on the Faces' Far East tour, about $300–$500 a week and a bonus of $1,000 or something, doing Kenney's drums. Kenney was so quiet and non-committal, you know, 'Give me my cognac and 7-Up, make sure the hairdresser's there and turn the monitors up in the drums.' He had the drum monitors so fuckin' loud, we used to fake turning it up just to keep him happy. Kenney agreed to pay me £50 a week to stay with the Faces, which was double what I'd made before. I thought, 'Fuck, yeah!' Then Ronnie and I kissed and made up but I used the lever to get more wages. I think he paid me £60 a week.

"Ronnie was doing OK then. He was in the throes of selling Wick Cottage back to Woody at the time, the LMS was going out for something like £1,200 a week, and he had some money from his Faces buy-out. He was the only one of the band who got paid for his equipment. [After Lane left the Faces] all the gear they owned was valued and he got a fifth share of it. They paid him off – he got his guitars and two or three nice little Ampeg amps."

After eight low-key British dates with the seven-piece Slim Chance (featuring Kate jigging about the stage as a cancan dancer on certain numbers), Ronnie, Kate and their children Alana and Luke moved to Fishpool Farm in the spring with the LMS in tow to start recording *Anymore For Anymore* with assorted musicians, roadies, and their families. "Ronnie had hired all of these caravans to live in," says Schlagbaum. "It was all strange and bizarre to me. I stayed in Twickenham – work had to be done in London and I hated seeing Ronnie and Kate play at being farmers."

Anymore For Anymore presented Ronnie's talent in the best possible light with great tunes – a form of English folk infused with hints of Dylan, blue-grass, Cajun, Dixie, music hall and skiffle – and simple production. 'Anymore For Anymore' was recorded al fresco with the sound of the wind on the mikes, while 'Bye & Bye (Gonna See The King)' featured a back-up chorus of whoever was around including the Montgomery Tanners who helped to build the farm. Ironically a beauteous 'Roll On Babe' was written by Derroll Adams, a favourite of Rod Stewart's – in fact *Anymore For Anymore* shared much in common with Stewart's early solo recordings.

The album was mixed and mastered at IBC in May and released on GM

Records in July.* GM paid £6,000 to LMS Ltd for the sessions but Billy Gaff was annoyed to discover that Lane had signed a deal with A&M in America. "[GM Records] were establishing Ronnie and we worked extremely hard," Gaff says. "I hadn't got round to having a contract with him and he fucked off to A&M Records behind my back. I called Jerry Greenberg at A&M because we were friends and I said, 'What the fuck are you doing?' He said, 'Billy, he's going to leave you anyway. What choice have I got?' Ronnie fucked himself by leaving me because we had a handle on it and we were devoted."

Be that as it may, GM Records' lifespan was short-lived with the label folding in 1975. "As I recall, Billy actually negotiated the deal with A&M," says Schlagbaum. "Ronnie used the $50,000 advance and the receipts from selling Wick Cottage to buy Fishpool Farm and record that first album. The contract was for three albums with a second $50,000 advance payable, hinging on the US release of *Anymore For Anymore*." GM's last act of faith on behalf of Lane was to extract 'The Poacher' in June but despite the song's beguiling quality, it failed to emulate the success of 'How Come', partly due to a valuable *TOTP* slot being lost because of a technicians' strike at the BBC. By the following week the single had slipped down the charts.

Ronnie hardly noticed – on Friday, May 31, the Passing Show debuted in the Buckinghamshire countryside at Marlow, very near to where he, Mac and Steve had once lived communally. The idea was to set up the tent – which featured rows of benches, a central circus ring and stage – in selected towns off the usual rock circuit, staying approximately a week at each with shows on Friday and Saturday nights to feature local talent, as well as invited friends like Ron Wood and Pete Townshend (although neither showed). The title came from a Meher Baba saying, "life is just a passing show", in other words the only thing that matters is beyond normal existence. This belief was reflected in the lackadaisical regard to practicalities behind the whole exercise. As a testament to Lane's quixotic nature, the ambitious enterprise was innovative but a chronic lack of logistical planning became its ultimate undoing.

Russ Schlagbaum: "We got pawned off to the wrong people. Ronnie first went to Chipperfield's but they couldn't take it on. Then he asked Gerry Cottle who said, 'I can't do it but I know a fellow who has all this gear in storage. He's been off the road for a while.' What he didn't say is

---

* The front sleeve shot of the rag and bone men heading into the sunset on horse and cart first appeared among the *A Nod Is As Good As A Wink . . .* poster montage.

that he'd been off the road for 20 fuckin' years! So he put Ronnie on to Wally Luckins and of course, right away, Wally charms Kate and she says, 'Ooh he's lovely, Wally's lovely' so Ronnie falls for it. He was following what Kate wanted and Kate was in his ear all the time that you should take the music to the people – that whole spiel had started.

"We were resorting to the old circus ways. When I met the circus blokes I thought, 'These guys are criminals' but I had no idea how criminal they were. Luckins took £6,000 as advance, with something like £800 a week to provide a tent, transport, etc. He must have thought, 'Here comes this gullible pop star with a lot of dough, he'll never make it past the first week,' because when we started to move from Marlow to Bath this guy was physically shaking. The trucks he supplied belonged in the London Transport Museum. I got the dubious pleasure of driving this 1947 Bedford flatbed truck from Marlow to Bath overloaded to the gills with canvas, with my living van behind it, a little four-cylinder gas job. I never even got down the motorway. I pulled in to the first service area and went into the garage and told the mechanic, 'I don't know what's wrong but start by changing the points and plugs.' The guy pulled out a spark plug and said, 'I've been a mechanic for 25 years and I've never seen one like this.' I finally managed to coax this fucker to the Bath site. I was fuming because I'd spent all fuckin' night just to travel 100 miles. I'd left Sunday afternoon and this was Monday afternoon. I was pissed off, tired and I thought, 'Christ, this is not the way to do it.' I passed three of the other trucks broken down, blown up on the side of the M4.

"Ronnie was jumping with glee because finally somebody made it. He was towing this gypsy living van on a low loader with his Land Rover. In fact if it weren't for the Range Rover and the two Land Rovers we would have never got that show from one point to the other. It was a quadruple journey with the Land Rovers towing shit off the road.

"At Bath we were going to be shut down because we didn't have any fire equipment but the Bath Arts Council got behind us and sent this licensed fireman named Hutch Hutchinson, out to the site with a fire truck. The tent would hold a maximum of about 900 people and in Bath we had maybe six or seven hundred. That was our best audience but it was just magic."

In spite of outmoded transport, officialdom, and scant attendances thanks to little advance publicity, Ronnie was determined to see his vision through.

"Ronnie wanted to carry on," says Russ, "it was, 'Wally will make it work.' Anyway they brought in this guy, Captain Hill [Peter Hill] whose main job was to keep this circus rolling. He had his living van and his truck with acetylene torches and tools and everything he needed but even he couldn't keep it going. One by one these trucks would break down . . . the Bedford that I had nursed to Bath blew up in Shrewsbury so we left it. One of the three circus clowns, we left him there, too and said, 'Find your own way home, we're leaving.'

"One morning we woke up to find [sax player] Jimmy Jewell had left a note on Ronnie's trailer saying 'Goodbye Cruel Circus, I'm Off To Join The World'. His wife and Bruce Rowland's wife worked the box office and I would use the proceeds to buy groceries or diesel fuel, whatever. It might only be a couple of hundred quid in some cases – we were only charging £1.10 admission. The audiences weren't that big – in Carlisle we had about 15. It seemed some nights there were more people in the band than in the audience. It was pretty bad but Ronnie insisted on continuing. He thought he could handle the setbacks but he was absolutely over-whelmed so he would just disappear – go fishing or something and they would all come to me and being the farm boy that I am I just grabbed hold and tried to solve the problems but they were insurmountable.

"Ronnie's brother Stan, who stayed with us for a week in Carlisle, took one look and said to me, 'What the fuck is going on here?' Stan restored cars, he drove trucks so he knew something about the subject. He tried telling Ronnie but of course, Ronnie wouldn't listen. The one good thing in the middle of all this, Andy Knight, who was the engineer on *Anymore For Anymore*, arrived to mix the sound. I mean the sound he got in that tent was exceptional."

It seems inexplicable that the LMS wasn't utilised to record the shows but as Schlagbaum explains: "We couldn't deal with it. That was another fuckin' trailer to tow around. But we couldn't have recorded the shows even if we had the opportunity because Paul Lambert, Kate's brother, who was looking after Ronnie Lane Enterprises had booked it out. It was just one nightmare after another."

The Passing Show ground to an abrupt halt midway through the itiner-ary at Newcastle. "Ronnie's 1947 London Transport country bus blew up and that's what finally done him in. He just loved that bus especially the little Indian hood ornament, which he took off and kept. And the day his father died, that fucking bus left him stranded up in the gypsy horse fair somewhere in north Wales. He was supposed to get down and catch the train but his fucking bus wouldn't run."

The remaining dates were cancelled leaving Lane, disillusioned and financially drained, to ponder his next move. "Ronnie was a difficult boy," says Billy Gaff. "And like all difficult people he eventually blew it with everybody to the point that it never did him any good."

1975 would prove an eventful year for the Faces, beginning with a resolution to the complicated legal contretemps surrounding Rod's recording contract. Mercury and Phonogram Records jointly appealed against a preliminary High Court ruling by Mr. Justice Willis concerning their rights to future Stewart solo recordings but it was dismissed with costs by a panel of appeal court judges that included Lord Denning.

Billy Gaff explains: "The Mercury deal had expired [on October 8, 1973] but under the terms they could extend their option and call for another album.* Warner Bros. claimed they had papers on Rod effective as of the expiry date. To cut a long story short Mercury and Phonogram lost the case – not on the grounds of contract law but the Landlord and Tenant Act, which states that if you are a tenant and the landlord sells the building then he has a duty to inform the tenant of the new landlord. When Mercury was dissolved [in October 1972] Rod's contract was assigned to a company called New Mercury Corporation that changed its name to Phonogram Inc. Because it was a personal services contract, the court ruled that Phonogram had an obligation to notify Rod of the Mercury assignment which they failed to do, and the law was very specific."

This left Stewart a free agent to sign exclusively with Warner Bros., which by now was a decidedly different company from the pleasantly genial operation he had joined with the other Faces five years earlier. "I'd left Warners and so had Ian [Ralfini] before Rod signed his solo deal with Warners," says Martin Wyatt. "Joe Smith took that over completely. It started to get so political at Warners with different people in the States leaning on you. Plus we'd gone through three name changes – Warners to Kinney to WEA – you didn't know who you were working for half the time. So Ian and I left in '74 and went to ABC Records where we created Anchor Records, more because we wanted to get some sanity back into it and have a direct relationship with acts."†

During the promotional junket for *Smiler*, Stewart had told Harvey Kubernik, "Woody and I don't relish the idea of doing another Faces

---

* Which they received in the form of *Smiler*.
† The first success Ralfini and Wyatt had at Anchor was in late 1974 with Ace's 'How Long', later covered by Rod Stewart in 1982.

album. What I wanted to do was make singles, because I think they're such a great singles band." In his *Sounds* column, 'You Can Make Me Dance . . .' topped John Peel's list of Top 40 singles of 1974 (Rod's 'Farewell' came ninth). The Faces and particularly Rod remained on good terms with their early British champion and several members had attended his wedding (to 'The Pig' as he affectionately referred to Sheila Gilhooly) on August 31.

"['You Can Make Me Dance . . .'] really was a good step towards how we're all feeling now," Wood told Barbara Charone. "I'd love to see a good Faces album. It's just that we're all a bit scared to jump in there. The single was a good teaser, it came together quickly and I see no reason why the album can't because we've got a load of material."

That may have been the case but it wasn't evident when the Faces reconvened at AIR Studios on London's Oxford Street in the New Year to cut tracks with Ron Nevison engineering. "We weren't actually set up to record," says McLagan, "we were set up to rehearse. We were all in a circle and Rod was in the middle so his voice is all over the guitar and drums." A ramshackle medley of Tommy Tucker's 'Hi Heel Sneakers' and Solomon Burke's 'Everybody Needs Somebody To Love' sounded like a garage band learning their chops.

"It seemed like they were mailing it in," says Nevison. "They were performing in a perfunctory manner. I think it was something that Mac and Kenney wanted but I don't think Woody and Rod did. At that point, Billy Gaff was really tugging at Rod to go solo and Woody was looking at joining the Stones so everybody had reasons not to make this album happen. Rod wasn't providing songs, and it was a half-hearted effort to get something going."

An unexpected choice to cover was 'Gettin' Hungry', a 1967 Beach Boys song from *Smiley Smile* credited to Brian Wilson and Mike Love. "I had it on a single and I used to play it all the time," says Mac. "We only ran through it a couple of times." Of the few originals, 'Rock Me' was a directionless boogie, credited to McLagan when released in 2004, but 'Open To Ideas' was of greater merit, another tender soul ballad in the vein of 'As Long As You Tell Him', and a title conveying unintended irony in view of the Faces' state at the time.

Ron Nevison: "I'd been using AIR Studios over the past year and those were the last sessions I did there. One morning, after we'd been in a couple of days I got called in by the head guy who was pissed off that we had a bar set up. We had a table with a few bottles. Can you imagine that? If we'd been running around, breaking stuff I can see where there could be a problem. I was flabbergasted and I told him so, you know, 'I'm not taking it down, kick us the fuck out of here if you want'. It didn't really matter anyway because I think the sessions only lasted a couple of weeks."[*]

Nevison decided to take up Gary Kellgren and Chris Stone's offer to be chief engineer at the Record Plant in Los Angeles. "It was just too good to pass up so I left Mac's place and moved to LA. So that pretty much broke the ties between the Faces and myself."

Ronnie Wood continued recording at his home studio in the Wick – on songs for his second solo album but also outside projects for family and friends. In the latter category was ex-Birds singer, Ali MacKenzie, now out of the music business as a glazier.

"Ronnie had a lovely Victorian greenhouse [at the Wick] and I was doing some repairs on it for him," Ali recalls. "We were chatting one day and he said, 'The studio's being finished off at the moment so if you've got any new bands or anything you think might be good, let me know.' As I was leaving that day, he remarked, 'And of course if there's anything you want to do, let me know.' Anyway, weeks or months went by and we were talking about something else and the studio cropped up again and he said, 'Why don't we do something then?' It ended up being Terry Mordue, a friend of mine, on drums, Mick Jagger on guitar, Tetsu on bass and Ronnie on guitar. We put down two tracks including 'Travellin' In Style' [by Free] and one other that I can't remember. These were just demos which were just kicked about in the studio. Ronnie still has them I think."

While the MacKenzie recordings remained uncompleted, a single for Ronnie's brother Ted Wood was issued in the UK on the Penny Farthing label in September. Ted, who had been playing trad jazz with the Temperance Seven since the early Seventies sang lead on a version of the old Billie Holiday song, 'Am I Blue' while the B-side, 'Shine' featured a backing chorus of Rod Stewart, Gary Glitter and Bobby Womack.

For the first time in 14 months, the Faces returned to the States for a sold out, five-week coast-to-coast tour. "We're playing as one now like our life depended on it," Stewart told Barbara Charone before departing. "This American tour is a turning point for the Faces. If we can get that rapport going with our audience that we had four years ago, then I'll say we've accomplished something . . . The whole band has improved. We used to be horrible, have to be blind drunk to walk onstage. But now

[*] The AIR tapes were shelved until 'Open To Ideas' was first exhumed for the Warners compilation *Good Boys When They're Asleep* in 1999. The other tracks were mixed by McLagan and released on the *Five Guys Walk Into A Bar . . .* box set in 2004.

the confidence is there. Now we drink afterwards. Suddenly we've all grown up."

The 20-date tour took in the East Coast, mid-West, West Coast and Pacific Northwest, playing 18 cities, earning $1,500,000, breaking all the band's previous records, regardless of the recession affecting the US rock industry with reduced attendances and ticket prices. While the box offices were as busy as ever, the travelling was mind numbing. The ever-ready drink, drugs and women helped alleviate the boredom as did humour such as when a middle-aged woman approached Woody and Tetsu on the flight to Indianapolis. "Excuse me," she said, "are you a group?" "You must be joking Madam," a poker-faced Wood replied. "This is one of the most dangerous men on earth. Stand well clear. I'm escorting him to Sing Sing."

Regardless that the band weren't touring behind any new product and with essentially the same show, the excitement they conveyed won over such notoriously demanding critics as Lester Bangs who wrote in *Creem*: "I had to admit I had not seen the tiredness in the onstage Faces that I expected from this tour. I'd been amazed, in fact at how tight and excited they continued and manage to be," although he did worry, "It just may be that the Faces have seen their day because they're too *natural*. Or maybe they haven't and I'm more paranoid than Rod."

With Tony Toon shielding his charge against press interviews while at the same time fabricating an unlikely romance between Rod and Susan Ford, the American President's 17-year-old daughter, attention inevitably moved to Wood and the persistent Stones rumours. "I suppose in another time and in another era . . . I would join the Stones," he told Barbara Charone. "Aesthetically I would because a lot of my roots and influences are there. But . . . it just couldn't happen while I'm with the Faces. The Stones know that, that's why they wouldn't ask me. Cause, ya know, they dig the Faces too. It's just a very tempting little carrot to be dangled." The fact that Ronnie spent the evening before the tour opened nightclubbing in New York with Mick and Bianca only added fuel to the flames.

Now promoted to road manager was Charlie Fernandez: "They had wanted somebody to work with John Barnes and travel with the band and Chuch thought that would be a good position for me since we all got along well. I think he and Mac were instrumental in moving it forward so that worked out great. John left after about a year and then I came into position in 1975 – that last year – of moving the band around, and dealing with luggage, which was a full-time job almost, for departures out of hotels and things. As tour manager Pete Buckland did all the advance arrangements with the hotels, charter planes, transportation, etc. and I did the day to day. Before every show the band all loved jamming in the dress-ing room. Getting them from the dressing room to the stage on time was a chore because they liked playing music so much."

While the playing had tightened up, the shows had gained an air of predictability with the band entering to the strains of 'The Stripper', a time-honoured Faces ritual for the past 18 months. Much to Mac's chagrin, at Stewart's behest, the string section introduced at the Kilburn shows was expanded to a 10-piece orchestra at selected dates on the tour, picking up and rehearsing the musicians at the venues in question.

Sunday Mirror journalist Colin Wills and photographer Bill Vetell accompanied the tour for nine days. Wills described the scene at the Chicago show on February 18. "Each shows the strain in different ways. Kenney Jones makes little coughs, Mac yawns, Woody who normally chatters continually is silent, Tetsu, who generally utters about five words a day starts rabbiting on. Rod Stewart in a glittering gold suit keeps walking over to me, asking: 'All right gal, all right?' (Rod calls all his mates "gal", male or female) . . . They tune up and then comes the call to go on. 'Right,' yells Woody. 'Let's slaughter the lot of them.'"

The *Mirror*'s images capture life on the road from the mundane – Mac and Ronnie shopping for suitcases, lying in luggage-strewn hotel rooms – to the glamorous – backstage luminaries Andy Warhol, David Bowie (deep into his Jerome Newton *The Man Who Fell To Earth* persona), Gary Glitter and 19-year-old banking heiress Sabrina Guinness watching from the wings at Madison Square Garden on February 24. Rod considered it an improvement over the last two occasions the band played the vast venue but in his *Melody Maker* review Chris Charlesworth noted a lack of finesse: "Each and every tune came to a ragged close with the five musicians glancing at each other warily as if to see who would close a song and when. Invariably there was an odd drum-beat or piano chord after four fifths of the band had decided to abandon."

A capacity crowd of 20,000 sat in the dark holding lighted matches. "For ten minutes New York requested a return," Charlesworth wrote, "but the house lights went up and the cheers soon turned to hearty boos. An odd ending."

When the tour moved over to the West Coast, Rod sent for Dee to join him. As she recalls. "He rang and said, 'I'm on my way to LA.' Los Angeles was our special place because it was where we met and where we flew after we got engaged. He said, 'Will you get on the next plane, I'll organise the flight'. I told him I'd arranged for this team of cleaners to come in because the house was so huge, it needed all this stuff doing to it and he put the phone down on me. So then Tony Toon rang back because he would always be trotting behind. He was even living at the house by then. He said, 'Oh Dee, Rod's really upset.' So I said, 'I'll tell you what, Tony, I won't come tomorrow, I'll get all this stuff sorted and I'll arrive the day after.' Really, on the face of it I should have just gone, 'OK see you tomorrow' and just cancelled the cleaners."

Among the glitterati backstage at the Faces' first LA Forum show on March 3 were Joan Collins and her husband, former Apple Records executive Ron Kass, who had brought along 32-year-old actress Britt Ekland as their guest. Stewart and Ekland had fleetingly met at a function in London. After being reintroduced Rod was entranced but pretended to ignore the "Swedish sex-kitten", as the British tabloids invariably described her. Two nights later at the second concert, with Britt standing in the wings, Rod made his move and invited her out to dinner.

With bittersweet irony, the day before she had her final showdown with Rod, the *Daily Mail* in Britain ran a Q&A with Dee. "I don't care if we're not married as long as we're together," she said. "Obviously Rod gets attracted to other women sometimes and I don't mind because it keeps him in touch. But I think he knows that I'm the right one for him . . . Whatever anyone says, I'm the one he comes home to, aren't I?"

Dee Harrington: "When I got to LA Rod accused me of having an affair back in London because 'that was the reason why I wouldn't get the first plane out.' He told me he had to go meet Bobby Womack or Billy Gaff or someone like that. He'd rented this Mercedes sports car so that when he was busy I could see friends of mine. I said to Tony Toon, 'Come on, let's go for a drive.' As we drove down the Strip, ahead of us, I spied Rod getting out of a limo with who I thought was Krissie Wood because I knew she was in town and they walked into this club. I got out to go in to find out what was happening and there he was with Britt Ekland. I didn't recognise her at first. I said to him, 'What are you doing? What's going on? Are you mad? Why did you even bother to ask me to come here?' [to LA] He just looked at me and went, 'It works both ways.' I said, 'I'm out of here.' I actually flew back to London on the same plane that I came over on. It went up to San Francisco, turned around and came back. The longest round trip I'd ever done.

"It was almost like somebody was giving me the opportunity to leave because Rod and I had tried to leave each other before and it hadn't worked. I'd kind of rush off and stay away and then he'd go round and get a picture printed of himself with another woman, thanks to Tony Toon. That kind of ridiculous behaviour went on in the six months before we split up. But the writing was on the wall for us because of this kind of separate stuff that had gone on and it was unpleasant. Rod's existence was different therefore *our* existence was different. I still wanted to do something with my life. He'd achieved what he wanted to do. There was such an imbalance going on. I didn't stay out all night and party like everybody else and Rod felt he had to join in and create some other kind of existence to actually deal with his world. I kind of see how that needed to happen for him but I definitely wasn't going there."

Over their four-year relationship Dee endured the worst of Rod's lothario behaviour. "[Dee] knew very well what the form was," Stewart told Michael Cable, offhandedly. "I used to tell her that was the way it was going to be and that it would get worse before it got better."

Nevertheless, she retains no bitterness towards him. "I always had everything I ever wanted," Dee says today. "I had my stable block and horses, the fields were fenced. I drove around in a four-seater Lamborghini and a two-door Rolls-Royce. How bad could it be? Rod wanted to make life great for me."

The former wife of Peter Sellers (with whom she had a child, Victoria), Britt Ekland had only just split from record and film producer Lou Adler, the father of her two-year-old son Nicholai. Two days later, she and Rod were officially an item, parading before the press. "I feel fantastic," Ekland gushed. "The future isn't important for either of us. It's only the present that counts for us now."

Rod cut to the heart of the matter: "What do you think of her, then? She's a nice bit of fluff, ain't she?"

While Rod and Britt canoodled around Hollywood, Faces studio time booked at the Record Plant turned into all-night jamming and partying with guests like Bobby Womack, or nervously looking for an escape route from Ike and Tina Turner's heavily fortified Bolic Sound Studio. It wasn't the first time they had encountered Ike. Back in November 1971, he joined in on an all-night jam session with Mick Jagger, Ronnie Wood, and Ronnie Lane at the Beverly Wilshire. "It was after one of the Forum shows," says Mac. "Mick asked if we wanted to go round there because being Inglewood, it was nearby. I wished we hadn't. It took us ages to get in, going through this security and then Ike ended up making us record this track for him. We didn't get out of there until the next morning."

The show at the Swing Auditorium, San Bernardino on March 7 was professionally recorded for the *King Biscuit Flower Hour* syndicated radio

357

show (three tracks appear on *Five Guys Walk Into A Bar . . .*) and five days later the tour reached Seattle.

Ian McLagan: "We stayed at the Edgwater Inn where the rooms over-look the water. I'd scored a load of blow in LA and the next day we had an early flight to Vancouver so obviously I wasn't going to take any with me so I decided to have a party after the show. We did as much damage as we could to this coke but there was so much of it left over. Eventually I got to bed about six and thought the wise move would be to order my breakfast at that point so I wouldn't have to wake up in the morning and be hungry if I had to rush. I was lying in bed with the breakfast tray, promptly fell asleep and coffee, tea, juice, eggs, everything went all over the bed. I woke up covered in this mess so I opened the window and threw the bedsheets out and the tray of food, cups and saucers, everything. Then I threw the empty bottles out, a chair and a table and eventually I biffed most of the things in the room out the window. I was in such a hurry . . . basically what I was trying to do was to see what was my stuff and what was the hotel's.

"Charlie Fernandez was banging on the door and I said, 'OK I'm coming, I'm coming.' I'd either slammed my clothes into suitcases or thrown stuff out the window and eventually there were chairs and tables drifting out to sea and picture frames, everything floating away. There was hardly anything left in the room. The telephone, that went out because it kept ringing. As I finally left the room, the manager of the hotel was facing me against the opposite wall in the corridor and he was smiling. I was ready to give him some shit but he just smiled. Well, eventually I got a bill for the hotel telephone because the company charged them but all the rest . . . but in a letter it said you're very welcome to come back any time; he'd obviously found my handiwork entertaining which was nice of him. I actually had that letter framed in my kitchen in England years ago. I thought it was pretty classy. Pretty unclassy of me, though."

At tour's end in Vancouver, Tony Toon attempted to involve McLagan in a tacky exposé about his relationship with Kim, now that she and Keith Moon were about to be divorced, but Mac was an unwilling accomplice. Regardless the British press was full of the story by the time he arrived home. On April 11, Mac accompanied Kim to the London Divorce Court where she was granted an uncontested decree nisi, custody of Mandy, and a one-time settlement of £40,000, the approximate value of their Chertsey home that Keith had put on the market after uprooting to Los Angeles.

Rod and Britt flew back to London to supervise the sale of the Mayfair flat given to her by Sellers, and while awaiting its sale, Rod moved out of his Berkshire estate and into the apartment with Britt. The Toon machine went into overdrive and throughout the month of March the British tabloids were full of pictures and stories about the couple. "I am overwhelmed by his affection," she cooed to the *Sun* one minute, "My heart just keeps on thumping and crunching," Britt breathlessly revealed to the *Mail* the next. And most implausibly of all [to the *Daily Express*]: "We've got a pact to be faithful to each other."

Still nursing her wounds at a friend's home, a hurt and jilted Dee told David Wigg of the *Express*, "It's just a game. And so silly when there are so many other important things going on in the world."

When his accountant pointed out he was paying 83p in the pound Stewart was advised to become a tax exile. With the recording sessions for a new album, his first for Warner Bros., due to take place in America anyway, the move took on more sense. "I do intend to leave the country," Rod told *Disc*. "Unless there is a change of government . . . it's so unfair. I've worked all my life and they're going to take it all away in taxes. Anyone who has the initiative to get up and do something for themselves loses it all."

On April 5 he and Ekland flew back to Los Angeles. "I'd gone over and rented a house there before Rod did," says Billy Gaff, "so he was staying with me for about a month before he moved with Britt into his own place [at 391 Carolwood Drive] in Beverly Hills."

A week later it was formally announced that Ronnie Wood would be joining the Rolling Stones on a temporary basis for their forthcoming American tour while a replacement for Mick Taylor was sought. On April 1, appropriately enough, Wood had flown to Rotterdam where the Stones were auditioning possible replacements for Taylor including Rory Gallagher, Jeff Beck, Steve Marriott, Robert A. Johnson, Harvey Mandel and Wayne Perkins. According to Wood in his autobiography, when he walked into the studio, cajoling the other Stones to help him out on a riff he'd written called 'Hey Negrita', Charlie Watts remarked, "He's only just walked in and he's bossing us around already."

Woody could not believe his luck at being in the right place at the right time – being asked to play with his all-time favourite band, although he had to keep up the pretence of loyalty to the Faces. "At first I could not accept the job, because it would have meant leaving the Faces," he declared in a press statement. "I am too close to the whole idea of the Faces ever to turn my back on them. And I think Mick Jagger understood this as well as anybody. But finally we arrived at a formula. I will become a part-time Rolling Stone. I'll remain a full-time member of the Faces and still be free to carry on with my own musical projects."

These included *Now Look*, his second solo album co-produced with Bobby Womack and Ian McLagan, recorded at the Wick and in Amsterdam, featuring the core crew that assisted Ronnie on *I've Got My Own Album To Do*. Wood's voice was still an acquired taste and many of the songs were rough-hewn but there was some tasty slide playing to compensate. Dave Marsh in *Rolling Stone* was encouraging: "While there are some rough edges here, with some of the melodies only half-formed, *Now Look* is as fresh and buoyant a super-session as anyone has ever done."

Things were looking up for Woody in other areas too. After the recording of *Now Look*, he holidayed in Jamaica with Keith Richards. When Krissie's requests to commence divorce proceedings went unanswered, she followed him out there and stayed, and when the couple arrived home she moved back into the Wick. In line with the unconventional world of premier league rock'n'roll that they inhabited, she and Ronnie had remained on good terms throughout her relationship with Jimmy Page, and now that was over they simply carried on as before. (On February 13, at Nassau Coliseum, Wood even got up and jammed with Led Zeppelin – a band he had never professed much love for – on an interminable version of 'Communication Breakdown'.)

The Stones jaunt started on May 1 with a press preview in New York. The media had assembled at Feathers restaurant in the Fifth Avenue hotel at 9th Street where they were led to believe that a press conference would take place, when suddenly their attention was drawn to a commotion outside. Incredibly, it was the Stones playing 'Brown Sugar' on the back of a flatbed truck being driven down Fifth Avenue towards Washington Square Arch – an idea of Charlie Watts from New Orleans jazzers who used to advertise shows in the same fashion. The 41 dates, 25-city tour proper started in Baton Rouge, Louisiana on June 1. It was Ron Wood's 28th birthday and he couldn't have wanted for a better gift, despite receiving only $100,000 for his services over the next 10 weeks.

During a six-show run at Madison Square Garden at the end of June, Bill Wyman was interviewed by Barbara Charone: "If something goes wrong Ronnie has to run over and kind of suss out what's going on. He doesn't know Keith that well yet. But if he plays with us long enough he will do. But he's got his own band and he's got his solo career. It's nice to have him on the tour but I don't know about the future."

If the Stones' laconic bassist was reluctant to make predictions, the future was plainly evident to others, including Pete Buckland. "I went to see the Stones at the LA Forum in July. They played five nights and I saw every show. I thought 'This is it, Woody's going.'"

CHAPTER 20

Atlantic Crossing

"I'd always said I'd never be with another band, that the Faces was my last and final band, and I meant it. Yeah I could have gone out on my own and – I tell you what – I'd have been a total failure. There's no question in my mind that 90 per cent of the reason I've been successful is because of the band – the support from them."

– Rod Stewart, *Sounds*, 1972

"If we weren't in the group, I'm sure we'd still be together somewhere. Maybe we'd spend our time drinking in a pub instead of making music on a stage. But I'll tell you one thing with this bunch of guys, whatever we were doing we'd be enjoying ourselves. This band won't slowly die; we'll have a good time right up to the last show."

– Kenney Jones, *New Musical Express*, 1972

BLOODIED but unbowed from the chastening Passing Show debacle, Ronnie Lane put a new version of Slim Chance together in late 1974 with a fluid line-up featuring Brian Belshaw (bass), Ruan O'Lochlain (sax, keyboards) and "the Fishpool Philharmonic", fiddle players Charlie Hart (a multi-instrumentalist formerly of Pete Brown's Battered Ornaments and Kilburn & The High Roads) and Steve Simpson, who doubled on guitar and mandolin. Bruce Rowland was replaced by Glen Le Fleur. "Bruce left to undertake session work to get some much needed money," says Russ Schlagbaum. "Ronnie was devastated when he left. He wouldn't talk about it, nobody had the feel for Ronnie's music like Bruce."

Billy Gaff had transferred Lane's management on to Brian Adams from British Lion Music. "Billy had tried really hard to help," says Russ, "but Ronnie was not prone to listen and of course Billy was preoccupied with Rod Stewart's career and that really pissed Ronnie off! We didn't have a contract with British Lion so after we slipped away from them in August '74, through Ruan O'Lochlain's connection, Ronnie got hooked up with

Trentdale Music Management, a company run out of a flat in Hasker Street, Chelsea by two Welsh guys, Hywel and Ceredig Davies."

Trentdale coerced Lane into not releasing *Anymore For Anymore* in the US. Instead they arranged a worldwide deal (excluding the States and Canada) with Island Records for a £25,000 advance. "A&M in America agreed to release Ronnie's second album [his first for Island], but because the second advance of $50,000 hinged on the release of *Anymore For Anymore*, he never got his next payment and they consequently dropped the contract. This, in my opinion, was Ronnie's biggest career gaffe."

In March Island issued *Ronnie Lane's Slim Chance*, recorded at Stargroves using the LMS and a single 'Brother Can You Spare A Dime?', cut at Basing Studios and used on the title sequence of the film of the same name, released that year, containing Depression-era archive. However, just as the single started receiving attention the Beeb blacklisted it because of the current economic climate.

Russ Schlagbaum: "All these mishaps kept affecting Ronnie. Disorganisation, mismanagement, bad timing happened to him all the time. Ronnie would always say, 'What do you think, Russell?' I couldn't tell him what I really thought because he was the boss and I was still young and naïve. What I did try to tell him for a long time was to take that band to the States. If we'd have gone to Austin, Texas in 1975 we'd have been right there with Willie Nelson and all those outlaw artists. It was all happening there and Slim Chance was a great band."

After an abrupt falling-out with Trentdale Management, Russ handled Ronnie's business affairs for a few months, from his address in Twickenham. Eventually Lane was introduced to EG Management which looked after ELP, King Crimson and Roxy Music. "David Enthoven was very good with Ronnie," says Russ, "but Ronnie was in a frame of mind where he didn't want managing, only when he really needed it and if he had his mind made up nobody was going to talk him into things. So EG had a hard time with him, although David liked Ronnie and vice versa."

EG funded a second album for Island, *One For The Road*, made at Fishpool and produced by Chris Thomas. Again it was a critical if not commercial success. Throughout 1975, Slim Chance continued to gig throughout the country at colleges, universities, halls and ballrooms but with the hands he was being dealt, Lane was broke and feeling disillusioned. "There are so many obstacles to overcome that the band is only working to half its true capacity all the time . . . doing tour after tour, without it going anywhere or turning into anything – that's when it pisses me off . . ." he railed to *Sounds*' Mick Brown.

"There was a time when rock music seemed to stand for a sort of freedom against all those restrictions, but now it's just turned right back on itself and invented its own . . . This generation ain't done nothing new, although it thinks it has. In actual fact, I'm very disappointed in it.

"All this revolutionary business that went on in the late Sixties – we're going to change the world – it's come to a lot, ain't it? I don't excuse myself either, but for Christ's sake, let's try and do something about it . . ."

"I'm not unmaterialistic in the sense that I won't try and earn a bob or two," he concluded. "I've got to. But it's what you do with it that's important. If you really are in music for the right reason then you don't spend all the money you earn on yourself."

Many of his friends and associates can attest to Lane's unconcerned attitude towards money, including Billy Nicholls. "Once while Ronnie was away, I was looking after Molly, his pet mongrel. I was so broke because I wasn't working and I'd run out of money to feed the dog. I had to look around the house to find money to buy dog food. In a drawer, I found this bunch of airline tickets that hadn't been used. It amounted to something like £600. So I sent them back to British Airways or whoever it was and got back a cheque for 600 quid made out to Ronnie Lane. When Ronnie got back I explained and he just went, 'Oh, cheers mate' and popped the cheque in his pocket without any idea what I'd been through.

"Another time, after he'd got back from the States, we were driving along the motorway and he opened up his wallet and the wind caught all this money which blew it out everywhere. I said, 'Ronnie, aren't you going to go back and get it?' He wasn't even fazed. 'No, must keep going.'"

Lane's disillusionment with the music business clearly revealed him to be among the minority from the old guard who were in touch with the next generation of musicians, disenchanted with how dismal and remote rock had become. One of these was Ronnie Lane fan Glen Matlock, who in 1974 started rehearsing with a bunch of fellow Faces fans from west London.

"I first met Steve Jones and Paul Cook from when they used to come into Malcolm McLaren's shop where I worked and try and nick stuff. They already had a band together and were trying to get Malcolm to manage them. I overheard him saying to them, 'How's the band going?' and they'd go, 'Oh, our bass player never turns up' and I piped up, 'Well, I've got a bass' and they said, 'Oh yeah, what bands do you like?' I said,

'The Faces' and they said, 'Can you play?' In fact, the only song I knew all the way through was 'Three Button Hand Me Down'.

"When I went round there, Steve was still the singer and they had a guitarist called Wally Nightingale who thought he was Ron Wood but he had horrible glasses and bad teeth. Around that time I went and saw Ron Wood do his solo gig at the Kilburn Gaumont. I was up in the gods somewhere and all of a sudden these blokes I'd kind of half-met were coming down from this staircase that came from nowhere – they'd bunked in through the skylight. So the Faces were our common ground."

Unable to afford proper equipment the light-fingered Jones and Cook purloined it from various music shops and rock stars. "The story goes that Steve used to break into Ron Wood's house and have a go on his guitars," says Matlock. "Even though he wasn't in the band, Nick Kent used to knock around with us. He was the star writer for *NME* at the time and was mates with Malcolm. We were these oiks without a pot to piss in and Nick used to come and jam with us and we'd play 'I Can Feel The Fire' and stuff. But when John [Lydon] joined it became a different kind of band but we still got the Faces' influence. Steve's guitar sound, he had a Les Paul guitar through an Ampeg originally because the Faces had that."

The Sex Pistols were still in their infancy but within a year they became the spearhead of a new seditious movement known as punk rock that would tear at the barricades of the smug complacency and spiritually bankrupt world represented by dinosaur behemoths like ELP, Pink Floyd and Led Zeppelin and superstar tax exile sell-outs like Mick Jagger and . . . Rod Stewart.

"I think if people do leave the UK because of money, they can't love their country or be true-blooded Britons," an unashamedly patriotic Rod had told *Popswop* readers. On May 9, 1975 Stewart confirmed via a press statement that he had been forced out of Britain thanks to Chancellor Denis Healey's crippling tax laws. "I have reluctantly made up my mind to stay [in America] and I am applying for American citizenship." Once a tentative Liberal supporter for Jeremy Thorpe, he was now a confirmed Tory. Having put his Windsor mansion on the market for £400,000 to conform with the rules of Britain's punitive tax system, Stewart decamped to the hedonistic Hollywood of the mid-Seventies, aged 30, now set to unveil the next stage of his career.

In June, Stewart announced that he had signed a worldwide recording contract with Warner Bros. and was also in the process of forming his own label (Riva Records) with distribution handled by Warners. "I'm very confused as to what I'm going to do on the next album," Rod told *Penthouse* in January 1975. "I want to do a big sweeping change. I want to use different people. I want to do something completely different."

Names like the Meters and Bobby Womack's band were bandied about. Ian McLagan: "On the flight home [in March '75] from the US tour Rod said he was going to record in LA and I said, 'Cool,' you know, I wasn't bothered that I wasn't going to be on the album. He said, 'Do you have any suggestions for musicians?' I said, 'Yeah. Booker T. Jones, Steve Cropper, Duck Dunn and Al Jackson.' Years later, Steve Cropper told me, 'Oh yeah, that was the strange thing, we got the call from Rod and then Rod said, 'Hey, could you play more like Ronnie Wood?!' Ronnie Wood plays *like* Steve Cropper!"

The MGs and Memphis Horns played among the Muscle Shoals crew while the LA sessions featured the cream of the West Coast's players including Fred Tackett, Lee Sklar, Willie Smith, Bob Glaub and Jesse Ed Davis who impressed Stewart enough to be invited to join the forthcoming Faces' American tour.

Atlantic Crossing was intentionally symbolic of the changes in Rod Stewart. Of equal significance, it was the first of his solo albums not to feature input from any of his Faces comrades and to utilise the services of an outside producer, overlooking Lou Reizner's indistinct role on Rod's early albums. The choice of Tom Dowd was sound, and using the Muscle Shoals wrecking crew alongside the Memphis Rhythm Section could have resulted in a smooth yet down-home album. Thanks to Dowd's sure touch, Dusty Springfield's *Dusty In Memphis* and Lulu's *New Directions*, both distinctive British vocalists like Stewart, had been transformed from conventional pop backgrounds into mature and credible interpreters of Southern soul – if only for one album. However Warner Bros. wanted more bang for their bucks and Dowd delivered a slick, string-laden package. Staggeringly successful yet creatively moribund, it set the template for Rod's tenure with the label. Warners released the mawkishly sentimental 'Sailing', written by Gavin Sutherland of the Sutherland Bothers, as a single, which rewarded Stewart with a simultaneous number one album and single over the summer (and reached the Top 5 again the following year).

In July, Rod, Britt and entourage were on the way to Dublin from Nice for the European launch of the album when their plane was diverted to Heathrow. Unable to transfer flights without clearing customs, Stewart refused to leave the VIP international lounge because of his current tax situation. The party flew back to Amsterdam from where they took a direct flight to Dublin a day late. At a chaotic press conference Stewart became furious at the media probing and momentarily stormed out. On returning, he snapped: "The tax people haven't sent me a bill. When they do, I'll pay up in full."

Stewart gave interview after interview at his Gresham Hotel suite – from the rock press to the teen weeklies – and most of them alternately praised and disparaged his fellow Faces, often within the same conversation, intensifying the gap between singer and band. A conversation that appeared in lightweight girl's magazine *Jackie* of all places revealed Stewart's contrariness. "I think we [the Faces] were becoming just a pale imitation of ourselves last Christmas in our concerts. I think people have a right to come along and hear our music played as well as it is on the album. They should see a good stage show as well, and I don't think we were giving them all that. I think that's where we were going wrong . . .

"The boys and I have a big gap between us now. And it's not helped by me being in America and them being over here. I don't know exactly what's going to happen but certainly we've got to have a long talk about it."

To the *Sun*: "I don't think I want to make any more albums with the Faces. Simply because the fans don't seem willing to accept the albums I do with the band. My position at the moment obviously puts enormous pressure on them . . . Woody is touring with the Rolling Stones and that could change his outlook on things too.

"I have said many times I would never leave the Faces and that is still true. If we split up it will be after we have worked things out together."

But it was his caustic comments to *NME*'s Steve Clarke that gave most indication the Faces were in freefall: "I've got no idea what's going to happen to the band after this [forthcoming US] tour. I don't even know if our guitar player is still alive. I've spoken to him three times while he's been touring with the Stones, twice he was sounding really on top of the world and then the last time he sounded really down . . .

"So I might see Woody, but I very much doubt it. I don't know what shape he's in. I hope he's in good health cause he's got to finish a tour with them and start a tour with us. That's not the two easiest bands to tour with on the road. We'll all be down in Miami in three weeks and we'll start rehearsing and obviously there's going to be a lot of ego floating about. It's not just me and the band, they're all personalities in their own right. They've all got their own lifestyles.

"See, I want desperately to recreate what I've done on [*Atlantic Crossing*] onstage and I'll do anything to do that, literally anything . . . Anyway, we'll see what happens. We've got to feel each other out. If we don't break up within the next few months we'll never break up 'cos we're probably as near [to it] now as we've ever been."

Meanwhile further salt was applied to the wound in a *Daily Express* interview when Kenney blurted his disappointment at Rod's Stateside defection and that his decision to pull the plug on several proposed open air summer concerts at British football grounds had evidently left Jones out of pocket to the tune of £80,000. *NME* reported that the Faces' management were intervening after the contents of Jones' outburst were telexed to Stewart in the South of France. A spokesman told the paper: "There hasn't been any official reply and there isn't going to be one. The matter is being dealt with internally. The problem seems to have been a lack of communication, and I understand that Rod is speaking to Kenney on the phone to sort things out. And that's the end of it!"

When asked about Jones' stance, Stewart told Clarke, "That was so unfair 'cos [the band] were all going to leave England and live in America, all of us. Now, as it happens, me and Woody are the only two. The rest [have] stayed behind. Now I don't know if Woody is going to live there or live where. Plus the fact that those British gigs were never on 'cos Woody was touring the States with the Stones."

Stewart's comments were indicative of his impervious attitude to discretion, using the press to communicate directly with the other Faces, a point he was willing to concede: "There's a lot of bullshit goes down. We have a go at each other behind each other's backs. We never say the best things about each other, but when we're together we're the best of mates always. If that was to change then I'd be very surprised. If we're going to have a go at each other we go round the back ways, through PR people or managers or send telegrams .·. . You've got to look at it like this. Woody might want to join the Stones, I'd be very surprised if he did – he could have done it two years ago. A lot rests on his decision."

In August the Faces rendezvoused in Miami to rehearse before commencing the second part of their US tour – a two-month trek scheduled to commence at West Palm Beach Auditorium on August 15. The Stones' trek had been extended by six days causing the cancellation of three Faces dates in West Palm Beach, Tampa and Atlanta at a cost of $200,000, which only fed the tension. "We've had to cancel the concerts because there won't be enough time to rehearse the new numbers with Ronnie," said a band spokesman. "Rod is particularly fed up because he feels that the

Stones should have let him know about the extension much sooner." A Stones spokesman fired back: "The decision to extend the tour was taken a fortnight ago, I was not aware that the Faces had not been informed in good time."

While waiting for their guitarist to arrive, the others relaxed at a rented house at 461 Ocean Boulevard where Eric Clapton recorded his album of the same name the previous year.

Ian McLagan: "Woody was all full of it when he arrived in Miami. We were ready to go ahead and just carry on as normal but Rod thought Ronnie couldn't play without a rhythm guitarist so he got Jesse Ed Davis in."

Born a full-blooded Native American Indian in Oklahoma on September 21, 1944, Jesse Edwin Davis III dropped out of Oklahoma University and moved to Los Angeles playing sessions through his friendship with Leon Russell, and joined Taj Mahal in 1967. Davis released three solo albums featuring various musical luminaries while going on to be the LA session guitarist *du jour*, playing on albums by John Lennon, George Harrison, Ringo Starr, Eric Clapton, Jackson Browne and Gene Clark among numerous others.

"What Rod didn't realise," says Mac, "was that Jesse Ed was *our* friend and he was no more a rhythm guitarist than Ronnie was. I mean, Ronnie was both but Jesse was a lead guitarist so it was really odd to get a lead guitarist in when we already had one. So we didn't need Jesse but it was great to have him on tour. For a joke we got Bobby Womack in to help Rod out with his singing!"

If the addition of an extra guitarist was an unnecessary but bearable burden for Mac and Woody, Stewart's other embellishment – the addition of a 12-piece string section in tuxedos and black ties under the direction of Jimmy Horowitz – was beyond the pale, being seen as more of a theatrical device for the singer, especially by the opprobrious McLagan. "I never saw the need for strings," he says. "I hated the idea; Jimmy Horowitz standing up there conducting, looking like a fucking idiot in a penguin suit. The string players had these Barcus Berry pick-ups, Pete Buckland would attach them onto each violin. Early on in the tour, I overheard one guy complain that the pick-up scratched his instrument. Then I found out that if one player unplugged his Barcus Berry all of the others went out [of tune] so I would make a point and so would Ronnie of saying, 'You know make sure that pick-up doesn't scratch your instrument, you just unplug it if you don't like it.' Sabotage! It had to be done. It was such a joke and it sounded crap."

The lines were being drawn within the Faces entourage now split into two distinct camps with the party animals – Mac, Woody, and Tetsu – on one side and Rod's circle which included Billy Gaff, Tony Toon and Pete Buckland on the other. Jones remained on the fence. "It started to get a little odd during the first tour of '75," says Buckland, "but that last tour was the only tour I did with the Faces that I didn't enjoy. It was just a horrible tour. Everything started to fall apart."

The additional personnel required three jets to transport the entourage, creating extra expense. "It worked out well," considers Gaff. "There was never a disaster considering the bloody string players had to be hired and rehearsed by Jimmy. It wasn't like we travelled with the same string section, they had to be hired at every stop but it generally worked out fine except that you could barely hear them at some places."

"On that last tour everybody was going in so many different directions," says Charlie Fernandez. "I'd be on the phone quite a bit of the time, juggling ground transportation needs that kept changing from hour to hour and other things. Getting the band up in the morning to catch a plane was horrible, not only that but they'd wake up at, like, three in the afternoon and expect to be served breakfast and sometimes it would be crazy. If they didn't get breakfast in a hotel they would act up by breaking things and if they did and it wasn't perfect things would get broken. I'd listen for the trolley going down the hallway and think, 'OK, is the door going to open and am I going to hear a plate smash against the wall and then a door slam or what?' There were some hotels where we'd have to really do our best to persuade them to keep the kitchen open all day long – one particular place in Asheville, North Carolina, where we opened on that last tour. We rehearsed there and I persuaded them to let me go in and cook breakfast myself for the couple of days we stayed."

The tour moved through the south and mid-West on to California for a round of football stadium shows, using the Tower Of Power horn section supported by the likes of Loggins & Messina and the fast-rising Fleetwood Mac, now fronted by Stevie Nicks and Lindsay Buckingham.

"We based ourselves at the Beverly Hilton Hotel and flew out to do the shows," says Charlie Fernandez. "We did Anaheim Stadium [on August 30] and our truck had an accident in the Arizona desert and the band weren't able to use their gear. It was all rental gear from SIR and half of it worked, half of it didn't. It was just horrific, that was the worst, as the band walked off they knocked all the amps over. But usually the shows were great, every night was party night, you couldn't help enjoying yourself, it was so great."

Throughout the tour, Britt Ekland was never far from Stewart's side. When asked if Ekland's constant presence created any bad vibes, the ever-diplomatic Fernadez says: "It was not a problem. As far as I could see, she never interfered with anything that had to be done as far as logistics with the show and she kept Rod happy."

For others on the road – inevitably enough, the wives – she needed bringing down a peg or two. "Britt was not popular on that [last] tour," says Jan Jones. "We were cross that she was getting special treatment. She could stay in the dressing room longer than we could before a show because she was doing Rod's make-up and she was also 'the official photographer'. I think it was in California . . . We were livid enough that we had to leave the dressing room first and we said, 'Why is she staying behind?' Charlie promised us that she'd be out in a minute. Then when she didn't show and we looked up and saw Britt rising up in this cherry picker, taking photos, we were even more livid."

On September 8 the entourage arrived in Honolulu for two shows as well as a brief holiday. "In Hawaii, at this Warner Bros. dinner do on two massive tables full of record company execs, Britt was facing Tony Toon at the table behind us so I had my back to them facing Kenney with Woody and Mac either side of me. Britt was having a row with Tony and she picked up this great big pineapple full of prawn cocktail and threw it at Tony who ducked and it landed on my head. Both Woody and Mac simultaneously grabbed each of my arms and held me back because they knew I was going to go berserk. All the wives were just waiting for an opportunity to get Britt. And Woody and Mac were whispering at me, 'Don't worry, we got her, we got her.' Rod had to tell her off because it was embarrassing for him. I think what was embarrassing for him was that he was hoping I'd speak out and make a spectacle of myself.

"The silence spoke volumes. The cocktail lounge musicians stopped playing, put everything down and walked off quietly. The Hawaiian waiters and waitresses lining up serving people, they just all stopped. I suppose the manager of the hotel must have said, 'That's it.' We were still at the prawn cocktail stage and everybody left and Britt was hiding behind a curtain. We went and partied in Jesse Ed Davis' room and the next day Rod made her come up and apologise to me on the beach which must have been pretty hard for her since she always thought she was better than us."

During the first concert at Honolulu's HIC Arena Rod saw red when a security guard tried to remove a girl standing in front of the stage and swung his mike stand at the man, narrowly missing his head. However the most notable flashpoint on the Hawaiian stop involved Jeff Wald, singer Helen Reddy's husband and manager, which occurred at the plush Kahala Hilton. As Jan recalls: "Rod and Britt were about to check out but it wasn't soon enough for Jeff Wald and Helen Reddy who always had that particular suite. The normal check-out time was like noon and I think Rod had asked for another couple of hours or maybe he just stayed in there. Anyway Rod wasn't too pleased when Jeff Wald came banging on the door, demanding they get out. Rod came down to where we were on the beach and told the others what had happened. He, Mac and Woody went back up there and wrecked the room – clogged the drains so the water overflowed, ripped the TV out, dismantled the phone, broke the bed. Then they came back down to the beach very pleased with themselves. Rod was waiting for his limo to take him to the airport and everyone was by the bar.

"We kept popping up to the lobby to see what was going on and that's when Jeff Wald went berserk. He was shouting at the manager and then he went for Mac who was standing there watching. It was like a Marx Brothers film when Mac punched [Jeff Wald] and he went sliding back, landed on the sofa and the framed picture on the wall just fell on his head."

When the police arrived Wald told them he had been assaulted while McLagan claimed Wald had threatened him, saying he wouldn't leave the Island alive. Neither was arrested and according to the *Honolulu Advertiser* both were advised to swear out warrants if they wished to pursue the issue which both fully intended on doing although the matter was eventually dropped by either side. Judging by her former husband's behaviour in Reddy's 2006 autobiography *The Woman I Am*, it seems Mac got off lightly.

The Hawaiian sojourn offered some light relief on an otherwise fraught tour. "I think everybody in management was putting Rod into a position where as the front man, he had the brightest future as a solo star," says Charlie Fernandez. "And you get to that point, after a while, you keep hearing it over and over . . . [Rod] looked at things from a very business-like point of view and he did start separating his time spent with the band." There were other problems to contend with – in Arizona, Rod banged his knee against an amp and upset a cartilage, resulting in shows in El Paso and Abilene being cancelled. Towards the end of the tour Mac fell off the stage while it was being set up by the road crew and badly strained his wrist.

The final display of Faces' bad behaviour occurred on October 17 when a motel room in Lakeland, Florida got trashed. Jan Jones, who came along for part of the itinerary with three-year-old Dylan, recalls: "Mac, Woody, and Tetsu were going on to Miami the night before on a coach but Rod, Billy, Kenney and I stayed behind so we could fly there. They literally trashed a room, threw stuff into the pool and stole all the pillows and blankets for the coach. The police came banging on our chalet doors looking for 'this group the Faces.' 'No,' we said, 'they've all gone to Miami.' Kenney was standing behind the cops in his Esso jumpsuit, just looking like a mechanic. He wasn't so flamboyant or recognisable but Rod certainly was.

"So what we did was . . . we smuggled Rod over to the cafe restaurant across the road where he got a car to the airport. Billy, Kenney and I were the last to leave because we had a problem covering the damages and I struggled to pay the bill on my American Express card. Meanwhile there was chaos when Woody & co got to the hotel in Miami because nobody was being given a room. I think the manager had heard about the destruction in Tampa and wanted a great big deposit. So Billy had to get to Miami to put a deposit down and then they got put on the seventh floor where nothing worked anyway – the air conditioning didn't work – in case they decided to start breaking things."

As if there was a sixth sense that this was to be the last grand slam, more dates were added to the end of the itinerary before what turned out to be the final Faces show at the Labor Temple, Minneapolis on November 1.

With the majority of the shows being billed as Rod Stewart & The Faces any pretence of the band being a democratic unit had all but gone, particularly when they were expected to perform 'Three Time Loser', a song concerning VD off *Atlantic Crossing* which none of the band played on. In the interests of fairness, Wood was able to perform 'Take A Look At The Guy' and 'Big Bayou' off his solo albums but for McLagan, "that was probably Rod's way of saying, 'Well, you should do some, too, then I won't look such an asshole.'"

"I don't think there was any kind of power shift [in the Faces]," Pete Buckland declares. "Rod didn't really exert any sort of control. I think it was more in other people's perceptions and it was all down to Rod having gotten more and more famous. I think that's really what it was and earlier on the Faces benefited from that. Don't forget, as well as Rod being very good for the Faces, the Faces were very good for Rod. The Faces were, during that period, *the* best rock'n'roll band in the world, though they were loose and everything, they were a phenomenal rock'n'roll band.

Even with Tetsu, musically it wasn't as good but they were still doing great business and it was an excellent showcase for Rod and his songs so why would he want to change that? There was no reason for him to even want to upset the apple cart at that stage and it was only really that last tour where it became a problem."

A rumour suddenly surfaced in the British music press that the Faces were to play a farewell concert the first week of December in Dublin to be close-circuited to British cinemas. Stewart responded: "When we do break up there'll be no bloody farewell tour. It'll end with a punch-up. Our last concert will be a televised show of us kicking the shit out of each other."

Pete Buckland: "Things have to come to an end, it was just a shame that it ended in the way it did because it was a completely unnecessary process that went on during that last American tour – from a group of people that had been so closely knit together to being divided like that. When it all fell to pieces there was a lot of bad feeling and unfortunately Billy Gaff got blamed for stuff which was nothing to do with him. Gaff is a much-maligned character actually. The boys in the band, all of them, had been through so much shit in the past with the Don Arden–Peter Grant sort of manager. I don't think any one of those hardcore types of people would have survived with the Faces. They all knew what they wanted, they were each very smart guys. They wanted someone that they had a bit of control over. Even though we all used to gang up on Gaff a bit and were quite vile to him at times, I actually had a huge respect for Billy because he did a great job in terms of a manager. He certainly did a fantastic job for the Faces. You'll hear different from other people but . . ."

Billy Gaff: "To be honest with you I couldn't have survived if Woody hadn't been there, he was the go-between, he kept things on an even keel. Being a Gemini like me he kept both sides happy. It was very difficult at times. The problems I had were basically with McLagan and [when he was in the band] Ronnie Lane who always felt I was siding with Rod which I wasn't. It was called business. I wasn't the one who wrote the fucking riffs but I got the blame! The proof in the pudding was when Rod left the Faces and wanted me to go with him. I suppose that was the end justifying the means. There was no choice – Rod was going anyway, there was no doubt about that and I wasn't fucking stupid either!"

While Wood was away in Montreux recording with the Stones, the front page of the December 19 edition of the *Daily Mirror* announced: "Why rock star Rod is quitting Faces." The paper's music correspondent Stan Sayer wrote: "Rock superstar Rod Stewart decided last night to quit the Faces pop group – and go it alone. The 30-year-old singer is also planning to start his own band in the New Year: 'I have only just made up my mind. But I'm definitely quitting this time.'" Tony Toon added his own bitchy contribution: "Rod feels he can no longer work in a situation where the group's lead guitarist Ron Wood seems to be permanently 'on loan' to the Rolling Stones."

Jones and McLagan were both quoted in the article. "I won't believe [Rod] is leaving the Faces until I hear it from his own lips," said Mac, while Jones nonchalantly remarked, "If this means the end of the Faces, I'm not bothered. I expect I will survive."

For Faces fans that were hoping for the traditional UK Christmas tour it was sad to see their heroes dissolving in columns of newsprint. "I'd still like to work with Woody again," Rod told the *Mirror* in the following day's edition, "although I'm a bit annoyed with him, the silly sod . . . Working with the Faces wouldn't be the same without Woody. If he wants to talk to me he can. He knows my phone number. Any of the Faces can ring me. The ball is in their court."

CHAPTER 21

Glad And Sorry

"It isn't a question of wanting to be a star or anything else. It's simply that I can't do anything else but be a musician and it's a job I want for life . . . I don't want to be rich and retire at 35. This is my work, my livelihood. I haven't got a lot of pressure, I'm not setting the world alight. I just want to be an entertainer and earn a living like those musicians in New Orleans who, at 50 and 60, are still playing their music and having a good time."

– Ronnie Lane, *Sounds*, 1974

"I'm happy playing music. I just get by at doing it. What can you do if you stop playing?"

– Ian McLagan, in conversation with author, 2010

THE Faces were effectively defunct but in the New Year of '76, McLagan and Jones (with Tetsu in tow) clung to the hope that the band could continue to operate in some form. "After I heard through the front page of the *Daily Mirror* that Rod was quitting, Kenney, Tetsu, Woody and I started figuring out what we were going to do and thought we'd make an album with Woody and I singing," recalls Mac. "We couldn't record in England so we rented a studio in France, somewhere near the coast. Warner Bros. were footing the bill and then Mo Ostin came to London and Kenney and myself had a meeting with him and Derek Taylor [then MD of Warner Bros. UK division].

"Because Mo knew a little bit more than we did, he told us, 'Look, Ronnie Wood is going to join the Stones, there's no point in recording,' and I said, 'But Ronnie's keen to do it. That's what we've been talking about.' And Mo said, 'Yeah, Ronnie was *talking* about it but he isn't actually thinking of *doing* it.'"

In early January Wood flew to Nassau for a holiday with Krissie and then on to New York to complete work on the Stones' *Black And Blue* album. In an interview published in the January 24 edition of *Sounds*, Wood let slip to Barbara Charone that Stewart had advised him to join the Stones during the Faces' last US tour. "Then again, if I had gone and joined the Stones he would have called me all the names under the sun . . . I'll be quite interested to hear Rod's reaction when he finds out [the Faces are] gonna do an album without him. He'll be surprised that I'm gonna do it. He probably thinks I've severed all ties with the Faces like he has. But there's no reason for me to do that. If I had a good reason I'd tell ya."

That good reason came a month later when Wood was officially confirmed as a permanent addition to the Rolling Stones. A reported Faces' tour of Japan, Australasia, Europe and the UK planned for the first half of 1976 subsequently failed to materialise.

Ian McLagan: "At the meeting with Mo and Derek, Mo said, 'Why don't you and Kenney and Tetsu get together with Steve [Marriott].' And we said, 'Now excuse me, we've done that, that'd be going backwards' and what did we fucking do?"

Although their albums never sold in huge quantities in Britain, hard work had turned Humble Pie into one of America's top live attractions during the early half of the decade but after five years of gruelling, non-stop tours, the band had burnt out by 1975 with little to show for their efforts. When his solo album that year stiffed Marriott, skint and on a self-destructive spiral, was open to offers.

Reports of a Small Faces reunion had first surfaced during the Faces' inactivity in 1974. "Ronnie Lane and I were talking about the old band recently," Jones told *Disc* in June that year, "and thought we'd like to do a reunion gig. Then we talked to Steve [Marriott] and Mac and they agreed. I don't know when we will get the time, that is the only problem."

In late '75 Lane invited Jones and McLagan down to Fishpool Farm to play together and discuss ideas. "Ronnie wanted to form [a new version of] Ronnie Lane and Slim Chance and we'd be in Slim Chance," says Mac. "I looked at Kenney and I looked at Ronnie and I said, 'No fucking way, are you mad? Fuck that shit.'" Despite his antipathy to the idea, Mac did sit in on several Slim Chance gigs and a John Peel BBC session.

On Wednesday, January 7, as noted in Russ Schlagbaum's detailed diary, all four original Small Faces met up for the first time since 1969 at Jones' home in Kingston to discuss the reunion proposal. They agreed to rehearse a set, do some shows, record them on Ronnie's mobile and hopefully make some money at last.

Ian McLagan: "It was all done by a kind of fluke, there wasn't a plan. It came about because Tony Calder offered us £1,000 each to make videos for 'Itchycoo Park' and 'Lazy Sunday' because he was now working for NEMS and they'd bought the rights to Immediate and reissued those songs."

"I remember Don Arden rang Ronnie at Fishpool and asked him to come back and help promote the old material," says Russ. "Ronnie told him to fuck off and slammed the phone down on him."

Considering the song was so redolent of the hippie summer of '67 'Itchycoo Park' became a surprise UK hit when re-released, reaching number nine that month.

Ian McLagan: "We all had a meeting at EG Management and they agreed to back the project. That same day [January 19] we did the videos at Island Studios in Hammersmith for *Top Of The Pops* but they didn't show them," says Mac. "And we never got paid."

While the meetings and filming had passed pleasantly, Lane was still reluctant. "It's like going back to your old school," he was quoted. "You don't mind visiting, but who'd go back permanently?" But a moment later: "If someone called up and said, 'It's on in Yeovil next week,' then I'd do it."

He had good reason to be wary. On January 17, a typically boisterous Marriott appeared as a surprise guest during the encore at Slim Chance's gig at Essex University and basically took over. While it was great to see the old muckers reunited, Lane looked visibly embarrassed when Marriott loudly demanded of the enthusiastic punters, "Let's hear ya, this is Marriott and Lane! Get yer fucking hands together!"

While Marriott and Lane tentatively rehearsed in Steve's home studio at Beehive Cottage – an ironic setting considering it was Lane's former home and where their partnership had foundered in acrimony – Mac kept his chops up by touring Europe in Bobby Womack's band. Kenney, meanwhile, had been invited to be part of the band Rod Stewart was putting together, featuring three guitarists Jim Cregan, Billy Peek and ex-Strider axeman Gary Grainger, and Phil Chen, the bass who was almost a Face.

"Billy Gaff phoned me and said we were going to rehearse in the States," Jones told John Gray. "I didn't relish the idea of going, but eventually I decided I would . . . When we rehearsed in Britain it was really good, very tight . . . [but] I was constantly asking myself if I could go on stage with Rod. I knew it was going to end up as Rod Stewart and backing band, and it did . . . The other players were great but every time I looked round it wasn't Mac and it wasn't Woody so it wasn't the same.

"Pete Buckland came and collected my drums in their flight cases and took them to the airport and I thought that was it. I'd made the decision and I was going. But after a couple of hours had past, I realised I couldn't do it. The drums were due to fly out that evening, so I got in the biggest car I had and went to the airport to get my gear back. Then I called up Billy Gaff and told him."

Jones was replaced by Carmine Appice, formerly of Vanilla Fudge, Cactus, and Beck, Bogert & Appice.

The Small Faces reunion was still on the agenda but Lane continued to feel uneasy. Russ Schlagbaum: "EG got excited and Mark Fenwick flew to New York and was negotiating a $1m five album deal of which the band would get 25 per cent but Ronnie said, 'No, I've done the Small Faces.' EG tried strong-arming him into doing it because he owed £35,000 unrecouped royalties on *One For The Road*. Each of the guys, David Enthoven, Mark Fenwick and the accountant Sam Alder came down to the farm at different times and tried to coerce him but Ronnie said, 'Fuck the money, you're talking about my life here' and he stood his ground."

Lane's decision was final after a disastrous few days at Joe Brown's studio, Grange Sound in Chigwell, Essex.

Ian McLagan: "We started recording an album but after one night of that Ronnie had enough and he quit. We stayed up all night and went to the pub the next day and Ronnie got drunk and stroppy. We went back to the studio and we were doing a backing vocal and he just said, 'Oh fuck this.' He told me years later that was the first sign of MS he had, he didn't know what was going on but his legs were giving way. He was angry with himself for getting so pissed. In fact he wasn't really drunk. He was a year or so from diagnosis."

According to Schlagbaum's diary, the incident occurred on June 17: "Huge fight breaks out at SF rehearsals between SM & RL. L rings me: '. . . Russell, come get me out of here, fucking Marriott is insane.' I take RL [back] to Wales."

It was a low period for Lane – practically bankrupt, at loggerheads with his old mates and to add to his bad luck, his original Black Zemaitis bass was stolen among other items when thieves broke into his storage garage in East Twickenham.

"Ronnie was sitting by the fire at the cottage," says Russ, "twisting his neck curls as he always did when deep in thought. He said, 'What am I gonna do? I've been boxed into a corner.' He said, 'I think I'll call Pete [Townshend] and maybe I can get him to produce an album.' Ronnie hoped that with Pete on board, a record company would cough up a big advance and get him out of the financial shit so he could start again. It was a vicious circle. So he called Townshend and Pete said, 'Why don't you come down to London and we'll talk about it.'

"The next day we drove to London in the old '65 Ford Thames van that Ronnie's dad gave him and had Sunday lunch at Pete's in Twickenham to discuss it. Pete said, 'I can't produce you, Ronnie, I need a producer as badly as you do but why don't we do an album together and we'll get Glyn to produce it.'"

"When I got the call from Pete," says Glyn Johns, "I thought it was a great idea but at the time I was concerned that they might be doing it for the wrong reason. I said I wasn't interested in producing the record unless they were both committed to making it a really fine piece of work. If they were just doing it to raise money for Ronnie, then I wasn't interested."

Russ Schlagbaum: "After meeting with Glyn and he agreed to do it Ronnie had this crisis meeting scheduled with EG. I just remember it as being so funny because he went in there with this huge ace up his sleeve but he didn't tell them to start with. EG were still trying to pressure him into the Small Faces' reunion so there was all this terrible tension building up in this meeting. Ronnie kept saying, 'I'm not going do it and because you're my managers you're supposed to come up with Plan B,' but there was no Plan B. So there was dead silence – he just let them stew.

"Then Ronnie piped up, 'A fuckin' great lot of managers you are. I'm paying you 25 per cent and in the meantime I've made arrangements to make an album with Pete Townshend, Glyn Johns is gonna produce it, and we start recording in September. There, art thou happy?' Well, these guys fell out of their chairs in disbelief. I believe EG agreed they were not eligible to receive a percentage from the project and they quit funding Ronnie at that point so we were dependent on the £10,000 advance from Atlantic [Townshend and the Who's manager] Bill Curbishley was negotiating."

The sessions for what became *Rough Mix* continued intermittently throughout September and November '76 and into the New Year with a cast of friends including Charlie Watts, Ian 'Stu' Stewart, Charlie Hart, Billy Nicholls and Gallagher & Lyle. Playing a significant part was Eric Clapton with whom Lane had recently become acquainted.

Russ Schlagbaum: "Ian Stewart called Ronnie one day and mentioned, 'Oh, by the way I ran into Eric the other day and he asked how you were.' And Ronnie was mystified. He said to me, 'What the fuck does Eric Clapton want? I don't even know him that well.' Stu kept saying Eric's been asking after you so Ronnie asked Stu for his number. I was there when he made the call. 'Eric? This is Ronnie Lane, just what the fuck do you want?!' It was that blatant and that's what started their whole friendship."

Glyn Johns: "*Rough Mix* was a perfect title – apart from the obvious pun – because it had never occurred to me that Ronnie and Pete would ever work together and I don't think it had ever occurred to them either. They were good friends through their mutual interest in Meher Baba but they were completely independent in their careers although they respected one another. I'd known both of them for a long time independently and had a friendship as well as a working relationship with them. They fought like cats and dogs on a couple of occasions so there was some stress while it was being made."

"Ronnie always had a way of pushing people's buttons," says Russ. "The sessions started at 11 every day so Pete could leave early to be with his wife and daughters. This particular morning, from the beginning, Ronnie and Pete entered into this big discussion. It started in the control room, then the overdub booth, then the hallway, the toilet. Glyn did what he could, a little editing work or whatever but finally by about six o'clock, Glyn said, 'We're not going to get any work done today. Sod this, I'm going home.' Pete and Ronnie literally spent all day in this intense conversation.

"Everyone else had gone and I was sitting there in the reception area waiting for Ronnie when suddenly I heard this commotion starting, shouting and screaming. I looked and Ronnie and Pete were in the long hallway that connected the studios. Ronnie was curled up in a ball on the floor and Pete was kicking the shit out of him with those big Doctor Marten's boots of his. I'm thinking, 'What the fuck? Townshend's kicking the shit out of my boss, what am I gonna do?' Because the next day we were due to pick up the advance from Bill Curbishley. Great timing, Ronnie!

"As I went to break it up, Pete stops, walks past me and as he did, he stopped and looked me straight in the face and shouted, 'Tell that to the fucking cunt when he sobers up in the morning,' slammed the door almost breaking the glass and screamed off in his long stretch Mercedes. I go back inside and Ronnie's uncurled himself and he says in this timid voice, 'Has he gone?' I said, 'Christ, what did you say to him?' And he says, 'I don't know but it must have really pissed him off!' The next morning Ronnie brought in a box of chocolates as a peace offering, they kissed and made up and the sessions carried on as normal."

Rough Mix was released in September 1977 to critical praise but modest sales. "As far as I'm concerned *Rough Mix* is a fantastic album," says Johns. "Both Ronnie and Pete worked together well and it was a great vehicle for both of them. It's one of the best records I made in my career, yet it was the one that got away."

While Lane and Townshend were making *Rough Mix*, Jones, McLagan and Marriott ill-advisedly soldiered on as the Small Faces with bassist Rick Wills, a friend of Marriott's, who'd previously been in Cochise, Frampton's Camel and just recently, Roxy Music. In September '77 the volatile personality of Jimmy McCulloch was also added to the mix. "We signed for a huge advance with Atlantic," says Mac, "and then we discovered that Steve was still tied to A&M Records and Dee Anthony. That's when the penny dropped that Steve needed us and this deal to bail him out of the mess he was in."

The reconstituted Small Faces made two mediocre albums *Playmates* and *'78 In The Shade* but whatever spark was there had long been extinguished. While the band toured around Britain and Europe (with P.P. Arnold on occasion), the prevalent spirit of punk made them look even more of an anachronism – although the Small Faces' early Mod look and feisty energy of their records shared much in common with the fashion, speed and excitement of the movement.

After leaving the Sex Pistols in early 1977, Glen Matlock had formed a new band, Rich Kids.

"Mick Ronson was producing our album at Johnny Kongos' studio in Barnes," Matlock recalls, "and there was a track that needed some piano on it. Ronson was more of a classical pianist and I wanted something more rock'n'roll, 'like Ian McLagan.' The engineer said, 'Oh, he was down here last week. I've got a number for him.' So we got Mick Ronson to call Mac up and we sat there all excited. Ronson was like (*adopts Yorkshire accent*), 'Hello, is Mac there? It's Mick here.' 'Mick who?' 'Mick Ronson.' 'Who?' 'I used to play with David Bowie.' Anyway they had a chat and Mac came down the next day and we just clicked, we got on like a house on fire.

"The Rich Kids had a tour coming up and I asked him if he'd play with us and he said he'd love to. I don't think he was doing anything at the time. The reformed Small Faces had spilt up and the Rich Kids were falling apart, too. I actually asked Mac to join the band and he said, 'I'll think about it.' The next morning, we came down to breakfast at this hotel. I said, 'Had any further thoughts?' He said, 'You won't believe this but I called home last night and I had a phone call and this band have asked me to tour with them.' I said, 'Well, who is it?' and he said, 'The Rolling Stones.' I said, 'You'd better do it then.' "

As with Ronnie Wood, McLagan needed no further urging to play with his favourite band. In December '77 he'd gone to Paris to play on the Stones' sessions for *Some Girls* – his Wurlitzer prominent on the hit single 'Miss You' – and was invited to join them on their summer '78 US tour. Mac flew in and made his debut with scant rehearsal at Lakeland, Florida on June 10. He also recorded tracks with the Stones at RCA Studios in Los Angeles at the end of the tour.

"Nothing much was happening for me in England at that time," says Mac, "and Kim and I talked about moving to LA where there seemed to be more opportunities to work. Ronnie's manager at the time, Jason Cooper, suggested Kim and I get married to sort out the Green Card situation for her and Mandy."

On September 7 Keith Moon died, aged 32, at his Mayfair flat from an accidental overdose of medication prescribed by his doctor to combat alcoholism. The night before he'd been at a party thrown by Paul McCartney to mark Buddy Holly Week, and among the other guests at the Peppermint Park reception in Covent Garden were David Frost, John Hurt and, ironically, Kenney Jones.

Just over four weeks later, on October 9, Mac married Kim in a civil ceremony at Wandsworth Town Hall. Mandy Moon acted as bridesmaid.

"[The Faces] is the first band that I've been with in which I've actually earned a lot of money," Kenney Jones told *Disc* in 1973, "and when it finishes I shall be able to sit back with a lot more ease and wait for the right thing to come along. Rather than panicking because I've got no money and taking the first offer that comes along."

However, by September 1978, Kenney's coffers were running low. He, Jan, Dylan and new addition, Jesse Kaylan Jones, had moved from Kingston to a house adjoining the Osborne family residence in Gainesborough Gardens, Hampstead. "We were on our uppers at the time," Jan recalls, "and the house was a leasehold and we'd just done it up. It would have been out of our price range had it been freehold." Kenney's services were still in demand as a session drummer and thanks largely to Glyn Johns, he played on albums by artists including Andy Fairweather-Low and Joan Armatrading. Jones was about to join Lazy Racer, a studio AOR band that Johns discovered when he received the fateful call from Bill Curbishley asking him to join the Who, now that they had rashly decided to continue without Keith Moon.

Inviting Jones to replace Moon was largely down to Pete Townshend. He and John Entwistle had played with Kenney (and Ron Wood) on the *Tommy* film soundtrack sessions in 1974 and the fact that the Who and the Small Faces had close links going back to the Sixties helped seal the deal.

Jan Jones: "When Kenney was asked to join the Who, he spoke to Glyn and asked, 'What shall I do?' Glyn was always the voice of reason and common sense and he said, 'Take the Who.' He had a meeting with Curbishley and then the band met for a musical discussion or something at which point Kenney said to me, 'Go out and buy all the Who's albums.' Because he didn't know their stuff – I mean, he knew the singles and stuff like that but we really didn't listen to the Who's music at home so it was like, panic, 'Go out and get them' and it was hard work with headphones on with click tracks coming in at different times. I'll never know how he would know when to come in. I thought that was quite clever and fascinating."

Jones made his Who debut at London's Rainbow Theatre on May 2, 1979 and over the next four years played major – and lucrative – American and European tours with them. He also drummed on two lacklustre albums, *Face Dances* (1981) and *It's Hard* (1982), both of which were slated by the critics, and in a case of déjà vu, as he had done with Rod Stewart, Jones accused Townshend of holding his best material back for his solo albums. "My inner reaction was, 'Who the fuck are you? You're only in this fucking band 'cos I wanted you in it,'" Townshend told John Harris in 1996. "Roger [Daltrey] had never wanted him in, in the first place."

"I felt that Keith was such an extraordinary drummer, to try and replace him was just ridiculous," Daltrey explained to Ken Sharp in 1994. "We had the chance to be completely free to do literally anything . . . People were expecting nothing because the Who that people had known at that point had stopped. We just filled the gap and pushed it back into the same slot with a drummer who was quite obviously the completely wrong drummer. I'm not saying he's a bad drummer. I'm not saying he's a bad guy. I didn't dislike the guy, but I just felt he wasn't the right drummer for the Who. It's like having a wheel off a Cadillac stuck onto a Rolls-Royce. It's a great wheel but it's the wrong one."

Many cite the fact that Jones was on an equal cut rather than a wage – Ronnie Wood was on a retainer with the Stones – as another reason for Daltrey's dissatisfaction. Apart from playing one-offs at Live Aid in 1985 and the BPI Awards in 1988, the Who finally split (for the time being, anyway) in 1982, leaving Kenney in a much-improved financial position. After he and Jan divorced, Jones bought a 14th century farmhouse set in 70 acres of Surrey countryside, complete with helicopter landing pad now that he had his licence. When the adjoining 180-acre property went on the market, Jones set up the Hurtwood Park Polo Country Club in Ewhurst Green.

"I blame Steve Marriott," Jones told the *Glasgow Herald* in 1999. "One summer's afternoon before the Small Faces even had a name, we were rehearsing in a room above a London pub, and Steve said he'd got friends with horses in Essex, and we should bunk off out of the city and have a go. So we did. I was 14 [*sic*] I'd barely seen a horse, let alone ridden one, but I took to it like a duck to water. I've ridden ever since."

A dyed-in-the-wool Tory, remarried with four children, Jones nowadays rubs shoulders with the likes of Prince Charles along with his old mates from the rock aristocracy. It's a long way from Havering Street as the author saw for himself while conducting an interview with Jones at his clubhouse in 1998, watching the drummer present polo prizes to a bunch of chinless Hooray Henrys. "I want polo to be more accessible to the general public," Kenney told (who else?) *Hello!* magazine without any apparent sense of irony. "Many people are put off it because they think it is out of their reach. But it's affordable to people who have one or two horses."

As well as polo Jones continues to spend time and money unravelling the labyrinthine web around the Small Faces recordings and publishing as well as overseeing their ongoing legacy with McLagan. In 1991, Jones formed the Law with ex-Free and Bad Company singer Paul Rodgers, made up of various musicians, and achieved a *Billboard* hit with 'Laying Down The Law'. In 2005, the Jones Gang, with Robert Hart (ex-Bad Company) and Rick Wills, were more successful, achieving a surprise US number one with the AOR ballad 'Angel'.

"Kenney turned out to be incredibly shrewd," says Jan Jones. "When I first met him, he was the quietest shyest, least confident person you could possibly imagine. He had an easy, laid-back temperament. The others were terrible, at rehearsals they would shout, 'Shut up, Ken' because they couldn't hear themselves think when he was rat-tat-tatting away. But at the time people underestimated him and I think he always knew more than he let on. He started to wise up and it suited him to play the dumb drummer. He astonished me, I thought, 'Fair play to you Kenney, I wouldn't have thought you could have done it but you did.'"

"I think that Kenney developed as a person as well a musician," says his former brother-in-law Gary Osborne. "He'd gone from sweeping up on the pickle factory floor to being a proper pop star. He was very conscious of the fact that he'd had a scrappy education. Kenney was considered to be easy-going, almost a bit simple, not the brightest guy in the band. He didn't cause scenes, he wasn't a prima donna. The aggro if there was any aggro was between the others. Kenney's got a basic common sense and I think now they would consider he is the brightest guy out of the lot of them. He's confident, entrepreneurial, an interesting development."

The process of Ronnie Wood stepping out from behind the shadows of Rod Stewart was complete by the time he came to join the Rolling Stones. "Ron Wood was a fresh shot in the arm," Bill Wyman told Barbara Charone in 1976. "He added something new, different and exciting. We're not quite so pretty but much funkier now, much raunchier. New blood is good for the band. We're kickin' more now." While much was gained, something was lost. As a one-guitar band the Faces highlighted Wood's multi-faceted musicianship from slide, pedal steel, harmonica to plain old lead. Practising what Keith Richards calls "the ancient art of weaving", the twin-guitar Stones approach has resulted in Wood's abilities being submerged under the collective identity of 'being a Rolling Stone'.

With the Faces, there was a veneer of equality but in the Stones there was no mistaking who ran the show; Wood acting as an emollient between the competing egos of Jagger and Richards, particularly once Richards cleaned up his act. Whereas Stewart and Wood had an effective creative partnership, as Mick Taylor found out before him, it was nigh on impossible to break the lucrative Jagger-Richards songwriting hegemony.

Krissie was the first to fall by the wayside under her husband's upswing in fortunes. While Woody was away in Munich recording with the Stones, drug squad detectives raided the Wick and discovered traces of cocaine as well as Krissie and dressmaker friend Audrey Burgon crashed out together in the master bedroom. The pair were arrested and appeared at Kingston Crown Court in December on charges of possessing cocaine to which they pleaded not guilty and Krissie denied a further charge of possessing cannabis resin. The cannabis charge was dropped, and the two women were cleared of possessing cocaine following a retrial in April 1976. Four months later Ronnie and Krissie moved to Los Angeles and on October 30, their son Jesse James Wood was born there.

In March '78 Krissie filed for divorce, citing Ronnie's relationship with model (and eventually, second wife) Jo Howard who was expecting their first child, Leah. "To be honest Krissie couldn't handle everyday life," says Sandy Sarjeant who kept in touch after her marriage to Mac ended. "Ronnie knew that and he said that he'd always look after her no matter what. She did get maintenance money for Jesse but it wasn't an awful lot. Krissie ended up with the Wick Cottage but she had to sell that. She started selling off bits and pieces of Ronnie's that were in the stables garages. She was living on scrapings really."

Her reduced allowance was attributed to Ronnie's failed business investments, resulting in her moving into a small flat in Kings Road, Richmond. In 2003, Krissie put her issues with Ronnie aside to stand as proud parents when Jesse married Catherine 'Tilly' Boone, daughter of a Gloucestershire accountant. The couple's eldest child, Arthur, was named in honour of Jesse's beloved uncle.

Sandy Sarjeant: "One rainy Friday night, I was feeling nostalgic and I got in the car and just started driving and ended up in Richmond. I thought, 'I'll go and see Krissie.' I couldn't remember what number she lived at because it had been years since I'd been there but I found it. I rang the doorbell and Krissie's voice said, 'Hello.' I said, 'It's Sandy, Sandy Sarjeant.' There was a squeal at the other end and she buzzed me in, bless her. She was alone in the flat, there was no heating because she couldn't afford to pay the bill, the television had conked out and I just found it quite horrendous.

"I sat there for the rest of the night and we brought each other up to speed and told [each other] what was happening in our lives. I just felt incredibly sad because here was a girl who sometimes I could have murdered, a girl who sometimes drove me up the bloody wall, a girl I used to sometimes think, 'God you're so selfish.' But there was this other thing about Krissie that I always liked and when I did see her, I just wanted to shake her and say, 'For God's sake', you know? I had this completely different life, I was working up to six days a week to support four children whereas Krissie was still this social butterfly who turned up on people's doorsteps and would sort of camp out for the week or whatever. She hadn't moved on. She seemed healthy, she was not drinking or drugging, she hadn't been for a while and she had this younger boyfriend. That was the last time I saw her."

On June 11, 2005, Krissie was found dead, aged 57, of a suspected Valium overdose at an associate's west London home. She was in the process of selling her flat because she could no longer afford the mortgage and according to newspaper obituaries, apparently tried to find work in a supermarket, telling friends she had hit an "all-time low". Krissie was cremated at Mortlake Cemetery at a ceremony attended by 150 mourners including Ronnie, Rod, Kenney, and assorted former Faces women.

Ever since the death of his girlfriend Stephanie De Cort in 1964, Woody had become accustomed to seeing close friends and family slip away, including his brothers Art and Ted. "If there was a bad thing going on, Ronnie would try to avoid it, would put on his big smile, you know, 'Let's have some fun,'" says Russ Schlagbuam. "When Chuch died, Woody could not talk about it, he didn't want to know about something as dreadful as that."

During final rehearsals at Toronto's Crescent School for the Stones' '40 Licks' tour, Chuch Magee suffered a fatal heart attack on July 18, 2002, aged 54. "He died on his road case," says Charlie Fernandez who was about to fly out and meet up with his buddy. "Chuch died where he felt most comfortable, where he loved to be."

Charlie and Russ joined Chuch's widow Clare among the mourners at Magee's memorial service at the Messiah Lutheran Church in Marquette, Michigan. "The church was packed and I sat next to Tom Wright and his mother, Jan," says Russ. "They had driven all the way up from Birmingham, Alabama. Charlie and Suzie Fernandez were in the bench behind me and Charlie and I just held hands and tried to hold back the tears. The pastor talked about all the charity work Chuch and Clare did for the community. The life Chuch had there was completely opposite to the life he'd led on the road after all the years of self-abuse with the Faces and Stones. In the middle of the service Ronnie, Keith, Mick, Chuck Leavell and Darryl Jones got up, walked to the grand piano and played an acoustic version of 'Amazing Grace', with Woody on slide. It was very moving."

Still the 'new boy' in the Stones, advancing years failed to curb Ronnie's excessive lifestyle, and a poor business head ensured the riches he earned had a tendency to slip through his fingers. His ventures into the art world and the periodic call to get back on the road with the Stones have helped to restore the balance. Almost alone among rockers of his vintage, Woody plays up to the rock star cliché, dishevelled, craggy, prone to escorting ladies more tender of age (his second marriage ended in 2009 after 24 years) with repeated stints in rehab. As of writing, he is admirably clean, living with his Brazilian girlfriend in Surrey, and hosts a weekly digital radio show. His infectious zest for life is best summed up in the title of his latest album, *I Feel Like Playing*.

In 1979 Mac and Kim moved to California, settling into Keith Moon's old beach home at Victoria Point Road, Malibu. Woody wasn't far away. Facing a substantial tax bill he had sold the Wick – which Pete Townshend would eventually buy in the Nineties – and bought a house in Mandeville Canyon. That year Mac toured in the New Barbarians, a name suggested by Neil Young for an extracurricular Stones side project put together by Wood, featuring Keith Richards, Bobby Keys and a rhythm section of Stanley Clarke and Ziggy Modeliste. Mac played on Wood's third solo album *Gimme Some Neck* cut in LA that year utilising a familiar pool of musician friends, while the Barbarians and Ringo Starr appeared on *Troublemaker*, the first of two McLagan solo albums for Mercury, Rod Stewart's old label.

During the sessions McLagan and Wood were introduced to freebase cocaine, an epidemic that was hitting the wealthy Californian rock community. While Mac eventually managed to kick the habit, Ronnie entered a deep trough to the extent that by June 1981, when the Stones were preparing for a major US tour, he was told in no uncertain terms to sort himself out with an incentive of $500,000 to do the tour – but it would take some time. After trying out Chuck Leavell, the Stones hired McLagan for the tour, their longest to date with 50 shows in 28 cities which grossed over $36 million.

In '81 Mac released a second solo album *Bump In The Night* and formed his ongoing Bump Band. To make a living he moved into playing sessions including recordings by Renee Geyer, Bonnie Raitt, Jackson Browne, Bruce Springsteen, and Joe Cocker to name but a few of the many artists who have eagerly sought his services. He also toured with Bob Dylan, the Everly Brothers, David Lindley, Ronnie Wood, and Billy Bragg.

On May 3, 1993, from his home in Pasadena, by arrangement with the radio host, Mac called up the live *Rockline* show while Stewart and Wood were being interviewed to promote Stewart's *Unplugged . . . And Seated* collection, resulting in him being invited to become part of Stewart's touring band. The two men had barely spoken since the Faces' split and relations were not exactly improved whenever McLagan ventured a forthright opinion on the singer. When Mac's original Hammond B3 – stored during all this time with Stewart – was shipped from California to Texas, McLagan received the bill for the freight charges.

Mac remains close to Woody and has played on all his solo albums. "I realised when I was going back on things for the book that I should have been mad at Woody not Rod for the Faces split," he says, "but it's hard to stay angry with him for long."

The book in question, *All The Rage* – changed from Pete Townshend's original suggestion *Autobiography Of A Short Arse* – published in 1998 was a breezy, blunt and frequently hilarious traipse through McLagan's life, loves and laughs to that point and what it sometimes lacked in tact and diplomacy it made up for with affection. "It's been a life stuffed with tales of naughtiness and [this] chunky memoir coughs them up with relish . . ." wrote Peter Kane in his review for *Q*. "McLagan's penned a chirpy insider's portrait of some crazy times and even crazier people."

In 1994, tired of the smog, violence and earthquakes, Mac and Kim packed up and moved to Manor near Austin, Texas, where they soon became much-loved members of the local community. Mac continued to release albums with the Bump Band including *Best Of British* (1999), featuring speed skating cover star Alec McLagan. When not on the road, Mac was playing in the city's bars, an anecdote and a Guinness close at hand. Kim, still as lovely as ever, opened up a health and beauty parlour.

On August 2, 2006, Kim tragically died in an automobile accident in Travis County – a terrible shock as shown by the outpouring of sympathy from people who'd never known her in the condolence book opened on Mac's website. "Kim was already an angel," he posted days after the tragedy. "Now she has wings. We thank you so much for all your love." No tribute was more fitting than that paid by Charlie Fernandez: "Kim changed Mac's life and made him a better person. She brought out the good side of him and made him more patient than he knew he ever could be."

McLagan continues to reside in Texas, constantly on the road, recording and playing his Thursday night residency at the Lucky Lounge, Austin. "It's a rotten business in many ways," he reflects wearily. "If you're getting into music for the fun of it, that's fine but if you think you'll make lots of money out of it, think again! If I'd taken an accountancy course when I started out at 18, I might have been all right but then again if I'd treated it just as a business, I wouldn't have been on some great records. It shouldn't be about money but unfortunately the music business is set up for others to take advantage of those that don't know any better. That's the way it goes. Some people are just luckier than others."

During the *Rough Mix* sessions Ian Stewart and his wife Cynthia persuaded Ronnie Lane to see a doctor when he was exhibiting all the symptoms of multiple sclerosis. "Ronnie would wake up in the morning and his hand would be numb and he couldn't hold a pen, couldn't write," says Russ.

"He put it down to drink and drugs and everything else. His mother had MS but Ronnie never for a moment would admit that perhaps that's what it was."

The £10,000 advance for *Rough Mix* had sorted out Lane's financial plight and in 1977 Eric Clapton's manager Roger Forrester invited Ronnie and Slim Chance to be Clapton's support act around the UK and Europe. "Ronnie was still drinking heavily and the MS had started," says Russ. "He would get so drunk and obnoxious. He hated being a support act.

"I was getting homesick and I'd handed in my notice but Roger convinced me to stay on. Ronnie wasn't talking to me – he thought I'd taken sides with Clapton's road crew. Ronnie demanded loyalty. When he rang me at 3am in the morning, asking, 'Russell, this is Ronnie, I just want to know who's fucking side are you on?' that was the final straw. The next morning I'm checking out of my room, waiting for the lift, the doors open and it's Ronnie and Kate. There's this awkward silence and Ronnie pipes up, 'Just who do you work for?' In actual fact Roger Forrester had been paying my wages for the past few months.

"While we were in Europe I found out that Ronnie's storage space had been broken into and the mobile vandalised. They stole the video equipment and hacked through the cabling and stole the Studer and Revox [tape machines]. I didn't tell Ronnie until the tour ended – he was depressed enough already – so I stayed on in England until the insurance claim was settled."

After Lane was officially diagnosed, Pete Townshend convinced him and Kate to leave the Welsh wilderness and return to London where Ronnie could be among friends and receive proper treatment. Ronnie sold the farm and he, Kate, Alana, Luke and newborn son Reuben Jack Lane moved to a large house in east Twickenham. Mafalda Hall, the wife of respected promotions man Tony Hall, looked after Ronnie's bookings and in November 1979, a Townshend-produced single, 'Kuschty Rye' (a Romany expression meaning 'good gentleman'), appeared followed by an album, *See Me*, on the small Gem label the following year.

In 1981 Russ Schlagbaum returned to London from Ohio and started working for Townshend's Eel Pie operation. "Ronnie was in a very bitter, negative frame of mind," says Russ, "saying, 'I can't even drink myself to death.' He asked me to go back and work for him but I was with Pete."

That September Marriott and Lane reunited to record an album's worth of material on the LMS in Loughton, Essex with the tentative titles *The Mijits Strike Back* and *Majic Mijits*. They flew to New York to shop for a deal but no label was interested unless they were prepared to tour to promote it, an impossibility in view of Lane's worsening condition, and the tapes were shelved.*

At a low ebb, Ronnie walked out on Kate and was taken in by Boo Oldfield, a friend of the Faces' circle who lived in Kentish Town, north London. Attractive as well as compassionate, Boo curbed Lane's drink and drug intake and persuaded him to exercise and eat healthily to delay the onset of the disease. In early 1982, Ronnie and Boo flew to Florida for Ronnie to undergo experimental treatment. A ray of hope appeared when they'd read about the use of snake venom injections to arrest MS symptoms. However the practice, financed by Rolling Stones associate Freddie Sessler, ran counter to the United States Food & Drug Administration which shut the operation down shortly after their arrival. On top of which the treatment actually worsened Ronnie's condition.

A year on, Lane approached Eric Clapton with the idea of playing a benefit to raise money for ARMS (Action into Research for Multiple Sclerosis) to purchase a Hyperbaric Oxygen Decompression Unit that had made an improvement to his state. "Eric asked me to put a band together," Glyn Johns recalls, "and my original idea was to get Stu, Charlie Watts, maybe Bill [Wyman] and Kenney [Jones] but then it grew and grew. I started off by asking Stu and a few days later, he saw Jeff Beck and invited him to play. And once Jeff was on board, Jimmy Page offered to do it. And then Eric wanted to get Steve Winwood so all of these people came forward to help."

Advance rumours had Rod Stewart as being among the all-star line-up. "The first I heard about Rod playing," said Lane, "was when I read it in the papers. That was also the last I heard about it!" Stewart felt slighted at what he considered a deliberate exclusion, not just because of his former connection to Lane but because since the early Sixties his sister Peggy had been stricken with the disease, which eventually claimed her in 1985.

After the successful ARMS concert at the Royal Albert Hall on September 21, 1983, at which Ronnie was helped on to lead an emotional 'Goodnight Irene' finale, American concerts were undertaken, starting in Dallas. Says Johns, "I felt it would be better that rather than the money made from the American concerts being brought back into Britain that an ARMS research facility be established in America and that's what led to the office being set up in Houston."

* According to Lane's version of events Keith Richards loaned them an amount to finish the album but Marriott reputedly used the money to restart Humble Pie.

In late 1984, Lane left England and moved to Houston, Texas for treatment. Within a year it came to light that of the million dollars that had been invested into the ARMS America organisation a large amount of the funds had been misappropriated. "Ronnie spoke to the Attorney General in Texas," says Russ Schlagbaum, "and the case was going forward but the state of Texas had to investigate Ronnie as well and because charitable funds had been used to pay the rent on his apartment which was illegal, it had to be dropped or he'd have been prosecuted. I said, 'Holy shit, Ronnie, how do you get into these scrapes?'"

On December 12, 1985, Ronnie and a host of others in the rock world lost their dear friend Ian Stewart. Attending his doctor's surgery complaining of respiratory problems, Stu died of a heart attack, aged 47.

After living in Houston for a year, Lane moved to Austin where he was a welcome addition to the musical community. No longer able to play guitar and mostly confined to a wheelchair, he was backed by various bands, including a five-piece called the Tremors who featured Bobby Keys on occasion. At a Halloween party in 1987, Ronnie met Susan Gallegos, an electrologist of Hispanic–Native American origin, who became his third wife on April 9, 1988.

They lived in Susan's modest apartment, Ronnie's medical bills being covered by the likes of the Stones, Pete Townshend and Rod Stewart. In spring 1990 the Ronnie Lane band toured Japan with Mac playing keyboards.

Ian McLagan: "When Ronnie was living with Jo Rae Di Menno, who was his caregiver during those years in Houston [and is now my publicist], she got him exercising every day and so did I when I stayed with him and when he with me. Ronnie had been on a strict diet he wasn't supposed to eat wheat or dairy, and Jo Rae had him walking and he was doing really well . . . I came to rehearse here in Austin before we went to Japan and he'd been left strapped to his wheelchair with nothing but wheat crackers and cheese, the very stuff that weakened him.

"The Japanese tour wasn't a very pleasurable experience. Ronnie was not happy and Susan wasn't happy. He wasn't singing well and it was pretty awful. I wouldn't do 'Itchycoo Park' so he wasn't pleased with me and we left on bad terms but we made it up."

On April 20, 1991 Lane received the news that Steve Marriott had died in a fire at his home in Arkesden, Essex, aged 44. A year later Ronnie performed his last gig, singing 'Ooh La La' during Ronnie Wood's 'Slide On This' tour (with McLagan) at the Terrace, in Austin. In a poignant moment Wood sat in Lane's lap and kissed him on the cheek.

In 1994, when Mac and Kim moved from LA to Austin, McLagan discovered his old mate was moving to Trinidad, Colorado, a city lying approximately 200 miles to the south of Denver in the Rocky Mountains, with less humidity to affect his MS. It was also known as 'the Sex Change Capital of the World' thanks to a local doctor renowned for performing gender reassignment surgery – something that no doubt made Ronnie smile through his final days. His battle against the debilitating disease ended on June 4, 1997. He was 51.

"I saw Ronnie about a month before he died in the hospital in Trinidad," says Mac. "Susan thought it was serious and I flew out there and drove up to the hospital. He hadn't been well but he was quite chirpy and very funny. It was lovely. I went to their house and saw his bedroom and on the wall was that picture of his dad that's in *Spiritual Boy* [McLagan's album of Ronnie Lane songs]. He always had that on his bedroom wall.

"Ronnie came over for lunch about a month or so before he left Austin and it was about a month after I'd moved in. We couldn't lift him into the house because he went all stiff and we couldn't get him through the doors because his arms were sticking out. So we ended up taking him in his wheelchair out to the garage, which was full of packing cases and everything – it's now my studio – and we had lunch there. It was great. I said, 'Why did you ever leave the Faces?' He said, 'I don't know!'"

"When my band came to cut *Spiritual Boy* it was perfect because if he'd only come in the house there'd be no spirit but he'd been in this room. I put photographs all around the walls where everyone was sitting so they could picture him. It was kind of sweet."

"I'm glad I heard the news from Mac," Kenney Jones told Rupert Williams. "He called me up and said, 'Ronnie's gone.' Very tearful occasion . . . I used to speak to Ronnie a lot by phone and the sad thing is, towards the end, I couldn't have a conversation . . . When I used to phone, Sue would hold the phone to his ear and I'd say, 'Ronnie, I know you can't speak but this is what I think you'd like to ask me and this is my reply.' Sue used to say that he's beaming, he's smiling like crazy . . . and that's how it ended up."

CHAPTER 22

Simply Rod

"I'd say I was a crooner in the old fashioned style. It's smooth ain't it? . . . Well it makes a change, dunnit? Saying I'm a rock singer is really generalising."

— Rod Stewart, *Record Mirror*, 1972

"What we loved about Mick Hucknall was his voice range was just like Rod's in the Seventies . . . It's exciting to be on this path again. I hope Faces fans are as excited as we are."

— Ron Wood, quoted in press release, May 2010

O F the many people and places, and heroes and villains associated with the Faces' story, to borrow a line from the Beatles' 'In My Life', "some have gone and some remain". Don Arden continued to inspire fear and loathing among all who he encountered until his death from Alzheimer's in 2007. Shortly after a green plaque honouring Arden and the Small Faces was unveiled on the address in Carnaby Street where the whole saga began. Pulling the velvet rope was Kenney Jones. One hopes he saw the irony in that it was the same building where he and his fellow Small Faces were allegedly fleeced.

Andrew Oldham fought his personal demons throughout the Seventies and Eighties, relocating to Bogota, Columbia before finally becoming drug free, penning two entertaining autobiographical volumes *Stoned* and *2Stoned* of his life in the Fifties and Sixties with the odd detour beyond. He and Tony Calder unsuccessfully attempted to resurrect the Immediate label in the early Nineties.

Billy Gaff has retired from the music business and is now a globetrotter based in the South of France. He continued to manage Rod Stewart throughout the late Seventies and early Eighties until they parted painfully in 1982. Gaff sued the singer for £4 million for alleged wrongful termination of their business relationship but the following year he was forced to relinquish Stewart's publishing, recording, television and video rights as well as hand over an undisclosed sum. "When I finally split with Rod it was an emotional problem," says Gaff. "It was nothing to do with money. I was burnt out to be honest with you." Nevertheless, he and the similarly spurned Tony Toon used the tabloid press to vent their spleen. In 2003, Gaff was reported to be working on a candid Stewart biography with journalist Chris Hutchins. Nowadays, he is considerably more benign.

"Of all the shits I've met in the business, Rod is not one of them," Gaff states. "He could have gone solo long before the Faces split but he was incredibly loyal, much more loyal than he's ever given credit for. He'd never buy you a drink but when it came to songwriting he'd share the credits . . . I've had my ups and downs with Rod but one thing he's not is unfair, though," Gaff counters with a laugh, "not to his women."

After his time with the Faces and Rod, Gaff's management and publishing interests spanned John Cougar Mellancamp to Kajagoogoo singer, Limahl. "I've seen Woody and Kenney a few times since [the Faces] and we get on extremely well. I kept bumping into Woody in Dublin. Every time I saw him for an evening, I had to take three days off to recover. I ran into Mac in Adelaide in the Eighties. I was doing a lot of the Grand Prix circuits with McLaren at the time. That's the only time I've seen him. He was quite vile in his book but it's called rock'n'roll and nobody's ever terribly grateful for anything, you know."

Pete Buckland also left Stewart's orbit acrimoniously in 1982, moving on to work with Bow Wow Wow, Janet Jackson, Paul Young, TLC, the Eagles, Joni Mitchell and his current employer, Diana Krall. "Overall, the Faces was a fantastic experience for everyone that was involved from the musicians on down," Buckland says. "I still count Mac and Woody as friends. I haven't seen Kenney for bloody donkey's years but I know we're on good terms. It's a shame it just got to be the way it got because it was such fun for so long.

"I'm fortunate in as much as I've only ever worked with musicians or musical groups that I've really liked. Really, really good people. I couldn't do it otherwise, it would drive me bloody mad."

The other mainstays of the Faces' road crew carried on in the business; after the Eagles Richard Fernandez became tour manager for Bob Dylan and Tom Petty while younger brother Charlie looks after Jimmy Buffett, Joni Mitchell and Dan Fogelberg. Mickey Heyes worked for Billy Joel. John Barnes' whereabouts remain a mystery. Charlie Daniels, the Master Blaster, can be found in Massachusetts still taking pictures and checking out live music. Equally, Tom Wright lives in Michigan, continually photographing and documenting. His entertaining memoir, *Roadwork*, was published in 2007. At the time of writing he is working on a new book, "while all the music and good times I had with the Faces plays in my head".

Jeff Beck continues to be his own man, wilfully eclectic, releasing albums encompassing jazz-fusion to rockabilly and, on his last CD, instrumental versions of 'Nessun Dorma' and 'Over The Rainbow'. He and Stewart reunited for a US tour in the mid–Eighties but Beck lasted only six shows. "The whole audience was made up of blue rinse Vegas type women," he observed, "all sneering and leering at Rod's bum, you know. It was terrible."

After playing with Quicksilver Messenger Service, Nicky Hopkins returned to England in early 1971 to tour with the Rolling Stones. He resumed playing on recordings by rock's crème de la crème including John Lennon, George Harrison, the Stones and the Who, throughout the Seventies. Hopkins died on September 6, 1994, aged 50, in Nashville, Tennessee of complications from intestinal surgery. No better tribute can be paid to his talent than the vast treasury of important recordings that feature his playing.

Tony Newman resides in Las Vegas, three of his children being drummers.

"Mickey [Waller] has never bought me a drink in all the time I've known him, through three groups and all those years," Stewart told Penny Valentine in 1972, without any apparent hint of irony. "He's the only guy I know who comes out on Friday night with 30p for an evening out, he's a real character."

In 1978 Waller sued Stewart in the High Court for £6,000 unpaid royalties he claimed were owed to him for his work on *Smiler*. The claim was settled out of court. All was forgiven enough for Waller to be invited to play on Rod's 1980 album *Foolish Behaviour* although his work wasn't used. "I remember being at Rod's house in Windsor," Waller told John Gray in 1989, "and he said to me, 'It's all right for you being a drummer, you can go on until you're 70, but I can't.'" In the Nineties Waller took a law degree to recover royalties he believed were due to him and played with various blues bands but problems with alcohol hastened his death on April 29, 2008. He remains a most underrated drummer and the best to play behind Stewart.

Another musician from Rod's Mercury past to face him in court was Lindisfarne's Ray Jackson who claimed the mandolin hook he had written for 'Maggie May' was a fundamental part of the song's success and that he was therefore entitled to a composer's credit and royalties beyond the meagre £15 session fee he'd received in 1971. A spokesman for Stewart dismissed Jackson's claim as "mind-boggling", indicating that it was first brought up in the mid-Eighties, 14 years after the song was recorded. "Any contributions he [Jackson] may have made were fully paid for at the time as 'work-for-hire'."

By 2005 Jackson was forced to abandon any legal action against either Stewart or his publishers Warner Chappell when the cost of an insurance policy to cover him against losing in court (estimated to be over £100,000) was potentially as much any award for damages.

Martin Quittenton's royalties from 'Maggie May' alone presumably keep him in quiet fortitude. Gary Grainger was part of the Rod Stewart Band until 1981 and has continued in the industry, writing TV and radio theme music, alongside playing with various musicians including Kenney Jones.

Glyn Johns is still involved with production – mixing and mastering *Never Say Never* for Ian McLagan in 2008 and an archival live Thin Lizzy CD with Scott Gorham the following year. "I have four albums to do this year [2011] already," says Johns. "It's fair to say that I've done very little in the last few years but I have never lost the desire to make records, it's just the business I can't be bothered with."

Ron Nevison carved a highly successful career producing AOR bands. Jimmy Horowitz fought a long battle with the bottle and now lives in Texas, Jesse Ed Davis died of a heroin overdose aged 43 in Venice Beach on June 23, 1989. Lou Reizner died, aged 44, of stomach cancer, on June 26, 1977.

Ian Ralfini and Martin Wyatt continued to prosper in the music industry; Ralfini moved to the States working for Atlantic and EMI and is now president of Blue Note. He was recently awarded an OBE for services to the music industry. Wyatt has his own publishing company and looks after business affairs for Fleetwood Mac and the Moody Blues. John Peel's legacy as a much loved, eternally idiosyncratic broadcaster (and Faces fan) has outlasted his untimely passing from a heart attack on October 25, 2004. No DJ was ever more deeply mourned.

Gary Osborne moved from session vocalist to successful songwriter – penning English words for Kiki Dee's 'Amoreuse', co-writing several Elton John hits and the lyrics to Jeff Wayne's *The War Of The Worlds*.

"Because I now chair the Ivor Novello Awards I kind of engineered the Small Faces to receive an Outstanding Contribution to Popular Music Award [on May 30, 1996]," says Gary. "I knew that the guy at the Performing Rights Society who had that decision in his power was a Faces fan so I only had to say, 'Well, how about the Small Faces?' Obviously it was too difficult for Ronnie Lane to attend so Kenney invited Ron Wood to represent him with Ronnie's brother, Stan. I hadn't seen Woody for 10 years. We shook hands and he whispered, 'I think we have you to thank for this,' in my ear. I also ensured that Rod got a Lifetime Achievement Award [in 1999]." At the age of 72, Stan Lane still runs an Essex market stall and restores cars and trucks, an East End character through and through.

Key venues where the Faces played like the Marquee, the Edmonton Sundown, the Eastown Theater in Detroit, Boston Tea Party and Fillmores East and West have long since gone. Similarly, the digital age has seen the closure of many of the studios where the band recorded; De Lane Lea is now a Sainsbury's supermarket, Morgan a block of flats and Olympic closed its doors in 2009, evidently to become an independent cinema. The Lane Mobile Studio (LMS) has been restored and is still in operation. In 1998, Rod Stewart bought Stargroves, Mick Jagger's mansion, for £2.5 million. He never lived there, however, and sold it a few months later as part of his divorce settlement from second wife Rachel Hunter.

Of the Meher Baba community, Billy Nicholls is a successful songwriter and continues to release well-crafted solo albums. His songs have been covered by Roger Daltrey, Leo Sayer and Phil Collins and he acts as musical director/backing vocalist for the Who and Pete Townshend. Mike McInnerney produces illustration for a range of media clients, publishing and exhibiting work both nationally and internationally. Kate McInnerney resides in Wales.

After her split from Ronnie, Sue Lane moved to LA where she married musician Steve Humphreys in the Seventies. She has since remarried and teaches drama at the Meher Baba School in Walnut Creek, California. "Ronnie really was a unique and special person," she says. "He had a deep beauty that I think came from his connection to God or the Divine that he was mostly unconscious of. It shone through in his songs of course. He was a seeker. I am very grateful for finding Meher Baba with Ronnie."

Dee Harrington briefly married ex-Thin Lizzy guitarist Brian Robertson, who also dated Krissie Wood, worked in the music business managing Climie Fisher, had a son and now owns and operates a thriving Pilates business in west London. Jan Jones left the rat race and moved to Gloucestershire and is now a grandmother, as is Sandy Sarjeant who lives quietly in west London. "I look back on those times and I think, we were kids, big kids," says Sandy. "[It was] a great life but it's not natural for people to be thrown together like that and expect that everything's going to be wonderful. But then here I am, at 62," she adds, laughing, "and I don't really give a shit about it all anymore anyway."

And what of Rod?

Rod Stewart went on to become one of the most famous and successful rock singers ever, selling well over 100 million records – and still counting – by the time of writing. Stewart's personal life involved a succession of leggy blondes, four of whom bore him children,* and became as note-worthy as the music. After the end of his second marriage, when asked if he would remarry, he remarked, "Instead of getting married again, I'm going to find a woman I don't like and just give her a house." But while his fans remained loyal, he became a press pariah in the process, critics feeling he had irreparably damaged his credibility with his choice of songs, sound and image. Stewart even conceded as much in an interview with the *LA Times* in 1989: "In those days, I didn't really concentrate on singing. I was definitely more concerned with showing off the anatomy than in trying to prove my vocal prowess . . . 'Do Ya Think I'm Sexy?' hurt my rock'n'roll credibility, that's for sure . . ."

By the early Eighties, after a decade of phenomenal success, his career had slightly ebbed, which is when rumours of a Faces reunion started to appear. In a *Sun* newspaper interview from August '83, Kenney Jones claimed that the ARMS benefit concert was originally born out of a drunken evening with Stewart when the pair discussed plans for a Faces reformation.

Considering Bob Geldof's powers of persuasion, it was surprising the Faces' coming together didn't happen at Live Aid in 1985. Regardless, on May 14, 1986, the *Evening Standard* confirmed the reunion was on, amid mutterings that it might have been motivated by sluggish ticket sales for Stewart's concert at Wembley Stadium on July 5 – the climax of his first British tour in three years.

Ian McLagan: "We had about two days of rehearsals – or should I say drinking – about a couple of hours each but with no Rod. He only turned up to the run-through the day before [the show]." It was the first time Stewart and Lane had seen each other since 1973.

---

* Kimberly (born 1979) and Sean (1980) to Alana Hamilton; Ruby (1987) to Kelly Emberg; Renée (1992) and Liam (1994) to Rachel Hunter; and Alistair (2005) and Aiden (2011) to Penny Lancaster.

Backstage at Wembley, Rod, Woody and Kenney were interviewed by MTV. Amid the gurning and clowning between Stewart and Wood, Rod allowed himself one brief moment of seriousness. "One of the reasons we're here tonight is for Ronnie Lane," Rod said, "because as I've said so many times really he was the spirit behind the Faces. It wasn't us, it was Laneole." When asked if the event was successful, would they consider touring America, he replied, "Yeah, I'm up for it, I'd love to."

As the grand finale before 66,000, Rod brought on the other four original Faces, with Bill Wyman, standing in on bass for Lane, who was helped to a stool by his Texan carer Jo Rae Di Menno to a crowd chorus of *"we love you Ronnie, oh yes we do . . ."* With Stewart's band beefing up the sound, they performed '(I Know) I'm Losing You' (in which an extremely uncomfortable looking Lane was coaxed into handling the "mm mmm mmm" harmony), 'Stay With Me', 'Twistin' The Night Away', and 'Sweet Little Rock 'n' Roller'.

It was almost like old times with Chuch handing Wood his Zemaitis Disc Front guitar and slide except this time there was no bar on stage.

Ian McLagan: "After the show Rod told us, 'Don't go anywhere, we've got this party.' We got on this bus – Bill, Kim and I, Ronnie and Jo Rae and Woody and Jo – we were only going to another part of the Wembley complex. We got there and we weren't allowed in because our names had not been left on the door. I didn't see Rod again for some years after that."

The concert raised a generous £25,000 for the MS research fund. The following month a spurious story ran in the *Mirror* saying the Faces were about to embark on a world tour with Jones being quoted, "We will be playing absolutely everywhere, and all the money will go to Ronnie Lane's multiple sclerosis campaign. The tour should begin early next year, although Rod is trying to persuade us to start off in the Far East in November."

If the world tour had started in the Pacific then Tetsu Yamauchi might well have reappeared out of obscurity. After the Faces split and the aborted album session in 1976, he returned to Japan and continued in music, releasing an album *Tetsu And The Good Times Roll Band* and in the Eighties playing with the Easy Music Band and OPE. Through the mid to late Nineties, he was part of the Kamadoma-Poly Breath Percussion Orchestra who after various changes shortened their name to Poly Breath Percussion Band.* All through this time Yamauchi invariably kept a low profile – a state

---

* For a more detailed examination of Yamauchi's pre and post Faces recorded activities, consult http://www.the-faces.com/tetsu/index.html

of affairs that continues to this day. "Whenever I'm in Japan, which is about every two years or so I always ask around if people have seen Tetsu and yeah, he's been seen," says Pete Buckland. "No one seems to know completely what he's up to but I hope he's well, he was a particularly nice guy."

"When the Stones were on tour in Japan Tetsu showed up and Woody didn't recognise him initially," says Gary Grainger. "Apparently he was a lot older. And Woody said you were the same age as us and Tetsu said 'No, I lied!'"

According to Wood, in a 2004 newspaper interview, "Last time I saw [Tetsu], he tried to punch me out. He's torn between religion and alcohol. He is probably the only tramp in Japan!"

It was not until the 1993 BRIT Awards at London's Alexandra Palace on February 16 where Rod received an Outstanding Contribution honour that the next Faces reunion occurred. Rehearsals at John Henry's in north London were interrupted with 'Going To The Pub', in this case, the Balmoral Castle on Caledonian Road.

With Wyman again on bass, they closed the ceremony with a ragged 'Stay With Me' and 'Sweet Little Rock 'n' Roller', although the UK broadcast went off the air before the latter. As an added surprise for Rod the organisers asked Long John Baldry to present him with his award. Stewart never forgot the debt he owed his mentor, who had relocated to Vancouver, Canada where he continued his musical adventures and moved into doing television voiceovers. Baldry died on July 21, 2005, aged 64, of a lung infection.

Ian McLagan: "When we got back together for the BRIT Awards we agreed to reconvene and go through what there was of the Faces' unreleased tracks at Woody's studio in Ireland, which is where I mixed 'Open To Ideas'. But Rod never arrived. His line was, 'I never promised I was going to Ireland.'"

By the early Nineties, the Faces had received their due as a touchstone for the new breed of swaggering rock'n'roll revivalists into rhythm 'n' booze including the Georgia Satellites, the Replacements, Dogs D'Amour, Guns 'N Roses, the Quireboys and the Black Crowes to list the more prominent examples.

With their name also being dropped as an influence by some of the mid-Nineties Britpop bands and Rod's reputation going some way to being rehabilitated thanks to the likes of British author Nick Hornby extolling the virtues of his early Seventies work, the timing was perfect for a Faces tour. The fact that the well-received *Unplugged . . . And Seated*, featuring Ronnie Wood, mainly consisted of his best work from that period didn't hurt either. In the autumn of 1994, Rod told fanzine *Smiler* that he and Jones had gone to dinner on September 15 to discuss the matter but with Wood heavily committed to the Stones' 'Voodoo Lounge' tour, it would definitely take place after his own tour due to begin the following May. An impromptu reunion occurred at Stewart's concert in Dublin on December 6, 1995, with McLagan already part of Stewart's touring band, Wood and Jones as guests and Carmine Rojas from Rod's band on bass. However, by early 1996, when a tour was scheduled to happen, all had gone quiet again.

When asked by John Gray about the low estimation in which Stewart had held the Faces during his 'Beverly Hills phase' Rod conceded, "As the years go by you grow up a little bit and I've realised how good they were. They were badly good! . . . We were never great on record, a great live band, but I don't think we ever captured it in the studio . . .

"I think there's more of an audience for it now than there probably was two years ago. I say that because I went to see Woody play on his ['Slide On This'] solo tour and the Faces' songs went down better than the Stones things he did."

The passing of Ronnie Lane brought the Faces into sharp focus for Stewart. Having mostly given up writing his own material – astounding when considering the sheer quality of his early work – as a tribute to Laneole, on his 1998 album *When We Were The New Boys*, he covered 'Ooh La La' which entered the UK Top 20 that same year. For some Faces observers the irony was overwhelming. "I just remember thinking, 'Wait a minute, Rod was running this song down in the studio at the time and didn't want to sing it,'" says Russ Schlagbaum. "Then years later he says it's one of the greatest songs ever written . . ."

Back in 1991 Stewart had made news when the tabloid press conjectured whether he would have to cancel a world tour because of a viral infection that affected his vocal cords. In May 2000, Rod was diagnosed with thyroid cancer for which he underwent treatment in LA that same month. The surgery was successful but it affected that distinctive voice and by his own admission it was touch and go whether he would be able to sing again. "I seriously considered becoming a landscape gardener," was Stewart's flippant reaction. After painstakingly re-learning to sing, his ability to belt out rockers at the top of his range over a loud backing band was somewhat compromised.

In 1974, Stewart had told *Record Mirror*, "I'm lucky in that there aren't many things I can't sing." When asked if he would consider moving into the Sinatra league he groaned, "Oh no, I haven't got the voice have I? I've got to sing rock'n'roll otherwise I'm lost. I don't want to do that anyway."

Time makes fools of us all and in 2002, leaving Warners after 25 years and signing with Clive Davis' J Records (distributed through Sony), Stewart released the first instalment of *The Great American Songbook*, a collection of interpretations of classic standards from the pens of Irving Berlin, Cole Porter and the Gershwins.

It became an unexpected success; reaching number four on the *Billboard* album chart (eight in the UK) and paving the way for a further four (to date) albums of similar interpretations which were equally successful (the third volume alone sold 200,000 in its first week of release in late 2004).

Although his reinvention as a pinstriped Vegas lounge crooner appeared at odds with his previous devil-may-care, booze and blondes rock star image, on the threshold of 60 Rod still entertained the notion of a Faces reunion with either Bill Wyman or Carmine Rojas to fill Ronnie Lane's considerable shoes.

Mac had other ideas. "Glen Matlock is my first choice [to play bass] if ever there will be a Faces reunion . . ." McLagan told Steve Gardner in October 2000, "which is so unlikely that Queen Victoria may come back and rule England again . . . Ronnie Lane was a fine bass player. He never rated himself, but he played so melodic and solid . . . He [Matlock] loves Ronnie Lane's playing. And that was one of the things we talked about the first day we met and it's something I always remembered."

While Faces fans and Matlock waited for the Empress of India to resume her throne, the Faces' reputation was enshrined with two important McLagan-compiled archive releases for reissue specialists Rhino Records. The first, *Good Boys . . . When They're Asleep* – from another of Ronnie Lane's favourite sayings – was released in 1999, and featured the previously unreleased 'Open To Ideas' from the final Faces sessions. With a generous playing time of nearly 80 minutes, it superseded previous Faces compilation available, the poorly compiled *Snakes And Ladders* (1976), and *The Best Of The Faces* (1977) and redressed the bias towards Stewart with three Ronnie Lane vocals and 'Ooh La La'.

At that point Rhino were reluctant to green light a full-blown Faces retrospective but with the groundswell of interest surrounding the band, its members and its legacy, a four-CD set, produced by McLagan, appeared in 2004 with, as the result of a competition, the self-referential title *Five Guys Walk Into A Bar . . .* The 67 tracks spanning 1969–75 encompassed the band's single A & B-sides, album tracks, studio out-takes, BBC sessions, and rehearsal and live tracks – but arranged in scattershot order. "I did arrange them [chronologically] at first," Mac wrote in his breezy intro, "but listening to the songs in the order we recorded them was about as interesting to me as reading a phone book." Fair point, it was his party and he could compile how he wanted although the juxtaposition was sometimes jarring – the poignant mood established by 'Glad And Sorry' intruded on by a lo-fi run through of 'Shake, Shudder, Shiver' from an early Faces rehearsal. But then as McLagan pointed out in his notes, thanks to the digital age, "You're welcome to play them in any order you like."

If McLagan's disdain for chronology was refreshing, his choices – or more to the point, omissions – were sometimes questionable. 'Tell Everyone', 'Memphis', 'Devotion' and the unavailable-on-CD alternate single version of 'Had Me A Real Good Time' were left out at the expense of no less than four versions of 'Miss Judy's Farm' and an abysmal quality recording of 'Too Bad' from a 1972 Tampa, Florida show.

Still the set, with its 62-page book of photos, essays and tributes, sounded superb with much to savour and was well received with *Mojo* magazine awarding it 'Best Box Set Of 2004' while Stephen Erlewine of the online *All Music Guide* went out on a limb, saying, "There has never been a better box set . . . There has never been a box that captures an artist so perfectly, nor has a box set taken greater advantage of unreleased and rare material, to the point where it seems as essential and vital as the released recordings."

During 2004 and early 2005 there were several partial reunions following Stewart's gruff insistence that "There will never, never be a Faces reunion, Ronnie Lane is dead and that's the end of it." In May 2004, Jones and Wood were surprise onstage guests for the encore of McLagan's gig at the Mean Fiddler (aka LA2) in London. Three months later Wood and McLagan played with Stewart at the Hollywood Bowl. In March 2005 McLagan guested with Wood's band at Shepherd's Bush Empire, which also featured Jones on drums for the final encore.

On June 11, 2008 Stewart, now a CBE, announced that the surviving Faces were discussing a possible reunion, performing at least one or two concerts with plans to record. When interviewed for BBC digital station 6 Music the following month, McLagan said, "We're hoping to get together later this year to play and then we may have some news, but I want it to happen, badly . . . Rod hasn't wanted to do it for a long time. He didn't see the need in it but I think he really wants to now." With the band's 40th anniversary looming, on November 15, Jones and Wood, joined by McLagan the following day, started four days of rehearsals in Bermondsey, where it all originally started, "just to check if they can remember the songs." Stewart turned up for just the one run-through on the 18th.

"When we rehearsed in 2008, Rod was talking about bringing in another guitarist," says McLagan. "He wanted to get Jim Cregan in but Ronnie doesn't need it, we've never needed another guitar player."

However, as hopes intensified, in January 2009, a Stewart spokesperson scotched them with a statement via *Billboard*: "There are no plans for a Faces tour this year." Reports started to filter out as to why. One had it that Stewart insisted that certain songs be played in different keys to accommodate his voice. Considering that, for example, on 'Stay With Me', Wood plays slide in open tuning this would have been difficult, thereby robbing the songs of what made them special in the first place. Others suggested it had to do with revenue, particularly how it would be divided.

On October 25, 2009, billed as the Faces, Mac, Kenney and Woody got together for the PRS For Music Members Benevolent Fund at the Royal Albert Hall with Bill Wyman on bass, Andy Fairweather-Low (guitar), Paul Carrack (keyboards) and singer Mick Hucknall who came to fame in the Eighties with his soul lite, million-selling outfit Simply Red.

Among the family and friends present was Sandy Sarjeant: "Lee phoned me up saying they were doing this thing and Mac had told him, 'Please bring your mum.' I really wasn't in the mood but I went because I just thought, 'Well, how often do you get asked to go and there's no reason why I can't.'"

Sandy and Lee took their places in the box that had been reserved for Mac's friends, including John Pidgeon and Glen Matlock. "During the interval," said Sandy, "Glen leaned across and said to me, 'When you lived in Kensal Green, I used to be on my bike with my mates and somebody would say, "Ian McLagan's come round to pick up Sandy Sarjeant" and we'd all cycle round there.' When Mac, Kenney and Woody came on, I wasn't expecting anything but they were absolutely great. It was the sound, I'd forgotten what the sound was like."

The brief three-song set featured guest vocals from Carrack ('Cindy Incidentally'), Fairweather-Low ('Ooh La La') and Hucknall ('Stay With Me'). When a cry of 'Where's Rod?' rang out, Wood shot back, "That's what we want to know." At the end, PRS For Music chairman Ellis Rich presented the band with a Lifetime Achievement Award. *Classic Rock* magazine sent along reviewer Ian Fortnam whose "inner tartan scarf was holding out for a tearful reunion of Ronnie, Mac and Kenney with dear old Rod the Mod".

He and many others could only be disappointed. In a waspish review, wittily headlined 'Holding Back The Jeers' (a play on the Simply Red hit 'Holding Back The Years'), Fortnum observed, "And then, the world goes momentarily supernova as the riff to 'Stay With Me' rends the firmament in twain . . . but who is this we espy trotting sure-footedly toward the microphone? We clutch our chest as our popping eyes threaten to dislodge our misty spectacles, for it is none other than Mick Hucknall, and unless a sniper intervenes he's going to start singing. Which he does; he sings quite well actually, but he's no Rod Stewart. But it's not his fault, Rod should be here. What excuse can he possibly have? Surely three songs wouldn't kill him."

The Albert Hall appearance was adjudged enough of a success for an announcement to be made on May 25, 2010 that the Faces would be reforming – with Hucknall and Matlock – to perform at the inaugural Vintage at Goodwood festival at the Goodwood Estate in West Sussex via a rhetorical press release.

Ronnie Wood: "We got together to receive a PRS Lifetime Achievement award last year and very simply the magic was still there. Playing with the boys again just felt right so we thought, 'Well, why not?' It's exciting to be on this path again and I hope that the Faces' fans are as excited as we are – I'm just really looking forward to seeing them this summer – bring it on!"

Kenney Jones: "When we realised at the PRS Awards we hadn't played a live gig since 1975 [*sic*] we just couldn't believe it! The timing is just right, we can feel the excitement and we cannot wait to be back onstage playing to a live audience again. Expect the classics and also some incredible guests when we get back on the road, it's going to be lots of fun."

Ian McLagan: "Frustrated Faces fans can finally feel the heat as Ronnie Wood, Kenney Jones and me hit the stage with Mick Hucknall and Glen Matlock fanning the flames!"

Hucknall and Matlock certainly fanned the flames – in fact the inclusion of the flame-haired singer was enough to drench them in petrol, judging by the reaction in the media, websites and fan forums with one wag dubbing them 'Cod Stewart & The Red Faces'.

Born June 8, 1960 in Denton, Lancashire, Hucknall was too young to have properly experienced the Faces first time round although he was a fan of the music. "I know this is a bit of weird one," he admitted, "but I had a poster of the Faces on my wall when I was 11 years old."

Four days after the announcement, Rod Stewart was appearing at London's 02 Arena. When introducing its one rock'n'roll moment, 'Stay

With Me', he announced, "You know what I saw on the TV the other day? There's gonna be a Faces reunion without me. Mick Hucknall of Simply Red is the new lead singer." Whether Stewart was stating this as a point of fact or trying to stir a reaction, a large section of the crowd started to boo in sympathy. "He's a great little shouter," he insisted. "Give them a chance, I'll get back there some time."

One Faces project Stewart did get involved with was *Faces 1969–1975*, another in the series of limited edition rock photography books published by Genesis Publications. The book was compiled as a lavish illustrated account of the band's history with memorabilia and first-hand recollections from the ex-members, and signed by Wood, McLagan and Jones with a foreword by Wood's pal, Slash. With a retail price of around £300, one wonders what proportion of the aging tartan hordes could forego that month's mortgage payment to afford one.

At a press conference on August 4 to announce a hastily scheduled warm-up gig at the British Music Experience two days before Goodwood, Hucknall was quick to point out that the door had been left open for his predecessor if he so desired: "People don't understand how high Rod sings. I'm known for hitting high notes but this boy is up there all the time, yet the miracle of Rod's voice is it sort of sounds deep. I am standing in for the great man but if he wants to pop down and have a sing-song, I'll stand on the side of the stage any time." When asked about the rumour that Rod wanted a lion's share of the profits, Wood snorted, "Oh yeah, he made us an offer we could refuse, very easily! Silly things get in the way, but we're still pals. I talk to him on the phone. It was all happening in rehearsals and then there'd be some stumbling block, red tape, commitments; we just got fed up putting it on the back burner. The flame was still burning: it never went out on the Faces."

On August 11 a Q&A was held before the 75-minute warm-up at the 02. Like many critics present, Rick Pearson, reviewing for the London *Evening Standard*, had his knife sharpened: "Last night's show at the BME was as much an audition as it was a gig: could Hucknall really pull this off? From the opening line of 'Miss Judy's Farm', the answer was resounding: yes. Unveiling a vocal with more gravel than a driveway, Hucknall's rock'n'roll makeover was startling. If you closed your eyes . . . it could almost have been Stewart circa 1975. The rest of the Faces . . . were authentically shambolic throughout. Endings were botched and verses missed. Nothing, however could derail old-time rock'n'roll numbers like 'Cindy Incidentally' and 'Stay With Me'. If this was a musical audition, the Faces (and Hucknall) passed with flying colours." Two days later they closed the first night of the Goodwood Festival with Ronnie's eldest son Jesse playing additional guitar. Woody's five minute solo slide spotlight was the show-stopper, and now that he was in his own words "clean and serene", it sounded sharper than ever.

Rod fans and Faces purists inevitably continued to carp but then sacred cows in rock'n'roll are a dying breed. Brian May and Roger Taylor are shameless enough to tour without a retired John Deacon by adding Paul Rodgers – ironically, Stewart's vocal hero, calling themselves Queen. Pete Townshend and Roger Daltrey tour as the Who with four others onstage. Ray Manzarek and Robbie Krieger took a version of the Doors out with Cult singer Ian Astbury until they were sued by a naturally indignant John Densmore, while rumours of a Led Zeppelin tour without Robert Plant were buoyant in the wake of their reunion concert at London's 02 in 2007.

Without the creative engine of Ronnie Lane and Rod Stewart – a fundamental part of the band's dynamic – it stretches credibility to use the name 'Faces'. But then in an age where record sales have declined and the money lies in live appearances, it's easy to see the rationale behind it. 'Ronnie Wood & Friends' or the 'Ian 'Mac' McLagan All-Stars' doesn't translate into ticket sales and there's no one who deserves a substantial reward for his services to rock'n'roll more than Mac.

But then money was only a small consideration behind what made the Faces so great, at least in the beginning when, just over 40 years ago, they came together in that dingy rehearsal space and unleashed their unbridled, good-time brand of boozy bonhomie on an unsuspecting but welcoming world.

As of writing a Faces tour with special guests is planned to commence in January 2011. "It was a jolly joy ride," says McLagan of the band's legacy. "It was fun at least until Ronnie Lane left and then it was a different sort of fun and then it fizzled out. It ran its course but now the phoenix shall rise from the ashes and all those who wish to play step forward."

Epilogue

Saturday, September 5, 2015; a field in Surrey attached to a polo club. After years of rumours, an expectant crowd of 5,000 are about to get the closest they ever will to a Faces "reunion". The road leading to this hotly anticipated moment has been long and frequently potholed with unexpected obstacles.

Over the summer of 2011, during a run of 'Faces' festival shows featuring Mick Hucknall in the UK, Holland, Belgium and Japan, frequent assurances were made – not least by Hucknall himself – that the door was ajar if Rod wished to reclaim his place centre stage. Stewart dropped encouraging hints, but when it seemed that schedules were clear and the planets were aligned, nothing happened. Stewart continued to blame Wood. "It's something that I would want to do," he told rollingstone.com, "but it's getting a commitment from Ronnie who is hanging onto what the Stones are going to do. He'll suddenly say, 'Hey, let's tour next week!' I'll say, 'Hold on Ronnie, I've got commitments for the next year.' If we all sat around and said, 'Let's do it next summer, or let's do it for charity' or whatever reason, I would do it. It's not totally ruled out."

Rod's prevarication over the Faces did little to affect his pre-eminence. His concerts continued to sell-out, adding to a personal fortune estimated at upwards of £350 million, with album sales totalling over 100 million. In October 2011, it was announced that Random House had bagged the rights to his autobiography, set for 2012 publication. "I thought long and hard before committing to write my book," Stewart said via a press release. "It is a funny old thing telling my life story but I truly intend to hold nothing back. I've had quite a life, known some extraordinary people and had some amazing experiences. I've waited all this time, until my 50th year in the business and realize I can no longer put it off. Forget skeletons in the closet; this one's going to be socks and knickers under the bed."

Rod: The Autobiography was predictably a light, breezy read including brief, tongue-in-cheek chapters that concentrated on topics closely associated with the Stewart legend – barnet, cars and a love of trains and Scottish football. In parts, it heavily relied on previously published accounts. However, this was forgivable thanks to Rod's impish humour and the odd nugget of new info which included the puncturing of several commonly-held stories such as his employment as a gravedigger. He also admitted to embellishing the circumstances surrounding his brush with Brentford FC, confirming he never signed as an apprentice footballer.

In other selected quirks, he moved the year he lost his virginity at Beaulieu jazz festival forward to 1961, credited short-lived Beck Group bass player Doug Blake for inspiring his familiar stage move of flinging microphone stands in the air, and revealed that his remodelling of 'Street Fighting Man' (on *An Old Raincoat . . .*) was originally worked up from a version of Little Richard's 'The Girl Can't Help It'. "For no particular reason I started singing 'Street Fighting Man' over the top of it, and we took it from there."

He expressed mixed emotions regarding the Faces: "On a good night, the Faces were something special. On a bad night, we were bloody awful. But with the Faces, being bloody awful could sometimes be even more special than being good . . . while it worked – God, it was brilliant." He also confirmed the perception of an edge to his and Ian McLagan's personal dynamic: "I always sensed there was an undercurrent, something that prevented us from relaxing entirely in each other's company." Rod realised the band's cocaine consumption was a problem when after the triumphant Sunderland gig in April 1973, beside the pitch at Sunderland Football Club, Wood showed him the passage admitting daylight where his nasal septum used to be. Suppositories containing the devil's dandruff became the quick fix in preserving Rod's voice and Woody's beak.

To celebrate Rod's show business anniversary and to promote his latest album *Time*, a 90-minute, BBC *Imagine* documentary entitled *Rod Stewart: Can't Stop Me Now* was broadcast on July 9, 2013. The special was hard viewing in parts, not least due to presenter Alan Yentob's obsequious manner, but made worthwhile by the inclusion of some excellent rare footage. This included clips from the long-thought-lost *Rod The Mod* film, directed by Francis Megahy, shown once on British television in 1965 and recently excavated from the vaults of the British Film Institute. These remarkable excerpts showed the 19-year-old star-in-waiting, only weeks after joining Long John Baldry's Hoochie Coochie Men, as well as on the soccer pitch and performing at the Marquee, Eel Pie Island and the Manor House pub, north London.[*]

Researcher Lorna Lithgow, whose diligence resulted in the film being

---

[*] The whole film was shot over Easter weekend 1964 – hence its alternative title *An Easter With Rod*.

restored, revealed: "When we travelled to interview Rod in LA, we presented him with the film. Viewing this footage for the very first time, Rod was visibly emotional, watching himself as a young man finding his feet in life and seeing his much missed mum and dad interviewed in their sweet shop on the Archway Road where he grew up."

Elsewhere, family members talked on camera, including Rod's adopted daughter Sarah Streeter, with whom he had made a rapprochement. Rod and Ronnie were filmed at Stewart's house recounting their back pages; the first meeting at the Intrepid Fox, the Jeff Beck Group and Faces days. Harking back to Rod's folkie past, they busked a version of the traditional 'Worried Man Blues'. It was quite evident that the years had not diminished the pair's blood brotherhood.

On December 7, 2011 it was officially announced that the Faces – together with the Small Faces – were to be jointly inducted into the Rock'n'Roll Hall of Fame at the 27th annual ceremony in Cleveland, Ohio. Other artists being honoured that year included Guns N' Roses, the Red Hot Chili Peppers, the Beastie Boys, and Donovan.* After years of making snide comments about the nebulous, corporate institution, Mac expressed his ambivalence to rollingstone.com when first hearing the news.

"I was not happy that the Small Faces and the Faces were lumped together . . . You know, the Small Faces was such a different band than the Faces. I know three of us are the same, but when you take Steve Marriott out, it's a very different band. But in the end, I'm knocked out that Steve Marriott and Ronnie Lane, as well as Kenney Jones and I will be honoured . . . It's a damn big deal. It's going to be fun. I tell you, with the Chili Peppers, Guns N' Roses and the Faces . . . Look out, there's going to be some room-wrecking."

On April 13, 2012, Mac, Woody and Kenney appeared at the newly opened Rock'n'Roll Hall of Fame and Museum's Library and Archives, giving a press conference as well as signing copies of Genesis Publications' photo tome *Faces: 1969–75*. (Wood later revealed that Stewart's over-protective lawyers prevented Rod from adding his signature to the print run.)

The following evening, the ceremony itself was held at Cleveland's Public Auditorium. The band, in both guises, were represented by Ron

* Faces producer, Glyn Johns, was among those receiving an Award for Musical Excellence.

Wood, Ian McLagan, Kenney Jones and Mollie Marriott in place of her father Steve. Curiously, Ronnie Lane remained unrepresented. The induction speech was handled by 'Little' Steven van Zandt. "Not many bands get two lives," he announced. "In this case I'm sure it helped having not just one, but miraculously two of the greatest white soul singers in the history of rock and roll . . . After all is said and done, both the Small Faces and the Faces had one thing very much in common – for a bunch of guys who never took themselves seriously, they made some of the most soulful, beautiful music anyone's ever made."

The conspicuous absentee from the occasion was Rod. He had fully intended on being there and performing with his former comrades as he had missed his own induction as a solo artist back in 1994 due to the disruption caused by the Northridge earthquake in LA.*

"I was absolutely over the moon [about the Faces' induction], as one should be," he told rollingstone.com. "I never thought that would happen. I was a little disappointed with Ian McLagan's remarks about how the two bands shouldn't be lumped in together. I think that was a little out of order. I think Mac should think himself lucky that he's in the Rock'n'Roll Hall of Fame. I'll knock him into shape when I see him . . . Hopefully the band is going to get together. I said that I'd do it if we can get the rest of the band together."

However, just one day before the event, a bout of strep throat struck him down and he was unable to attend. At the eleventh hour Mick Hucknall was again called upon to deputise. The band rehearsed with Stewart bassist Conrad Korsch, on the Friday evening at Cleveland's Lava Room Recording studio in preparation for their induction performance; Mac handling the vocals until Hucknall's arrival. The band's three-song set consisted of 'All Or Nothing', 'Ooh La La' and a rendition of 'Stay With Me' "that featured some of the most blistering guitar work of the night, courtesy of Wood," according to classicrock.com Matt Wardlaw's report. ". . . Although they've been defunct as a performing unit for many years, Saturday night's near-Faces reunion performance begs for the possibility of a future raincheck from Stewart. It would be great to see this classic bunch of musicians, a huge inspiration for so many, take the stage one more time."

---

* This was the same quake that motivated Ian and Kim McLagan to relocate to Texas in May 1994.

Ronnie Wood was enjoying a rejuvenated middle age. He remained on the wagon and after splitting with Brazilian model Ana Araujo, he married his third wife, theatre director Sally Humphreys, who was nearly 31 years his junior. Ronnie seemed to enjoy playing more than ever, whether it be with early heroes like B.B. King, Buddy Guy and Jerry Lee Lewis or as godfather to new bands like the Faces-influenced Saint Jude with whom he got up to jam at two of their 100 Club gigs in 2010.* On the other end of the scale he was just as content to appear with young whippets One Direction and James Bay as he was with Paul Weller and Paul McCartney.

His ability to move into other media was ably illustrated by *The Ronnie Wood Show*, a weekly showcase on Absolute Radio, where all he had to do was act naturally – open his address book and invite various heavy friends (including Rod, Mac and Kenney at various times) to hang with him in the studio, tell yarns, play (and play along to) his cherished oldies alongside his own recordings throughout the years, including the Birds, Jeff Beck Group and the Faces, mixed with contemporary tracks. The programme, which began in April 2010, won Ronnie a Sony Gold Award (as Music Radio Personality Of The Year 2011) and two trophies at the 2012 Arqiva Commercial Radio Awards. The Sky Arts television counterpart was also well-received.

That other band of his rumbled back into action in 2012 to celebrate their 50th anniversary with a '50 And Counting' world tour. Wood's predecessor Mick Taylor was along as a guest and, in November 2013, Wood and Taylor played gigs together in London and New York. As an unexpected blast from the past, Ronnie's recently rediscovered hand-written 1965 diary during his spell in the Birds was published in August 2015 as *How Can It Be*. The book was augmented by his drawings, personal photographs and a re-recording of the Birds' B-side, 'How Can It Be'.

Kenney Jones carried on his charity work as well as playing with the Jones Gang and overseeing various reissues of the Small Faces' back catalogue. The year 2013 turned out to be Jones' *annus horribilis* – not only did his 89-year-old mother Violet pass away but the same month, at the time of his 65th birthday, he was diagnosed with prostate cancer during a routine health check.

Following advanced radiotherapy treatment at the Royal Surrey County Hospital, Guildford, which caught the cancer early, Kenney told

---

* Wood also contributed slide guitar to a track on their debut album *Diary Of A Soul Fiend*, released that same year.

413

the *Daily Mail*, "Now is the time for me to enjoy my wife and family in a more relaxed way. I intend to live to a ripe old age."

Ian McLagan preferred a life on the road with the Bump Band than staying for too long in his adopted home of Austin, Texas – by his own admission memories of his cherished life with Kim were hard to disregard. Whether it was at his regular Lucky Lounge gig or on club stages around the globe, Mac's personality lit up the room.

Because he was such a vocal champion of this book, I proudly advised him that it had received a Certificate of Merit in the 2012 Association for Recorded Sound Collections Award for Excellence in Historical Research. Mac wrote straight back to offer his congratulations as well as informing me that his son Lee had just become a father, making him and first wife Sandy grandparents. In 2014 McLagan released a new album *United States* for indie label Yep Roc and collaborated with Texan musician Alejandro Escovedo on a cover of the Kinks' 'I'm Not Like Everybody Else'.

In response to reports that Stewart and Wood had put aside 2015 for a proposed Faces tour, McLagan told *Uncut* that he and Jones would first be focusing on some form of Small Faces reunion to mark that band's 50th anniversary. "Why would we fuck around with the Faces when we've got bigger fish to fry? We've done the Faces and Rod didn't turn up," Mac vented. "Rod's says he's keen to do it now, and I believe him," he added. "But he'll have to wait until 2016 because 2015 is the Small Faces' year."

With tantalising plans ahead, it seemed Mac had years of playing left, making those closest to him totally unprepared for the shock news that broke on December 3, 2014. Ian McLagan had passed away of a massive stroke at the age of 69.

Two days before, he was due to fly to Chicago to rehearse for a pre-Christmas tour with Nick Lowe. "Something told me I should check on the house," Jo Rae Di Menno, Mac's friend, press agent and former assistant to Ronnie Lane, told the *Austin Chronicle*. "Then I thought, 'No, that's silly. I was just there the day before.'" When Mac uncharacteristically failed to show, on December 2, Di Menno and Jon Notarthomas, Mac's bassist and road manager, raced back to Manor, asking a neighbour to check the house ahead of their arrival. McLagan was discovered unconscious in the bath tub and airlifted to University Medical Center Brackenridge in Austin where he was put on life support.

Mac's good buddy, local journalist and radio personality Jody Denberg, recalled: "When my airshift ended I made my way to the hospital with my wife Barbara, where a few other close friends had already gathered. The doctors asked if Mac had expressed any wishes about being resuscitated in an event like this. He'd had some heart problems a couple years prior and had said he would not want to be kept on life support if he was to be ultimately compromised. The doctors said he would not be functional in the unlikely event that he did survive being taken off the artificial respirator.

"Mac's son Lee and brother-in-law Dermot had been notified in the UK. The doctors asked if there was anyone else Mac would have wanted to have the chance to say goodbye to and we all agreed that would be his guitarist of 20 years, 'Scrappy' Jud Newcomb. But 'Scrappy' had just arrived in Marfa, eight hours away. It was decided to keep Mac on the respirator until Jud made his way back to Austin the next day.

"Alejandro Escovedo called me the next morning – December 3 – and asked if Mac was still with us. When I told him yes he asked if I would go with him to the hospital so he could say goodbye. I declined as I'd already said my final goodbyes and couldn't begin to deal with that cold reality again. But Al insisted and I acquiesced. When we got to Mac's room the female nurses tending to him nodded in recognition as we came in and left the three of us alone. Alejandro took out his phone and called up a rocker from *Ooh La La* – 'Cindy Incidentally', I believe – and turned it up nice and loud. Mac's leg twitched. The two of us smiled at that. Then we rocked to 'Borstal Boys' and bid our friend adieu. Hours later he was gone."

Among the first to be notified was Kenney Jones. "I'm so proud and so honoured that life introduced me to Steve Marriott, Ronnie Lane and Ian McLagan. They've been a major part of my life – over half of it – and I miss all three of them. It's lonely, being here on my own. Rod, Woody, and me are still going to do the Faces this year. It's more important now than ever."

Ronnie Wood: "There's got to be a heavy dose of humour in everything we do. Mac epitomized the funny side of things, even in the most dire conditions."

Rod dispatched a tribute to *Uncut*: "I'm absolutely devastated. Ian McLagan embodied the true spirit of the Faces. Last night I was at a charity do, Mick Hucknall was singing 'I'd Rather Go Blind', and Ron Wood texted to say Ian had passed. It was as if his spirit was in the room. I'll miss you, mate."

Various friends, musicians and contemporaries the author approached in the wake of Mac's passing were unstinting in their appraisals.

Glyn Johns: "I always had a great respect for Mac as a musician when we worked together with the Small Faces and Faces, but we did not become really close friends until more recently when he asked me to mix his last two solo albums. Totally unabated by the years, his energy, enthusiasm and unique style of playing reminded me of the extraordinary contribution he made to both of those bands and to all the other artists that had the pleasure of working with him. All of these attributes, along with his unfailing sense of humour, will be sadly missed by all who knew him. We have lost one of the best from our generation. It is comforting to know that he leaves behind the legacy of a lasting impression on popular music."

Billy Nicholls: "Mac was an old friend who whenever we met, tried to make me laugh. That was one of his attributes."

Sandy Sarjeant: "The last couple of years had been good and we had seen a lot more of each other due to Lee having a daughter. So gramps Mac and nana Sand were absolutely delighted. Mac enjoyed his time here with us so much last Christmas that he had booked a ticket for this Christmas. Lee and I are both devastated but now he is with Kim who he missed so very much."

The cruel blow of Mac's passing was a sobering reminder of life's impermanence. In a triple whammy, just the day before McLagan's death, after a life of hell-raising, Bobby Keys succumbed to cirrhosis of the liver at his home in Franklin, Tennessee, and a month later Faces photographer and friend Tom Wright suffered a serious stroke and is currently being cared for by his son.

On March 18, 2015, the Austin Music Awards paid affectionate tribute to McLagan with a stirring finale featuring Charlie Sexton, Patty Griffin and Steven van Zandt. A film about Mac's life is in the pipeline, produced by Wes Orchoski – director of documentaries on Lemmy and the Damned – with the aid of Lee McLagan and Rupert Williams, the force behind *The Passing Show* documentary tribute to Ronnie Lane.

As for Ronnie Lane, his artistic reputation continues to grow thanks to the reformed (but unrepentant) Slim Chance and the reissue of his back catalogue, alongside the DVD and CD release of the all-star memorial concert staged in Lane's memory at the Royal Albert Hall in 2004.

On January 10, 2015, Rod Stewart's 70th birthday party held at his Beverly Hills home provided the setting for an impromptu set by the three surviving Faces as part of the evening's entertainment. What had been an essentially private affair was to become more fully realised once Kenney Jones' determination won through. Back in June 2014, in order to raise awareness of the charity Men United (Prostate Cancer UK), he organised a Rock 'n' Horse Power fundraising show (A Day Of Polo, Music & Motors) at his Hurtwood Park Polo Club in Ewhurst, reuniting him with the Who for the first time since 1988. The event was enough of a success for Jones to start planning an equally spectacular follow-up.

On August 5, 2015, it was confirmed the Faces reunification of sorts – without Lane and McLagan, it could never be considered a fully fledged 'reunion' – was definitely happening.

In a remarkable interview with *Uncut*, instead of his usual default position of blaming Wood's schedule, Stewart now cited McLagan as the culprit behind the failure of previous reunion attempts. "Mac was a bit of a fly in the ointment when it came to getting the band back together, so once he passed, it became a lot easier, because every time I'd say, 'Right, we're going to do it next year,' Mac would go, 'No, you're not doing it next year because we're not ready. We've got a Small Faces album coming out.' Or something like that. So it was always a bit of negativity with Mac. Funny guy but . . ."

Never the shrinking violet, admittedly Mac had sounded off at the singer in his 2014 interview with the same magazine. However, considering it was common knowledge that McLagan longed for a Faces reunion more than anything and, at the time of his death, was reportedly planning a special Small Faces-Faces show with Slim Chance supporting, Rod's comments appeared unfair. Mac, of course, no longer had the right of reply.

The show announcement coincided with the long-promised Warner/Rhino remastered reissues of the band's four studio albums, released on August 28 as *1970–1975: You Can Make Me Dance, Sing Or Anything . . .* in both CD and vinyl box sets. While the vinyl faithfully replicated the original records' packaging – gimmick sleeves, posters and inserts (albeit the US versions in the case of *First Step, Long Player* and *A Nod. . .*) – the CD counterparts left a lot to be desired, being housed in single card sleeves inside a brown box featuring a plain seventies Warner Bros Faces graphic and a foldout insert with no accompanying liner notes and scant recording information. Considering the care and attention that was lavished upon the *Five Guys Walk Into A Bar . . .* packaging it was something of a disappointment.

Of the unreleased bonuses on the CDs, the highlight by a country mile was 'Behind The Sun' (on *First Step)*, its sharp, sleazy riff a close cousin of Howlin' Wolf's 'Smokestack Lightning' containing some great Rod rhyming couplets ("would you strangle my youth for a glass of vermouth?"). It was cut during the aborted Western Recorders sessions in Los Angeles (see page 181), along with the five-minute grinding slide instrumental 'Mona – The Blues' (itself revived for Lane and Wood's *Mahoney's Last Stand* soundtrack in 1972). 'Behind The Sun' would have been a worthy addition to *Long Player* or as a substitute for one of the ill-fitting live tracks, while Mac's opening piano flourish to 'Mona' uncannily predicts his intro to 'Cindy Incidentally' by three years.

The *Long Player* bonuses included a previously unheard rampage through Marvin Rainwater's 'Whole Lotta Woman' featuring some hilarious studio badinage before the song unsteadily takes off, providing full disclosure on how booze-soaked the sessions were. An instrumental 'Sham-Mozzal' is basically a dry run for 'Had Me A Real Good Time' and an early take of 'Tell Everyone' features its composer Ronnie Lane's more delicate lead vocal. Two live tracks from the 1970 Fillmore East gigs filled out the disc. The sensible thing would have been to issue the two Fillmore sets as a double Warner Archive project – or at the very least, the highlights from both as a standalone live release – rather than dribbling out tracks on yet another Faces compilation as bait for fanatics to invest.

Of most frustration was the lack of offcuts from *A Nod Is As Good As A Wink . . .* It had long been rumoured that there was considerable material left in the can and at one point a tape of rehearsals or recordings from the sessions was said to be imminently surfacing on the underground market. In the absence of such a thing, the compilers were forced to fall back on two BBC tracks from the September 1971 *Top Gear* session.

While the sound was an improvement on previous reissues, there were some annoying oversights: 'Around The Plynth' lost its final, jokey "that's yer lot" sign-off, Ronnie Lane was credited as the writer of Ike Turner's 'Too Much Woman (For A Henpecked Man)', and a lacklustre live version of 'Jealous Guy' from the 1973 Reading Festival featuring Tetsu was added to *Ooh La La* at the expense of existing Lane-era recordings. In addition, the alternate single mix of 'Had Me A Real Good Time' was left off the bonus disc *Faces: Stray Singles & B-Sides* whose *raison d'être* was to mop up such things.

A Warners spokesman stated: "These releases are the first hurdle in rebuilding the relationship with the management and factions within the band. Because of our on-going discussions with Rod, at the moment we are having to focus on securing that relationship and product before looking again at further options on the Faces. That relationship is key to whatever we try to do in the future. Once we get over these, hopefully with no issues, we can open up dialogue on other releases."

Hurtwood, September 5: after a full day of entertainment featuring Chris Jagger, Steve Harley, Midge Ure and Paul Carrack, Rod, Ronnie, Kenney and band took to the stage. "We've only had a few hours' rehearsal so there's bound to be a few cock ups," Stewart apologised up front. "Just like the old days," Wood affirmed. Truth spoken in jest, the band of nine musicians (mostly from Rod's backing band) including female backing vocalists and a three-piece horn section could hardly disguise the fact, no matter how slick.

There were sloppy starts and wavering tempos with the autumn chill affecting tunings and vocals – the sluggish opener 'I Feel So Good' functioned more as a rehearsal with the lower key obviously altered to assist Stewart's larynx. "Have I got the right key?" Ronnie asked at the start of '(I Know I'm) Losing You'. The finale 'Sweet Little Rock'n'Roller' had to be restarted after Rod messed up the intro.

As predicted a full show was off the menu, just seven songs rehearsed: 'I Feel So Good', 'You Can Make Me Dance, Sing Or Anything . . .', 'Ooh La La', 'I'd Rather Go Blind', '(I Know) I'm Losing You', 'Stay With Me' and 'Sweet Little Rock'n'Roller'. Ultimately, any shortcomings with the ramshackle 45-minute performance failed to have a bearing on the audience's rapturous approval.

Under the headline of 'worth the 40-year wait' the *Telegraph*'s Neil McCormick gave the performance an unqualified five-star review. "The long-awaited reunion of one of Britain's best loved bands was a glorious shambles, a wonderful reminder of the joyous spirit that still exists beneath the increasingly respectable facade of rock and roll."

Classic Rock's Ian Fortnam declared that "no other band has ever made the business of conjuring up rock'n'roll mayhem seem like such casual, joyous and irresistibly infectious fun . . . Even at 60 per cent of their number Rod's Faces are nothing short of unmissable."

Speaking after the gig Stewart told Adrian Deevoy, "It was so loose. I was thinking, 'If this is what it's like when we're all relatively sober what must it have been like when we were completely pissed?!' "

It was perhaps this concern over professionalism that prevented the reunion being reprised as part of Rod's televised 'Festival In A Day' concert at Hyde Park the following weekend. (Wood had been a guest when Stewart performed at the park in June 2011, playing on the inevitable 'Maggie May' and 'Stay With Me'.) The set-list deliberately delved into the dustier corners of Rod's history, notably 'Gasoline Alley', 'Angel', 'In A Broken Dream', and, most surprising of all, Muddy Waters' 'Rollin' And Tumblin''. Evidently his band were not too familiar with the material – at one point, Stewart insisted 'Angel' be restarted after a fluffed chord. Clearly the rough and ready Faces would have gone down a treat. Perhaps another time then?

The final word is, and always has been, Rod's. "If Ronnie Wood and I can find a window, I'd love to do a couple of festivals with the Faces in the UK or the US. I think that'd be the best way to go."

APPENDICES

The Faces & Related
Selective Discography

A comprehensive discography of all appearances on record by the five musicians who made up the Faces from the early Sixties to the present day would occupy an inordinate amount of space and incorporate not just the Faces but records by the Rolling Stones, the Who and numerous other celebrated groups and artists. For that reason this discography is restricted to recordings made by the members of the Faces before and during their career together (and subsequent compilations that include material from this period), and a listing of key albums that followed. This approach precludes inclusion of guest appearances but the most important of these, for example, Rod Stewart's Python Lee Jackson recordings, are dealt with in detail in the main text.

My thanks to John Gray and Neal Webb for their invaluable help in constructing this listing.

FACES

UK Singles
Flying/Three Button Hand Me Down
(Warner Bros WB8005, 1970)

Had Me A Real Good Time*/Rear Wheel Skid
(Warner Bros WB8018, 1970)

Stay With Me/Debris
(Warner Bros K16136, 1971)

Cindy Incidentally/Skewiff (Mend The Fuse)
(Warner Bros K16247, 1973)

* = different to album version

Pool Hall Richard/I Wish It Would Rain
(Warner Bros K16341, 1973)

Cindy Incidentally / Memphis / Stay With Me / Pool Hall Richard
(Warner Bros K16406, 1974)

You Can Make Me Dance Sing Or Anything (Even Take The Dog For A Walk,
Mend A Fuse, Fold Away The Ironing Board, Or Any Other Domestic
Shortcomings)/As Long As You Tell Him
(Warner Bros K16494, 1974)

UK Albums

First Step
Wicked Messenger / Devotion / Shake, Shudder, Shiver / Stone /
Around The Plynth / Flying / Pineapple And The Monkey / Nobody Knows /
Looking Out The Window / Three Button Hand Me Down
(Warner Bros WS3000, 1970)

Long Player
Bad 'N' Ruin / Tell Everyone / Sweet Lady Mary / Richmond /
Maybe I'm Amazed (live) / Had Me A Real Good Time / On The Beach /
I Feel So Good (live) / Jerusalem
(Warner Bros WS3011, 1971)

A Nod's As Good As A Wink . . . To A Blind Horse
Miss Judy's Farm / You're So Rude / Love Lives Here / Last Orders Please /
Stay With Me / Debris / Memphis Tennessee / Too Bad / That's All You Need
(Warner Bros K56006, 1971)

Ooh La La
Silicone Grown / Cindy Incidentally / Flags And Banners / My Fault / Borstal
Boys / Fly In The Ointment / If I'm On The Late Side / Glad And Sorry / Just
Another Honky / Ooh La La
(Warner Bros K56011, 1973)

Coast To Coast Live! /Overture And Beginners
It's All Over Now / Cut Across Shorty / Too Bad-Every Picture Tells A Story
/Angel / Stay With Me / I Wish It Would Rain / I'd Rather Go Blind /Borstal
Boys-Amazing Grace / Jealous Guy / (I Know) I'm Losing You★
(Mercury 9100 001 (LP) / Warner Bros K456027 (cassette), 1974)

★ = cassette version only

US Singles

Around The Plynth / Wicked Messenger
(Warner Bros. 7393, 1970)

Had Me A Real Good Time/Rear Wheel Skid
(Warner Bros. 7442, 1970)

Maybe I'm Amazed/Oh Lord I'm Browned Off
(Warner Bros. 7483, 1971)

Stay With Me/You're So Rude
(Warner Bros. 7545, 1971)

Cindy Incidentally/Skewiff (Mend The Fuse)
(Warner Bros. 7681, 1973)

Ooh La La/Borstal Boys
(Warner Bros. 7711, 1973)

You Can Make Me Dance . . . /As Long As You Tell Him
(Warner Bros. 8066, 1975)

US Albums

First Step (Warner Bros WB 1851, 1970)
Long Player (Warner Bros WB 1892, 1971)
A Nod Is As Good As A Wink . . . To A Blind Horse (Warner Bros WB 2574, 1971)
Ooh La La (Warner Bros WB 2665, 1973)
Coast To Coast Live!/Overtures And Beginners (Mercury SRIM 1-697, 1973)

1970–1975: You Can Make Me Dance, Sing Or Anything . . . (5 CD Box Set)

Disc 1: **First Step** (or **The First Step**)
Tracks 1 to 10 as per original album
BONUS TRACKS (*all previously unreleased*):
Behind The Sun (Outtake) / Mona – The Blues (Outtake) / Shake, Shudder, Shiver (BBC Session recorded 9 March 1970, broadcast *Top Gear* 28 March 1970) / Flying (Take 3) / Nobody Knows (Take 2)

Disc 2: **Long Player**
Tracks 1 to 9 as per original album
BONUS TRACKS (*all previously unreleased*):
Whole Lotta Woman (Outtake) / Tell Everyone (Take 1) (Lane) / Sham-Mozzal (Instrumental – Outtake) / Too Much Woman (live, The Fillmore East, New York City, 10 Nov 1970) / Love In Vain (live, The Fillmore East, New York City, 10 Nov 1970)

Disc 3: *A Nod Is As Good As A Wink . . . To A Blind Horse . . .*

Tracks 1 to 9 as per original album
BONUS TRACKS (*both previously unreleased*):
Miss Judy's Farm (live) / Stay With Me (live)
(BBC session recorded 28 September 1971, broadcast *Top Gear* 6 October 1971)

Disc 4: *Ooh La La*

Tracks 1 to 10 as per original album
BONUS TRACKS (*all previously unreleased*):
Cindy Incidentally (BBC Session recorded 12 February 1973, broadcast *In Concert* 1 March 1973) / Borstal Boys (Rehearsal) / Silicone Grown (Rehearsal) / Glad And Sorry (Rehearsal) / Jealous Guy (live, recorded at the Reading Festival, 25 August 1973)

Disc 5: *Stray Singles & B-Sides*

Pool Hall Richard (single A-side, 1973) / I Wish It Would Rain (With A Trumpet) (live, Reading Festival, 1973 / Rear Wheel Skid (non-album B-side to 'Had Me A Real Good Time', 1970) / Maybe I'm Amazed (studio version, US 7″ single, 1971) / Oh Lord I'm Browned Off (non-album B-side to Maybe I'm Amazed, 1971) / You Make Me Dance, Sing Or Anything (Even Take The Dog For A Walk, Mend A Fuse, Fold Away The Ironing Board, Or Any Other Domestic Shortcomings) (single A-side, 1974) / As Long As You Tell Him (non-album B-side to You Can Make Me Dance, Sing Or Anything . . ., 1974) / Skewiff (Mend The Fuse) (non-album B-side to Cindy Incidentally, 1973) / Dishevelment Blues (non-album exclusive track issued on a one-side flexi-disc with the *New Musical Express*, April 1973)
(Warner Brothers / Rhino R2 550009, 2015)

VARIOUS

'Dishevelment Blues' (& excerpts from *Ooh La La*)
(*New Musical Express* flexi, 1973)

Reading Festival 1973 – Various Artists

(I Know) I'm Losing You★
(GM GML1008, 1974)

★ *This version also appears on the cassette version of Coast To Coast Live! / Overture And Beginners*

Compilations

The Best Of The Faces ★
(Riva RVLP3, 1977) charted at #24 in UK; *The Faces EP* was extracted from the album and made #41 on the UK singles chart.

The Best Of Faces: Good Boys... When They're Asleep... ★★
(Warner Archives-Rhino, 8122-75830-2, 1999) charted at #32 (UK) thanks to a belated television advertising campaign

Changing Faces: The Very Best Of Rod Stewart & The Faces ★★★
(Warner-Universal, 9812604, 2004) charted at #13 (UK)

Stay With Me: The Faces Anthology ★★★★
(Warner Bros/Rhino 8122797179, 2012)

★= includes It's All Over Now from *Gasoline Alley*

★★ = first release for previously unissued track Open To Ideas

★★★ = features seven Faces tracks mixed with Rod Stewart Mercury material and Python Lee Jackson track (In A Broken Dream)

★★★★ = double CD featuring three previously unreleased live tracks – Too Much Woman (For A Henpecked Man)/ Love In Vain/ Gasoline Alley – from Fillmore East, NYC, November 10, 1970

Five Guys Walk Into A Bar . . . (4 CD Box Set)
Disc 1: Flying / On The Beach / Too Bad / If I'm On The Late Side / Debris / Jealous Guy / As Long As You Tell Him / Evil (rehearsal) / Maggie May ★ / Cindy Incidentally (alternate mix) / Maybe I'm Amazed ★ / Insurance / I Came Looking For You (rehearsal) / Last Orders Please / Wyndlesham Bay (Jodie) (outtake) / I Can Feel The Fire (live) / Tonight's Number / Come See Me Baby (The Cheater) (outtake)

Disc 2: Pool Hall Richard / You're My Girl (I Don't Want To Discuss It) ★ / Glad And Sorry / Shake, Shudder, Shiver (rehearsal) / Miss Judy's Farm ★ / Richmond / That's All You Need / Rear Wheel Skid / Maybe I'm Amazed / (If Loving You Is Wrong) I Don't Want To Be Right (rehearsal) / Take A Look At The Guy (live) / Flags And Banners / Bad 'N' Ruin ★ / Around The Plynth / Sweet Lady Mary / Had Me A Real Good Time / Cut Across Shorty ★

Disc 3: You're So Rude / (I Know) I'm Losing You ★ / Love Lives Here / I'd Rather Go Blind (live) / Hi-Heel Sneakers-Everybody Needs Somebody To Love / Gettin' Hungry / Silicone Grown / Oh Lord I'm Browned Off / Just Another Honky / Open To Ideas / Skewiff (Mend The Fuse) / Too Bad (live) / Rock Me Baby /Angel ★ / Stay With Me ★ / Ooh La La

Disc 4: The Stealer ★ / Around The Plynth-Gasoline Alley ★ /
You Can Make Me Dance Sing Or Anything (Even Take The Dog For A Walk,
Mend A Fuse, Fold Away The Ironing Board, Or Any Other Domestic
Shortcomings) / I Wish It Would Rain / Miss Judy's Farm ★ / Love In Vain ★ /
My Fault ★ / I Feel So Good (rehearsal) / Miss Judy's Farm / Three Button
Hand Me Down / Cindy Incidentally / Borstal Boys / Flying ★ / Bad 'N' Ruin /
Dishevelment Blues / Stay With Me
(Warner Archives-Rhino 8122-78233-2, 2004)

★ = BBC recording

QUIET MELON

(Art Wood, Rod Stewart, Ron Wood, Ronnie Lane, Ian McLagan, Kenney Jones)

Art Wood's Quiet Melon
Diamond Joe / Engine 4444 / Instrumental
(CD: Lost Moment LMCD 051; 12″ single: LM12051, 1994)

ROD STEWART

UK Singles
Good Morning Little Schoolgirl/ I'm Gonna Move To The Outskirts Of Town
(UK: Decca F11996, 1964)

The Day Will Come/Why Does It Go On
(Columbia DB7766, 1965)

Shake/I Just Got Some
(Columbia DB7892, 1966)

Little Miss Understood/So Much To Say
(Immediate IM060, 1968)

It's All Over Now/Jo's Lament
(Vertigo 6086 002, 1970)

Reason To Believe/Maggie May
(Mercury 6052 097, 1971)

You Wear It Well/Lost Paraguayos
(Mercury 6052 171, 1972)

Angel/What Made Milwaukee Famous (Has Made A Loser Out Of Me)
(Mercury 6052 198, 1972)

Oh! No, Not My Baby/Jodie
(Mercury 6052 371, 1973)

Farewell/Bring It On Home To Me – You Send Me
(Mercury 6167 033, 1974)

Sailing/Stone Cold Sober
(Warner Bros K16600, 1975)

This Old Heart Of Mine/All In The Name Of Rock 'n' Roll
(Riva 1, 1975)

UK Albums

An Old Raincoat Won't Ever Let You Down
Street Fighting Man / Man Of Constant Sorrow / Blind Prayer / Handbags And
Gladrags / An Old Raincoat Won't Ever Let You Down / I Wouldn't Ever
Change A Thing / Cindy's Lament / Dirty Old Town
(Vertigo VO4, 1970)

Gasoline Alley
Gasoline Alley / It's All Over Now / Only A Hobo / My Way Of Giving/
Country Comforts / Cut Across Shorty / Lady Day / Jo's Lament / You're My
Girl (I Don't Want To Discuss It)
(Vertigo 6360 500, 1970)

Every Picture Tells A Story
Every Picture Tells A Story / Seems Like A Long Time / That's All Right /
Amazing Grace / Tomorrow Is A Long Time / Henry / Maggie May /
Mandolin Wind / (I Know) I'm Losing You / Reason To Believe
(Mercury 6338 063, 1971)

Never A Dull Moment
True Blue / Lost Paraguayos / Mama You Been On My Mind / Italian Girls /
Angel / Interludings / You Wear It Well / I'd Rather Go Blind / Twistin' The
Night Away
(Mercury 6499 163, 1972)

Smiler
Sweet Little Rock 'n' Roller / Lochinvar / Farewell / Sailor / Bring It On
Home To Me-You Send Me / Let Me Be Your Car / (You Make Me Feel
Like) A Natural Man / Dixie Toot / Hard Road / I've Grown Accustomed To
Her Face (instrumental) / Girl From The North Country / Mine For Me
(Mercury 9104 001, 1974)

Atlantic Crossing ★

Three Time Loser / Alright For An Hour / All In The Name Of Rock 'n' Roll / Drift Away / Stone Cold Sober / I Don't Want To Talk About It / It's Not The Spotlight / This Old Heart Of Mine / Still Love You /Sailing
(Warner Bros K56151, 1975)

★ *2009 reissue features alternative version of the album and three outtakes:* To Love Somebody / Holy Cow / Return To Sender

US Singles

Good Morning Little Schoolgirl/ I'm Gonna Move To The Outskirts Of Town
(Press 9722, 1964)

Handbags And Gladrags/An Old Raincoat Won't Ever Let You Down
(Mercury 73009, 1970)

Handbags And Gladrags/Man Of Constant Sorrow
(Mercury 73031, 1970)

It's All Over Now/Jo's Lament
(Mercury 73095, 1970)

Only A Hobo/ (B-side unconfirmed)
(Mercury 73115, 1970)

Gasoline Alley/Cut Across Shorty
(Mercury 73156, 1970)

Lady Day / My Way Of Giving
(Mercury 73175, 1971)

Country Comforts/Gasoline Alley
(Mercury 73196, 1971)

Reason To Believe/Maggie May
(Mercury 73224, 1971)

(I Know) I'm Losing You/Mandolin Wind
(Mercury 73244, 1971)

You Wear It Well/True Blue
(Mercury 73330, 1972)

Angel/Lost Paraguayos
(Mercury 73344, 1972)

Twistin' The Night Away/True Blue/Lady Day
(Mercury 73412, 1973)

Oh! No, Not My Baby/Jodie
(Mercury 73426, 1973)

Mine For Me/ Farewell
(Mercury 73636, 1974)

Let Me Be Your Car/Sailor
(Mercury 73660, 1974)

What Made Milwaukee Famous . . . / Every Picture Tells A Story
(Mercury 73802, 1975)

Sailing/All In The Name Of Rock 'n' Roll
(Warner Bros. 8146, 1975)

This Old Heart Of Mine/Still Love You
(Warner Bros 8170, 1975)

US Albums

The Rod Stewart Album (a.k.a. *Thin*) (Mercury SR 61237, 1969)
Gasoline Alley (Mercury SR 61264, 1970)
Every Picture Tells A Story (Mercury SRM 1-609, 1971)
Never A Dull Moment (Mercury SRM 1-646, 1972)
Sing It Again Rod (Mercury SRM 1-680, 1973)
Smiler (Mercury SRM 1-1017, 1974)
Atlantic Crossing (Warner Bros. BS-2875, 1975)

Rod Stewart And The Faces
Compilation featuring two previously unreleased Rod Stewart Sixties tracks:
Just A Little Misunderstood [sic] (demo) / Baby Come Home
(Springboard SPB 4030, 1975)

A Shot Of Rhythm And Blues
Compilation featuring six previously unreleased demo tracks from 1964:
Keep Your Hands Off Her / Don't You Tell Nobody / Just Like I Treat You /
Bright Lights, Big City / Ain't That Lovin' You Baby? / Mopper's Blues
(Private Stock PS 202, 1976)

Rod Stewart And Steampacket
Compilation featuring otherwise unreleased 1964 live track recorded by Giorgio Gomelsky:
Bright Lights, Big City (live)
(Springboard SPB 4063, 1976)

Handbags And Gladrags
Compilation featuring five previously unreleased Mercury tracks from 1973–74:

You Put Something Better Inside Of Me / Crying Laughing Loving Lying /
So Tired / Every Time We Say Goodbye / Missed You
(Mercury 528 823-2, 1995)

Storyteller
Box set featuring Atlantic Crossing *outtake (different version to that on the 2009 reissue and* The Rod Stewart Sessions 1971–1998)
To Love Somebody
(Warner Bros 9259871, 1989)

The Rod Stewart Sessions 1971–1998 (Disc One)
Box set featuring 15 outtakes from 1971–1975
Maggie May (early version) / Seems Like A Long Time (alt. version) / Italian
Girls (early version) / You Wear It Well (early version) / Lost Paraguayos (alt.
version) / I'd Rather Go Blind (alt. version) / Angel (alt. version) / Think I'll
Pack My Bags (Mystifies Me – early version) / Farewell (early version) / Girl
From The North Country (alt. version) / (You Make Me Feel Like A) Natural
Man (alt. version) / So Tired (early version) / This Old Heart Of Mine (alt.
version) / To Love Somebody (early take) / Sailing (alt. version)
(Warner Archives-Rhino, 8122 79853 8, 2009)

Rarities
*Double CD compilation featuring previously unreleased Faces BBC track recorded 15
September 1970, broadcast* Top Gear *19 September 1970*
Country Comforts
(Mercury/Universal 0602537285136, 2013)

LONG JOHN BALDRY & THE HOOCHIE COOCHIE MEN
Up Above My Head (B-side of You'll Be Mine)
(United Artists UP 1056, 1964)

Looking At Long John Baldry: The UA Years 1964-1966
Up Above My Head (Take 3) / Got My Mojo Working
(from LJB session with Ottilie Patterson, 4/3/64)
(EMI 094635089929, 2006)

STEAMPACKET
Rock Generation Vol. 6
Can I Get A Witness / Baby Take Me / Oh Baby Don't You Do It / Lord
Remember Me
(BYG 529 706, 1971)

SHOTGUN EXPRESS

I Could Feel The Whole World Turn Round / Curtains
(Columbia DB8025, 1966)

JEFF BECK GROUP

Singles

Hi Ho Silver Lining/Bolero
(UK: Columbia DB8151, 1967)
(US: Epic 5-10157, 1967)

Tallyman/Rock My Plimsoul
(UK: Columbia DB8227, 1967)
(US: Epic 5-10218, 1967)

Love Is Blue/I've Been Drinking
(UK: Columbia DB8359, 1968)

All above singles credited simply to Jeff Beck

Plynth (Water Down The Drain)/Jailhouse Rock
(US: Epic 5-10484, 1969)

Albums

*Truth**

Shapes Of Things / Let Me Love You / Morning Dew / You Shook Me / Ol'
Man River / Greensleeves / Rock My Plimsoul / Beck's Bolero / Blues Deluxe
/ I Ain't Superstitious
(UK: Columbia SX (mono)/SCX 6293, 1968)
(US: Epic PE 26413, 1968)
Extra tracks on 2006 CD reissue:
I've Been Drinking (Stereo Mix) / You Shook Me (Take 1) / Rock My
Plimsoul (alternate, B-Side of Tallyman single) / Beck's Bolero (Mono Mix) /
Blues Deluxe (Take 1) / Tallyman (Single) / Love Is Blue (Single) / Hi Ho
Silver Lining (Single)

* Credited to Jeff Beck

Beck-Ola (Cosa Nostra)

All Shook Up / Spanish Boots / Girl From Mill Valley / Jailhouse Rock /
Plynth (Water Down The Drain) / The Hangman's Knee / Rice Pudding
(UK: Columbia SX (mono)/SCX 6351, 1969)
(US: Epic BN 26478, 1969)
Extra tracks on 2006 CD reissue:
Sweet Little Angel (live) / Throw Down A Line / All Shook Up (early version)/
Jailhouse Rock (early version)

RON WOOD

THE BIRDS

Singles

You're On My Mind/You Don't Love Me (You Don't Care)
(Decca F12031, 1964)

Leaving Here/Next In Line
(Decca F12140, 1965)

No Good Without You Baby/How Can It Be
(Decca F12257, 1965)

(as Birds' Birds)

Say Those Magic Words/Daddy Daddy
(Reaction 591005, 1966)

Album

The Collectors' Guide To Rare British Birds CD

You're On My Mind/You Don't Love Me (You Don't Care)/ Leaving Here/
Next In Line/ No Good Without You Baby/ How Can It Be/ You're On My
Mind (demo)★/ You Don't Love Me (You Don't Care) (demo)★/ Say Those
Magic Words (stereo mix)★/ Daddy Daddy (stereo mix)★/ Run Run Run
(version 1)★/ Good Times★/ Say Those Magic Words (early backing track)★/
Daddy Daddy (alternate version)★/La Poupee Qui Fait Non / Run Run Run
(version 2)/ Daddy Daddy (early backing track)★/ Granny Rides Again★/ That's
All That I Want You For (hidden track – from *The Deadly Bees* soundtrack)★
(Deram 564 139-2, 1999)

★ = previously unreleased

THE CREATION

Midway Down The Girls Are Naked
(Polydor 56246, 1968)

For All That I Am/Uncle Bert
(Germany, Hit-ton HT 300235, 1968)

Available on *Our Music Is Red – With Purple Flashes* CD (Diablo Records DIAB
857, 1998)

RON WOOD

Singles

I Can Feel The Fire/Breathe On Me
(Warner Bros K16463, 1974)

If You Don't Want My Love/I Got A Feeling
(Warner Bros K16679, 1975)

Albums

I've Got My Own Album To Do

I Can Feel The Fire / Far East Man / Mystifies Me / Take A Look At The Guy /
Act Together / Am I Grooving You? / Shirley / Cancel Everything / Sure The
One You Need / If You Gotta Make A Fool Of Somebody / Crotch Music
(UK: Warner Bros K56065, 1974)
(US: Warner Bros BS 2819, 1974)

Now Look

I Got Lost When I Found You / Big Bayou / Breathe On Me / If You Don't
Want My Love / I Can Say She's Alright / Caribbean Boogie / Now Look /
Sweet Baby Mine / I Can't Stand The Rain / It's Unholy / I Got A Feeling
(UK: Warner Bros K56145, 1975)
(US: Warner Bros BS 2872, 1975)

The First Barbarians: Live From Kilburn (CD & DVD) ★

Disc 1 (CD): Intro / Am I Grooving You? / Cancel Everything / Mystifies Me/
Take A Look At The Guy / Act Together / Shirley / Forever / Sure The One
You Need / I Can't Stand The Rain / Crotch Music / I Can Feel The Fire
Disc 2 (DVD): Intro/ Am I Grooving You? / Cancel Everything / If You Gotta
Make A Fool Of Somebody / Mystifies Me / Take A Look At The Guy / Act
Together / Shirley / Forever / Sure The One You Need / Crotch Music / I
Can Feel The Fire
(Wooden Records CDWDN4, 2007)

★ = Wood-approved release of material from Kilburn Gaumont State 14/7/74

RON WOOD & RONNIE LANE

Mahoney's Last Stand

Tonight's Number / From The Late To The Early / Chicken Wire / Chicken
Wired / I'll Fly Away / Title One / Just For A Moment (Instrumental) / Mona'
The Blues/ Car Radio / Hay Tumble / Woody's Thing / Rooster Funeral /
Just For A Moment
(UK: Atlantic K50309, 1976)
(US: Atco SD 36126, 1976)

KENNEY JONES

Ready Or Not/Woman Trouble (GM GMS027, 1974)

IAN McLAGAN

THE MULESKINNERS

Back Door Man/Need Your Lovin' (Fontana TF527, 1965)

Knockout R&B With The Muleskinners EP
Need Your Lovin'/Back Door Man/Why Don't You Write Back To Me/Untie Me
(Acid Jazz AJX235S, 2010)

THE SMALL FACES

UK Singles

What'cha Gonna Do About It/What's A Matter Baby
(Decca F12208, 1965)

I Got Mine/It's Too Late
(Decca F12276, 1965)

Sha La La La Lee/Grow Your Own
(Decca F12317, 1966)

Hey Girl/Almost Grown
(Decca F12393, 1966)

All Or Nothing/Understanding
(Decca F12470, 1966)

My Mind's Eye/I Can't Dance With You
(Decca F12500, 1966)

I Can't Make It/Just Passing
(Decca F12565, 1967)

Patterns/E To D
(Decca F12619, 1967)

Here Come The Nice/Talk To You
(Immediate IM050, 1967)

Itchycoo Park/I'm Only Dreaming
(Immediate IM057, 1967)

Tin Soldier/I Feel Much Better
(Immediate IM062, 1967)

Lazy Sunday/Rollin' Over
(Immediate IM064, 1968)

The Universal/Donkey Rides A Penny A Glass
(Immediate IM069, 1968)

Afterglow Of Your Love/Wham Bam Thank You Mam
(Immediate IM077, 1969)

UK Albums

Small Faces
Shake / Come On Children / You Better Believe It/ It's Too Late / One Night
Stand / What'cha Gonna Do About It / Sorry She's Mine / Own Up Time/
You Need Loving / Don't Stop What You're Doing / E To D / Sha La La La Lee
(Decca LK 4790, 1966)

Extra tracks on 2006 CD reissue:
What's A Matter Baby/ I've Got Mine/ Grow Your Own/ Hey Girl/ Almost
Grown/ What'cha Gonna Do About It★/ Come On Children★/ Shake★/ Own
Up Time★/ E Too D★/ Hey Girl★

★ = alternate version

From The Beginning
Runaway / My Mind's Eye / Yesterday, Today And Tomorrow / That Man /
My Way Of Giving / Hey Girl / (Tell Me) Have You Ever Seen Me / Come
Back And Take This Hurt Off Me / All Or Nothing / Baby Don't You Do It /
Plum Nellie / Sha La La La Lee / You've Really Got A Hold On Me /
What'cha Gonna Do About It
(Decca LK 4879, 1967)

Extra tracks on 1996 CD reissue:
My Mind's Eye (French EP version) / Hey Girl (French EP version) / Come
Back And Take This Hurt Off Me (alternate version) / Baby Don't You Do It
(alternate version) / What'cha Gonna Do About It (BBC recording)

Small Faces
(Tell Me) Have You Ever Seen Me / Something I Want To Tell You / Feeling
Lonely / Happy Boys Happy / Things Are Going To Get Better / My Way Of
Giving / Green Circles / Become Like You / Get Yourself Together / All Our
Yesterdays / Talk To You / Show Me The Way / Up The Wooden Hills To
Bedfordshire / Eddie's Dreaming
(Immediate IMLP 008, 1967)

Extra tracks on 2002 2–CD mono/stereo mixes reissue:
Disc One: I Can't Make It★/ Just Passing★/ Here Come The Nice★/ Itchycoo
Park★/ I'm Only Dreaming★/ Tin Soldier★/ I Feel Much Better★/ Don't Burst
My Bubble/ Things Are Going To Get Better (alternate version)/ Green Circles
(slow version)
Bonus Disc: I Can't Make It★★/ Just Passing★★/ Here Come The Nice★★/
Itchycoo Park★★/ I'm Only Dreaming★★/ Tin Soldier★★/ I Feel Much
Better★★/ (Tell Me) Have You Ever Seen Me (alternate version)/ Green Circles
(USA mix)

★ = stereo ★★ = mono

Ogdens' Nut Gone Flake
Ogdens' Nut Gone Flake / Afterglow (Of Your Love) / Long Agos And Worlds
Apart / Rene / Song Of A Baker / Lazy Sunday / Happiness Stan / Rollin' Over
/ The Hungry Intruder / The Journey / Mad John / Happy Days Toy Town
(Immediate IMLP 012, 1968)

2006 3-CD Castle Music Deluxe Edition features mono mix, stereo mix & 1989
BBC *Classic Albums* documentary

The Autumn Stone
Here Come The Nice / The Autumn Stone / Collibosher / All Or Nothing
(live) / Red Balloon / Lazy Sunday / Call It Something Nice / I Can't Make It
/ Afterglow (Of Your Love) / Sha La La La Lee / The Universal / Rollin' Over
(live) / If I Were A Carpenter (live) / Every Little Bit Hurts (live) /My Mind's
Eye / Tin Soldier (live) / Just Passing / Itchycoo Park / Hey Girl / Wide Eyed
Girl On The Wall / What'cha Gonna Do About It / Wham Bam Thank You Mam
(Immediate IMAL01/2, 1969)

Extra tracks on 1996 CD reissue:
Donkey Rides A Penny A Glass / All Or Nothing (live) / Tin Soldier (live)

The BBC Sessions
Whatcha Gonna Do About It (*Saturday Club* 23.8.65) / Jump Back (*Saturday
Club* 23.8.65) / Baby Don't You Do It (*Saturday Club* 23.8.65) / Shake (*Saturday
Club* 14.3.66) / Sha La La La Lee (*Saturday Club* 14.3.66) / You Need Loving
(*Saturday Club* 14.3.66) / Hey Girl (*Saturday Club* 3.5.66) / E To D (*Saturday
Club* 3.5.66) / One Night Stand (*Saturday Club* 3.5.66) / You Better Believe It
(*Saturday Club* 30.8.66) / Understanding (*Saturday Club* 30.8.66) / All or
Nothing (*Saturday Club* 30.8.66) / You Better Believe It (*Saturday Club* 30.8.66)
/ If I Were A Carpenter (*Top Gear* 9.4.68) / Lazy Sunday (*Top Gear* 9.4.68) /
Every Little Bit Hurts (*Top Gear* 9.4.68) /Steve Marriott/Kenney Jones
interviews (from *Saturday Club*/ *Top Gear*)
(Strange Fruit SFRSCD087, 1999)

Here Comes The Nice: The Immediate Years 1967–69
Four CD limited edition box set includes rare and previously unreleased
material, unheard recording sessions from Olympic, IBC & Trident Studios,
outtakes, early mixes, alternate versions and live tracks.
(Immediate/Sanctuary, CHARLYBX170, 2014)

Small Faces: The Decca Years
Five CD limited edition box set collecting all Small Faces recordings made for
Decca, including rarities and alternative versions alongside a disc of the group's
BBC sessions including several previously unavailable tracks.
(UMC 4734296, 2015)

Small Faces (reformed line-up)
Playmates (Atlantic K50375, 1977)
'78 in The Shade (Atlantic K50468, 1978)

A Selection Of Key Post-Faces Albums:

Rod Stewart

A Night On The Town (Riva RVLP1, 1976)
Foot Loose & Fancy Free (Riva RVLP 5, 1977)
Tonight I'm Yours (Riva RVLP 14, 1981)
Out Of Order (Warner Bros 925 684-2, 1988)
Unplugged . . . And Seated (Warner Bros. 9362-45289-2, 1993)★
A Spanner In The Works (Warner Bros. 9362-45867-2, 1995)
When We Were The New Boys (Warner Bros. 9362-46792-2, 1998)

★ = features Ron Wood

Ron Wood

Gimme Some Neck (CBS 83337, 1979)
1234 (CBS 85227, 1981) ★
Live At The Ritz With Bo Diddley (JVC/Victor VDPZ-1329 – Japan 1988) ★★
Slide On This (Continuum 19210-2, 1992)
Slide On Live: Plugged In And Standing (Continuum 19309-2, 1993)
Not For Beginners (SPV 085-72762, 2001)
Anthology: The Essential Crossexion (EMI 5639552) ★★★
I Feel Like Playing (Eagle EAGCD 428, 2010)

★ = features one track produced by Rod Stewart
★★ = not released in UK/US
★★★ = includes 'You Strum And I'll Sing' featuring Rod Stewart's vocals

Ronnie Lane

Anymore For Anymore (GM GML 1013, 1974)
Ronnie Lane's Slim Chance (Island ILPS 9321, 1975)
One For The Road (Island ILPS 9366, 1976)
Rough Mix (with Pete Townshend) (Polydor 2442 147, 1977)
See Me (Gem GEMLP 107, 1980)

Ian McLagan

Troublemaker (Mercury 9100 072, 1979)
Bump In The Night (Mercury SRM-1-4007, 1980)
Last Chance To Dance EP (Barking Dog GWD90505, 1985)
Best Of British (Maniac MRCD 0001, 2000)
Rise & Shine (When WENCD 222, 2004)
Spiritual Boy (Maniac MRCD 0006, 2006)
Never Say Never (Proper Records PRPCD 039, 2008)
United States (Maniac MRCD 0008, 2014)

The Faces (& Rod Stewart) At The BBC 1970–1975

BBC RADIO SESSIONS 1970–73:

(All sessions recorded in London and broadcast on Radio 1 unless otherwise stated)

DLT (initials for show host Dave Lee Travis)
Recorded: 10/3/70 (8:30 pm–12:00 pm)
Studio: The Camden Theatre
Producer: Paul Williams
Transmitted: 15/3/70 10:00–12:00pm
Songs: 'Three Button Hand Me Down', Flying', 'Wicked Messenger'

Top Gear
Recorded: 9/3/70 (2 sessions 2:30–6:00 pm; 6:00–9:30 pm)
Studio: Playhouse Theatre
Producer: John Walters
Transmitted: 28/3/70 3:00 pm–5:00 pm
Songs: 'Wicked Messenger', 'Devotion', 'Pineapple And The Monkey', 'Shake, Shudder, Shiver'

John Peel Concert
Recorded: 25/6/70 (Rehearsal 4:00 pm; recording 9:00–10:30 pm)
Studio: Paris Cinema
Producer: Jeff Griffin
Transmitted: 5/7/70 4:00 pm–5:00 pm
Songs: '(I Don't Want To Discuss It) You're My Girl', 'Wicked Messenger', 'Devotion', 'It's All Over Now', 'Feel So Good'
(Argent were other show guests)

Sounds Of The '70s
Recorded: 27/8/70 (8:00–12:00 pm)
Studio: Aeolian 2
Producer: Malcolm Brown
Transmitted: 1/9/70 6:00–7:00 pm
Songs: 'It's All Over Now', Three Button Hand Me Down', 'Around The Plynth'
(The Groundhogs were other show guests)

Top Gear
Recorded: 15/9/70 (6:00–9:30pm)
Studio: Maida Vale 4
Producer: John Walters
Transmitted: 19/9/70 3:00–5:00 pm
Songs: 'Had Me A Real Good Time', 'Around The Plynth', 'Country Comforts'
(Hawkwind and Brett Marvin & The Thunderbolts were the other guests)

John Peel's Sunday Concert
Recorded: 19/11/70 (9:00–10:30 pm)
Studio: Paris Cinema
Producer: Jeff Griffin
Transmitted: 29/11/70 7:00–8:00 pm
Songs: 'Country Comforts', '(I Don't Want To Discuss It) You're My Girl',
'I Need A Woman', 'Maybe I'm Amazed', 'Around The Plynth'

Top Gear 1970
Recorded: 8/12/70 (2:30–6:00 pm)
Studio: Maida Vale 4
Producer: John Walters
Transmitted: 26/12/70 5:30–7:30 pm
Songs: The Faces were among a chorale including Marc Bolan, John Peel,
Robert Wyatt, Mike Ratledge, and Ivor Cutler singing Christmas carols – no in
session songs apart from 'Gasoline Alley' and 'Cut Across Shorty' (both from
record)
(All other artists were taken from previous *Top Gear* sessions)

Sounds Of The 70s – Bob Harris
Rec: 20/4/71 (6:00–9:30pm)
Studio: T1, Transcription Studio, Kensington House, Shepherd's Bush
Producer: John Muir
Transmitted: 3/5/71 6:00–7:00 pm
Songs: 'Had Me A Real Good Time', 'Love In Vain', 'Browned Off' [sic],
'Maybe I'm Amazed

John Peel's Sunday Concert
Recorded: 13/5/71 (9:00–10:30 pm)
Studio: Paris Cinema
Producer: Jeff Griffin
Transmitted: 23/5/71 7:00–8:00 pm
Songs: '(I Don't Want To Discuss It) You're My Girl', 'Maybe I'm Amazed' (not
broadcast), 'Cut Across Shorty', 'Love In Vain', 'Bad 'N' Ruin', 'It's All Over
Now', 'Had Me A Real Good Time', '(I Know) I'm Losing You', 'Feel So Good'

Top Gear
Recorded: 28/9/71 (2:30–11:00pm)
Studio: Maida Vale 4
Producer: John Walters
Transmitted: 6/10/71 10:00–12:00 pm
Songs: 'Stay With Me', 'Miss Judy's Farm', 'Maggie May'
(also with repeat of Family *Top Gear* session from 2/7/71)

Sounds Of The '70s – In Concert
Recorded: 17/2/72 (3:30 pm rehearsal; recording 9:00–10:30pm)
Studio: Paris Cinema
Producer: Jeff Griffin
Transmitted: 26/2/72 6:30–7:30 pm
Songs: 'Three Button Hand Me Down', 'Miss Judy's Farm', 'Memphis', 'Give
Me The Moonlight' (20 second version), 'Too Bad', 'Last Orders Please',
'Devotion', 'That's All You Need', '(I Know) I'm Losing You', 'Stay With Me',
'Had Me A Real Good Time', 'Underneath The Arches' (25 second version),
'Every Picture Tells A Story'

In Concert
Recorded: 8/2/73 (3:30 pm rehearsal; recording 9:00–10:30pm)
Studio: Paris Cinema
Producer: Jeff Griffin
Intended transmission date/times: 24/2/73 6:30–7:30 pm
Songs: 'Silicone Grown', 'Cindy Incidentally', 'Angel', 'Memphis', 'True Blue',
'I'd Rather Go Blind', 'You're My Girl (I Don't Want To Discuss It)', 'Twistin'
The Night Away', 'It's All Over Now', 'Miss Judy's Farm', 'Maybe I'm
Amazed', 'Three Button Hand Me Down', 'I'm Losing You'

N.B: The above session was never broadcast because it was felt that the tape
"was not as good as we would all have wished" (see Chapter 16 for further
explanation). The original BBC contract for the Faces was cancelled on 22/2/73
and a make-up session was scheduled for 29/3/73. (The original aborted session
received an inadvertent airing on BBC digital channel Radio 6 in January 2003.)

In Concert
Recorded: 29/3/73
Studio: Paris Cinema
Producer: Jeff Griffin
Transmitted: 21/4/73 6:30–7:30 pm
Songs: 'Silicone Grown', 'Cindy Incidentally', 'Memphis', 'If I'm On The Late
Side', 'My Fault', 'The Stealer', 'Borstal Boys', 'Angel', 'Stay With Me', 'You're
My Girl (I Don't Want To Discuss It)', 'True Blue', 'Twistin' The Night Away',
'Miss Judy's Farm', 'Jealous Guy', 'Too Bad'

BBC Television Appearances
1970–1974

All transmitted BBC 1 unless otherwise stated

Top Of The Pops
Recorded: 11/3/70 7:30 pm
Studio: Television Centre
Transmitted: 12/3/70
Song: 'Flying'

Disco 2
Rehearsals: 2:30 pm 14/3/70
Studio: Presentation B, Television Centre
Transmitted: BBC 2 14/3/70
Songs: 'Flying', 'Pineapple And The Monkey'

Top Of The Pops
Recorded: 2/12/70 9:30 pm
Studio: Television Centre
Transmitted: 3/12/70
Song: 'Had Me A Real Good Time'

Disco 2
Rehearsals: 3:00 pm 22/4/71
Studio: Television Centre
Transmitted: BBC 2 22/4/71
Songs: 'Tell Everyone', 'Sweet Lady Mary', 'Bad 'N' Ruin'

Top Of The Pops
Recorded: 28/4/71 7:30–10:00 pm
Studio: Television Centre
Transmitted: 29/4/71
Songs: 'Richmond', 'Bad 'N' Ruin' (in show's LP slot)
N.B: The group received a special fee of £150

Top Of The Pops
Recorded: 18/8/71 7:30–10:00 pm
Studio: Television Centre
Transmitted: 19/8/71 (2nd showing: 16/9/71; 3rd showing 14/10/71)
Song: 'Maggie May'

Top Of The Pops
Transmitted: 9/9/71
Song: 'Maggie May' (visual dubbed Pan's People dance troupe)

Top Of The Pops
Recorded: 29/9/71 7:30–10:00 pm
Studio: Television Centre
Transmitted: 30/9/71 (2nd showing: 7/10/71 – only half was shown due to time constraints; also clip shown on *Ask Aspel* TX: 15/10/71; 3rd showing; 28/10/71)
Song: 'Maggie May'

Top Of The Pops
Recorded: 20/10/71 7:30–10:00 pm
Studio: S8, Television Centre
Transmitted: 21/10/71 (2nd showing: 4/11/71)
Songs: 'Maggie May'

Sounds For Saturday
Recorded: 26/10/71
Studio: Television Theatre
TX: BBC 2 1/4/72
Note: Programme had a working title of *Festival* and was due to be recorded at Television Theatre from 10:30 onwards
Producer: Stanley Dorfman
Songs: 'Three Button Hand Me Down', 'Maybe I'm Amazed', 'I Wanna Be Loved', 'Miss Judy's Farm', 'Love In Vain', 'Stay With Me', '(I Know) I'm Losing You'

Top Of The Pops '71 – Part Two
'Maggie May'
TX: Mon 27/12/71
Repeat of telerecording first transmitted on 21/10/71

Top Of The Pops
Recorded: 5/1/72 7:30–10:00 pm
Studio: 8, Television Centre
Transmitted: 6/1/72
'Stay With Me' from *Sounds Of Saturday* was used (2nd showing: 20/1/72)

Top Of The Pops
Transmitted: 13/1/72
Song: 'Stay With Me' (visual dubbed Pan's People dance troupe)

The Old Grey Whistle Test
Content: 16-mm film insert supplied by Kinney shot at the Faces' Rainbow concert – either 10, 11 or 12/2/72
TX: BBC 2 15/2/72
Song: 'Stay With Me'

Top Of The Pops
Transmitted: 10/8/72
Song: 'You Wear It Well' (visual dubbed Pan's People dance troupe)

Top Of The Pops
Recorded: 16/8/72
Studio: Television Centre
Transmitted: 17/8/72 (2nd showing: 31/8/72)
Song: 'You Wear It Well'
Note: Used for BBC radio broadcast as well

Top Of The Pops
Recorded: 15/11/72
Studio 8, Television Centre
Transmitted: 16/11/72 (2nd showing: 30/11/72)
Song: 'Angel'
Note: Used for BBC radio broadcast as well

Top Of The Pops '72 (Part 1)
Recorded: 21/12/72
Studio: 8, Television Centre
Transmitted: 25/12/72
Song: 'You Wear It Well'

Top Of The Pops
Recorded: 7/2/73
Studio: 8, Television Centre
Transmitted: 8/2/73
Song: 'Cindy Incidentally'
Note: Used for BBC radio broadcast as well

Top Of The Pops
Transmitted: 15/2/73
Song: 'Cindy Incidentally' (visual dubbed Pan's People dance troupe)

Top Of The Pops
Transmitted: 13/12/73
Song: 'Pool Hall Richard' (visual dubbed Pan's People dance troupe)

Top Of The Pops
Recorded: 18/12/73
Studio: B, Television Centre
Transmitted: 20/12/73
Song: 'Pool Hall Richard'

Top Of The Pops
Transmitted: 27/12/73
Repeat of 'Maggie May' first recorded for *TOTP* on 20/10/71
(BBC paperwork erroneously states 29/9/71)

Top Of The Pops
Content: 16-mm film insert supplied by Mike Mansfield shot at Lewisham
Odeon 17/11/74
Transmitted: 12/12/74
Song: 'You Can Make Me Dance . . .'

The Faces: Concert File
1969–1975

The following is a comprehensive list of all the concerts the Faces played between their formation in 1969 and split at the end of 1975. Thanks to the notes and diaries of Faces chief road manager Pete Buckland who worked for the band throughout this time, it is as accurate as possible. Many concerts and tours were pre-advertised in the British and American music press but were subject to change and cancellation often at the eleventh hour so if a gig that was widely listed doesn't appear here, the chances are it didn't occur for whatever reason. However I am happy to be proved otherwise and would welcome any updates or additions (with documentary evidence) to this listing for a future reprint at facesgigs@hotmail.com or c/o the publisher's address.

My thanks go to Pete Buckland, Russ Schlagbaum, Doug Hinman, Olle Lundin, Christopher Hjort, John Madsen, Genero Alberto, John Gray and Neal Webb for their invaluable assistance in researching this concert file.

1969

circa December: First Faces gig in a gymnasium on a USAF base, Cambridgeshire (exact details unknown)

1970

Sat 31/1/70: Great Hall, University of Surrey, Guildford (billed as 'The Small Faces' with Grisby Dyke)
Mon 2/2/70: Top Rank Suite, Southampton, Hampshire. Southampton Students' Charity Week: Flush '70' (billed as 'the New Small Faces' with the Taste, the Nite People, Brownhill Stamp Duty)
Sat 7/2/70: Refectory Hall, University, Leeds, Yorkshire (billed as 'Small Faces', with Keef Hartley Band)
Sat 14/2/70: Uppsala, Sweden (billed as 'Small Faces')
Sun 15/2/70: Cue Club, Gothenburg, Sweden (billed as 'Small Faces')
Wed 18/2/70: University, Studentkåren, Stockholm, Sweden (billed as 'Small Faces')
Sat 21/2/70: Tinghallen, Viborg, Denmark (billed as 'Small Faces')

Sun 22/2/70: Revolution Club, Copenhagen, Denmark (billed as 'Small Faces')

Fri 27/2/70: Anson Room, University, Bristol, supporting Free

Sun 1/3/70: The Lyceum, London, with Silver Metre, Brian Auger, Illes and Silas (billed as First London Performance: Faces with Silver Metre And – A Special Sunday Surprise A Faces-Silver Metre Production)

Fri 6/3/70: Royal Agricultural College, Cirencester, Gloucestershire

Sat 7/3/70: The Belfry, Wishaw, nr. Sutton Coldfield, Warwickshire

Mon 16/3/70: Cook's Ferry Inn, Edmonton, north London

Sat 21/3/70: Mothers, Birmingham, Warwickshire, with Clarke-Hutchinson Band

First US tour

Wed 25/3/70: Varsity Arena, Toronto, Ontario, Canada, supporting MC5 and Canned Heat

Thurs 26–Sat 28/3/70: The Boston Tea Party, Boston, MA (Poster has The Faces opening for Lee Michaels; with Zephyr)

Mon 30/3/70: Northern Virginia Community College, Annandale, VA (billed as 'Rod Stewart and The Small Faces')

Tues 31/3/70: Wheaton Youth Center, Wheaton, MD

Fri 3–Sat 4/4/70: Eastown Theater, Detroit, MI, with Argent and Zephyr

Sun 5/4/70: Fillmore North, Toronto, Canada (*without Ian McLagan*)

Wed 8–Thurs 9/4/70: Ungano's, New York City

Fri 10–Sat 11/4/70: Electric Factory, Philadelphia, PA

Wed 15–Thurs 16/4/70: Beaver's, Chicago, IL

Fri 17–Sat 18/4/70: Palladium, Birmingham, MI

Sun 19/4/70: Labor Temple, Minneapolis, MN

Mon 20/4/70: Boston Garden, Boston, MA

Thurs 23/4/70: The Warehouse, Ithaca, NY

Fri 24–Sat 25/4/70: Action House, Island Park, Long Island, NY, with Velvet Night (billed as 'Small Faces with Rod Stewart')

Fri 1–Sun 3/5/70: Eastown Theater, Detroit, MI, with Savoy Brown

Thurs 7–Sun 10/5/70: Fillmore West, San Francisco, CA, supporting Lee Michaels (billed as 'Small Faces with Rod Stewart')

Fri 15–Sat 16/5/70: Eagles Ballroom, Seattle, WA

Sun 17/5/70: Strawberry Mountain Fair, Garden Auditorium, Vancouver, British Columbia, Canada

Sat 23/5/70: University of California, Irvine, CA

Sun 24/5/70: Lansing University, Lansing, MI

Tues 26/5/70: Stanley Warner Theatre, Jersey City, NJ

Thurs 28/5/70: University, Scotch Plains, NJ

Fri 29 & Sat 30/5/70: Capitol Theatre, Port Chester, NY

Fri 5/6/70: Castle Rock, Castle Grounds, Dudley Zoo, Worcestershire, with Tyrannosaurus Rex, Edgar Broughton Band, Quintessence and Sam Apple Pie. MC: Jeff Dexter. Proceeds in aid of World Wildlife Fund; light show by Proteus

Mon 15/6/70 Cooks Ferry Inn, Edmonton

Wed 17/6/70: Victoria Rooms, Bristol

Fri 19/6/70: Great Hall, University, Lancaster, Lancashire

Sat 20/6/70: Civic Hall, Dunstable, Bedfordshire
Fri 26/6/70: Top Rank Suite, Swansea, Glamorganshire, Wales

Wed 5/8/70: The Boston Tea Party, Boston, MA
Thurs 6/8/70: Capitol Theatre, Springfield, MA
Fri 7/8/70: International Music Festival, Goose Lake Park, Jackson, MI
Sun 9/8/70: Milwaukee Arena, Milwaukee, WI (unconfirmed)
Mon 31/8/70: Charlton Park, Bishopsbourne, near Canterbury, Kent (billed as 'The
    Small Faces with Rod Stewart', below headliners Pink Floyd. Also appearing:
    Mott The Hoople, Edgar Broughton Band, Stoneground, Silver Metre, Linda
    Lewis, Shawn Phillips, Daddy Longlegs, and Al Stewart. Comperes: Wavy Gravy,
    General Wastemoreland MC: Jeff Dexter)

Wed 2/9/70: Folkets Hus, Oslo, Norway
Thurs 3/9/70: Liseberg, Stora Scenen, Gothenburg, Sweden (billed as 'Small Faces')
Fri 4/9/70: Rødovre Statsskole, Copenhagen, Denmark
Sat 5/9/70: 'Love And Peace Festival', Isle of Fehmarn, West Germany
On same day: Canned Heat, Mungo Jerry, Taste, Keef Hartley Band, Cat Mother &
    The All-Night Newsboys, Total Music Company and Colosseum (Jimi Hendrix
    was billed to play but didn't until the following day – his last ever concert
    appearance)
Fri 11/9/70: Country Club, Hampstead, north London, with Spyrogyra
Sun 13/9/70: Black Prince Club, The Black Prince Hotel, Bexley, Kent (billed as
    'The Faces featuring Rod Stewart')
Fri 18/9/70: Lyceum Ballroom, London 'Klooks at the Lyceum' – The Kinks were
    due to headline over the Faces but Dave Davies was ill so Faces play with Daddy
    Longlegs and T2 in support
Sat 19/9/70: Eliot College, University of Kent, Canterbury
Fri 25/9/70: Marquee Club, London, with Fail Safe

Second US tour
Thurs 1/10/70: Goddard College, Plainfield, VT
Fri 2 – Sat 3/10/70: Capitol Theatre, Port Chester, NY
Mon 5 – Wed 7/10/70: The Boston Tea Party, Boston, MA
Fri 9/10/70: The Club, Rochester, NY (2 shows)
Sat 10/10/70: Wagner College, Staten Island, NY
Mon 12/10/70: Kingston Armory, Wilkes-Barre, PA
Fri 16 – Sat 17/10/70: Eastown Theater, Detroit, MI, with Savoy Brown
Sun 18/10/70: The Scene, Milwaukee, WI
Fri 23/10/70: Quaker City Rock Festival, The Spectrum, Philadelphia, PA
    'Quaker City Rock No.4' with Grand Funk Railroad, The Small Faces with Rod
    Stewart, Eric Burdon & War & Elizabeth, Isaac Hayes, Mongo Santamaria, and
    Esther Phillips
Sat 24/10/70: Action House, Island Park, Long Island, NY
Tues 27/10/70: Palladium, Birmingham, MI
Wed 28/10/70: Fillmore West, San Francisco, CA (billed as 'Small Faces with Rod
    Stewart')

Fri 30/10/70: Civic Auditorium, Santa Monica, CA (with Roxy featuring Miss Rita
    Coolidge)
Sat 31/10/70: Kinsmen Field House, Edmonton, Alberta, Canada
Sun 1/11/70: PNE Agrodome, Vancouver, Canada (billed as 'Rod Stewart & Small
    Faces', with Redbone and the Legendary Seeds of Time)
Tues 3/11/70: Dewey's Club, Madison, WI
Thurs 5/11/70: Stony Brook College, Stony Brook, Long Island, NY
Fri 6/11/70: Chapin Hall, Williams College, Williamstown, MA (billed as 'Small
    Faces with Rod Stewart', with Poco and Chapin)
Sat 7/11/70: Olympia Stadium, Detroit, MI
Sun 8/11/70: The Depot, Minneapolis, MN
Tues 10/11/70: Fillmore East, NYC. Two shows (recorded for *Long Player*), with
    Black Sabbath, If And Pig Light Show
Wed 11/11/70: The Club, Rochester, NY
Fri 13/11/70: The Syndrome, Chicago, IL
Sat 14/11/70: O'Hara Arena, Dayton, OH
Sun 15/11/70: Commodore Ballroom, Lowell, MA

Fri 20/11/70: Marquee Club, London
Sun 22/11/70: The Wake Arms, Epping, Essex
Sat 28/11/70: University, Leicester, Leicestershire
Sun 29/11/70: The Greyhound, Croydon, Surrey
Sat 5/12/70: Lower Refectory, University, Sheffield, with Terry Reid (introduced
    as 'The Small Faces')
Sun 6/12/70: Black Prince Club, The Black Prince Hotel, Bexley
Mon 7/12/70: Marquee Club, London (private gig filmed for WDR-TV, Germany)
Sat 12/12/70: Sisters Club, 834 Seven Sisters Road, north London
The Faces with Patto

1971

Wed 20/1/71: City Hall, Newcastle, Northumberland, with Dorris Henderson's
    Eclection
Fri 22/1/71: Trent Polytechnic, Nottingham, Nottinghamshire
Tues 26/1/71: La Taverne de l'Olympia, Paris, France
Sat 30/1/71: Westfield College, Hampstead, north London
Sun 31/1/71: Winter Gardens, Bournemouth, Hampshire, with Steamhammer and
    Dorris Henderson's Eclection
Mon 1/2//71: Marquee Club, London, with Dorris Henderson's Eclection

Third US tour with Savoy Brown and The Grease Band

Fri 5/2/71: Mosque Auditorium, Richmond, VA
Sat 6/2/71: Appalachian State Teacher's College, Boone, NC
Sun 7/2/71: Civic Auditorium, Salem, VA
Tues 9/2/71: Music Hall Theatre, Boston, MA (billed as 'Small Faces with Rod
    Stewart')

Wed 10/2/71: Stanley Warner Theatre, Jersey City, NJ (two shows)
Fri 12 & Sat 13/2/71: Pirates World, Dania, FL
Tues 16 & Wed 17/2/71: Fillmore East, NYC
Sat 20/2/71: Metropolitan Sports Arena, Bloomington, MN
Sun 21/2/71: Kiel Opera House, St. Louis, MO
Tues 23/2/71: Cobo Hall, Detroit, MI
Thurs 25/2/71: Civic Auditorium, Knoxville, TN
Sat 27/2/71: The Warehouse, New Orleans, LA (with Savoy Brown and Southern Comfort)
Sun 28/2/71: Shady Grove Musical Theater, Gaithersburg, MD

Wed 10/3/71: The Forum, Inglewood, Los Angeles, CA
Thurs 11/3/71: Berkeley Community Theatre, Berkeley, CA
Fri 12/3/71: Memorial Auditorium, Sacramento, CA
Sat 13/3/71: Selland Arena, Fresno, CA
Sun 14/3/71: Denver Coliseum, Denver, CO
Thurs 18/3/71: San Diego Sports Arena, San Diego, CA
Sat 20/3/71: San Jose Civic Auditorium, San Jose, CA
Sun 21/3/71: Portland Civic Auditorium, Portland, OR
Mon 22/3/71: University of Washington, Tacoma, WA
Tues 23/3/71: Kinsmen Field House, Edmonton, Canada
Wed 24/3/71: PNE Agrodome, Vancouver, Canada, with The Grease Band
Sat 27/3/71: Sam Houston Coliseum, Houston, Texas (billed as 'Rod Stewart & Small Faces', with Savoy Brown)
Sun 28/3/71: Will Rogers Auditorium, Fort Worth, TX
Tues 30/3/71: Atlanta Civic Center, Atlanta, GA
Fri 2/4 & Sat 3/4/71: Capitol Theatre, Port Chester, NY

Wed 14/4/71: Rheinhalle, Dusseldorf, West Germany, with May Blitz and Patto
Thurs 15/4/71: Musikhalle, Hamburg, West Germany, with May Blitz and Patto
Fri 16/4/71: Festhalle, Frankfurt, West Germany, with May Blitz and Patto
Sat 17/4/71: Circus-Krone-Bau, Munich, West Germany, with May Blitz and Patto

Sat 24/4/71: University, Nottingham
Thurs 29/4/71: Camden Festival, The Roundhouse, Chalk Farm, north London, with Dorris Henderson's Eclection
Thurs 6/5/71: Town Hall, Watford, Hertfordshire, with Philip Goodhand-Tait
Sat 8/5/71: The Polytechnic, Leicester, with Atomic Rooster & Roy Young Band
Sat 15/5/71: Crystal Palace Garden Party, Crystal Palace Concert Bowl, south London. 1:30 – 8pm, with Pink Floyd, Mountain and Quiver. Compere: Pete Drummond
Tues 18/5/71: Town Hall, Birmingham, with The Grease Band (*make-up date from 27/1/71*)
Fri 21/5/71: Edward Herbert Building, University, Loughborough, Leicestershire
Sat 22/5/71: The Liverpool Stadium, Liverpool, Lancashire, with Man
Mon 24/5/71: Brighton College of Education, Sussex, with Beggars Death and Fernhill

Wed 26/5/71: Winter Gardens, Bournemouth, with Atomic Rooster
Thurs 27/5/71: The Nag's Head Pub, Wollaston, Northamptonshire (*gig finally played after being cancelled on 15 January and 14 May*)
Fri 28/5/71: 'Fillmore North', Mayfair Ballroom, Newcastle
Sun 30/5/71: The Greyhound, Croydon
Sat 3/7/71: Kingston Polytechnic, Kingston-upon-Thames, Surrey

Fourth US tour with Deep Purple and Southern Comfort

Fri 9/7/71: The Spectrum, Philadelphia, PA
Sat 10/7/71: Public Auditorium, Cleveland, OH
Sun 11/7/71: Minneapolis Auditorium, Minneapolis, MN
Tues 13/7/71: Coliseum, Quebec City, Quebec, Canada
Wed 14/7/71: Milwaukee Auditorium, Milwaukee, WI
Fri 16/7/71: Syria Mosque, Pittsburgh, PA
Sat 17/7/71: Dayton Hara Arena, Dayton, OH (billed as 'The Faces featuring Rod Stewart')
Sun 18/7/71: Toledo Sports Arena, Toledo, OH
Tues 20 & Wed 21/7/71: Auditorium Theatre, Chicago, IL
Fri 23/7/71: Pirates World, Dania, FL (billed as 'Rod Stewart & Faces')
Sat 24/7/71: Orlando Sports Stadium, Orlando, FL
Sun 25/7/71: The Warehouse, New Orleans, LA
Tues 27/7/71: San Antonio Municipal Auditorium, San Antonio, TX
Wed 28/7/71: Sam Houston Coliseum, Houston, TX
Fri 30/7/71: Long Beach Arena, Long Beach, CA
Sat 31/7/71: Salt Palace, Salt Lake City, UT
Sun 1/8/71: Berkeley Community Theatre, Berkeley, CA
Wed 4/8/71: Mississippi River Festival, SIUE, Edwardsville, IL
Thurs 5/8/71: Municipal Auditorium, Atlanta, GA
Fri 6/8/71: Boston Common, Boston, MA
Sat 7/8/71: Washington D.C. National Armory, Washington D.C. (billed as 'Rod Stewart & The Faces'), with Grin

Sun 22/8/71: Jazz Bilzen Festival, Bilzen, Belgium
Fri 27/8/71: Mayfair Ballroom (aka Fillmore North), Newcastle upon Tyne
Sun 29/8/71: Weeley' 71 Festival, Weeley, near Clacton-on-Sea, Essex
Sunday line-up (in order): Mott The Hoople, Groundhogs, Being, Caravan, Lindisfarne, Julie Felix, Quintessence, Head, Hands & Feet, Faces, T. Rex, the Grease Band, Country Jug, Van der Graaf Generator, and Stray

Sun 5/9/71: Queen Elizabeth Hall, London, with Ricotti-Alburquerque
Sat 18/9/71: 'Goodbye Summer' (in aid of Bangla Desh), The Oval, south London, 11am – 9:30 pm, with the Who, Atomic Rooster, Eugene Wallace, America, Mott The Hoople, Quintessence, Lindisfarne, the Grease Band & Cochise MCs: Rikki Farr & Jeff Dexter
Fri 8/10/71: Starkers Club, Royal Ballroom, Boscombe, Hampshire, with Thin Lizzie (*sic*). Promoted by Mel Bush
Sat 16/10/71: Refectory Hall, University, Leeds

Fri 22/10/71: Kinetic Circus, Mayfair Ballroom, Birmingham
Mon 25/10/71: Free Trade Hall, Manchester, Lancashire

Fifth US tour – Bull Angus support on first 10 dates according to *Billboard*:

Tues 23/11/71: Kiel Auditorium, St Louis, MO
Wed 24/11/71: Canton Memorial Civic Center, Canton, OH
Fri 26/11/71: Madison Square Garden, NYC, with Cactus (sold-out show before
    20,000 people) MSG grosses $120,000 tickets $5.50–$7.50
Sun 28/11/71: San Diego Sports Arena, San Diego, CA
Tues 30/11/71: Swing Auditorium, San Bernadino, CA with Cactus and Bull Angus
Wed 1/12/71: Seattle Center Coliseum, Seattle, WA
Fri 3/12/71: P.N.E. Coliseum, Vancouver, Canada, with Cactus and Bull Angus
Sat 4/12/71: Veterans Memorial Auditorium, Des Moines, IA
Sun 5/12/71: Omaha Civic Auditorium, Omaha, NE
Wed 8/12/71: Cobo Hall, Detroit, MI (Audience and Cactus support for rest of
    tour)
Thurs 9/12/71: Maple Leaf Gardens, Toronto, Canada
Fri 10/12/71: The Forum, Montreal, Quebec, Canada
Sun 12/12/71: Baltimore Civic Center, Baltimore, MD
Tues 14/12/71: College Of William and Mary, Williamsburg, VA
Wed 15/12/71: University of Virginia, Charlottesville, VA
Thurs 16/12/71: Memorial Auditorium, Buffalo, NY
Fri 17/12/71: International Amphitheatre, Chicago, IL

1972

Sun 6/2/72: Dacorum Pavilion, Hemel Hempstead, Hertfordshire
Mon 7/2/72: Top Rank Suite, Brighton, with Nazareth and Byzantium
Thurs 10–Sat 12/2/72: Rainbow Theatre, Finsbury Park, north London, with
    Ashton, Gardner & Dyke and Byzantium
Sat 26/2/72: The Ahoy, Rotterdam, Holland
Sun 27/2/72: Martinihal, Groningen, Holland

Sun 5/3/72: Fillmore North, Top Rank Suite, Sunderland, Durham, with
    Byzantium
Fri 10/3/72: Stadhalle, Offenbach, West Germany
Sat 11/3/72: Deutschlandhalle, Berlin, West Germany
Sun 12/3/72: Philipshalle, Dusseldorf, West Germany

Mon 3/4/72: Mar Y Sol Festival, Vega Baja, Puerto Rico.
Three-day festival 1–3/4/72; Monday line-up includes: Nitzinger, Cactus and the
    J. Geils Band

Sixth US tour with Free

Fri 21/4/72: Mid-South Coliseum, Memphis, TN
Sat 22/4/72: Littlejohn Coliseum, Clemson University, Clemson, SC

Mon 24/4/72: Freedom Hall, Louisville, KY
Tues 25/4/72: Auburn Memorial Coliseum, Alabama, AL
Wed 26/4/72: Jacksonville Veterans Memorial Coliseum, Jacksonville, MS
Fri 28/4/72: Hollywood Sportatorium, Hollywood, FL
Sat 29/4/72: Scott Stadium, Charlottesville, VA
Sun 30/4/72: Tampa Stadium, Tampa, FL, (billed as 'Rod Stewart And The Faces')
    and jam with Free

Sat 6/5/72: The Roundhouse, Chalk Farm, north London, with Nazareth
Sat 27/5/72: Great Western Express, Bardney, Lincolnshire
Also on Saturday's bill: Stone The Crows, Strawbs, Head, Hands And Feet, Ry
    Cooder, Persuasions, Helen Reddy, Legs Larry Smith, Steve Goodman, Roxy
    Music, Locomotive GT, Nazareth, Ollie Ollie Ollie DJ: John Peel
Sun 28/5/72: London Coliseum, London, with Badfinger. Charity concert for the
    Sir Malcolm Sargent Cancer Fund for Children
Sun 18/6/72: Free Trade Hall, Manchester (*rescheduled from 31/5/72*)
Sun 25/6/72: Green's Playhouse, Glasgow, Lanarkshire, Scotland (*rescheduled from
    2/6/72*)

Seventh US tour (Rock & Roll Circus Summer Tour '72)
Sat 1/7/72: Boston Garden, Boston, MA
Sun 2/7/72: The Spectrum, Philadelphia, PA
Mon 3/7/72: Rubber Bowl, Akron, OH
Wed 5/7/72: Chrysler Arena, Ann Arbor, MI
Thurs 6/7/72: Onondaga War Memorial Auditorium, Syracuse, NY, with
    Badfinger
Sat 8/7/72: 'Concert 10', Pocono Festival, Pocono International Raceway, Pocono
    Mountains, Long Pond, PA.
Ten-hour festival including Mother Night, Claire Hammill, The Groundhogs,
    Cactus, Edgar Winter, Humble Pie, J. Geils Band, Three Dog Night and ELP
Sun 9/7/72: Civic Arena, Pittsburgh, PA
Mon 10/7/72: Dillon Stadium, Hartford, CT, with Badfinger

Fri 28/7/72: Starkers Club, Corn Exchange, Devizes, Wiltshire, with Demick and
    Armstrong, and Willie Cochrane (bag-piper) Promoter: Mel Bush
Sat 29/7/72: Guildhall, Southampton
Tues 1/8/72: Sherwood Rooms, Nottingham (*in lieu of cancelled Stoke gig on 7/8/72*)
Mon 7/8/72: Trentham Gardens Ballroom, Stoke-on-Trent, Staffordshire
    (*rescheduled from 31/7/72*)
Sat 12/8/72: 11th National Jazz, Blues, & Rock Festival, Reading, Berkshire
Faces topped the bill on the second day. Saturday line-up includes: ELO, Focus, the
    Edgar Broughton Band, If, Linda Lewis, Man, Jonathan Kelly and the Johnny
    Otis Show

Eighth US tour
Sat 19/8/72: Cotton Bowl, Dallas, TX with Three Dog Night

Sun 20/8/72: Atlanta Stadium, Atlanta, GA, with Three Dog Night
Tues 22/8/72: Cessna Stadium, Wichita, KA, with John Kay
Wed 23/8/72: Denver Coliseum, Denver, CO
Fri 25/8/72: Hollywood Bowl, Hollywood, CA, with Ballin' Jack
Sat 26/8/72: San Diego Sports Arena, San Diego, CA, with Ballin' Jack
Sun 27/8/72: Hollywood Palladium, Hollywood, CA
Tues 29/8/72: Las Vegas Stadium, Las Vegas, NV
Wed 30/8/72: Oakland Coliseum, Oakland, CA, with Tower Of Power (billed as
    'Faces with Rod Stewart')
Sat 2/9/72: Seattle Center Coliseum, Seattle, WA
Wed 6/9/72: Cobo Arena, Detroit, MI
Thurs 7/9/72: Maple Leaf Gardens, Toronto, Canada
Fri 8/9/72: Baltimore Civic Center, Baltimore, MY
Mon 11/9/72: Madison Square Garden, with Rory Gallagher

Sat 21/10/72: Winter Gardens, Weston-super-Mare, Somerset
Sun 22/10/72: Kinetic Circus, Mayfair Ballroom, Birmingham
Sun 29/10/72: The Wembley Festival Of Music, Empire Pool, Wembley,
    Middlesex with the Pink Fairies and the New York Dolls. MC: Emperor Rosko

Faces UK tour with special guests Vigrass & Osborne with Stumble

Thurs 7/12/72: Caird Hall, Dundee, Angus, Scotland
Fri 8/12/72: City Hall, Newcastle upon Tyne
Sun 10/12/72: Opera House, Blackpool, Lancashire
Tues 12/12/72: Stadium, Liverpool
Thurs 14/12/72: Town Hall, Leeds
Sat 16/12/72: Sundown Theatre, Brixton, south London
Sun 17 & Mon 18/12/72: Sundown Theatre, Edmonton, north London
Fri 22/12/72: City Hall, Sheffield
Sat 23/12/72: Free Trade Hall, Manchester

1973

Sat 10/3/73: 'Pop Gala', De Vliegermolen Sportshal, Voorburg, The Hague,
    Holland.
Saturday line-up: Colin Blunstone, Argent, Rory Gallagher, Gary Glitter, Chi
    Coltrane, the Faces, the Who.

UK dates (Sutherland Brothers & Quiver support unless otherwise stated)

Sun 8/4/73: Hippodrome, Bristol
Mon 9/4/73 New Theatre, Oxford, Oxfordshire
Tues 10/4/73: Gaumont Theatre, Worcester, Worcestershire
Fri 13/4/73: Fillmore North, Locarno Ballroom, Sunderland, with Beckett
    (*rescheduled from 23/3/73*)

Ninth US tour with Jo Jo Gunne

Mon 23/4/73: Minneapolis Auditorium, Minneapolis, MN
Tues 24/4/73: Kiel Auditorium, St Louis, MO
Thurs 26/4/73: Auditorium Theatre, Chicago, IL
Sat 28/4/73: Ohio State University, Columbus, OH
Mon 30/4/73: Cobo Arena, Detroit, MI
Wed 2/5/73: Boston Gardens, Boston, MA
Thurs 3/5/73: Providence Civic Center, Providence, RI
Sat 5/5/73: Hampton Rhodes Coliseum, Hampton, VA
Mon 7/5/73: Springfield Civic Center, Springfield, MA
Wed 9/5/73: The Spectrum, Philadelphia, PA
Thurs 10/5/73: Nassau Coliseum, Uniondale, Long Island, NY
Sat 12/5/73: Roanoke Civic Center, Roanoke, VA
Sun 13/5/73: Indiana State Fair Coliseum, Indianapolis, IN

Fri 1/6/73: Sundown Theatre, Edmonton, north London
Sun 3/6/73: Sundown Theatre, Edmonton, north London
Mon 4/6/73: Sundown Theatre, Edmonton, north London
Wed 6/6/73: Sundown Theatre, Edmonton, north London

European tour – first dates with Tetsu Yamauchi on bass

Mon 16/7/73: Palasport, Turin, Italy
Tues 17/7/73: Palasport, Bologna, Italy
Wed 18/7/73: Palasport, Rome, Italy (Area support on all Italian dates)
Sun 22/7/73: '2. Sommer Rock Festival', Radstadion, Frankfurt, West Germany
    (Introduced by Keith Moon) Sunday line-up includes: Chuck Berry, Rory
    Gallagher, Sly & The Family Stone, Nazareth and Blue MC: Rikki Farr
Sun 29/7/73: Hard Rock, Manchester (first UK gig with Tetsu; Kenney collapses
    and Willy Wilson from Sutherland Brothers & Quiver replaces him for end of set)

Sat 11/8/73: Kursaal Ballroom, Southend, Essex
Fri 17/8/73: Top Rank Suite, Doncaster, Yorkshire
Sat 25/8/73: 12th National Jazz, Blues & Rock Festival, Reading
Faces topped the bill on the second day. Saturday line-up includes: Status Quo,
    Andy Bown, Magma, Caravan, Fumble, Jack the Lad, Strider, Claire Hammill,
    Tasvallan Presidenti, Riff Raff and Dave Ellis

Tenth US tour with Rory Gallagher

Sat 15/9/73: Bayfront Center, St. Petersburg, FL (billed as 'Rod Stewart & The
    Faces')
Wed 19/9/73: Duke University, Durham, NC
Thurs 20/9/73: Richmond Coliseum, Richmond, VA
Sat 22/9/73: Roberts Stadium, Evansville, IN
Sun 23/9/73: University of Tennessee, Knoxville, TN
Tues 25/9/73: LSU Assembly Center, Baton Rouge, LA
Thurs 27/9/73: Sam Houston Coliseum, Houston, TX

Fri 28/9/73: Convention Center Arena, San Antonio, TX
Sat 29/9/73: Tarrant County Convention Center, Fort Worth, TX
Mon 1/10/73: El Paso County Coliseum, El Paso, TX
Tues 2/10/73: Johnson's Gym, University of New Mexico, Alberquerque, NM
Wed 3/10/73: Denver Coliseum, Denver, CO
Fri 5/10/73: Tucson Convention Center, Tucson, AZ
Sat 6/10/73: Veterans Memorial Coliseum, Phoenix, AZ
Tues 9/10/73: Cow Palace, San Francisco, CA
Wed 10/10/73: San Diego Sports Arena, San Diego, CA
Thurs 11/10/73: Selland Arena, Fresno, CA
Sat 13/10/73: Campus Stadium, UCSB, Santa Barbara, CA, with Rory Gallagher
    and Dalton & Dubarri
Mon 15/10/73: Long Beach Arena, Long Beach, CA
Tues 16/10 & Wed 17/10/73: Anaheim Convention Center, Anaheim, CA
Thurs 18/10/73: Hollywood Palladium, Hollywood, CA

UK tour, supported by John Baldry and band replaced midway through by Strider

Thurs 29/11/73: Granada, East Ham, east London
Fri 30/11/73: Kilburn Gaumont State, Kilburn, north London
Sun 2/12/73: Hippodrome, Bristol
Mon 3/12/73: Gaumont Theatre, Worcester
Fri 7/12/73: Odeon Theatre, Birmingham
Sat 8/12/73: Queens Hall, Leeds
Sun 9/12/73: Empire Theatre, Liverpool
Tues 11/12/73: Free Trade Hall, Manchester
Wed 12/12/73: Opera House, Blackpool
Sat 15/12 & Sun 16/12/73: Apollo Theatre, Glasgow
Mon 17/12/73: Odeon Theatre, Newcastle upon Tyne
Wed 19/12/73: Winter Gardens, Bournemouth
Thurs 20/12/73: Granada Theatre, Sutton, Surrey
Sun 23/12/73: New Theatre, Oxford
Mon 24/12/73: Sundown Theatre, Edmonton, north London

1974

Australasian & Far East tour

Sun 27/1/74: Western Springs Stadium, Auckland, New Zealand
Fri 1/2/74: Randwick Racecourse, Sydney, New South Wales, Australia (billed as
    'The Faces')
Sun 3/2/74: South Melbourne Football Ground, Melbourne, Victoria, Australia
    (billed as Rod Stewart/The Faces). *As with Auckland, this was the only daytime
    concert on the tour.*
Tues 5/2/74: Memorial Park Drive, Adelaide, South Australia
Fri 8/2/74: Festival Hall, Melbourne, Australia (billed as 'The Faces with Rod
    Stewart')

Sat 9/2/74: R.A.S. Hordern Pavilion, Sydney, Australia (billed as 'Faces with Rod Stewart')
Tues 12/2/74: Hong Kong Football Club Stadium, Hong Kong
Fri 15/2/74: Kosei-Nenkin Hall, Osaka, Japan
Tues 19/2/74: Budokan Hall, Tokyo, Japan
Wed 20/2/74: Budokan Hall, Tokyo, Japan

Sat 6/7/74: Buxton Festival, with Humble Pie (Memphis Horns guest with Faces)
Saturday line up includes: Humble Pie, Lindisfarne, Chapman/Whitney, Trapeze, Strider and National Flag
Sat 13/7 & Sun 14/7/74: Kilburn Gaumont State, Kilburn, north London (Ron Wood & Friends) supported by Chili Willi & The Red Hot Peppers

Sat 17/8/74: Jazz Bilzen Festival, Bilzen, Belgium

European tour with Strider

Fri 13/9/74: Palais de Sports, Paris, France
Tues 24/9/74: Donauhalle, Ulm, West Germany
Wed 25/9/74: ATSV-Sporthalle, Saarbrucken, West Germany
Sat 28/9/74: Musikhalle, Hamburg, West Germany
Sun 29/9/74: Niedersachsenhalle, Hanover, West Germany
Tues 1/10/74: Stadhalle, Karlsruhe, West Germany
Wed 2/10/74: Stadhalle, Frankfurt, West Germany
Fri 4/10/74: Kongressaal Deutsches Museum, Munich, West Germany
Sun 6/10/74: Messehalle, Nuremberg, West Germany
Sat 12/10/74: Concert Hall, Rotterdam, Holland
Sun 13/10/74: Martinihal, Groningen, Holland
Fri 18/10/74: Tivolis Koncertsal, Copenhagen, Denmark
Sat 19/10/74: Vejlby-Risskov Hallen, Århus, Denmark
Wed 23/10/74: Konserthuset, Stockholm, Sweden
Thurs 24/10/74: Olympen, Lund, Sweden

UK tour supported by Strider

Fri 15/11, Sun 17/11 & Mon 18/11/74: Odeon Theatre, Lewisham, south London
Sat 23/11 & Sun 24/11/74: Belle Vue, Manchester
Tues 26/11 & Wed 27/11/74: Odeon Theatre, Newcastle upon Tyne
Fri 29/11 & Sat 30/11/74: Odeon Theatre, Birmingham
Sun 1/12/74: Trentham Gardens, Stoke-on-Trent
Tues 3/12 & Wed 4/12/74: Odeon Theatre, Taunton, Somerset
Fri 6/12/74: Winter Gardens, Bournemouth
Sun 8/12/74: New Theatre, Oxford
Tues 10/12 & Wed 11/12/74: Opera House, Blackpool
Fri 13/12/74: Odeon Theatre, Edinburgh, Scotland
Sat 14/12, Mon 16/12–Wed 18/12/74: Apollo Theatre, Glasgow, Scotland
Sat 21/12–Mon 23/12/74: Kilburn Gaumont State, Kilburn, north London

1975

Eleventh US tour

Tues 11/2/75: War Memorial Auditorium, Rochester, NY
Wed 12/2/75: Wings Stadium, Kalamazoo, MI
Fri 14/2/75: Cobo Hall, Detroit, MI
Sat 15/2/75: Capital Centre, Largo, MD, with Blue Oyster Cult
Sun 16/2/75: Civic Center, Philadelphia, PA, with Duke Williams & The Extremes
Tues 18/2/75: International Amphitheatre, Chicago, IL
Thurs 20/2/75: Indiana Convention Center, Indianapolis, IN
Fri 21/2/75: Charleston Civic Center, Charleston, VA
Sat 22/2/75: Cincinnati Gardens, Cincinnati, OH
Mon 24/2/75: Madison Square Garden, NYC, with Blue Oyster Cult
Tues 25/2/75: Providence Civic Center, Providence, RI
Wed 26/2/75: New Haven Veterans Memorial Coliseum, New Haven, CT
Sun 2/3/75: Cow Palace, San Francisco, with Foghat
Mon 3/3 & Wed 5/3/75: The Forum, Inglewood, LA, with Foghat
Thurs 6/3/75: Anaheim Convention Center, Anaheim, CA
Fri 7/3/75: Swing Auditorium, San Bernadino, CA, with Foghat
Sun 9/3/75: Veterans Memorial Coliseum, Phoenix, AZ
Wed 12/3/75: HEC Edmundson Pavilion, Seattle, WA
Thurs 13/3/75: PNE Coliseum, Vancouver, Canada, with Foghat

Twelfth (and final) US tour (featuring Jesse Ed Davis on additional guitar & 12-piece string orchestra)

Tues 19/8/75: Asheville Civic Center, Asheville, NC
Wed 20/8/75: Norfolk Scope Arena, Norfolk, VA, with Elvin Bishop and Uriah Heep
Fri 22/8/75: Roosevelt Stadium, Jersey City, NJ, with Ten Years After and Lynyrd Skynyrd
Sat 23/8/75: Cleveland Stadium, Cleveland, OH, with Uriah Heep, Blue Oyster Cult, Aerosmith and Mahogany Rush
Sun 24/8/75: Mesker Amphitheatre, Evansville, IN
Tues 26/8/75: Kiel Auditorium, St Louis, MO
Wed 27/8/75: Mid-South Coliseum, Memphis, TN
Thurs 28/8/75: Myriad Convention Center, Oklahoma City, OK
Sat 30/8/75: 'Sunshine Festival', Anaheim Stadium, Anaheim, CA, with Loggins & Messina and Fleetwood Mac
Sun 31/8/75: Balboa Stadium, San Diego, CA, with Loggins & Messina
Mon 1/9/75: Madera Speedway, Fresno, CA, with Black Sabbath and Lynyrd Skynyrd
Sat 6/9/75: Spartan Stadium, San Jose, CA
Sun 7/9/75: 'Sunshine Festival', Hughes Stadium, Sacramento, CA, with Loggins & Messina and Peter Frampton
Tues 9/9 & Wed 10/9/75: H.I.C. Arena, Honolulu, HI, with Peter Frampton
Fri 12/9/75: McNichols Sports Arena, Denver, CO

Sat 13/9/75: Johnson's Gym, University of New Mexico, Alberquerque, NM

Mon 14/9/75: University of Arizona Stadium, Tucson, AZ

Fri 19/9/75: Convention Center Arena, San Antonio, TX, with Blue Oyster Cult

Sat 20/9/75: Hofheinz Pavilion, Houston, TX, with Blue Oyster Cult

Sun 21/9/75: Convention Center Arena, Ft. Worth, TX, with Blue Oyster Cult

Tues 23/9/75: Municipal Auditorium, New Orleans, LA, with Hammersmith

Wed 24/9/75: Municipal Auditorium, Atlanta, GA

Fri 26/9/75: Municipal Auditorium, Nashville, TN, with the James Gang

Sat 27/9/75: Charlotte Coliseum, Charlotte, NC, with Uriah Heep

Sun 28/9/75: University of South Carolina, Columbia, SC

Tues 30/9/75: Ohio State Fairgrounds Coliseum, Columbus, OH, with Charlie
   Daniels

Wed 1/10/75: The Spectrum, Philadelphia, PA, with Gary Wright

Fri 3/10/75: Assembly Hall, Indiana University, Bloomington, OH

Sat 4/10/75: ACC South Bend, Indiana, IN

Sun 5/10/75: University of Dayton Arena, Dayton, OH

Wed 8/10/75: Toledo Sports Arena, Toledo, OH

Thurs 9/10/75: Civic Arena, Pittsburgh, PA

Sat 11/10/75: Cole Field House, University of Maryland, College Park, MD

Sun 12/10/75: Nassau Coliseum, Uniondale, Long Island, NY

Mon 13/10/75: Boston Garden, Boston, MA, with Peter Frampton (*rescheduled from
   10/10/75*)

Wed 15/10 & Thurs 16/10/75: Lakeland Civic Center, Lakeland, FL, with Jeff
   Beck and Aerosmith

Sat 18/10/75: Gulfstream Race Track, Hallandale Beach, FL

Sun 19/10/75: The Omni, Atlanta, GA with Jeff Beck and Aerosmith

Tues 21/10 & Wed 22/10/75: Cobo Arena, Detroit, MI

Fri 24/10/75: The Forum, Montreal, Canada

Sat 25/10/75: Ottawa Civic Centre, Ottawa, Canada with Sha Na Na

Mon 27/10/75: Maple Leaf Gardens, Toronto, Canada

Thurs 30/10/75: Kolf Sports Arena, University of Wisconsin, Oshkosh, WI

Fri 31/10/75: Chicago Stadium, Chicago, IL

Sat 1/11/75: Labor Temple, Minneapolis, MN (last ever Faces concert)

Acknowledgments

Back in late 2008 when my editor Chris Charlesworth proposed I take on the task of chronicling the Faces story, little did I realise to what gargantuan lengths it would grow in doing the subject adequate justice. With the possible exception of Crosby, Stills, Nash & Young, no other group presents the biographer with such a considerable challenge of unravelling the individuals' various backgrounds, previous musical journeys and subsequent careers.

An intensive year of development began with a trawl through virtually every major UK and US music publication from the mid-Sixties into the Seventies, as well as certain regional papers, being undertaken at the British Library, St. Pancras, and the British Newspaper Library, in Colindale, north London. Certain addresses and events were identified with the help of Samantha Letters in the Local Studies department at Uxbridge Library, Valerie Crosby at Bruce Castle Museum & Archives (Haringey Culture, Libraries & Learning) and Julian Carr at the London Metropolitan Archives in Clerkenwell. The radio and television research was conducted thanks to Jeff Walden at the BBC Written Archives Centre in Caversham, Berkshire.

In a concurrent operation, considerable effort went into tracking down and making approaches to the supporting characters in the Faces story – some of whom had never previously spoken about their association with the group and that incredible time in their lives.

Of those sharing their memories I am indebted to (in alphabetical order): Keith Altham, Brian Auger, Andrew Bown, Pete Buckland, Peter 'Dougal' Butler, Phil Chapman, Chris Charlesworth, Phil Chen, Ron Chimes, Richard Cole, Charlie Daniels, Jeff Dexter, Bob Edkins, Charlie Fernandez, Richard Fernandez, Billy Gaff, Mick Gower, Gary Grainger, Dee Harrington, Mickey Heyes, Glyn Johns, Jan Jones, Stan Lane Jr., Glen Matlock, Mike McInnerney, Ali MacKenzie, Tony Munroe, Ron Nevison, Billy Nicholls, Gary Osborne, Craig Petty, Jonathan Rowlands, Sandy Sarjeant, Russ Schlagbaum, Jerry Shirley, Don Stewart, Sue Tacker, Chris Welch, Peter Whitehead, Tom Wright, Martin Wyatt.

While the actual subject's input can validate a biography it can also throw up confusion, especially as living within the vortex can often involve, in this example, five differing accounts of what really happened – a case of "when the legend becomes fact, print the legend". In an attempt to sift through myth and fact, approaches were made to Rod Stewart, Ronnie Wood, Kenney Jones and Ian McLagan for their input.

Rod's PR was most helpful but because he was touring through much of 2010 his schedule was unfortunately not compatible with my deadline. Additionally it transpires he has plans for an autobiography for which he would doubtless prefer to keep his best memories of the period.

Through the Rolling Stones' office, Ronnie Wood felt he'd said all he had to say about the Faces via his contributions to Genesis Publications' limited edition photographic doorstopper. While I have no wish to denigrate him, having read both of his heavily ghost written and often uncharacteristically self-aggrandizing autobiographies, and hearing some of the anecdotes related throughout his weekly digital radio show, the ravages of nearly four decades in the eye of the rock 'n' roll hurricane have meant Ronnie's memory is not the most reliable, as he admits in the front pages of McLagan's autobiography, *All The Rage* . . . "You never said anything about writing a book . . . It's just as well you are, because I wouldn't remember a bloody thing!"

If, as buddy and bandmate Keith Richards claimed for his 2010 auto-biography *Life*, "This is the life. Believe it or not I haven't forgotten any of it," Woody is the opposite, bless him.

Kenney Jones redirected my enquiry to his manager who, after keeping me on hold for several weeks, eventually asked, "What's in it for Kenney?" It brought to mind what Ernest Hemingway is alleged to have remarked to Scott Fitzgerald when the latter said, "The rich are different from you and me." "Yes," replied Hemingway, "they have more money." Fortunately I was able to fall back on an unpublished interview I did with Jones from 1998 covering his childhood, through the Small Faces up to the formation of the Faces, quotes from which are used in the first part of this book.

Ian McLagan was enthusiastic and supportive of the project from the outset and my grateful thanks go to him for being generous with his time, sitting for three lengthy phone interviews to his studio in Texas and numerous e-mail follow-ups as well as passing on contact details for other individuals connected with the story. My special thanks go to Mac and his manager Lynne Rossi for all their help. (Visit www.ianmclagan.com and www.macspages.com for all up-to-date info on Mac and more.)

I had a lead to Tetsu Yamauchi in Japan but as he is currently no longer involved with music, I respected his stated wish not to speak about his time in the Faces. Through an intermediary, Faces secretary Shirley Arnold politely turned down my request for an interview, as did the band's early studio engineer Martin Birch but I thank them for considering it.

I am grateful to the following who assisted along the way with help and information, no matter how minor or major: David Bainbridge, John Baker, Moira Bellas, Will Birch, Jerry Bloom, Alex Budnyj, Murray Cammick, Gordon Chilvers, Dave Clark, Sherry Daly, Jody Denberg, Tim Derbyshire, Jeff Dexter, Steve Ellis, Richard Evans, Brian Finlay, Pete Frame, Kate Gadd, Bill Harrison, Tony Haslam, Richard Havers, Paolo Hewitt, Clinton Heylin,

Doug Hinman, Chris Hjort, Becky Hutton, Bruce Jarvis, Spencer Kelly, Matt Kent, Tony King, Mike M. Koshitani, Mark Lewisohn, Nick Logan, Olle Lundin, Nick Maingay, Dave Marsh, Gareth Millard, Chris Morphet, Billy Nicholls, Gary Osborne, John Reed, Nigel Reeve, Johnny Rogan, Keith Smart, Simon Smith, Bob Solly, Mike Stax, Leigh Stephens, Don Stewart, Nick Warburton, Neal Webb, Simon Wells, Trevor Williams, Philip Windeatt, Ali Zayeri, Clive Zone.

Certain individuals deserve specific commendation, namely Russ Schlagbaum for opening his diaries and an almost total recall of his time with the Faces and Ronnie Lane; Pete Buckland, for trawling his memory to answer my request for minutiae no matter how trivial and generously allowing me access to his original tour schedules; to Rupert Williams and James Mackie for copies of interviews conducted for their excellent Ronnie Lane documentary *The Passing Show* – if you haven't seen it, I highly recommend that you do – and to Dan Valentine for permission to quote extensively from interviews conducted by his late, lamented mother Penny.

To Dave McNarie, webmaster of the fab Faces site www.the-faces.com for help in various areas and John Hellier for supplying ready answers to various queries and permission to reproduce quotes from interviews in *The Darlings Of Wapping Wharf Launderette*. For the last word in all things Small Faces and related, go to: www.wappingwharf.com

A special thank you above all must go to John Gray of Smiler – The Rod Stewart/Faces Fan Club (www.rodstewartfanclub.com) for invaluable access to his extensive collection of scrapbooks and interview material relating to the Faces, and his work with Neal Webb on the discography and concert listing. Also to Chris Charlesworth, my editor, for his enthusiasm, encouragement and patience – as deadlines came and went – and providing the opportunity in the first place and lastly but by no means least, to my darling Felicia, the sweetest Face of all, who spent the first year of our married life, putting up with my non-stop keyboard tapping while I was adrift in Faces land.

Let me lift a glass and say a big "Cheers" to you all.

See you at the bar!

Andy Neill,
London
January 2011

Bibliography

Bacon, Tony: *London Live* (Balafon Books, 1999)

Badman, Keith & Rawlings, Terry: *Quite Naturally: The Small Faces* (Complete Music, 1997)

Bangs, Lester & Nelson, Paul: *Rod Stewart* (Putnam Publishing Group, 1981)

Burton, Peter: *A Life On The Town* (New English Library, 1977)

Charlesworth, Chris: *Deep Purple: The Illustrated Biography* (Omnibus Press, 1983)

Chesterton, GK: *All Things Considered* (Quiet Vision Publishing, 2004)

Cohn, Nik: *Awopbopaloobop Alopbamboom: Pop From The Beginning* (1969, reprint edition Pimlico Books 2004)

Davies, Ray: *X-Ray An Autobiography* (Overlook Press, 1995)

Ewbank Tim & Hildred, Stafford: *Rod Stewart: A Biography* (Headline, 1991)

Fletcher, Tony: *Dear Boy: The Life Of Keith Moon* (Omnibus Press, 1998)

Gray, John: *Rod Stewart: The Visual Documentary* (Omnibus Press, 1992)

Hewitt, Paolo & Hellier, John: *All Too Beautiful: Steve Marriott* (Helter Skelter, 2004)

Hinman, Doug: *The Kinks: All Day And All Of The Night* (Backbeat Books, 2004)

Hjort, Christopher: *Strange Brew: The British Blues Boom* (Jawbone, 2007)

Hjort, Christopher & Hinman, Doug: *Jeff's Book* (Rock 'n' Roll Research Press, 2000)

McLagan, Ian 'Mac': *All The Rage* (Sidgwick & Jackson, 1998)

Melly, Jim: *Last Orders Please: The Faces* (Ebury Press, 2003)

Miles: *The Rolling Stones: A Visual Documentary* (Omnibus Press, 1994)

Neill, Andy & Kent, Matt: *Anyway Anyhow Anywhere: The Complete Chronicle Of The Who 1958–1978* (Friedman/Fairfax, 2002)

Oldham, Andrew: *Stoned* (Secker & Warburg, 2000)

Oldham, Andrew: *2Stoned* (Secker & Warburg, 2002)

Palmer, Alan: *The East End* (John Murray, 1989)

Paytress, Mark: *Bolan: The Rise And Fall Of A 20th Century Superstar* (Omnibus Press, 2002)

Pidgeon, John: *Rod Stewart & The Changing Faces* (Panther, 1976)

Rawlings, Terry: *Rock On Wood: The Origin Of A Rock & Roll Face* (Boxtree, 1999)

Repsch, John: *The Legendary Joe Meek* (Woodford House Publishing Ltd, 1989)

Rogan, Johnny: *Starmakers & Svengalis: The History Of British Pop Management* (Macdonald/Queen Anne Press, 1988)

Rylatt, Keith & Scott, Phil: *CENtral 1179: The Story Of Manchester's Twisted Wheel Club* (Bee Cool Publishing, 2001)

Sandbrook, Dominic: *State Of Emergency: The Way We Were 1970–74* (Allen Lane, 2010)

Selwood, Clive: *All The Moves (But None Of The Licks)* (Peter Owen, 2003)

Stewart, Rod: *Rod: The Autobiography* (Century, 2012)

Taylor, Derek: *It Was Twenty Years Ago Today* (Bantam Press, 1987)

Tobler, John & Grundy, Stuart: *The Guitar Greats* (BBC Books, 1983)

Tremlett, George: *The Rod Stewart Story* (Futura, 1976)

Twelker, Uli & Schmitt, Roland: *Happy Boys Happy! A Rock History Of The Small Faces And Humble Pie* (Sanctuary Publishing, 1997)

Warwick, Neil, Kutner, Jon & Brown, Tony: *The Complete Book Of The British Charts Singles And Albums* (Third Edition) (Omnibus Press, 2004)

Wood, Ron with German, Bill: *The Works* (Harper Collins Publishers, 1987)

Wood, Ronnie: *Ronnie: The Autobiography* (St Martin's Press, 2007)

Wright, Tom, with Susan van Hencke: *Roadwork: Rock 'n' Roll Turned Inside Out* (Hal Leonard, 2007)

Wyman, Bill: *Rolling With The Stones* (Dorling Kindersley, 2002)

Source Notes

The main text includes secondary quotes given by the Faces and associates to various interviewers for assorted publications over the years. These were used by the author because the individual in question was unavailable or to maintain objectivity on a matter untainted by hindsight. Accordingly, a listing of these follows (where no writer appears, none was credited on the source material) to stand alongside the preceding Bibliography:

Chapter One:
NME 25/2/66: 'Small Faces: Big Problems!' by Alan Smith
The Darlings of Wapping Wharf Launderette #14: Ronnie Lane interview by
    Allan Vorda 5/4/87, Houston, TX
The Passing Show transcript of Kenney Jones interview by Rupert Williams
    2004
My Generation: The Small Faces: Kay Marriott interview by Len Brown
    Granada Television 1995
Rave July 1966: 'Facts On Faces' by Alan Freeman
The Darlings of Wapping Wharf Launderette # 10: Jimmy Winston interview
    by John Hellier 1996
NME 15/10/65: 'Small Faces Get Their Fans Going' by Norrie
    Drummond
Storytellers: David Bowie (Bowie re: Steve Marriott) VH-1 1999
The Darlings of Wapping Wharf Launderette # 27: 'Windows, Rockets And
    Ronnie Lane!'/ www.vintagehofner.co.uk re: Selmer quotes
Steve Marriott transcript interview by John Hellier 24/2/84

Chapter Two:
Sounds 3/8/74: 'Where Was We?' Ronnie Lane interview by Penny
    Valentine
The Darlings of Wapping Wharf Launderette # 12: Jimmy Winston interview
    by John Hellier 1996
Beat Instrumental # 36 April 1966: Player Of The Month: Ian McLagan
Beat Instrumental # 32 December 1965: 'A New Small Face'
Melody Maker 12/2/66: 'Small Faces get hung up – on sounds'
Fabulous 208 20/8/66: fan letter from 'Dulcie Row'
Melody Maker 26/9/70: 'The two Faces of Rod . . .' by Mark Plummer

Chapter Three:

Melody Maker 25/1/64: 'After Cy Davies – Long John and the Hoochie Coochies' by Bob Dawbarn

Record Mirror 14/9/74: 'Smiler – Rod talks to Pete Harvey'

Melody Maker 13/1/73: Rod Stewart column re: Al Jolson – as told to Peter Burton

Disc & Music Echo 18/9/71: 'The amazing Mr. S' by Caroline Boucher

Record Mirror 3/10/70: 'How Rod's Old Raincoat Didn't Let Him Down . . .' by Rob Partridge

Penthouse Vol. 10 No. 2 1975: Interview with Rod Stewart by Patsy Ledger

The Sun 16/5/74: 'Rod's so soccer crazy he wants to buy Hampden!' by Frank Clough

Smiler # 13 autumn 1987: 'A Chat With Mary [Stewart]' by John Gray & Alison Knight

Mojo May 1995: 'Rod Stewart: The Graveyard Shift' by Will Birch

Melody Maker 5/10/74: Rod Stewart re: Ramblin' Jack Elliott

Melody Maker 26/9/70: 'The two Faces of Rod . . .' by Mark Plummer

Melody Maker 10/7/71: 'Hot Rod' by Roy Hollingworth

Rolling Stone 24/12/70: Rod Stewart interview

Zigzag #19 May 1971: 'Face to face with a Face' by Pete Frame

Sounds 19/12/70: 'The *Sounds* Talk-In: Rod Stewart' by Royston Eldridge

Smiler # 35 spring 1993: John Baldry interview by John Gray & Steve Holmes

Melody Maker 30/5/64: 'Baldry blasts R&B greats' by Bob Dawbarn

NME 13/11/71: Rod Stewart interview (Part 1) by Nick Logan

Record Mirror 20/11/71: 'Rod's Life And Hard Times' by Bill McAllister

Hampstead & Highgate Express October 1964: 'Rod, The Hoochie Koochie Man From Highgate' by J.O.

Zoo World 30/8/73: 'Rod Stewart Cockerel Haired Working Class Hero' by Michael Wale

Chapter Four:

Daily Express 26/10/72: Ron Wood interview with David Wigg

Melody Maker 13/7/74: 'The Faces – it's like a marriage!' by Geoff Brown

Disc & Music Echo 29/1/72: 'Ron Wood: larfin' all the way to the bank' by Caroline Boucher

Evening News 24/4/74: 'With a little help from his friends . . .' by John Blake

Ugly Things # 13 1994: 'The Birds . . . Uncaged' by Mike Stax

Uxbridge Weekly Post 4/8/65: 'Byrds V. Birds Clash in Local Pop Row'

Sounds 11/9/71: 'Ronnie Wood in The *Sounds* Talk-In' by Penny Valentine

Chapter Five:

The New York Times 15/6/68: 'Jeff Beck Group Cheered In Debut: British Pop Singers Delight Fillmore East Audience' by Robert Shelton

Sounds 10/10/70: 'Rod Remains A Face' by Penny Valentine

More Golden Eggs album: Keith Relf interview by William Stout 1974

Sounds 7/7/73: 'The Jeff Beck Story' by Steve Rosen

King Biscuit Flower Hour Jeff Beck radio interview with Scott Muni 13/8/89

Trouser Press # 22 October 1977: Jimmy Page interview (Part 2) by Dave
  Schulps

Rolling Stone # 120 26/10/72: 'Third time around: Jeff Beck: Back in the
  fudge again' by Paul Bernstein

Dancing In The Street: 'Crossroads' (Jeff Beck interview re: Jimi Hendrix)
  BBC Television 1996

Disc & Music Echo 29/1/72: 'Ron Wood: larfin' all the way to the bank' by
  Caroline Boucher

Hit Parader July 1967: 'Jeff's Future Beckons' by Valerie Wilmer

NME 27/5/67: 'Jeff Beck not nearly so wicked as he thinks he is' by Keith
  Altham

Guitar Vol. 3 No. 4 June 1993: Jeff Beck interview by Douglas J. Noble

Melody Maker 11/3/67: 'Beck Leaves Tour – Disastrous Debut' by Chris
  Welch

Sunday Mirror 12/3/67: 'Pop Groups, Sex-Mad Girls And 'Don't Care' Parents' by Jack Bentley

Sounds 16/11/74: 'Rod The Haystack In LA' by Harvey Kubernik & Justin
  Pierce

Record Mirror 29/4/67: 'Jeff won't be making another disc like 'Hi Hi Silver
  Lining'. . .' by Peter Jones

Beat Instrumental # 91 November 1970: Player Of The Month: Ron Wood

Melody Maker 6/5/67: ''Hi Ho Silver Lining' Is Just Not Jeff'

Melody Maker 25/12/71: Rod 'the Face of 1971' interview (Part 1)

NME 20/11/71: Rod Stewart interview (Part 2) by Nick Logan

Sounds 15/9/73: 'Reizner Citizen Of The World' by Martin Hayman

Ugly Things # 15 1997: 'The Creation!' by Mike Stax

Zigzag # 20 June 1971: 'My Beck Pages' by Pete Frame

Rolling Stone 24/12/70: Rod Stewart interview

Sounds 26/5/73: 'Nicky Hopkins In The Talk-In' by Chuck Pulin

Rolling Stone 1/2/69: 'It Happened In 1968'

Chapter Six:

Sounds 1/7/72: 'Oldham – still going strong' by Penny Valentine

Steve Marriott transcript interview by John Hellier 24/2/84

Record Mirror 28/8/65: 'Nico leads Andrews's Off Beat Company . . .' by
  Peter Jones

Sounds 19/12/70: 'The *Sounds* Talk-In: Rod Stewart' by Royston Eldridge

The Darlings of Wapping Wharf Launderette # 31: Pete Townshend interview
  1969 (no source/writer credited)

Ronnie Lane interview with Jody Denberg KLBJ-FM Austin 9/4/86
Disc & Music Echo 20/4/68: Small Faces 'Lazy Sunday'
Rave November 1966: 'Little Stevie Wonders . . .' by Dawn James
NME 17/4/71: 'The Faces Of '71' Ronnie Lane interview by Nick Logan

Chapter Seven:
Rolling Stone 25/11/71: 'Ronnie Lane – the Story of a Face' by Andrew
    Bailey
NME 20/11/71: Rod Stewart interview (Part 2) by Nick Logan
Steve Marriott transcript interview by John Hellier 24/2/84
Melody Maker 4/1/69: 'Stevie Marriott is alive and well and living in Essex'
    by Chris Welch
Sounds 19/2/72: 'Memories And Mr. Lane' Ronnie Lane interview (Part 1)
    by Penny Valentine
Melody Maker 21/6/69: 'At least Mac still has his sense of humour' by Chris
    Welch
Disc & Music Echo 8/2/69: 'Is Steve Marriott quitting the Small Faces?'
Disc & Music Echo 22/2/69: 'Steve Marriott – Small Faces Split 'Within A
    Month''
Jersey Evening Post 10/3/69: 'The end of the Small Faces? New group on the
    way'
Melody Maker 26/4/69: 'Pop Giants' Supergroup: Steve Marriott-Peter
    Frampton tie-up' by Chris Welch
NME 17/4/71: 'The Faces Of '71' Ronnie Lane interview by Nick Logan
NME 14/3/70: 'It's Music, Not Faces That Count' by Gordon Coxhill
Melody Maker 7/3/70: 'Mickey Waller: diary of an international drummer'
    by Bob Dawbarn
Zigzag #19 May 1971: 'Face to face with a Face' by Pete Frame
NME 19/10/74: 'Escape routes for lead guitar . . .' Ron Wood article
Sounds 10/7/71: ''umble Rod takes a bow' by Penny Valentine
NME 14/9/74: 'Spare the Rod' Rod Stewart interview by James Johnson
Sounds 11/9/71: 'Ronnie Wood in The *Sounds* Talk-In' by Penny Valentine
Rolling Stone 24/12/70: Rod Stewart interview
Sounds 26/5/73: 'Nicky Hopkins In The Talk-In' by Chuck Pulin
Sounds 19/12/70: 'The Sounds Talk-In: Rod Stewart' by Royston Eldridge
I'm In A Rock 'n' Roll Band: Jeff Beck interview BBC Television 2010

Chapter Eight:
Music Now 15/8/70: 'It means a lot to us to get recognition in England . . .'
    by Tony Norman
Record Collector # 153 May 1992: 'Quiet Melon'
Melody Maker 21/6/69: 'At least Mac still has his sense of humour' by Chris
    Welch

Mick Liber/David Montgomery/David Bentley interviews
  www.nickwarburton.com
NME 5/8/72: 'Working class hero Rod' by Nick Logan
NME 21/10/72: 'For Rod – a snake bite from the past' by Danny Holloway
NME 20/11/71 Rod Stewart interview (Part 2) by Nick Logan
Melody Maker 7/3/70: 'Mickey Waller: diary of an international drummer'
  by Bob Dawbarn
Smiler # 20 summer 1989: Mickey Waller interview by John Gray
Rolling Stone 24/12/70: Rod Stewart interview
Sounds 19/12/70: 'The Sounds Talk-In: Rod Stewart' by Royston Eldridge
Disc & Music Echo 18/9/71: 'The amazing Mr. S' by Caroline Boucher
NME 28/2/70: *An Old Raincoat . . .* review
IT/# 74 27/2 – 13/3/70: *An Old Raincoat . . .* review
Rolling Stone 7/2/70: *The Rod Stewart Album* review by Greil Marcus
Sounds 11/9/71: 'Ronnie Wood in The *Sounds* Talk-In' by Penny
  Valentine
Sounds 19/2/72: 'Memories And Mr. Lane' Ronnie Lane interview (Part 1)
  by Penny Valentine
NME 20/11/71: Rod Stewart interview (Part 2) by Nick Logan

Chapter Nine:
NME 14/3/70: 'It's Music, Not Faces That Count' by Gordon Coxhill
Disc & Music Echo 18/9/71: 'The amazing Mr. S' by Caroline Boucher
I'm In A Rock 'n' Roll Band: Jeff Beck interview BBC Television 2010
Music Now 15/8/70: 'It means a lot to us to get recognition in England . . .'
  by Tony Norman
Rolling Stone 25/11/71: 'Ronnie Lane – the Story of a Face' by Andrew
  Bailey
Smiler # 33 autumn 1992: Kenney Jones interview by John Gray
Sounds 10/8/74: 'Where Was We?' Ronnie Lane interview (Part 2) by
  Penny Valentine
NME 3/10/70: 'Hot Rod' by Nick Logan
Rolling Stone 24/12/70: Rod Stewart interview
Sounds 10/10/70: 'Rod Remains A Face' Rod Stewart interview by Penny
  Valentine
Sounds 19/12/70: 'The *Sounds* Talk-In: Rod Stewart' by Royston Eldridge

Chapter Ten:
Sounds 11/9/71: 'Ronnie Wood in The *Sounds* Talk-in' by Penny Valentine
Rolling Stone 21/2/70: 'Rod Stewart Does A Neil Young'
The Darlings of Wapping Wharf Launderette # 22: Jenny Marriott interview by
  John Hellier 1999
Melody Maker 21/2/70: 'New Faces in the old band' by Chris Welch

Sounds 19/2/72: 'Memories And Mr. Lane' Ronnie Lane interview by
   Penny Valentine
Melody Maker 21/2/70: New Pop Singles by Chris Welch
Music Now 15/8/70: 'It means a lot to us to get recognition in England . . .'
   by Tony Norman
Melody Maker 7/3/70: Caught In The Act by Bob Dawbarn
NME 14/3/70: 'It's Music, Not Faces That Count' by Gordon Coxhill
NME 14/3/70: 'Free's simple sound' by Jan Nesbit
NME 3/10/70: 'Hot Rod' by Nick Logan
Sounds 10/10/70: 'Rod Remains A Face' Rod Stewart interview by Penny
   Valentine
Record Mirror 23/10/71: 'Poker-Face Speaks' Kenney Jones interview by Bill
   McAllister
Melody Maker 25/4/70: 'A Face From The States' Ian McLagan interview by
   Chris Welch
Rolling Stone 28/5/70: *First Step* review by Joel Selvin
Sounds 1/7/72: 'Oldham – still going strong' by Penny Valentine
Rolling Stone 13/12/69: 'Immediate Sues CBS for $7,200,000'
Rolling Stone 19/3/70: 'Immediate Records Down for Count'
Rolling Stone 16/4/70: 'Immediate Records Swan Song'
Melody Maker 4/7/70: 'Face to Face with Ronnie' by Chris Welch

Chapter 11:
Disc & Music Echo 21/3/70: 'Rod thinks the new Faces won't be small' by
   Penny Valentine
Sounds 26/2/72: 'Memories And Mr. Lane' Ronnie Lane interview by
   Penny Valentine
NME 25/8/73: 'Tartan Hordes' Rod Stewart interview by James Johnson
Rolling Stone 24/12/70: Rod Stewart interview
Zigzag #19 May 1971: 'Face to face with a Face' by Pete Frame
NME 3/10/70: 'Hot Rod' by Nick Logan
Melody Maker 18/9/71: 'Now Rod's face fits' by Richard Williams
Melody Maker 4/7/70: 'Face to Face with Ronnie' by Chris Welch
Sounds 16/1/71: 'The Sounds Talk-In: Steve Marriott' by Penny Valentine
NME Mailbag 20/6/70
Rolling Stone 3/9/70: *Gasoline Alley* review by Langdon Winner
Melody Maker 12/9/70: '100 octane Rod Stewart' *Gasoline Alley* review by
   Richard Williams
Sounds 24/10/70: 'Guitar Maker, By Accident' by Jerry Gilbert
The Passing Show transcript of Kenney Jones interview by Rupert Williams 2004
Record Mirror 29/8/70: 'Faces Ditch Producers' by Valerie Mabbs
NME 4/8/73: 'In Frankfurt With The Faces' by James Johnson
Sounds 19/12/70: 'The Sounds Talk-In: Rod Stewart' by Royston Eldridge

Sounds 17/4/71: 'Here comes Britain's biggest rock and roll band' Ronnie Wood interview by Penny Valentine

Disc & Music Echo 2/1/71: 'Cool appraisal of the 'uncool' Faces' by Caroline Boucher

Sounds 28/11/70: 'Faces and the future' by Royston Eldridge

Music Now 10/10/70: 'Stewart's evolution' by Dai Davies

Melody Maker 25/12/71: Rod Stewart interview (Part 1)

Sounds 5/1/74: The John Peel Column

IT/94 17-31/12/70: 'Rod The Mod' interview by J. Mandelkau

Disc 25/8/73: 'We Are The Boozers' Rod Stewart interview by Peter Erskine

Hull Times 11/12/70: 'Hot Rod's Powering Along Pop Tracks'

Chapter 12:

Sounds 11/9/71: 'Ronnie Wood in The *Sounds* Talk-In' by Penny Valentine

LA Times 12/3/71: 'Faces Make Rock Scene First Time' live review by John Mendelsohn

NME Annual 1973: 'Why Rod wants to stay in the shadows' by Nick Logan

Sounds 10/10/70: 'Rod Remains A Face' by Penny Valentine

Rolling Stone 24/12/70: Rod Stewart interview

Melody Maker 13/7/74: 'The Faces – it's like a marriage!' by Geoff Brown

Zigzag #19 May 1971: 'Face to face with a Face' by Pete Frame

NME 17/4/71: 'The Faces Of '71' by Nick Logan

Record Mirror 27/3/71: 'The best band in this land?' *Long Player* review by Bill McAllister

Rolling Stone 18/3/71: *Long Player* review by John Mendelsohn

NME 20/11/71: Rod Stewart interview (Part 2) by Nick Logan

Sounds 30/10/71: 'Rod's Success – Sweet And Sour' by Penny Valentine

The Passing Show transcript of Bruce Rowland interview by Rupert Williams 2003

Melody Maker 20/2/71: 'Rod Raises A Riot In Boston' live review by Richard Williams

It Ain't Easy John Baldry CD liner notes by Sid Griffin

Record Mirror 3/4/71: 'Wait till they get back home' Ronnie Wood interview by Bill McAllister

LA Free Press 19/3/71: 'Five Faces flatten Forum fans' live review by Richard Cromelin

Music Now 10/10/70: 'Stewart's evolution' by Dai Davies

Melody Maker 8/5/71: 'Funky, funny Faces are here' live review by Chris Charlesworth

Record Mirror 8/5/71: live review by Bill McAllister

Sounds 8/5/71: 'Faces don't light up' live review by Steve Peacock

Watford Evening Echo 7/5/71: 'Varied Faces have a rave-up' live review by Patrick Stoddart

The Nag's Head Story documentary (Part 2) BBC Radio Northampton 2006

Sounds 22/5/71: 'A bowl full of secrets at the Palace' live review by Steve Peacock

NME 9/10/71: 'Rod Chart Sensation'

Chapter 13:

NME 3/7/71: 'Rod And The Faces The Hope For Rock' Rod Stewart interview by Nick Logan

Disc & Music Echo 29/1/72: 'Ron Wood: larfin' all the way to the bank' by Caroline Boucher

Smiler # 87 February 2010: Pete Sears interview by Mike Walton

Sounds 10/7/71: ''umble Rod takes a bow' by Penny Valentine

Zigzag #19 May 1971: 'Face to face with a Face' by Pete Frame

Melody Maker 15/5/71: 'Rod: artistry with roots' by Richard Williams

Sounds 3/7/71: 'Rod Stewart – Out Front' *EPTAS* review by Penny Valentine

Melody Maker 3/7/71: 'Rod: a touch of genius' *EPTAS* review by Richard Williams

Rolling Stone 8/7/71: *EPTAS* review by John Mendelsohn

Financial Times 1/7/71: *EPTAS* review by Michael Wale

Sounds 29/5/71: Ian Paice interview by Jerry Gilbert

NME 4/9/71: 'A One Group Festival - And they were the Faces . . .'

Melody Maker 25/9/71: 'Who retain title at Oval' live review by Chris Charlesworth

Melody Maker 9/10/71: Open Letter by Roy Hollingworth

Sounds 30/10/71: 'Rod's Success – Sweet And Sour' by Penny Valentine

Rolling Stone 3/2/72: '1971 Vanishes . . . But There's Still Hope'

Chapter 14:

Sounds 22/1/72: 'A Nod's As Good As A Wink To The Faces . . .' Ron Wood interview by Penny Valentine

NME 19/2/72: 'Rod Stewart Was Over-Exposed' Kenney Jones interview by Tony Norman

NME 20/11/71: 'A Nod's As Good As A Wink For The Faces – Know What I Mean??' Kenney Jones interview by Julie Webb

Record Mirror 31/7/71: 'Now Rod Will Help The Faces Score' by Bill McAllister

Sounds 10/7/71: ' 'umble Rod takes a bow' by Penny Valentine

Record Mirror 23/10/71: 'Poker-Face Speaks' Kenney Jones interview by Bill McAllister

Sounds 28/9/74: 'Woody And The Street Feel' Ron Wood interview by Barbara Charone

NME 18/12/71: 'Finest Faces' *A Nod Is As Good* . . . review by John Wells

Melody Maker 11/12/71: 'Year of The Faces' *A Nod Is As Good* . . . review by Roy Hollingworth

Rolling Stone 6/1/72: *A Nod Is As Good* . . . review by Jon Landau

Sounds 30/10/71: 'Rod's Success – Sweet And Sour' by Penny Valentine

Record Mirror 19/2/72: 'In The Land Of Nod' by Bill McAllister

NME 4/12/71: 'Fantastic Faces Drive New York Wild!' by Nancy Lewis

Melody Maker 4/12/71: 'Booze, bears and football on stage as The Faces knock 'em out in New York' Kenney Jones interview by Chris Charlesworth

Beat Instrumental # 107 April 1972: 'Not All Of Us Are Stars . . . Faces' by Derek Abrahams

Cream March 1972: 'Roddd-Neee: Kop Idol' by Pete Roche

Record Mirror 14/9/74: 'Smiler – Rod talks to Pete Harvey'

Disc 3/6/72: 'Everything Stops For Baldry' John Baldry interview by Mike Ledgerwood

Chapter 15:

Melody Maker 25/12/71: Rod Stewart interview (Part 1)

Sounds 30/10/71: 'Rod's Success – Sweet And Sour' by Penny Valentine

Record Mirror 27/11/71: 'Rod Stewart: Tired of being alone' Rod Stewart interview (Part 2) by Bill McAllister

Creem July 1972: 'The Festival That Never Should Have Been'

Rolling Stone 8/6/72: 'Rod Stewart at Work and Play in the Holiday Inns of America' by Robert Green

NME 27/5/72: 'A little bit on Rod Stewart: 'Never A Dull Moment' by Nick Logan

Daily Express 28/10/72: Rod Stewart interview with David Wigg

Disc & Music Echo 12/2/72: 'Stewart on booze and Baldry' by Andrew Tyler

Melody Maker 13/5/72: live review by Chris Charlesworth

NME 12/8/72: 'A question of flash' Rod Stewart interview (Part 2) by Nick Logan

Daily Express 27/10/72: Ronnie Lane interview with David Wigg

Sounds 5/8/72: Rod Stewart interview (Part 1) by Penny Valentine

NME 5/8/72: 'Working class hero Rod' by Nick Logan

Sounds 22/7/72: 'It's Max Miller with soul' *Never A Dull Moment* review by Penny Valentine

Smiler # 20 summer 1989: Mickey Waller interview by John Gray

Melody Maker 7/10/72: 'The snaky tale of Python Lee Jackson' by Mark Plummer

Sounds 15/7/72: 'Faces In Philly' by Peter Burton

Sounds 22/7/72: Pocono festival review by Chuck Pulin

Sounds 19/8/72: 'Reading Report . . . Boring or just relaxed?' by Steve Peacock
Record Mirror 16/9/72: 'Faces, USA' by Peter Burton

Chapter 16:
Disc 5/8/72: Rod Stewart interview by Mike Ledgerwood
Sounds 17/2/73: 'The Silent Face' Ian McLagan interview by Ray Telford
Record Mirror 5/8/72: 'I'm a crooner' Rod Stewart interview by Charles Webster
Melody Maker 13/1/73: Rod Stewart column re: Denis Law – as told to Peter Burton
Sounds 7/4/73: 'Penny Valentine talks to Ronnie Wood and asks: when's the looning going to stop?'
Sounds 17/2/73: 'Cindy Incidentally' review by Penny Valentine
Sounds 14/4/73: 'Something Amiss With The Boys' *Ooh La La* review by Billy Walker
NME 7/4/73: 'Private lives, public faces' by James Johnson
Melody Maker 21/4/73: 'Rod: Our new album is a disgrace . . . a bloody mess' by Roy Hollingworth
NME 27/5/72: 'A little bit on Rod Stewart: 'Never A Dull Moment' by Nick Logan
Circus June 1973: 'Rod Stewart mellows the Faces in 'Ooh La La'' by Barra Greyson

Chapter 17:
NME 16/6/73: 'A Mod's Progress' Rod Stewart interview by James Johnson
Sounds 25/8/73: 'Swashbuckler Rod' Rod Stewart interview by Penny Valentine
NME 25/8/73: 'Tartan Hordes' Rod Stewart interview by James Johnson
The Times 29/8/73: Reading Festival review by Michael Wale
Disc 29/12/73-5/1/74: 'Rod Reigns' Rod Stewart interview by Rosalind Russell
Rolling Stone 16/8/73: 'Rod's hits: The great and not so great' *Sing It Again Rod* review by Jon Landau
Music Scene 1973: 'Rod The Mod' article
Disc 25/8/73: 'We Are The Boozers' by Peter Erskine
Record Mirror 28/9/74: 'Ron Wood Is... Just one of the boys'
Sounds 27/4/74: 'Get Your Kicks In Room Sixty Six' Ian McLagan interview re: Tucson hotel incident
Evening News 21/5/74: 'Sipping Into Something Nice' Rod Stewart interview re: Joanna Lumley
Sounds 22/12/73: 'A debonair twinkle in a working man's eye' Ron Wood interview by Rob Mackie

Sounds 29/12/73: 'Faces: live and refined' *Overture and Beginners* review by Pete Erskine

Rolling Stone 28/2/74: *Overture and Beginners* review by Jon Landau

Chapter 18:

NME 16/6/73: 'A Mod's Progress' Rod Stewart interview by James Johnson

Melody Maker 16/11/74: 'Wood: it's a family affair' by Brian Harrigan

Disc 25/8/73: 'We Are The Boozers' Rod Stewart interview by Peter Erskine

Sounds 17/11/73: 'Romantic Ron Knows Where He's Going . . .' Ronnie Lane interview by Pete Erskine

Record Mirror 28/9/74: 'Ron Wood Is . . . Just one of the boys'

Melody Maker 16/2/74: 'Bored Faces' Ian McLagan interview

NME 14/9/74: 'Wood: I've got my own promo tour to do' by Lisa Robinson

Sounds 13/7/74: 'Wood Within Wood' Ron Wood interview

Sounds 28/9/74: 'Woody And The Street Feel' by Barbara Charone

Smiler # 20 summer 1989: Mickey Waller interview by John Gray

Sunday Express 20/1/74: 'I don't waste my money, says Rod Stewart' by Peter Dacre

Disc 27/7/74: 'Sunshine, Love, Death & McLagan' by Rosalind Russell

NME 4/1/75: 'The Episodic Adventures Of Rod Kool & The Tartan Gang' by Nick Kent

Chapter 19:

Rolling Stone 27/2/75: 'Raunchy Faces Back on Tour' by Barbara Charone

Sounds 16/11/74: 'Rod The Haystack In LA' by Harvey Kubernik & Justin Pierce

Sounds 11/1/75: 'No, I Won't!' Ron Wood interview by Barbara Charone

Sunday Mirror 2/3/75: 'In America With Rod Stewart: Let's Slaughter 'Em!' by Colin Wills

Creem May 1975: 'The Faces, Who Are Still Kicking' by Lester Bangs

Melody Maker 8/3/75: 'Faces bring back the fun' live review by Chris Charlesworth

Daily Mail 5/3/75: 'The harsh truth about living with a pop star' by Roderick Gilchrist

Daily Express 31/3/75: 'It's just a game says 'jilted' Dee' by David Wigg & Michael O'Flaherty'

Disc 6/7/74: 'Costa del Rod' Rod Stewart interview by Rosalind Russell

The Sun 15/4/75: 'The new Rolling Stone' by Bob Hart

Rolling Stone 14/8/75: *Now Look* review by Dave Marsh

Chapter 20:
Sounds 12/8/72: Rod Stewart interview (Part 2) by Penny Valentine
NME 19/2/72: 'Rod Stewart Was Over-Exposed – Kenny Jones' by Tony
  Norman
Sounds 26/4/75: 'All Roads Lead To The Big Top' by Mick Brown
Popswop Annual 1974: 'Rod Appeal . . . That's The Stewart Secret'
Daily Mirror 9/5/75: 'Exit Rod The Rock Star' by Stan Sayer
Penthouse Vol. 10 No. 2 1975: Interview with Rod Stewart by Patsy
  Ledger
Daily Mirror 24/7/75: 'I'll pay the tax, says angry Rod' by Stan Sayer
Jackie # 615 18/10/75: 'Why I Left Britain'
The Sun 25/7/75: 'I Don't Fit The Faces Now, Says Rod' by Bob Hart
NME 2/8/75: 'You can make Rod Stewart, dance, sing, or do any old
  thing . . .' by Steve Clarke
NME 26/7/75: 'Rod leaving Britain lost me £80,000' Says Kenny Jones'
Daily Mirror 29/7/75: 'Faces v Stones In Big Rock Battle' by Jack Lewis
Honolulu Advertiser 12/9/75: 'Reddy's man: Rod's pianist: Hitting it off?' by
  Terry McMurray
Sounds 18/10/75: Jaws column Rod Stewart comment re: Faces farewell
  concert
Daily Mirror 19/12/75: 'Why rock star Rod is quitting the Faces' by Stan Sayer
Daily Mirror 20/12/75: 'Rod's plea to 'missing' pop star' by Stan Sayer

Chapter 21:
Sounds 10/8/74: 'Where Was We?' Ronnie Lane interview (Part 2) by
  Penny Valentine
Sounds 24/1/76: 'Cast your fate to the wind, the Faces or the Rolling Stones'
  Ron Wood interview by Barbara Charone
Disc 29/6/74: 'For one night only – Small Faces to reform!'
Smiler # 34 winter 1992: Kenney Jones interview (Part 2) by John Gray
Disc 14/4/73: 'Face To Face With A Face' Kenney Jones interview by Peter
  Erskine
Q # 117 June 1996: Pete Townshend interview by John Harris
Goldmine # 364 8/7/94: 'Look Who's Talking: A Conversation with Roger
  Daltrey' by Ken Sharp
The Herald (Glasgow) 5/3/99: 'Big Lift for Small Faces' by David Belcher
Hello! #330 12/11/94: Kenney Jones article
Sounds 6/3/76: 'Lone Stone' Bill Wyman interview by Barbara Charone
Q #149 January 1999: *All The Rage* review by Peter Kane
Melody Maker 1/10/83: Talk Talk column Ronnie Lane quote re: Rod
  Stewart and ARMS concert
The Passing Show transcript of Kenney Jones interview by Rupert Williams
  2004

Chapter 22:

Record Mirror 5/8/72: 'I'm a crooner' Rod Stewart interview by Charles Webster

Sounds 5/8/72: Rod Stewart interview (Part 1) by Penny Valentine

Smiler # 20 summer 1989: Mickey Waller interview by John Gray

LA Times 29/7/89: Rod Stewart interview by Paul Grein

MTV interview 5/7/86 with Rod Stewart

Daily Mirror 8/8/86: 'Faces set to tour the world'

Smiler # 41 autumn 1994: Rod Stewart interview by John Gray

Record Mirror 14/9/74: 'Smiler – Rod talks to Pete Harvey'

Five Guys Walk Into A Bar . . . Ian McLagan sleeve note 2004

BBC Radio 6 *Roundtable* 10/7/08: Ian McLagan interview

Classic Rock 26/10/09: 'Holding Back The Jeers: Hucknall Sings With Faces' review by Ian Fortnam

Evening Standard 11/8/10: 'Rod's former band takes the Mick at The Faces launch' by Rick Pearson

Epilogue

RollingStone.com 7/12/11: Rod Stewart: 'I'll Definitely Make Myself Available' for a Faces Reunion by Andy Greene

BBC website: Behind The Scenes of *Rod Stewart - Can't Stop Me Now* by Lorna Lithgow July 2015

Rolling Stone.com 7/12/11: Faces/Small Faces' Ian McLagan Warming to Hall of Fame Induction by Andy Greene

UltimateClassicRock.com 16/4/12: The Full Text of Steven Van Zandt's Small Faces/Faces Hall of Fame Induction Speech by Dave Swanson

UltimateClassicRock.com 15/4/12: The Faces Perform Blistering Set Following Rock and Roll Hall Of Fame Induction by Matt Wardlaw

Daily Mail.co.uk 22/7/14: How magic beads saved a rock star's love life: Drummer Kenney Jones of The Who on the new op that destroyed his prostate cancer

Uncut.co.uk 13/12/13: Ian McLagan dismisses any chance of The Faces reuniting in 2015

The Austin Chronicle.com 20/3/15: All Or Nothing Ian McLagan article by Tim Stegall

Uncut.co.uk 4/12/14: Rod Stewart pays tribute to Ian McLagan: "I'll miss you, mate"

Uncut #222, November 2015: 'You Wear It Well' Rod Stewart interview by Jaan Uhelszki

Telegraph.co.uk 6/9/15: The Faces, Hurtwood Park Polo Club, review: 'worth the 40-year wait' by Neil McCormick

ClassicRockMagazine.com, 11/15: Faces Hurtwood Park review by Ian Fortnam

Sunday Mail 11/10/15: 'Some Guy Had All The Luck' by Adrian Deevoy

Index

Singles releases are in roman type and albums/books are in italics.

1970–1975: You Can Make Me Dance, Song or Anything . . . (box set) (Faces), 417–418

A Wop Bop A Loo Bop A Lop Bam Boom – Pop From The Beginning (book) (Nik Cohn), 20

Abadi, Ivor, 17

Abadi, Philip, 17

Academy In Peril, The (John Cale), 256

Ace, 351*n.*

Acquaye, Speedy, 276

Act Together (Ron Wood), 334

Action, The, 70

Adams, Berle, 85

Adams, Brian, 361

Adams, Derroll, 347

Adler, Lou, 96, 290, 357

Adler, Sam, 378

Ad-Lib, The, 52

Afterglow (Of Your Love) (Small Faces), 105, 115

Ain't That Lovin You Baby (Rod Stewart), 49

Ain't That Lovin' You Baby (Jimmy Reed), 333

Akido, 276*n.*

Alder, John 'Twink', 86

Alice Cooper, 98, 263, 277*n.*

All Day And All Of The Night (Kinks), 276

All Or Nothing (Small Faces), 33, 103, 412

All Our Yesterdays (Small Faces), 98

All Shook Up (Elvis Presley), 123

All Shook Up (Jeff Beck Group), 123

All The Rage (autobiography) (Ian McLagan), 151*n.*, 389

All The Young Dudes (Mott The Hoople), 277*n.*

All Things Must Pass (George Harrison), 224

All You Need Is Love (Beatles), 99

Allman Brothers, The, 263

Allman, Duane, 122, 160

Almost Grown (Small Faces), 33

Altham, Keith, 77, 94, 178

Am I Blue (Billie Holiday), 353

Am I Blue (Ted Wood), 352

Am I Grooving You? (Freddie Scott), 334

Am I Grooving You? (Ron Wood), 334

Amazing Grace (Judy Collins), 221

Amazing Grace (Rod Stewart), 221

Ambrose, Dave, 55, 81, 150

Amen Corner, 177*n.*

America, 234

Amoreuse (Kiki Dee), 397

An Old Raincoat Won't Ever Let You Down (Rod Stewart), 138, 161, 183

An Old Raincoat Won't Ever Let You Down (Rod Stewart) (see *The Rod Stewart Album*)

Anderson, Ted, 221

Andes, Mark, 300*n.*

Angel (Jones Gang), 384

Angel (Rod Stewart), 275, 288, 420

Animals, The, 22, 30, 77

Another Side Of Bob Dylan (Bob Dylan), 275

Anthony, Dee, 279, 381

Antonioni, Michelangelo, 75*n.*

Anymore For Anymore (Ronnie Lane), xii, 347–348, 350, 362

Anyway Anyhow Anywhere (Who), 22

Apache (Shadows), 6

Apostolic Intervention, 97, 111

Appice, Carmine, 127, 148, 251, 378

Arden, David, 22

Arden, Don, 19, 21–23, 24.*n,* 30–35, 77,
  95–96, 99, 102, 108, 112–113, 124,
  152, 373, 377, 394
Armatrading, Joan, 382
Armitt, Ian, 210, 225
Arnold, Billy Boy, 65*n.*
Arnold, P.P., 56, 79, 97, 130, 381
Arnold, Shirley, 273–274, 308
Around The Plynth (Faces), 123, 160,
  175, 207, 225, 245, 418
Artwoods, The, 60, 67, 71*n.*, 86, 129, 225
As Long As You Tell Him (Faces/Rod
  Stewart), 342, 352
As Safe As Yesterday Is (Humble Pie), 118
Asher, Peter, 229
Ashton, Gardner & Dyke, 86, 129, 257
Ashton, Tony, 86
Astbury, Ian, 408
Astley, Edwin 'Ted', 131
Astley, Karen, 131–132, 285, 287
At Newport 1960 (Muddy Waters), 26
Atlantic Crossing (Rod Stewart), 288*n.*,
  365–366, 372
Atlas, Charles, 204
Atomic Rooster, 234–235, 273
Attack, The, 80
Audience, 251
Auger, Brian, 52–54, 81, 150, 168
Autumn Stone, The (Small Faces), 115
Azzara, Steve, 314

Baba, Meher, 107, 130, 132–133, 160,
  162, 176, 189, 203–204, 207, 247,
  262, 272, 286–287, 297, 348, 380
Bacharach, Burt, 151
Back Door Man (Howlin' Wolf), 28
Back Door Man (Muleskinners), 28
Back, Terry, 59
Bad 'N' Ruin (Faces), 202–203, 214, 242
Bad Company, 307, 326, 384
Bad Company (Bad Company), 307, 326
Badfinger, 278
Baez, Joan, 275
Bagaris, Bob, 178
Baker, Ginger, 117
Baldry, Long John, 36, 74, 44–55, 130,
  149–150, 152, 208, 210, 220–221,
  225, 258, 263, 273, 320, 322, 401,
  410

Band, The, 122–123, 159, 183, 185, 315
Bangs, Lester, 354
Barabajagal (Donovan), 126
Barber, Chris, 45, 337
Bardens, Peter, 55
Barnes, Cyril, 279
Barnes, John, 279–281, 301, 317, 354, 395
Barrett, Syd, 84
Barrie, Jack, 29
Bart, Lionel, 14, 55, 222*n.*
Barton, Cliff, 46–47
Bassey, Shirley, 66, 103
Bay, James, 413
Bay City Rollers, The, 331
Beach Boys, The, 70, 95, 181, 352
Beastie Boys, The, 411
Beatles, The, 10–12, 31–33, 44, 48, 60,
  64, 91, 94, 99, 101, 151*n.*, 164, 211,
  216, 236, 241, 261, 268, 331, 346,
  394
Beck, Bogert & Appice, 378
Beck, Jeff, ix–x, 35, 72–92, 98*n.*, 106,
  111, 121–124, 126–130, 133,
  135–140, 147–148, 150, 160, 166,
  168–169, 173, 179, 186, 195–196,
  203, 210–211, 221*n.*, 251, 257, 295,
  336, 359, 391, 396, 413
Beck's Bolero (Jeff Beck), 80, 88
Beck-Ola (Jeff Beck Group), 123, 159–160
Bee Gees, The, 134, 150
Beefheart, Captain, 160–161
Behind The Sun (Faces), 417–418
Beiderbecke, Bix, 58
Belchamber, Edwin, 247
Bell, Graham, 108*n.*, 290
Bell, Madeline, 84, 221
Bell, Maggie, 210, 221, 290
Belshaw, Brian, 361
Bennett, Kenny, 7
Bentley, David, 133–135
Berg, Ron, 273
Berlin, Irving, 403
Berry, Chuck, 12, 22, 27, 59, 245, 256,
  275, 321, 337
Best Of British (Ian McLagan), 389
Best Of The Faces, The (compilation)
  (Faces), 403
Best Of The Immediate Years (Various
  Artistes), 115*n.*

Bethell, Lord, 250
Between The Buttons (Rolling Stones), 241
Big Bayou (Ron Wood/Rod Stewart & The Faces), 372
Billy's Bag (Billy Preston), 32
Bingenheimer, Rodney, 231
Birch, Martin, 157–158, 202
Birch, Will, 39, 44
Birds Birds, 71
Birds, The, ix, 56–57, 61–72, 78, 125, 129, 134, 151, 298, 312, 353, 413
Black And Blue (Rolling Stones), 375
Black Crowes, The, xi, 401
Black Girl (John Baldry), 210
Black Sabbath, 278
Black, Cilla, 32*n*., 151
Blackberry Way (Move), 116
Blackburn, Tony, 214
Blackmore, Ritchie, 129, 225–226
Blackwell, Chris, 95
Blaikley, Alan, 149
Blake, Doug, 122, 410
Blake, John, 61
Blake, William, 205
Bland, Bobby 15
Blind Faith, 117, 164, 256
Blind Prayer (Rod Stewart), 137
Blonde On Blonde (Bob Dylan), 222
Bloomfield, Mike, 117
Blossom Toes, 62
Blow-Up (film), 75*n*.
Blue Cheer, 88, 122
Blue Eyes (Don Partridge), 108
Blue Monk (Thelonius Monk), 26
Blues Anytime (Jeff Beck & The All Stars), 91*n*.
Blues Anytime Volume 3 (Anthology), 86*n*.
Blues Deluxe (Faces), 196
Blues Incorporated, 45–46, 60
Bluesbreakers, The, 55–56, 81–82, 94, 126, 129, 157
Bluesology, 150–151
Bo Street Runners, The, 64
Boat That I Row, The (Lulu), 79
Bob Dylan's Dream (Bob Dylan), 222*n*.
Bobak, Mike, 182, 219, 337
Boffey, Suzannah, 43, 186
Bogert, Tim, 127, 148, 251
Boilerhouse, 157

Bolan, Marc, 189, 198, 214, 233, 266, 268, 270, 303, 331
Bolero (Jeff Beck), 87, 91
Bond, Graham, Organisation, 68
Boney Moronie (Larry Williams), 296
Bonham, John, 91
Bonnet, Graham, 150
Bonzo Dog Doo-Dah Band, 60
Booker T., 15, 28, 33, 86*n*., 116, 124, 161, 242, 365
Booker T. & The MG's, 16, 28, 31, 86*n*., 161, 177, 365
Boone, Catherine 'Tilly' (see Catherine 'Tilly' Wood)
Booth, Pat, 103*n*.
Bootleg Series Volumes 1–3, The (Bob Dylan), 184*n*., 275*n*.
Borstal Boys (Faces), 294, 297, 312, 321, 415
Boucher, Caroline, 38–39, 41–42, 48, 58, 77, 139, 147, 195, 198, 200
Bow Wow Wow, 395
Bowie, David, 18, 135, 150, 200, 210, 231, 266, 268, 270, 307, 315, 321, 323, 333, 338, 355, 381
Bown, Alan, 149–150, 156–157, 273, 303
Bowyer, Peter, 233–234, 269
Boyd, Franklyn, 64
Boyd, Joe, 202*n*.
Boyd, Pattie, 103*n*.
Boz & The Boz People, 24, 29–30, 32, 67*n*.
Bradford, Geoff, 46–47
Bragg, Billy, 388
Brave New World (Steve Miller Band), 127, 241
Brennan, Terry, 28
Breslau, Marty, 267
Brewer & Shipley, 221
Bricusse, Leslie, 55
Bridge Over Troubled Water (Simon & Garfunkel), 239
Briggs, Vic, 53
Bright Lights, Big City (Jimmy Reed), 47
Bright Lights, Big City (Rod Stewart), 49
Bring It On Home To Me (Sam Cooke), 337
Bring It On Home To Me – You Send Me (Rod Stewart), 337

Bring It To Jerome (Birds), 65*n*.
Bring It To Jerome (Bo Diddley), 65*n*.
Brinsley Schwartz, 165
Broonzy, Big Bill, 45, 47, 51
Brother Can You Spare A Dime? (Ronnie Lane), 362
Brother Can You Spare A Dime? (St Valentine's Day Massacre), 71*n*.
Broughton, Edgar, Band, 187–188, 198–199, 232, 280
Brown Sugar (Rolling Stones), 243, 360
Brown, Denny, 194
Brown, Geoff, 58, 203
Brown, James, 15, 17, 33, 207
Brown, Joe, 53, 378
Brown, Len, 14
Brown, Maxine, 314
Brown, Mick, 362
Brown, Pete, 27, 105, 361
Brown, Rich, 210
Brown, Ricky, 53
Brown, Stewart A., 151
Browne, Jackson, 340, 368, 388
Bruce, Jack, 45
Bruford, Rose, 148
Bruvvers, The, 53
Buckingham, Lindsay, 369
Buckland, Peter, 157–158, 170, 181, 187, 191, 198, 212–213, 234, 246, 248, 279, 290, 308, 317, 322, 326–329, 341–342, 344–345, 354–355, 360, 368–369, 372–373, 377–378, 395, 401
Buckley, Lord, 97–98
Buffalo Springfield, 101, 117
Buffett, Jimmy, 395
Bull Angus, 251
Bump In The Night (Ian McLagan), 388
Bundrick, John 'Rabbit', 307–308
Burdon, Eric, 45
Burgon, Audrey, 385
Burke, Solomon, 22, 352
Burns, Tito, 95
Burrell, Boz, 117, 232
Burton, James, 74
Burton, Peter, 278
Burton, Trevor, 116
Butler, Dougal, 319, 333
Butts Band, The, 308

Bye & Bye (Gonna See The King) (Ronnie Lane), 347
Byrds, The, 66–67, 71, 116
Byzantium, 273

C'mon Everybody (Eddie Cochran), 40
Cable, Michael, 357
Cactus, 251, 263, 378
Cagney, James, 34
Calder, Tony, 35, 90, 94–95, 97, 106, 108, 113, 118, 154, 156, 377, 394
Cale, J.J., 142
Cale, John, 256
Call It Something Nice (Small Faces), 116
Cambridge, George, 13, 16
Cambridge, George, & The Telstars, 13
Camp, Hamilton, 184, 221
Can You Please Crawl Out Your Window? (Bob Dylan), 223
Can't Stop The Want (Sandy Sarjeant), 102
Canned Heat, 170
Capaldi, Jim, 293
Caraeff, Ed, 274
Caravan, 143
Carpenter, Mick, 27
Carr, Roy, 57
Carrack, Paul, 405, 419
Carter, John, 82
Cash, Johnny, 275, 330, 338
Cattini, Clem, 79
Cennamo, Louis, 44*n*.
CENtral 1179 (Keith Rylatt & Phil Scott) (book), 17
Chain Gang (Sam Cooke), 48
Changing Of The Guard, The (Marquis Of Kensington), 97*n*
Chanter, Doreen, 337
Chanter, Irene, 337
Chapman, Phil, 241, 294, 297*n*.
Chapman, Tony, 149
Charles, Prince, 384
Charles, Ray, 15, 48, 51
Charlesworth, Chris, 215, 225–226, 235–236, 253, 267, 269, 318, 339
Charone, Barbara, 244, 333, 352–353, 360, 376, 385
Chas & Dave, 106
Cheater, The (Faces), 298

Checker, Chubby, 66
Chen, Phil, 308–309, 377
Cherokees, The, 27
Chest Fever (Band), 159
Cheynes, The, 55
Chicken Shack, 83, 276
Child, June, 198
Chimes, Ron 'Ben', xi, 7–8, 10–13, 16
Chisnall, Arthur, 43
Chkiantz, George, 99
Christie, Agatha, 68
Cindy Incidentally (Faces), 294–296, 405, 407, 415, 418
Cindy's Lament (Rod Stewart), 138, 186
Cissy Strut (Meters), 177
Clapton, Eric, 28, 45, 60–61, 73–76, 88, 117, 191, 200, 204, 293, 332, 335–336, 368, 379–380, 390–391
Clark, Dick, 75, 99
Clark, Gene, 368
Clark, George, 131
Clark, Petula, 153
Clark, Terry, 149
Clarke, Stanley, 388
Clarke, Steve, 366–367
Clash, The, 108*n*.
Class, Barry, 229, 249
Class, Sylvia, 229, 249
Clayman, Barry, 22
Clayton Squares, The, 30
Clayton, Lucie, 229
Clayton, Merry, 290, 314
Cleave, Maureen, 64
Clifton, Peter, 269
Cloud Nine (Temptations), 135
Clough, Frank, 38
Coasters, The, 297
Cocaine (J.J. Cale), 142
Cochise, 234, 381
Cochran, Eddie, 40–41, 74, 122z, 185, 221
Cocker, Joe, 127, 195, 204, 209, 233, 327, 388
Cockney Rebel, 62
Cohen, Nat, 229
Cohn, Nik, 20
Coletta, John, 226
Collectors' Guide To Rare British Birds, The (Birds), 72*n*.

Collibosher (Small Faces), 116
Collins, Grenville, 97
Collins, Joan, 356
Collins, Joe, 67
Collins, Judy, 221
Collins, Phil, 398
Colosseum, 232
Colyer, Ken, 44
Come Back Again (Daddy Cool), 258
Come Back Again (John Baldry), 258
Come Home Baby (Rod Stewart & P.P. Arnold), 56
Come Home Baby (Wilson Pickett), 56
Come On Children (Small Faces), 33
Comin' Home Baby (Booker T. & The MGs), 31
Comin' Home Baby (Mel Torme), 31
Comin' Home Baby (Small Faces), 31
Communication Breakdown (Led Zeppelin), 360
Conn, Mervyn, 67
Cooder, Ry, 160, 207
Cook, Martin, 162
Cook, Paul, 363–364
Cook, Ray, 78–79
Cooke, Sam, 48, 54, 70, 276, 337
Cooley, Alex, 263–264
Coombes, Rod, 81
Cooper, Jason, 382
Corbett, Bill, 32
Corriston, Shakey Pete, 314
Cosby, Bill, 152
Cottle, Gerry, 348
Cotton, Mike, Sound, 68
Country Comforts (Rod Stewart), 185, 257
Country Honk (Rolling Stones), 212
Country Line Special (Cyril Davies R&B All-Stars), 46
Coward, Noel, 258
Coxhill, Gordon, 121, 169
Coz I Luv You (Slade), 239
Crabby Appleton, 212
Craig, John, 274
Cramer, Floyd, 123
Crazy Horse, 288*n*.
Cream, 56, 78, 80, 82–83, 88, 100–101, 117, 150, 179
Creation, The, ix, 78, 85–86, 125, 129

Cregan, Jim, 62, 377, 405
Crerand, Paddy, 322
Crewe, Bob, 175
Crickets, The, 293
Crocker, John, 18
Cromelin, Richard, 211
Cropper, Steve, 223, 343, 365
Crosby, David, 117
Crosby, Stills & Nash, 155
Crossley, Ian, 50
Crudup, Arthur 'Big Boy', 221
Cry Of Love (Jimi Hendrix), 275
Crying Laughing Loving Lying (Rod
    Stewart), 338*n*.
Culley, Patrick, 191, 248
Cult, The, 408
Cum On Feel The Noize (Slade), 295
Curbishley, Bill, 379–380, 382–383
Curved Air, 198
Cut Across Shorty (Eddie Cochran), 185,
    221
Cut Across Shorty (Rod Stewart), 221
Cutler, Ivor, 198

d'Abo, Mike, 84, 137
Dacre, Peter, 339
Daddy Cool, 258
Daddy Daddy (Birds), 71
Daddy Rides Again (Birds), 72*n*.
Dainty, Paul, 328
Dallon, Miki, 135, 277
Daltrey, Roger, 104, 231, 315, 383, 398,
    408
Daly, Brian, 51
Daniels, Charlie, 164, 172, 180, 231, 252,
    254–255, 265–266, 278–281, 317,
    395
Dantalion's Chariot, 56
Dave Clark Five, The, 95, 100
Dave Dee, Dozy, Beaky, Mick & Tich,
    80, 149
David Live (David Bowie), 321
Davies, Ceredig, 361
Davies, Cyril, 44–46, 53, 60, 91
Davies, Dave, 40, 194
Davies, Hywel, 361
Davies, Ray, 38, 40, 242, 307
Davies, Ron, 210
Davis, Clifford, 154

Davis, Clive, 177, 403
Davis, Jesse Ed, 365, 368, 370, 397
Davis, Martin, 52
Davis, Spencer, 95
Davison, Harold, 35, 62–63, 95, 112
Dawbarn, Bob, 122, 136, 168
Day Will Come, The (Rod Stewart), 54
de Clerck, Leo, 62, 64, 66–67, 69–70
De Cort, Stephanie, 61–62, 387
de Leon, Delia, 132, 247
Deacon, John, 408
Dean, Elton, 150
Debris (Faces), 244–245, 247, 297
Dee, Kiki, 397
Deevoy, Adrian, 419
Deep Purple, 129, 225–226, 307
Delaney & Bonnie And Friends, 186, 204
Deltones, The, 74
Denberg, Jody, 107, 414–415
Denny, Sandy, 290
Densmore, John, 408
Dent, Terry, 11
Derbyshire, Tim, 217
Derek & Clive, 295
Desdemona (Marsha Hunt), 140
Deviants, The, 132
Devotion (Faces), 159–160, 188, 404
Dexter, Jeff, ix, 23, 234–235, 262
Di Menno, Jo Rae, 392, 400, 414
Diamond Joe (Quiet Melon), 140
Diamond, Neil, 79
Diary Of A Soul Fiend (Saint Jude), 413*n*.
Diddley, Bo, 12–13, 22, 62–65
Dillards, The, 263, 285
Dimensions, The, 44
Dion & The Belmonts, 32*n*.
Dirty Old Town (Rod Stewart), 138, 224
Dissatisfied, The, 62
Distel, Sacha, 153
Dixie Cups, The, 258
Dixie Toot (Rod Stewart), 337
Dixon, Willie, 33, 85, 142, 258
Do Ya Think I'm Sexy? (Rod Stewart),
    399
Dogs D'Amour, 401
Doing Fine (Python Lee Jackson), 135
Domino, Fats, 58, 314*n*.
Don't Talk To Me Of Love (Outcasts), 13
Don't Try To Lay No Boogie Woogie

On The King Of Rock And Roll
(John Baldry), 210
Don't You Tell Nobody (Rod Stewart),
49
Done This One Before (Ronnie Lane),
298, 325
Donegan, Lonnie, 6, 9, 38
Donovan, 126, 411
Doonican, Val, 49, 101
Doors, The, 101, 408
Dorsey, Lee, 55
Dowd, Tom, 365
Downliners Sect, 44
Dreja, Chris, 74
Drinking Again (Dinah Washington), 84
Driscoll, Julie, 53–55, 150, 258
Dudgeon, Gus, 86n.
Dunbar, Aynsley, 81–82, 157
Duncan, Lesley, 208, 273
Dunn, Duck, 161, 365
Dunnage, Reg, 60
Dury, Ian, & The Blockheads, 108n.
Dusty In Memphis (Dusty Springfield), 365
Dyke, Roy, 86
Dylan, Bob, 41, 94, 127, 131, 137–138,
159, 164, 183–183, 221–224, 242,
255, 275–276, 284–285, 295, 297,
315, 338, 346–347, 388, 395

E To D (Small Faces), 17
Eagles, The, 255, 283, 395
East Wind Band, 331
Easton, Eric, 27–28, 94
Easy Music Band, The, 400
Easybeats, The, 134, 337–338
Eaton, Johnny, 27–28
Eddie's Dreaming (Small Faces), 98
Eddy, Duane, 85
Edkins, Bob, 7
Edmunds, Dave, 210
Egan, Joe, 338n.
Ekland, Britt, 356–359, 365, 370–371
Ekland, Nicholai, 357
Eldridge, Royston, 44, 47, 53, 106, 127,
138, 141, 162, 195, 197
Electric Light Orchestra, 280
Electric Warrior (T. Rex), 233, 257
Elliott, Ramblin' Jack, 41, 138
Ellis, Terry, 91

Ellison, John, 161
Elmer Gantry's Velvet Opera, 149
ELP (see Emerson, Lake & Palmer)
Emberg, Kelly, 399n.
Emerson, Keith, 138
Emerson, Lake & Palmer, 193, 263, 279,
364
Engine 4444 (Quiet Melon), 140
English, Scott, 79
Eno, Brian, 307
Enthoven, David, 362, 378
Entwistle, John, 80, 104, 383
Epstein, Brian, 134
Eric Clapton's Rainbow Concert (Eric
Clapton), 293
Erlewine, Stephen, 404
Erskine, Peter, 200, 321, 324–325
Ertegun, Ahmet, 211, 261
Ertegun, Mica, 261
Escovedo, Alejandro, 414, 415
Essex, David, 331, 342
Evans, Bobby, 38
Eve Of Destruction (Barry McGuire), 54
Everly Brothers, The, 21–22, 152, 225,
285, 388
Every Picture Tells A Story (Rod
Stewart), 220, 234, 275, 290n.
Every Picture Tells A Story (Rod Stewart),
x–xii, 186, 192, 216–225, 231, 233,
236–237, 239, 247, 250, 262, 274,
276–277, 324, 338
Every Time We Say Goodbye (Rod
Stewart), 338n.
Everybody Needs Somebody To Love
(Faces), 352
Everybody Needs Somebody To Love
(Solomon Burke), 22, 352
Everything Stops For Tea (John Baldry), 258
Evil (Faces), 142
Evolution (Ronnie Lane), 204
Exile On Main Street (Rolling Stones),
221, 241
Eyes Of Blue, 85
Eyes, The, 67

Face Dances (Who), 383
Faces 1969–1975 (book), 407, 411
Faces: Stray Singles & B-Sides, 418
Fairport Convention, 183, 189

Fairweather-Low, Andy, 382, 405
Faith, Adam, 64, 104
Faithfull, Marianne, 66, 101
Falcons, The, 61
Fame, Georgie, 51, 53, 55–56, 98, 105
Family, 62, 153, 256
Farewell (Rod Stewart), 337, 352
Farlowe, Chris, 95–96, 137, 185, 222n.
Farlowe, Chris, & The Thunderbirds, 55, 61
Farr, Rikki, 234
Farrell, Colin, 62, 69
Farren, Mick, 132, 199
Feel So Good (Faces), 142, 188, 196
Feel So Good (Shotgun Express), 55
Female Eunuch, The (book) (Germaine Greer), 243
Fenson, Ricky, 46
Fenwick, Mark, 378
Ferguson, Jay, 300n.
Fernandez, Charlie, xiii, 212, 278–279, 300, 316, 328–330, 354, 358, 369–371, 387, 389, 395
Fernandez, Richard, 212–213, 255, 278, 395
Fernandez, Suzie, 387
Ferry, Bryan, 315
Fields, Gracie, 103
Findlay, Christine (see Christine Wood)
First Step (Faces), 126, 159–162, 165, 167, 175, 202, 417
Fisher, Climie, 398
Five Guys Walk Into A Bar . . . (box set) (Faces), 142, 228n., 295n., 298, 353n., 358, 403–404, 417
Five Proud Walkers, 149
Flack, Roberta, 332
Flags And Banners (Faces), 296
Flee-Rekkers, The, 53
Fleetwood Mac, 83, 153–154, 156–157, 159, 264, 316, 369, 397
Fleetwood, Mick, 55, 157
Flirtations, The, 177
Fly In The Ointment (Faces), 297
Flying (Faces), 141, 155n., 161, 167, 210
Flying Burrito Brothers, The, 204
Focus, 280
Fogelberg, Dan, 395
Fool, The, 132

Fool To Cry (Rolling Stones), 243
Foolish Behaviour (Rod Stewart), 396
Foot Loose & Fancy Free (Rod Stewart), 186n., 295
For All That I Am (Creation), 86
Ford, Gerald, President, 354
Ford, John, 149
Ford, Susan, 354
Fordyce, Keith, 64
Forrester, Roger, 390
Fortnam, Ian, 405–406, 419
Fortnight Of Furore, A (book) (Andy Neill), 106n.
Fortunes, The, 54
461 Ocean Boulevard (Eric Clapton), 368
Four Tops, The, 82
Fowler, Bill, 261
Fowler, Harry, 246
Frame, Pete, 44, 185, 205, 214, 221
Frampton, Peter, 109, 111–112, 118–119, 149–150, 159
Francis, Freddie, 68
Franklin, Aretha, 122, 230, 332, 337
Franklin, Jeff, 165, 264
Frantics, The, 15
Fraser, Andy, 308
Freddie & The Dreamers, 334n.
Free, 169, 224, 264, 294, 307, 309, 321, 353, 384
Freed, Harvey, 103
Freeman, Alan A., 153
Freewheelin' Bob Dylan, The (Bob Dylan), 222n., 338
Friday On My Mind (David Bowie), 338
Friday On My Mind (Easybeats), 337
Frijid Pink, 227
Frost, David, 382
Frosty, 172
Funk Brothers, The, 224

Gaff, Billy, 148–152, 154–156, 158, 165, 167, 170–171, 178, 184, 192, 194, 207–208, 213, 225–226, 234, 251–253, 258, 260, 264, 273, 278–279, 289, 291, 303, 310, 319, 322, 325, 336, 339–340, 345, 348, 351–352, 356, 359, 361, 369, 372–373, 378, 394–395
Gallagher & Lyle, 263, 379

Gallagher, Benny, 263, 325
Gallagher, Mick, 108*n*.
Gallagher, Rory, 273, 316, 359
Gallegos, Susan (see Susan Lane)
Gallows Pole (Led Zeppelin), 123
Gallup, Cliff, 74
Gamble & Huff, 314
Gardner, Kim, 59, 61–64, 66, 68–69,
    71–72, 78, 85–86, 129
Gardner, Steve, 403
Garland, Judy, 103
Garner, Bob, 85
Gasoline Alley (Faces), 195, 213
Gasoline Alley (Rod Stewart), 183–184,
    195, 220
Gasoline Alley (Rod Stewart), xii, 170,
    179, 182–186, 190, 194–195, 198,
    201, 216, 220, 276, 290, 324
Gaye, Marvin, 67, 70
Geffen, David, 165
Geils, J., Band, 263
Geldof, Bob, 399
Genesis, 331
Genevieve (Susanna Hunt), 103
Georgia Satellites, The, 401
Gerry & The Pacemakers, 99
Gershwin, George, 152, 403
Gershwin, Ira, 152, 403
Get It On (T. Rex), 233
Get Yer Ya-Ya's Out (Rolling Stones), 206
Get Yourself Together (Small Faces),
    97*n*., 98
Gettin' Hungry (Beach Boys), 352
Gettin' Hungry (Faces), 352
Geyer, Renee, 388
Gibb, Russ, 179
Gilbert, Jerry, 225
Gill, Mike, 208, 267
Gillan, Ian, 307
Gilliam, Terry, 296
Gimme Some Neck (Ron Wood), 388
Ginger Baker's Air Force, 193
Girl Can't Help It, The (Little Richard),
    38, 410
Girl From Mill Valley (Jeff Beck Group),
    123
Girl From New York (Billy Nicholls), 119
Girl From The North Country (Bob
    Dylan), 338

Girl From The North Country (Rod
    Stewart), 338
Girls Are Naked, The (Creation), 86
Give Her My Regards (Steve Marriott), 15
Giving It All Away (Roger Daltrey), 315
Glad And Sorry (Faces), 283, 297, 404
Glaub, Bob, 365
Glitter, Gary, 331, 344, 353, 355
Glover, Johnny, 308
Glover, Roger, 225–226, 307
Gods, The, 72
Goffin, Gerry, 314
Golden Apples Of The Sun, 94
Goldsmith, Charlie (Ronnie's great
    uncle), 6
Gomelsky, Giorgio, 52–54, 74, 77*n*.
Gonna Make You A Star (David Essex),
    342
Goo Goo Barabajagal (Donovan with the
    Jeff Beck Group), 126
Good Boys . . . When They're Asleep
    (archive compilation) (Faces), 403
Good Morning Little Schoolgirl (Rod
    Stewart), 51, 65
Good Morning Little Schoolgirl (Sonny
    Boy Williamson), 51
Good Morning Little Schoolgirl
    (Yardbirds), 51
Good, Jack, 48
Goode, Clifford, 13
Goodwin, Keith, 208
Gordy, Berry, 94, 224
Gorham, Scott, 397
Got My Brand On You (Faces), 142
Got My Mojo Working (Faces), 142
Got My Mojo Working (Muddy Waters),
    26
Gouldman, Graham, 82
Gower, Mike, 11
Graham, Bill, 178, 180, 192, 195
Graham, Bobby, 50
Graham, Davy, 191
Grainger, Gary, 322, 340–341, 344, 377,
    397, 401
Grand Funk Railroad, 161
Grant, Cornelius, 224
Grant, Julie, 27
Grant, Peter, 77, 81, 89–92, 122, 127,
    135, 154, 373

Grateful Dead, The, 87, 153, 196
Gray, John, 39, 44, 47–48, 136, 156, 277, 337, 377, 396, 402
Gray, William, Sir, 344
Grease Band, The, 209, 234
Great American Songbook, The (Rod Stewart), 403
Grech, Ric [Rick], 117, 256–257, 293, 337
Green Circles (Small Faces), 97–99
Green Onions (Booker T. & The MG's), 28
Green, Al, 342
Green, Irving, 84–85, 136
Green, Peter, 55–56, 83, 154, 157, 191
Green, Robert, 264–265
Green Tea (Samurai), 307
Greenberg, Jerry, 348
Greenfield, Robert, 264
Greenslade, 273
Greensleeves (Jeff Beck Group), 87
Greer, Germaine, 243
Greyson, Barra, 302
Griffin, Jeff, 294
Griffin, Patty, 416
Griffiths, Derek, 60
Griffiths, Mark, 340
Grimes, Hamish, 74
Grin, 230
Grow Your Own (Small Faces), 33
Growing Closer (Faces), 141
Growing Closer (Humble Pie), 118
Grundy, Stuart, 91
GTOs, The, 91, 244
Guest, Reg, 51
Guinness, Sabrina, 355
Gunnell, John, 55, 90, 154
Gunnell, Rik, 55, 90, 154
Guns N' Roses, xi, 401, 411
Guthrie, Woody, 41, 138
Guy, Buddy, 74, 82, 413

Ha! Ha! Said The Clown (Yardbirds), 89
Had Me A Real Good Time (Faces), 197, 204, 217, 223n., 234, 243, 245, 404, 418
Haley, Bill, & His Comets, 25, 38, 320
Hall, Mafalda, 390
Hall, Tony, 390
Hallyday, Johnny, 110

Hamilton, Alana, 399n.
Handbags & Gladrags (compilation) (Rod Stewart), 338n.
Handbags And Gladrags (Chris Farlowe), 137, 185
Handbags And Gladrags (Double Trouble), 137
Handbags And Gladrags (Love Affair), 137
Handbags And Gladrags (Rod Stewart), 137, 185
Handbags And Gladrags (Stereophonics), 138n,
Hang On Sloopy (McCoys), 94
Hangman's Knee, The (Jeff Beck Group), 123
Happenings Ten Years Time Ago (Yardbirds), 75
Happiness Stan (Small Faces), 104, 106
Happydaystoytown (Small Faces), 104
Hard Rain's A-Gonna Fall, A (Bob Dylan), 315
Hard Rain's A-Gonna Fall, A (Bryan Ferry), 315
Hard Road (Rod Stewart), 337
Hardin, Tim, 116, 138, 224, 231
Hardin, Ty, 7
Harley, Steve, 419
Harrigan, Brian, 332
Harrington, Dee, 229–230, 232–234, 249–250, 253–254, 256, 261, 267, 270, 284, 320, 330, 334, 337, 355–357, 359, 398
Harris, Jet, 6, 78
Harris, John, 383
Harris, June, 76
Harris, Richard, 290
Harrison, George, 118, 191, 204, 224, 239, 292, 312, 320, 332–333, 336, 368, 396
Harrison, Pattie, 312, 320
Hart, Charlie, 361, 379
Hart, Robert, 384
Hartley, Keith 'Keef', 60, 129
Harty, Russell, 314, 343
Harvey, Les, 290n.
Harvey, Pete, 258
Hathaway, Donny, 294, 332
Hats Off To Roy Harper (Led Zeppelin), 160

Havens, Richie, 290
Hawkwind, 277*n.*
Hayman, Martin, 85
Hayward, Philip, 62*n.*
Hazlewood, Lee, 85
Head, Hands & Feet, 232
Healey, Denis, 364
Heart Full Of Soul (Yardbirds), 75
Heath, Andrew, 273
Heath, Edward, Prime Minister, 268, 272
Heatley, Spike, 275
Heavies (Gary Osborne), 193
Hellier, John, 16, 19, 23, 93, 96, 100, 109, 112, 166
Helman, John, 133
Hendrix, Jimi, 76–79, 81, 83, 88, 100–101, 179, 193–194, 267, 275, 341
Hennessey, Brian, 254
Hensley, Ken, 72
Herd, The, 109, 111, 116, 149
Here Come The Nazz (Lord Buckley), 97
Here Come The Nice (Small Faces), 97–98
Here Today (Beach Boys), 70
Here Today (Birds), 70
Herman's Hermits, 77, 80, 101
Heron, Mike, 202
Herron, Allan, 332*n.*
Hey Girl (Small Faces), 33
Heyes, Mickey, 266, 278, 280–281, 395
Hi Heel Sneakers (Faces), 352
Hi Heel Sneakers (Tommy Tucker), 352
Hi Ho Silver Lining (Attack), 80
Hi Ho Silver Lining (Jeff Beck), 79–83, 89
High Heel Sneakers (Shotgun Express), 55
Hill, Jesse, 17
Hill, Peter, 349–350
Hitchcock, Alfred, 61
Hocking, Pete (aka Pete McDaniels), 62, 68–69
Hogman, Peter, 44*n.*
Hold On I'm Coming (Shotgun Express), 55
Holding Back The Years (Simply Red), 406
Holiday, Billie, 185, 353
Holland, Eddie, 65
Holland–Dozier–Holland, 65

Hollies, The, 95, 116
Hollingworth, Roy, 41, 235–236, 247–248
Holloway, Danny, 135
Holly, Buddy, 14–15, 26, 28, 74, 382
Honeycombs, The, 149
Honky Tonk Women (Faces), 207
Hoochie Coochie Man (Faces), 142
Hoochie Coochie Man (Muddy Waters), 26
Hoochie Coochie Men, The, ix, 47–52, 149, 210, 410
Hoover's Not Working, The (Faces), 243
Hope, Bob, 330
Hopkins, John 'Hoppy', 131
Hopkins, Nicky, 46, 80, 84, 87, 90–91, 115, 121, 123, 126, 127*n.*, 137, 396
Hopkinson, Tom, 132
Hornby, Nick, 401
Horowitz, Jimmy, 149–152, 208, 273, 276, 314, 337–338, 368–369, 397
Horricks, Ray, 50–51
Horton, Ralph, 150
Hot Love (T. Rex), 215
House Of The Rising Sun (Frijid Pink), 227
How Blue Can You Get (Python Lee Jackson), 135
How Can It Be (Birds), 67, 413
How Can It Be (Ronnie Wood book), 413
How Come (Ronnie Lane), 324–325, 348
How Long (Ace), 351*n.*
How Long (Rod Stewart), 351*n.*
Howard, Jo (see Jo Wood)
Howard, Ken, 149
Howerd, Frankie, 49, 150
Howes, Arthur, 109
Hucknall, Mick, 394, 405–407, 409, 412, 415
Hudson, Brian, 13
Hudson, Garth, 159, 222
Hudson, Richard, 149
Humble Pie, 112, 116–117, 119, 142, 159, 170, 187, 335, 376, 391*n.*
Humperdinck, Engelbert, 54, 81, 84, 101
Humphreys, Sally, 413
Humphreys, Steve, 398
Humphreys, Susan (see Susanna Tacker)
Hungry Intruder, The (Small Faces), 104

Hunt, Marsha, 140

Hunt, Susanna (see Susanna Tacker)

Hunter, Rachel (Rod's second wife), 398, 399*n.*

Huntley, Colin, 149

Huntley, Gordon, 275

Hurt, John, 382

Hutchins, Chris, 395

Hutchinson, Hutch, 349

Hutton, Alan, 7, 12

I Ain't Got You (Billy Boy Arnold), 65*n.*

I Ain't Got You (Birds), 65*n.*

I Ain't Superstitious (Jeff Beck Group), 82, 87

I Can Feel The Fire (Ron Wood), 333

I Can Feel The Fire (Sex Pistols), 364

I Can't Make It (Small Faces), 96

I Can't Stand The Rain (Ann Peebles), 334

I Can't Stand The Rain (Ron Wood), 334

I Could Feel The Whole World Turn Round (Shotgun Express), 56

I Don't Believe You (Bob Dylan), 295

I Don't Want To Talk About It (Crazy Horse) 288*n.*

I Don't Want To Talk About It (Rod Stewart), 288*n.*

I Feel Like Playing (Ron Wood), 387

I Feel Much Better (Small Faces), 295

I Feel So Good (Faces), 205, 419

(I Know) I'm Losing You (Faces), 82, 216, 253–254, 309, 311, 321*n.*, 400, 419

(I Know) I'm Losing You (Jeff Beck Group), 82

(I Know) I'm Losing You (Rod Stewart), 186, 216, 223, 275

(I Know) I'm Losing You (Temptations), 216, 223

I Lied To Auntie May (Next Change), 150

I Was Only Joking (Rod Stewart), 186*n.*

I Wish It Would Rain (Faces), 311

I Wish It Would Rain (Temptations), 311

I Wouldn't Ever Change A Thing (Rod Stewart), 138, 183

I'd Rather Go Blind (Chicken Shack), 276

I'd Rather Go Blind (Etta James), 276, 342

I'd Rather Go Blind (Faces), 309, 344, 415, 419

I'd Rather Go Blind (Rod Stewart), 266, 276

I'll Fly Away (Ronnie Lane & Ronnie Wood), 263

I'm Gonna Move To The Outskirts Of Town (Big Bill Broonzy), 51

I'm Gonna Move To The Outskirts Of Town (Rod Stewart), 51

I've Been Drinking (Jeff Beck Group), 84, 91, 295

I've Got Mine (Small Faces), 23, 31–32, 105

I've Got My Own Album To Do (Ron Wood), 324, 332–336, 360

I've Grown Accustomed To Her Face (Rod Stewart), 315, 338

Idle, Eric, 246*n.*

If I'm On The Late Side (Faces), 294, 297

If Loving You Is Wrong (I Don't Want To Be Right) (Faces), 295

If Loving You Is Wrong (I Don't Want To Be Right) (Luther Ingram), 295

(If Paradise Is) Half As Nice (Amen Corner), 177*n.*

If You Gotta Make A Fool Of Somebody (Freddie & The Dreamers), 334*n.*

If You Gotta Make A Fool Of Somebody (James Ray), 334

If You Gotta Make A Fool Of Somebody (Ron Wood), 334–335

Iko Iko (Dixie Cups), 258

Iko Iko (John Baldry), 258

I'm Not Like Everybody Else (Alejandro Escovedo), 414

Imagine (John Lennon), 259

Impressions, The, 70, 153

In A Broken Dream (Python Lee Jackson), 134–135, 277, 419

In Memoriam (Small Faces), 115

In My Life (Beatles), 394

In Newport (Muddy Waters), 142

In The Midnight Hour (Shotgun Express), 55

Incredible String Band, The, 202

Ingram, Luther, 295

Insurance (Faces), 298
Isley Brothers, The, 19, 342
It Ain't Easy (Dave Edmunds), 210
It Ain't Easy (David Bowie), 210
It Ain't Easy (John Baldry), 210
It Ain't Easy (John Baldry), 210, 220, 258
It Ain't Easy (Ron Davies), 210
It Ain't Easy (Three Dog Night), 210
It Was Twenty Years Ago Today (book)
    (Derek Taylor), 101
It's All Over Now (Faces), 188, 207, 221,
    234, 269, 311
It's All Over Now (Rod Stewart), 184,
    190, 207
It's All Over Now (Rolling Stones), 184
It's All Over Now (Valentinos), 184
It's Alright (Birds), 70
It's Alright (Impressions), 70
It's Hard (Who), 383
It's Only Rock 'n' Roll (Rolling Stones),
    333
Italian Girls (Rod Stewart), 266, 275
Itchycoo Park (Small Faces), 99–102, 108,
    166, 175, 377, 392

Jackson, Al, 161, 365
Jackson, Aunt Molly, 184
Jackson, Janet, 395
Jackson, Ray, 210, 219–220, 223, 225,
    236, 266, 276, 337, 396–397
Jagger, Bianca, 216, 292, 354
Jagger, Chris, 273, 419
Jagger, Mick, 28, 43–45, 55–56, 72,
    94–96, 100, 125, 126*n*., 137, 202,
    207, 216, 243, 264, 285, 292, 299,
    311–312, 315, 325, 332–336, 344,
    353–354, 357, 359, 364, 385, 387,
    398
Jaguar And The Thunderbird (Chuck
    Berry), 59
Jailhouse Rock (Elvis Presley), 123, 297
Jailhouse Rock (Jeff Beck Group), 123
James Gang, The, 248
James, Elmore, 82, 98*n*., 160
James, Etta, 276
James, Jimmy, 308
Jealous Guy (Donny Hathaway), 294
Jealous Guy (Faces), 294, 321, 418
Jealous Guy (John Lennon), 294, 321

Jefferson Airplane, 101, 126, 127*n*.
Jeggo, Roger, 71
Jerome, Jerome K., 107
Jerusalem (Faces), 205
Jethro Tull, 153, 192, 195, 331
Jewell, Jimmy, 325, 350
Jimmy James & The Vagabonds, 308
Jo Jo Gunne, 300
Jo's Lament (Faces), 183, 186, 190
Joel, Billy, 395
John Wesley Harding (Bob Dylan), 159*n*.
John, Elton, 150–151, 185, 187, 202, 208,
    210, 224, 258–259, 268, 315, 320,
    331, 337, 343–344, 397
Johns, Glyn, 32, 97–99, 101, 104, 110,
    124–125, 127, 155*n*., 159, 202,
    240–242, 244, 247–248, 255,
    262–263, 274, 283–284, 293–294,
    299, 311, 323, 325, 379–383, 391,
    397, 411*n*, 415–416
Johnson, Colin, 273
Johnson, James, 123, 315, 339
Johnson, Johnnie, 321, 337
Johnson, Lonnie, 45*n*.
Johnson, Robert, 160, 207
Johnson, Robert A., 359
Jolson, Al, 37–38, 195, 199
Jones Gang, The, 384, 413
Jones, Brian, 45, 61, 100, 124–125, 126*n*.,
    267
Jones, Darryl, 387
Jones, Dylan (Kenney's son), 272, 372,
    390, 382
Jones, Jack, 85–86
Jones, Jan, 103–104, 111, 119–120, 130,
    156, 190, 207, 211, 216, 233–254,
    256, 261, 272, 292, 302, 310–311,
    313, 323, 334, 338, 370, 372,
    382–384, 398
Jones, Jesse Kaylan (Kenney's son), 382
Jones, John Paul, 51, 79–80, 87
Jones, Kenney, ix, xi, xii, 8–16, 18–19,
    21–23, 31, 33–34, 96–98, 103–104,
    106, 111–114, 116–121, 123, 125,
    129, 141–143, 151, 156–157,
    159–161, 167, 170–174, 178, 181,
    185–186, 190, 192–195, 207, 211,
    214–216, 224–225, 229–232, 237,
    239–241, 244, 247, 251–253, 256,

Jones, Kenney (*contd.*)
262, 272, 276, 279, 284, 289,
296–297, 301–303, 309–311, 313,
315, 323, 326–327, 333–334, 338,
340–341, 347, 352, 355, 361, 367,
372–378, 382–385, 387, 391, 393,
395, 397–400, 402, 404–407,
411–412, 413–414, 415, 416
alcohol use, 32, 104, 162, 170, 187, 195
as object of fun/condescension, 311,
323, 384–385
birth, 9
birth of son, Dylan, 272
birth of son, Jesse, 382
cancer scare, 413–414
charity fundraising, 416–417
drug use, 34–35
drumming skill/style, 11, 98, 119–120,
168, 197, 225, 245, 311, 347
dyslexia, 9
early groups, Pioneers/Outcasts, 11–12
early jobs, 18
extravagances, 112–113, 157, 272
financial state, 22, 112–113, 117, 120,
156–157, 171, 193, 382, 384
first drum-kit, 10
first Faces album (*First Step*),
contribution to, 159–162
first gig, 10
heat exhaustion, 310
Immediate Records, signing to, 35, 113
Lane, Ronnie, first meeting with, 8,
10–11
Law, The, formation of, 384
mod influence, 21–23, 112, 114
musical inclinations, 9–10
Osborne, Jan, marriage to/relationship
with, 103–104, 119–120, 190, 210,
256–257, 292, 313, 323, 384
political affiliations, 384
polo, interest in, 384
professionalism/career advancement,
284, 323, 382–385
Rod Stewart band, turns down offer of
work, 377–378
schooling, 9
session work, 174, 193, 256, 333, 382
shyness, understated personality, 11,
178, 252, 262, 372, 384

Small Faces first album, 32
Small Faces, formation of, 15–16
solo single, 340
teen zine fame, 34
Warner Bros signing, 154–157
Who, recruitment to, 382–384
Jones, Patsy, 229–230, 254
Jones, Paul, 45, 84
Jones, Peter, 80
Jones, Quincy, 85
Jones, Raymond 'Wizz', 42
Jones, Samuel Thomas (Kenney's father),
9–10
Jones, Steve, 363–364
Jones, Tom, 54, 101
Jones, Violet Elizabeth (Kenney's
mother), 9–10, 272, 413
Joplin, Janis, 210, 221, 267
Jordan, Louis, 51
Journey, The (Small Faces), 104
Jubilee Cloud (John Baldry), 258
Jubilee Cloud (John Kongos), 258
Judy Collins Fifth Album (Judy Collins),
221
Juicy Lucy, 81
Jump Back (Rufus Thomas), 17
Just Another Honky (Faces), 294, 297
Just For A Moment (Ron Wood &
Ronnie Lane), 263, 298
Just Like I Treat You (Rod Stewart), 49

Kajagoogoo, 395
Kamadoma-Poly Breath Percussion
Orchestra, 400
Kane, Peter, 389
Kanner, Alexis, 262–263
Karstein, Jim, 293
Kass, Ron, 356
Keary, Vic, 49
Keep Your Hands Off Her (Rod Stewart),
49
Kellgren, Gary, 318, 332, 353
Kelly, Jo-Ann, 191
Kenny, Sean, 94
Kent, Nick, 331, 344, 364
Kenton, Phil, 11
Kern, Jerome, 152
Kerouac, Jack, 42, 325
Keys, Bobby, 204, 263, 388, 392, 416

Khan, Inayat, 107
Kilburn & The High Roads, 361
King, Albert, 82
King, B.B., 82, 135, 413
King, Carole, 236, 314
King Crimson, 232, 362
King, Maurice, 22
King, Reg, 319
Kingwell, Colin, 60
Kinks, The, 15, 91, 97, 101, 116, 194,
    215, 276, 307, 414
Kirke, Simon, 169, 307–309
Kirwan, Danny, 157
Kitt, Eartha, 103
Klein, Allen, 151*n.*
Kleinow, Sneaky Pete, 204
Klingberg, John, 189
Knight, Andy, 350
Knight, Bob, 27, 217
Knight, Gladys, & The Pips, 167
Knight, Marie, 50
Knock On Wood (Shotgun Express), 55
Kongos, John, 258, 381
Kool Kats, The, 38
Kooper, Al, 117
Korner, Alexis, 45, 60, 110
Korsch, Conrad, 412
Kossoff, Kirke, Tetsu, Rabbit (Kossoff,
    Kirke, Tetsu, Rabbit), 307–308
Kossoff, Kirke, Tetsu, Rabbit, 307–308
Kossoff, Paul, 224, 307–308
Krall, Diana, 395
Krell, Gene, 267
Kresge, S.S., 227
Krieger, Robbie, 408
Kristina, Sonja, 198
Kronfeld, Eric, 96
Kubernik, Harvey, 80, 351
Kuschty Rye (Ronnie Lane), 390

L'Amour Est Bleu (Vicky Leandros), 83
Ladwig, Jim, 295
Lady Day (Faces), 183, 185, 213
Lamb Lies Down On Broadway, The
    (Genesis), 331
Lambert, Annie, 262, 286
Lambert, Kit, 21–22, 70, 262
Lambert, Paul, 350
Lancaster, Penny, 399*n.*

Landau, Jon, 247–248, 314, 322
Lane, Charlie (Ronnie's uncle), 4
Lane, Elsie May (Ronnie's mother), 4–8,
    120–121, 133
Lane, Ethel (Ronnie's aunt), 4
Lane, Lenny (Ronnie's uncle), 4
Lane, Luke Kito (Ronnie's son), 326,
    347
Lane, Rene (Ronnie's aunt), 4, 242
Lane, Reuben Jack (Ronnie's son), 390
Lane, Ronnie, ix, xi–xii, 5–8, 10–16,
    18–19, 21, 23, 30–34, 81*n.*, 95–99,
    102–107, 109, 111–114, 116–121,
    124–126, 129–133, 141, 143, 147,
    151, 157–162, 166–167, 169–173,
    175–178, 181–182, 185–191,
    193–198, 201–206, 211–217,
    223–224, 228–229, 231–232,
    236–237, 240, 242–247, 251–252,
    255, 257, 262–264, 266, 269,
    272–273, 276, 279–281, 283–292,
    294, 296–303, 307–309, 312,
    314–316, 320, 324–327, 332,
    346–348, 357, 361–363, 367–368,
    375–381, 389–393, 398, 400,
    402–404, 408, 412, 414, 415, 416
amorous exploits, 8
Anymore For Anymore, recording/
    release, 347–348
benefit concert, 391–392
birth, 5
birth of son, Reuben Jack, 390
brother, Stan, relationship with, 7–8,
    302, 350
catchphrases, love of, 6, 246
country music, interest in, 263, 285
death, 393, 402
drinking, x, 15–16, 32, 126, 162, 170,
    177, 187, 195, 262, 264, 299,
    390–391
drug use, 34–35, 391
early groups, 7–8, 12
Faces, leaving of, 301–303, 307
final gig with Faces, 303
financial state, 112–113, 117, 120,
    156–157, 171, 272–273, 324, 363,
    390
first Faces album (*First Step*),
    contribution to, 159–162

Lane, Ronnie (*contd.*)
  Gallegos, Susan, marriage
    to/relationship with, 392–393
  guitar, learns to play, 6–7
  hippie/gypsy lifestyle/image, 288–289,
    300, 325–326, 346
  'How Come' chart success with, 325,
    348
  Hunt, Susanna, marriage
    to/relationship with, 102–103, 109,
    120–121, 130–133, 190, 203, 207,
    217, 285–287, 297, 398
  Immediate Records, signing to, 35, 95
  jobs, early, 8, 12–13, 18
  last gig, 392
  Mahoney's Last Stand, contribution to
    soundtrack, 262–263
  Marriott, Steve, fractious relationship,
    rivalry/conflict with, 103,112, 116,
    120, 223, 302, 377–378
  McInnerney, Kate, relationship with,
    131, 283, 285–289, 291–292, 300,
    302, 325–326, 347, 349, 390–391
  McLagan, Ian, onstage fracas with,
    300–301
  Meher Baba/Sufism, involvement with,
    107, 130–133, 160, 176–177, 190,
    203–204, 207, 272, 286, 348, 380,
    398
  mod influence, 21–23, 31, 112, 114, 147
  mood swings, 120–121
  multiple sclerosis, 121, 223, 378,
    389–393, 400
  music business, disillusionment
    with/bitterness, 362–363, 390
  musical inclinations, 5–6
  non-materialist tendencies, 272–273,
    324–325, 363, 375
  Ogdens' Nut Gone Flake, contributions
    to, 104–108
  origin of 'Plonk' nickname, 7
  Passing Show concept, 346, 348,
    350–351
  pluckiness/charisma, bubbly
    confidence, 5, 7, 11, 262, 291
  pranks, love of, 18, 291
  Ronnie Lane's Slim Chance, release, 362
  Rough Mix, recording/release of,
    379–381

  schooling, 7
  See Me solo album, 390
  sensitivity/moodiness, ix, 103
  singing style, 141, 245, 418
  Slim Chance, formation of, 114,
    324–325, 347, 361–362
  Small Faces first album, 32
  Small Faces, formation of, 15–16
  Small Faces, resentment, disaffection
    with/leaving of, 109–110
  solo single 'Kuschty Rye', 390
  songwriting, ix, 23, 33, 98–99, 101,
    105–106, 159–160, 156, 185,
    203–204, 242–243, 245, 288,
    296–298, 302
  Stewart, Rod, conflict with, x–xi, 223,
    251, 288, 299–302
  teen zine fame, 34
  Townshend, Pete, friendship/working
    relationship with, 106–107, 114, 132,
    160, 202, 243, 273, 287, 348,
    379–380, 390
  Warner Bros signing, 154–157
Lane, Rosie (Ronnie's aunt), 4
Lane, Stanley Frederick (Ronnie's father),
    4–6, 8, 14, 58, 105, 120–121, 244,
    393
Lane, Stanley, Jr (Ronnie's brother),
    4–10, 13, 32, 105, 120–121,
    302–303, 350, 398
Lane, Susan (Ronnie's third wife),
    392–393
Langham, Bob, 59, 62
Langtry, Lillie, 132
Langwith, Esta (Jimmy Winston's
    mother), 16
Langwith, William (Jimmy Winston's
    father), 16
Last Date (Floyd Cramer), 123
Last Orders Please (Faces), 228*n.*, 243
*Last Orders Please: The Faces . . . And The
    Britain We Forgot* (book) (Jim Melly),
    xii
Law, Denis, 270, 292–293, 322
Law, Don, 88, 172
Law, The, 384
Lawrie, Billy, 193*n.*, 340
Laying Down The Law (Law), 384
Lazarus, Bill, 211

Lazy Racer, 382
Lazy Sunday (Small Faces), xii–xiii, 9*n*.,
    106, 108, 110, 157*n*., 377
Le Fevre, Mylon, 320
Le Fleur, Glen, 361
Leadbelly (Huddie Ledbetter), 6, 210
Leandros, Vicky, 83
Leavell, Chuck, 387–388
Leaving Here (Birds), 65–67
Leaving Here (Eddie Holland), 65
Leaving Here (Who), 66
Led Zeppelin, x, 80, 86*n*., 91, 123, 127,
    160, 167, 174, 179, 188, 195, 241,
    264*n*., 268, 278, 316, 326–327, 331,
    334, 360, 364, 408
Led Zeppelin III (Led Zeppelin), 160
Ledgerwood, Mike, 259, 284
Lee, Albert, 232
Lee, Alvin, 143, 320
Lee, Peggy, 151
Leiber, Jerry, 297
Leigh, Suzanna, 68
Lennon, John, 198, 244, 294, 320–321,
    368, 396
Let 'Em Say What They Will (Alvin Lee
    & Mylon Le Fevre), 320
Let It Be (Beatles), 241
Let It Bleed (Rolling Stones), 212
Let Me Be Your Car (Rod Stewart), 337
Let Me Love You, Baby (Jeff Beck
    Group), 82
Let The Heartaches Begin (Long John
    Baldry), 150
Let's Burn Down The Cornfield (John
    Baldry), 210
Let's See Action (Who), 161
Lewis, Jerry Lee, 16, 22, 58, 256*n*., 288,
    413
Lewis, Ken, 82
Lewis, Linda, 189
Liber, Mike, 133–135
Liberace, 268
Liddell, Billy, 38
Limahl, 395
Lin, Cara, 94
Lindisfarne, 210, 234, 396
Lindley, David, 388
Lindsay, Peter, 69, 72
Lithgow, Lorna, 410

Little Beaver, 343
Little Eva, 177
Little Games (Yardbirds), 89
Little Miss Understood (Rod Stewart), 84,
    137
Little Richard, 22, 38, 53, 410
Little Walter, 28, 52
Little Wing (Jimi Hendrix), 341
Little Wing (Strider), 341
Little, Carlo, 46
Live Aid, 399
Live! (Mott The Hoople), 321
Live! Coast To Coast Overture And Beginners
    (Rod Stewart/Faces), 321–322
Livsey, Billy, 324
Lochinvar (Rod Stewart), 337
Lofgren, Nils, 230
Logan, Nick, 47, 53–55, 84, 88, 109, 120,
    127, 134, 136, 139–140, 142, 159,
    170, 185–186, 194, 198, 206,
    221–222, 266, 269–270, 276, 302
Loggins & Messina, 369
London Chuck Berry Sessions, The (Chuck
    Berry), 256
Long Player (Faces), 181, 194*n*., 202–206,
    209, 214, 216, 240–242, 245, 298,
    325, 418
Look Ka Py-Py (Meters), 177
Looking Out The Window (Faces), 161
Lord Of The Rings (book) (J.R.R.
    Tolkien), 132
Lord Remember Me (John Baldry), 258
Lord, Jon, 60, 86, 129, 225
Lorraine, Gary And Jan, 104, 156
Lost Paraguayos (Rod Stewart), 275
Love In Vain (Faces), 311
Love In Vain (Robert Johnson), 207
Love In Vain (Rolling Stones), 207, 311
Love Is Blue (Jeff Beck), 83, 295
Love Is Blue (Paul Mauriat & His
    Orchestra), 84
Love Lives Here (Faces), 242, 244
Love Me Do (Beatles), 94
Love Songs (Billy Nicholls), 273
Love, Mike, 181, 352
Love's Just A Broken Heart (Cilla Black),
    32*n*.
Love's Made A Fool Of You
    (Muleskinners), 28

495

Loving You Is Sweeter Than Ever (Jeff Beck Group), 82
Lowe, Nick, 414
Luckins, Wally, 349
Lulu, 77, 79, 81, 151, 193*n*., 340, 365
Lumley, Joanna, 320, 323, 330
Luvvers, The, 81
Lydon, John, 364
Lyle, Graham, 263, 325
Lynch, Kenny, 15, 24*n*., 32–33, 67*n*.
Lyttelton, Humphrey, 26, 47

Mabbs, Valerie, 192
Macauley, Tony, 150
MacColl, Ewan, 138
MacKenzie, Ali, 57, 59, 61–72, 353
MacKenzie, Josie, 70
Mackie, Rob, 321
Macleod, John, 150
Macmillan, Ian, Prime Minister, 20
Magee III, Roydon Walter ('Chuch'), 180, 191–192, 227–228, 248–251, 278–281, 291, 300, 309–310, 317, 322–323, 328, 332, 334, 341–342, 354, 387, 400
Magee, Clare, 387
Magee, Nicky, 249
Maggie May (Rod Stewart), x–xi, 129, 218, 220–223, 231, 234, 236–237, 239, 250, 276, 280, 337, 396–397, 419
Maggie's Farm (Bob Dylan), 242
Magic Band, The, 160
Mahoney's Last Stand (soundtrack), 262–263, 266, 295, 418
Mama Weer All Crazee Now (Slade), 277
Mama You Been On My Mind (Bob Dylan), 275
Mama You Been On My Mind (Joan Baez), 275
Mama You Been On My Mind (Johnny Cash), 275
Mama You Been On My Mind (Rod Stewart), 275
Man In Black (Skip Bifferty), 108*n*.
Man Of Constant Sorrow (Rod Stewart), 137–138
Man Of The World (Fleetwood Mac), 154

Man, 280
Mandel, Harvey, 359
Mandelkau, J., 198–199
Mandolin Wind (Rod Stewart), 220, 223
Manfred Mann, 28, 84, 314
Manish Boys, The, 18
Mann, Barry, 56
Manning, Rufus, 140, 158
Mansfield, John, 62*n*.
Mansfield, Mike, 302, 340, 343, 345
Manzarek, Ray, 408
Marbles, 150
Marcus, Greil, 139
Margain, Art, 326–327
Marks, Milton, 156, 250, 270
Marquis Of Kensington, The, 97*n*.
Marriott, Bill (Steve's father), 14–15
Marriott, Jenny (Steve's wife), 103, 166, 176
Marriott, Kay (Steve's mother), 14–15
Marriott, Mollie (Steve's daughter), 412
Marriott, Steve, ix, 3, 13–19, 22–23, 30–35, 80, 93, 95–117, 119–121, 124, 133, 141–142, 159, 166, 168, 174, 176–178, 185, 187, 206, 272, 302, 335, 348, 359, 376–378, 381, 384, 390–392, 412, 415
acting/radio/TV appearances, 14
ambition, 15
Beehive Cottage, purchase of, 109
birth, 14
chirpiness/cheekiness, ix,14, 17, 103
death, 392
drama school, 14–15, 104
drinking, 15–16, 32
drug use, 34–35, 97–98
early groups, 15–16, 18
financial state, 108–109, 112, 376
first meeting with Ronnie Lane, 13
guitar playing, 14
Humble Pie, involvement with, 111–112, 116–117, 142, 159, 335, 376
Immediate Records, signing to, 35, 113
Lane, Ronnie, rivalry/conflict with, 103, 377
Lynch, Kenny, friendship with, 32
marriage, 102
mod influence, 21–23, 31, 112–114

Ogdens' Nut Gone Flake, contributions to, 104–108
Rylance, Jenny, marriage to, 103, 176
Small Faces first album, contribution to, 32
Small Faces formation of, 15–16
Small Faces, leaving of, 111–113, 115–116
Small Faces reunion, 376–377, 381
solo album, 376
songwriting, 23, 33, 97–98, 105–106, 108
soul music, love of, 15
teen zine fame, 34, 111
vocal power, 33, 101, 105, 141
Marsden, Beryl, 55
Marsh, Dave, 360
Martin, Dean, 153
Martin, John, 207
Marvin, Hank, 6, 84
Marx Brothers, ix, 296, 371
Marx, Karl, 42
Mason, Barry, 54
Masters, Robert, 208, 273
Matlock, Glen, 268–269, 287, 363–364, 381, 403, 405–406
Matthews Southern Comfort, 189, 340
Mauriat, Paul, 84
May Blitz, 127
May, Brian, 408
Mayall, John, 55–56, 63, 81–82, 94, 126, 129, 157
Maybe I'm Amazed (Faces), 176, 195, 205, 211–212, 257, 269, 302, 321
Maybe I'm Amazed (Paul McCartney), 176, 211, 321
Mayfield, Curtis, 153
MC5, 170, 192
McAllister, Bill, 206, 240–241, 262
McCartney (Paul McCartney), 176
McCartney, Linda, 333, 343
McCartney, Paul, 176, 211, 315, 321, 333, 338, 343, 382, 413
McCarty, Jim, 74
McCormick, Neil, 419
McCoys, The, 71, 94
McCulloch, Jimmy, 333, 340, 381
McCullough, Henry, 209
McDevitt, Chas, 38

McGhee, Brownie, 45*n.*
McGoohan, Patrick, 263*n.*
McGovern, George, Senator, 280
McGuinness, Tom, 28
McGuinness-Flint, 263
McGuire, Barry, 54
McInnerney, Alana, 285, 287, 289, 326, 347, 390
McInnerney, Kate, 131–133, 162–163, 214, 246, 271, 283, 285–289, 291–292, 297, 300, 302, 326, 347, 349–350, 390–391, 398
McInnerney, Mike, 131–133, 162–163, 189, 207, 213–214, 216, 244, 246–247, 252, 271, 283, 285–287, 289, 325, 398
McLagan, Alec (Ian's father), 24, 30, 389
McLagan, Ian 'Mac', ix, xi, 20, 24–34, 43, 46–48, 52, 60, 79*n.*, 95, 97–102, 105–108, 110, 112, 114–115, 117–121, 123–126, 129, 136–138, 141–143, 151, 156–162, 166, 170–178, 180–182, 184, 186, 189–190, 192–197, 200, 204–205, 207–208, 211–215, 219, 223–224, 226, 228*n.*, 229, 232, 234, 237, 239–242, 245–248, 251–252, 254–256, 262, 264, 266, 270–271, 276, 278, 281, 283–284, 288–290, 296–298, 300–302, 307, 309, 312–313, 315–319, 321–322, 326–330, 332–333, 335–336, 340–341, 348, 352–355, 357–358, 360, 365, 368–378, 381–382, 384, 388–389, 392–393, 395, 397, 399–405, 407–408, 410, 411–412, 414–417
alcohol use, 162, 170, 174, 177, 187, 195, 264, 317, 335
All The Rage autobiography, 388–389
antipathy towards Rock'n'Roll Hall of Fame, 411
antipathy towards Stewart's extravagances, 319, 388
Australia, contemptuous attitude towards, 330
birth, 24
birth of son, Lee, 166

McLagan, Ian 'Mac' (*contd.*)
 Boz & The People, involvement with, 24, 29–30
 Bump Band, work with, 300*n.*, 388–389, 414
 Bump In The Night solo album, 388
 childhood, 25
 cockiness, 27
 death, 414–416
 death of wife, Kim, reaction to, 389
 drug use, 29, 34–35, 100–101, 170, 388
 drugs bust, 100–101, 170, 173
 early groups, 26–29
 finances, 30–31, 108–109, 112, 114–115, 117–118, 156–157, 171, 388
 first Faces album (*First Step*), contribution to, 159–162
 groupies, involvement with, 173–174
 homesickness, 174
 Immediate Records, signing to, 35
 industriousness, 20, 115
 joining Small Faces, 30–31
 keyboard/organ playing, 159, 161, 168, 172, 184, 223–224, 245, 276
 Lynch, Kenny, friendship with, 32
 managing Muleskinners, 27–29
 marital discord, 197
 Marriott, Steve, conflict with, 115
 mod influence, 31, 112
 Moon, Kim, involvement with/marriage to, 312–313, 319, 358, 382, 388–389, 412*n.*, 414, 416
 musical inclinations, 25–26
 New Barbarians, touring with, 388
 Ogdens' Nut Gone Flake, contributions to, 104
 Rolling Stones, touring with, 381–382, 388
 Sandra Sarjeant, marriage to, 102, 117–118, 173–174, 176, 189–190, 196–197, 207, 255–256, 270–271, 405
 session work, 388
 Small Faces first album, 32
 songwriting, 104, 161, 242, 352
 Spiritual Boy recording, 393
 stage fall/sprained wrist, 371–372
 teen zine fame, 34

 Texas, relocation to, 388–389, 412*n*
 Troublemaker solo album, 388
 Warner Bros signing, 154–157
McLagan, Kim, 119, 312–313, 319, 358, 382, 388–389, 400, 414
McLagan, Lee (Ian's son), 166, 169, 174, 190, 196–197, 207–208, 255–256, 270–271, 287, 405, 414–416
McLagan, Michael, (Ian's brother), 24–25
McLagan, Susan (Ian's mother), 24–26
McLagan's Bump Band, Ian, 300*n.*, 388–389, 414
McLaren, Malcolm, 268, 363
McLester, Campbell 'Cam', 178
Me, You And Us, Too (Small Faces), 115*n.*
Meaden, Peter, 21
Meehan, Pat, Jr, 19, 22
Meek, Joe, 40, 225
Megahy, Francis, 49, 410
Mellancamp, John Cougar, 395
Melly, Jim, xii
Memo From Turner (Mick Jagger), 207
Memphis (Chuck Berry), 221, 245, 257
Memphis Horns, The, 337, 365
Memphis Rhythm Section, 365
Memphis Tennessee (Faces), 245, 251, 295, 303, 404
Mendelsohn, John, 201, 206
Mendl, Hugh, 50
Meters, The, 177, 197, 212, 365
Michaels, Lee, 172, 180
Michel, Jean 325
Midway Down (Creation), 86
Miles, Barry, 131
Miles, Buddy, 85
Miller, Steve, 88, 127, 241
Millie, 44*n.*
Milligan, Spike, 49, 105
Mills, Hayley, 293
Mills, John, 272
Mimms, Garnet, 15
Mine For Me (Rod Stewart), 338, 343
Miracles, The, 70, 243
Miss Judy's Farm (Faces), 236, 242–243, 251, 404, 407
Miss You (Rolling Stones), 382
Missed You (Rod Stewart), 338*n.*
Mitchell, John 'Mitch', 103–104

Mitchell, Joni, 165, 183, 395
Mitchell, Sam, 210, 219–221, 225
Moby Grape, 88
Modeliste, Joseph 'Zigaboo', 197, 388
Mona – The Blues (Faces), 418
Money, Zoot, 55–56
Monk, Thelonius, 26
Montagu, Lord, 38
Montgomery Tanners, The, 327, 347
Montgomery, David, 133–134
Moody Blues, The, 105, 202, 340, 397
Moon, Keith, 31, 80, 119, 202, 235, 299,
    312–313, 317, 319, 340, 358,
    382–383, 388
Moon, Kim (see Kim McLagan)
Moon, Mandy, 313, 319, 358, 382
Moondance (Van Morrison), 189
Moondog Matinee (Band), 315
Moondogs, The, 15
Moonlites, The, 15
Moontrekkers, The, 40
Moore, Scotty, 74
Moppers Blues (Rod Stewart), 49
Mordue, Terry, 353
Morice, Barbara, 300, 346–347
Morley, Robert, 77
Morning Dew (Jeff Beck Group), 87
Morning Dew (Tim Rose), 87
Morrison, Bryan, 52
Morrison, Jim, 267
Morrison, Van, 189
Most, Mickie, 77–81, 83–84, 89–90, 126,
    154, 159, 295
Mother Ain't Dead (John Baldry), 258
Mott The Hoople, 234, 264n., 277n., 307,
    321
Mountain, 192, 217
Move It (Cliff Richard & The Drifters),
    19
Move, The, 76, 116
Mr Tambourine Man (Byrds), 67
Mud, 331
Muleskinners, The, ix, 7, 12–13, 15,
    27–29, 46, 52, 60
Muni, Scott, 75
Munro, Terry, 25–26
Munroe, Tony, 58–61, 63, 67–72
Murray, Charles Shaar, 57
My Boy Lollipop (Millie), 44n.

My Fair Lady (soundtrack), 315, 338
My Fault (Faces), 294, 296
My Generation (Who), 241
My Mind's Eye (Small Faces), 35
My Sweet Lord (George Harrison), 239
My Way Of Giving (Chris Farlowe), 96
My Way Of Giving (Rod Stewart), 185
My Way Of Giving (Small Faces), 98, 185
Mylne, Robert, 272
Mystifies Me (Ron Wood), 334–335

Napier-Bell, Simon, 77, 80–81
Nash, Graham, 116
Nashville Skyline (Bob Dylan), 338
Nashville Teens, The, 22, 30, 77
Natural Born Bugie (Humble Pie), 142
Nazz Are Blue, The (Yardbirds), 98
Neat Change, The, 150
Nelson, Paul, 184, 275, 287
Nelson, Ricky, 74
Nelson, Willie, 362
Nesbit, Jan, 169
Nessun Dorma (Jeff Beck), 396
Never A Dull Moment (Rod Stewart), xi,
    260, 264, 274–277, 288n., 290n.,
    302, 336–338
Never Say Never (Ian McLagan), 397
Neville, Richard, 133
Nevison, Ron, 273, 288, 292–295, 311,
    313, 326, 332, 352–353, 397
New Barbarians, The, 388
New Directions (Lulu), 365
New Vaudeville Band, The, 77
New York Dolls, The, 287
Newcomb, 'Scrappy' Jud, 414
Newhart, Bob, 152
Newley, Tony, 153
Newman, Randy, 210
Newman, Terry, 12–13, 16
Newman, Tony, 122, 127, 160, 396
Newmark, Andy, 332–333
Next In Line (Birds), 66
Nice, The, 97
Nicholls, Billy, 118–119, 121, 132,
    175–177, 202, 214, 235, 262–263,
    273, 285–287, 326, 346, 363, 379,
    398, 416
Nicks, Stevie, 369
Nico, 94

Night Time Is The Right Time (Cyril Davies R&B All Stars), 47
Nightingale, Wally, 364
Nightshift, The, 74
Nilsson, 89
Nitty Gritty Dirt Band, The, 296
Nixon, Malcolm, 44, 52
Nixon, Richard, President, 198, 280
No Expectations (Rolling Stones), 160
No Good Without You Baby (Birds), 67
Noble, Douglas J., 78
Nobody Knows (Faces), 161, 297
Nod Is As Good As A Wink . . . To A Blind Horse, A (Faces), xi, 158n., 227n., 228, 239–248, 251, 253, 257, 260, 272, 274, 283–284, 298, 348n., 418
Nod's As Good As A Wink . . . , A (Faces) (see *A Nod Is As Good As A Wink . . . To A Blind Horse*)
Noir, 199
Not Fade Away (Rolling Stones), 28
Notarthomas, Jon, 414
Nothing In The World (Geneveve), 103
Now Look (Ron Wood), 333n., 360

O'Connor, Des, 49
O'Lochlain, Ruan, 361
O'Sullivan, Gilbert, 331
Oddie, Bill, 150, 208
Ogdens' Nut Gone Flake (Small Faces), 102, 104–106, 111, 115, 119, 133, 241
Oh Lord, I'm Browned Off (Faces), 212
Oh Pretty Woman (Jeff Beck Group), 82
Oh Well Parts 1& 2 (Fleetwood Mac), 159
Oh! No, Not My Baby (Manfred Mann), 314
Oh! No, Not My Baby (Maxine Brown), 314
Oh! No, Not My Baby (Merry Clayton), 314
Oh! No, Not My Baby (Rod Stewart), 314
Ol Man River (Jeff Beck Group), 87
Oldfield, Boo, 391
Oldham, Andrew, 35, 53, 55–56, 93–97, 100, 106, 108, 112–113, 118, 124, 134, 142, 152, 154, 156, 170, 175–177, 394

Oliver! (musical), 14, 222n.
Oliver, Jack, 229–230
On The Beach (Faces), 204–205
On The Beach (novel) (Neville Shute), 204
On The Road To Freedom (Alvin Lee & Mylon Le Fevre), 320
Once (Geneveve), 103
One Direction, 413
One For The Road (Ronnie Lane), 362
Only A Hobo (Hamilton Camp), 184, 221
Only A Hobo (Rod Stewart), 183–184, 221
Ono, Yoko, 289
Oo Poo Pah Doo (Jesse Hill), 17
Ooh La La (Faces), 297–298, 325, 392, 403, 405, 412, 419
Ooh La La (Faces), xi, 283–285, 288, 294–302
Ooh La La (Rod Stewart), 402
OPE, 400
Open To Ideas (Faces), 352, 401, 403
Orbison, Roy, 35, 78
Orchovski, Wes, 416
Ormond, Willie, 332
Ormsby-Gore, Alice, 293
Osborne, Gary, 104, 113, 119, 130, 151, 156, 193, 275, 289–290, 325n., 333, 340, 342, 385, 397–398
Osborne, Jan (see Jan Jones)
Osborne, Tony, 103–104, 119
Ostin, Mo, 147, 153, 375–376
Out Demons Out (Edgar Broughton Band), 187
Out Of Time (Chris Farlowe), 95, 222n.
Outcasts, The, ix, 12–13, 16
Over The Rainbow (Jeff Beck), 396
Own Up Time (Small Faces), 33

Page, Jimmy, 74–76, 80, 86n., 89, 91, 160, 336, 360, 391
Paice, Ian, 225
Painter Man (Creation), 86
Pallenburg, Anita, 312
Palmer, Tony, 54
Paper Lace, 331
Parker, Johnny, 47
Parkes, Larry, 37
Parnes, Larry, 49

Partridge, Don, 108
Partridge, Rob, 38, 40, 47
Passing Show, The (documentary film), 416
Passing Show, 346, 348, 350–351
Passion Play, A (Jethro Tull), 331
Paths Of Victory (Hamilton Camp), 184, 221
Paul, Les, 73
Peacock, Steve, 215, 217, 280
Pearson, Rick, 407
Peebles, Ann, 334
Peek, Billy, 377
Peel, John, 133–135, 188–189, 198, 216, 236, 270, 299, 352, 376, 397
Peel, Sheila, 352
Pentangle, 224
Perfect, Christine, 276
Perkins, Carl, 22
Perkins, Wayne, 359
Permanent Damage (GTOs), 91
Perry, Fred, 21
Pet Sounds (Beach Boys), 70, 106
Pete Brown's Battered Ornaments, 361
Peter B's Looners, 55
Peter, Paul & Mary, 152
Peters & Lee, 314
Pether, Dave, 27–28
Petrolini, Ettore, 296
Petty, Craig, 227, 251–252
Petty, Tom, 395
Peverett, John 'Pee Wee', 194, 248
Phillips, Eddie, 85–86
Phillips, John, 96
Philosopher, The (John Cale), 256
Physical Graffiti (Led Zeppelin), 326
Pickett, Kenny, 85–86
Pickett, Wilson, 15, 56
Pidgeon, John, xii, 290, 405
Pinball Wizard (Rod Stewart), 290, 321
Pineapple And The Monkey (Faces), 161
Pink Fairies, The, 287
Pink Floyd, The, 76, 84, 100–101, 174, 217, 331, 364
Pin-Ups (David Bowie), 315, 338
Pioneers, The, 11
Plant, Robert, 188, 408
Platz, David, 153
Play It Again Fats (Fats Domino), 314*n*.
Playmates (Small Faces), 381

Plummer, Mark, 35, 41, 277
Plynth (Water Down The Drain) (Jeff Beck Group), 123, 160
Poacher, The (Ronnie Lane), 348
Poly Breath Percussion Band, 400
Pomus, Doc, 32*n*., 71
Pool Hall Richard (Faces), 321, 342
Pool, Malcolm, 60
Poor Miner's Farewell (Aunt Molly Jackson), 184
Poor Miner's Farewell (Bob Dylan), 184
Popcorn Double Feature (Searchers), 80*n*.
Porter, Cole, 338*n*., 403
Posta, Adrienne, 97*n*., 104
Potter, Brian, 22
Powell, Dick, 184–185, 222, 224, 266, 275–277
Powell, Enoch, 199–200
Powell, Jimmy, & The Five Dimensions, ix, 44
Powell, Tony, 262
Presley, Elvis, 32*n*., 64*n*., 73–74, 123, 221, 236, 281, 297
Press, Perry, 250
Preston, Billy, 32
Pretty Things, The, 28, 52, 63, 78
Price, Jim, 263
Pridden, Bob, 157
Prince, 78
Principal Edwards Magic Theatre, 232
Procol Harum, 100–101, 135, 193
Pugh, Martin, 136
Pulin, Chuck, 91, 126, 279
Python Lee Jackson, 133–134, 188, 277

Quadrophenia (Who), 294, 331
Quaife, Pete, 40, 116
Quant, Mary, 94
Queen, 408
Quick One, A (Who), 70
Quicksilver Messenger Service, 126, 396
Quiet Melon, 129–130, 140, 142, 158
Quintessence, 187, 234
Quireboys, The, ix, 401
Quittenton, Martin, 136, 138, 182, 184–185, 219–220, 222, 266, 275–277, 314–315, 337–338, 397
Quiver, 310
Quotations, The, 81

R&B Chartbusters Volume 3 (EP) (Various Artistes), 65
Rafferty, Gerry, 338*n*.
Rainwater, Marvin, 418
Raitt, Bonnie, 388
Ralfini, Ian, 153–156, 205, 211, 260, 351, 397
Ralphs, Mick, 307
Ranglin, Ernest, 44*n*.
Ray, James, 334
Read, Frankie, & The Casuals, 134
Ready Or Not (Kenney Jones), 340
Rear Wheel Skid (Faces), 181, 197
Reason To Believe (Rod Stewart), 224, 231
Reason To Believe (Tim Hardin), 224, 231
Red Balloon (Small Faces), 116
Red Balloon (Tim Hardin), 116
Red Hot Chili Peppers, xi, 411
Redding, Otis, 54, 230, 274
Reddy, Helen, 371
Redfern, Anthea, 103*n*.
Reed, Jimmy, 15, 27, 47, 51, 333
Regan, Russ, 289
Reizner, Lou, 84–85, 90, 135–136, 138–139, 183, 290, 397
Relf, Keith, 61, 73–74, 76
Renaissance, 44
Rene (Small Faces), 105
Renegades, The, 59
Replacements, The, xi, 401
Repsch, John, 40
Resurrection Shuffle (Ashton, Gardner & Dyke), 257
Revolution (Beatles), 91
Reynolds, Jack, 185
Reynolds, Joshua, Sir, 272
Rhinoceros, 186
Rich, Ellis, 405
Rich Kids, The, 381
Richard, Cliff, 64*n*.
Richard, Cliff, & The Drifters, 19
Richards, Keith, 45, 56, 94–96, 100, 160, 206, 299, 312–313, 331, 333–337, 344, 360, 385, 387–388, 391*n*.
Richmond (Faces), 204, 214, 245
Ricotti & Alburquerque, 234, 322
Ridley, Greg, 112, 118

Riot In Cell Block # 9 (Coasters), 297
Rivers, Tony, & The Castaways, 13
Roadwork (book) (Tom Wright), 396
Robertson, Brian, 398
Robinson, Lisa, 332
Robinson, Smokey, 70, 243
Roche, Pete, 257
Rock Around The Clock (Bill Haley & His Comets), 25
Rock Island Line (Lonnie Donegan), 6
Rock Me (Faces), 352
Rock Me Baby (B.B. King), 82
Rock My Plimsoul (Jeff Beck Group), 82
Rockwell, Norman, 320
Rod Stewart Album, The (Rod Stewart), 136–140, 166, 186, 190, 195, 198, 216, 224, 410
Rod Stewart And The Changing Faces (book) (John Pidgeon), xii
Rod Stewart Sessions 1971–1998, The (Rod Stewart), 222, 334*n*.
Rod Stewart: Can't Stop Me Now (television documentary), 410–411
Rod The Mod (television documentary), 36, 49, 410–411
Rod: The Autobiography (book), 409–410
Rodgers, Paul, 221, 308, 384, 408
Rogan, Johnny, 22*n*., 217
Rojas, Carmine, 402–403
Roll On Babe (Ronnie Lane), 347
Rollin' And Tumblin' (Rod Stewart), 419
Rollin' Over (Small Faces), 105
Rolling Stones, The, xi, 12, 22, 26–28, 33, 43–44, 46, 53, 56, 60–61, 72, 91, 93–96, 99, 124–126, 137–138, 141, 149, 151*n*., 155*n*., 160, 164–165, 170, 184, 187, 202, 204, 212, 216, 221, 241, 243, 273, 268, 278, 299, 311–312, 319, 325, 327, 331, 333–334, 344–345, 352, 354, 359–360, 366–368, 374–376, 382–383, 385, 387–388, 391–392, 396, 401–402, 413
Rolling Stones, The (Rolling Stones), 95
Rolling Thunder Revue, 346
Ronnie Lane's Slim Chance (Ronnie Lane), 362
Ronson, Mick, 381
Ronstadt, Linda, 229

Roosters, The, 28
Rose, David, 322
Rose, Tim, 87
Rosen, Steve, 74, 88
Rosie (Don Partridge), 108
Rough Mix (Ronnie Lane/Pete Townshend), 379–381, 390
Row, Dulcie, 34
Rowe, Dick, 64
Rowland, Bruce, 209, 263, 325, 350, 361
Rowland, Steve, 256*n.*
Rowlands, Jonathan, 48–49, 51, 54, 74, 85, 90, 136
Roxy Music, 307, 362, 381
Rubettes, The, 331, 342
Ruffin, David, 135, 184, 224, 254
Run Run Run (Birds), 70
Run Run Run (Who), 70
Rundgren, Todd, 98
Rush, Pepi, 49
Russell, Leon, 209, 368
Russell, Rosalind, 311
Rylance, Jenny (see Jenny Marriott)
Rylatt, Keith, 17

Safe As Milk (Captain Beefheart & The Magic Band), 160
Sailing (Rod Stewart), 365
Sailor (Rod Stewart), 337
Saint Jude, 413, 413*n*
Sam Apple Pie, 187
Samurai, 307
Samwell, Ian 'Sammy', 19, 22–23, 152, 154–155, 261
Samwell-Smith, Paul, 74–75
San Francisco (Scott McKenzie), 99
Santa Barbara Machine Head, 86*n.*
Sarjeant, Sandra (Ian McLagan's wife), 102, 117–118, 120, 165, 169, 173–174, 176, 189–190, 196–197, 207–208, 253, 255–256, 270–271, 287, 313, 386, 398–399, 405, 414, 416
Savages, The, 46, 91
Savoy Brown, 171, 173, 209
Say Those Magic Words (Birds), 71
Say Those Magic Words (McCoys), 71
Sayer, Leo, 315, 331, 398
Sayers, Tom, 18

Schiffer, Liesel, 336
Schlagbaum, Russell, x, 191–192, 227–228, 248–250, 279–281, 288–291, 294, 297, 300, 302, 309–310, 319, 326–329, 334, 347–350, 361–362, 376, 378–380, 387, 390, 392, 402
School's Out (Alice Cooper), 277*n.*
Scott, Freddie, 334
Scott, Keith, 46
Scott, Ken, 87
Scott, Phil, 17
Scott, Ronnie, 119
Scrimshaw, Robin, 59, 61
Searchers, The, 66, 80*n.*, 95
Sears, Pete, 182, 219–221, 224–225, 266, 314–315, 337
See Me (Ronnie Lane), 390
Seeger, Peggy, 41
Seeger, Pete, 41
Seeker, The (Who), 222*n.*
Seems Like A Long Time (Rod Stewart), 221
Seger, Bob, 192
Sellers, Peter, 257
Selvin, Joel, 175
Selwood, Clive, 133–134
Session, The (Jerry Lee Lewis), 256*n.*
Sessler, Freddie, 391
Seventh Sons, 88
'78 In The Shade (Small Faces), 381
Sex Pistols, The, 381–382
Sexton, Charlie, 416
Sgt Pepper's Lonely Hearts Club Band (Beatles), 101, 105–106
Sha La La La Lee (Small Faces), 32–33, 80
Shadows, The, 6, 10–12, 78
Shady Grove (Quicksilver Messenger Service), 126
Shake (Otis Redding), 54
Shake (Rod Stewart), 54
Shake (Sam Cooke), 54
Shake, Shudder, Shiver (Faces), 141–142, 155*n.*, 160–161, 404
Sham-Mozzal (Faces), 418
Shapes Of Things (Jeff Beck Group), 87, 123
Shapes Of Things (Yardbirds), 75, 87, 123, 137

Sharp, Ken, 383
Shaw, David, 208
Shaw, Russ, 211, 226
She Trinity, The, 77
Shelton, Robert, 73, 88
Shine (Ted Wood), 353
Shirley, Jerry, 97, 111, 119
Shot Of Rhythm & Blues, A (Rod Stewart), 49n.
Shotgun Express, 55–56, 81, 130, 150
Shrimpton, Chrissie, 43, 55
Shrimpton, Jean, 43
Shuman, Mort, 32, 71
Shute, Nevil, 204
Siffre, Labi, 338n.
Silent Song Through The Land (Ron Davies), 210
Silicone Grown (Faces), 294, 296
Sill, Lester, 94
Silver Machine (Hawkwind), 277n.
Silver Metre, 168, 182, 185
Simmonds, Kathy, 320
Simms, Ken, 45
Simon & Garfunkel, 239
Simon & Marijke, 132
Simon, Paul, 131
Simper, Nick, 72
Simply Red, 405, 407
Simpson, Steve, 361
Sinatra, Frank, 153, 327, 403
Sing It Again Rod (compilation) (Rod Stewart), xi, 314
(Sittin' On) The Dock Of The Bay (Otis Redding), 274
634–5789 (Shotgun Express), 55
Skewiff (Mend The Fuse) (Faces), 295
Skip Bifferty, 108n.
Sklar, Lee, 365
Slade, xii, 239, 277n., 295, 331
Slade In Flame (book) (John Pidgeon), xii
Slash, 407
Slater, Terry, 19
Slatus, Teddy, 213
Slim Chance, 114, 276n., 324–325, 347, 361–362, 376–377, 390, 416, 417
Slim, Memphis, 42, 52
Sly & The Family Stone, 88, 193, 332
Small Faces (Small Faces), 32, 98
Small Faces, The, ix–xii, 7, 9n., 16–19,

21–25, 30–35, 63, 69, 78–80, 86, 93, 95–116, 119–121, 124, 127, 129–130, 133, 140, 148, 151, 153, 156–159, 162, 166–168, 170, 173, 175, 178, 180, 185, 187–189, 194, 198, 206, 241, 251, 257, 262, 267, 269, 271, 296, 323, 328, 336, 346, 370, 378–379, 381, 383–384, 397–398
Smeeth, Clifford, 11
Smiler (Rod Stewart), 331, 336–339, 343–344, 351, 396
Smiler (television documentary), 343
Smiley Smile (Beach Boys), 352
Smiling Men With Bad Reputations (Mike Heron), 202
Smith, Chris, 105
Smith, Joe, 154–155, 166–167, 208, 262, 351
Smith, Terry, 170
Smith, Willie, 365
Smokestack Lightning (Howlin' Wolf)
Snakes And Ladders (compilation) (Faces), 403
So Much To Say (Rod Stewart), 84
So Tired (Rod Stewart), 338n.
Soft Machine, 198
Some Girls (Rolling Stones), 382
Some Kind Of Wonderful (Jeff Beck Group), 83, 161
Some Kind Of Wonderful (Soul Brothers Six), 83, 161
Song Of A Baker (Small Faces), 105
Songer, Dick, 191–192
Sorry She's Mine (Jimmy Winston & The Reflections), 24n.
Sorry She's Mine (Small Faces), 33
Soul Agents, The, 52, 74
Soul Brothers Six, 83, 161
Soulful Dress (Shotgun Express), 55
Sounds Incorporated, 122
Space Oddity (David Bowie), 135
Spanish Boots (Jeff Beck Group), 123
Spanish Harlem (Aretha Franklin), 230
Spear, Roger Ruskin, 60
Spector, Phil, 54, 94–95, 241
Spiders From Mars, The, 307
Spirit, 300n.
Spiritual Boy (Ian McLagan), 393

Spooky Tooth, 112, 325*n*.

Springfield, Dusty, 19, 95, 151, 208, 365

Springsteen, Bruce, 247, 388

St John, Bridget, 133

St Valentine's Day Massacre, 71*n*., 129

Stamp, Chris, 21, 70

Stanley, Ron, 11

Stardust, Alvin, 331

Starkey, Maureen, 320

Starmakers & Svengalis: The History Of British Pop Management (book) (Johnny Rogan), 22*n*.

Starr, Ringo, 31, 114, 290, 299, 320, 368, 388

Start, John, 40

Status Quo, 273

Stax, Mike, 63, 66, 86

Stay With Me (Faces), 222*n*., 236, 241–244, 251, 257, 295–296, 400–401, 405–407, 412, 419

Stealer (Faces), 294, 321

Stealer (Free), 294, 321

Stealers Wheel, 81

Steam Packet, ix, 36, 52–55, 68, 130, 150, 169, 258

Steamhammer, 44, 136

Steele, Tommy, 49, 58

Steeled Blues (Yardbirds), 75

Steinberg, Irwin, 183, 237

Stephen, John, 23

Stephens, Leigh, 122, 124–125, 136, 168

Steve Marriott's Moments, 13, 15, 17*n*., 25*n*.

Stevens, Cat, 81

Stevens, Don, 107

Stevens, Guy, 15

Stewart, Aiden (Rod's son), 399*n*.

Stewart, Alistair (Rod's son), 399*n*.

Stewart, Al, 131

Stewart, Chrissy, 325

Stewart, Cynthia, 389

Stewart, Donald (Rod's brother), 36–37, 40, 42–43, 53

Stewart, Elsie Gilbart (Rod's mother), 36–37, 43, 48–51, 411

Stewart, Ian, 124–126, 141, 379, 389, 391–392

Stewart, Joseph Robert (Rod's father), 36–40, 42–43, 49–50, 411

Stewart, Kimberly (Rod's daughter), 399*n*.

Stewart, Liam (Rod's son), 399*n*.

Stewart, Mary (Rod's sister), 37, 39, 50

Stewart, Peggy (Rod's sister), 37, 391

Stewart, Renée (Rod's daughter), 399*n*.

Stewart, Robert 'Bobby' (Rod's brother), 37, 39, 41, 189, 250, 331

Stewart, Rod, ix–xii, 35–56, 62, 65, 70, 72–73, 78–85, 87–90, 103, 106, 111, 122–123, 125–130, 134–143, 147–152, 155, 157–163, 165–169, 172–173, 179–186, 188–190, 192, 194–210, 213–226, 229–245, 247, 249–271, 274–280, 283–285, 287–292, 294–303, 307–312, 314–316, 318–324, 326, 328–332, 334–344, 345*n*., 346, 351–359, 361, 364–368, 370–374, 376–377, 383, 387–388, 391, 394–396, 398–408, 412, 415, 416–417

alcohol use, x, 78, 87, 126, 162, 170, 187, 195, 236, 265

America, reception in, 139, 165–175, 179–181, 192, 195, 198, 200, 206, 210, 219, 236, 239, 251–253, 274, 288, 316

Atlantic Crossing, release/reaction to, 365

awards, 198, 236–238, 315, 344, 398

Baldry, (Long) John, friendship/ working involvement, 44–48, 50–52, 150, 208, 210, 258–259, 401, 410

beatnik phase, 41–42, 50

birth, 36

Boffey, Suzannah, relationship with, 43, 186

chauvinist lyrics/persona, 243–244

childhood, 37

children, list of, 399n.

credibility, loss of, 399

credibility, restoration of, 401

defensiveness, 163, 166

distancing from Faces, culminating in departure, 330, 352, 366–367, 371–374

drug use, 320, 329, 334–335, 410

Dylan, Bob, as preference for cover versions, 137, 159, 183–184, 221–223, 275, 338

Stewart, Rod (*contd.*)

Ekland, Britt, relationship with, 357–359, 365, 370–371

Every Picture Tells A Story, recording and reception, 219–225, 236, 239

Faces, asked to join, 129, 141–143, 147

Faces reunions, 399–400, 404–405, 409, 412, 414, 417, 419–420

fame and divisive effect on Faces, 219, 231, 236–237, 239–240, 247, 251, 260–262, 271, 274–275, 283–285, 311, 316–317, 366

financial canniness/frugality 49, 51, 127, 135–136, 156–157, 183, 189, 207–208, 250–251, 255, 267, 339, 342, 388, 395, 407

first child, Sarah (Thubron/Streeter), 43, 43*n*, 410

first Faces album (*First Step*), contribution to, 159–162

first single, 50–51

first solo album, recording of, 136–139

folk music, fascination with, 41, 137, 183, 222, 247

football, love of, 39–40, 249–250, 270, 292–293, 322, 330–332, 335, 343, 409–410

Gaff, Billy, sued by, 394–395

Gasoline Alley (Rod Stewart), 419

Gasoline Alley, recording/release of, 179, 182–186, 190, 194–195, 198, 201, 216, 220, 276, 290, 324

girlfriends/amorous adventures, 38, 43, 89, 103, 165, 186, 229–230, 234, 266, 312, 320, 354, 357, 399

Great American Songbook recordings, 403

Harrington, Dee, relationship with, 229–230, 232–233, 249–250, 253–254, 256, 320, 330, 337, 355–356, 359

Hucknall, Mick, reaction to his joining Faces, 406–407

image/dress sense, 36, 38, 40, 50. 234–236, 253, 277, 280, 303, 314–315, 318, 338–339, 343, 355, 399, 401

Jagger, Mick, friendship/rivalry with, 55–56

Jeff Beck Group, involvement with, 35, 78–79. 81–83, 111, 122–123, 127–128, 135

Johns, Glyn, attitude towards, 284, 294

Jolson, Al, influence of, 37–38, 199

Lumley, Joanna, relationship with, 320, 322, 330

Marriott, Steve, negative comments about, 166

Mercury Records, signing to, 90, 135

mod influence, 36, 50

mortality, 'obsession with', 30–31

musical influences, 37–38, 47–48, 70

Never A Dull Moment, analysis and reception, 274–277

Ooh La La, public criticism of, 299–300

Peel, John, friendship with, 133–134, 188, 198, 236, 270

political views/support of Enoch Powell, 199–200, 243

post Faces litigation, 394–397

press statements/interviews, 166, 183–186, 194–195, 199–203, 217–218, 220–222, 237, 274. 299, 315–316, 351–352, 366–367

Python Lee Jackson, involvement with, 134–135, 188, 277

reunions, ambivalence towards, 404–405, 409

Riva Records, formation of, 365

Rod The Mod documentary, starring in, 36, 49, 410–411

Rylance, Jenny, relationship with, 103

schooling, 38–39

Scottish heritage/identity, 38–39, 183, 314–315, 320–321, 331–332, 344

sense of humour, 189, 214, 226, 291, 341

Shotgun Express, involvement with, 55–56

Simmonds, Kathy, relationship with, 320

slicker Seventies' sound, 314, 338, 365

Small Faces, first meeting with, 35

Smiler, release of/reaction to, 336–339

solo recordings, pre-Faces, x, 50–51, 84–85, 136–139

Stewart, Rod (*contd.*)
  songwriting, 84, 136, 138–139,
    161–162, 183–185, 203, 220, 223,
    242–244, 274–275, 294–295, 297,
    321, 338, 342
  stage fright, 87–88, 130
  stagecraft, 196, 200, 215, 410
  Steam Packet, involvement with, 36,
    52–55
  surliness, 329, 339
  tax exile, 359, 364. 366–367
  thyroid cancer diagnosis, 402
  Tommy, guest appearance in adaptation
    of, 290
  topless shots of fiancée, attempts to
    prevent, 254
  Troupe, Sarah, relationship with, 89,
    165, 228
  turns professional, 47
  Unplugged . . . And Seated, reaction to,
    388, 401
  virginity, loss of, 38, 410
  vocal style, ix, 35, 37–38, 40, 48, 54,
    88, 138–139, 141, 159, 161, 168,
    181, 224, 233, 245, 258, 402–403
  Warner Bros signing, 154–157, 351,
    364
  When We Were The New Boys solo
    album, 402
  wives and lovers, post Faces, 399
  Wood, Ron, first meeting with, 65,
    130, 169, 213, 411
Stewart, Ruby (Rod's daughter), 399n.
Stewart, Sean (Rod's son), 399n.
Sticky Fingers (Rolling Stones), 202
Stigwood, Robert, 70–71, 149–151,
  165n., 208, 344
Still I'm Sad (Yardbirds), 75
Stills, Stephen, 117
Stoddart, Patrick, 216
Stoller, Mike, 297
Stone (Faces), 160, 204
Stone Crazy (Jeff Beck Group), 82
Stone The Crows, 210, 290n.
Stone, Chris, 353
Stoned (autobiography) (Andrew Loog
  Oldham), 177n., 394
Stooges, The, 192
Storms, The, 61

Stout, William, 73
Strangeloves, The, 94
Strawbs, The, 81
Street Fighting Man (Rod Stewart),
  137–138, 207, 410
Street Fighting Man (Rolling Stones), 137
Streeter, Sarah (see Sarah Thubron)
Strider, 322, 340, 344, 377
Stringfellow, Geoff, 17
Stringfellow, Peter, 17
Stripper, The (David Rose), 322, 355
Strzelczyk, Lee, 322, 344
Stumble, 289, 325n.
Substitute (Who), 243
Sugar Baby Love (Rubettes), 342
Sumlin, Hubert, 28
Summerbee, Mike, 322
Summertime Blues (Eddie Cochran), 122
Super Session (Mike Bloomfield, Al
  Kooper, Steve Stills), 117
Sure The One You Need (Ron Wood),
  334
Sutch, Screaming Lord, 46, 74, 91, 103
Sutherland Brothers And Quiver, 310,
  340
Sutherland Brothers, The, 310, 315, 365
Sutherland, Gavin, 365
Sway (Rolling Stones), 202
Sweet Lady Mary (Faces), 204, 214
Sweet Little Angel (Jeff Beck Group), 82
Sweet Little Rock 'n' Roller (Chuck
  Berry), 337
Sweet Little Rock 'n' Roller (Faces), 344,
  400–401, 419
Sweet Little Rock 'n' Roller (Rod
  Stewart), 337
Sykes, Eric, 49
Sylvain, Sylvain, 287

T. Rex, 187, 214–215, 232–233, 257,
  259, 331
Tacker, Susanna, 102–103, 105, 107, 109,
  118, 120, 124, 130, 132, 143, 159,
  190, 203, 207, 217, 254, 273,
  285–289, 297, 398
Tackett, Fred, 365
Taj Mahal, 368
Take A Look At The Guy (Ron Wood),
  335

Take A Look At The Guy (Ron Wood/ Rod Stewart & The Faces), 372
Tales From Topographic Oceans (Yes), 331
Talk To Me Baby (Jeff Beck Group), 82
Talk To You (Small Faces), 98
Talking About My Baby (Birds), 70
Tallyman (Jeff Beck), 82–83
Talmadge, Arthur, 85
Talmy, Shel, 70, 86, 241
Tapestry (Carole King), 236
Tarkio (Brewer & Shipley), 221
Taste, 193
Tati, Jacques, 180, 214
Tatum, Art, 58
Taupin, Bernie, 151, 185, 337
Taylor, Derek, 101, 261, 375–376
Taylor, Eve, 104
Taylor, Gary, 149
Taylor, James, 220, 229, 244
Taylor, Mick, 72, 82, 125–126, 332, 344, 359, 385, 413
Taylor, Roger, 408
Taylor, Steve, 7–8, 11, 13
Telford, Ray, 283
Tell Everyone (Faces), 202–203, 214, 325, 404, 418
Tell Everyone (Ronnie Lane), 325
Tell Me (Rolling Stones), 95
Tell Me (Steve Marriott), 95
(Tell Me) Have You Ever Seen Me (Apostolic Intervention), 97
(Tell Me) Have You Ever Seen Me (Small Faces), 98
Temperance Seven, 353
Tempest, Roy, 150
Temptations, The, 82, 135, 184, 216, 223–224, 311
Ten Little Indians (Yardbirds), 89
Ten Years After, 83, 91, 143, 192–193, 195
Terry, Sonny, 45*n*.
Tetsu And The Good Times Roll Band (Tetsu Yamauchi), 400
Thacker, Clive, 150
Tharpe, Sister Rosetta, 45*n*., 50
That's All Right (Elvis Presley), 221
That's All Right (Rod Stewart), 221
That's All That I Need For You (Birds), 68
That's All You Need (Faces), 242, 245

Them, 55, 67*n*.
Then Play On (Fleetwood Mac), 159
These Foolish Things (Bryan Ferry), 315
Thin Lizzy, 397–398
Think (James Brown), 17
Think I'll Pack My Bags (Rod Stewart), 334*n*.
Third Power, The, 180, 191
32nd Street (Ronnie Lane), 346
This Old Heart Of Mine (Isley Brothers), 342
This Wheel's On Fire (Julie Driscoll & The Brian Auger Trinity), 150
Thomas, Chris, 362
Thomas, Rufus, 17
Thompson, Danny, 224
Thornton, Eddie 'Tam Tam', 98
Thorpe, Jeremy, 364
Three Button Hand Me Down (Faces), 138, 161–162, 168, 196, 225, 364
Three Day Nation (Gary Osborne), 193
Three Dog Night, 210
Three Men In A Boat (book) (Jerome K. Jerome), 107
Three Time Loser (Rod Stewart & The Faces), 372
Thubron, Sarah aka Sarah Streeter (Rod's daughter), 43, 43*n*, 411
Thunderbirds, The, 59–60
Thunders, Johnny, 287
Thyrds, The, 64
Tillotson, Johnny, 19
Times They Are A-Changin', The (Bob Dylan), 184
Tin Soldier (Small Faces), 101, 103, 108, 115, 241
Tiny Tim, 153
TLC, 395
Tobler, John, 91
Tolkien, J.R.R., 105, 132
Tolliday, Ray, 118
Tommy (Who), 106, 119, 132, 290, 383
Tomorrow, 44*n*., 86
Tomorrow Is A Long Time (Bob Dylan), 221
Tomorrow Is A Long Time (Hamilton Camp), 221
Tomorrow Is A Long Time (Judy Collins), 221

Tomorrow Is A Long Time (Rod
  Stewart), 221
Too Bad (Faces), 245, 251, 404
Too Much Woman (For A Henpecked
  Man) (Faces), 418
Toon, Tony, 339, 354, 356–358,
  369–370, 374, 395
Torme, Mel, 31
Toussaint, Allen, 177
Townshend, Pete, xii, 21, 60, 70, 76, 104,
  106–107, 113–114, 118, 131–133,
  160–161, 178, 193, 202, 213, 231,
  235–236, 243, 246–247, 263, 273,
  285, 287, 290, 293–294, 319, 348,
  378–381, 383, 388–390, 392, 398,
  408
Tracks Of My Tears (Birds), 70
Tracks Of My Tears (Miracles), 70, 243
Traffic, 92, 101, 179, 293
Travellin' In Style (Free), 353
Tremlett, George, 55, 135, 183
Tremors, The, 392
Tridents, The, 74, 78
Trifle, 81
Troublemaker (Ian McLagan), 388
Troupe, Sarah, 89, 165, 229–230,
  232–233
Troy, Doris, 22, 221
Trudeau, Margaret, 263*n*.
True Blue (Rod Stewart), 274–275, 298,
  314
Truth (Jeff Beck), 80*n*., 82, 87–88, 90–92,
  123, 133
Tucker, Tommy, 352
Tumbleweed Connection (Elton John), 224
Tungate, Rene, 105–106
Turner, Ike, 357, 418
Turner, Ike & Tina, 53, 56, 357
Tweddell, Nick, 27, 105
Twistin' The Night Away (Faces), 344,
  400
Twistin' The Night Away (Rod Stewart),
  276, 280, 337
Twistin' The Night Away (Sam Cooke),
  276, 337
2Stoned (autobiography) (Andrew Loog
  Oldham), 177*n*., 394
Tyrannosaurus Rex, 187
Tyrell, Ricky & The Presidents, 241

Uncle Bert (Creation), 86
United States (Ian McLagan), 414
Universal, The (Small Faces), 108, 262
Unplugged . . . And Seated (Rod Stewart),
  388, 401
Unwin, Stanley, 'Professor', 105
Up Above My Head (Long John Baldry &
  The Hoochie Coochie Men), 50,
  258
Up The Wooden Hills To Bedfordshire
  (Small Faces), 96
Ure, Midge, 419
Uriah Heep, 269

Valentine, Penny, ix, 21, 72, 112, 114,
  122, 124, 126, 141, 157–158, 162,
  167–168, 171, 173, 177, 187,
  195–196, 198, 201, 206–207, 217,
  220, 237, 240, 248–249, 251, 257,
  274, 277, 293, 295, 298, 308, 310,
  315, 396
Valentinos, The, 184
Vallon, Larry, 212
Van Der Graaf Generator, 85
Vanda, Harry, 337
Vanilla Fudge, 92, 127, 148, 251, 378
Vaughan, Frankie, 101
Vee, Virginia, 151
Velvettes, The, 46
Vernon, Mike, 50
Vertue, Beryl, 150, 208
Vigrass, Paul, 289–290, 325*n*., 340, 342
Vincent, Gene, 22, 26, 40, 73–74
Volunteers (Jefferson Airplane), 126
Vorda, Allan, 7, 13, 15

Wace, Robert, 97
Waddell, Willie, 38
Wages Of Sin, The, 111
Wald, Jeff, 371
Wale, Michael, 51, 311
Walker Brothers, The, 22, 33, 81
Walker, Billy (boxer), 104
Walker, Billy (critic), 298
Walker, Brenda, 103*n*.
Walker, John, 84
Walker, T-Bone, 75
Wall, Max, 254*n*., 296
Wallace, Eugene, 234

Waller, Fats, 98, 197, 281
Waller, Mickey, 53, 79, 83, 87–89, 92,
    121–123, 125, 136, 140, 168, 182,
    184, 210, 219–221, 225, 266,
    275–277, 314–315, 337, 396
Walsh, Jill, 8, 242
Walton, Mike, 220
War Of The Worlds (Jeff Wayne), 397
War Of The Worlds, The (Small Faces),
    116*n.*
Warburton, Nick, 134
Wardlaw, Matt, 412
Warhol, Andy, 355
Waring, Eddie, 217
Warm Heart Pastry (Mike Heron), 202
Warner, Jack, 152
Warren, Phil, 328
Warwick, Dionne, 70
Washington, Dinah, 84
Waters, Muddy, 15, 26, 33, 45, 142, 419
Watson, Bernie, 46
Watson, Doc, 221
Watts, Charlie, 45, 53, 126*n.*, 333,
    359–360, 379, 391
Way You Do The Things You Do, The
    (Birds), 70
Wayne, Jeff, 397
We Can Make It (Peters & Lee), 314
We Love You (Rolling Stones), 137
We'll Meet Again (Faces), 303
Weatherburn, Gillian, 25–26, 29
Weatherburn, Joe, 24–25
Weatherburn, Paddy, 24–25
Weatherburn, Phil, 29–30
Webb, George, 52, 55
Webb, Janet, 258
Webb, Julie, 240, 245
Weberman, A.J., 198
Weedon, Bert, 38
Weeks, Willie, 332
Weight, The (Aretha Franklin), 122
Weight, The (Band), 122
Weil, Cynthia, 56
Weir, John, 18
Weiss, Larry, 79
Weiss, Steve, 127
Welch, Bruce, 6
Welch, Chris, 79, 112, 116, 130,
    167–168, 174–175, 181, 187–188

Weller, Paul, 413
Westwood, Vivienne, 268
Whales And Nightingales (Judy Collins),
    221
Wham Bam Thank You Mam (Small
    Faces), 115
What Hit Me (Birds), 70
What Made Milwaukee Famous (Has
    Made A Loser Out Of Me) (Jerry
    Lee Lewis), 288
What Made Milwaukee Famous (Has
    Made A Loser Out Of Me) (Rod
    Stewart), 288
Whatcha Gonna Do About It (Small
    Faces), 22–23, 30
Whelan, Bernadette, 331
When We Were The New Boys (Rod
    Stewart), 402
When Will I Be Loved (Everly Brothers),
    225
When Will I Be Loved (Faces), 225
White, Barry, 342
White, Eric, 39
Whitehead, Peter, 95
Whitehouse, Mary, 237
Who Came First (Pete Townshend), 160
Who, The, x, 21–22, 31, 63, 66, 70, 75*n.*,
    80, 91, 100–101, 104, 114, 119, 132,
    157, 161, 178–179, 202, 215, 222*n.*,
    231, 234–236, 241, 248, 268, 278,
    290, 294, 312, 316–317, 319, 325,
    327, 331, 334, 379, 383–384, 396,
    398, 408
Who's Next (Who), 241
Whole Lotta Woman (Faces), 418
Wicked Messenger (Faces), 159, 161, 188
Wicked Messenger, The (Bob Dylan),
    159*n.*
Wide Eyed Girl On The Wall (Small
    Faces), 116
Wigg, David, 58, 267, 272, 359
Wilde, Marty, & The Wildcats, 53
Williams, Andy, 32*n.*
Williams, Joe, 47
Williams, Larry, 296
Williams, Richard, 186, 190, 209, 215,
    222
Williams, Rupert, 11, 192, 209, 416
Williamson, Sonny Boy, 28, 47, 51–52

Willis, Justice, Mr, 351
Willis, Mickey, 11
Wills, Colin, 355
Wills, Rick, 381, 384
Wilmer, Valerie, 77
Wilson, Brian, 352
Wilson, Don, 60
Wilson, Harold, Prime Minister, 20, 268
Wilson, Jackie, 70
Wilson, John 'Willie', 310
Winchester Cathedral (New Vaudeville
    Band), 77
Wings, 333
Winner, Langdon, 190
Winston, Frank (Jimmy Winston's
    brother), 16, 23
Winston, Jimmy (Jimmy Langwith),
    16–17, 23–24, 30–31
Winston, Jimmy, & The Reflections, 24*n*.
Winter, Johnny, 171, 213
Winwood, Steve, 80, 117, 164, 290, 293,
    391
Wolf, Howlin', 28, 52, 82, 142
Womack, Bobby, 184, 342, 353,
    356–357, 360, 365, 368, 377
Woman I Am, The (autobiography) (Helen
    Reddy), 371
Woman Is The Nigger Of The World
    (John Lennon), 244
Woman Trouble (Kenney Jones), 340
Wombles, The, 331
Wonder, Stevie, 230, 255–256, 330
Wood, Art, Combo, 60
Wood, Arthur (Ron's brother), 58, 60,
    62, 67, 71*n*., 129–130, 140, 336,
    386–387
Wood, Arthur (Ron's grandson), 386
Wood, Arthur 'Archie' (Ron's father),
    57–58, 236
Wood, Catherine 'Tilly' (Ron's
    daughter-in-law), 386
Wood, Christine (Ron's wife), 61, 71–72,
    76–77, 89, 92, 124, 126, 166, 169,
    190, 207, 214, 216, 236, 253–254,
    256, 261, 292, 312, 320, 323, 336,
    356, 360, 375, 385–387, 398
Wood, Doreen (Ron's sister-in-law), 336
Wood, Edward (Ron's brother), 58, 60,
    353, 387

Wood, Jesse James (Ron's son), 385–386,
    408
Wood, Jo, 386, 400
Wood, John 'Junior', 44*n*., 86
Wood, Leah (Ron's daughter), 386
Wood, Mercy Leah Elizabeth 'Lizzie'
    (Ron Wood's mother), 57–58, 336
Wood, Peter, 340
Wood, Ron, ix–xi, 56, 58–62, 76–78,
    81–83, 85–89, 92, 106, 116*n*.,
    121–127, 129–130, 134, 136–138,
    140–143, 147, 151, 157–163, 164,
    167–173, 179, 181–184, 186,
    189–191, 193, 195–197, 201–207,
    210–216, 219–225, 229–230, 232,
    234, 236–237, 242–249, 251–253,
    256–258, 262–263, 265–266, 272,
    276, 280–281, 284, 287, 289,
    291–293, 296–299, 301–302, 309,
    312–319, 321, 323–324, 326,
    329–350, 352–355, 357, 359–360,
    364–376, 382–383, 385, 387–388,
    392, 394–395, 398–402, 404–407,
    409, 411–412, 413, 414, 415
alcohol use, x, 61–62, 65, 87, 138, 170,
    195, 236, 262, 265, 299, 413
America, first trip to, 89
art work, 58, 60, 387
bass playing, 81, 83, 137–138, 159, 184,
    196, 203, 206
Birds, naming of/involvement with,
    61–72
birth, 58
bottleneck/slide playing, 159–161,
    184–185, 189, 196, 203–204,
    206–207, 225, 243, 245, 405,
    407–408
Brazilian girlfriend, 387, 413
Clapton, Eric, guest appearance on
    'comeback' show, 293
Creation, The, involvement with,
    85–86
Decca Records, signing to, 64
drug use, 318, 388, 410
early groups, 59–60
enduring rock 'n' roll lifestyle, 387
Faces, confirmation of leaving, 359
Faces, recruitment to, 124–125
failed business investments, 386–387

Wood, Ron (*contd.*)
  financial state, 127, 156–157
  Findlay, Christine (Krissie), relationship
    with, 61, 71–72, 76, 92, 207, 214,
    236, 256, 292, 336, 360, 375,
    385–386
  first Faces album (*First Step*),
    contribution to, 159–162
  first girlfriend, death of, 61–62, 387
  first stage appearance, 58
  fun-loving nature, 124, 163, 169, 181,
    214, 262, 291, 354, 387
  Howard, Jo, relationship with/marriage
    to, 385–386
  Humphreys, Sally, marriage to, 413
  I Feel Like Playing, solo album, 387
  I've Got My Own Album To Do,
    recording of, 332–334, 336
  Jeff Beck Group, joining/leaving of,
    77–78, 121–122, 126–127
  Mahoney's Last Stand, contribution to
    soundtrack, 262–263
  mortality/death, attitude to, 61–62,
    387
  musical influences, 58
  Now Look, recording of/reaction to,
    353, 360
  'Ooh La La', lead vocal on, 297–298
  pedal steel guitarist, 203–204, 214
  purchase of Georgian mansion, the
    Wick, 272
  Rolling Stones, involvement with, xii,
    125–126, 141, 202, 207, 216, 312,
    331, 333–334–336, 344–345, 354,
    359, 366–368, 374–375, 385,
    387–388, 402
  Ronnie Wood Show, The (radio show),
    387, 413
  Romany image/influences, 37, 65
  schooling, 58–59
  solo shows, 335–336
  songwriting, 321, 342
  stage presence, 86
  Stewart, Rod, relationship/interaction
    with, 65, 129–130, 143, 169, 213,
    236, 265, 291, 302, 336, 366, 385,
    400, 411
  Warner Bros signing, 154–157
Wood, Sir Henry, 205

Working In The Coal Mine (Lee Dorsey),
  55
Working In The Coal Mine (Rod
  Stewart), 55
Works, The (book) (Ron Wood), 206
Worrell, Alan, 25–26
Worth, Suzy, 229
Worried Man Blues (Stewart/Wood),
  411
Would You Believe (Billy Nicholls), 119
Would You Believe (Billy Nicholls), 119
Wrapping Paper (Cream), 80
Wright, Biddy, 276n.
Wright, Chris, 91
Wright, Geoff, 48–49, 51, 54, 90
Wright, Tom, 178–180, 191–192,
  227–228, 248–249, 279, 281, 296,
  387, 395–396, 416
Wyatt, Martin, 147, 153–156, 159, 167,
  205, 260–262, 351, 397
Wyman, Bill, 61, 360, 385, 391, 400–401,
  403, 405
Wyndlesham Bay (Faces), 298
Wynter, Mark, 94

Yamashta, Stomu, 331
Yamauchi, Tetsu, xi, 307–310, 312,
  315–316, 322, 326, 329–330, 344,
  353–355, 369, 372–373, 375–376,
  400–401, 418
Yardbirds, The, 47, 51, 53, 60–61, 63,
  72–78, 80, 82, 86n., 87, 89, 98n.
Yentob, Alan, 410
Yes, 331
You Better Believe It (Small Faces), 33
You Can Make Me Dance, Sing Or
  Anything (Even Take The Dog For
  A Walk, Mend A Fuse, Fold Away
  The Ironing Board, Or Any Other
  Domestic Shortcomings) (Faces/Rod
  Stewart), 342–343, 352, 419
You Can't Judge A Book (John Baldry),
  258
You Don't Love Me (You Don't Care)
  (Birds), 63–64
You Don't Love Me (You Don't Care)
  (Bo Diddley), 63
(You Make Me Feel Like A) Natural Man
  (Rod Stewart), 337

(You Make Me Feel Like A) Natural Woman (Aretha Franklin), 337
You Must Believe Me (Birds), 70
You Need Love (Willie Dixon), 33
You Put Something Better Inside Me (Rod Stewart), 338*n.*
You Really Got Me (Kinks), 15, 276
You Really Got Me (Steve Marriott's Moments), 15
You Send Me (Sam Cooke), 337
You Shook Me (Jeff Beck Group), 82
You Shook Me (Led Zeppelin), 91
You Wear It Well (Rod Stewart), 276–277, 280, 337
You'll Be Mine (Long John Baldry & The Hoochie Coochie Men), 50
You're Messing Up A Good Thing (Bobby Womack), 342

You're My Girl (I Don't Want To Discuss It) (Faces), 188, 225
You're My Girl (I Don't Want To Discuss It) (Rod Stewart), 186
You're On My Mind (Birds), 63–64
You're So Rude (Faces), 242
You're Too Much (Eyes), 67
Young, George, 38, 337
Young, Neil, 155, 165, 220, 388
Young, Paul, 395
Your Saving Grace (Steve Miller Band), 127, 241

Zandt, 'Little' Steven van, 412, 416
Zappa, Frank, 91
Zemaitis, Antanus 'Tony', 190–191, 195, 341
Zoot Money's Big Roll Band, 55–56